The Financial Development of
Japan, Korea, and Taiwan

The Financial Development of Japan, Korea, and Taiwan

Growth, Repression, and Liberalization

Edited by

HUGH T. PATRICK
YUNG CHUL PARK

New York   Oxford
OXFORD UNIVERSITY PRESS
1994

Oxford University Press

Oxford   New York   Toronto
Delhi   Bombay   Calcutta   Madras   Karachi
Kuala Lumpur   Singapore   Hong Kong   Tokyo
Nairobi   Dar es Salaam   Cape Town
Melbourne   Auckland   Madrid

and associated companies in
Berlin   Ibadan

Library of Congress Cataloging-in-Publication Data
The Financial development of Japan, Korea, and Taiwan :
growth, repression, and liberalization /
edited by Hugh T. Patrick and Yung Chul Park.
p.   cm.
Includes bibliographical references and index.
ISBN 0-19-508766-6
1. Finance—Japan.   2. Finance—Korea (South).
3. Finance—Taiwan.   4. Banks and banking—Japan.
5. Banks and banking—Korea (South).
6. Banks and banking—Taiwan.
I. Patrick, Hugh T.
II. Park, Yung Chul.
HG187.J3F557   1994   332'.095—dc20   93–31448

Preface

The extraordinarily successful economic growth and development of Japan, Korea, and Taiwan have brought about, and been intertwined with, profound changes in economic structure. The three countries share common economic and institutional circumstances and patterns of development, and they also have certain significant differences. Yet relatively little attention has been paid to understanding the workings and the evolutionary process of development of their financial systems.

The central issue in this book is how, and to what degree, finance matters. The financial intermediation process affects savers, investors, entrepreneurs, and consumers. The historical realities of the processes of economic and financial development make for complex interactions and feedbacks among real and financial factors. At the very least, effective finance supports and facilitates the real factors driving economic development and growth. And in some circumstances financial development itself is a significant causal force.

Policymakers in Japan, Korea, and Taiwan have certainly believed that finance matters, and they have been deeply involved in the functioning of their respective financial systems. They have understood that effective and efficient financial intermediation in the long run is built on macroeconomic stability, particularly control over inflation; an appropriate institutional framework and structure; effective prudential regulation and system safety; and competitive financial markets. At the same time policymakers have recognized that finance is a powerful instrument to achieve economic objectives and have, to one degree or another and by one means or another, channeled funds to finance investment in priority sectors. Essentially they encouraged the creation and growth of bank-based financial systems. Only in the last decade or so have capital markets begun to play a significant role in financing business investment, and then only for large companies.

The postwar financial development of Japan, Korea, and Taiwan has occurred in two phases. In the first phase the monetary authorities regulated interest rates at below-market levels, restricted entry of new financial institutions and creation of new financial instruments, segmented financial markets, and insulated domestic finance from world financial markets. This financial repression was rather modest in comparison with many developing countries in Latin America and elsewhere, but it had important effects on these three economies.

The second phase, yet to be fully achieved, is that of a highly competitive, market-based financial system where government regulation focuses on prudential regulation for system safety and protection against various forms of moral hazard, while leaving the allocation of financial resources to the marketplace. The transition from one phase to the other has taken place at different periods of time, so the degree to which each economy has entered the second phase as of the early 1990s differs. In general, deregulation and liberalization—the unfettering—of financial markets and institutions has been a deliberate, gradual, piecemeal process. The authorities in all three economies have issued timetables and more or less implemented them—a process that to many participants and foreign critics, has moved all too slowly and unevenly, albeit in the right direction.

The book's evaluation in a long-run development context of the financial development of Japan, Korea, and Taiwan provides understanding of and lessons applicable for the countries themselves as the 1990s progress, as well as for other economies that have repressed their financial systems for economic or political reasons and are now wondering what to do. The analysis is made in the broader context of the evolution of the financial system and its relationship to the superior performance of the real economy in each country, and in the more focussed context of the efficiency, effectiveness, and internal management of commercial banks as the major financial intermediaries.

In Chapter 1 Park provides a framework for considering the issues, including an examination of the theoretical literature on the role of finance. The next six chapters—two each on Japan, Korea, and Taiwan—provide detailed description and analysis by specialists on the macro aspects of the financial system and its development and on the more micro aspects, particularly commercial banking. These important studies offer both new insights and significant new data, helping fill what have been major voids in the literature available in English. A common set of appendix tables for each country follow chapters 2, 4, and 6. In the concluding chapter Patrick draws some comparisons and contrasts in their processes of financial development and addresses their implications for several broader issues of finance and development.

A note on terminology: This is a book on finance and economics, not international relations. Accordingly, we have followed the generally used terminology in referring to these three economies. We use Korea to refer to the Republic of Korea, or South Korea. We use Taiwan to refer to the Republic of China, or Chinese Taipei in the terminology of the Asian Development Bank. Clearly these are three autonomous, self-governed economies that have become significant players in the international economy. The international political status of the three is not an issue here.

Financial Development of Japan, Korea, and Taiwan is the product of a truly international collaborative project—in conception, execution, and funding. Perhaps most distinctive is not just the high degree of interaction and cooperation among the scholars participating in this project but in the extensive and intensive rewriting of chapters through the process. We met four times as a team: at an initial planning workshop in New York in early 1989, at a follow-up meeting in Tokyo in the fall, then a preliminary workshop in Seoul in the late spring of 1990, followed by a full-fledged conference in Taipei in the late summer of 1990 to obtain the insights of a wider range of participants, including bankers and government officials as well as scholars. We worked assiduously on revising and updating the chapters through the summer of 1992, particularly in light of the very recent dramatic changes in financial markets, policies, and institutions in all three countries.

This book would not have been possible without the efforts of Larry Meissner, to whom we owe a special debt of gratitude. He went far beyond the call of duty, and of the limits of budget, in providing an intensive and extensive editing of all the chapters, as well as updating and improving the presentation of the desirably large amounts of data provided readers in the tables. Throughout our lengthy editorial process he has provided his own knowledge and insight as well as the assiduous attention to detail of a perfectionist. We also thank Donna Keyser, Associate Director of the Center on Japanese Economy and Business at Columbia University, for carefully shepherding the manuscript through the final page proof stages.

This collaborative study would not have been possible without the sincere and insightful efforts of our colleagues who wrote these chapters—Dong Won Kim, Hiroshi Kitagawa and Yoshitaka Kurosawa, Jia-Dong Shea, Juro Teranishi, and Ya-Hwei Yang. The Park–Patrick collaboration in organizing and managing this project has been truly balanced and equal; neither of us would have attempted this project without the other. We are particularly indebted to Professors Shea and Teranishi for organizing meetings and arranging funding in Taiwan and Japan respectively.

We also feel deep appreciation for the financial and other support provided by institutions in each of our countries. They are, at Columbia University, the Pacific Basin Studies Program, the Taiwan Studies Program, the Center for Korean Research, and the Center on Japanese Economy and Business; in Japan, the Twenty-First Century Fund; and in Taiwan, the Institute of Economics of Academia Sinica and the Ministry of Finance. In Korea, we are grateful to Mr. Hun Jai Lee, commissioner of the Securities and Exchange Committee of Korea, who encouraged and provided financial support for Korea Studies when he was president of Korea Investors Service.

New York   H. T. P. and Y. C. P.

Contents

Contributors

EDITORS

HUGH T. PATRICK is R. D. Calkins Professor of International Business, director of the Center on Japanese Economy and Business, and codirector of the Pacific Basin Studies Program at Columbia University. He is also chair of the International Steering Committee of the Pacific Trade and Development Conference (PAFTAD). He was previously a professor of economics and director of the Economic Growth Center at Yale University, and visiting professor at Hitotsubashi University (Tokyo), University of Tokyo, and University of Bombay. Among other works, he is the general coeditor of the three-volume series *The Political Economy of Japan,* and he edited and wrote the overview chapter for *Pacific Basin Industries in Distress,* which won the 1992 Masayoshi Ohira Prize.

YUNG CHUL PARK is a professor of economics at Korea University, Seoul, and the president of the Korea Institute of Finance. In addition, he is a member of the Ministry of Finance's Financial Development Committee and chair of its Financial Reform Subcommittee. He previously served as the chief economic adviser to President Doo Hwan Chun, as president of the Korea Development Institute, and as an academic member of the Bank of Korea's Monetary Board. He also was the director of the Institute of Economic Research at Korea University and a visiting professor at Harvard University, its Institute for International Development, and a research economist at the International Monetary Fund. After completing undergraduate work at Seoul National University, he received his Ph.D. from the University of Minnesota.

OTHER CONTRIBUTORS

DONG WON KIM is a professor of economics at the University of Suwon in Suwon, Korea, and a visiting scholar at the Salomon Center, Stern School of Business, New York University. He has been a special research fellow at the Korea Institute of Finance (KIF) in Seoul. He has written many papers on financial reform in Korea for the Bank of Korea, Korea Development Insitution (KDI), Korea Economic Research Institute, and KIF. These include (with Sang Woo Nam) "The Principal Transaction System in Korea" (World Bank, 1993).

HIROSHI KITAGAWA is an associate professor of economics at Seikei University, Tokyo. He trained at Hitotsubashi University. He participated in the Economic Planning Agency's working group studying financial market regulation and contributed working papers. He recently has been concentrating his research on the relationship between economic development and the financial system.

YOSHITAKA KUROSAWA is a professor of international finance at Nihon University, Tokyo. He is a former senior manager at the Japan Development Bank and served as chief of the bank's Research Insititute of Capital Formation. While at the bank he was a member of the working group that established a bond rating system in Japan. His Ph.D. is from Hokkaido University.

JIA-DONG SHEA is the director of, and a research fellow at, the Institute of Economics of Academia Sinica (IEAS) and a professor in the economics department of National Taiwan University, both in Taipei. He served as an adjunct research fellow at Chung-Hua Institution for Economic Research, as well as on the Tax Reform Committee and National Security Council, and he has taught at several universities in Taiwan, including Cheng-Chi, Chung-Hsiang, and the Open University. He earned his Ph.D. in economics from Stanford University in 1978 and joined IEAS as an associate research fellow. In 1982 he was promoted to research fellow, and he became director in 1991. During the 1980s he authored many theoretical and empirical articles on the phenomenon of financial dualism in Taiwan. In the 1990s his focus has been on the welfare effects of economic liberalization in an economy with an imperfect financial market.

JURO TERANISHI is a professor of economics at the Institute of Economic Research, Hitotsubashi University, Tokyo. He is the author of a number of works on Japanese finance, including *Money, Finance and Economic Development in Japan* (in Japanese), which won the Ekonomisuto Prize and the Nikkei Prize in 1982. He contributed to and is a coeditor of *Japanese Experience of Economic Reforms* (Macmillan, 1993).

YA-HWEI YANG is at the Chung-Hua Institution for Economic Research, Taipei, where she serves as director of the Taiwan Economy Division and as a research fellow. An adjunct professor at Catholic Fu-Jen University, she also has taught at National Taiwan University, Central University, and Tong-Hai University. She earned her Ph.D. from National Taiwan University in 1984 and pursued postdoctoral research at Harvard University in 1987. Her work has been on monetary policy and the financial system—both at a theoretical level and in the case of Taiwan. She has written more than thirty papers, some of which have attracted considerable attention.

The Financial Development of
Japan, Korea, and Taiwan

1

Concepts and Issues

YUNG CHUL PARK

For all the scrutiny the exceptional economic performance of Japan, Korea, and Taiwan has attracted, relatively little attention has been paid to understanding the workings and development of their financial systems. But finance matters— these countries' financial systems and their evolutionary development—have been a fundamental component of the overall development process. This process has been driven by real economic growth and the attendant growth and change in demand for various types of financial services, by institutional development within the financial system, and by changes in government policies concerning finance. Thus, the experience of these three countries is useful in understanding the relationship between finance and real economic performance, as well as the efficiency and effectiveness of finance.

This chapter begins with an overview of the historical legacies and the basic similarities and differences of the three economies and their financial systems. I then review the theoretical literature on financial development. All this provides a setting for the country chapters. They are detailed, richly informative, insightful studies, at times strikingly graphic, of the evolution of the respective financial and commercial banking systems of Japan, Korea, and Taiwan over the postwar period.

In all three countries the financial authorities initially pursued policies to ensure relatively low interest rates, segmented financial markets, limited entry, domestic insulation from world financial markets, and system safety at the expense of competition. This is one theme of this book. The process of real economic growth was increasingly market-oriented and competitive, and the presumed benefits of financial repression were undermined at the same time the pressures to develop a more market-based financial system intensified in what were becoming ever more complex economies in an increasingly inter- dependent world.

In all three countries the response to the changing needs their financial systems had to meet was a conscious decision by policymakers to deregulate and liberalize. This provides the second main theme that runs through the book: the causes, process, and degree to which each of the countries has moved from relatively mild financial repression to a less regulated and more competitive financial system. Both macro and micro issues of markets and financial institutions are taken up.

The country chapters offer significant evidence on important general issues in finance theory as it pertains both to advanced industrial economics and to the financial development of developing market economies. Examples are the effects of financial structure on real economic performance; the dominance of relationship banking over securities issue in corporate finance; competition, oligopoly, and stability in the financial system; the realities of and adjustments to imperfect information, asymmetrically distributed, in evaluating borrower creditworthiness; issues of bank ownership and control; incentive systems for risk taking and risk avoidance; and moral hazard problems. They stand on their own, so it is not the aim of this chapter, or of Patrick's concluding chapter, to summarize the country case studies.

CONTEXT

The economic and financial policies of every country are strongly shaped by certain fundamental assumptions and objectives, at times not fully articulated, that determine the mind-set of policymakers and the public alike. Usually these come from historical experiences that have, in one way or another, been traumatic.

The experience of hyperinflation on mainland China in the 1940s and Japan's postwar inflation until 1949 has meant double-digit inflation has been intolerable to policymakers and society alike in Taiwan and Japan. In contrast, in the 1960s and 1970s Korea had inflation rates on the order of 20 percent. The dramatic success in containing inflation in the 1980s suggests Korean policymakers are now less willing to accept inflation, although renewed increases in prices in the early 1990s indicate the limit may be somewhat higher than the experience of the mid- to late 1980s suggests.

Safety and the stability of the financial system have been accorded high priority, as they are in most countries. The fear of bank runs or other sources of financial panic is particularly pervasive in these countries. In Japan this can be traced to the 1927 banking crisis, while in Taiwan and Korea it derives from both the Japanese prewar and their own historical experiences.

Japan has been a model for financial system institution building in Taiwan and Korea. In part this is because both were ruled by Japan until 1945 (Taiwan from 1895, Korea from 1905), and the banks were Japanese-owned. With independence, both countries sought to overcome the historical legacies of Japanese colonial rule, and among other measures, both nationalized these banks. Government majority ownership has persisted into the 1990s in Taiwan, although the government has inaugurated a policy of privatization and has licensed a number of new banks. In Korea the banks were sold to wealthy businessmen in 1957, nationalized again in 1961, and reprivatized in the early 1980s.

The basic economic characteristics of the three economies in 1960 and 1990 are provided in Table 1.1. Much more detailed tables and other data accompany and support the analyses in the country chapters.

Table 1.1. *Summary Data*

	Year	Japan	Korea	Taiwan
Population (millions)	1960	93.4	24.7	10.6
	1990	123.6	42.8	20.4
GNP (billion US$)	1960	43.02	3.77	1.59
	1990	3109.80	237.99	161.73
GNP per capita (US$)	1960	457	153	150
	1990	25158	5561	7887
GDP growth rate	1960–70	10.50	8.50	9.20
(% per annum, compound)	1970–79	4.02	9.50	10.20
	1980–89	4.10	9.70	7.70
Gross domestic savings	1960	34.00	1.00	17.80
as % of GDP	1990	34.00	37.00	29.20
Current account	1960	140	33	−125
(million US$)	1990	35761	−2172	10866
Current account	1960	0.33	0.88	−7.86
as a % of GNP	1969	1.15	−0.91	6.72
Inflation rate	1960–70	5.10	16.70	4.10
(% per annum, compound)	1970–79	8.20	19.50	8.90
	1980–89	1.50	5.10	3.10
Ratio of financial assets	1960	3.66	0.89	1.61
to GNP (FIR)	1990	6.62	4.55	4.95
Ratio of M2 to GNP	1960	0.67	0.11	0.17
	1990	1.17	1.14	1.47
Exchange rate	1960	360 yen	65 won	39.5 NT$
(local currency per US$)	1990	138 yen	708 won	26.9 NT$

Major Similarities

It has been the demand by savers and borrowers for more services—both more scale and more types—that has driven financial development in general and liberalization and deregulation in particular in all three countries. The monetary authorities in each country belong to a respected technocratic elite that has quite consciously used its control of the financial system to achieve macroeconomic goals. The extraordinarily successful economic development and growth performance of the three economies over the past 30 years or more, with high GNP growth and considerable equity in income distribution, is well known and raises the question, pursued later and in the country chapters, of the relationship between that growth and the way the financial system has operated.[1]

The economies share similar resource endowments: poor in natural resources and initially abundant in unskilled labor. The path to growth has been that of industrialization. Improving the skills of the labor force has been essential and it has been achieved through both formal education and on-the-job training of managers and engineers as well as of skilled workers. Indeed, education has been the route to economic success and social status, and it is meritocratic. The people of Japan, Korea, and Taiwan are ambitious and hardworking, and risk-taking entrepreneurs are plentiful.

The capital stock has grown very rapidly in all three economies. High rates of domestic investment, made profitable by importing technology and increasing domestic R&D, were a major engine of growth. Although firms have retained most of their earnings, and cash flow from depreciation has been significant, external sources of funds have been essential to achieve such rapid rates of investment growth. The financial system, broadly defined, in one way or another has successfully transferred savings to investments although this was by no means an automatic or easy process.

All three pursued an export-oriented development strategy while concurrently protecting most of their domestic production from imports. They pursued similar macroeconomic policies to support their preeminent objective of rapid growth. The government's sector has comprised a relatively low share of GNP. Government fiscal policy on the whole has been conservative in that it has not been a source of inflation; Taiwan's government sector has run a large financial surplus since World War II, and Korea has had a surplus since 1975. Monetary policy has been accommodative. Taiwan and Japan have maintained price stability from the late 1950s, except temporarily during the oil crisis shocks. Korea achieved price stability only in the 1980s; the inflation rate averaged 18.4 percent between 1965 and 1980 (World Bank 1992, p. 219).

Significant Differences

While there are broad similarities in economic structure, performance and policies, their differences—some major, some more of nuance—also are significant. Perhaps most important, Japan is qualitatively different in its economic size and level of economic development. Japan has a population of 124 million; Korea, 43 millon; and Taiwan, 20 million. Japan's GNP per capita as of 1990 was more than 3 times larger than that of Taiwan and 4 1/2 times that of Korea (at market exchange rates; somewhat less on a relative purchasing power basis). Japan has been the world's second largest market economy since the early 1970s, when its GNP per capita also reached European levels (and its growth rate slowed). Japan's economy (1990 GNP) was 13 times larger than that of Korea and 19 times that of Taiwan. Japan started developing far earlier, beginning in the last quarter of the nineteenth century and accordingly has chronologically preceded the other two.

1. There is a large literature on the growth and transformation of these countries' real economies. For studies in English of the postwar period see for Japan: Patrick and Rosovsky 1976, Yamamura and Yasuba 1987; for Korea, Song 1990; for Taiwan, Wade 1990, Ranis 1992.

Taiwan and Korea were colonies of Japan for some 50 years until the end of World War II. Although the two countries' colonial heritage produced similar financial systems, it has posed immense problems for the ownership and control of their banking systems. Japan was never colonized, but the postwar Allied Occupation reforms between 1945 and 1952 brought about major political and economic change, although considerably less to the financial system.

Accordingly, the political systems and policy environments have been rather different in each country. Japan has had a democratic system of government since the Occupation. Only in the mid- to late 1980s did Korea and Taiwan start to make substantial progress toward evolving from their previous authoritarian regimes into democratic states. In practice, financial liberalization has been associated with a broader process of political as well as economic liberalization in both economies, together with the considerable turmoil characterizing this transition process. At the same time, the sense of external threat to domestic security has been very different—high for Korea and Taiwan, low for Japan. It is noteworthy that both Korea and Taiwan were able to achieve very rapid economic growth despite very high defense expenditures (greater than the United States as a share of GNP). In contrast, under its "peace" constitution and security treaty with the United States, Japan's defense expenditures as a share of GNP have been low.

Significant differences in the patterns of savings have enabled high investment rates. National and household savings rates have been high in Taiwan and Japan since the early 1960s, but in Korea, only from the early 1980s. Korea relied substantially on foreign loans between 1965 and 1985, averaging about 5 percent of GNP. In the early 1980s it had one of the highest ratios of foreign debt to GNP of any developing country, but it did not have debt-servicing problems because of its large and growing share of exports in GNP. In contrast, neither Japan nor Taiwan has relied significantly on foreign loans.

Because the Japanese economy and domestic market are so large, its manufacturing production structure is considerably more diversified than those of Korea or Taiwan. Exports were given priority, but mainly to overcome the balance of payments (import) constraint on growth until 1970 or so. Accordingly, the share of exports in Japan's GNP has been relatively low, only 10 to 15 percent. In contrast, both Taiwan and Korea are among the most successful examples of export-led growth, with export shares in GNP some three times as high as Japan's.

Patterns of finance are strongly associated with the nature of corporate structure, especially firm size and the role of business groups. Korea's industrialization has been based on large-scale enterprises organized in family-owned conglomerates (*chaebol*). In contrast, small and medium firms predominate in Taiwan, although some family-based large conglomerates have emerged, and large-scale government enterprise dominates the basic industries. In Japan, large firms are important, but most manufacturing is done by small firms, about 60 percent through subcontracting arrangements. The prewar family-owned conglomerates (*zaibatsu*) were dissolved by the Allied Occupation authorities and have been replaced by professionally managed companies organized in business groups of equals. (Some are more equal than others, but there is no central control within any horizontal business group.)

Maturing Economies

The era of rapid growth in all three economies can be characterized as neoclassical in the sense that growth was determined essentially by the ability to expand productive capacity. Beginning in the mid-1970s, however, following the first oil crisis, the decline in private demand relative to growing supply capacity created in Japan a new, Keynesian condition in which private savings were greater than private investment. Between 1975 and 1980 Japan relied increasingly on government deficit spending to cover the Keynesian gap and maintain growth, albeit at a slower rate. Then in the 1980s, the country relied on an increasing current account surplus until the yen appreciated substantially. By the late 1980s Japan had become the world's largest net creditor nation according to the standard cost-measure basis, with extensive participation by private financial institution's in foreign and international markets.

Taiwan's increasing success in developing exports, coupled with persisting restrictions on imports, capital flows, and the exchange rate, suddenly produced in the 1980s an immense current account surplus, averaging some 11 percent of GNP. By 1990 Taiwan had also become a major creditor nation, although most of its external assets have been held by the central bank. Given Taiwan's export competitiveness, it probably is not appropriate to think of the 1980s as a Keynesian period, even though domestic investment was substantially below savings; after all, the government did not feel compelled to engage in deficit spending.

Korea also developed a substantial current account surplus in the mid-1980s, although it had (probably only temporarily) disappeared by 1990. It was more like Taiwan than Japan in that growth continued to be constrained more on the supply side than on the demand side. In contrast to Taiwan and Japan, Korea's current account surplus was used to reduce its net foreign debt position. It is ironic that U.S. policymakers criticized Korea for repaying its debt too rapidly (that is, running too large a current account surplus) and at the same time criticized a number of other debtor developing countries for not solving their debt servicing problems. In any case, the generation of current account surpluses enabled Korea and Taiwan to liberalize imports and foreign capital flows as it had for Japan earlier and, indeed, stimulated foreign pressures to do so.

FINANCIAL FACTORS IN ECONOMIC DEVELOPMENT

A financial system is an economic sector that uses productive factors to provide the services of a payments system, financial intermediation, and access to securities markets. It also provides financial instruments that meet the diverse tastes, needs, and circumstances of lenders and borrowers. It has its own industries—commercial banking, investment banking, and insurance—and also a superstructure of regulatory authorities.

Historical experience shows that financial development in general proceeds from simple lending and borrowing arrangements to a system dominated by commercial banking and eventually to a broader system complemented by a variety of nonbank financial institutions and well-functioning money and capital markets. Thus, in most developing countries, largely because of problems of information and uncertainty, open capital markets for primary securities such as stocks, bonds, mortgages, and commercial bills are insignificant channels for mobilizing and allocating savings. Therefore, for all practical purposes, the banking system—broadly defined to include a variety of depository institutions—dominates the financial system and is usually the only organized credit market available.

The observed correlation between economic development and financial sophistication suggests financial institutions and markets play important roles in economic growth and development. However, it has been difficult to explain theoretically either the importance or the evolutionary process of financial structure. This difficulty stems largely from the lack of understanding of the mechanism of interactions between the financial system on the one hand and the real sector of the economy on the other. As a result, both the quantitative and the qualitative importance of the efficiency of financial structure remains controversial. Views range from those arguing the irrelevance of finance to those attaching strategic importance to it. This controversy has made it difficult to identify financial policies for developing countries that are consistent with the objectives of growth and industrialization.

During the 1950s and 1960s there were two lines of thought in the literature concerning the link between financial factors and real economic growth. Gurley and Shaw (GS) (1955) focused on "financial capacity" as an important determinant of aggregate demand. According to GS, financial intermediaries could extend borrowers' financial capacity as they transformed primary securities issued by firms into the indirect securities desired by savers. This enabled certain classes of borrowers to obtain greater quantities of credit at better terms than they could otherwise obtain from issuing securities. The GS argument was more or less ignored, in part because it was not presented in a "rigorous" manner, and in part because it was outside the period's mainstream of development economics—with its heavy Keynesian influence and dismissal of financial factors.

The dominant position was reinforced by the formulation of the Modigliani–Miller (MM) proposition (1958) that real economic decisions are independent of financial structure. Consistent with the neoclassical world of perfect markets, MM's work was felt to provide a rigorous justification for abstracting from financial considerations in microeconomic analysis. This, in turn, provided a basis for Keynesian macroeconomics' devoting attention to the market for money for transaction purposes (the medium of exchange) but ignoring financial factors, including credit markets.

The prevailing view in the 1960s was that interest rates should be kept relatively low to stimulate capital formation. This implicitly means an expansionary monetary policy as a means of promoting economic growth in developing countries. A similar message was carried by the monetary growth models that flourished in the 1960s. In these models, real cash balances were treated as part of wealth and as substitutes for physical assets. Economic agents could therefore satisfy their savings objectives by accumulating either one. Inflation is a tax on holding money, and thus encourages accumulation of physical assets. Given the propensity to save, inflation then increases the GNP growth rate if it speeds up fixed capital formation. Long (1983) argues such models provided a rationale for inflationary policies and the theoretical underpinning for aggressively expansionary fiscal policies that allocated a large share of resources to development expenditures in the 1950s and 1960s.

In the 1960s, while various development strategies and models ignored the financial sector, economic historians examined the experiences of financial development in search of clues that might shed light on how finance affects real economic activity (Cameron 1967, 1972). In a classic contribution, Goldsmith (1969) documented that as real income and wealth increase, in the aggregate and per capita, the size and complexity of the financial superstructure also grow. He could not, however, determine the direction of causality. He observed (p. 48) that underlying causality is likely to differ among and within countries from stage to stage of industrialization. In short, causality can run in both directions. The growth and diversity of financial instruments, markets and participants can stimulate savings and investment, as well as improve the economy's allocative efficiency. Or financial development can simply be an aspect of economic growth whose main causes are elsewhere.

Gerschenkron (1962) emphasized a major role for banking. Based on his examination of Central Europe, Germany, and Russia, he argued that the banking system could play a key role at certain development stages, because it served as the prime source of both capital and entrepreneurship. A modern interpretation of this thesis is that financing through banks is less costly and more advantageous than financing directly from anonymous, organized markets. This argument, of course, rests on the assumption that banks can reduce the problems of adverse selection and moral hazard stemming from asymmetric information between lenders and borrowers, because the banks can economize on the costs of monitoring and controlling the activities of borrowers. Gerschenkron also contended that firms strongly prefer self-finance, thereby suggesting that the importance of internal finance rises with economic development.

The leading role of financial intermediaries was further elaborated by Patrick (1966), who developed the hypothesis of supply-leading and demand-following finance. Demand-following means that as an economy grows, it generates additional and new demands for financial services, which brings about a supply response in the growth of the financial system. Patrick further suggested that the creation of financial institutions and the supply of their financial assets, liabilities, and services in advance of demand for them can induce growth by generating incentives to savers to increase their savings rate and to entrepreneurs to increase their investment level. Emphasizing the relevance of supply-leading finance in the early stages of development, Patrick advocated realistic interest rate policies and promotion of the efficiency of financial intermediation through private market mechanisms in developing countries.

In many developing countries in the 1960s, inflationary development policies did not promote capital formation or economic growth. Many of them also had inward-looking development strategies, focused on import substitution. Characterized by restricted trade flows and distorted prices, interest rates, and exchange rates, large parts of the developing world suffered slow growth, high inflation, and balance of payments difficulties.

In sharp contrast, those countries that undertook trade liberalization and monetary reform aimed at encouraging holding financial assets paying positive real interest rates displayed sustained rapid growth. The historical case studies of already developed countries including Japan, combined with the experiences of Taiwan and Korea—often cited as the archetypal outward-looking development cases that also benefited from monetary reform—led to a reassessment of the tenets of Keynesian development theory. By the mid-1970s there was general acceptance that finance mattered. Progress in theory, particularly the application of information theory, has made it possible to provide rigorous proofs of the propositions of GS and others (Gertler 1988).

Unfortunately, one of the first applications of the new approach—the economic liberalization that swept Argentina, Chile, and Uruguay (the Southern Cone)—was superimposed on failed populist economic policies (see Sjaastad 1983 and Edwards 1985). In all three, economic liberalization was taken as an alternative economic philosophy, and this generated expectations that economic liberalization would not only improve microefficiency but also solve macrodifficulties, and quickly. This misunderstanding was probably the reason for the ready acceptance of liberal economic policies by authoritarian military regimes that had traditionally subscribed to populist ideology.

Nothing in the theory, however, indicates that liberalizing financial and trade regimes by themselves will stabilize an economy, reduce unemployment, or redress current account problems. The 1970s experience of the Southern Cone was bitter, but it cannot be used simply to dismiss liberalization. It does, however, provide the basis for a critique that I make in a later section.

The rapid pace of financial deregulation in advanced countries undoubtedly helped sustain the momentum for financial liberalization in developing countries. Although not without negative effects, discussed later, the process of financial innovation and deregulation in the United States, United Kingdom, Japan and other developed countries appears to have strengthened the position of, and given more confidence to, the supporters of financial liberalization in developing countries.

THE ROLE OF FINANCIAL INTERMEDIARIES

The observed importance of financial variables and the phenomenon of financial deregulation in both developed and developing countries beginning in the late 1970s has meant an upsurge in the attention given the role of financial factors in explaining real output growth and fluctuation. This has spawned a vast and often highly technical literature, which is excellently surveyed by Gertler (1988).

From the early 1980s on, most of the studies on the interaction between finance and real economic variables are particularly concerned with informational asymmetries as determinants of the behavior of financial markets and institutions. This application of information theory shows that—in a setting that specifies the behavior of economic agents, informational imperfections and environment and initial endowment—financial contracts and institutions are endogenously and simultaneously determined together with real variables. It shows that the spending decisions of individual consumers and firms are influenced by financial variables such as rationed credit, balance sheet positions and cash flows.

The theory also implies information asymmetries reduce the level of financial market activity and increase the market's sensitivity to exogenous disturbances, thereby making the economy susceptible to financial crises. The greater the degree of moral hazard and adverse selection problems, the greater the reduction in intermediation activity, and hence the lower the level of real investment and output.

Financial intermediaries are regarded as optimal institutional responses to financial market inefficiencies that result from asymmetric information between lenders and borrowers. In seeking to overcome these imperfections, institutions perform two closely related activities: They process information and they assess risk. There are scale economies to information gathering and processing. More precisely, acting on behalf of many depositors (ultimate lenders), only the intermediary needs to gather and assess a piece of information.

Risk processing relates to qualitative asset transformation. An intermediary is able to transform, at a low transaction cost, large denomination assets, such as loans and investments, into smaller and more liquid ones, such as bank deposits. Because the intermediary holds a large and diversified asset portfolio, it can reduce the overall risk involved in lending. When transforming assets, however, the intermediary's balance sheet becomes "mismatched"—the offset for long-term assets (loans and investments made) are short-term liabilities (deposits received). This poses risks to the intermediary beyond the credit risk of borrower default. Foremost among these are liquidity risk (deposits can be withdrawn faster than loans can be called) and interest rate risk (at least in an unregulated environment). Interest rate "risk" can also be an opportunity—as demonstrated in the early 1990s as banks worldwide cut the rates they paid for deposits much more quickly than they cut loan rates, thereby substantially boosting their margins.

This assessment of financial intermediaries as overcoming frictions from indivisibilities in financial assets and as exploiting of scale economies in transaction technologies that could otherwise limit the degree of risk sharing and diversification go back to Gurley and Shaw (GS).

In seeking further understanding of the role of banks and other financial intermediaries, Jensen and Meckling (1976) and Diamond (1984) developed the view that they served as "delegated monitors." In a world of imperfect information, banks are able to minimize agency problems as they reduce the moral hazard related to asymmetric information in the relation between borrowers and lenders.

Financial intermediaries screen and monitor borrowers more efficiently (less expensively) than individual lenders do.

In several advanced countries, however, where there has been substantial financial deregulation, such as the United States, financial intermediaries try to match the maturities of their assets and liabilities, including securitizing their loans and insulating themselves from interest rate risk by floating rates paid and charged in ways that lock in spreads. All this shifts risks to the ultimate lenders and represents an abandonment of any delegated monitor role the intermediaries may have played (see Hellwig 1990).

In contemplating the delegated monitor hypothesis, the intermediaries may use the information they collect to influence or control the activities of their borrowing firms. Indeed, Mayer (1990) suggests that they even went beyond monitoring to actual control. He argues that this control approach provides a basis for understanding a variety of financing patterns observed in eight advanced countries, including the dominant role of retained earnings in corporate finance and the predominance of banks as a source of external finance.

Another approach, built on information theory and Mayer's (1988) observations on the role of banks in Japan and Germany, regards financial intermediation as a device for establishing a long-term relationship between borrowers and lenders (Hellwig 1990). Simple observation and "common sense" are reasons to believe that such long-term relationships are valuable to both parties and to society, but in a competitive environment they may not develop because of the time inconsistency problem. That is, although the long-term relationship may be initially regarded as desirable, after it is established, each party has an incentive to breach. Because both parties recognize this temptation, they may never establish a long-term relationship at all. Mayer and Hellwig both emphasize the difficulty of writing a complete and binding agreement covering all future actions and outcomes over a long period of time.

Financial intermediaries can mitigate the time inconsistency problem because they have more information about their clients than outside financiers. In other words, exclusive financing of a firm by one financier can reduce possible conflicts among financiers. According to this reasoning, competition in financial markets can undermine the ability of a firm to commit itself to a bank, and a bank to a firm (Mayer 1988). In Mayer's framework, when capital is available from many sources, exclusive financing is possible and efficient through intermediation. The Japanese main bank system represents a successful effort in overcoming these problems through a particularly intensive form of relationship banking.

These ideas have a number of implications for an optimal financial policy regime. One is that the more pronounced the information asymmetries, the more preferable banking arrangements are to direct securities markets. In developing economies, where informational problems are severe because accounting and auditing systems are typically less reliable, the role of banks is thus more important than in advanced economies. In the course of development, institutions specializing in gathering and disseminating information appear, as do regulatory agencies that can enforce greater disclosure by firms. This makes it possible to develop bond and stock markets. As larger firms turn to direct financing, banks and other intermediaries shift their loan-customer base to medium and small firms. In practice, however, banks have remained the dominant source of external finance, even in advanced countries.

Related to this is the implication that intermediaries are a more efficient arrangement for supplying long-term finance to industry than open securities markets. In fact, intermediaries could lengthen the investment horizon of firms as the intermediary monitors the activities of its borrowers. Banks can also enter repeated relationships with borrowers in order to mitigate informational distortions. This, in turn, can facilitate provision of long-term (or at least ongoing) credit. Coming at this from the other direction, Mayer (1988) argues that competition in financial markets can have time inconsistency costs that result in a decline in long-term financing. Yanelle (1989) feels scale economies and Bertrand oligopolistic competition imply unfettered competition in financial intermediation is not likely to be realized and that deregulated banking may not lead to an efficient allocation of resources.

Having reached a consensus that finance matters in some way—at least in the sense that financial intermediaries have a positive role to play in real economic activity—we are still a long way from understanding just how this comes about, both at the theoretical level and in our attempts to understand what has happened historically in ways that are useful to policymakers and others involved in financial markets. I return to this in my critique of liberalization.

THE CASE FOR GOVERNMENT INTERVENTION
IN FINANCIAL MARKETS

The financial system has historically been subject to substantial public regulation in all countries. Entry into financial industries requires government charters. The capitalization, ownership, types of assets and liabilities, deposits and lending rates, and other activities of financial intermediaries are governed by regulations and sometimes by statutes. A natural and important question arises as to what characteristics and roles of the financial markets and institutions make them so different from other sectors that they are the object of public regulation.

One of the major reasons rests on the argument that the payments system, in particular, and public confidence in financial institutions and instruments, in general, bear the qualities of public goods. At one time, even Friedman (1959, p. 8) observed that the market itself cannot provide the stable monetary framework that is a prerequisite for the effective operation of a private market economy and "hence the function of providing one is an essential government function on par with the provision of a stable legal framework." More recently, in a study with Schwartz, Friedman (1986) is no longer so positive on public regulation of financial institutions, although he believes the forces preventing free banking will continue to prevent it.

The conventional wisdom has been that because unfettered competition among intermediaries is likely to increase the probability of bank failures and hence the

Concepts and Issues

15

risks of default and breakdown of the payments system, banks should be subject to at least prudential regulation. Financial industries, and fractionally reserved banking in particular, are viewed as inherently unstable and therefore subject to breakdown. In addition, information asymmetries among participants may also lead to market failures.

In a banking industry characterized by fractional reserves, liquidity creation through the transformation of illiquid assets into liquid liabilities gives rise to the possibility of multiple equilibria, one of which is a bank run (Diamond and Dybvig 1983). Even if a bank is solvent, if depositor confidence is broken, all of them—including those who would prefer to leave their funds in place if not for the concern with bank failure—will withdraw their money immediately, thereby precipitating a liquidity crisis. Assets liquidated under such circumstances typically sell at a discount from the nondistressed price. News of withdrawals may trigger runs on other banks and even, in the extreme, can bring down the entire system. Because of this risk of withdrawal if there are no well-functioning secondary markets for bank assets, there may be a case for government intervention (Fama 1985 and Bhattachary and Gale 1987).

Governments and their central banks routinely act as lenders of last resort and have established deposit insurance schemes. These may encourage banks to assume more risk than they would if they were held more accountable for their actions. In this way, the moral hazard problem associated with the government guarantees provides a justification for public regulation.

Natural barriers to entry to banking are small, and the technology of intermediation requires little specific physical and financial capital. But should anyone be able to set up a bank anytime they choose? JP Morgan noted that banking is built on trust. There must be confidence in the integrity of both financial institutions and instruments including the confidence that contracts will be honored. There is strong logic for government having some control over who opens financial institutions and how they operate them.

The case for some sort of government regulation is solid. The question is the degree and nature. The gamut runs from basic prudential regulation plus a legal system concerned with the sanctity of contracts, to closely controlled, heavily repressed systems that are tools of government policy, and to complete state control in the case of socialist economies.

In Chapter 4, in discussing Korea, I make a case for controls and repression under certain circumstances in the early development. Still, history clearly shows that at some point the costs of controls exceed any benefits, and so the financial system must move on. Indeed, change came in Japan, Korea, and Taiwan only when the monetary authorities decided the costs of maintaining the status quo were too great. As each country achieved substantial balance of payments surpluses and the United States put pressure on them to open their financial markets, the forces for change were nonetheless primarily domestic—the results of the growthing size and complexity of the real economy and thus the expanding of demand for more and additional services. The continued accommodation of these new needs transformed the system and made deregulation and liberalization the logical next step.

Although one can contend that an allocatively neutral financial system is neither desirable nor optimal for a developing country, the heavy emphasis on the use of finance as the instrument a government uses in directing economic development efforts reduces the scope and effectiveness of monetary policy. This is because it forces banks and other intermediaries to hold extremely illiquid asset portfolios dominated by policy (government-directed) loans.

The use of finance as a handmaiden to growth also can compromise—conflict with—prudential regulation of financial institutions. Perhaps the need for such regulation is not well understood in developing countries. But they may in fact have more of a problem with banks failing to keep honest books, being involved in self-dealing, concentrating their lending to a limited number of borrowers, and committing other improprieties in part because they are regulated by development planners, not by independent and well-trained bank examiners. In addition, the opportunities for rent-seeking activities are greater in a repressed financial system.

MONETARY REFORM

McKinnon and Shaw were the two most influential economists in advancing the cause of financial liberalization in the early 1970s. They provided a theoretical basis for, as well as empirical evidence of, the benefits of a liberal financial regime in developing countries. Combining a number of country experiences, including those of Brazil, Korea, and Taiwan, McKinnon (1973) develops a framework in which a monetary reform—an exogenous increase in bank deposit and lending interest rates to close to an equilibrium level—is shown to be conducive to a high rate of capital accumulation and economic growth through financial deepening (an increase in the ratio of financial assets to GNP). Shaw (1973) is equally convinced of the positive effects of financial liberalization, although he does not explicitly define what he means by the term. According to him, financial liberalization can raise the level of private domestic savings relative to income, open the way to superior allocation of resources by widening and diversifying the financial markets in which investment opportunities compete for savings, and even promote equalization of the distribution of income (pp. 9–12).

In most developing countries the insignificance of institutionalized markets for stocks and bonds implies that the financial instruments available for savings are limited to currency plus demand, time, and savings deposits—the sum of which is often defined as "broad money," or M2. McKinnon contends that an increase in the nominal (and real) interest rate on time and savings deposits induces increased savings because it means a higher rate of return on savings. After an interest rate reform, more investment resources will be allocated through the banking system than before. This is because wealth owners have shifted to M2 (a flow effect) from inventories, precious metals, foreign currencies and lending in informal credit markets into bank savings deposits, which have been made more attractive by the interest rate increase (a stock adjustment effect).

Assuming banks have scale economies and experience in collecting and processing information, they will be more efficient in seeking out good borrowers with investment projects yielding high real returns. Because investment opportunities with high yields abound in developing countries, the high real cost of financing stimulates investment through a greater availability of credit. An interest rate reform thus has the effect of enhancing growth by both increasing the savings ratio and reducing the capital-output ratio (Long 1983).

In theory, the effect of an exogenous increase in real interest rates on savings can be either positive or negative. McKinnon (1973, ch. 6) argues that, during the early stages of development, money (M2) and physical assets are likely to be complements rather than substitutes in savers' asset portfolios. If this is true, then an increase in the real interest rate on time and savings deposits will lead to an increase in the real demand for M2 and a corresponding increase in real savings. Fry (1978, 1980, 1988) shows empirically that for a sample of developing countries, savings is positively affected by real interest rates for deposits, as is demand for real M2. Other studies find the impact of real interest rates on savings to be negligible, although all are subject to various theoretical and estimation problems (Mikesell and Zinser 1972, Giovannini 1985).

Using Korea as an example, McKinnon (1973, pp. 105–11) cites its 1964–66 monetary reform, in which real deposit and lending rates were raised in a remarkable policy shift. In the wake of the reform there were sharply increased savings as well as buoyancy in investment and output. But Cole and Park (1983, pp 204–11) believe that the effect of the reform was ambiguous because it was only one of many changes that contributed to an upward shift in the savings function.

While the sensitivity of savings to interest rates remains an unresolved empirical question, others have emphasized the efficiency gains from a high interest rate policy (Patrick 1966, Galbis 1977). Improvements in the process of financial intermediation, such as those brought about by higher real interest rates, can result in a high rate of economic growth because they help shift resources from low-yielding investments to higher-yielding ones. The efficiency gain is claimed to be sizable in developing countries where disparities in the rates of return to capital are wide, and indivisibilities of physical assets are substantial.

The validity of this argument rests, of course, on the assumption that banks actually lend on the basis of an objective evaluation of an investment's expected return. In particular, it requires that they have some competence in gathering and analyzing information on alternative investment projects. As McKinnon himself points out (1982, p. 383), banks that are tightly controlled by the government may have neither incentive nor expertise in screening good borrowers who can pay high real interest rates on their loans. Moreover, in the absence of asset portfolio regulation, banks can use the greater availability of their loanable funds to finance consumption rather than investment, a possible consequence of decontrol that concerned Patrick (1966).

In countries where informal credit markets are extensive and efficient, high interest rates on bank deposits can lead to an overall credit contraction. This is because funds are shifted from the informal markets, which have no lending restrictions, to the organized banking sector, where reserve requirements and credit ceilings are strictly enforced (Taylor 1983, p. 197). However, the central bank can readily offset any such contractionary effects.

Improvements in efficiency hinges critically on who controls the banking system. In many developing countries, financial markets are dominated by a few oligopolistic commercial banks, which often are connected with large industrial groups through ownership or management. The banks often channel a large share of their resources to affiliated firms (Long 1983). Given these market distortions, a high interest rate policy may not result in any improvement in credit allocation.

A monetary reform can invite greater direct government involvement in credit allocation, as it did in Korea, unless it is accompanied by a relaxation of other regulations governing bank asset management. Insofar as the government has a strong inclination to intervene in resource allocation, increasing the share of credit available to the banking system may only persuade policymakers of a need to tighten their grip on the banking industry. The effects of reform on the autonomy of the financial system therefore can be more negative than positive.

FINANCIAL LIBERALIZATION

Beginning in the 1970s and 1980s a number of OECD countries took steps to deregulate or liberalize their financial markets and institutions by abolishing credit and interest rate ceilings, capital movement controls, and other relations governing lending and borrowing activities. It was widely expected that deregulation would reduce the operating costs of financial intermediaries and hence the costs of their loans and other services. This, together with a reduction in credit rationing, would then improve the allocative efficiency of the financial system. Deregulation would also provide greater flexibility for smoothing shocks to incomes and expenditures through the use of credit and financial markets and also would make the economy more resilient to short-run fluctuations of financial asset prices.

An OECD study in 1990 asserts that although these benefits have been substantial, there also have been a number of undesirable macroeconomic outcomes associated with deregulation. These are increased financial fragility, greater asset price volatility, inflation and balance of payment difficulties stemming from the slower speed with which goods markets adjust relative to financial markets, and decreased effectiveness of monetary policy.

The study finds that with reduced liquidity constraints, private consumption has become less sensitive to changes in transitory income in the United States, Canada, and Japan, whereas in other countries the sensitivity remains high. There was an inverse correlation between household borrowing and saving ratios among most OECD countries in the early to mid-1980s. There is no longer any evidence in most OECD countries of a stable long-run relationship between nominal income and money, whether money is narrowly or broadly defined.

The liberalization of financial markets can, as noted earlier, curtail the long-term loan supply and hence may favor short-term investment. The greater volatility of financial prices may contribute to this outcome although there is no theory explaining the effects of volatile financial prices on business investment. The authors of the OECD study felt the effects of stock market volatility on industrial production were significant in the 1970s for the United States, Japan, and the United Kingdom. Even for these countries, the significance disappeared in the 1980s.

The Southern Cone Experience

Few developing countries have ever attempted to develop laissez-faire finance. Hong Kong and Singapore are exceptions, and they never engaged in financial repression. The closest any others have come was in the mid 1970s when three Latin American countries—Argentina, Chile, and Uruguay (the Southern Cone)—embarked on a course of extensive and radical economic and financial liberalization. The important element was a wide-ranging deregulation in which state-owned financial intermediaries were privatized; interest rates were freed to be determined in financial markets; control over bank asset management was lifted; and foreign banks were allowed to operate in domestic financial markets.

Contrary to expectations, financial liberalization in the Southern Cone ended in chaotic financial markets, reimposition of banking regulations, and renationalization of the banks. The radicalness and traumatic results of the region's experience have generated a great deal of research interest and a voluminous literature on just what went wrong.

My reading suggests the following possible adverse consequences of financial liberalization:

- Insofar as fiscal deficits are financed by money creation and are growing, financial liberalization serves to accelerate inflation, and this combined with an overvalued exchange rate, promotes capital flight.
- Liberalization does not help mobilize domestic savings, although deregulation does raise real interest rates to a positive level and results in an increased diversity of financial instruments being made available to savers.
- Liberalization does not necessarily enhance competition in the financial sector. Instead, it can lead to domination of the financial system by big-business groups that have market-controlling powers in other sectors of the economy.
- Distortion in credit allocation because of any inflation and any self-dealing by those controlling banks reduces any efficiency gains from deregulation, and can actually increase inefficiency.
- Deregulation shortens the economic horizons of savers and investors so much that banks are forced to match their assets and liabilities, thereby drying up long-term finance.
- Financial liberalization generates incentives for destabilizing and imprudent behavior by banking institutions. More specifically, it invites moral hazard problems. In developing countries, the consequences of this can be magnified because informational asymmetries, and hence adverse selection problems, are likely to be more serious than they would be in economies with a stable financial system. In addition, in a deregulated, liberalized environment,

banks are prone to speculate or lend excessively in areas such as real estate, stocks and commodities.

What lessons can be drawn from the Southern Cone experience? Clearly, deregulation can generate forces that undermine the stability and safety of the financial system in countries where public confidence in financial institutions and instruments is weak, and this can be compounded in countries where deposit insurance systems are instituted to overcome the confidence problem.

A high degree of business concentration interferes with financial liberalization, at least in small and medium-size developing countries. This is particularly true when the concentration is in groups of affiliated companies operating in many sectors of the economy, as is the situation in many developing countries. Governments seeking to take advantage of minimum efficient firm size, indivisibilities in production processes, increasing returns to scale and the like often encourage the emergence of large firms. Such firms have preferential access to credit from the banking system, and deregulation alone cannot end that. This is especially if a business group controls a bank (which does not require actual ownership, just friendly relations with management). Moreover, relaxation of barriers to entry is not an answer to the problem of concentration of bank and industrial-group control. Business groups can control the new banks and thereby compound the problem more than resolving it.

REALITIES, PROBLEMS, AND ISSUES OF FINANCE

What have we learned from the developments in financial theory and the experience of financial development and liberalization in various countries, including particularly the Southern Cone and the three of this book? First, it seems completely unregulated, laissez-faire finance is neither feasible nor desirable. Beyond that, Japan, Korea, and Taiwan show that financial repression and closedness notwithstanding, it was possible to achieve financial expansion as measured by various ratios of financial assets to GNP or to wealth, as well as remarkably high rates of GNP growth and industrial development. This was particularly true in regard to Taiwan and Korea.

Reality raises a number of questions about this theory, some of which are taken up in the country chapters—particularly Chapter 4 on Korea—and others that are simply beyond the scope of this book. Consider the following questions: Has the high degree of financial control in Korea and Taiwan been dictated by and effective in mitigating the adverse consequences of financial market failure in the two countries? Can we infer from their experience that finance does not matter in promoting economic development, or at least does not matter as much as is claimed, or matters only in some circumstances but not others? Does the mounting evidence on financial instability and institutional failures associated with financial deregulation in developed and developing countries justify restrictive financial policies?

Is there an alternative to laissez-faire finance? What is needed is prudent regulation by the government in order to maintain a balance between the competitive efficiency and the safety of the banking system. Policymakers in developing countries are prone to adopt activist development policies, so they can easily succumb to the temptation of crossing the line between prudent regulation and intervention in credit allocation. In so doing, the government becomes a monopoly in the main capital market available, namely, the bank credit market.

The public good nature of the financial system may explain why monetary reform—that is, a partial liberalization—has been successful in mobilizing savings and in allocating them to efficient uses, whereas full-scale liberalization has not. Financial deregulation may succeed initially in inducing savers to save more and to do so using financial assets. But at some point it this process is bound to threaten the safety of the system, particularly the payments system. Once public confidence in the system has eroded and moral hazards begin to spread, financial liberalization efforts will in all likelihood come to an end. Especially when liberalization efforts are made in an economically difficult situation, the moral hazards triggered by the accumulation of nonperforming loans virtually ensure disaster.

The application of information theory to finance has revolutionized the theoretical approach to the role of financial markets, financial institutions, and corporate finance. According to this approach, financial intermediaries evolve to mitigate the information asymmetries of open securities markets and direct investment by savers. Our studies suggest that until countries are quite highly developed, the theoretical choice between banking markets and securities markets is not really relevant.

The real question is the role of the financial system, including its panoply of banks and nonbank financial intermediaries, in allocating funds. This is a complex story in each country, with considerable differences in the degree of government intervention, including its nature, specificity, enforcement mechanism, and effects. Moreover, in each of these countries informal markets historically played an important part, although they were no longer relevant in Japan by the early 1950s. Thus, for example, Shea argues in Chapter 6 that informal markets improved resource allocation in Taiwan.

Although there seems to be a certain inevitability to financial deregulation and liberalization in the course of financial development, it is important to remember that each of these is different. It is especially important to keep in mind that deregulation and the promotion of competitive markets (liberalization) are distinct. In particular, even though markets may become fully competitive, it is doubtful any financial system will ever be fully deregulated. Because of its nature as a public good, such systems will continue to be subject to prudential supervision.

I have alluded to the theoretical possibility of the difficulty of ensuring unfettered competition in financial markets. Moreover, what we know so far about the workings of finance does not fully account for the repressive nature of finance in these three countries. It is difficult to come up with a credible rationale for the government's intervention for such a long time. Nor do the existing theories adequately explain why the system remained relatively closed in Japan until the early 1980s and until far more recently in Taiwan and Korea.

Financial Deepening in Perspective

McKinnon (1991, p. 30) cites a number of empirical studies that he feels demonstrate achieving financial liberalization has a real payoff in terms of rapid financial and real output growth. However, as far as Japan, Korea, and Taiwan are concerned, there is no clear evidence suggesting the causality runs from financial liberalization to financial deepening and hence to higher output growth.

It is true that during the 1980s, when Korea and Taiwan were deregulating, the stocks of M3 and total financial assets grew faster than nominal GNP, resulting in a large increase in M3/GNP and the financial intermediation ratio (FIR) in both countries. But neither ratio appears to be an adequate measure of financial deepening or of the effect of substitution between financial and real assets, especially in the latter half of the decade. The presence of a strong substitution effect favoring the holding of financial assets associated with the financial liberalization would, other things being equal, have moderated the increase in the nominal value of real assets. In both countries, holdings of land, individual housing, and commercial buildings accounted for a major portion of total wealth.

As shown in Table 1.2, in the second half of the 1980s in all three countries the nominal values of these real assets far outstripped increases in nominal supplies of M2 and of total financial assets. Measured by equity prices, the nominal value of capital goods such as plant and equipment rose faster than the nominal supply of M2 and of total financial assets in the last half of the 1980s and, in Japan, in the decade's first half as well. Overall, during the 1980s the proportion of total financial assets in total wealth, including capital goods and real property, does not appear to have increased as much as M2/GNP or FIR, and it actually decreased during the 1986–90 speculative asset booms in all three countries.

Table 1.2. *Indexes of Land Prices, Stock Prices, Financial Assets, and M2 in Japan, Korea, and Taiwan (1985 = 100)*

Japan Year	All urban land	Largest cities	Six stock index[a]	Financial assets	M2 + CDs
1980	77.3	72.9	54.7	63.2	66.4
1981	84.1	79.1	59.8	69.9	73.7
1982	90.0	84.4	58.9	76.0	79.5
1983	94.3	88.5	70.1	83.4	85.3
1984	97.3	93.1	84.2	92.4	92.0
1985	100.0	100.0	100.0	100.0	100.0
1986	102.9	114.2	130.5	107.6	109.2
1987	108.4	143.8	184.6	120.4	120.9
1988	119.3	184.0	215.1	131.3	133.3
1989	128.3	228.9	271.1	142.2	149.2
1990	146.4	297.7	308.3	154.0	160.3

Table 1.2.   (Cont'd)

Korea Year	All city land	Seoul land	Stock prices	Financial assets	M2
1980	59.8	42.7	78.3	36.4	43.9
1981	64.0	44.0	90.9	47.5	54.9
1982	68.1	48.6	87.8	60.7	69.7
1983	79.1	71.7	91.9	72.2	80.3
1984	89.8	90.7	95.0	84.8	86.5
1985	100.0	100.0	100.0	100.0	100.0
1986	104.1	104.6	164.0	113.9	118.4
1987	114.1	108.8	300.6	133.3	141.0
1988	143.8	132.9	499.0	163.2	171.3
1989	192.5	180.5	661.3	199.1	205.3
1990	232.9	231.4	537.7	245.7	240.5

Taiwan Year	All city land	Nominal housing (Taipei)	Stock prices	Financial assets	M2
1980	65.9	109.2	73.3	49.8	36.2
1981	88.7	118.3	73.6	57.9	43.0
1982	94.5	109.7	64.0	66.9	53.5
1983	98.2	103.2	87.7	76.0	67.5
1984	99.6	105.2	117.0	87.5	81.1
1985	100.0	100.0	100.0	100.0	100.0
1986	103.9	101.2	126.7	116.2	125.3
1987	109.3	138.4	286.4	143.0	158.6
1988	124.0	272.0	697.7	170.5	186.9
1989	174.0	484.9	1155.6	201.3	215.4
1990	345.8	555.4	908.7	222.5	236.6

Note: Each country has a somewhat different definition of M2: Japanese data are for M2+CDs, Japanese land data are for Mar. 31 of year shown and are the average of three categories—commercial, residential, and industrial—as compiled by the Japan Real Estate Institute.

a. Nikkei Index of 225 Tokyo Stock Exchange issues.

Source: Japan: BOJ *Economic Statistics Annual* 1990, p. 199 Table 102 (stock prices); p. 321, Table 170 (1) (land prices); p. 1 (M2+CDs). Korea: BOK *Economic Statistics Yearbook* 1991, p. 15, Table 4 (1) (M2); BOK *National Accounts* 1990. Taiwan: All City Land 1980–86 is from Lin 1989 and 1987–90 is from Japan Institute for Real Estate Research 1991; Wu 1989 (nominal housing, Taipei); MOF, *Yearbook of Financial Statistics* 1990, p. 437, Table 119 (M2); CBC, *Financial Statistics Monthly*, various issues.

In regard to the means by which financial growth exerts a positive effect on output growth, McKinnon (1973, 1991) and others (for example, World Bank 1989), emphasize the savings incentives and investment efficiency effect generated by financial deepening. However, my review of the evidence shows no indication that financial deepening measured by M3/GNP or FIR has increased private savings as a proportion of GNP or improved the allocative efficiency of the economies of Taiwan and Korea (see Park 1992).

Concluding Thoughts

Japan started earlier and has gone farther along the road of deregulation and liberalization than Taiwan and Korea. However, in all three countries, in certain important respects the markets have remained fettered. After the speculative bubbles burst in each country, concern about the very stability of the systems has been thrust to the fore to an extent that has not been seen since the late 1940s and early 1950s, and this will color events throughout the 1990s. However, there is a recognition that the bubbles may well have been exacerbated by adjustments brought on by the transitions from the repressive systems. Thus, while there has been some talk that the monetary authorities in these countries are actually not displeased about what could be seen as a mandate for the continuation of their guidance, it seems highly unlikely the process of liberalization and deregulation will be reversed.

An interesting question is whether Korea and Taiwan will telescope the evolution of their financial systems as they did the development of their real economies. In some senses they have and will—the very act of integrating into international markets means moving toward further deregulation and liberalization in a number of areas. Financial development is something else. Financial systems cannot be readily ranked along some continuum of betterness. Until such theoretical judgments are possible, the relevant question is, How can the system work better in the context of the real economy? In a very conscious way, this is the issue that has occupied the monetary authorities and other players in the financial systems of these countries, and it will continue to do so.

REFERENCES

(The word "processed" describes informally reproduced works that may not be commonly available through libraries.)

Bhattachary, S. and D. Gale. 1987. "Preference Shocks, Liquidity and Central Bank Policy." In W. A. Barnett and K. Singleton, eds., *New Approaches in Monetary Economics*. Cambridge: Cambridge University Press.

Cameron, Rondo. 1972. *Banking and Economic Development*. New York: Oxford University Press.

———. with the collaboration of Olga Crisp, Hugh T. Patrick and Richard Tilly. 1967. *Banking in the Early Stages of Industrialization*. New York: Oxford University Press.

Cole, David C. and Yung Chul Park. 1983. *Financial Development in the Republic of Korea 1945–1978*. Studies in the Modernization of the Republic of Korea, 1945–1975. Cambridge, MA: Harvard University, Council on East Asian Studies.

Diamond, David W. 1984. "Financial Intermediation and Delegated Monitoring." *Review of Economic Studies* 51:393–414, July.

Diamond, D. W. and D. H. Dybvig. 1983. "Bank Runs, Deposit Insurance, and Liquidity." *Journal of Political Economy*, June, pp. 401–19.

Edwards, Sebastian. 1985. "Stabilization with Liberalization: An Evaluation of Ten Years of Chile's Experiment with Free Market Policies, 1973–83." *Economic Development and Cultural Change*, January.

Fama, E. 1985. "What's Different about Banks?" *Journal of Monetary Economics*, January.

Friedman, Milton. 1959. *A Program for Monetary Stability*. Bronx, NY: Fordham University Press.

———, and A. J. Schwartz. 1986. "Has Government Any Policy in Money." *Journal of Monetary Economics*, January, pp. 37–62.

Fry, Maxwell J. 1978. "Money and Capital or Financial Deepening in Economic Development." *Journal of Money, Credit and Banking*, November.

———. 1980. "Saving, Investment, Growth and the Cost of Financial Repression." *World Development*, August.

———. 1988. *Money, Interest and Banking in Economic Development*. Baltimore: Johns Hopkins University Press.

Galbis, V. 1977. "Financial Intermediation and Economic Growth in Less Developed Countries: A Theoretical Approach." *Journal of Development Studies*, January.

Gerschenkron, Alexander. 1962. *Economic Backwardness in Historical Perspective*. Cambridge, MA: Harvard Univeristy Press.

Gertler, M. 1988. "Financial Structure and Aggregate Economic Activity." *Journal of Money, Credit and Banking*, August. Also National Bureau of Economic Research, Working Paper 2559.

Giovannini, A. 1985. "Interest Elasticity of Savings in Developing Countries: The Existing Evidence." *World Development* 11 (7).

Goldsmith, Raymond W. 1969. *Financial Structure*. New Haven, CT: Yale University Press..

Gurley, J. G., and E. S. Shaw. 1955. "Financial Aspects of Economic Development." *American Economic Review* 45 p 515–38.

Hellwig, Martin F. 1990. "Banking, Financial Intermediation and Corporate Finance." In A. Giovannini and Colin Mayer, eds., *Financial Integration*. Cambridge, MA: Cambridge University Press.

Japan Institute of Real Estate Research. 1991. *Survey of Land Prices in Foreign Countries*. Tokyo: Japan Institute of Real Estate Research.

Jensen, M. C., and W. H. Meckling. 1976. "Theory of the Firm: Managerial Behavior, Agency Cost and Ownership Structure." *Journal of Financial Economics* 3.

Lin, Yuan-Hsin. 1989. "On Methods of Compiling Price Indexes for Real Estate." *Journal of National Chengchi University*. In Chinese.

Long, M. 1983. "Review of Financial Sector Work in the World Bank." Processed. World Bank.

Mayer, Colin. 1988. "New Issues in Corporate Finance." *European Economic Review* 32: 1167–89.

———. 1990. "Financial Systems, Corporate Finance, and Economic Development." In R. Glen Hubbar, ed., *Asymmetric Information, Corporate Finance, and Investment*. Chicago: University of Chicago Press.

McKinnon, Ronald I. 1973. *Money and Capital in Economic Development*. Washington, DC: Brookings Institution.

———. 1982 Autumn. "The Order of Economic Liberalization: Lessons from Chile and Argentina." In *Economic Policy in a World of Change*. Carnegie–Rochester Conference Series on Public Policy.

———. 1991. *The Order of Economic Liberalization: Financial Control in the Transition to a Market Economy*. Baltimore: Johns Hopkins University Press.

Mikesell, R. E., and J. E. Zinser. 1972. "The Nature of the Savings Function in Developing Countries." *Journal of Economic Literature*, December.

Modigliani, Franco and M. Miller. 1958. "The Cost of Capital, Corporate Finance, and the Theory of Investment." *American Economic Review* v, June.

OECD (Organisation for Economic Co-operation and Development). 1990. *Macroeconomic Consequences of Financial Liberalization*. Paris:OECD.

Park, Yung Chul. 1992. "The Role of Finance in Economic Development in South Korea and Taiwan." In A. Giovannini, ed., *Finances and Development: Issues and Experiences*. London: Center for Economic Policy Research (CEPR).

Patrick, Hugh. 1966. "Financial Development and Economic Growth in Underdeveloped Countries." *Economic Development and Cultural Change*, January.

———, and Henry Rosovsky, eds. 1976. *Asia's New Giant: How the Japanese Economy Works*. Washington, DC: Brookings Institution.

Ranis, Gustav, ed. 1992. *Taiwan: From Developing to Mature Economy*. Boulder, CO: Westview Press.

Shaw, Edward S. 1973. *Financial Deepening in Economic Development*. New York: Oxford University Press.

Sjaastad, L. A. 1983. "Failure of Economic Liberalization in the Cone of Latin America." *World Trade*, March.

Song, Byung-Nak. 1990. *The Rise of the Korean Economy*. New York: Oxford University Press.

Taylor, L. 1983. *Structuralist Macroeconomics*. New York: Basic Books.

Wade, Robert. 1990. *Governing the Market: Economic Theory and the Role of the Government in East Asian Industrialization.* Princeton, NJ: Princeton University Press.

World Bank. 1989. *World Development Report 1989.* New York: Oxford University Press.

———. 1992. *World Development Report 1992.* New York: Oxford University Press.

Wu, De-Hsien. 1989. "The Study of Business Cycles in the Construction Industry and Their Relation to Housing Supply." Ph.D. dissertation, National Chengchi University, Taipei. In Chinese.

Yamamura, Kozo and Yasukichi Yasuba, eds. 1987. *The Political Economy of Japan.* Vol. 1: *The Domestic Transformation.* Stanford, CA: Stanford University Press.

Yanelle, M. O. 1989. "The Strategic Analysis of Intermediation." *European Economic Review* 33.

2

Japan: Development and Structural Change of the Financial System

JURO TERANISHI

In the first three decades after World War II Japan can be regarded as a developing economy that, starting as a middle-income economy with chronic balance of payment pressures and Lewisian surplus labor, accomplished a successful transformation into a highly industrialized economy. This chapter examines the interaction between this development and the financial system.

A brief summary of Japan's macroeconomic performance between 1955 and 1990 forms the first section. The second section discusses the formation of the basic framework of the financial system of the high-growth period (1956–70) with special reference to the economic problems and financial conditions of the early 1950s. It also explores how and why the need to fill the gap between the demand and the supply of long-term funds, as well as for information, resulted in a highly regulated financial system based on indirect finance instead of a system of competitive money and capital markets.

Why the system had such seemingly paradoxical characteristics as competitive banking under regulation, high levels of intermediation with deposit rate regulation, rapid economic growth without reliance on foreign capital inflows, and effective monetary policy with an accommodating credit supply are explained in the third section.

The relationship between development and the financial system during the high-growth period is analyzed in the fourth section. The system seems to have contributed to rapid growth by helping realize dynamic scale economies through the supply of long-term funds and by successfully coping with unemployment through improving access to funds for declining industries and small and medium firms.

The fifth section deals with the two decades after the high-growth period—the 1970s and 1980s—which are characterized by expanding current account surpluses and more moderate levels of private sector investment, although the surge of private investment after 1987 is quite remarkable. During this period, the financial system underwent a gradual transformation from regulated to deregulated. Three causes of deregulation are examined: the issuance of large amounts of government bonds, increased sensitivity to interest rates by asset holders, and

internationalization. Although internationalization as a result of the globalization of world financial markets is important as a driving force of deregulation,
the first two factors—related to change in real economic activity—are nonetheless more fundamental, and internationalization itself is partly explained by
these real factors. The major causes of deregulation in Japan seem to lie in the
transformation of the real economy.

AN OVERVIEW OF THE MACROECONOMY

Around 1950 –51, immediately after Japan had come out of its war-related confusion, there was an active controversy over development strategy between
Marxian economists who insisted on promoting heavy and chemical industries
within the framework of a more or less socialistic planned economic system, and
neoclassical economists who espoused an outward-oriented policy based on
exporting light manufactures such as textiles within the framework of a market
economy. (The Marxists were led by Hiromi Arisawa, the neoclassicalists by
Ichiro Nakayama.)

The discouraging prospects for the growth of world trade due to the cold war
seemed to support the Marxists, while the democratic atmosphere prevailing in
society favored the neoclassists. In hindsight, the actual strategy was intermediate: in regard to trade, Japan eventually embarked on import substitution based
on an appreciated exchange rate and heavy protection of industries through
import quotas, but in regard to the economic regime, there is no doubt Japan has
chosen a market-based, competition-oriented framework.

Table 2.A1 summarizes the macroeconomic statistics over the 35 years under
study. The growth rate of real GNP was frequently in double digits during the
so-called rapid growth period of 1955 to 1970. Since the first oil shock, Japan's
growth has never been higher than the slowest rate of the rapid-growth period,
which was 5.9 percent. The slowdown after 1974 can be explained by termination of the shift of excess labor out of agriculture and the narrowing of the gap
between domestic and foreign technological levels (see Teranishi 1986a). Inflation was modest throughout the period except for 1973 and 1974. As a result, the
real rate of interest generally was positive.

In terms of components of aggregate demand, the very high share of gross capital formation is impressive. It rose to over 38 percent in 1970 and has been over
30 percent every year since 1967, except one. A rising trend since 1985 is worth
noting. By comparison, for all OECD countries, the average level during the
1960s and 1970s was around 20 percent (OECD 1984).

Adding the second and fourth columns of Table 2.A1 gives the share of gross
savings in real GNP. It was generally very high and rose until 1970 and also during the late 1980s. The savings rate of households also has been high, rising until
1974 and declining thereafter. The average figure for household savings for all
OECD countries also shows the same time pattern, but the level is 5 to 6 percentage points lower than for Japan: 9.0 percent in 1960, 11.5 percent in 1970,
and11.9 percent in 1980.

Exports have been a relatively modest part of total demand, less than 10 percent until 1973. There was a rising trend until 1984. The average figures for all OECD countries are much higher: 11.6 percent in 1960, 13.5 percent in 1970, and 20.2 percent in 1980. The current account was positive in nominal terms after 1968 except for the two years of oil shock, although in real terms the account was negative until 1981.

EMERGENCE OF THE FINANCIAL SYSTEM
DURING THE HIGH-GROWTH PERIOD

Japan's economy in the early 1950s can be viewed as a middle-income developing economy in two senses. First, there was underemployment in the traditional sector. Second, the balance of payment deficits was an effective constraint on growth.

Due to wartime devastation of cities, the work force in agriculture increased 26 percent during 1940–47, and most of these people were still in rural areas in the early 1950s. Thus agriculture provided 46 percent of total employment in 1951. This work force was underemployed in the Lewisian sense (Minami 1973), and the wage differential by firm size tended to increase.

The exchange rate of 360 yen to the dollar adopted in 1949 and maintained until 1971 was considerably overvalued, especially during the early postwar period. For example, in 1953 the ratio of the Japanese yen price to the U.S. dollar price of typical industrial products was five or more for energy, steel, and chemicals; almost five for nonferrous metals; and more than three for textiles. Consequently, the trade balance was in serious deficit through 1957, and the current account was in deficit in the years 1953–57 (except 1955) and 1961–64 despite severe quota and tariff restrictions on imports.

Japan's trade deficits before the Korean War were financed by foreign aid (which appears as a surplus in the transfer account), and those during 1952–57 were covered by special U.S. military procurement related to the Korean War and its aftermath (a surplus in the service account).

When the financial system was restructured during 1950–55, the new system was naturally expected at the least to alleviate these problems. The most important role assigned to the system was supplying sufficient long-term funds for industries to realize dynamic scale economies. Although endowed with a rich supply of experienced labor, including engineers and managers, Japan was backward in the level of industrial technology, partly owing to its isolation during and just after the war. Consequently, growth with borrowed technology was considered the most efficient way to enhance the international competitiveness of industries.

Introduction of advanced technology is effective only when sufficient time and resources are devoted to the learning process, so an ample supply of long-term funds is crucial to inducing entrepreneurs to pursue internal economies of scale. However, long-term fund markets were highly imperfect in the 1950s. Mainly because of inflation during and immediately after the war, the ratio of private financial assets to GNP had fallen to 1.07, the level of around 1910, and consequently, the term structure of bank deposits and bank loans had considerably shortened (see Table 2.1).

The financial system was also expected to alleviate underemployment by enhancing the availability of funds in low-productivity and traditional areas. In view of the huge number of small and medium firms—partly a legacy of wartime promotion of subcontracting (Hondai 1988)—efficient procurement of information regarding them was considered crucial to preventing inefficient credit rationing and adverse selection in financial markets.

Table 2.1. *Long-Term Deposits and Loans as a Percentage of Total Deposits and Loans at Zenkoku Banks and at City Banks*

Mar. 31 [a]	Loans[b]		Deposits[c]	
	Zenkoku	City	Zenkoku	City
1951	8.2	2.1	—	—
1956	14.0	5.1	—	54.9
1961	16.9	6.4	79.1	77.0
1966	20.3	10.0	82.4	79.3
1971	25.4	13.6	85.8	83.8
1976	38.2	29.3	84.9	82.4
1981	40.8	33.5	85.4	81.0
1984	39.1	32.1		
1985	39.9	34.6		
1986	39.0	32.7		
1987	41.6	37.4		
1988	44.7	41.9		
1989	48.0	47.5		
1990	52.7	52.9		

— Not available.

Note: Zenkoku banks are called "all banks" in English in the source.

a. Fiscal year-end. Fiscal 1950 ended Mar. 31, 1951, etc.

b. There is a lamentable asymmetry between loans and deposits in the source. Loans of exactly 1 year are in a 3 to 12 month category, so the data here are for loans over 1 year.

c. "Ordinary" time deposits of 1 year or more in source. Before Sep. 1970, 1 year was the maximum term. Before Mar. 1973 it was 18 months, at which point 2-year deposits were introduced. Excludes "maturity-designated" and "liberalized interest rate" time deposits, money market certificates, nonresident yen, and foreign currency deposits. Until 1982 the excluded categories were not significant. However, as discussed in the text, because of the introduction of new instruments, "ordinary" time deposits have become a smaller share of total time deposits—62% in Mar. 1985, but less than 12% in Mar. 1990. Unfortunately the source does not disaggregate the new instruments by term.

Source: Bank of Japan, *Economic Statistics Annual,* various issues. For example, data for 1982–90 are on p. 127 (deposits) and p. 129 (loans) of the 1990 edition.

Finally, the financial system itself had to be safe and stable. This was an indispensable requirement derived from the bitter memory of the seriously unstable banking system, plagued with chronic bank runs, in the prewar period. (See, for example, Teranishi 1990. There is little in English that covers prewar banking in Japan except in descriptive terms or as part of a discussion of its development.)

A Highly Regulated Financial System

Faced with playing these three roles, the financial system of the rapid growth period was gradually built during 1950 –55. Although the new system was established on the foundation of a wartime controlled system, inheriting such techniques of credit allocation as bond issuance committees and such structural characteristics as a two-tier banking system of city and local banks, I do not feel much emphasis should be put on the wartime legacy (see Teranishi 1992).

Table 2.A12 shows the structure of postwar Japan's financial system. The system is made up of both private and government institutions. In terms of assets, commercial banks—and city banks in particular—loom large. (City banks nominally operate nationwide but generally have branches only in the larger cities.) In number, however, the institutions aimed at small and medium firms and agriculture rank first.

In April 1989, the principal group of intermediaries for small and medium firms, *sogo banks*, were almost all converted into commercial banks called second-line local banks (*daini chigin*). (The last sogo bank merged out of existence in April 1992.) There have been a few conversions of local banks into city banks, and at the end of the 1980s what appears to be a wave of mergers of banks of all sizes was getting underway. However, generally speaking, the number of institutions was stable throughout the period discussed here.

The postal savings system has over 20,000 branches covering every town, village, and neighborhood in the country. The Trust Bureau of the Ministry of Finance is mainly in charge of the investments and loans of these funds. The main conduits are two government banks—the Japan Development Bank and the Export–Import Bank of Japan—and several special corporations such as the Housing Finance Corporation and the Finance Corporation for Small and Medium Firms. (Despite subsequent changes, Suzuki (1987) presents a useful and detailed discussion of financial institutions and markets.)

Until the mid-1970s these institutions were subject to strict governmental regulation. Within the intricate structure of implicit and explicit regulation that prevailed during the high-growth period, six stood out, those pertaining to

1. Establishment of both new institutions and new branches.
2. Entry into such markets as bond issuance, stock listing, and short-term money.
3. Creation of new instruments—for deposits, and in money and capital markets.
4. Interest rates on deposits, loans, and newly issued bonds.
5. Brokerage commissions charged by securities firms.
6. International capital movements—portfolio and direct, inflow as well as outflow.

7. Specialization of lending areas. Private and government institutions specialized in small and medium firm lending, long-term credit supply, and agricultural lending.

The alternative to this highly regulated approach is, of course, a competitive
financial system. Competitive capital and money markets can solve the problem of long-term fund supply either through the direct issue of bonds or through
facilitating liquidity adjustment by nonbanks by means of sales and purchases
of securities in the secondary market. With the development of an efficient
money market, commercial banks can also supply long-term funds through
term transformation activity. If money markets work well, there is no threat to
bank safety in terms of liquidity risk, and the solvency risk can be reduced by
adherence to minimum capital ratio requirements and adequate supervision by
means of auditing and the like, perhaps in association with a deposit insurance
system.

In this regulated system, however, the money market was strictly confined to
be interbank and was not open to nonbanks until the emergence of the *gensaki*
(repo) market in the late 1960s. The banking sector was heavily protected by
deposit rate regulation and Bank of Japan credits. This system of protection is
sometimes referred to as a "convoy system." All institutions, even the most inefficient, were led to grow at the same speed, and none was allowed to go bankrupt.

The corporate and government bond markets also were strictly controlled.
Interest rates on newly issued bonds were kept artificially lower than the prevailing market rates, providing implicit subsidies to the issuer. This had consequences. Not surprisingly an excess supply of bonds arrived, and was met by
rationing under government guidance. Only firms in basic industries such as
electricity were allowed to issue bonds. Second, bonds purchased by bank syndicates through assignment were rarely resold—doing so entailed realized losses. As a result, the secondary market for bonds remained extremely underdeveloped throughout the rapid growth era.

One reason the market solution was not adopted in the 1950s was probably the
general atmosphere of disbelief in the market mechanism nurtured through the
experience of the Great Depression, and respect for the effectiveness of policy
intervention à la Keynesianism. But, the more basic and immediate reason
prompting policymakers at that time seems to have been the fear that the scarcity of both long-term funds and information was so serious there would be market failures. It was felt the price of long-term funds would be too high to undertake long-term investment if it was determined by the market. In addition, if
information production was left to the normal activities of bond rating companies and commercial banks, the problem of information asymmetry would be
aggravated, eventually leading to serious bank insolvency.

It can be argued that these two problems were even more serious than was
imagined initially. This is suggested by the rise to a strategic role of Bank of
Japan (BOJ) credits in two areas.

The supply of long-term credit did not go smoothly. Debentures issued by long-term credit banks were not absorbed by the public because of its low asset levels, so the debentures were allocated to city banks at below-market interest rates. BOJ credit was then used to subsidize the city banks. Throughout the high-growth period, the official BOJ discount rate was kept lower than the interbank deposit rate (the call loan rate). BOJ loans were rationed to banks, city banks being the exclusive recipients, and this was a major tool of base money control. (Base money is the usual term in Japan for "high-powered money"—currency in circulation plus central bank deposits held by banks.) The continuing dependence of the banking sector on BOJ loans was called "overloan."

Because the information problem and the resulting credit rationing to small and medium firms were considered so serious, the Ministry of Finance (MOF) adopted a policy of more generous licensing of branches to the private special institution such as sogo banks and *shinkin banks*, which were aimed at small and medium firms. But this policy had a side effect: a greater increase in their deposits than in their loans, as only the lending was subject to specialization requirements. Moreover, special institutions for agriculture obtained large deposits from using their advantage in nonprice competition based on close relationships in rural areas.

On the other hand, city banks faced a huge demand for loans from large businesses. Because they dealt mainly with large customers, city banks did not need a large number of branches to gather information about their borrowers, so MOF licensing was less generous to city banks. As a consequence, they had a smaller deposit absorption capability. Another result of this has been that the city banks' ratio of loans to deposits has been consistently higher than that of other banks, and on the interbank deposit market (call market), city banks have thus always been on the borrower side and other banks on the lender side. This phenomenon, called an "imbalance of bank liquidity" (*shikin henzai*), had the effect of assigning to the interbank deposit market the role of adjusting structural deficits and surpluses of funds. Consequently, to reduce the volatility of the interbank rate, BOJ's credit came to be assigned a role of adjusting the banks' short-term liquidity position.

Actual implementation of branching policy took into account "the safety and avoidance of excess competition among financial institutions" as well as the profitability of new branches (Kinyuseido Chosakai 1970). Profitability seems to have been judged roughly by the following formula: The lending rate times lending, minus the deposit interest rate times deposits, minus the fixed cost of opening the branch. In this formula, since the lending rate is the average of the bank as a whole and thus is a constant for each individual bank, the profitability of a new branch seems higher whenever the volume of lending surpasses that of deposits. This seems to confirm the MOF's concerns with the ability of new branches to assess the creditworthiness of new borrowers in new geographical areas.[1]

1. I have changed my view about the cause of *shikin henzai* from my earlier work (1982, 1990). Previously, the difference of generosity in MOF's branch licensing policy was simply assumed. Now, I believe the difference is related to the differences in the information needs of city and other banks.

HOW THE FINANCIAL SYSTEM OF THE
HIGH-GROWTH PERIOD WORKED

The financial system of the rapid growth era had several rather astonishing properties, which can be considered paradoxical from the viewpoint of orthodox neoclassical ideas about the efficiency of free competition. (This section is a complete revision of Teranishi 1986b.)

Severe Competition Under Regulation

Although there were ceiling rates on bank loans during the high-growth period, it was usual to require deposits (compensating balances) to evade the ceiling. In addition, the regulation was applicable only to loans over 1 million yen with a maturity of less than a year, so about 60 percent of bank loans were beyond the scope of the regulation. It might therefore be safe to say the effective loan rate—the regulated rate adjusted for compensating balances—cleared the market.

Regulation of deposit rates, on the other hand, was quite effective. Although nonprice competitive "services," such as giving small presents to depositors, were common, their effect seems to have been only marginal.

City banks were free to compete in the lending market, and their customers were large businesses with a huge appetite for funds. At the same time, there is strong evidence that banking operations had increasing return to scale (Royama and Iwane 1973, Tsutsui 1988). It follows that the subjective equilibrium of a bank is such that it is profitable to expand as much as possible, that is, there is no equilibrium.[2]

The size of a bank's operations were determined only by MOF branching policy. The immediate result was fierce competition for deposits among city banks. Because corporate deposits comprised one-third of their total deposits, this meant competition for new corporate firms as customers. (The changes in a

---

2. The subjective equilibrium for a typical city bank can be described as follows. Let D denote deposits—which is equal to loans—and R(D) and C(D) total revenue and noninterest cost, respectively. Profit π can be written as $\pi = R(D) - \bar{l}D - C(D)$ where $\bar{l}$ represents the regulated deposit rate. Maximization yields $R' = \bar{l} + c'$.

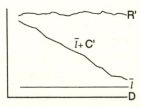

For the reasons given in the text, R' for an individual bank can be regarded as constant over the relevant range. The subjective equilibrium of a bank is something like the one shown in the adjoining figure.

firm's main bank found by Horiuchi and Fukuda [1988] and Horiuchi and Pack-er (1987) can be partly understood from this kind of competitive environment: Their definition of a main bank is the bank with the largest share of lending over the previous three years. Other definitions show fewer changes in main banks because they take into account such factors as interlocking directors.

Murakami (1984) used the term "compartmentalized competition" (*shiki-rareta kyoso*) for a similar phenomenon in a more general setting of industrial competition under increasing economy of scale in postwar Japan. Incidentally, it can be argued that using college graduates to collect deposits door-to-door from corporate clients was a serious misallocation of human resources. But, it should be emphasized that by collecting deposits in this way, the new hires indirectly fulfilled the important role of producing information about potential new bor-rowers as well as grassroots views of economic conditions.

There also was competition for deposits between private banks and postal sav-ings (government finance). Bank deposit rates are determined by MOF, while postal savings rates are set by the Ministry of Postal and Telecommunication Ser-vices, so this competition entailed a stiff political struggle among bureaucrats.

Despite this severe competition, there was a rather clear-cut complementary relationship between private financial intermediaries and the government finance system. Thus, there was a division of labor in terms of deposit maturity. The effective rate of interest on postal savings was kept higher for long-term (more than 2 years) deposits and lower for short-term deposits (6 to 18 months) than the deposit rate at private banks. (Interest on postal savings is compound-ed every 6 months.) As a consequence, account activity (turn-over, measured as the ratio of total withdrawals to average balance during a year) was much lower for postal savings than for private bank deposits: In 1965, it was 0.26 for the for-mer and 1.18 for the latter.

Most of the funds of private financial intermediaries were directed towards firms in the growing or modern sectors, especially those producing investment goods and exports. This was more or less the result of the free play of market forces. Government guidance and intervention have never been truly effective. On the other hand, although the flow of government finance was concentrated in key industries immediately after the war, later the emphasis was on the declin-ing traditional sectors and on social overhead investment. Similarly, smaller manufacturing firms depended more on government finance than did larger ones—in the late 1950s firms with fewer than 20 employees obtained 9 to 10 per-cent of their borrowings from government sources, compared to less than 3 per-cent for firms of 300 or more workers (see Teranishi 1982, ch. 6). The shares of funds earmarked for modernizing low-productivity sectors (agriculture and small and medium firms) and providing overhead capital for industries (mainly railways and electricity) were becoming more significant, and the share set aside for promoting key industries was low and decreasing (see Table 2.2).

The emphasis on declining sectors is apparent in Table 2.3. Such stagnating industries as mining, textiles, agriculture, and marine transportation depended heavily on government finance for investment funds, whereas such growing

Table 2.2. *Composition of Fiscal Investments and Loan Programs by Purpose*
(percent)

Fiscal years (begin April 1)	1953–55	1956–60	1961–65	1966–70	1971–75
Promotion of key industries	23.6	16.6	9.9	6.3	3.7
Foreign economic aid and export promotion	2.8	4.3	7.9	10.4	8.8
Overhead capital for industries	26.4	21.6	26.1	24.3	23.2
Modernization of low-productivity sectors[a]	18.6	20.9	19.0	20.1	19.6
Regional development	5.7	9.0	7.5	4.6	3.7
Improvement of living conditions	22.9	27.6	29.6	34.3	41.0

a. Agriculture and small and medium firms.
Source: Ogura and Yoshino 1984.

industries as steel, machines, and chemicals relied less and less on it. (These
points were originally suggested by Ouchi (1962) and recently confirmed and
emphasized by Ogura and Yoshino (1984) and Horiuchi and Otaki (1987).)

To summarize, the division of labor was as follows: The growing, modern sector obtained ample funds from private financial intermediaries at market interest rates, and the declining, traditional sector and social overhead were financed
by the government at regulated interest rates. Also, areas such as housing, consumers credit, and small firms in declining industries were generally left out by
both private financial intermediaries and government finance.

Table 2.3. *Share of Government Funds and Bond Financing in Total Fixed
Investment by Industry*
(percent)

		Government funds				Bond financing	
		1954–60		1961–70			
	1951–55[a]	Total	JDB	Total	JDB	1954–60	1961–70
Agriculture and fishery	n.a.	52.9	0.5	47.9	0.4	0.5	0.7
Mining	n.a.	25.7	17.0	39.9	18.8	2.3	2.8
Textiles	n.a.	14.2	2.1	14.7	2.2	5.0	6.9
Chemicals	n.a.	8.1	3.4	7.1	3.8	3.6	4.2
Steel	9.1	4.6	2.5	3.6	1.0	6.1	9.2
Machinery	n.a.	11.3	2.6	9.5	3.1	5.5	8.9
Land transport	n.a.	10.4	0.7	21.9	2.2	10.7	8.5
Marine transport	n.a.	33.9	29.5	50.9	39.0	0.1	0.1
Electricity	18.4	32.4	13.1	19.7	8.3	7.0	19.6

n.a. Not applicable.
Note: Data are for fiscal years, which begin Apr. 1.
a. All supplied through Japan Development Bank (JDB).
Source: Horiuchi and Otaki 1987 and Japan Development Bank, *Twenty-five Year History.*

High Intermediation under Deposit Rate Regulation

The high level of financial intermediation in postwar Japan can be traced with the help of Table 2.A10, which shows the composition of sources of private sector funds. A major portion of the outside funds were raised through the private financial system, and only a small part through issuance of bonds and equities. This high intermediation ratio implies a very limited role for direct lending and an underdeveloped securities market.

The role of direct lending, a typical method of traditional financing before the development of a modern financial system, diminished considerably after World War II. In 1957, the share of traditional financing was only 10.3 percent but in 1932, it had been 39.2 percent (Teranishi 1982, ch. 6). Traditional financing was almost perfectly replaced by the well-developed financial system, aimed at small and medium firms and agriculture. Even the smallest firms obtained almost two-thirds of their funds through the modern system.

An important reason for this can be found in drastic changes in the level and distribution of asset holdings due to inflation during and immediately after the war. From 1940 to 1950, every index of prices rose 100 to 300 times. As a consequence, private financial assets accumulated through the prewar period lost most of their value. Asset distribution became more equitable during the process. Small farmers were emancipated from the heavy burden of prewar agricultural debt, and the landlords and other wealthy classes virtually disappeared—partly owing to the inflation and partly owing to land reform and the dissolution of the zaibatsu. Because traditional financial methods were essentially means for the rich to profitably finance the poor, it was inevitable that these changes considerably reduced the role of such direct financing.

It may be easy to understand why the securities market remained underdeveloped. One reason lies in the reduced level of asset accumulation. At low levels of total wealth, asset holders (with utility functions characterized by decreasing absolute risk aversion) become less inclined to take risks, and hence they reduce their investment in risky assets. Government regulation has contributed to the risk. Japanese institutions and corporations have been allowed liberal use of their security holdings as collateral—a fact which incidentally reduces any burden of being a stable shareholder. In contrast, margin transactions (purchases on credit and short sales) by individuals must be closed within a specified time period—12 months since 1990, just 6 months before then. This has contributed to the perception of the stock market as a place for speculation rather than investment. (In the United States, the rules applied to individuals and institutions are more or less the same. Margin positions, including short sales, can run indefinitely, and loan balances are secured by all assets held in the account.)

The reduced role of traditional financing, the underdevelopment of the securities market, and limited access to foreign asset holdings have been the three main reasons for the high level of financial intermediation. In other words, because the availability of alternative assets was limited, people had no other choice but to hold deposits, the low level of interest paid on them notwithstanding. At least the real rate generally was positive until the mid-1960s. There was some disintermediation, particularly by businesses using investments in inventories, land, and equities as alternatives (Patrick 1984).

Rapid Growth without Foreign Capital

In view of the developing country debt problem in the 1980s, a natural question is why Japan could successfully accomplish import substitution without significantly relying on foreign capital inflow. First, it is not precise to say Japan did completely without foreign capital. In addition to relying on foreign aid and U.S. military demand immediately after the war, Japan began issuing foreign currency bonds in 1957, and there was short-term bank borrowing by large corporations from Japanese branches of foreign banks (impact loans). Borrowing from the International Bank for Reconstruction and Development (IBRD) also came to a considerable amount. But, it is also true that the overall balance of the long-term capital account remained in deficit throughout this period.

There are several factors that kept Japan's reliance on foreign capital so low. First, its balanced budget policy (adopted in 1949 and continued until 1975) and a relatively low share of government expenditures in GDP are most responsible because they eliminated capital inflow through sovereign borrowing. Because Japan's growth depended essentially on private initiatives, there emerged a virtuous circle in the government budget: Realized tax revenues always exceeded planned expenditures, and the tax reduction based on this surplus further promoted private sector development.

Second, underdevelopment of international capital markets during this period may be another reason. Japan could borrow only from the World Bank (IBRD)—and in fact was the second largest borrower in the 1950s, after India. Nonetheless—although important for infrastructure (railroads and Tokyo expressways) and certain industries such as steel and electricity—the amount was marginal to the system as a whole. Usually, the Japan Development Bank borrowed from the World Bank and then relent the money. Japan borrowed all together about $857 million during the 1950s and 1960s.

Third, Japan suffered from a scarcity of foreign exchange reserves. Throughout the period of rapid growth, the economy followed a stop–go policy, alternating between an acceleration of growth with the replenishment of reserves through a trade balance surplus, and a deceleration with the exhaustion of reserves due to the increased amount of imports induced by rapid growth.

Fourth, the rapid growth of exports reduced the necessity of replenishing foreign exchange by way of importing capital. The growth of exports can be explained either by the expansion of world trade under the GATT or by the high income elasticity of exports (Houthakker and Magee 1969). It is important to note that Japan resorted to export promotion policies only marginally. As Table 2.4 shows, implicit subsidies to exports by means of both special tax treatment and preferential credits comprise only a small fraction of the export value, particularly compared to Korea, for example.

Japan's strict regulation of international capital transactions seems to have provided a necessary condition for sustaining the financial system during this

Table 2.4. *Implicit Subsidies to Export*

	Subsidies (million US$)		Subsidies as a percentage of exports	
	Tax reduction[a] from preferences	Preferential credit[b]	Japan[b]	Korea[c]
1955	9.7	0.6	0.5	n.a.
1956	12.5	0.6	0.5	n.a.
1957	20.8	12.1	0.8	n.a.
1958	34.7	5.2	1.4	2.3
1959	27.8	5.0	1.0	2.5
1960	31.9	6.8	1.7	1.9
1961	30.6	12.7	1.0	6.6
1962	59.7	31.7	1.9	16.5
1963	65.3	24.8	1.7	15.1
1964	66.1	55.4	1.8	12.8
1965	68.3	n.a.	0.8	14.8
1966	72.5	n.a.	0.7	19.0
1967	71.6	n.a.	0.7	23.0
1968	104.2	n.a.	0.8	28.1
1969	139.7	n.a.	0.9	26.1
1970	210.8	n.a.	1.1	27.8

n.a. Not applicable.

a. Accelerated depreciation, special deductions on overseas income, and reserves for overseas markets.

b. The preferential credit was discontinued in Dec. 1971, but data are not available after 1964, so the subsidy rate is just tax preferences as a percentage of exports. The credit subsidy is calculated as the volume of Bank of Japan preferential loans related to exports multiplied by the difference between the call rate and the rate charged on the loans. The call rate is the average of the highest and lowest rate for unconditional call loans. Yen amounts are converted to dollars at the annual average of daily rates.

c. Direct subsidies, domestic tax concessions, tax rebates on exports, and interest subsidies.

Source: The amounts for tax reduction and value of exports, and Korean subsidy rates are from Iton and Kiyono 1984 (p. 172, Table 6, in the English edition). The volume of BOJ loans is from *One-Hundred Year History of Bank of Japan,* vol. 5.

period: first, by closing loopholes in interest rate regulations and, second, by stabilizing the money supply. As for the first point, it is apparent that without restricting international capital inflows, the various regulations governing the bond markets would have been largely ineffective. Because interest rates in Japan were comparatively high by international standards during the rapid-growth period, without the restrictions every business firm deemed creditworthy enough would have floated bonds abroad, and the rationing system of the domestic bond market would have collapsed. The argument here assumes there was a sufficient foreign demand for Japanese corporate bonds, which in fact may not have existed. Because the exchange rate was fixed during the period, hedging was not necessary.

As for the international outflow of funds, what would have happened in the absence of regulation is less clear. Because returns on investments were very high in Japan, it can be argued that eliminating regulation would not have had any significant impact on actual outflow. However, in view of the considerable disintermediation by the corporate sector into land and inventories, a possibility of disintermediation toward overseas objectives cannot be ruled out.

With high returns on domestic assets, there was a strong tendency for inflating the money supply by means of capital imports. (Recall the Korean experience in the mid-1960s, during which the liberalization of interest rates in the absence of regulations on the import of foreign capital caused a significant monetary expansion.) Moreover, the accommodating stance of the Bank of Japan toward domestic credit also implied possible inflationary pressure. Therefore, in order to control the money supply, restrictions on foreign capital imports seem to have been crucial. (For example, during 1972–73 the amount of medium- and long-term impact loans approved by the Ministry of Finance was drastically reduced in order to control the money supply.)

Effective Monetary Policy with Accommodating Credit from the Bank of Japan

With the balance of payments more or less balanced in the medium term and an open security market not sufficiently developed, base money during the rapid-growth period was mainly supplied through Bank of Japan (BOJ) direct credits to city banks at a preferential rate.

What is particularly interesting about this is that BOJ took quite an accommodating stance in its credit supply, increasing credit whenever the demand for it increased. As a result, BOJ credit supply moved in the same direction as the call money rate. This feature was emphasized by Teranishi (1982) and tentatively confirmed by Kuroda (1988) by means of causality tests. Such an accommodating stance toward credit supply is liable to amplify swings during the business cycle.

The reason BOJ did this seems to lie in the illiquidity of commercial banks, a problem that had several causes. First, some of the banks' assets were devoted to holding bonds that could not be resold except at a loss. Second, the banks supplied investment funds to growing sectors using relatively short-term deposits. On this last point I have already noted the difference in the average maturity at commercial banks compared to postal savings. The maturity period of deposits was considerably shortened due to the loss of wealth caused by the postwar inflation. The lowering of the wealth to income ratio increased the share of the remaining wealth held in liquid forms, and in inflationary periods, of course, more liquid financial assets naturally are preferred.

BOJ used another very direct measure of restrictive policy in combination with this basic stance—"window guidance," which set ceilings on the quarterly rate of increase of city bank loans. The complementarity of window guidance and accommodation accounts for the effectiveness of monetary policy during the rapid growth period. This point was first suggested by Suzuki (1974), who confirmed that BOJ used the call rate and the rate of increase of city bank loans as operating targets of its monetary policy.

A basic characteristic of monetary policy during the rapid growth period can be summarized as follows: To alleviate the illiquidity of banks, BOJ credit was supplied passively in accordance with demand by banks. Window guidance was an effective tool of restrictive monetary policy under this accommodating stance of credit supply. Indeed, it can be shown that a sufficient condition for the effectiveness of window guidance is the accommodating stance of BOJ credit. This is done in Table 2.5.

Two additional comments are in order. First, another sufficient condition for the effectiveness of window guidance is a low interest elasticity of demand by the banks for reserves. (This point can be readily confirmed by assuming a case of elastic reserve holding. In Table 2.5's Equations 1 and 2, letting $\gamma = \gamma(\rho)$, with $N = \bar{N}$, we obtain $dA/d\bar{A} > -1$.) Owing to accommodating credit supply by BOJ and the strong demand for funds by business firms, reserve holding by banks tended to be kept at a minimum level. Therefore, I am somewhat skeptical about the elasticity of reserve holdings. However, this point must be settled empirically and so is still open to question (Teranishi 1982, pp. 600 – 603).

Second, the degree of effectiveness of window guidance depends on the degree of loan market segmentation vis-à-vis noncity banks (that is, on the magnitude of the partial derivative $\delta A/\delta i$). The more segmented the loan market is, the more effective window guidance is. Although most noncity banks are required to specialize in their loan clients, this restriction tended to become ineffective owing to the development of arbitrage techniques such as lending through agent banks. This weakness in the effectiveness of window guidance led BOJ to place some of the noncity banks under window guidance, and the number of such banks rose during this period. Window guidance was formally discontinued after the April–June quarter of 1991.

EFFECTS OF THE SYSTEM

In view of the successful transformation of Japan from a middle-income developing economy into a full-fledged industrialized one, it seems safe to say the financial system so far articulated had some favorable effects on growth and employment. Let us look at the specifics of how finance contributed.

Realization of Dynamic Scale Economies

Although we should not ignore the contribution of domestic R&D (Goto and Wakasugi 1984), there is no doubt that during its rapid-growth period Japan benefited immensely from the introduction of foreign technology. Growth by means of imported technology is effective only when sufficient time and resources are devoted to learning. When the dynamic scale economies attributable to learning are external, it is well known that subsidies are necessary to prevent market failure. On the other hand, the supply of long-term funds is crucial to realizing

Table 2.5. *The Effectiveness of Window Guidance*

Consider an asset market model with base money market, deposit market, call loan market, and securities market, and decompose the banking system into city and noncity banks. In the interbank call market, city banks behave as borrowers and noncity banks as lenders. The portfolio of private asset holders contains base money, deposits, and securities. The rate of interest rate on securities i represents the cost of capital of the economy; a decrease in i has expansionary effects on economic activity. In the deposit market, the interest rate is assumed to be fixed, and equilibrium is to be attained on the demand function of deposits by asset holders. It is also assumed the deposits of city banks are a fraction β of total deposits, and the remaining fraction $1-\beta$ is held with noncity banks. The coefficient β is a constant, presumed dependent on branch office licensing policy. For the sake of simplicity, assume the demand for deposits and base money by private asset holders are given by $C(i)$ and $D(i)$, and $dC/di < 0$, $dD/di < 0$. Also assume base money is supplied solely through BOJ credits to city banks.

Denoting the call rate and Bank of Japan credits by r and N, the demand for call loans by city banks can be written

$$\overline{A} + \gamma\beta\, D(i) - N - \beta\, D(i)$$

where γ is a fixed coefficient of bank reserve holdings and $\overline{A}$ a constant, represents the constrained demand for securities by city banks regulated by window guidance. (For convenience, window guidance is assumed to be related to the stock instead of the flow of securities.) N takes the following values depending on the policy stance: $\overline{N}(r)$ with $dN/dr > 0$ is accommodating, N (constant) is otherwise.

The supply of call loan by noncity banks is represented as

$$(1 - \beta)D(i) - A(i,r) - g(1 - \beta)D(i)$$

where $A(i,r)$ is the demand for other assets by noncity banks, $\delta A//\delta i > 0$, and $\delta A\,\delta \rho > 0$. (For simplicity, the same coefficient of reserve holding as city banks is used.)

Equating the supply and demand of call loans gives

$$\overline{A} + A(i,\rho) = N + (1 - \gamma)D(i) \tag{1}$$

The equilibrium condition in the base money market is

$$N = \gamma\, D(i) + C(i) \tag{2}$$

These two equations represent a general equilibrium of assets markets for the model. The equilibrium condition for other assets can be deleted in light of Walras law.

Window guidance is ineffective in the absence of an accommodating stance. If $N = \overline{N}$ in (2), it follows $di/d\overline{A} = 0$, $d\rho/d\overline{A} > 0$, and $da/d\overline{A} > -1$.

A reduction of A due to window guidance is exactly offset by an increase in A and has no effect on the cost of capital i. This is because a reduction of A decreases the demand for call loans by city banks, and the consequent fall of the call rate induces non-city banks to shift their asset holding from call loans to securities. This proposition was originally shown by Horiuchi (1980).

The effectiveness of window guidance under the accommodating stance of BOJ credit supply can be readily shown. Substituting $N = N(\rho)$ in (2) yields $di/d\overline{A} < 0$, $d\rho/d\overline{A} > 0$, $dA/D\overline{A} > -1$.

With the accommodating stance, the fall in the call rate due to window guidance is smaller owing to the decrease in BOJ credits. Consequently, the offsetting increase of the demand for securities by noncity banks becomes smaller in absolute value than the reduction in $\overline{A}$. Therefore there is a net decrease in total demand for other assets $A + \overline{A}$, and the cost of capital is increased.

42

the internal part of dynamic scale economies whenever financial markets are imperfect.

In the rapid growth period long-term funds were rationed to particular sectors at subsidized rates. As for corporate bonds, key industries such as steel and electricity were able to issue bonds for interest rates lower than the market rate. Bonds of private long-term credit banks were also sold at a preferential rate, and funds obtained by those banks were lent mainly to heavy and chemical industries. Both kinds of bonds were sold by allocation to city banks, which in turn were subsidized by a cheap and elastic supply of BOJ credit.

City banks also absorbed deposits from other banks. In this sense, the short-term deposits of the banking sector were partly converted into long-term funds and rationed to particular industrial sectors. Similarly, long-term funds obtained by the government financing system through the postal savings system were rationed to key industries in the early period and later to declining industries and social overhead areas.

Because successful introduction of new technology depends on the accomplishment of learning which in turn can be facilitated by the availability of long-term funds, a positive relationship is expected between the allocation of long-term funds and the rate of increase in productivity. This has been confirmed by means of a cross section analysis of industries (Teranishi 1982). The positive relationship is especially clear for 1965–70. But, the analysis suffers from an obvious drawback in that it uses labor productivity instead of total factor productivity as a proxy for the result of learning.

Table 2.6 reports a time series analysis conducted by Horiuchi and Otaki (1987). They assume total factor productivity depends on the ratio of long-term funds (corporate bonds and long-term borrowing from financial intermediaries) to total assets F with respect to a Cobb–Douglas production function. For many industries—such as textiles, pulp and paper, primary metals, transportation equipment, metal products, and mining—F is seen to be highly significant, although several cases seem to suffer serial correlation in error terms. Horiuchi and Otaki note that a similar regression for the period 1971–80 yielded insignificant effects from F.

Allocation Under Uncertainty

During the rapid-growth period, information production was important in two senses. First, information about individual firms was needed. This is because the period was characterized by the birth and death of a large number of firms, and the dynamics of the economy depended on the innovative activities of small and medium firms. Because the owners and managers of small and medium firms are often the same people, their aversion to disclosing information has always been strong, so information asymmetry was a serious issue. Second, because the technology, as well as the industry, to be transplanted could be chosen from a wide menu of those available existing in advanced countries, information was needed about the general direction of industrial organization and industrial structure.

Table 2.6. *Productivity Growth and Long-Term Funds:
Time Series Regression by Horiuchi and Otaki*

	$ln(L)$		$ln(F)$		R^2	DW
Mining	−0.26	(−5.27)	0.94	(3.05)	0.95	0.77
Food	1.54	(4.94)	0.01	(0.00)	0.85	0.74
Textiles	−1.57	(−2.80)	8.05	(10.78)	0.94	1.66
Paper and pulp	1.04	(3.09)	2.11	(2.35)	0.81	1.25
Chemicals	0.40	(0.83)	4.24	(1.84)	0.85	0.83
Primary metals	0.00	(0.02)	4.09	(8.37)	0.85	1.58
Metal products	0.31	(2.11)	9.00	(2.44)	0.49	1.26
General machinery	0.75	(2.59)	0.50	(0.07)	0.52	0.62
Electrical machinery	1.23	(6.36)	0.15	(0.04)	0.85	1.66
Transportation equipment	−1.19	(−1.42)	14.84	(2.99)	0.78	1.01

Note: t values in parentheses.

Assume a Cobb–Douglas production function $V = AK^b L^a$ where V is value added; A, total factor productivity; K, capital stock; L, labor. Because

$$ln(V/L) - bln(K/L) = lnA + (a+b-1)lnL$$

the following equation is estimated by OLS on time series data for 1956–70:

$$ln(V/L) - bln(K/L) = \alpha_0 + \alpha_1 lnF + \alpha_2 lnL + u$$

where u is an error term and b is assumed to be equal to the income share of capital.

Source: Horiuchi and Otaki 1987.

In regard to the first problem, financial intermediaries (especially banks) seem to be able to claim special merit on this point. This is because they are constantly investing in obtaining information in order to maintain proper lender–borrower relationships and because they can produce information about borrowers jointly with the provision of other services, such as transaction accounts. Intermediaries' accumulated information capacity—that is, the experience of the staff as individuals and the data they have on various firms and industries—is most useful in the face of a massive emergence of new firms.

It can be argued, therefore, that the high degree of financial intermediation during the rapid growth process has had growth-promoting effects through efficient production of information. In this regard, competition among city banks deserves special attention. Through their competition for corporate deposits, banks sought promising new customers among small and medium firms. Banks used to be criticized for devoting too many human resources to collecting deposits but the close relationship between this activity and producing information suggests the expenditure may have been warranted.

The second problem is related to industrial policy. If industrial policy is interpreted as intended to change or adjust industrial organization, I am quite skeptical about the effect of government provision of such information or of indicative planning in general. The attempts to develop coal mining and marine transportation as key industries failed (Kosai 1986), and aluminum smelting is also felt to have suffered since the 1970s from policy mistakes by the government.

If, on the other hand, industrial policy is interpreted as a policy dealing with market failure (Komiya 1984), it can have some positive effects. For example, in oligopolistic situations, providing information not embodied in price variables could improve welfare (Itoh and others 1984). Still, although some growing strategic industries were supplied with long-term funds by the government in the form of loans from the government financial system and the rationing of bond issuance, and there is no doubt these industries benefited from the availability of long-term funds and the implicit subsidies accompanying them, I am skeptical about the necessity of such a rationing scheme. That is, these growing industries would probably have received sufficient funding even if they had been left to the market mechanism.

Effects on Employment

The financial system of the rapid-growth period seems to have contributed to the alleviation of unemployment and underemployment in two ways. First, owing to the nationwide development of the financial institutions for small and medium firms, virtually everyone could have access to bank borrowing—although at high effective interest rates even for good borrowers, reflecting serious information asymmetry. This access helped generate jobs. Second, the system helped declining industries retain workers. In the case of coal mining, the trauma of industrial adjustment was eased. On the other hand, the result has been an unnecessarily prolonged adjustment period for agriculture.

Generally, the market-oriented private financial system has two drawbacks in supplying adequate funds to a declining sector. Whenever there is lack of malleability of production factors, the market rate of return of a declining sector during the adjustment period tends to be lower than otherwise. It follows that the supply of funds through the free market, whether direct or indirect, is also likely to be inadequate. (This is a part of the general problem of adjustment aid; see Mussa 1982 and Sekiguchi and Horiuchi 1984.)

Second, because building up information channels between a firm and a bank has the property of a fixed investment, banks are particularly reluctant to establish such channels with a declining industry because of the risk of being unable to recover the costs. (Thus, for example, promising young bankers are not assigned jobs related to declining industries.) Consequently, even if the short-term rate of return of some firms within such industries is high, adequate information often is not conveyed to the banks.

In the case of Japan during the rapid growth era, government finance is seen to have played the role of supplying funds to declining sectors. This role can be understood as the remedy for the two market failures cited earlier. In this sense, the characteristic division of labor between government and private financial systems can claim special merit for its growth-promoting effect.

Costs and Benefits of Regulations

No regulation is free from some sort of distortion. One of the important effects of this highly regulated system is its impact on income distribution. (This problem was first taken up rigorously by Iwata and Hamada 1980.) Depositors probably provided a huge subsidy to private financial institutions (deposit banks). This is quite straight-forward, as seen by looking at the nature of the commercial banks' asset–liability management under this system.

On the asset side, some assets were used for compulsory purchases of bonds at below-market interest rates, but the bulk were devoted to business loans at (effectively) freely set interest rates. On the liability side, some funds came from BOJ credits at a preferential rate, but the bulk were from private deposits at regulated rates. BOJ credits took the form of either rediscounting commercial bills or repurchasing of bonds from banks at a preferential price (*riron kakaku*). In the latter case, the banks were able to liquidate year-old bonds without a loss.

Within this framework there are implicit subsidies from borrowing from BOJ (equal to the call rate minus the official discount rate, times borrowing from BOJ) and from the regulation of deposit rates (equal to 1 minus the reserve ratio, times the call rate, minus the deposit rate, times deposits), as well as implicit taxation of bond holdings (equal to the market interest rate minus the issue rate, times bond holdings). Table 2.7 provides estimates of these for city banks.

Estimates of the subsidy from deposit rate regulations are quite large—essentially the same as net subsidies, about one-fifth of the total subsidies (explicitly) supplied to various industries, and more than one-third of estimated city bank profits. (It is important to note here, however, that there are similar implicit subsidies due to price controls in many other areas; rice is perhaps the archetypal example.)

It is difficult to say how these implicit subsidies were used. There are three possibilities. They could have been distributed to bank employees in the form of high wages, transferred to bank clients in the form of low-interest loans, or used to expand the level of loans. Banks have been preferred employers in Japan, but (except briefly during the bubble period) not because of the generosity of their

Table 2.7. *Estimates of Implicit Subsidies to and Taxation of City Banks, and Total Subsidies to Private Industries* (annual average, billion yen)

	1966–70	1971–75
Implicit subsidy due to regulation of		
Official discount rates	20	19
Deposit rates	85	242
Implicit taxation due to regulation of		
Bond yields	17	31
Net estimated subsidy	88	230
Estimated profit of city banks[a]	251	488
Total industrial subsidies	451	1006

a. Estimated as follows. In 1970 city banks held 63% of total deposits in ordinary banks. This percentage is applied to the total profits of all ordinary banks to estimate city bank profit. (Disaggregate data are not available.)

Source: Teranishi 1982 and Ogura and Yoshino 1984.

compensation packages. In view of the market-determined nature of bank loan rates, the second possibility is unlikely. Bank dividends were strictly regulated (in the form of a maximum rate). So, by elimination the third possibility remains: The extra retained earnings provided a larger capital base for intermediation. (Stockholders did benefit from the buildup of asset value.)

In the case of the postal savings system, where the deposit rate also was regulated, it is clear that the implicit subsidies were largely transferred to borrowers through government financial institutions. Their loan rates were below market—after all, subsidizing them was the primary point.

Table 2.A2 shows that throughout most of the period until the mid 1970s the share of assets held by the corporate sector was larger than that of the personal sector, and it rose during the 1960s. For comparison, in the United States the corporate share is only one-fifth to one-fourth of total assets. Thus, perhaps the most serious legacy of the fiancial system during the rapid-growth period is the huge financial asset holdings of corporate businesses. Hugh Patrick suggested two reasons for this phenomenon: the deposits corporations were forced to hold as compensating balances for loans, and hedging against the possible curtailment of bank credit. As one aspect of this, Table 2.8 shows that the equity held by nonfinancial corporations increased during the 1950s, 1960s, and early 1970s.

Two points are significant. First, bank credit seems to have had a considerable impact on the expansion of asset holdings by the business sector. In regard to the early 1960s, it can be shown that rapid expansion of bank credit financed the increase of corporate assets in the form of trade credits. Because the corporate sector was more or less under conditions of increasing returns to scale, expansion of business activity—and hence this leveraging—was profitable. After 1968, when the trade credits were liquidated, the proceeds were invested in other forms of financial assets rather than in reducing leverage equivalently (Kosai 1986, Teranishi 1982, p. 555).

Second, financial disintermediation by the corporate sector into land, inventory, and equities also seems to be responsible: The accumulation of assets by the corporate sector was accelerated by profitable investments in these areas.

DEREGULATION AND INTERNATIONALIZATION

After two decades of rapid growth, Japan had accomplished a remarkable transformation into a highly industrialized economy. The share of agriculture in employment was below 9 percent in 1985 and underemployment, together with any serious unemployment problem, had disappeared. The chronic trade balance deficits had been replaced by huge current account surpluses, and Japan was the world's largest capital exporter.

These changes were accompanied by significant shifts in the aggregate demand component and sectoral IS balances. The share of capital formation in GNP, over 39 percent in 1973, has gradually decreased in the 1980s, with a concomitant rise of the share of exports (see Table 2.A1). On the other hand, the savings and investment balance by sectors has changed considerably. The deficits

Table 2.8. *Distribution of Shareholdings by Type of Shareholder*

Mar. 31	Nonfinancial companies	Securities firms	Financial institutions	Investment trusts	Individuals[a]	Foreigners[b]
1951	11.0	11.9	12.6	0	61.3	0
1956	13.2	7.9	19.5	4.1	53.2	1.7
1961	17.8	3.7	23.1	7.5	46.3	1.3
1966	18.4	5.8	23.4	5.6	44.8	1.8
1971	23.1	1.2	30.9	1.4	39.9	3.2
1976	26.3	1.4	34.4	1.6	33.5	2.6
1981	26.0	1.7	37.3	1.5	29.2	4.0
1984	25.9	1.9	38.0	1.0	26.8	6.3
1986	24.1	2.0	40.9	1.3	25.2	5.7
1988	24.9	2.5	42.2	2.4	23.6	3.6
1989	24.9	2.5	42.5	3.1	22.4	4.0
1990	24.8	2.0	42.3	3.7	22.6	3.9
1991	25.1	1.6	41.6	3.6	23.1	4.1

Note: Data cover all listed companies. Government and public corporation holdings are not shown, so rows do not add to 100%.

Through fiscal 1984 (ended Mar. 31, 1985), based on actual number of shares held. Subsequently, based on transaction units (round lots) held, with odd lot holdings excluded. A transaction unit is 1,000 shares for 50 yen par value stocks, 100 shares for 500 yen par value stocks. Nippon Telegraph and Telephone was privatized in 1985, with the shares still all held by the government, with a par value of 50,000 yen and a transaction unit of one share. As a result, the government's share on Mar. 31, 1986, went from 0.187% (old method) to 0.753% (new method). Not many companies have 500 yen par —the electric utilities, KDD (the principal international telecommunications carrier), the Long-Term Credit Bank, Nippon Credit Bank, a few regional banks, and some others. These all happen to be the sorts of things insurance companies like to own; hence financial institutions also increased share slightly under the new system.

a. Includes unincorporated organizations.

b. Individual and corporate entities.

Source: Data are compiled by the National Conference of Stock Exchanges and published in a variety of places, including the *Tokyo Stock Exchange Fact Book* and the Bank of Japan's *Economics Statistics Annual* (e.g., 1990 ed., p. 200, provides annual data for fiscal years ending in 1973–89). WARNING! In many sources, including BOJ, the data are for Mar. 31 of the year *following* the year shown because they are fiscal year-end data. Also, the financial institutions entry sometimes includes investment trusts.

(investment minus savings) of the corporate sector, measured as a percentage of GNP, gradually fell and were replaced by increases in the deficits of the government sector during 1975–85 and of the overseas sector after 1980. In 1988 government turned into a surplus sector, and beginning in 1987, private investment shows a remarkable surge, resulting in an increase in the corporate deficit. Data are in Table 2.A3.

The financial environment had also changed significantly. The level of accumulation of financial assets increased rapidly, especially with respect to the personal sector after 1975 (Table 2.A2). Consequently, the term structure of deposits lengthened (Table 2.1) and the supply of long-term credit from the banking sector increased considerably.

Globalization and integration of international financial markets are other important environmental changes in this period. Such phenomena as the emergence of round-the-globe, round-the-clock trading, the formation of multilateral settlement systems such as SWIFT and SHPS, the worldwide spread of financial innovation based on electronics and information processing, and the homogenization of financial systems across countries all have had significant effects on the Japanese financial system (Bryant 1987). Expansion of overseas economic activities, such as trade and foreign direct investments have also helped make inevitable the internationalization of the financial system.

Aspects of Deregulation

These changes in real-growth patterns as well as in the financial environment are the context in which the financial system has been drastically transformed since 1970. This transformation has occurred on four fronts: money markets, deposit markets, and the government bond market each developed and underwent deregulation, and there were reduced requirements for specialization of activities.

The expansion of the money market was triggered by the spontaneous emergence of gensaki markets among nonbank economic units during the late 1960s. Since then, several new instruments have been introduced: certificates of deposit (1979), bankers' acceptances (1985), treasury bills (1986) and commercial paper (1987). Judged by the ratio of money market assets to GNP, the development of the money market has accelerated since 1980 (see Table 2.9, column 1). The share of open market instruments to total money market instruments seems to have risen rather slowly.

Deregulation of deposits began in 1981 when new types of financial instruments were approved for commercial banks, trust banks, long-term credit banks, and the postal savings system—a different type for each. Although these new instruments still had regulated rates, entirely deregulated deposit substitutes with market determined rates were introduced: CDs (1979), money market certificates (1985), and large-denomination time deposits (1985). In addition, the minimum sizes have been lowered gradually but fairly regularly. However, the deregulation of small and demand deposits has been repeatedly put off. Still, the index of deregulation of this market—the percentage of deposits with market-determined interest rates in total commercial bank deposits—seems to be accelerating upward.

Since the issuance of large amounts of revenue-financing bonds in 1975, the once strictly regulated government bond market has been deregulated, gradually at first but then rapidly. Since 1977, restrictions on sales of bonds held by banks have been progressively relaxed, as indicated by the rise in the ratio of transactions to end-of-year outstanding balances, especially after 1984. The conditions for issuing bonds have also been softened: After 1980 the issue rate has closely followed a market rate.

Specialization requirements were relaxed for the various types of financial intermediaries, and this has intensified competition among them. Ordinary (city and local) banks were allowed to issue 30-month time deposits in 1971. In 1973, Sogo banks were allowed to enter the foreign exchange business, and in 1989, to convert into ordinary banks. In 1973 shinkin banks were allowed to lend to

Table 2.9. *Indexes of Deregulation of Financial Markets*

Year	Securities markets 1	Securities markets 2	Money markets 3	Money markets 4	Deposit markets 5
1967	n.a.	n.a.	2.6	12.2	n.a.
1968	n.a.	n.a.	2.6	21.2	n.a.
1969	n.a.	n.a.	2.8	22.8	n.a.
1970	n.a.	n.a.	3.1	26.8	n.a.
1971	n.a.	1.11	3.5	30.3	n.a.
1972	n.a.	0.00	2.9	44.7	n.a.
1973	n.a.	0.90	4.9	30.3	n.a.
1974	n.a.	0.02	5.0	24.1	n.a.
1975	n.a.	0.30	5.9	20.4	n.a.
1976	0.1	0.39	5.7	21.7	n.a.
1977	0.7	−0.28	6.2	26.3	n.a.
1978	1.6	0.44	6.3	32.1	n.a.
1979	2.0	0.35	6.9	37.2	n.a.
1980	2.3	0.69	6.6	42.7	0.0
1981	2.4	−0.76	6.5	48.2	0.0
1982	2.2	−0.83	7.4	46.6	0.0
1983	2.7	−1.28	8.4	43.6	0.0
1984	4.5	−0.40	9.4	45.8	11.6
1985	12.6	−1.04	12.2	40.2	17.5
1986	19.6	−0.46	14.2	44.0	25.7
1987	25.6	−0.14	15.8	44.2	42.0
1988	18.5	−0.06	19.7	44.6	55.1
1989	15.6	0.42	23.5	47.1	73.6

n.a. Not applicable.

Column 1: Ratio of fiscal year's volume of transaction to outstanding balance of government bonds at fiscal year-end (Mar. 31 of year following).

Column 2: Difference in percentage points between the market rate and the issue rate for government bonds at calendar year-end.

Column 3: Calendar year-end ratio of money market assets to GNP. These are either interbank or open market instruments. The former include call loans and bill transactions (1973–). Open market instruments are *gensaki,* CDs (1979–), government short-term bonds (1981–), bankers acceptances (1985–), treasury bills (1986 –), and commercial paper (1987–).

Column 4: Open market instruments as a percentage of total money market assets at calendar year-end.

Column 5: Unregulated interest rate deposits as a percentage of total time deposits at *zenkoku ginkō* (usually translated as "all banks") at fiscal yearend (Mar. 31 of year following). Also called "free interest rate deposits." Includes money market certificates (MMC, 1985–), large-denomination time deposits (1982–), nonresident yen deposits, and foreign currency deposits.

Source: Various issues of *Koshasai yoran* and Bank of Japan, *Economic Statistics Annual,* plus Kuroda 1988.

"graduate" firms (former members that had grown above the normal ceiling for using shinkin).

The wall between the banking and security businesses has been lowered since 1980. For example, in 1980 securities companies were allowed to issue medium-term government bond funds (called *chukoku*) that were virtual substitutes for deposits and in 1983 banks were in turn allowed to broker government bonds.

Derivative instruments also were introduced: futures on long-term government bonds in 1985, stock index futures in 1988, and stock options in 1989.

Causes of Deregulation

Let us try to clarify the possible qualitative effects of the basic economic forces behind the deregulation that has been and is taking place in Japan's financial system. Three points are discussed—the issuing of large amounts of government bonds, the increased sensitivity of asset holders, and the internationalization of finance.

Government Bond Issue

The slowing of growth led by the expansion of private investment in equipment had significant repercussions on both the investment–savings balance and the asset–liability management in each sector. With respect to the IS balance, the general government budget has changed from being balanced to having a large deficit, resulting in the issuance of a large volume of government bonds. The deficits were not caused by an increase in investment expenditure such as normally occurs when counter-cyclical measures are taken, but rather by increases in various categories of current expenditure. The ratio of government final consumption expenditure to GNP rose from 6.8 percent in 1970–72 to 9.6 percent in 1982–84, and the ratio of transfer expenditure (subsidies and social security expenditures) rose from 5.4 percent to 12.5 percent over the same period.

The reason for the increase in current government expenditure is not difficult to understand. First, the termination of rapid growth meant that attention turned to how to share a less expansive pie and the government began adjusting the distribution of income. Second, the earlier high aggregate growth had resulted in a rapid change in industrial structure, so it was inevitable there would be expenditures for smoothing the adjustment of those industries and regions that had been left behind. (See Sekiguchi 1991 for more on Japan's policy toward declining industries.) In short, after 1970 the movement in the equilibrium in the goods and services market was controlled by the move toward "large" government.

The effect of government bonds on financial markets can be understood in terms of market pressure effects. (See Feldman 1986. His original concept of market pressure is broader than the one used here, as he also considers overseas deficits. Here only domestic ones are treated as "pressure.")

The necessity of accommodating large amounts of bonds is considered to have caused the deregulation of their conditions for issue and, through arbitrage, the relaxation of regulations in other assets markets as well. This pressure can be conveniently captured by the savings–investment balance of the sectors. Table 2.A3 shows that the sum of deficits (investment minus savings) of the government and corporate sectors as a percentage of GNP was quite high after 1974 through 1982, suggesting a continuing pressure on the bond issue market.

On the other hand, Table 2.10 shows the stock of government bonds absorbed by private asset holders became enormous after 1980, with the consequent rise of the share of bonds in total private assets. This was partly caused by the end of increases in the amount of bonds held by the commercial banking system. The timing corresponds exactly to the change in the relationship in the issue and market rate of bonds (Table 2.9, column 5). When banks finally became resistant to accepting unprofitable bonds, the issuer (the government) was obliged to turn to the public by increasing the coupon rate to a market yield.

Increased Sensitivity of Asset Holders

The effects of changes in portfolio selection are most evident in the corporate business sector, where asset holdings showed significant increases during the rapid-growth period. That the corporate sector engages in integrated portfolio selection between real and financial assets has been confirmed by many authors with respect to business cycles (for example, Teranishi 1982, Horiye and Naniwa 1989).

During boom periods with large investments in equipment, the relative share of inventory and securities holdings rises because of the expectation of higher prices, and during slump periods the share of trade credits increases, reflecting the high rate of return from promoting sales by financing them (sales promotion

Table 2.10. *Government Bond Supply and Demand*
(trillion yen)

Fiscal year-end[a]	Outstanding balance	Amount held by			Percentage of private assets[e]
		Zenkoku ginko[b]	Other[c]	Private sector[d]	
1971	4.7	1.1	0.3	1.0	0.6
1973	8.3	1.3	0.4	1.5	0.6
1975	15.8	4.3	1.1	2.2	0.6
1977	32.8	11.4	3.4	6.5	1.5
1979	57.3	15.6	8.6	2.7	0.5
1981	84	16	16	27	4.1
1983	112	17	31	32	4.0
1986	147	23	46	26	2.7
1988	159.	29	47	18	1.3

a. Fiscal year-end is Mar. 31 of following year.
b. Usually translated as "all banks."
c. Other private financial intermediaries.
d. Nonfinancial private sector.
e. Amount held by the nonfinancial private sector as a percentage of the sector's total financial assets.

effects). During inflationary periods such as the 1950s or the oil shock years, the inventory share goes up, and during rapid-growth periods, when every firm tries to increase market share to realize (static) scale economies, the sales promotion effects of trade credits become large.

Since the end of rapid growth, the principal component of aggregate demand has shifted from private domestic demand to either public or overseas demand. For either type, the sales promotion effects of trade credit are small, so the share of trade credit dropped quickly after 1970. Since 1974 (through 1987, the most recent data) it has been volatile but basically trendless. The end of rapid growth also explains the low rate of return on inventories in the long run, as the price level is expected to be more or less stable.

These seem to be the principal reasons for the shifts in the composition of asset holdings after 1970, plus, in the 1980s, more deposits with a market interest rate. As a result, the percentage share of nonoperating profits to total profits of large corporations has risen (see Table 2.11).

Looking at the composition of liquid assets held by large corporations, since the early 1970s securities have increased and inventories have decreased share, while trade credits and cash and deposits have been trendless. It can be argued that these changes imply the benefits of evading regulations on financial instruments had become larger than the cost of complying with them. The emergence of the gensaki market is a typical example of arbitrage activity induced under such conditions.

Overall, the arbitrage of financial assets by the corporate sector seems to be the basic driving force of deregulation. The process was started around 1970 when the implicit return on trade credits had fallen owing to changes in the demand structure. However, the high inflation of the 1970s, interrupted the

Table 2.11. Nonoperating Income of Large Corporations as a Percentage of Operating Profits (fiscal year)

1960	22.9	1971	44.3	1982	44.7
1961	27.9	1972	43.2	1983	45.6
1962	34.2	1973	35.5	1984	41.1
1963	30.3	1974	42.9	1985	50.4
1964	32.1	1975	62.5	1986	60.4
1965	37.5	1976	51.4	1987	50.5
1966	32.4	1977	61.8	1988	42.0
1967	29.1	1978	55.6	1989	48.9
1968	29.9	1979	34.9	1990	54.0
1969	29.3	1980	43.0	1991	54.2
1970	33.0	1981	41.5		

Note: Fiscal years begin on Apr. 1. Firms in all industries with paid-in capital of more than one billion yen. Nonoperating income comprises interest and dividend income, bill discounting fees, and realized capital gains on securities.

Source: Hōjin kigyō tōkei nenpō.

process because the funds freed from trade credit supply were invested in real assets, including inventory and real estate. Financial arbitrage by the corporate sector was resumed after 1980 when prices stabilized.

To this must be added the effects of increases in personal asset holdings in the 1980s. As Table 2.12 on flow savings shows, this entailed an increase in the

Table 2.12. *Composition of Personal Financial Assets (Flow Savings)* (percent)

Year	Currency	Deposits[a]	Trust funds	Insurance	Securities	All else[b]
1955	4.1	69.7	8.4	13.3	4.7	−0.2
1956	7.0	63.5	1.6	12.5	15.3	0.1
1957	1.4	54.5	0.9	13.3	17.8	12.1
1958	3.2	60.4	4.0	14.8	18.7	−1.1
1959	5.9	56.0	4.1	13.2	17.0	3.8
1960	6.9	54.9	3.9	13.5	25.1	−4.3
1961	7.5	49.9	4.0	13.4	37.6	−12.4
1962	4.0	41.9	4.2	11.8	17.3	20.8
1963	4.7	56.4	5.9	11.8	14.7	6.5
1964	6.1	59.6	6.9	11.8	15.6	0.0
1965	6.2	61.8	7.9	12.8	6.4	4.9
1966	6.2	57.6	7.4	13.0	8.3	7.5
1967	6.7	56.7	6.5	12.2	7.0	10.9
1968	5.7	60.0	6.6	13.9	8.4	5.4
1969	6.6	61.2	5.8	13.2	10.8	2.4
1970	6.5	57.6	6.1	14.9	13.4	1.5
1971	6.0	60.3	6.7	14.6	13.8	−1.9
1972	8.6	68.5	6.4	11.5	6.9	0.1
1973	5.8	69.0	5.3	11.5	8.3	0.1
1974	7.0	65.7	7.2	14.0	9.6	−3.5
1975	2.7	64.8	7.1	12.7	12.3	0.4
1976	3.8	60.9	7.4	12.7	14.1	1.1
1977	3.6	61.6	7.0	13.5	13.7	0.6
1978	5.6	62.4	5.9	13.5	12.9	−0.3
1979	2.1	67.0	6.4	16.3	9.1	−0.9
1980	1.0	65.0	5.6	18.0	9.7	0.7
1981	2.5	61.5	7.6	17.4	11.2	−0.2
1982	2.5	52.7	10.2	18.8	17.0	−1.2
1983	1.5	47.5	8.8	19.3	17.0	5.9
1984	3.0	46.6	8.4	21.2	17.0	3.8
1985	2.8	52.2	8.6	27.5	7.7	1.2
1986	5.4	47.8	5.5	33.4	6.4	1.5
1987	4.0	48.0	3.8	33.8	24.4	−14.0
1988	5.0	44.9	11.9	44.9	5.6	−12.3
1989	5.8	53.3	8.4	33.0	2.3	−2.7
1990	0.5	49.9	10.7	30.5	10.4	−1.9

a. Demand, time, and CDs.

b. "All else" is a residual that includes foreign currency deposits, nonresident yen deposits, and "other assets," as well as any statistical discrepencies. Because of inherent problems in collecting consistent data, particularly over time, these numbers are "best guesses."

Source: Bank of Japan, flow-of-funds accounts.

shares of such long-term contractual saving instruments as insurance and pension funds. (Financial asset holdings are shown in Table 2A.9.) There seems no doubt that this offered another channel of arbitrage with government bonds and deposits, and promoted the deregulation process.

Internationalization of Finance

The rapid progress of internationalization of Japan's economy is indicated in Table 2.13. Both gross assets and liabilities have expanded continuously. Although the movement of net assets is governed by the current account situation, the level of gross balances is mainly determined by financial transactions.

Around 1980 when a new Foreign Exchange Law was enacted, gensaki transactions by foreigners were approved and regulations on impact loan and foreign currency deposits were eliminated. In 1984, under pressure from U.S. financial firms, itself a manifestation of globalization, basic regulations on transactions in Euromarkets were relaxed.

One of the interesting points regarding the effect of the internationalization of real economic activity on the internationalization of the financial system can be found in the relationship between the banks and foreign direct investment by

Table 2.13. *Assets and Liabilities of Japanese Residents in Relation to Nonresidents* (billion US$)

	1976	*1977*	*1978*	*1979*	*1980*	*1981*	*1982*
Total assets	68	80	119	135	160	209	228
Total liabilities	58	58	83	107	148	198	203
Total net assets[a]	10	22	36	29	12	11	25
Long-term assets	19	23	34	47	40	47	62
Short-term assets	−9	−1	2	−19	−29	−36	−37
Increase in net assets	3	12	14	−7	−17	−1	14
Current account	4	11	17	−9	−11	5	7

	1983	*1984*	*1985*	*1986*	*1987*	*1988*	*1989*
Total assets	272	341	438	727	1,072	1,469	1,771
Total liabilities	235	267	308	547	831	1,178	1,478
Total net assets[a]	37	74	130	180	241	292	293
Long-term assets	68	116	179	284	410	521	572
Short-term assets	−31	−42	−49	−104	−170	−229	−279
Increase in net assets	13	37	56	50	61	51	1
Current account	21	35	49	86	87	79	57

Note: The difference in the change in net assets and current account arises from the following reason: Because claims on residents by nonresidents are mainly denominated in yen, an appreciation of the yen increases the dollar value of gross liabilities. An increase in stock prices held by nonresidents works in the same direction.

a. Net assets are the differences between assets and liabilities in each of the categories.

Source: Ministry of Finance, *Kokusai kinyu kyoku nenpa* More detailed annual data for 1985–89 are in Bank of Japan, *Economic Statistics Yearbook* 1991, p. 250.

business firms. It is said that most Japanese firms retain their main bank relationship when they go abroad, so banks must follow. When banks go abroad, they usually borrow from the local money market to finance their Japanese clients. This is closely related to the phenomenon of international financial intermediation—borrowing in short-term instruments and investing in long-term assets.

As a result of the deregulation of international financial transactions, such transactions by corporate businesses have considerably expanded: The percentage share of foreign financing in total outside financing of large businesses increased from 7.8 percent during 1975–79 to 22.7 percent during 1980 – 83, and the share of foreign currency assets in total financial assets rose from 2.4 percent to 33.0 percent during the same period (*Chosa geppo* May 1985). One particularly interesting aspect of this is that the buyers of the bonds issued overseas were mainly Japanese institutions. In other words, domestic regulation moved Japan's corporate bond market to London (primarily). It also induced arbitrage activity between the regulated domestic and unregulated offshore systems.

There are several points regarding the impact of this on deregulation of domestic markets. The number of companies eligible for bond financing without collateral in the domestic market has increased considerably—from 2 in March 1979, to 175 in July 1985, and to about 240 in February 1988. This relaxation of regulation seems to be related to the overall rise in the share of the foreign market in total bond financing as indicated in Table 2.14.

Table 2.14. *Japanese Corporate Financing through Bond Issuance* (trillion yen)

Year	Straight		Convertible		Warrant	
	Domestic	Foreign	Domestic	Foreign	Domestic	Foreign
1979	1.25	0.17	0.37	0.65	n.a.	n.a.
1980	1.05	0.15	0.10	0.46	n.a.	n.a.
1981	1.26	0.10	0.36	0.74	0.02	n.a.
1982	1.15	0.36	0.45	0.62	0.04	0.09
1983	0.65	0.63	0.83	1.05	0.01	0.13
1984	0.81	0.65	1.21	1.39	0.02	0.48
1985	0.65	1.34	1.90	0.86	0.01	0.59
1986	0.97	1.24	2.74	0.27	0.12	1.96
1987	0.94	0.94	5.26	0.34	0.03	2.66
1988	0.91	0.55	6.64	0.64	0.00	3.61
1989	1.10	0.65	7.64	1.64	0.92	8.72
1990	2.92	1.35	0.91	0.84	0.40	3.03
1991	4.08	4.50	1.28	0.87	0.38	3.98

n.a. Not applicable.

Note: With respect to foreign market isues, the dollar value is converted into yen at the year-end exchange rate.

Source: Ministry of Finance, *Kokusai kinyū kyoku nenpō*

Decreases in foreign financing by convertible bonds in the late 1980s also seem to be related to deregulation. Active use of overseas bond markets by large corporations caused the authorities to recognize as real the possibility that the domestic convertible bond market could dry up, and they were thus obliged to relax domestic regulations (Horiuchi 1989). (However, the same theory does not seem to apply to straight bonds, for which the number of eligible firms also increased. This point will be explained later.)

As asset holders become more sensitive to the rates of returns on various financial assets, financial intermediaries were forced to pursue more profitable portfolios by means of international diversification. The increase in international investments by insurance companies is an example.

In the early 1980s when the internationalization of banks was proceeding rapidly, a cross-section analysis of 12 city banks (excluding the Bank of Tokyo) regarding the relationship between domestic deregulation and internationalization of activities is instructive. Table 2.15 reports simple correlation coefficients among six variables based on the average data of five 6-month accounting periods covering September 1982 through March 1985 (Teranishi 1987).

It can be seen that variable 5, indicating the effects of domestic deregulation, is positively correlated with variables 1 and 2, indicating the internationalization of activities. The reason for this seems to be related to the following fact. When a bank's involvement in international activities is high (variables 1 and 2), both the level of profits (variable 6) and their riskiness (variable 4) are high. Also, note that variables 1 and 2 are inversely correlated with variable 3. This seems to imply that those banks with a high degree of internationalization, in the sense of a large value of variables 1 and 2, are expanding their business by tak-

Table 2.15. Cross-Section Analysis of City Banks
(correlation coefficients of variables)

	1	2	3	4	5	6
1 Percentage share of deposits and CDs at overseas branches in total deposits and CDs	1.00	0.72	−0.76	0.72	0.63	0.67
2 Ratio of profits related to international activities to total bank operating revenue		1.00	−0.55	0.76	0.65	0.59
3 Ratio of lendings and security investments to deposits and CDs at overseas branches			1.00	−0.52	−0.38	−0.32
4 Percentage share of risky sovereign loans (for which special overseas reserves are allowed) in total lendings and security investment of banks				1.00	0.50	0.50
5 Percentage share of free interest rate deposits (large denomination, MMC, and foreign currency deposits held by residents) in total deposits					1.00	0.60
6 Profit rate (current profit divided by total assets)						1.00

Note: For details, refer to Teranishi 1987.
Source: Data are from various issues of *Shukan kinyū zaisei jijū*.

ing part in the Eurolending business, which was high risk and high return in light of developing countries' debt problems. (Note that at overseas branches the amount of deposits and CDs roughly equals the sum of lending and investments to overseas customers and Eurolending.)

Characteristics of Deregulation

It is sometimes claimed that the process of deregulation in Japan has been slow and piecemeal because it is essentially governed by the logic of political struggle—with both domestic and foreign (especially U.S.) pressure and players. There is no doubt that actual change in the system occurs through political processes, in which conflict among interest groups, bureaucrats, and politicians influence the speed, degree, and direction of changes. In a Japanese context this idea is emphasized in Hamada and Horiuchi (1987) and aptly analyzed in Rosenbluth (1989).

To understand the seemingly slow and piecemeal process in Japan, however, it is necessary to consider two of its basic characteristics. First, deregulation has been essentially motivated and preceded by the transformation of the real economy. As Cargill and Royama (1988) stressed, the course of Japan's deregulation has had a close relationship with changes in the pattern of the flow of funds since the end of rapid growth. Thus the rise of the government as a deficit sector necessitated development of a government bond market; the fall of the rate of return on domestic investment impelled financial intermediaries to look abroad in pursuit of profitable investment opportunities; and there was increasing arbitrage based on increased asset accumulation by nonfinancial units. All worked as driving forces to develop new financial instruments.

It is natural that institutional changes so motivated occur slowly and in tandem with changes in the real economy. This pattern in Japan contrasts strongly with the experiences of deregulation in the United States and in developing countries. In the United States, one explanation of deregulation is that it took place because failure of monetary policy in the mid- and late 1970s brought about an inflation level that widened the gap between regulated deposit rates and the unregulated alternatives such as money market funds (Cargill and Royama 1988). In most developing countries, deregulation has been effected in pursuit of efficient resource allocation—based on theory advanced by McKinnon (1973) and endorsed by the World Bank and IMF—and the necessity of coping with free market forces from domestic informal credit markets and offshore intermediation.

In Japan neither of these has been important. For one thing, inflation in the mid-1970s was quickly brought under control. For another, although there was strong advocacy for unleashing market forces on the financial system during the 1960s (*kinyu seijokaron*), it never led to drastic liberalization attempts.

Domestic deregulation has occurred in tandem with deregulation on the international front. As an example, in May 1979 short-term impact loans (in this instance, foreign currency lending to firms financed either through the dollar call market or Eurodollar markets) was liberalized. It may appear that this change had the effect of offering banks access to funds with uncontrolled interest rates, because neither the dollar call rate nor the Eurodollar rate is regulated. But, this was not the case: There was another regulation called the real demand principle (*jitsuju gensoku*) prohibiting forward exchange transactions except for real trade demand (export or import). Because hedging or swapping was not allowed, the use of impact loans had an exchange risk, and consequently the degree of substitutability with domestic deposits was limited. This seems to explain why liberalization of domestic deposit interest rates did not take place at that time.

However, in June 1984 when short-term Euroyen loans to residents were liberalized under U.S. pressure (the Yen–Dollar Committee), the authorities understood that it was useless to insist on the real-demand principle because the banks had access to unregulated interest sources without an exchange risk. So the principle was abandoned, and immediately after this (in 1985) domestic deposit instruments with unregulated rates, such as large-denomination deposits and money market certificates, were introduced.

When regulations remain in the domestic market, related de facto regulations are kept intact on the international front. A good example is the separation of long-term and short-term financing in the domestic system. According to this principle, long-term credit banks are the only institutions that conduct financial intermediation in long-term funds. Although short-term Euroyen lending to residents by commercial banks was liberalized in June 1984, long-term lending is not yet allowed, and although commercial banks could issue Euroyen CDs with less than 6-month maturity was approved in December 1984, longer maturity CDs are still not allowed.

The number of firms eligible for the straight bond market increased considerably (from 2 in March 1979, to 57 in October 1985, and to about 120 in February 1987). But domestic issue of straight bonds has not shown any significant increase (Table 2.14). This is because long-term credit banks have pressured the authorities to nullify the deregulation of bond issue conditions (*tekisai kijun*) in order to preserve the separation of long-term and short-term credits. It is said issuing firms have been asked to collateralize their bonds, despite being eligible to issue uncollateralized bonds. This raises the effective interest rate, because in order to collateralize, the firms must pay additional fees (*shintaku hoshu tesuryo*).

When domestic deregulation is conducted as part of a delicate balance with opening up on the international front, it seems inevitable that the process must proceed slowly and seemingly piecemeal. This is because authorities must seek ways to satisfy demands from both domestic and international interest groups. Japan's domestic and international in-tandem liberalization seems to be in contrast to the sequential liberalization espoused by Edwards (1984) and McKinnon and Mathieson (1981).

Consequences of Deregulation

What have been the costs and benefits of deregulation? It certainly has cost a lot. Physical investment has been enormous, especially in computer equipment and software. For example, the complicated accounting and settlement of chukoku funds (a deposit substitute issued by security companies) would not be possible without a huge investment in computers. Investment in human capital has also been significant. In the 1980s many natural sciences graduates preferred working in finance rather than in manufacturing. As for the benefits, efficiency gains in the financial industry are to be expected, and there are noticeable signs of greater competition among intermediaries belonging to different groups. There will be some positive impact on income distribution from the liberalization of interest rates.

Deregulation is ongoing, so it is still too early to judge the final consequences. Still, two salient phenomena deserve comment. These are the more diverse funding sources available to large business firms and the increased risk exposure of the banking sector.

Increased diversification in the fund-raising instruments available to large business firms is a direct consequence of liberalization. Large firms now have access not only to such short-term financing as gensaki and commercial paper, but also to long-term bonds offered in foreign markets. Moreover, an active market for Japanese convertible and warrant bonds has increased the availability of equity financing, and at least in the late 1980s such money came very cheaply. As a result, large businesses have become increasingly independent of bank control. They are now subject to rating in Euromarkets, in addition to still being subject to monitoring by their main banks. However, because they can choose between domestic and Euromarket sources of funds, they have more freedom than they did before, say, the mid-1980s. Japanese firms were already more or less free of corporate control by stockholders, so this situation raises a serious question of how to maintain corporate governance.

For banks, this implies a reduction in their lending opportunities. Any resulting excess supply of bank funds is especially significant when a loose monetary policy prevails.

The asset market bubble and its bursting seems to be closely related to these situations. The bubble was launched by the accommodating monetary policy adopted after the 1985 Plaza Accord. To increase the value of the yen against the dollar, BOJ lowered its discount rate from 5.0 percent to the historically low level of 2.5 percent in February 1987 and maintained it there until May 1989. Because the discount rate had already been falling since 1980 and the level of investment had already been high for years, the additional supply of high-powered money largely resulted in additional demand for such assets as land and equities, thus fueling the bubble with expectations of further capital gains.

The demand for equity was met by increased supply, as companies took the opportunity to lower their cost of capital. Table 2.16 shows a surge in equity issues, including convertible and warrant bonds. Although most of the warrant bonds were issued abroad, they were largely bought by Japanese investors. High stock and land prices, increasing the value of collateral, allowed an expansion of bank lending to finance further demand for stock and land, especially by business firms, and this led to a self-feeding rise.

The percentage of stock (at book value, excluding shares in related firms) in total financial assets of large manufacturing firms increased to 58 percent

Table 2.16. *Sources and Uses of Funds by Large Manufacturing Firms* (fiscal year, trillion yen, and percent)

	1981–85 average		1986		1988		1989	
	yen	%	yen	%	yen	%	yen	%
Distribution of sources of funds								
Internal funds	4.8	73.8	5.3	78.6	7.1	69.9	7.8	47.9
Depreciation	3.6	55.0	4.4	64.7	4.7	46.4	5.1	31.2
Retained earnings	1.2	18.9	0.9	13.9	2.4	23.5	2.7	16.7
External funds	1.7	26.2	1.4	21.4	3.0	30.1	8.5	52.1
Borrowings	0.1	1.3	−1.2	−18.1	−2.5	−24.9	−2.7	−16.5
Straight bonds	0.0	−0.2	0.4	6.2	−0.5	−4.5	−0.4	−2.5
Equity	1.6	25.0	2.2	33.3	6.0	59.6	11.6	71.1
Convertible bonds	0.6	9.2	0.6	9.5	0.9	9.0	2.6	15.9
Warrant bonds	0.2	2.5	0.6	8.5	2.1	21.1	4.0	24.7
Stock	0.9	13.3	1.0	15.3	3.0	29.5	5.0	30.5
Distribution of uses of funds[a]								
Real investments	4.7	72.0	3.0	44.0	6.8	67.0	9.2	56.4
Equipment and real estate	4.7	71.6	5.0	74.8	5.9	58.1	7.9	48.2
Inventories	0.0	0.4	−2.1	−30.8	0.9	8.9	1.3	8.2
Financial investments[b]	1.6	24.8	3.0	44.7	3.9	38.6	6.6	40.3
Cash and deposits	0.6	8.9	1.6	23.6	2.1	20.3	2.9	17.8
Short-term securities	0.2	3.0	1.0	14.3	−0.1	−1.4	0.5	2.9
Long-term securities[c]	0.2	3.0	−0.1	−0.9	0.4	4.9	0.6	3.9
Related firms[d]	0.5	7.0	0.6	8.7	1.5	14.4	2.3	14.2

Note: Flow financing and asset investment of large manufacturing firms (379 in 1986, 381 in 1988, 387 in 1989), for fiscal years ending Mar. 31 of following year.

  a. Real + financial uses do not total 100%; the difference is investment in other assets, such as intangibles.

  b. The four detail rows do not add to this row because of nonitemized items such as trade credits.

  c. Excludes investment in related firms.

  d. Long-term investment only (that is, excludes trade credits and the like).

Source: Percentages are computed by the author from absolute data in Bank of Japan, *Chōsa geppō* (Research monthly) Nov. 1990 and unpublished BOJ data. Many of these series for the previous fiscal year generally appear in Nov. issues of *Shuyō kigyō keiei bunseki* (Financial statements of principal enterprises).

in 1989, compared to 38 percent in 1979. In the same period, land (at book value) climbed from 9 to 13 percent of total real investments. At market values these percentages would have been larger—much larger in 1979 and somewhat larger in 1989 (because of heavy purchases, particularly of stocks, in the late 1980s).

The bubble burst when the monetary authority lifted the discount rate in May 1989 and introduced quantitative controls on bank lending for real estate transactions. Banks and nonbank financial institutions that the banks used as conduits for real estate loans are now suffering under the weight of nonperforming loans backed by real estate. (Ironically, perhaps, loans collateralized by real estate increased as a percentage of total loans in the fiscal year ending in March 1992: Property is still considered to be the safest collateral as long as the loan is not too large a percentage of the value.) The collapse of stock prices has caused tremendous losses for investors, including business firms and financial institutions.

The turmoil of the burst bubble has shaken the financial sector, even if only a few firms are truly shaky. To this is added a direct consequence of liberalization: increased risk exposure for the banking sector. Credit risk seems to have grown as relatively more lending goes to consumers and small and medium firms—large firms, as noted, now relying less on banks (see Table 3.4). This has been partly offset by raising risk premiums: BOJ estimates 20 percent of short-term loans in mid 1992 were at premiums to city bank prime rates, compared to just 10 percent at the height of the bubble—but it will take time for the banks to become accustomed to the new circumstances.

The most serious risk comes from the greater mismatch of maturities. As deregulation progressed, the maturity composition of deposits rapidly became short-term. At the same time, as lending to large businesses fell, banks expanded long-term lending such as residential loans. Thus, in share terms, long-term liabilities have dropped dramatically since 1986, but long-term assets have steadily grown since after 1982 (see Table 3.3). This mismatching causes both interest rate and liquidity risk.

Interest rate risk can be reduced by changing to spread or variable rate lending or by using futures markets, whereas liquidity risk can be sloughed off by resorting to loan sales. But, it is conceivable that a more fundamental step will be needed such as allowing city banks to issue long-term debentures. This, however, would cause serious political turmoil, in view of the rivalry between city banks and long-term credit banks.

Another important effect of deregulation on the structure of the financial services industry is the greater presence of security firms in a previously bank-dominated system. All three causes of deregulation induced expansion of securities companies. Thus, issuance of large amounts of government bonds was a trigger for a surge of broker activity. The brokers went overseas far earlier than did the banks, mainly to underwrite Eurobond issues. Finally, increased corporate liquidity and emphasis on asset and liability management by nonfinancial firms offered a vast opportunity for securities companies.

Brokers, once heavily dependent on borrowings from banks and credits from the securities finance companies, have become largely independent of such sources. By using retained earnings as well as direct access to the money market, their capacity for risk taking (especially market making and underwriting) has considerably improved. It is important to note that their brokers' sizable internal financing capability is related to the oligopolistic market structure, which is based on fixed commissions and government-restricted entry. In view of the 1991 scandal over compensating clients for trading losses, some of the excess profits from regulation apparently have been shared with selected clients.

CONCLUDING REMARKS

Just as the evolution of Japan's financial system has been closely related to changes in the real economy, the future of the system will also be dependent on the pattern of real growth. Four points seems worth mentioning in this regard.

The role of the banking sector will certainly undergo considerable change. Owing to the lengthening of maturities of assets held by nonfinancial units and the development of secondary markets, the part banks play in maturity transformation will be reduced, although their role in producing information about borrowers will continue to be important. To the extent the main bank system works as a device for delegated monitoring, it may remain more or less intact.

Secondary securities markets will gain importance, even though there is uncertainty about the role of security markets in fund raising. Judging from Table 2.A10, although there is much year-to-year variability, there is no definite tendency for the shares of various sources of funds to change. In view of the importance of information production, it still seems possible that the dominance of bank lending will continue. Although it is possible securitization in the form of bank loan sales will gain importance, nothing definite can be said, if only because such sales have been permitted only since May 1990.

With respect to international aspects, it is difficult to say anything definite about the future of capital export from Japan. It depends on the course of demand management policies and the relative speed of productivity growth in Japan and the rest of the world. But, the role of Japan as an international financial intermediary will continue and probably grow, notwithstanding the need for the banks to adjust to BIS capital adequacy standards. As Table 2.13 indicates, Japan is lending long (row 5) while borrowing short (row 6), and this is becoming more pronounced.

Japan's monetary policy will need to shift its modus operandi toward a more market-based pattern. To this end, the Bank of Japan is actively trying to enhance the efficiency of money markets, and it is eager to introduce a treasury bill market in Japan. Its effort is reasonable in view of the changing financial environment.

If Japan is equipped with a full set of money and capital market instruments, it is feared in some quarters that Japan will dominate world financial markets, eclipsing not only Hong Kong and Singapore in the western Pacific but also partly replacing London and New York as the global center. I think that this is unlikely to happen, if only because global trading requires centers in several different time zones.

More fundamental is a domestic matter. Because the share of the financial sector in Japan's GDP reached 7.5 percent in 1988—greater than the share of construction (7.4 percent) and of transportation and communication (5.6 percent)—it may be worth rethinking whether Japan should exert further effort to expand its financial industry. There is a strong sentiment in Japan, which I share, that a healthy economy is based on real productive activity and that a tendency for more and more college graduates to work for the financial industry—lured by its readiness to pay high salaries—should somehow be avoided. In this regard, one cannot but feel the reduced new-hiring and downsizing by banks and securities firms are positive effects of the burst bubble.

This chapter owes much to studies by other researchers. Among the huge pile of literature covering the same period, the following five works seem especially relevant and complementary: Hamada and Horiuchi 1987, Suzuki 1987, Royama 1983–84, and Patrick 1984, 1972. I would like to thank Yoshio Suzuki, Shoichi Royama, Masaaki Komatsu, Kozo Horiuchi, and Hidenobu Okuda for their conversation, comments, and support.

REFERENCES

(The word "processed" describes informally reproduced works that may not be commonly available through libraries.)

Bryant, Ralph C. 1987. *International Financial Intermediation*. Washington, DC: The Brookings Institution.
Cargill, Thomas F., and Shoichi Royama. 1988. *The Transition of Finance in Japan and the United States: A Comparative Perspective*. Stanford, CA: Hoover Institution Press.
Edwards, Sebastian. 1984. "The Order of Liberalization of the External Sector in Developing Countries." Essays in International Finance 156. Princeton, NJ: Princeton University, International Finance Section.
Feldman, Robert. 1986. *Japanese Financial Markets*. Cambridge, MA: MIT Press.
Goto, Akira and Ryutei Wakasugi. 1984. "Gijutsu seisaku" ("Technology policy"). In Ryutaro Komiya and others, editors, *Nihon no Sangyo Seisaku*.
Hamada, Koichi, and Akiyoshi Horiuchi. 1987. "The Political Economy of the Financial Market." In Kozo Yamamura and Yasukichi Yasuba, eds., *The Political Economy of Japan*. Vol. 1: *The Domestic Transformation*. Stanford, CA: Stanford University Press.
Hondai, Susumu. 1988. "Subcontracting among Firms and Elasticities of Substitution—Japan's Machine Industries in the 1930s and the 1980s." Processed.
Houthakker, Hendrik S., and Stephen P. Magee. 1969. "Income and Price Elasticities in World Trade." *Review of Economics and Statistics* 51 (2) (May).
Horiuchi, Akiyoshi. 1980. *Nihon no Kin'yu Seisaku—Kinyu Mekanizumu no Jissho Bunseki (Monetary Policy In Japan)*. Tokyo: Toyo Keizai Shinposha.
———. 1989. "Informational Properties of the Japanese Financial System." *Japan and the World Economy* 1 (3).
Horiuchi, Akiyoshi, and Shinichi Fukuda. 1988. "Nihon no 'main bank' wa donoyo-na yakuwari o hatashita ka." Kinyu kenkyu 6 (3) (Oct).
Horiuchi, Akiyoshi, and Masayuki Otaki. 1987. "Kinyu: Seifu kinyu to ginko kashidashi no juyo-sei" (Finance: Government lending and the importance of bank loans). In Koichi Hamada, Masahiro Kuroda, and Akiyoshi Horiuchi, eds., *Nihon keizai no macro bunseki*. Tokyo: Todai shuppankai.
Horiuchi, Akiyoshi, and Frank Packer. 1987 Jul. "What Role Has the 'Main Bank' Played in Japan?" Processed.
Horiye, Yasuhiro, and Sadao Naniwa. 1989 Jun. "Kinyu hensu no jittai keizai katsudo e no eikyo ni kansuru kosatsu." Discussion Paper 403, Institute of Socioeconomic Planning, Tsukuba University.
Itoh, Motoshige, Kazuharu Kiyono, Masahiro Okuno and Kotaro Suzumura. 1984. "Shijo no shippai to hoseiteki sangyo seisaku" ("Industrial policy as a corrective to market failures"). In Komiya and others, eds., *Nihon no sangyo seisaku*.
Itoh, Motoshige, and Kazuharu Kiyono. 1984. "Boeki to chokusetsu- toshi" ("Foreign trade and direct investment"). In Komiya and others, *Nihon no sangyo seisaku*.
Iwata, Kazumasa and Koichi Hamada. 1980. *Kinyu seisaku to ginko kodo*. Tokyo: Toyo keizai shinposha.
Kinyuseido chosakai. 1970. *Zaisei kinyu jijo kenkyukai*. Vol. 4 of *Kinyu seido chosakai shiryo*.

Komiya, Ryutaro. 1984. "Josho" ("Introduction"). In Komiya and others, eds., *Nihon no sagyo seisaku.*

Komiya, Ryutaro, Masahiro Okuno, and Kotaro Suzumura, eds. 1984. *Nihon no sangyo seisaku.* Tokyo: Todai shuppankai. Translated in 1987 as *Industrial Policy of Japan.* San Diego: Academic Press.

Kosai, Yutaka. 1986. The Eve of High-Speed Growth: Notes on Postwar Japanese Economy. Tokyo: University of Tokyo Press.

Kuroda, Akio. 1988. Nihon no kinyu shijo. Tokyo: Toyo keizai shinposha.

McKinnon, Ronald I. 1973. Money and Capital in Economic Development. Washington, DC: Brookings Institution.

McKinnon, Ronald I., and Donald J. Mathieson. 1981. "How to Manage a Repressed Economy." Essays in International Finance 145. Princeton, NJ: Princeton University, International Finance Section.

Minami, Ryoshin. 1973. *The Turning Point in Economic Development: Japan's Experience.* Tokyo: Kinokuniya.

Miyauchi, Atsushi. 1988. "Kinyukikan no kinri risk ni tsuite." *Kinyu kenkyu* 7 (2) (Aug).

Murakami, Yasusuke. 1984. *Shin chukan taishu no Jidai.* Tokyo: Chuo koron-sha.

Mussa, Michael. 1982. "Government Policy and Adjustment Process." In Jagdish Bhagwati, ed., *Import Competition and Response.* Chicago: University of Chicago Press.

OECD (Organization for Economic Cooperation and Development). 1984. *Historical Statistics 1960–1982.* Paris: OECD.

Ogura, Seiritsu, and Naoyuki Yoshino. 1984. "Zaisei to zaisei-toyushi" ("The tax system and the fiscal investment and loan program"). In Komiya and others, eds., *Nihon no sangyo seisaka.*

Ouchi, Tsutomu. 1962. *Nihon keizairon.* Tokyo: Todai shuppankai.

Patrick, Hugh. 1972. "Finance Capital Markets and Economic Growth in Japan." In A. W. Samety, ed., *Financial Development and Economic Growth.* New York: New York University Press.

———. 1984. "Japanese Financial Development in Historical Perspective, 1868–1980." In Gustav Ranis and others, eds., *Comparative Development Perspectives.* Boulder, CO: Westview Press.

Rosembluth, Frances. 1989. *Financial Politics in Contemporary Japan.* Ithaca, NY: Cornell University Press.

Royama, Shoichi. 1983–84. "The Japanese Financial System: Past, Present and Future." *Japanese Economic Studies* 12 (2) (Winter).

Royama, Shoichi and Toshihiro Horiuchi. 1984. "Boeki to chosei enjo" ("Trade and adjustment assistance"). In Komiya and others, eds., *Nihon no sangyo seisaku.*

Royama, Shoichi and Toru Iwane. 1973. "Wagakuni ginkogyo no kibo no keizaisei" *Osaka daigaku keizai-gaku* 23.

Sekiguchi, Sueo. 1991. "Japan: A Plethora of Programs." In Hugh Patrick with Larry Meissner, eds., *Pacific Basin Industries in Distress, Structural Adjustment and Trade Policy in the Nine Industrialized Economies.* New York: Columbia University Press.

Sekiguchi, Sueo and Toshihiro Horiuchi. 1984. "Boek to Choseienjo" ("Trade and Adjustment Assistance"). In Komiya and others, eds., *Nihon no sangyo seisaku.*

Suzuki, Yoshio. 1974. *Gendai Nihon kinyuron.* Tokyo: Toyo keizai shinposha. Translated in 1980 as *Money and Banking in Contemporary Japan,* New Haven, CT: Yale University Press.

———, ed. 1987. *The Japanese Financial System.* New York: Oxford University Press.

Teranishi, Juro. 1982. *Nihon no keizai hatten to kinyu.* Tokyo: Iwanami shoten.

———. 1986a. "The 'Catch-up' Process, Financial System and Japan's Rise as a Capital Exporter." *Hitotsubashi Journal of Economics* 27 (special issue).

———. 1986b. "Economic Growth and Regulation of Financial Markets: Japanese Experience during Postwar High Growth Period." *Hitotsubashi Journal of Economics* 27 (2) (Dec).

———. 1987. "Nihon no shihonyushutsu kokuka to ginko no kokusaika." In S. Royama and R. Tachi, eds., *Nihon no kinyu.* Vol. 2. Tokyo: Todai shuppankai. (Processed English version available.)

———. 1990. "Financial System and the Industrialization of Japan: 1900 –1970. *Banca Nazionale del Lavoro Quarterly Review* 174 (Sep) pp. 309– 41.

———. 1992. "Financial System Reform after the War." In Yutaka Kosai and Juro Teranishi, eds., *Economic Reform and Stabilization Policy in Postwar Japan.* London: Macmillan.

Tsutsui, Yoshiro. 1988. *Kinyu shijo to ginko-gyo.* Tokyo: Toyo keizai shinposha.

Table 2.A1. Japan: Macroeconomic Indicators
(percent)

Year	Growth rate of real GNP	Gross investment (as % of real GNP)	Export of goods and services (as % of real GNP)	Current account (as % of GNP) Real	Current account (as % of GNP) Nominal	Household savings rate[a]	Rate of change in GNP deflator	Real interest rate[b]
1955	—	16.2	4.7	−2.4	0.9	11.9	—	—
1956	7.4	17.7	5.1	−3.5	−0.2	12.9	4.8	2.0
1957	8.1	20.2	5.3	−4.6	−1.9	12.6	6.5	7.7
1958	6.7	18.9	5.2	−2.9	1.5	12.3	−0.5	10.0
1959	9.3	20.6	5.4	−3.8	1.1	13.7	4.5	3.7
1960	13.6	24.2	5.3	−4.7	0.4	14.5	6.8	1.6
1961	11.9	27.6	5.0	−6.3	−1.8	15.9	7.8	5.7
1962	8.9	27.0	5.4	−5.0	−0.0	15.6	4.2	6.2
1963	8.4	28.0	5.3	−6.1	−1.1	14.9	5.5	2.2
1964	11.6	29.3	5.8	−5.9	−0.5	15.4	5.3	4.7
1965	5.9	28.6	6.8	−4.7	1.1	15.8	5.1	2.0
1966	10.7	29.2	7.2	−4.6	1.3	15.0	5.0	0.8
1967	11.1	31.9	6.9	−6.1	−0.0	14.1	5.5	4.0
1968	12.8	34.2	7.6	−5.4	0.8	16.9	4.9	3.0
1969	12.5	35.6	8.1	−4.9	1.3	17.1	4.4	3.3
1970	10.8	38.5	8.6	−5.8	1.1	17.7	6.5	1.8
1971	4.4	36.8	9.6	−4.9	2.6	17.8	5.5	0.9
1972	8.5	37.2	9.2	−5.4	2.3	18.2	5.6	1.1
1973	7.9	39.1	9.0	−7.8	0.0	20.4	12.9	−5.7
1974	−1.4	36.9	11.3	−6.7	−0.9	23.2	20.8	−8.3
1975	2.7	33.4	11.1	−4.7	−0.1	22.8	7.7	3.0
1976	4.8	33.1	12.4	−3.5	0.7	23.2	7.2	−0.2
1977	5.3	32.8	13.2	−2.5	1.6	21.8	5.8	−0.1
1978	5.2	33.4	12.4	−3.3	1.8	20.8	4.8	−0.4
1979	5.2	34.0	12.2	−4.4	−0.8	18.2	3.0	3.3
1980	3.5	30.1	12.1	−0.8	−0.9	17.9	4.6	6.3
1981	3.4	29.8	13.2	0.4	0.6	17.9	3.7	3.7
1982	3.4	28.7	12.8	1.0	0.8	16.1	1.7	5.3
1983	2.8	27.3	13.1	2.0	1.9	15.8	1.4	5.0
1984	4.3	27.7	14.4	2.8	2.9	15.8	2.3	3.8
1985	5.2	28.1	14.4	3.7	3.7	15.8	1.6	4.9
1986	2.6	28.5	13.4	2.7	4.3	15.5	1.8	3.0
1987	4.3	29.6	12.8	2.0	3.7	14.9	0.0	3.5
1988	6.2	31.7	12.9	0.8	2.9	14.4	0.4	3.2
1989	4.7	33.1	13.5	−0.1	2.1	13.8	1.9	3.0
1990	5.6	34.5	—	−0.3	1.4	—	2.1	5.1

— Not available.

a. Fiscal year ending Mar. 31 of following year.

b. The real interest rate is calculated as the average unconditional call rate (before 1969, the average of the minimum and maximum rate) minus the rate of change in the GNP deflator.

Source: Economic Planning Agency, *Annual Report on National Accounts* 1986 and 1991; *EPA Report on National Accounts from 1955 to 1969;* and Bank of Japan, *Economic Statistics Monthly,* various issues. All series in this table use the revised 1980s data introduced in EPA 1991.

Table 2.A2. *Japan: GNP Per Capita, GNP, and Financial Assets Outstanding*

Year	GNP per capita US$	GNP	Assets outstanding Total	Assets outstanding Personal	Assets outstanding Corporate	Assets to GNP ratio Total	Assets to GNP ratio Personal	Assets to GNP ratio Corporate
			trillion yen					
1965	917	32.7	120	30.7	38.1	3.66	0.94	1.16
1966	1056	38.0	140	36.1	44.5	3.70	0.95	1.17
1967	1225	44.5	166	42.4	53.2	3.73	0.95	1.19
1968	1436	52.8	193	50.4	60.5	3.65	0.95	1.15
1969	1672	62.1	230	59.8	73.8	3.71	0.96	1.19
1970	1948	73.2	268	70.5	83.1	3.66	0.96	1.14
1971	2189	80.6	313	83.5	95.2	3.89	1.04	1.18
1972	2855	92	393	103	116	4.25	1.12	1.25
1973	3836	113	479	121	152	4.26	1.07	1.35
1974	4206	134	539	144	154	4.02	1.08	1.15
1975	4466	148	627	172	178	4.23	1.16	1.20
1976	4955	166	713	201	195	4.28	1.21	1.17
1977	6031	186	823	233	198	4.44	1.25	1.07
1978	8383	204	930	266	219	4.55	1.30	1.07
1979	8736	222	1055	301	253	4.76	1.36	1.14
1980	9068	240	1165	334	277	4.85	1.39	1.15
1981	9898	257	1290	371	295	5.02	1.45	1.15
1982	9141	272	1402	412	306	5.15	1.51	1.12
1983	9905	298	1538	455	335	5.15	1.52	1.12
1984	10469	317	1704	496	363	5.37	1.56	1.15
1985	11014	321	1845	540	374	5.74	1.68	1.16
1986	16180	335	1985	588	406	5.93	1.76	1.21
1987	19553	351	2222	733	583	6.32	2.09	1.66
1988	23317	372	2422	814	620	6.50	2.18	1.66
1989	22342	399	2625	903	683	6.58	2.26	1.71
1990	25158	429	2841	935	645	6.62	2.18	1.50

Note: Unincorporated business included in corporate assets.

Source: IMF *International Financial Statistics;* BOJ *Economic Statistics Annual.*

Table 2.A3. *Japan: Financial Surplus or Deficit by Sector as a Percentage of GNP*

Year	Government Central	Government Other [a]	Private Corporate	Private Personal [b]	Rest of the world
1955	−0.62	−1.67	−5.11	7.80	−0.97
1960	1.45	−1.00	−9.82	8.60	−0.32
1965	0.29	−3.10	−4.35	7.66	−1.02
1970	1.30	−2.21	−6.91	7.89	−0.97
1971	0.89	−2.79	−6.22	9.40	−2.48
1972	0.65	−3.33	−7.97	11.54	−2.21
1973	1.8	−3.97	−7.62	8.89	0.03
1974	0.72	−4.46	−8.59	10.33	0.99
1975	−2.72	−4.64	−4.14	10.57	0.14
1976	−3.30	−4.15	−3.96	11.42	−0.65
1977	−3.96	−3.29	−2.58	11.09	−1.53
1978	−5.35	−3.71	−1.01	11.04	−1.70
1979	−4.45	−3.42	−3.03	9.08	0.89
1980	−3.17	−3.53	−3.46	8.16	1.07
1981	−3.75	−3.52	−3.03	10.93	−0.45
1982	−3.90	−2.99	−3.79	10.73	−0.66
1983	−3.90	−2.84	−3.02	10.29	−1.76
1984	−3.24	−2.50	−1.70	9.73	−2.77
1985 [c]	−2.08	−2.02	−1.85	9.67	−3.58
1986	−2.28	−1.81	−1.29	10.06	−4.22
1987 [d]	−0.55	−0.83	−2.20	7.81	−3.58
1988	0.41	0.17	−4.53	7.42	−2.73
1989	0.41	0.18	−6.74	9.13	−1.97
1990	0.60	0.18	−9.02	9.83	−1.21

Note: Rows do not sum to zero because of statistical discrepancies in the underlying data.

a. Public corporations and local authorities. Public corporations coming under private management are included in the private corporations column for subsequent periods; see notes c and d.

b. Households, noncorporate business firms, and nonprofit organizations.

c. Nippon Telegraph and Telephone and Japan Monopoly Corporation privatized beginning with the Apr.–Jun. quarter.

d. Japan National Railways privatized beginning with the Apr.–Jun. quarter.

Source: Computed by author from underlying data in Bank of Japan, *Economic Statistics Annual,* various years. Using the 1990 edition as an example, sectoral balances (for 1986–89) are in Table 108, panel 3 (pp. 213–14), and GNP (for 1983–89) is in Table 174, panel 1 (pp. 327–28).

Table 2.A4. *Japan: Savings by Sector and Investment as a Percentage of GNP*

	Gross domestic saving					Gross domestic investment[c]	Net foreign flow[d]
	Private						
Year	Personal[a]	Corporate	Total	Government[b]	Total		
1955	9.1	1.2	10.3	3.3	13.6	23.5	–1.0
1960	10.0	6.3	16.3	5.7	22.0	32.9	–0.3
1965	10.8	3.1	14.0	5.3	19.2	32.0	–1.0
1970	11.1	9.3	20.4	6.6	27.0	39.1	–1.0
1971	11.6	6.1	17.7	6.8	24.5	35.8	–2.5
1972	12.0	6.3	18.4	6.0	24.4	35.5	–2.2
1973	13.8	5.0	18.8	6.8	25.6	38.1	0.0
1974	16.4	0.4	16.8	6.3	23.1	37.4	1.0
1975	17.0	– 0.7	16.3	3.2	19.5	32.8	0.1
1976	17.4	0.7	18.2	2.0	20.2	31.9	– 0.6
1977	16.0	1.3	17.4	2.3	19.6	30.9	–1.5
1978	15.3	3.3	18.6	1.4	20.0	30.9	–1.7
1979	13.2	3.5	16.6	2.4	19.0	32.4	0.9
1980	12.9	2.8	15.8	2.6	18.3	32.2	1.1
1981	13.2	2.0	15.3	3.1	18.3	31.2	– 0.4
1982	12.0	2.4	14.4	2.8	17.2	29.9	– 0.7
1983	11.6	2.3	13.9	2.3	16.2	28.0	–1.8
1984	11.2	2.8	14.0	3.2	17.2	28.0	–2.8
1985	10.8	3.0	13.8	4.2	18.1	28.0	–3.6
1986	11.2	2.9	14.1	4.1	18.1	27.7	– 4.2
1987	10.0	2.8	12.8	5.7	18.5	28.5	–3.6
1988	9.6	3.3	12.9	6.8	19.7	30.4	–2.7
1989	9.6	2.3	11.8	7.7	19.5	31.5	–2.0
1990	9.5	1.9	11.4	8.4	19.7	32.6	–1.2

Note: Gross domestic savings plus net foreign flow does not equal gross domestic investment because of depreciation, as well as statistical discrepancies in the various underlying data series.

a. Households, noncorporate businesses, and nonprofit private organizations.

b. Including public corporations. Note that Nippon Telegraph and Telephone and the Japan Monopoly Corporation were privatized and hence are included in the private corporate sector, beginning with the Apr.–Jun. quarter of 1985. Japan National Railways was privatized beginning with the Apr.–Jun. quarter of 1987.

c. Gross domestic fixed capital investment plus increase in stocks (inventory) (codes 3.1 and 3.2 in the source).

d. Long-term capital account (direct investment plus loan disbursements minus loan repayments plus/minus minor items). Negative numbers represent capital outflows. In the source, this is the "net lending to the rest of the world" series (code 3.3).

Source: Computed by author from underlying data in Economic Planning Agency, *Annual Report on National Accounts,* various years, which are in Japanese. Using the 1991 edition (which has 1976 – 89 data) as an example, GNP is on pp. 80 – 81; investment and foreign flow are on pp. 82– 83; and savings are on pp. 86 –91.

Table 2.A5. *Japan: Sources of External Funds Raised by Nonfinancial Sectors* (percent)

	1970–74	1975–79	1980–84	1985–89	1985	1989
Distribution of funds by sector raising funds						
Central government	4.7	30.1	22.5	10.6	18.6	3.0
Other government[a]	10.7	13.0	13.2	−0.4	8.0	4.1
Corporate	67.0	37.2	44.3	64.2	54.9	62.9
Personal	17.7	19.7	20.0	25.6	18.5	30.0
Distribution of funds by source						
Borrowing from financial institutions	58.3	50.6	53.7	63.0	59.7	74.7
Securities issued	12.9	29.3	30.8	23.3	28.7	20.8
Foreign borrowing[b]	−0.1	0.8	1.1	6.5	5.1	12.4
Trade credits	28.8	19.3	14.4	7.3	6.4	−7.8
Borrowings from financial institutions (as % of total sources)						
Government institutions	10.4	17.1	16.6	10.7	10.8	11.5
Private institutions	47.9	33.5	37.1	52.3	48.9	63.2
Monetary institutions[c]	40.1	28.4	32.6	45.7	48.9	50.5
Trust banks	3.5	1.9	1.2	2.1	2.6	3.4
Insurance companies	3.5	2.1	2.9	4.3	3.1	8.3
Securities companies	0.1	0.3	0.4	1.4	−0.4	1.6
Other[d]	0.7	0.8	0.0	−1.2	−5.3	−0.6
Securities issued (as % of total sources)						
Government and public bonds	9.2	26.1	25.2	8.8	15.8	5.9
Corporate bonds	1.5	1.5	1.0	5.2	8.4	1.4
Bills and CPs (1987–)	n.a.	n.a.	n.a.	3.0	n.a.	3.6
Stocks and equities	2.3	1.6	4.6	6.2	4.6	9.8

n.a. Not applicable.

Note: Multiyear figures are computed by averaging the totals for the period. Excludes miscellaneous sources.

a. Public corporations and local authorities; see Table 2.8 regarding privatization of public corporations in 1985 and 1987.

b. Excludes direct investment.

c. Zenkoku banks plus financial institutions for small and medium firms, and for agriculture. Bank of Japan has not been a direct source.

d. Includes statistical discrepencies.

Source: Bank of Japan, flow-of-funds data from many different publications.

Table 2.A6. *Japan: Uses of Funds by Non-financial Sectors*

	1970–74	1975–79	1980–84	1985–89	1985	1989
Distribution of funds by sector investing funds						
Central government	6.2	7.2	6.8	6.0	9.1	2.7
Other government [a]	1.0	1.6	1.0	2.2	1.7	2.9
Corporate	47.3	33.9	36.4	39.8	36.3	28.9
Personal	45.4	57.3	55.8	52.0	52.9	65.4
Distribution of funds by uses						
Currency	3.7	2.5	1.2	2.1	1.5	3.1
Deposits and similar [b]	58.4	65.9	52.3	53.9	59.9	59.9
Securities purchased	6.8	10.2	31.7	35.0	24.7	38.8
Foreign lending [c]	0.3	0.2	1.8	4.3	9.1	3.2
Trade credits	30.8	21.3	12.9	4.7	4.8	−5.1
Deposits and similar claims on financial institutions (as % of total uses) [b]						
Monetary institutions	48.2	52.2	37.2	32.7	39.2	35.1
Demand deposits	14.1	9.7	3.0	2.5	2.0	−1.3
Other [d]	34.1	42.5	34.2	30.2	37.2	36.4
Nonbanks	10.2	13.7	15.1	21.2	20.7	24.8
Trust companies	4.0	5.1	5.3	7.5	7.2	8.8
Insurance companies	6.2	8.5	9.9	13.8	13.5	15.9
Securities purchased (as % of total uses)						
Bonds [e]	3.8	7.7	7.0	−1.1	4.6	−1.3
Bills and CPs (1987–)	n.a.	n.a.	n.a.	0.4	n.a.	0.6
Stocks and equities	2.1	1.3	22.1	31.2	18.1	38.1
Investment trusts	1.0	1.1	2.7	4.5	1.9	1.4

n.a. Not applicable.

Note: Multiyear figures are computed by averaging the totals for the period. Excludes miscellaneous uses.

a. Public corporations and local authorities. See Table 2.8 regarding privatization of public corporations in 1985 and 1987.

b. Excludes deposits and claims between financial institutions.

c. Excludes direct investment.

d. Time deposits and CDs.

e. Data are not available that separate corporate from government and public bond purchases.

Source: Bank of Japan, flow-of-funds data from many different publications.

Table 2.A7. *Japan: Distribution of Purchases and Issuance of Debt Instruments and Equity by Sector*
(percent)

	1970–74	1975–79	1980–84	1985–89	1985	1989
Short-term securities [a]						
Issuance by						
Financial sector	65.8	12.6	103.4	21.4	110.1	33.3
Government[b]	34.2	87.4	–3.4	32.4	–10.1	20.0
Businesses[c]	n.a.	n.a.	n.a.	46.2	n.a.	46.7
Purchases by[d]						
Financial sector	94.6	98.4	84.7	92.0	80.4	123.1
Central government	5.0	1.9	10.7	– 0.1	19.6	–34.9
Other government[e]	0.4	– 0.3	4.6	–1.6	0.0	– 0.0
Businesses[c]	n.a.	n.a.	n.a.	9.7	n.a.	11.8
Long-term securities						
Issuance by						
Financial sector	33.1	17.8	27.9	52.8	24.3	38.0
Central government	27.8	56.3	53.2	21.9	52.5	14.3
Other government[e]	28.7	20.6	8.4	–4.3	–9.0	4.6
Businesses	10.4	5.3	10.5	29.7	32.2	43.0
Purchases by						
Financial sector	72.2	73.0	69.1	82.0	79.9	77.9
Government[f]	– 0.1	2.4	– 0.7	– 0.2	–5.0	0.1
Businesses	3.2	4.8	6.7	– 0.4	8.1	0.2
Individuals	24.7	19.8	25.0	18.6	17.0	21.9
Equity (stock)						
Issuance by						
Financial sector	16.2	15.9	7.3	30.1	12.3	32.6
Businesses	83.8	84.1	92.7	69.9	87.7	67.4
Purchases by						
Financial sector	56.5	71.2	23.1	28.6	25.0	29.4
Government	1.5	0.8	1.6	– 0.1	4.1	0.0
Businesses	32.2	16.0	46.0	44.4	53.4	41.0
Individuals	9.8	12.0	29.4	27.1	17.5	29.7

n.a. Not applicable.

a. Excludes interbank transactions, such as call market loans.

b. All issuance was by the central government.

c. Businesses did not issue or purchase short-term securities (bills and commercial paper) until 1987.

d. Individuals (the personal sector) do not directly purchase items in short-term securities.

e. Public corporations and local authorities. See Table 2.A4 note b regarding privatization of public corporations in 1985 and 1987.

f. Virtually all by the central government; other government usually was less than ±0.1%, never more than ±0.4%.

Source: Bank of Japan, flow-of-funds data from many different publications.

Table 2.A8. *Japan: Distribution of Holdings*
of Outstanding Debt Instruments and Equity by Sector
(percent)

	1970–74	1975–79	1980–84	1985–89	1985	1989
Short-term securities [a]						
As an asset [b]						
Financial sector	95.8	94.8	92.0	89.9	92.8	92.4
Central government	3.8	5.0	6.4	7.0	5.6	2.7
Other government [c]	0.4	0.2	1.6	0.3	1.6	0.0
Businesses [d]	n.a.	n.a.	n.a.	2.7	n.a.	4.9
As a liability						
Financial sector	49.7	37.4	34.7	38.3	51.8	36.6
Government [e]	50.3	62.6	65.3	47.6	48.2	40.3
Businesses [d]	n.a.	n.a.	n.a.	14.1	n.a.	23.1
Long-term securities						
As an asset						
Financial sector	70.2	72.0	70.9	73.2	70.8	73.9
Government [f]	0.1	0.8	0.6	0.3	0.5	0.3
Businesses	4.5	3.9	5.4	4.4	5.5	3.9
Individuals	25.2	23.3	23.1	22.1	23.2	22.0
As a liability						
Financial sector	36.8	27.4	25.1	32.1	26.0	33.7
Central government	20.8	37.8	47.3	42.9	48.0	40.5
Other government [c]	29.9	25.9	20.1	12.3	17.0	10.8
Businesses	12.4	8.9	7.5	12.8	9.1	15.0
Equity (stock)						
As an asset						
Financial sector	41.7	50.2	26.8	25.2	21.6	26.2
Central government	0.7	0.5	0.3	0.3	0.7	0.2
Other government [c]	0.5	0.7	0.4	0.2	0.3	0.1
Businesses	26.7	24.6	39.0	44.5	43.8	44.2
Individuals	30.4	24.0	33.4	29.8	33.6	29.3
As a liability						
Financial sector	11.0	12.6	10.8	15.2	10.0	19.5
Businesses	89.0	87.4	89.2	84.8	90.0	80.5

n.a. Not applicable.

a. Excludes interbank transactions, such as call market loans.

b. Individuals (the personal sector) do not directly hold items in this category.

c. Public corporations and local authorities.

d. Businesses did not issue or hold short-term securities (bills and commercial paper) until 1987.

e. All by the central government.

f. All by the central government from 1983; before then, other government was less than 0.2%.

Source: Bank of Japan, flow-of-funds data from many different publications.

Table 2.A9. *Japan: Composition of Financial Asset Holdings of the Personal Sector*
(percent)

	1970–74	1975–79	1980–84	1985–89	1985	1989
Deposits and similar claims on financial institutions (as % of total holdings) [a]						
Currency	6.7	5.5	4.1	3.6	3.5	3.6
Deposits and similar[a]	80.6	82.4	80.7	75.2	77.3	73.7
Securities[b]	12.6	12.1	15.2	21.3	19.1	22.8
Monetary institutions	61.5	62.9	59.6	51.0	54.9	48.1
Demand deposits	13.2	10.7	7.6	6.1	6.3	6.2
Other [c]	48.4	52.2	52.1	44.8	48.7	41.9
Other financial institutions						
Trust banks	6.0	6.4	6.7	6.5	6.9	6.4
Life insurance[d]	13.1	13.1	14.4	17.7	15.5	19.2
Securities (as % of total holdings)						
Bonds of						
Government and public bodies	2.2	2.9	4.0	2.3	3.5	1.6
Financial institutions	3.7	4.1	3.6	2.8	3.5	2.3
Nonfinancial corporations	0.5	0.7	0.5	0.5	0.6	0.5
Stock and equities	4.5	2.5	4.9	11.5	8.5	13.9
Investment trusts	1.8	1.8	2.2	4.3	3.0	4.6

Warning: Data before 1985 are not comparable with later years because the method of valuing securities changed. See note b.

Note: The Personal Sector comprises households, noncorporate business firms, and nonprofit organizations. Excludes miscellaneous holdings. Multiyear figures are computed by averaging the totals for the period.

a. Excludes deposits and claims between financial institutions.

b. Bonds are included at face value. Stocks and equities are at market value after 1984; until then, at par value (generally substantially less than market value). Security investment trusts are at principal value, which approximates net asset value.

c. Time deposits, including certificates of deposit.

d. Life insurance and pension funds. Entry is for total operating funds.

Source: Bank of Japan, flow-of-funds data from many different publications.

Table 2.A10. *Japan: Distribution of Sources of Funds Raised by the Private Corporate Sector*
(percent)

	1970–74	1975–79	1980–84	1985–89	1980	1985	1989
Internal[a]	34.7	42.0	47.6	43.4	45.1	50.0	42.9
Equity	2.2	2.3	5.4	5.4	1.5	4.0	8.7
Debt securities[b]	1.4	2.2	1.2	7.1	1.1	7.3	4.5
Borrowings from							
Private financial institutions	33.2	27.6	29.1	28.2	25.3	31.3	32.3
Government financial institutions	3.0	4.2	3.3	5.7	3.7	2.3	5.6
Foreign sources[c]	−0.2	1.0	1.3	5.6	−1.7	4.6	11.0
Trade credits	25.7	20.7	12.1	4.5[d]	24.9	0.5	−5.0
Amount raised, in trillion yen (annual average of multiyear periods)	36,913	39,057	58,359	101,419	51,953	73,401	116,938

Note: Multiyear figures are computed by averaging the totals for the period. Excludes miscellaneous sources.

a. Internal funds are savings and gross fixed capital depreciation.

b. Bonds, commercial paper, and bills.

c. Bonds and other foreign liabilities.

d. In 1986 trade credits were −11.9%; this, combined with the negative value in 1989, contributes to the small number for 1986 – 89.

Source: Bank of Japan, flow-of-funds data from many different publications.

Table 2.A11. *Japan: Distribution of Uses of Funds Invested by the Private Corporate Sector*
(percent)

	1970–74	1975–79	1980–84	1985–89	1980	1985	1989
Real assets[a]	58.8	60.9	63.7	51.0	64.4	58.6	62.2
Financial assets (as % of total uses)							
Currency	0.3	0.3	0.1	0.2	0.1	0.1	0.4
Deposits at banks	12.8	12.6	9.8	11.8	4.9	11.7	6.2
Trust deposits	0.7	1.1	0.9	4.8	0.6	2.7	5.8
Equities	1.2	0.8	6.2	21.6	0.3	12.0	26.9
Debt securities	0.4	1.3	2.3	0.7	2.4	1.9	0.8
Foreign claims	0.2	0.2	2.1	4.7	0.3	8.5	3.9
Trade credits	25.4	22.9	14.9	5.2	26.9	4.5	− 6.2
Amount invested, in trillion yen (annual average of multiyear periods)	40,874	46,383	66,579	124,807	61,810	91,497	130,281

Note: Multiyear figures are computed by averaging the totals for the period. Excludes miscellaneous uses.
a. Includes gross fixed capital formation, inventory change, and purchases of land.
Source: Bank of Japan, flow-of-funds data from many different publications.

Table 2.A12. *Japan: Number of Financial Institutions*

	1960	1970	1980	1990
City banks	13	15	13	13
Regional banks	64	63	63	64
Daini chigin[a]	n.a.	n.a.	n.a.	68
Long-term credit banks	3	3	3	3
Trust banks	7	7	7	7
Foreign banks	—	—	64	82
Specialized intermediaries [b]				
Sōgō banks[a]	72	72	71	n.a.
Shinkin banks	538	502	461	451
Credit cooperatives (*shinren*)	461	532	476	407
Agriculture co-ops[c]	11635	6015	4490	3600
Life insurance companies	20	20	21	25
Non–life insurance companies	20	21	22	24
Securities companies[d]	503	251	227	210
Securities finance companies	3	3	3	3
Government institutions [e]				
Postal saving system[f]	16234	—	22287	23408
Special finance co-ops	8	8	10	9

n.a. Not applicable.

— Not available.

Note: In the source the first five are collectively called *zenkoku ginkō* ("all banks").

a. In Feb. 1989 sōgō banks became members of the Daini chigin (Second association of regional banks).

b. Intermediaries for small and medium firms and for agriculture. In addition to the groups listed there are the Shoko Chūkin Bank, the Zenshinren Bank, labor credit associations, the Nōrin Chūkin Bank, fishery cooperatives, and an assortment of credit federations.

c. Data are from Table 28 (p. 88) of the 1990 *Annual.*

d. Data for 1980 and 1990 from Table 36 (p. 93) of the 1990 *Annual.*

e. There are also a Japan Development Bank and an Export–Import Bank.

f. Number of post offices and agencies dealing in postal savings. The entry under 1990 is as of Mar. 31 (1989 fiscal year-end).

Source: Bank of Japan, *Economic Statistics Annual* and *Economic Statistics Monthly,* various issues. Annual data for 1977–90 for most of these, including number of branches, are summarized in the 1990 *Annual,* Table 77 (p. 160), except the numbers here differ slightly for securities companies and agricultural co-ops (see notes c and d).

Table 2.A13. *Japan: Assets at Financial Institutions*

	Trillion yen				Percentage of total			
	1960	*1970*	*1980*	*1989*	*1960*	*1970*	*1980*	*1989*
City banks	7.9	36.9	122.8	328.3	33.8	27.5	21.0	22.3
Regional banks	3.5	17.2	68.8	164.5	15.0	12.8	11.8	11.2
Daini chigin[a]	n.a.	n.a.	n.a.	62.7	n.a.	n.a.	n.a.	4.3
Foreign banks	—	—	7.5	15.3	—	—	1.3	1.0
Long-term credit banks	1.2	6.5	26.9	69.8	5.1	4.8	4.6	4.7
Trust banks	1.9	10.2	44.3	170.3	8.1	7.6	7.6	11.6
Agriculture co-ops	0.8	6.5	59.0	54.2	3.4	4.8	5.0	3.7
Nōrin Chūkin Bank	0.3	2.4	17.9	25.3	1.3	1.8	3.1	1.7
Life insurance companies	0.8	5.9	26.3	116.2	3.4	4.4	4.5	7.9
Non–life insurance companies	0.2	1.4	7.2	23.8	0.8	1.0	1.2	1.6
Securities companies[b]	0.3	0.6	2.3	12.9	1.3	0.4	0.4	0.9
Securities finance companies	0.1	0.3	1.1	3.0	0.4	0.2	0.2	0.2
Intermediaries for small and medium firms								
Sōgō banks[a]	1.2	11.5	33.0	n.a.	5.1	8.6	5.6	n.a.
Shinkin banks	1.2	9.4	40.9	87.4	5.1	7.0	7.0	5.9
Credit cooperatives	0.2	2.1	9.4	21.0	0.8	1.6	1.6	1.4
Shōkō Chūkin Bank	0.3	1.3	5.8	12.3	1.3	1.0	1.0	0.8
Government institutions								
Postal saving system[c]	2.1	14.6	100.1	227.6	9.0	10.9	17.1	15.5
Special finance co-ops	0.8	4.3	32.1	62.4	3.4	3.2	5.5	4.2
Japan Development Bank	0.5	1.7	5.1	9.1	2.1	1.3	0.9	0.6
Export–Import Bank	0.1	1.5	5.1	5.5	0.4	1.1	0.9	0.4

n.a. Not applicable.

— Not available.

Note: Loans and investments, bills discounted, call loans, deposits at other financial institutions, and currency—except as noted.

a. Sōgō banks became members of the Daini chigin in 1989.

b. Securities held for own account plus loans to clients.

c. Assets of the Trust Fund Bureau of the Ministry of Finance.

Source: Bank of Japan, *Economic Statistics Annual,* various issues. For example, the 1991 edition, Tables 16–50 (pp. 41–104), gives a variety of annual data series for most of these institutions.

Table 2.A14. Japan: Loans and Investments of Financial Institutions

	Trillion yen				Percentage of total			
	1960	1970	1980	1989	1960	1970	1980	1989
City banks	5.6	25.6	88.2	239.8	30.3	24.8	18.3	19.8
Regional banks	2.8	13.7	57.6	137.0	15.1	13.3	12.0	10.8
Daini chigin[a]	n.a.	n.a.	n.a.	52.6	n.a.	n.a.	n.a.	4.3
Foreign banks	—	—	4.8	10.1	—	—	1.0	0.8
Long-term credit banks	1.0	5.4	21.4	55.9	5.4	5.2	4.4	4.6
Trust banks[b]	1.6	8.3	39.9	161.6	8.6	8.0	8.3	13.3
Agriculture co-ops	0.3	3.3	13.1	15.3	1.6	3.2	2.7	1.3
Nōrin Chūkin Bank	0.3	2.1	11.8	23.3	1.6	2.0	2.4	1.9
Life insurance companies	0.6	5.2	23.7	95.9	3.2	5.0	4.9	7.9
Non–life insurance companies	0.1	0.8	4.6	16.6	0.5	0.8	1.0	1.4
Securities companies[c]	0.3	0.6	2.3	12.9	1.6	0.6	0.5	1.1
Securities finance companies	0.1	0.3	1.1	3.0	0.5	0.3	0.2	0.2
Intermediaries for small and medium firm								
Sōgō banks[c]	1.0	5.7	25.1	n.a.	5.4	5.5	5.2	n.a.
Shinkin banks	0.9	7.2	32.0	63.8	4.9	7.0	6.6	5.2
Credit cooperatives	0.2	1.8	7.8	15.9	1.1	1.7	1.6	1.3
Shōkō Chūkin Bank	0.2	1.2	5.7	12.1	1.1	1.2	1.2	1.0
Government institutions								
Postal saving system[d]	2.1	14.6	100.1	227.6	11.4	14.1	20.8	18.7
Special finance co-ops	0.8	4.3	32.1	62.4	4.3	4.2	6.7	5.1
Japan Development Bank	0.5	1.7	5.1	9.1	2.7	1.6	1.1	0.8
Export–Import Bank`	0.1	1.5	5.1	5.5	0.5	1.4	1.1	0.4

n.a. Not applicable.

— Not available.

Note: Loans and discounts plus securities. Excludes government bonds.

a. Sōgō banks became members of the Daini chigin in 1989.

b. Includes securities held for investment trust.

c. Securities held for own account plus loans to clients.

d. Assets of the Trust Fund Bureau of the Ministry of Finance.

Source: Bank of Japan, *Economic Statistics Annual,* various issues. For example, the 1991 edition, Tables 16 –50 (pp. 41–104), gives a variety of annual data series for most of these institutions.

Table 2.A15. *Japan: Indirect Instruments Issued by Financial Institutions*

	Trillion yen				Percentage of total			
	1960	*1970*	*1980*	*1989*	*1960*	*1970*	*1980*	*1989*
City banks	5.6	25.6	87.9	210.7	35.2	27.9	21.9	20.4
Regional banks	2.9	14.5	59.1	137.7	18.2	15.8	14.7	13.3
Daini chigin[a]	n.a.	n.a.	n.a.	55.1	n.a.	n.a.	n.a.	5.3
Foreign banks	—	—	1.5	2.4	—	—	0.4	0.2
Long-term credit banks	1.0	5.4	21.8	51.4	6.3	5.9	5.4	5.0
Trust banks[b]	0.6	4.5	16.5	102.9	3.8	4.9	4.1	10.0
Agriculture co-ops	0.8	6.2	27.5	51.5	5.0	6.8	6.8	5.0
Nōrin Chūkin Bank	0.3	2.3	11.0	25.7	1.9	2.5	2.7	2.5
Life insurance companies[c]	0.8	5.9	26.3	116.2	5.0	6.4	6.5	11.2
Non–life insurance companies[c]	0.2	1.4	7.2	23.8	1.3	1.5	1.8	2.3
Intermediaries for small and medium firms								
Sōgō banks[a]	1.1	6.4	27.4	n.a.	6.9	7.0	6.8	n.a.
Shinkin banks	1.0	7.7	34.5	74.8	6.3	8.4	8.6	7.2
Credit cooperatives	0.2	2.0	8.6	19.0	1.3	2.2	2.1	1.8
Shōkō Chūkin Bank	0.2	1.2	5.5	11.8	1.3	1.3	1.4	1.1
Government institutions								
Postal saving system	1.1	7.7	62.0	134.6	6.9	8.4	15.4	13.0
Special finance co-ops	0.1	0.8	5.3	14.5	0.6	0.9	1.3	1.4
Japan Development and Export–Import banks	n.a.	0.0	0.1	0.8	n.a.	0.0	0.0	0.1

n.a. Not applicable.

— Not available.

Note: Indirect instruments comprises deposits, savings deposits, CDs, financial debentures (yen and foreign currency–denominated), and installment savings.

a. Sōgō banks became members of the Daini chigin in 1989.

b. Includes money, pension, and loan trusts.

c. Total assets.

Source: Bank of Japan, *Economic Statistics Annual,* various issues. For example, the 1991 edition, Tables 16 –50 (pp. 41–104), gives a variety of annual data series for most of these institutions.

3

Japan: Development and Structural Change of the Banking System

HIROSHI KITAGAWA AND
YOSHITAKA KUROSAWA

Maximization of capital investment was a goal shared by all three major groups of players in Japan—large industrial corporations, banks, and the central government—during the 1950s and 1960s as the nation sought to rebuild in the wake of World War II (see Nakamura 1980). Big businesses and major banks were closely tied by means of a main bank and cross-shareholding relationships. The corporate sector was able to borrow at relatively low interest rates from the banking sector, while small business paid much higher interest rates. There was little left in the way of loanable funds for households that wanted to engage in housing investment or consumer finance.

The Ministry of Finance and the Bank of Japan provided banks with a favorable operating environment, in part made possible by the government's strict control of the banking sector. Safety was the principal explicit reason for this control, but the need to maintain the credit allocation system had far more to do with the actual forms regulation took than did the safety of the system. The low-risk low-return character of this approach served all three groups well during the reconstruction and high–economic growth period, which explains its survival into the mid 1970s. Deregulation has proceeded gradually since then—generally reacting to changed environments, although of course the deregulation process itself has been an important contributor to environmental change.

This chapter reviews the behavior and efficiency of Japanese banks on a micro basis through the tightly controlled period and the relaxation period, focusing especially on the city banks. Table 3.1 provides information on the city banks.

The first two sections take up regulation and deregulation. Relationship banking is extremely important in Japan, including cross-shareholding with clients and the main bank system. These are analyzed in the third section. Succeeding sections discuss liabilities, assets, nonperforming loans, off-balance sheet items, and the handling of financial crises. We then turn to operational efficiency, specifically in regard to economies of scale and scope, and the question of whether Japanese banks have sought to maximize scale or profits. Sections on the effects of liberalization and trends in the early 1990s conclude the chapter.

Table 3.1. *Japanese City Banks, Assets and 1992 BIS Ratio (trillion yen on Mar. 31 of year shown)*

By size in 1992	1962	1972	1982	1992	BIS ratio
Dai-Ichi Kangyo (1971)	n.a.	5.71	22.4	61.3	8.24
Sumitomo	1.01	4.55	19.1	60.2	8.43
Sakura (1990)	n.a.	n.a.	n.a.	59.6	7.92
Fuji	1.09	4.77	20.2	58.2	8.04
Mitsubishi	1.05	4.53	18.8	56.6	8.20
Sanwa	1.02	4.29	17.5	56.2	8.10
Tokai	0.77	3.31	13.0	35.0	8.38
Asahi (1991)	—	—	—	30.0	8.30
Bank of Tokyo	0.65	2.51	13.6	28.4	8.10
Daiwa	0.51	2.06	6.9	18.4	8.27
Hokkaido Takushoku	0.26	1.27	4.9	11.1	8.26
Kyowa	0.43	2.16	7.2		
Saitama (not a city bank in 1962)	—	1.46	6.2		
Mitsui	0.73	3.09	15.1		
Taiyo-Kobe (1973)	—	—	11.2		
Taiyo (not a city bank in 1962)	—	1.27	—		
Kobe	0.35	1.77	—		
Dai-Ichi	0.71	—	—		
Nippon Kangyo	0.67	—	—		
Total for all city banks	9.25	42.75	176.1	475.0	

n.a. Not applicable.

— Not available.

Note: Unconsolidated.

Excludes guarantees. (Customer liability for guarantees appears as an asset on balance sheets in Japan, offset by a liability for the guarantee.)

Fiscal years end Mar. 31 of the following calendar year, so 1992 Mar. 31 is the end of fiscal 1991, etc.

Dates in parentheses indicate mergers among city banks.

Throughout most of the period 1954–89 there were 13 city banks, but not always the same 13; during 1969–71 there were 15. In December 1968 the Japan Mutual Bank, by far the largest of the mutuals, became a city bank under the name Taiyo. In April 1969 the largest local bank, Saitama (based in a growing part of the Tokyo metro area), became a city bank. Mergers in 1971 (Dai-Ichi Kangyo) and 1973 (Taiyo Kobe) reduced the number back to 13. Mitsui and Taiyo–Kobe merged in April 1990 and adopted the name Sakura Bank in April 1992. Kyowa and Saitama merged in April 1991 and became Asahi Bank in September 1992. Ranked by assets, Dai-Ichi Kangyo has been the largest bank since its formation in 1971; Fuji was prior to that.

For more details on changes during the 1940s and Occupation, and on other types of banks, see the Bank of Japan, *Economic Statistics Annual* (e.g., 1990 edition, notes pp. 3–6). Histories of banking in Japan in English include Fuji Bank 1967 and (postwar only) Adams and Hoshii 1972.

Source: FBAJ, *Analysis of Financial Statements of All Banks,* issues for years shown.

REGULATION

Japanese banks have been strictly controlled by the Ministry of Finance (MOF) and the Bank of Japan (BOJ). The key regulatory tools were restriction of competition (by means of interest rate controls, entry restrictions, and segmentation of businesses), rigorous bank examination, and regulation of various operating and balance sheet ratios. Much of the regulation was what is termed administrative guidance rather than specific laws or explicit rules.

Gross profit margins were effectively guaranteed by the interest rate restrictions, so banks were able to increase profits simply by expanding loan volume. Banks were therefore competitive with one another in seeking new borrowers, and the monetary authorities basically supported their behavior. In accordance with government industrial policy, one key target of bank regulation was to channel funds toward investment in export and heavy industries. In this sense regulation was an active tool for economic development. Of course the authorities also sought to maintain the soundness of the banking sector in order to keep the payment system in good order.

Three interrelated regulations were used to achieve these two targets. The first was segmentation—separating financial services among different types of institutions and prohibiting entry in order to reduce competition. Second, banks were subject to direct regulation of interest rates, dividends, the opening of branches, and—through "window guidance" by BOJ—lending volume. The third was regulation based on operating and balance sheet ratios.

Segmentation

To separate commercial banking from long-term lending, the Long-Term Credit Bank Law was enacted in 1952, covering the Long-Term Credit Bank of Japan (LTCB, a newly established bank) and the Industrial Bank of Japan (IBJ, which was converted from being a special government financial institution). Two other special government banks—Nippon Kangyo and Hokkaido Takushoku—also were briefly long-term banks but became city banks in December 1953. There have been three long-term credit banks since the Japan Credit Bank was established in 1957 (under the name Hypothec Bank, later changed to Nippon Fudosan Bank; the present name was adopted in 1977). All are listed on the Tokyo Stock Exchange. The largest shareholders are mostly insurance companies and city banks. However, LTCB counts Kawasaki Steel, Toyota and Nippon Steel among its dozen largest holders, and 6 of IBJ's 10 largest are industrial companies.

These long-term banks and 10 government financial institutions relied mostly on 5-year coupon and 1-year discount "bank debentures" (*kinyu sai*), which could not be issued by other types of banks. In contrast, "ordinary banks" (city and regional) could offer only 3- and 6-month, and 1-, 2- and 3-year time deposits in accordance with MOF administrative guidance, although there are no legal provisions regarding the maturity of deposits. This separation of short- and long-term banking directly eliminated a good deal of competition on the deposit side. There are no controls by type of bank on maturities of loans, but lending maturities have tended to be set by the length of deposits, and thus the lending market also was segregated.

As a result of this separation policy, the loan market share among city banks (55 to 58 percent), regional banks (27 to 29 percent), long-term banks (12 percent), and trust banks (3 percent) remained relatively unchanged for the 15 years 1960 –75, except for a slight decrease in city bank share. Even within categories, the authorities did not want to change the market share of specific banks, so MOF gave permission to open branches according to current market share. Because city banks were eager to collect deposits, given the low interest rate on them, restrictions on opening new branches were an effective means of controlling bank behavior.

Trust banks and securities companies were also separated from the ordinary banking business. The Securities Exchange Act (1948) did not allow financial institutions other than securities firms to engage in securities businesses. Banking and trust activities were separated by means of administrative guidance, a policy regarded as an important measure in controlling long-term funds and maintaining the banks' soundness.

Regulators made opening new branches more difficult in 1949, and in 1953 MOF announced a general policy of no new branches. This was followed in 1954 by an announced policy of no new banks and the encouragement of mergers to improve the efficiency of existing ones. The number of banks had risen from 69 at the end of 1945 to 85 in 1952 and 87 in 1954, including 12 new regional banks in the period 1950 –54. Since 1954 there have been 85 to 88 banks. Under restrictions on branching, the number of city bank branches actually declined by 50 between 1953 and 1961. In 1962– 63 banks were allowed to open 130 branches, primarily to serve newly built-up areas. Table 3.2 has data on the number of the various types of banks.

Market segmentation enabled banks to raise deposits from individuals despite the low interest rates. The banks were not allowed to accept long-term deposits, but at the same time long-term and trust banks had few branches and thus could not easily take part in the short-term deposit business. In addition, the capital market was too immature to attract household savings. Therefore, the separation reduced competition and was a prerequisite for keeping interest rates at a low level. This of course had a direct negative effect on the welfare of depositors.

Interest Rate Controls

From the start of the high growth period in the 1950s, interest rates on commercial lending were artificially controlled to stimulate fixed capital investment in the private sector. A key instrument for this low interest rate policy was the Temporary Interest Rate Adjustment Law (TIRAL) implemented in 1947 and still effective in 1992 despite the "temporary" label. The purpose of the law was to prevent interest rate competition, which was considered detrimental to the profitability of financial institutions.

On the liability side of the balance sheet, controls brought an increased the compensating balances, a phenomenon called "overloan," and a maldistribution of loan funds—topics to which we return later.

Table 3.2. *Number of Banks and Branches*

Dec. 31	City Banks	City Units	Long-term [a] Banks	Long-term [a] Units	Trust [b] Banks	Trust [b] Units	Regional Banks	Regional Units	Sogo [c] Banks	Sogo [c] Units	Shinkin [d] Banks	Shinkin [d] Units
1952	11	1,583	4	[e]	6	62	64	3,571	70	1,513	634	244
1962	13	1,799	3	26	7	171	65	3,729	72	2,310	534	2,757
1972	14	2,395	3	39	7	268	63	4,369	72	2,941	485	4,103
1982	13	2,708	3	57	7	343	63	5,616	71	3,975	456	6,132
1991	11	3,067	3	74	7	384	64	6,792	68	4,474	443	7,526

Note: Because of mergers and change of status, these are not always the same banks.

Units includes home offices and domestic branches but excludes subbranches, etc.

Through 1988 city, long-term, trust, and local banks were collectively called "all banks" in discussions and data series. Beginning with 1989, as discussed by Ternanishi in his chapter, the sogo banks were "upgraded" and are now included in "all banks."

a. Long-term credit banks. Two of those in 1952 changed to city banks in 1953; the third currently existing bank was formed in 1957.

b. The seventh was created in 1959 from Sanwa Bank's trust division, the defunct Bank of Kobe, and the securities management division of Nomura Securities.

c. Members of the Second Association of Regional Banks. Called mutual loan and savings banks in early editions of the source. 1972 data are as of Sep. 30.

d. Called credit associations in early editions of the source.

e. Not comparable (see note a).

Source: Bank of Japan, *Economic Statistics Annual* has a table of annual data, generally covering 14 years, for these and several other types of financial institutions. Thus the 1990 edition, p. 160, Table 77, covers 1977–90, and the 1975 edition, p. 34, Table 15, covers 1961–74.

Deposits

Almost all deposits and savings interest rates were regulated through the 1960s and 1970s under TIRAL. MOF proposed rate levels and changes in rates and the BOJ Policy Board determined maximum rates. BOJ then published these guidelines and required that each financial institution observe them. For competitive reasons, deposit-taking institutions set their own deposit rates at the maximum guideline level, resulting in the same interest rate for a given type of deposit of a given maturity. Strict deposit interest rate restrictions applied not only to commercial banks but also to thrifts, cooperatives, and indeed all private financial institutions.

There was competition for deposits in the form of services. Bank employees would pick up deposits at people's homes and offices. If only as a gesture, customers were given facial tissue and towels. There was also an appeal to group loyalty: A bank's deposit collectors would canvass employees of firms that had a main-bank relationship with the bank.

Loans

Lending rates also were regulated, although not as strictly as deposit rates. Short-term rates at private financial institutions for individual loans under 1 year in maturity were determined within a band between the maximum interest rate set by TIRAL and the prime rate set by the Federation of Bankers Association of Japan (FBAJ). This prime was usually set 25 basis points above the official discount rate and served as the de facto lower limit for short-term lending rates. The primary factors determining the interest rate in individual cases were the credit-worthiness of the borrower and the closeness of the borrower's business relationship with the bank.

Neither TIRAL nor MOF set explicit maximum limits on long-term lending (maturity over 1 year). In fact, however, the "long-term prime rate" charged high-quality corporations such as electric power companies was determined by the parties concerned and government authorities, using implicit rules. When changes were made, all financial institutions would simultaneously change their rate.

The long-term prime's level was determined as a fixed spread above the fund-raising cost of 5-year fixed interest, bank debentures. This amounted to 90 basis points above the interest rate on the debentures and 88 basis points above the expected dividend rate on loan trusts for trust banks. Because the rate paid on debentures newly issued by all long-term credit banks was the same, as was the dividend rate for all trust banks, the long-term prime was, in practice, set. Banks make loans to corporate clients at rates above the prime or by requiring borrowers to maintain compensating balances for both short- and long-term loans. Horiuchi (1984, pp. 16–20) argues that compensating balances raised the effective loan rates to virtually market-clearing levels within each market segment (big business, small business, and the like).

Effects

Control of the interest rates banks paid and charged, as well as of bank dividend rates, was meant to keep all banks in a sound condition. The main purpose of interest rate control was to eliminate competition for deposits and to reduce the cost of funds for manufacturing industries and thereby encourage fixed capital investment. To collect deposits at low interest rates, it was necessary to ensure that housholds had few alternative financial assets available to them. The controls provided a guaranteed minimum spread for the banks. Rates were set to ensure survival of even the most inefficient bank, so banks had an opportunity to make sizable profits by expanding their loans. Moreover, effective interest rates were adjusted to some extent by requiring borrowers to maintain compensating balances.

Window Guidance

BOJ directly controlled the level of bank lending by varying the growth rate of loan volume. Called "window guidance," this practice was adopted in 1953 as a form of moral suasion to keep the increase in bank lending within the monthly limits BOJ felt appropriate to its overall monetary policy. At the same time it set a fixed lending share among banks in the same category.

Guidance was applied first to city banks and long-term banks. From 1964, lending levels were set quarterly, and trust and regional banks were included. The larger sogo banks (mutual banks) were included in 1967. Ultimately it extended not only to the larger *shinkin* banks (credit associations) and foreign banks but also to trading companies.

Reserve requirements were introduced in September 1959 at a level of 0.5 percent for time deposits and 1.5 percent for other deposits. The latter was cut to 1 percent for most of 1965–69 and changed frequently during 1973–77, reaching as high as 4.25 percent in 1974 –75; it has been 2.5 percent most of the time since 1977. Time deposit reserve requirements have risen relatively more—climbing from one-third to almost two-thirds of the level for other deposits.

The average ratio of loans to deposits for city banks was over 90 percent until 1975. This was quite high, particularly considering that the ratio of securities holding to deposits was 17 to 20 percent.

As a result of window guidance, the marginal ratio of loans to deposits wavered between 188 percent during 1973, a relaxed guidance period, and 53 percent when tightly squeezed in 1975.

There are theoretical and empirical studies suggesting window guidance was effective, although others have expressed doubt. Suzuki (1966) and Horiuchi (1977, 1978) provide the main analyses against effectiveness. The principal point of both is that during periods of window guidance, lending shifted from guided institutions to outsider institutions, resulting in no real change in lending overall. Horiuchi insists that as excess reserves accumulated at guided institutions as a result of implementation of window guidance, outsiders took advantage of the resulting lower call money rates to obtain funds to expand their lending. The increase in lending by outsiders relative to the increase of guided institutions during guided periods was 45.1 percent for 1973–74 and 52.3 percent for 1979–80. During the unguided period 1975–76 it was 34.8 percent, and for 1977–78, 19.0 percent (Furukawa 1985, p. 71).

There were two reasons individual banks went along with window guidance, even though it was a form of moral suasion with no legal basis (Furukawa 1985, pp. 61–65). First, the banks, especially city banks, feared they might not be able to borrow from BOJ, which provided credit at interest rates lower than the call rate. The second was a demonstration effect. Each bank tried to keep up with the others in maintaining its lending and deposit share because BOJ allotted lending increases to the banks during window guidance periods in accordance with their past lending or deposit shares. (For more on window guidance see Suzuki 1987, pp. 325–26.)

Other Controls

Dividends were controlled by MOF from 1956 so as not to exceed 12.5 percent of paid-in capital. This forced banks to accumulate retained earnings. In practice, administrative guidance kept the level the same for all city banks and at 10 percent or less. This was intended to avoid competition among them, which might cause a difference in the cost of their capital. The ratio of dividends to net profits also was regulated to be 40 percent or less. From the 1960s through the 1980s the level varied from 20 percent at Fuji, Mitsubishi, and some other banks to 40 percent at Daiwa and Taiyo Kobe.

In 1970 the banks were theoretically allowed to increase their dividends to 15 percent of their stock's par value. However, the 10 percent guided limit remained in place so none of the 76 banks affected increased its dividend. Finally in 1980 a few banks started paying more than 10 percent as government policy shifted from strict regulations to gradual relaxations. Out of 77 city and regional banks at the end of fiscal 1988 (March 31, 1989), 55 (no city banks) paid 10 percent, 5 (0) paid 12 percent, 8 (5) paid 14 percent, 2 (1) paid 16 percent, and 7 city banks paid 17 percent. Par is 50 yen per share, so these are very low yields based on stock price, less than 1 percent in almost all cases.

The opening of branches also was controlled. This undoubtedly reduced the number of branches there would otherwise have been, as the banks had an incentive to open as many as possible in a quest for more cheap (controlled rate) deposits.

Specifically to protect smaller banks from larger ones, in 1954 the FBAJ imposed restrictions on advertising to preempt government controls. The rules covered the amount of television ad time and where in newspapers and magazines ads could appear (not near the front). In early 1992 FBAJ announced the limits would be abolished in March 1993.

The monetary authorities also have formal rules such as restrictions on the size of loans, and controls on liquidity and equity levels.

Loan size restrictions were imposed on all banks by administrative guidance in 1974 and became law in 1981. Loans to one company must be less than 20 percent of bank equity for ordinary banks (city and regional), and 30 percent for long-term banks. All other credits and the value of any equity holdings involving the client are excluded from this restriction, as are loans to subsidiaries. It is, therefore, possible for a bank to have a greater exposure to a single company than that implied by the loan limit.

Equity (including reserves exceeding the required coverage of deposits and CDs) was mandated at 10 percent of total assets in 1954. However the average for city banks was always far less because otherwise-strict regulation was deemed sufficient to keep the banks sound (Hasui 1986, p. 133). As liberalization progressed in the late 1980s, the authorities recognized the need to enforce the equity regulation, particularly in the wake of the July 1988 BIS agreement, to which we return.

Liquidity regulations were imposed in 1959 to keep the level of current assets to deposits and CDs at 30 percent or greater. Neither city nor regional banks met this restriction until 1980 when city banks met it by taking time deposits in the Euromarket (which are not subject to liquidity requirements) and making call loans (which are a current asset for purposes of meeting the requirements) (Hasui 1986, p. 133).

MOF's Bank Inspection Department and BOJ's Examination Bureau take turns making annual examinations. Japanese bond-rating agencies—JCR (Japan Credit Rating Agency), NIS (Nihon Investors Service), and JBRI (Japan Bond Research Institute)—have rated Japanese banks since 1987.

Deposit Insurance

The Deposit Insurance Corporation was established in 1971 to provide deposit insurance. Capital was provided one-third each by MOF, BOJ, and private banks.

The corporation has no inspection or regulatory powers, in contrast to its U.S. counterpart. By law the governor is also a deputy governor of BOJ; most of the other directors come from member banks. An amendment in 1986 increased the insured limit from 3 million to 10 million yen of deposit principal (interest earnings are not covered) and premiums from 0.008 to 0.012 percent of deposits at the end of the previous fiscal year (March 31). The system applies per person per bank. In March 1989 the fund held some 440 billion yen, and in March 1991 holdings were 602 billion yen, about 0.1 percent of insured deposits in both years.

The deposit insurance system has never been called on to pay off depositors because regulators have stepped in at troubled financial institutions before they went bankrupt. In early 1992, however, the Deposit Insurance Corporation made loans in connection with the Toho Sogo and Toyo Shinkin rescues.

DEREGULATION

The deregulation process is chronicled in the Appendix.

In part because of the increase in government bond issuance and a decrease in the financial needs of the corporate sector in the 1970s, the regulatory system came under more and more pressure to change. In particular, the separation between different types of banking businesses began to weaken and controls on interest rates became less strict.

As the bank-intermediated financial needs of leading industrial companies declined, city, trust and long-term credit banks all sought to increase loans to small and medium companies. City banks extended their business to longer-term loans in an effort to improve profitability. As a result, long-term banks saw their share of total long-term loans drop. Tables 3.3 and 3.4 show these shifts in lending emphasis.

Table 3.3. *Long-Term Loans as a Percentage of Outstanding Loans and Discounts*

Type of bank	1961	1966	1971	1976	1981	1986	1989	1992
All	16.9	20.6	25.4	38.2	40.8	39.0	48.0	56.4[a]
City	6.4	10.0	13.6	29.3	33.5	32.7	47.5	57.2
Long-term	93.5	91.7	93.6	92.5	84.1	70.9	69.0	79.7
Trust	n.a.	21.4	33.1	42.0	37.3	24.4	35.5	41.4
Regional	8.4	11.1	18.6	31.7	36.8	40.1	43.4	48.4

n.a. Not applicable.

Note: Data are for Mar. 31 of year shown. Fiscal 1960 ended Mar. 31, 1961, etc.

Long-term means over 1 year in duration. Interbank lending is not included in total lending. Overseas branch offices included through Sep.1982, then excluded.

a. Includes Second Association of Regional Banks.

Source: Bank of Japan, *Economic Statistics Annual,* various issues. For example, the 1990 edition, pp. 129–30, Table 58, provides absolute data and percentage distribution by term for fiscal years ending in 1982–90, and the 1974 edition, pp. 108–10, covers 1966–74.

Table 3.4. *Loans to Small and Medium Firms as a Percentage of Outstanding Loans and Discounts*

Type of bank	1961	1966	1971	1976	1981	1986	1988	1992
City	26.6	23.7	25.8	29.0	37.7	44.4	51.2	57.9
Long-term	6.1	10.7	16.0	15.0	26.9	28.1	35.4	40.1
Trust	9.9	7.3	10.1	10.5	22.0	31.7	40.4	51.2
Regional	54.4	53.3	55.5	51.3	55.0	59.5	62.6	65.3

Note: Data are for Mar. 31 of year shown, which is the fiscal year-end. Fiscal 1960 ended Mar. 31, 1961, etc. The ceiling for "small and medium firms" has grown with time. From the latter part of the 1980s it has been firms with ≤300 employees or ≤100 million yen in capital, with lower limits for wholesalers and for retailers, restaurants, and service companies. The same group is also called "small enterprises" in some sources.

Source: EPA, *Henkakuki no kinyū system* 1989 has annual data through fiscal 1987. The Long-Term Credit Bank of Japan, *Economic Review,* periodically publishes data as a percentage of *domestic* loans, which of course make the numbers larger. See, e.g., Issue 99 (Apr. 1990), p. 21.

The city banks' search for clients among medium and small firms brought friction with sogo banks, resulting in sogo banks being allowed to convert to ordinary banks, starting in 1989.

The change in the maturity pattern of loans has brought competition between city banks and trust banks. Shortening of maturities on assets of trust banks and loan sales by city banks are the causes of the friction. Long-term assets as a percentage of total assets at trust banks declined to 79 percent in 1985 from 87 percent in 1975. Loan sales by city banks threaten trust banks with the possibility of losing out to asset securitization.

Separation of banking and the securities business has been weakened by allowing banks to engage in sales (1983) and to deal (1987) in government bonds, and to deal in commercial paper (1987).

Despite the change in the maturity pattern on loans, the main source of funds at long-term banks was regulated to be 5-year bonds and at city and regional banks was time deposits with maturities of less than 3 years. Remember that maturities of liability instruments had been carefully allotted by MOF to avoid competition among types of financial institutions. As a result, both long-term banks and city banks had trouble matching the maturities of their assets and liabilities. At the end of March 1985 city banks had a 30 trillion yen gap between 59 trillion yen of long-term loans and securities holdings and 29 trillion yen of deposits of 2 years or longer. Long-term city bank loans generally run 5 to 6 years except for housing loans, which that run to 15 years.

City banks therefore sought to circumvent the 3-year limit by using such things as interest rate swaps, dollar denominated 5-year CDs and floating rate loans. In addition, they took the proceeds of Euroyen bonds, which have been allowed for nonresident private issuers since 1984 and for residents since 1985, in exchange for shorter term liabilities. Sales of loans made to local governments, permitted since 1989, and of general loans, allowed since 1990, are additional tools to adjust term structure.

Interest Rates

Both spread and floating rate lending have been widely used, and a new short-term prime rate method was introduced in 1989 that fluctuates according to market rates for large-scale time deposits and CDs. The prime previously had changed with the official discount rate.

Deregulation of interest rates on bank liabilities started with foreign currency deposits in May 1972 in the wake of abolition of related foreign exchange controls, although an upper limit was set on how much a person could have in such deposits. CDs were introduced in May 1979. Besides internationally familiar types of deposits, novel ones were introduced, including BIG (June 1981) for trust banks and WIDE (October 1981) for long-term banks. These do not fall within the jurisdiction of TIRAL, although in practice the rates have not been freely set. Money market certificates (MMCs) appeared in March 1985, and interest paid on large time deposits was liberalized in October 1985. Table 3.5 outlines the characteristics of these instruments.

The share of funds garnered by the banking sector decreased from 60 to 80 percent in the 1960s and 1970s to 40 to 50 percent in the early 1980s—supplanted by increases in *gensaki* (a market-rate instrument), *chukoku* funds, and postal savings. Offered by securities firms, gensaki, similar to repurchase agreements in the United States, attracted short-term funds from industrial companies, beginning in the mid-1970s. Chukoku funds, made up of government long- and medium-term bonds, induced individuals to shift from bank accounts to security company accounts by providing higher returns without much sacrifice in liquidity.

It will have taken 14 years to fully deregulate bank time deposit interest rates. There seem to be two reasons for such a long time. First, MOF intended the slow pace in order to maintain orderly credit conditions. ("Orderly conditions" means avoiding bankruptcy or financial distress for weaker banks. Gradual removal of the benefits they received from regulated deposit rates meant the banks had time to adjust.) Second, it was 1990 before MOF, the Federation of Bankers Association, and the Ministry of Posts (MOP) agreed on how to deal with interest rates on postal savings, which represent one-third of personal savings. Postal saving rates will be based on an average of private deposit rates—but MOF and MOP will monitor the situation and adjust the rates if there is any considerable shifting of funds.

According to a MOF announcement in August 1990, all time deposits will have completely free rates in 1993, with no minimum size limit. This delay appears to be a decision by MOF not to disturb the current market shares of each of the various players. A request by smaller banks for a further 2 or 3 years of controls was rejected. As of mid-1992, demand deposits had still not been scheduled for deregulation—so banks continued to be prohibited from paying interest on demand deposits.

Especially in regard to small deposits, city banks fear the power of the postal savings system in setting competitive interest rates, and small and medium institutions such as regional banks, sogo banks, and shinkin fear bankruptcy from the loss of deposits.

Table 3.5. *Characteristics of Deposit Instruments Created during Liberalization*

Instrument	Offered by	Characteristics (including restrictions on term and minimum size as of June 1992)
CDs 1979	All banks	Interest rate is negotiated. 2 weeks to 2 years; 50 million yen.
BIG 1981	Trust banks	A loan trust that compounds interest semiannually but pays it at maturity (rather than semiannually, as is the usual case). The interest rates (classed as dividends for legal purposes) are exempt from TIRAL but in practice have been the same for all banks. 5-year, 10,000 yen minimums.
WIDE 1981	Long-term credit banks and 2 other special government financial institutions	Financial bond with 5-year maturity. Interest is compounded semiannually and paid at maturity. Rates are the same as for BIG. 10,000 yen minimum.
MMCs 1985	Any financial institution authorized to take deposits	Rates are CD rate minus 1.75 percentage points for 3-month MMCs), 1.25 (6-month), 0.75 (1-year), and 0.50 (2-year); and 0.70 less than the 10-year Treasury for 3-year MMCs. Minimum 500,000 yen.
Large time deposits 1985	Same as MMCs	These have completely free interest rates, which thus vary some among banks. Large meant just that—1 billion yen when created in 1985. The threshold has been substantially reduced since. 1 month to 2 years, 3 million minimum.
Super MMCs 1991	Same as MMCs	Rates are 80 to 94% of average interest paid on (unregulated) large time deposits, adjusted weekly. Various maturities, 1 million to 3 million yen, limited withdrawals.

Note: The year the instrument was first offered is shown in the first column. Changes in size and term are included in the Appendix.

Tax exemption of small savings started in 1963 and was abolished in April 1988. The exemption applied to postal savings deposits and all personal bank deposits up to 3 million yen, the maximum an individual may have in the postal saving system, although the limit was easily evaded by using fictitious names.

The postal system traditionally has attracted household savers, mainly because it has a unique product, which has represented the bulk of the postal system's total deposits—some 90 percent in March 1985. Called "fixed amount postal savings," they have a minimum term of 6 months, after which they can be withdrawn without notice. The attractive feature is that the interest rate in effect at the time of the deposit is guaranteed for up to 10 years (semiannual compounding). This means a saver is protected against falling rates—by simply leaving the money in place—but can capture a higher rate by closing the account and opening a new one. This was a common practice—named "postal deposit shift"—at the end of tight money periods. Helped by this product, the share of total postal deposits in total personal deposits (the sum of those in private banks and in postal deposits) rose from 20 percent in 1965 to 28 percent in 1975 and 32 percent in 1985 but then fell slightly, to stand at 30 percent in 1991.

The ongoing introduction of new instruments has led to changes in the composition of bank deposits. Not surprisingly, deposits with unregulated interest rates have steadily gained share, as shown in Table 3.6.

With the gradual relaxation of the minimum size and maturity to 10 million yen and 1 month to 2 years in 1990, large time deposits became the largest unregulated deposit source for city banks (44 percent of total deposits on March 31, 1990, compared with 26 percent the year before, 17 percent in 1988, and 7 percent in 1987). Virtually all of the shift has been from regulated deposit types. All city banks have been eager to attract large time deposits from business corporations. This seems to suggest that incentives in expanding lending volume might still be effective, even though the margins have narrowed since the introduction of nonregulated deposits.

RELATIONSHIP BANKING

The relationship between banks and business corporations is discussed in this section. The historical process of business group formation is analyzed, followed by a theoretical discussion of its merits. Cross-shareholding, the main bank system, and some hypotheses regarding bank behavior are also taken up.

Table 3.6. Deposits with Unregulated Interest Rates as a Percentage of Total Deposits by Type of Bank

Mar. 31 [a]	City	Local	Trust	*Sōgō*	Shinkin	All 5
1985	11.8	6.5	16.8	4.2	0.8	8.1
1986	15.9	9.6	24.9	8.6	2.1	11.8
1987	23.9	13.8	39.6	16.8	4.8	18.2
1988	34.7	21.4	47.2	22.3	9.5	26.3
1989	43.8	31.5	57.1	30.5	16.2	35.8
1990	60.2	48.6	71.4	46.0	—	55.2[b]
1991	66.9	60.6	72.9	61.7	—	64.3[b]
1992	61.9	55.4	69.1	56.1	—	59.0[b]

— Not available.

a. Fiscal year-ends. Fiscal 1984 ended Mar. 31, 1985, etc.

b. Excludes shinkin, includes long-term credit banks — i.e., "all banks." For comparison, all banks is 39.6% in 1989, 30.3% in 1988.

Source: Ministry of Finance, *Ginkō kyoku nenpō* through 1989, then FBAJ, *Analysis of Financial Statements of All Banks* 1992, p. 33.

Japanese Business Groups

Before World War II, groups of companies were owned by *zaibatsu* families such as Mitsubishi, Mitsui, Sumitomo, Yasuda, and Furukawa, and the companies acted on behalf of family members. After dissolution of the zaibatsu and elimination of the holding companies by American Occupation forces (SCAP) in 1945, the groups became independent of family ownership. However, in the late 1940s and early 1950s many former zaibatsu companies began to form groups, often referred to as *keiretsu*. (Hadley 1970 is a standard source on the zaibatsu, their breakup, and the early stages of keiretsu.)

Mitsubishi companies formed a group with 27 core member companies and in 1954 created a committee of their presidents called the *kin'yo-kai,* the Friday Club, because it met each Friday. Others formed similar clubs. The discussion here centers on the big six—Mitsubishi, Mitsui, Sumitomo, Sanwa, Fuyo (Fuji Bank), and Daiichi Kankin (Daiichi Kangyo Bank).

Until the 1970s such horizontal business groups were discussed in Japan mainly as problems of social power or of monopoly. Following Williamson's analysis (1975), however, there has been a growing tendency to reevaluate the rationality of business groups as a hierarchical response to market failure.

Direct corporate control of large firms based on ownership has been insignificant in Japan in the postwar period, for two reasons. The first is the necessity for corporations constantly to make technical innovations and to be constantly informed of consumer preferences. This can be attributed to the remarkably high pace of technical innovations and the change and diversification of consumer needs that have characterized the postwar world, particularly in Japan. When firms need to react to external changes quickly and flexibly, it is difficult for owners who do not have product knowledge or management know-how to provide useful input to corporate decisionmaking.

The second reason is structural: the wide dispersion of shares and cross-shareholding (the holding of one another's stock by members of a business group). Wide dispersion of a large percentage of shares decreases the influence of individual shareholders, and cross-shareholding enables the group shareholders collectively to have as much influence on management as could be referred to as "control." Still, it is misleading to attempt to understand Japanese industry in the 1980s and 1990s—that is, after the period of high economic growth—using the concept of control by post-zaibatsu big business groups as the mode of analysis. The groups played a somewhat important role until the early stage of Japan's rapid growth, but that role is only a small portion of the economic significance of keiretsu. The broader significance is discussed later. (Japanese business groups have been much studied from a variety of angles. In English, a useful evaluation and analysis is Gerlach 1992.)

The Economic Advantage of Group Formation

The advantages of group formation are closely related to the character of each industry. Three advantages are relevant from the viewpoint of information theory: Groups are a device (a) to supply information in the presence of interdependence among firms, (b) for the efficient production of information about new products, and (c) to secure high-quality parts.

Regarding supplying information, assume there are two firms whose products are complementary. Further assume that if both make new investments, both will profit as a result, but if only one invests, the investment may not pay off. Because of this uncertainty, it is possible that the investment will not be made. Because the exchange of information is beneficial to group performance, it is more likely there will be sharing of investment plans—for example, through meetings of group presidents—if both firms are within the same group than if they have no relationship. Such information exchange can explain the rationality of "one-set investment" (investments made by a whole group together) which groups often undertook, especially during the early stage of rapid economic growth. Information supplied by financial institutions and administrative guidance by the Ministry of International Trade and Industry (MITI) also enables a firm to determine whether another firm will make complementary new investments.

In industries where product differentiation has increased and technical innovations are taking place at a rapid pace, appropriate marketing based on the quick grasp of consumer preference changes is essential. In such a situation, prompt exchange of information through vertical integration of production, sales, R&D, and the like, is a great advantage. When product life cycles are short, being the first company to enter can lead to the greatest profit, although it can also lead to dead ends (as Sony and the Betamax VCR demonstrate). This type of group is typical in industries such as electronics and computers.

In manufacturing that involves assembling a large number of parts, it is important in terms of efficiency to ensure the quality of each component. In this case, a firm has a significant advantage in forming long-term relationships with parts makers. A case in point is the automobile industry, in which Japan is not alone in having many subcontractors but has taken the practice further than most other countries have (see Smitka 1991 and Odaka, Ono, and Adachi 1988).

Shareholding

Group formation was facilitated by cross-shareholding relationships, and the phenomenon is often considered a peculiarity of the Japanese equity market. The Antitrust Law enacted in 1947 prohibited industrial companies from owning shares of other companies, but it did allow financial institutions to hold up to 5 percent. The law was later amended to allow industrial companies to acquire shares as long as they were not in a competitive position, and in 1953 the law was changed to increase permitted bank holdings to 10 percent of a company. (The bank's level was reduced to 5 percent in 1977 with a 10-year grace period.) Once it had become legal to do so, companies from three prewar groups—Mitsubishi, Mitsui, and Sumitomo—bought one another's shares, which earlier had been sold in the market as part of the zaibatsu dissolution program.

During the recession in the early 1960s, two government financial institutions were established—Kyodo Shoken (Japan Joint Securities) and Shoken Hoyu Kumiai (Japan Securities Holding Association)—to support the stock market by buying the holdings of unsuccessful investment trust funds, securities firms, and individuals. These holdings were sold to companies in 1969 to encourage cross-holding relationships. During 1971 and 1972, group companies bought more stock, this time in the market, under government guidance. Both times the purpose was to make it difficult in practice for foreign companies to buy controlling interests in Japanese companies, now that they were to be allowed to do so in theory.

Two important points can be made about the distribution of share ownership by type of holder (see Table 2.8). First, the percentage of shares financial institutions hold is very high and had even increased over time. They have had the largest shareholdings since 1972, when they surpassed individuals, who have been a steadily diminishing presence since their peak share in 1949.

The second point is that when the percentage of shareholding by foreign investors went up, as in 1953, 1969, and the early 1980s, the weight of individual Japanese went down, and the weight of domestic institutions went up. How should this be analyzed? As a defensive measure against mergers by foreign investors, cross shareholding has undoubtedly protected management. There are two arguments concerning this. First, it is said that employment practices such as life-time employment and promotion by seniority have made human resources, including future managers and even general labor skills, firm-specific. Takeovers and mergers involve a great risk of destroying human capital. Therefore, this argument contends that labor as well as managers support measures to prevent the merging of their companies.

The second argument regards shareholding by banks as a way of maintaining long-term customer relationships. Bank holdings of client stock have helped maintain the company's existing management and thus have helped ensure that the firm remains a bank customer. According to this view, long-term customer relationships are a kind of cooperative game, and regarding increased investment by foreign investors as a threat to the relationship has made a cooperative solution to the game easier.

The first analysis is problematic. If the managerial skills are firm-specific, the market for managers would be noncompetitive, resulting in tremendous agency costs for both managers and shareholders (on this point, see Jensen and Meckling 1976 and Fama 1980). According to Pettway, Sicherman and Yamada (1990), empirical results show that agency costs in the Japanese capital market are not very different from those in the United States. There are no empirical studies to support the argument that Japanese employment practices influence the capital market. It is quite doubtful the second analysis alone can explain the extensive cross shareholding and expansion of corporate ownership of shares. This field needs further study.

Some 20 to 30 percent of the shares of each bank are held by members of the group it belongs to. Clearly a close relationship exists between financial institutions and business groups, although member companies have explicit and implicit relationships with members of other groups as well.

Two arguments are often made from this regarding Japan's high-growth period. One emphasizes group control over banks, while the other—the conventional wisdom—contends the banks were basically dominant within the group. The argument for bank dominance is based largely on the logic that the banks had the money and thus could call the tune. Further, the head of the bank sat at the head of the table when the group met. We have interviewed loan officers of many of the banks and to our surprise found they consistently reported they rarely had any say in whether or not a specific loan was granted to a group member. The word came down, and the loan officer had little more to do than make sure the collateral and paperwork were in order. This suggests that if banks were indeed dominant, the distribution and level of lending to the group were fairly high-level, strategic decisions.

That seems to be what more or less typically occurred. The availability of funds and regulatory oversight provided a constraint to how much the bank could lend to its group. In a series of negotiations, the bank and group members would work out how these funds were divided among them, taking into consideration each company's needs and government policy. The main bank lent a predetermined share—say 20 to 30 percent—and took responsibility for arranging with other financial institutions within the group plus other city banks for the remaining loans. Usually, the share of each institution was set and maintained on a stable, recurring basis.

One purpose of the groups was to share information and thereby attempt to use scarce resources and exploit opportunities more efficiently. If one is also coordinating investments and market niches, it makes sense to coordinate the financing. And no true believer in information asymmetry can argue that the banks knew more about where to invest than the other group members (although a group bank knew more about its fellow group companies than other banks did.) In addition, it seems to us more consistent with the idea of consensus building in Japan that the bank's role within the group was constrained. It is interesting that outside those involved, no one knows for sure what the process was—the system was far from transparent, one can only make inferences. Although for purposes of exposition, we have understated what we actually believe the bank's role to have been, we do feel the available evidence is such that it cannot simply be argued that banks were dominant within the group. Instead, we think the relation was one of interdependence between the bank and the other group members.

The Main Bank System

Specific banks have tended to continuously provide the largest share of lending to specific clients. This is called the "main bank relationship"; it is typically strengthened by cross-shareholding between the bank and the client. (For greater detail in English, see Hoshi, Kashyap, and Scharfstein 1990, Sheard 1989.) Sometimes the client's board includes members from the bank. Main banks play a central role in restructuring firms that get in financial trouble. Two hypotheses explain the function of main bank relationships.

The Risk-sharing Hypothesis

The risk-sharing hypothesis, advanced by Nakatani (1984), posits that banks and their clients share risks through implicit contracts. Banks play an insurance role, such as smoothing the volatility of interest rates for their clients and helping them when they get in trouble. To avoid moral hazard caused by such implicit insurance contracts, banks try to have a continuous relationship by exchanging equity shares and supplying board members. If the bank's degree of risk aversion is smaller than the firm's, provision of this implicit insurance is efficient.

Horiuchi, Packer, and Fukuda (1988), and Horiuchi (1988) point out that the risk-sharing hypothesis appears inconsistent with reality, for three reasons. First, firms have gotten only some 20 to 30 percent of their loans from their main bank, so borrowing from a main bank is not large enough to reduce financing risk. Second, the hypothesis cannot explain why main banks sometimes do not help a client in trouble. Finally, interest expense and other financing costs in manufacturing show no inverse correlation with net operating profits (all are measured as a percentage of assets), as they would if banks played an "insurance" role by increasing loans in the face of declining profits (see Horiuchi 1988). They therefore insist that the delegated monitor hypothesis better fits the evidence.

The Delegated Monitor Hypothesis

According to the delegated monitor hypothesis, having the largest share of loans to a client is regarded as a signal of client credibility. That is, the main bank functions as a provider of information to other lenders. Nonmain banks are beneficiaries of this information. An unchanged relative position in loans by a main bank is regarded as a safety signal, even when the absolute level of outstanding loans is declining.

Accumulated information on clients can be considered an intangible asset, and it will quickly dissipate if the relationship ends. Cross-holding shares and sending managers from the bank to the client promote efficiency in producing information. Main banks obtain most of client's fee business in return for providing nonmain banks with implicit information on creditworthiness. This saves the client financing costs when borrowing from other banks, which trust the main bank's judgment and, as a result, adjust their risk premiums down (relative to a less well known borrower).

The decision of whether or not a main bank rescues a client depends on the costs and benefits in each instance. Rescues can be costly. Main banks do not, therefore, bail out a client when bankruptcy is regarded as inevitable or when the bank's investment in information on the client is limited. But a rescue is likely if there is a probability of successful restructuring and a prospect of continued profits from being the main bank (that is, earning a return on the bank's investment in information about the client).

The main bank's decision is also affected by reputation costs. It is common for the main bank to bear a disproportionate share of the costs of a restructuring or failure—both by incurring the administrative costs of taking a leadership role in the process and by accepting a lower level of recovery on its claims than other lenders. This clearly lends credibility not only to the bank's plans for the troubled company but also to its general reputation as a trustworthy monitor (one that will, by taking over some or all of their loans, in effect partially insure any losses incurred by those who follow its lead).

The Hypotheses Together

These two hypotheses do not exclude each other. An insurance role in the risk sharing hypothesis works under the delegated monitor hypothesis. An empirical study by Tsutsui (1988) found that the main banks and their clients share the risk of interest rate volatility and that this relationship is stronger for larger banks than for smaller banks. The main bank system was effective in promoting economic growth by finding promising companies and continuously financing them.

During the high-growth period there were two reasons for banks and their clients to maintain a stable relationship. The first is that during the high-growth period there were no alternatives to bank loans for companies requiring outside financing. The capital market was immature, and bond issuance was strictly controlled by the Bond Issue Committee, even though it had no legal basis to do so. (The Bond Issue Committee consisted of the trustee banks, the four major brokerage houses, and some other members. It is descended from the Bond Issuance Adjustment Council established in 1947; see Adams and Hoshii 1972, pp. 49, 58, 83.)

Second, no information businesses such as rating agencies existed during this period. Having a good relationship with banks was the only way to gain a good reputation and funding for promising young companies. Financial liberalization since the 1980s has consequently made the main bank relationship less important to large firms seeking to raise funds. The role of a main bank has been changing toward being more of an advisory function, including assisting clients wishing to invest abroad.

LIABILITIES AND EQUITY

One feature of Japanese banks in the postwar period has been the low equity ratio. In the prewar period paid-in capital was some 13 to 14 percent, and total equity was 20 percent, of total assets. In the immediate postwar period these became 1.1 percent and 3.5 percent respectively and remained around those levels until the late 1980s. Tables 3.7 and 3.8 provide data on bank balance sheets.

MOF attempted through regulation to keep the ratio of equity (including reserves) to total deposits and CDs at 10 percent or more. But the ratio for most banks was around 4 percent for two practical reasons. The rapid growth of deposits and loans simply outran the ability of city banks to build an appropriate equity base. MOF restrictions on dividends made it difficult to raise new equity—the returns to shareholders were seen as minuscule. (In fact, even allowing for the 1990s market decline, along with the rest of the Japanese market bank stocks have enjoyed great price increases since the early 1950s. But it was not obvious in the 1950s and 1960s that this would happen.)

Taking the risk–return relationship into consideration, the equity ratio of city banks during the highly controlled period was not necessarily low. Insolvency risks were minimal because of cross shareholding with group member companies; a profitable spread between interest costs and income was largely ensured

Table 3.7. *Balance Sheet Structure by Type of Bank:*
Equity and Major Liability Items as a Percentage of Total

Fiscal year [a] and item	All	City	Regional	Trust	Long-term
1960					
Deposits	74	77	88	79	10
Bank debentures	7	0	0	0	80
Borrowed money[b]	6	9	0	2	1
Call money and bills sold	2	2	1	4	0
Foreign exchange	3	5	0	0	1
Reserves	1	1	2	1	1
All else	4	3	5	8	4
Equity	3	3	4	6	3
Guarantees[c]	8	11	4	6	6
Balance sheet total in trillion yen	12.9	7.9	3.4	0.4	1.2
1970					
Deposits	72	75	88	78	15
Bank debentures	8	0	0	0	76
Borrowed money[b]	5	8	0	1	1
Call money and bills sold	3	5	0	1	0
Foreign exchange	2	3	0	1	1
Reserves	2	2	2	2	2
All else	4	4	5	9	2
Equity	4	3	5	8	3
Guarantees[c]	12	16	5	12	7
Balance sheet total in trillion yen	60.7	35.2	16.7	2.5	6.4
1980					
Deposits	74	78	87	57	25
Bank debentures	8	1	0	0	64
Borrowed money[b]	3	4	0	1	1
Call money and bills sold	4	5	0	6	2
Foreign exchange	1	2	0	4	1
Reserves	1	1	1	1	1
All else	6	7	7	28	3
Equity	3	2	4	4	3
Guarantees[c]	8	10	4	8	8
Balance sheet total in trillion yen	258.3	144.3	70.1	15.1	28.9
1990					
Deposits	73	79	85	55	28
Bank debentures	7	1	0	1	56
Borrowed money[b]	2	2	1	0	2
Call money and bills sold	5	6	3	11	4
Reserves	0	0	1	0	0
All else	10	9	6	29	7
Equity	3	3	4	4	3
Guarantees[c]	8	9	2	8	9
Balance sheet total in trillion yen	865.6	449.7	188.4	75.6	84.9

a. Fiscal years end Mar. 31 of following year.

b. Money borrowed from BOJ and from other financial institutions.

c. Although they appear on bank balance sheets, guarantees are not included in the balance sheet total. For this reason, the percentage distribution totals 100% *without* the guarantees.

d. For fiscal 1990, All includes the Second Association of Regional Banks (the former sōgō banks).

Source: FBAJ, *Analysis of Financial Statements of All Banks,* for years shown. For example, data for 1986–90 are in the Mar. 31 1991, issue, p. 26. Data in Bank of Japan, *Economic Statistics Annual,* on "Banking Accounts of . . ." have different numbers for a variety of reasons.

Table 3.8. *Distribution of Equity and Major Liability Items among Types of Bank*

Fiscal year [a] and item	Item total (billion yen)	Percentage of item held by			
		City	Regional	Trust	Long-term
1960					
Deposits	9,489	64	31	4	1
Bank debentures	934	0	0	0	100
Borrowed money[b]	730	95	2	2	2
Call money and bills sold	194	76	12	10	2
Foreign exchange	402	98	0	0	2
Reserves	266	54	33	3	10
Equity	424	54	31	6	9
Total[c]	12,847	61	26	4	9
Guarantees[c]	1,086	81	11	2	6
1970					
Deposits	43,890	60	34	4	2
Bank debentures	4,950	3	0	0	97
Borrowed money[b]	2,939	95	2	1	2
Call money and bills sold	1,934	99	0	1	0
Foreign exchange	1,177	94	1	2	3
Reserves	1,254	59	27	4	10
Equity[c]	2,397	50	34	8	8
Total	60,737	58	27	4	11
Guarantees	7,246	77	13	4	6
1980					
Deposits and CDs	190,385	59.5	32.3	4.5	3.7
Bank debentures	19,884	7.0	0.0	0.0	93.0
Borrowed money[b]	4,129	90.1	2.8	1.4	5.6
Call money and bills sold	9,618	81.3	3.1	9.4	6.3
Foreign exchange	3,368	76.5	0.0	17.6	5.9
Reserves	2,694	60.0	28.0	4.0	8.0
Equity	7,318	43.8	37.0	8.2	11.0
Total	258,303	55.9	27.2	5.8	11.2
Guarantees[c]	19,777	69.2	13.6	6.1	11.1
1990					
Deposits and CDs	575,470	60.7	28.0	7.2	4.2
Bank debentures	51,494	7.9	0	0	92.1
Borrowed money[b]	13,175	73.0	13.6	1.6	11.8
Call money and bills sold	55,826	64.9	11.1	15.2	8.8
Foreign exchange	18,443	86.2	0.9	10.6	2.2
Reserves	4,394	55.4	24.2	9.1	11.3
Equity	27,722	52.0	25.8	12.3	10.0
Total[c]	798,511	56.3	23.6	9.5	10.6
Guarantees[c]	60,131	69.8	7.1	10.1	13.0

Note: Sum of items listed + all else (not listed) = entry for item total in yen.

a. Fiscal years end Mar. 31 of following year

b. Borrowed from BOJ and from other financial institutions.

c. Although they appear on bank balance sheets, guarantees and acceptances are not included in the total here.

Source: FBAJ, *Analysis of Financial Statements of All Banks,* for years shown. For example, underlying data for fiscal 1986 – 90 are in the Mar. 31, 1991, issue, p. 26. The data in Bank of Japan, *Economic Statistics Annual,* on "Banking Accounts of . . ." have different numbers for a variety of reasons.

by government regulations; and there were implicit guarantees by MOF and BOJ to prevent bank failures.

Sources of Funds

Most bank funds come from deposits. During the time period we are considering, city and regional banks were the main intermediaries, channeling household savings to the corporate sector. Only the three long-term banks and the Bank of Tokyo were allowed to issue bonds, and they comprised a small percentage of the totals. City banks were the main absorbers of call money and the main borrowers from BOJ.

Industrial companies deposited larger sums than individuals did, in part because of compensating balance requirements. The ratio of corporate to total deposits increased during the high-growth period, from 61.8 percent in 1956 to 68.8 percent at the end of March 1965, whereas personal deposits decreased from 38.2 percent in 1956 to 31.2 percent. The nature of long-term and trust banks made the share of corporate deposits extremely high: 99.0 percent and 92.6 percent, respectively in 1965. On the other hand, the smaller the bank, the greater its share of deposits from households. The ratios were 51.3 percent for regional banks, 41.5 percent for sogo banks, and 28.0 percent for *shin'yo kinko* (credit unions) in 1965.

Corporate clients recognized that deposits constituted a liquid asset against tight window guidance by the BOJ during booms. The ratio of company deposits to total deposits (excluding public and financial institution deposits) on an all-bank basis was still greater than 50 percent in the 1980s, even though compensating balances to total loans fell from just over 17 percent in 1974 to 7.4 percent in 1985, according to estimates by the Fair Trade Commission.

Deposits in city banks were not large enough to meet the financial needs of their clients. But other banks—regional, trust, thrifts, and agricultural financial units—had a surplus continuously until 1978. This reflected a regional imbalance in the demand for and use of funds. Large firms borrowed almost exclusively from city banks but paid employees and subcontractors in outlying areas. In addition, although taxes were collected largely from urban-based corporations, much of the government's spending was for infrastructure in rural areas in support of regional industrial development. Regional institutions with surpluses had no reason to subscribe to public and private bonds because of their low returns relative to the call money market rate. Table 3.9 shows the deficits and surpluses of funds by type of bank.

City bank dependence on external debt (that is, borrowings from BOJ, other financial institutions, and the call market)—measured as a percentage of funds available—increased into the mid-1960s. Borrowing from BOJ was the main source of city bank external debt for most of the 7 years between 1957 and 1963. Then BOJ changed its policy instrument from "lending" to bond purchases ("market operations"). BOJ lent to city banks within its overall monetary policy objectives as long as they had qualified collateral. In the mid-1960s, manufacturing capacity caught up with demand for the first time in the postwar period, and this reduced the need for banks to seek external funds.

Table 3.9. *Deficits and Surpluses of Funds by Type of Bank*

Mar. 31[a]	City	Regional	Trust	Long-term
Billion yen				
1956	−149	35	9	—
1957	−273	41	−1	—
1958	−672	46	19	—
1959	−575	70	37	—
1960	−656	91	72	—
1961	−809	104	97	—
1962	−1,518	56	112	—
1963	−1,763	147	159	—
1964	−1,816	116	132	—
1965	−2,442	168	196	—
1966	−2,496	215	200	—
Trillion yen				
1967	−4.8	0.2	0.0	0.0
1968	−5.3	0.4	0.0	0.0
1969	−5.8	0.5	0.1	0.0
1970	−7.3	0.5	0.2	0.0
1971	−9.0	0.8	0.3	0.0
1972	−6.6	0.8	0.4	0.2
1973	−9.1	0.5	0.5	0.2
1974	−15.7	1.1	0.0	−0.0
1975	−20.5	1.4	−0.3	−0.2
1976	−19.3	1.7	0.0	0.2
1977	−20.1	2.1	0.2	−0.0
1978	−10.2	1.1	0.0	0.1
1979	−11.9	1.4	0.0	0.3
1980	−12.6	1.6	−0.3	−0.1
1981	−10.2	1.5	−0.3	−0.3
1982	−8.3	1.9	−0.9	−0.5
1983	−11.5	2.2	−1.3	−0.6
1984	−11.3	3.1	−1.9	−1.0
1985	−15.7	3.3	−2.9	−1.2
1986	−20.3	3.0	−4.7	−2.7
1987	−26.5	2.6	−6.1	−3.5
1988	−27.9	1.7	−5.6	−3.8
1989	−33.0	2.1	−6.4	−4.9
1990	−35.9	−4.8	−6.5	−6.2
1991	−37.4	−4.4	−6.8	−6.1

— Not available.

Note: Call loans minus call money minus borrowed money.

a. Fiscal year-ends. Fiscal 1955 ended Mar. 31, 1956, etc.

Source: 1956–66: Watanabe and Kitahara 1966, p. 634; 1967– Federation of Bankers Assocs. of Japan, *Analysis of Financial Statements of All Banks,* various fiscal year-end issues.

The high ratio of BOJ loans to city banks is attributed by Goto to the lack of a fiscal policy (1966, p. 204). When the gap between government payments and collections, including foreign exchange, was positive, BOJ loans outstanding to city banks were reduced. When the gap was negative, loans increased. In 1955, 1958, and 1963, for example, net government payments to the private sector were positive and BOJ loans declined. In 1957 and 1961 the reverse occurred. Another way of looking at this is that BOJ set its expansion of credit to city banks on the basis of the net credit provided by foreign exchange inflows and by the government budget surplus of deficit.

City banks, therefore, played a role in central government fiscal policy. These BOJ loans were distributed to industrial companies so that they could continue to expand even during periods of tight fiscal policy. Borrowing from BOJ by noncity banks was very low in the 1950s and 1960s. For the years 1955 to 1970 the regional banks held just 1.6 percent of BOJ loans, trust banks 0.5 percent, and long-term banks 1.9 percent (based on the total of year-end outstanding balances during the period). This was because BOJ policy was to lend essentially only to city banks—they owed from 92 to over 98 percent of year-end outstanding balances in 1955–70.

BANK ASSETS

Banks traditionally are in the business of lending money, and in the 1960s and the 1970s some two-thirds of their assets were loans, while one-eighth or so were securities (at cost). Loans subsequently became relatively less important, as did foreign exchange, whereas securities and liquid assets (cash, deposits, call money) became larger percentages. Tables 3.10 and 3.11 provide data on assets.

Loans

The most common form of loans have been bill loans and discounted promissory notes, although long-term banks make loans through a loan agreement form. At the end of March 1966, bill loans and discounted promissory notes were 63 percent and 35 percent respectively, of city bank total outstanding lending. For regional banks, they were 60 percent and 35 percent. During the mid-1950s to early 1970s high-growth era, most of the city bank loans matured in 2–3 months but were continuously rolled over, so bill loans were convenient to handle. During this period promissory notes issued by industrial companies brought high liquidity to commercial banks because they were accepted as collateral and rediscounted by the Bank of Japan.

Loans by city banks were mostly for working capital at industrial companies, but a portion financed fixed capital investments (7.7 percent of outstanding loan balances at the end of 1965, 19.8 percent in 1975, and 20.8 percent in 1985). From the 1950s city banks steadily increased the share of their loans with a term of one year or more. Such loans climbed from 5.2 percent of outstanding loan

Table 3.10. *Balance Sheet Structure by Type of Bank:*
Major Asset Items as a Percentage of Total

Fiscal Year [a] and item	All	City	Regional	Trust	Long-term
1960					
Cash and deposits	11	13	9	15	3
Call loans	1	0	2	6	1
Securities	13	13	15	11	8
Loans	67	64	70	63	85
Foreign exchange	5	7	0	0	1
Operating assets	1	1	2	2	1
Balance sheet total in trillion yen	12.85	7.89	3.37	0.43	1.16
1970					
Cash and deposits	9	11	9	9	5
Call loans	1	0	3	9	2
Securities	12	11	12	19	11
Loans	68	66	72	55	79
Foreign exchange	6	9	0	2	1
Operating assets	2	2	2	3	1
Balance sheet total in trillion yen	60.74	35.17	16.70	2.48	6.38
1980					
Cash and deposits	14	18	7	17	11
Call loans	3	3	3	5	2
Securities	16	12	20	28	18
Loans	58	57	64	38	62
Foreign exchange	4	6	0	6	3
Operating assets	1	1	1	2	0
Balance sheet total in trillion yen	258.3	144.3	70.1	15.1	28.9
1990					
Cash and deposits	15	20	7	55	12
Call loans	2	2	4	2	1
Securities	16	12	20	24	18
Loans	60	59	63	45	65
Foreign exchange	1	2	0	1	0
Operating assets	1	1	1	1	0
Balance sheet total in trillion yen	865.6	449.7	188.4	75.5	84.9

Note: Total includes items not elsewhere classified, so percentages do not add to 100. Guarantees are excluded.

a. Fiscal years end Mar. 31 of following calendar year.

b. Includes members of the Second Association of Regional Banks (former sōgō banks) in 1990, but not in earlier years.

Source: FBAJ, *Analysis of Financial Statements of All Banks,* for years shown.

Table 3.11. Distribution of Major Asset Items among Types of Bank

Fiscal year [a] and item	Item total in billion yen	Percentage of item held by			
		City	Regional	Trust	Long-term
1960					
Cash and deposits	1,469	72	21	4	3
Call loans	115	5	60	23	12
Securities	1,650	60	32	3	5
Loans	8,666	58	27	3	12
Foreign exchange	103	98	0	0	2
Operating assets	168	62	31	4	3
Total	12,847	61	26	3	10
1970					
Cash and deposits	5,666	65	25	4	6
Call loans	891	4	56	26	14
Securities	7,142	55	29	7	9
Loans	41,773	56	29	3	12
Foreign exchange	3,403	96	1	1	2
Operating assets	1,070	59	30	7	4
Total	60,737	58	28	4	10
1980					
Cash and deposits	35,427	71	14	7	9
Call loans	7,415	54	26	10	10
Securities	41,849	43	34	10	13
Loans	150,701	54	30	4	12
Foreign exchange	10,591	80	3	9	8
Operating assets	2,954	54	33	8	4
Total	258,303	56	27	6	11

1990 Fiscal year [a] and item	Item total in trillion yen	Percentage of item held by				
		City	Regional [b]		Trust	Long-term
			1st	2d		
Cash and deposits	132,289	67	10	3	13	7
Call loans	19,556	38	42	9	7	4
Securities	135,726	40	27	8	13	11
Loans	521,661	51	23	9	7	10
Foreign exchange	9,529	86	4	1	5	4
Operating assets	5,830	40	30	14	12	4
Total	865,581	52	22	7	9	10

Note: Total includes items not elsewhere classified.

a. Fiscal years end Mar. 31 of following calendar year.

b. 2d means Second Association of Regional Banks (former sōgō banks), which are not included for previous years.

Source: FBAJ, *Analysis of Financial Statements of All Banks,* for years shown.

balances at the end of fiscal year 1955, to 6.9 percent in 1965, 13.8 percent in 1970, 29.7 percent in 1975, 34.2 percent in 1980, 35.2 percent in 1985, and 52.9 percent in 1990.

Collateral

Collateral was always required not only for bank lending but for interbank transactions and corporate bonds as well. The principle of collateralized transactions has its origins in the 1927 financial panic, which was brought on by uncollateralized call funds borrowed by the Bank of Taiwan.

Loan provisions and practices regarding collateral were standardized in 1962 when the Federation of Bankers Associations published uniform bank loan contracts. The standardized form gave banks the right to demand possession of the collateral at any time there were reasonable grounds to believe the integrity of an asset was in jeopardy.

During the 1970s, 60 to 70 percent of the money lent by banks was collateralized, although some of this represented third-party guarantees rather than hard assets. In the 1980s the volume of unsecured loans was somewhat larger. During the latter part of the decade banks increased lending secured by real estate more rapidly than overall lending. This was particularly true for city banks, as regional banks were less involved in the speculative bubble. Table 3.12 shows data on collateral.

The principle of collateralized transactions was strictly applied to corporate bond issues. The Law on Collateralization of Securities and Trust of 1905 applied to all corporate bonds after an agreement was reached in 1933 among banks, insurance and trust companies that corporate bonds must be collateralized and have sinking funds. Securities firms underwrote the bonds, but banks played an important role by administering the collateral as trustee for the bondholders. The banks bought back all outstanding bonds whenever the issuer was not able to pay the interest or principal. This insurance meant banks charged high fees and that the provision of collateral was essential to the banks. To get around these costs, starting in the early 1980s many firms began to issue bonds in the Euromarket without collateral.

Security Holdings

In the prewar period, securities holdings (at cost) were as high as 30 percent of the total assets of all banks. At the end of 1960 they accounted for 11.8 percent and in 1990 were 17.0 percent. The level of government bond issues explains a large part of the difference in share. During the first 20 years of the postwar period there were few government bonds. Then in 1966 holdings of government securities rose from 28.3 billion to 551.8 billion yen. In the 1970s such holdings generally increased more rapidly than total assets—the extremes being jumps of 160 percent from 1974 to 1975 and 122 percent from 1975 to 1976.

During the high growth period most bondholdings were issues of the three long-term banks. City banks bought the largest portion of these bonds despite their own lack of funds because they could use them as collateral when borrow-

*3.12. Distribution of Outstanding Loans of All Banks
by Kind of Collateral*
(percent)

Mar.31 [a]	Real estate	Securities	Other	Third-party	Unsecured	Total loans (billion yen)
1960	24.6	3.0	16.4	21.7	34.2	4.77
1965	25.4	4.1	15.8	21.5	33.2	11.88
1970	27.6	3.2	14.6	22.9	31.7	24.68
1975	31.1	2.3	9.2	24.9	32.0	67,410
1980	28.5	1.8	9.0	27.0	33.6	114,469
1982	25.7	1.6	9.0	26.4	37.2	145,540
1983	24.2	1.5	8.9	26.5	38.8	164,010
1984	22.8	1.7	8.8	27.1	39.7	185,519
1985	21.8	1.8	8.3	26.6	41.4	215,771
1986	21.7	2.0	9.6	26.3	40.4	240,093
1987	22.1	2.2	9.9	26.0	39.9	280,169
1988	23.2	2.4	9.4	25.6	39.4	320,414
1989	23.9	2.6	9.2	26.8	37.6	364,822
1990	24.6	2.9	9.0	27.2	36.2	420,625
1991	27.2	2.3	8.6	29.9	31.9	514,442

Note: Members of the Second Association of Regional Banks (former sōgō banks) are not included. Loans by overseas branches are included.

a. Fiscal year-ends. Fiscal 1959 ended Mar. 31, 1960, etc.

b. Includes vessels.

Source: Computed for the authors from absolute data in Bank of Japan, *Economic Statistics Annual.* The 1990 edition, p. 147, Table 68, covers fiscal years ending in 1982–90; 1974 edition, p. 121, Table 39, covers 1965–74; etc.

ing from BOJ. Such holdings have become less important. Table 3.13 shows the distribution of securities holdings by type.

NONPERFORMING LOANS

No continuous data regarding nonperforming loans have been published by regulatory agencies or banks. BOJ and MOF alternately examine all banks on site once a year. They categorize all lendings into four groups—no risk, slow or substandard (called *S satei*), doubtful (*D*) and loss or estimated loss (*L*). The ratio of S, D, and L to total lending is called the "cautious lending ratio" (CLR). Examined banks must respond to and incorporate the inspector's suggestions within a specified time. The broader ratios have never been disclosed to the public even for banks as a group, although in early 1992 the narrowest ratio, L, was released.

A time series reflecting changes in the level of the CLR appeared in *Kinyu Business* in November 1987. No absolute numbers were given. Rather, the arti-

Table 3.13. *Distribution of Securities Holdings by All Banks (percent)*

Year	Govt. debt	Local govt. debt	Public corp. bonds	Bank debentures	Other corp. bonds	Equity	Foreign [a]	All else [b]	Total holdings [c] (trillion) yen)
1955	12.5	5.7	8.1	29.5	32.7	10.6	n.a.	0.8	0.519
1960	3.0	7.1	14.7	29.3	29.9	15.2	n.a.	0.9	1.524
1965	0.7	8.0	17.0	29.9	25.2	15.5	n.a.	3.8	3.962
1966	11.6	7.6	13.4	25.8	23.4	15.7	n.a.	2.5	4.767
1969	10.9	11.1	14.4	19.5	22.8	19.5	n.a.	1.8	6.532
1972	16.1	12.0	12.7	19.0	15.2	21.3	n.a.	3.8	11.467
1975	18.0	17.2	11.2	16.2	11.7	18.6	n.a.	7.1	18.046
1978	44.8	13.1	8.8	9.4	5.5	14.1	n.a.	4.3	33.665
1981	36.1	14.7	12.4	8.3	4.9	17.5	3.3	2.9	43.448
1984	31.4	10.9	13.2	9.6	3.2	20.3	8.4	3.0	52.558
1987	28.7	7.6	10.9	9.4	3.0	20.8	14.0	5.7	76.098
1990	24.2	5.8	8.6	8.8	2.5	27.6	14.8	7.6	124.037

n.a. Not applicable.

a. Foreign securities are included in All else before 1980.

b. Before 1980, All else, called "others" in the source, includes beneficiary certificates and foreign securities. Beginning with 1980 the entries here are computed as residuals that include beneficiary certificates (which are no longer explicitly itemized in the source).

c. From 1983 "securities lent" are included. In the source these are distributed among the various security types. Absolute data on total securities lent during 1975–90 are available on p. 42, Table 16 of the 1990 source.

Source: Computed for the authors from absolute data in Bank of Japan, *Economic Statistics Annual,*1974, p. 71 (for 1955–72) and 1990, p. 45 (for 1975–90).

cle gave the ratios for fiscal 1973– 87 (inclusive) as an index relative to September 1980 (the midpoint in the period). The index for city banks rose from approximately 40 percent during 1973–76, dropped to 80 percent in 1981– 83, and then moved up to 150 percent in 1987. The relative ratio for regional and sogo banks was higher than for city banks until 1986.

A data series showing actual loan losses for Japanese banks is not very meaningful. In most years since 1970 banks have written off (removed from their balance sheets as worthless) only some 0.01 percent of outstanding loans each year. City banks have had somewhat higher levels, reaching 0.02 percent in several years. The exceptional year was 1977, when city banks wrote off 0.6 percent (0.5 percent for all banks). This reflected restructuring in the aftermath of the first oil shock. There are several reasons for the low reported ratio. First, there is no clear definition of a "bad loan." More important, losses cannot be deducted from profits for tax purposes until they are realized, including the sale of collateral. Essentially, a bank must satisfy MOF that a loan truly cannot be recovered. If there is any collateral, the taxing authorities are reluctant to allow a tax-deductible write-off, even if the current market precludes its being sold at all. Under U.S. accounting practices, similarly impaired loans would be written off.

During the 1980s banks paid 45 to 60 percent of their reported pretax income in income taxes, with the lower end of the range being more common at the end of the decade. The nominally comparable range for U.S. banks was 22 to 28 percent for 1981–86 (OECD 1992, pp. 101, 185), after which write-offs and other factors make the numbers somewhat meaningless; a rate around 30 percent on domestic income is considered normal by analysts. Bank taxes are a sizable source (some 2 to 3 percent) of government revenue in Japan, although at 1.3 trillion yen in fiscal 1990, the amount was well below the peak of 2.0 trillion yen in fiscal 1988.

Another reason for low write-off levels is that if a company gets in trouble and is unable to pay interest or principal, the members of its group will help—at least as long as the setback appears temporary. There seem to be several companies that might have defaulted without the assistance of their group's companies. The company's main bank negotiates a rescheduling of its loans and those of some or all other bank creditors. The banks usually extend the maturity and provide additional loans to restructure the business and pay interest during the period. This is done willingly as long as it is approved by other companies in the group because the interest is paid without suspension.

Industries supported by certain government industrial policies expect to be bailed out by the government under a broad industrial restructuring plan. As long as the banks cooperate with the plan, interest payments continue—paid by the government directly or indirectly. The coal-mining industry, to which bank loans were subrogated by the government in the 1960s and 1970s, is an early example. Textiles and shipping in the 1960s, and aluminum, shipbuilding, petrochemicals, and steel in the 1970s also are good examples. To a large extent banks lending in these areas avoided having interest and principal be in arrears.

During the early growth period the Japan Development Bank (JDB) and the Industrial Bank of Japan (IBJ) were the de facto syndicate leaders that judge the creditworthiness of a company or project. JDB or IBJ approval of a potential borrower was called a "cow bell" signaling other banks to join in lending, secure in the knowledge that the loans were what government policymakers wanted and thus were implicitly guaranteed by the government. These credit judgments were so reliable that private banks could enjoy very low nonperforming loan levels as long as they followed the bell. Horiuchi and Otaki (1987) tested this cow bell effect between the JDB and private banks and found that the loans by private banks for steel, transportation, electric power and shipping were led by JDB lending.

Shipping and shipbuilding were regarded as among the safest industries for banks to lend to in the 1960s because of various government protections. This faith was vindicated when the two industries fell on hard times. Shipping companies that participated in the government restructuring program were able to secure cargoes on a long-term basis, and the banks lending to the companies received interest subsidies from the government. Restructuring under government auspices became necessary again in the late 1970s, but the loans were paid back.

Low levels of consumer lending were another reason for the low nonperformance ratio. Until the speculative late 1980s most loans—probably more than 90 percent—were allotted to industrial companies, and less than 1 percent were given to consumers. In 1991, however, consumer credit had reached 5 percent of loans, and the share was expected to continue increasing. This phenomenon will have a serious impact on bank loan performance.

Rigorous examinations of banks by BOJ and MOF may have reduced the non-performing loan ratio. The Japanese oversight system generally worked well, and it was able to intervene before an institution got into serious trouble—the Heiwa case discussed later is a notable exception. Lifetime employment at BOJ and MOF facilitated this. Because the inspector who had previously analyzed a bank remained in the same institution, information could be accumulated.

Although some large-scale bankruptcies have occurred, the main and other banks were able to deal with such troubles as Ataka Industries (1975) and Sanko Shipping (1985). The system does not seem to work for loans to highly indebted middle-income, developing countries and in the early 1990s is being critically tested by the burst bubble of speculative real estate and securities lending. As discussed in the concluding section, these loans are expected to be a burden on Japanese banks.

OFF BALANCE SHEET AND FEE-BASED ACTIVITIES

Off balance sheet activities started to increase in the early 1980s as banks looked for ways to offset decreases in profits from lending activities. The BIS regulation of the risk–asset ratio also encouraged banks with foreign business to increase such activities. Thus fees from foreign branches and subsidiaries started to climb in 1982, representing guarantees for bonds issued by local governments in the United States, currency and interest swaps, merger and acquisitions advice, leveraged buyouts, and options and futures.

Main banks, especially the top five city banks (top six since the creation of Sakura Bank) have aggressively increased their fee-based services domestically as well. These include the handling of cash balances and the settlement of promissory notes. Clients save personnel costs and maintain liquidity. Charges for account transfers that are used to make business and personal payments—particularly to utility companies—are a main item. Compared to the United States, fees traditionally have been very high in Japan, although in the 1990s U.S. banks have been raising theirs aggressively.

Gains on sales of securities jumped in 1987 and 1988 as banks sold stock in order to meet the Anti-Monopoly Act requirement that they reduce their holdings in any one company from a maximum of 10 percent to 5 percent, in order to increase reserves for overseas loan losses, to retain additional earnings to meet the BIS risk–asset ratio, and to show higher profits.

HANDLING FINANCIAL CRISES

Most bank troubles in Japan have been caused by embezzlement and disguised loans. The troubles have often been attributed to distortions brought about by restrictive regulations: Disguised loans and fictitious name deposits were made because of restrictions on competition. The number of bank problems is not usually made available, but it was reported that there were 162 incidents of embezzlement by employees or officers of depository institutions in 1967 and 204 in 1969 (KGCK 1972, p. 84).

There have been no bankruptcies in banking since World War II, although several institutions have faced serious crises. Traditionally, when a bank gets into serious trouble, there are four ways to get it out: voluntary restructuring, special aid from specific financial institutions, mutual aid from institutions in the same category (such as other sogo banks), or merger with a larger bank. In all cases, MOF and BOJ are closely involved as soon as a problem is perceived.

There is a consensus that MOF should play a leading role in handling financial crises because it is responsible for maintaining orderly credit conditions (*Kinsei Toshin* June 5 1985, p. 38). MOF, therefore, prevents any bank from falling into bankruptcy.

Before the bursting of the speculative real estate and stock bubbles, which are happening as we write, the best-known banking crisis involved Heiwa Sogo Bank. How it was handled is illustrative. Heiwa was the fifth largest sogo bank at the time, actually larger than some of the regional banks. It got into trouble in 1985 because of the bankruptcy of two major clients—Sobutsusho and Taiheiyo. Heiwa was their main bank, and part of the problem was the result of disguised loans to related companies. The situation was complicated by a contentious struggle for control between some of the largest stockholders of the two companies and a group of the managers.

MOF examined of the bank and its 102 branches right after the trouble came to light. On advice from MOF, Heiwa skipped its dividend, installed as its new president a man retired from MOF (who had earlier been made chairman) and accepted two advisers—one each from BOJ and MOF.

The examination took 5 months, during which time the bank functioned normally as far as its depositors were concerned. The examination revealed that the bank had nonperforming loans amounting to 533 billion yen, 49 percent of its total loans. Of these, only 13 billion yen were deemed completely uncollectible, but another 170 billion yen were placed in a doubtful category that was also written off. In addition, there were 391 billion yen of loans for which interest was more than 6 months in overdue. There were 50 billion yen in unrealized securities gains not on the balance sheet, but this was clearly not enough to offset the losses.

At this point MOF concluded that the problems were caused by management negligence and indicated that restructuring was inappropriate. Ten days after MOF's announcement, Sumitomo Bank indicated it was ready to absorb Heiwa if MOF asked. Heiwa agreed. The merger was effective October 1, 1986. Sumitomo, based in Osaka, was able to double the number of branches it had in the Tokyo metropolitan area. Moreover, it was allowed to keep the old Heiwa branches open until 7:00 pm—a major competitive advantage (Yamashita 1986, p. 16).

MOF and BOJ clearly prefer that banks be restructured rather than go into bankruptcy, as this protects depositors directly—as well as indirectly, by maintaining confidence in the system. When the regulatory agencies find problems during routine annual inspections, they first offer detailed instructions and expect the bank to recover through its own efforts (a voluntary restructuring). It is not necessarily difficult for the regulators to foresee that a bank is likely to get in trouble in the near future, because MOF and BOJ often have close, continuous relationships with banks through sending retiring staff to serve on bank boards or as advisers, particularly at regional and other smaller banks.

In the Heiwa Sogo case, the problems were not found until the start of a regular examination in August 1985, even though the chairman was a former MOF staffer who had come to Heiwa in 1983 (*Keizaikai* September 24, 1985, pp. 44 – 46). MOF tried at first to restructure Heiwa by means of financial assistance. BOJ, the Sogo Bank Association, six city banks, and three long-term banks were ready to give support, but MOF abandoned this approach after the first 200 billion yen in nonperforming loans surfaced.

Emergency loans are not automatic. They were extended by BOJ to Yamaichi Securities in 1965, but not to Taiko Sogo Bank when it got in serious trouble in 1979, because it was reasoned that Taiko's problems would not significantly affect the overall credit system (Kusano 1986). Regulators sometimes ask troubled banks to get permission before paying dividends. Such data are generally not available, but there were 20 banks identified as troubled in 1983 (Saito 1983).

The number of mergers between 1955 and 1984 for city and regional banks was 10 (3 involving banks in a different category; the others were within a category). For sogo banks, the number was 25 (23); for shinkin, 99 (20); and 95 (35) for credit cooperatives (*shinren*). Subsequent mergers are discussed later.

PROFITABILITY

Interest rate margins in the banking industry were quite steady during period of the rapid economic growth in Japan. Several regulations contributed to this, with controls on deposit rates being especially important. But even if deposit rates are regulated, profitability can be depressed if the loan market is severely competitive or if the demand for loans is low. Fortunately for the banks, elaborate regulations and administrative guidance restrained competition in loan markets.

First was market segmentation by borrowing sector. Each financial institution in Japan had specific niches for its lending, which was reinforced by regulations. For example, for agriculture, Norin Chukin and the agricultural cooperatives were the central institutions. In loans to consumer and small and medium firms, sogo banks, shinkin, credit cooperatives and labor credit associations played a key role. In addition, government financial institutions helped support such industries as coal mining and textiles, which were depressed.

Second, the loan market was regionally segmented. City banks were severely restrained from establishing branches throughout Japan, despite their being called nationwide banks. Regional banks dominated local markets, and major firms in rural areas formed close relationships with them. In rural areas deposits exceeded the demand for loans, so the regionals were suppliers of funds in the call market. City banks borrowed from the call market and made loans to firms in big cities.

Third, interest rates had a stable yield curve during the rapid growth period. The long-term prime rate was set in such a way that the spread between it and the rate on debentures issued by long-term credit banks became constant. Therefore, long-term credit banks could earn steady profits.

Basic data on the profitability of city banks are in Table 3.14, while additional details on city and regional bank expenses are in Table 3.15.

Economies of Scale

The issue of economies of scale in banking in Japan has engendered a spirited discussion and a number of empirical studies. MOF has played a leading part in mergers of financial institutions—mostly small ones such as shinkin and credit cooperatives—since around 1970, on the grounds that economies of scale do exist. Many empirical studies show them. But there is some controversy as to whether they are large enough to justify mergers.

Tsutsui and Royama (1987) estimated economies of scale by different types of banks. According to their estimate, scale economies for city banks are far greater than those for regional banks and have been increasing rapidly since the mid-1970s. They attribute this increase to deregulation and technological innova-

Table 3.14. *Profitability of City Banks*
(percent of average balance sheet total)

Fiscal year [a]	Interest [b] Income	Interest [b] Expense	Net interest income	Net noninterest income	Provisions (net) [c]	Profit before taxes
1981	8.02	6.87	1.15	0.36	0.02	0.41
1982	7.14	5.90	1.23	0.29	0.07	0.45
1983	6.25	5.05	1.26	0.28	0.04	0.49
1984	6.81	5.74	1.07	0.32	0.04	0.46
1985	5.60	4.66	0.94	0.34	0.01	0.43
1986	4.87	3.86	1.01	0.33	0.03	0.50
1987	4.82	3.84	0.98	0.46	0.03	0.63
1988	5.22	4.28	0.94	0.63	0.16	0.68
1989	5.82	5.13	0.69	0.41	0.05	0.46
1990	6.47	5.87	0.61	0.34	0.03	0.33

Note: Profit before taxes = net interest income + net noninterest income − operating expenses − provisions.

a. Fiscal years end Mar. 31 of following calendar year. Thus, fiscal 1981 ended Mar. 31, 1982, etc.

b. Includes fees related to lending operations and dividend income on shares and participations. May also include amortization of premiums or discounts on bonds.

c. Net transfers to reserves for possible loan losses and to reserves for government securities price fluctuations. The former is the maximum allowed by tax regulations.

Source: OECD *Bank Profitability, Statistical Supplement 1981–90* (1992), p. 105 and Introduction. Also refer to the notes on Japan in the *Supplement 1980–84* (1987), pp. 131-35. Data provided to OECD by FBAJ.

Table 3.15. Bank Operating Expenses

Fiscal year [a]	Total as % of average total assets	Total (billion yen)	Percentage distribution		
			Personnel	Nonpersonnel	Taxes [b]
City banks					
1970	1.19	452	55.3	39.1	5.6
1975	1.40	1,267	61.2	33.0	5.8
1980	1.16	1,774	58.6	34.7	6.7
1982	1.01	2,019	56.2	33.6	10.2
1983	0.96	2,094	55.5	34.0	10.4
1984	0.90	2,197	54.1	35.5	10.4
1986	0.81	2,407	52.0	35.3	12.5
1988	0.73	2,856	44.7	c	c
1989	0.59	2,723	49.1	44.5	6.3
1990	0.59	2,937	47.9	46.2	5.8
Regional banks					
1970	1.54	252	62.5	31.1	3.3
1975	2.07	802	61.1	28.9	7.0
1980	1.87	1,315	64.2	29.0	6.8
1983	1.74	1,586	62.7	28.1	9.2
1986	1.53	1,843	60.2	30.5	9.3
1989	1.15	2,015	58.6	35.6	5.8
1990	1.14	2,146	57.2	37.4	5.4

Note: Excludes expenses (fees, commissions, etc.) specifically related to lending operations, securities, foreign exchange trading, etc.

a. Fiscal years end Mar. 31 of following calendar year. Thus, fiscal 1970 ended Mar. 31, 1971, etc.

b. Taxes are other than income and corporate taxes.

c. There is a discontinuity in the series because of statistical changes.

Source: All data are from FBAJ. For city banks for fiscal 1981–90, annual data on total and staff costs are found in OECD *Bank Profitability, Statistical Supplement 1981–90* (1992), pp. 104–5 and Introduction.

tions. Tsutsue and Royama hypothesized that easing limits on CD issue and relaxing the rules governing extension of foreign branches would work more favorably for large banks. Their analysis concluded the effect from CDs was not significant, but new foreign branches did work favorably for large banks.

As to technological innovation, Kasuya (1989) showed that the rate of technological development (measured as the growth rate of labor productivity) at city banks was much higher than regional banks. This seems to be due to the city banks' greater computerization, a substitution of capital equipment for labor. The percentage of personnel expenses in general and administrative expenses fell in the 1980s, and the trend was more pronounced at city banks than at regionals.

Economies of Scope

Studies of economies of scope are becoming more common. Banking and the securities business have been separated in Japan, but since the mid-1980s each has gradually been allowed to move into the other's fields, an overlap that was greatly expanded by the 1992 banking law. It is thus worth analyzing whether such convergence indeed makes sense.

Suda (1985) analyzed data for 1981–83, looking at two sources of earnings (and associated costs): the spread between deposit rates and lending rates, and earnings from fees and other nonlending transactions. He concluded there were no economies of scope.

On the other hand, Kasuya (1986) used 10 years of data (1975–85), with interest revenue from lending as one earning source and fee revenues plus interest and dividends (but not realized gains) on securities (other than government bonds) held as the second source. He concluded that there were economies of scope for city banks in all 10 years and that they were gradually increasing. For regional banks, the economies existed only for the final 2 years studied—1984 and 1985. Tachibanaki, Misui, and Kitagawa (1990) extended the study, using data from 1985–87, with the spread between deposit and lending as one revenue source, and earnings from all securities business (including profits from hidden assets) and fee revenues as the second. They confirmed economies of scope existed and were tending to increase.

Furukawa (1990) analyzed each year from 1981 through 1988, comparing wholesale loans and retail loans as revenue sources. Economies of scope were clearly observed in city banks, but not at regional banks.

None of these four studies looked at exactly the same data, and only Kasuya and Furukawa covered more than a few years. Because of the stock market boom in the 1980s, including stock market profits may distort the effects on profitability of a wider scope. Comparable results would no doubt be found if securities transactions were tested as an added activity to making, say, steel. Certainly the emergence of *zaitech* (financial speculation by nonfinancial firms) in the late 1980s suggests many manufacturing companies took the possibility seriously enough to act on it. Still, we feel economies of scope do exist in banking.

Whether or not there are economies of scope or scale, it is clear that the cost functions of banks are changing. These relate not just to the changed regulatory and competitive environments but also to new communications and information-processing technologies. Further empirical studies are necessary to assess their impact.

Scale or Profit Maximization?

In explaining Japanese bank behavior, it is often pointed out the object was not profit but scale (volume of deposits) or market share. Thus, staff promotions and other rewards often were designed as incentives for expansion of scale. A branch is a profit center and a branch manager expects to be promoted to the main office if he succeeds in expanding the scale of his branch. In some cases, a bank officer receives a higher bonus when he brings in a large deposit.

Why would a bank try to maximize its scale or share? There are several hypotheses. One relates to the controlled, low level of interest rates on deposits and the ensured spread on lending. In such a situation, profits increase as deposits increase; that is, profit maximization is consistent with scale maximization.

But even if the spread is positive, if there is an increasing real resource cost for collecting deposits, then "the more, the better"—that is, scale maximization—is consistent with profit maximization only if the cost of collecting deposits has scale economies. That is, deposits should be accepted only up to the point that their marginal cost (marginal real resource cost plus deposit rate) is equal to the interbank rate. In this case, the scale of a bank is determined by regulations such as limits on expanding the number of branches. These regulations are always binding on a bank and give it incentives to expand its scale.

Second, BOJ rationing of lending through window guidance was based on the size of the bank. Usually, borrowing from BOJ meant paying less than borrowing in the interbank market, and there is no real resource cost associated with borrowing from BOJ. In this sense borrowing from BOJ is a kind of subsidy. The amount of subsidy depends on the bank's size, so a bank had incentives to expand its scale.

Third, long-run profit maximization is said to be consistent with short-run scale maximization. For example, an increase of loans during the current period will result in the growth of the borrowing firm, which may lead to an increase in its borrowings and fee-based needs in subsequent periods. In addition, information accumulated through lending activities during each period will lower future credit analysis costs. Finally, expansion of the activity level of a bank improves the knowledge and know-how of its officers and managers, which may raise productivity in subsequent periods. In this way, if there are dynamic increasing returns to scale, it is natural that what really is profit maximization in the long run on the surface looks like scale maximization in the short run.

These three hypotheses propose that in essence banks are maximizing their profits but for various reasons appear to be maximizing their scale. In contrast, the fourth hypothesis is that a bank's objective function really is maximizing its scale or market share. Mechanisms to maximize scale are built into the organization and do not necessarily lead to profit-seeking behavior. This is because the scale of a bank is seen as expressing the social status of its staff. Moreover, an expanding scale generates more jobs for management, especially future opportunities for middle managers. Even though the management pyramid narrows toward the top, when the pyramid is growing, the narrowing at each level is slower.

Noma (1986) provides an instructive empirical analysis. He tested the first three hypotheses, based on profit maximization, and rejected them. The fourth, scale maximization for its own sake, he deduced from indirect empirical analysis. However he has not analyzed why scale maximization became the objective function.

Izawa and Tsutsui (1989) empirically analyzed whether bank managers have any objectives other than profit maximization and, if so, whether the expansion preference hypothesis held. Their results reject both profit maximizing and expansion.

The Financial Development of Japan, Korea, and Taiwan

In summary, clear-cut direct empirical tests of the four hypotheses do not exist—and are perhaps impossible. Our own feeling is that profit maximization is the eventual goal, but expansion as a means has sometimes become a goal in its own right—and as such has actually prevented profit maximization. Indeed, in the financial difficulties of the early 1990s Japan's banks have had to restrain their growth in order to meet the BIS capital adequacy requirements and to cover actual and potential loan losses.

EFFECTS OF LIBERALIZATION

In the 1980s bank behavior changed in accordance with deregulation and financial liberalization, and such changes are likely to be even greater throughout the 1990s. Among the changes, two deserving particular notice have already been discussed: Interest rates have become sensitive to market conditions and the degree of market segmentation among different categories of banks has lessened. This section looks at some of the other changes.

The large increase in asset prices, particularly for land and equities, during the latter half of the 1980s had a significant impact on the behavior of banks. The bursting of the bubble in the 1990s will no doubt cause more wrenching changes.

Balance Sheet Composition and BIS Requirements

The stock price run up enabled banks to increase their own equity by issuing new shares and convertible bonds. They also enjoyed huge increases in unrealized capital gains on their long-standing holdings of securities in other firms. Although these holdings are no secret, they are nonetheless called "hidden reserves" because the banks are not required to show unrealized capital gains on their balance sheets. This nonreporting has been justified on the grounds the holdings are an integral part of the banks' relationship with their clients, thus are unlikely to be sold, and thus are truly not available as a source of capital to the banks.

It is no secret that banks trade these accounts to dress up their earnings reports, and in the late 1980s banks tended to depend more on returns from securities holdings to make up for decreased profits from lending. Initially, stock profits made it look easy for the banks to meet the BIS capital requirement of 8 percent set for the end of March 1993. Indeed, banks increased their stock holdings during the stock boom period, as Tables 3.13 and 3.16 show.

Accordingly some of the hidden reserves disappeared in the stock market decline that began in 1990, and earnings from securities are anticipated to diminish to a large extent. This fact suggests it is risky for the banks to depend on securities holdings to meet the BIS ratio and to secure steady earnings. All but one city bank chose to reduce its asset base in the fiscal years ending March 1991 and March 1992 (Asahi in fiscal 1990, Daiwa in fiscal 1991).

Low equity ratios have been attributed to the high growth of lending and a strict control of dividend policy. Liberalization on liabilities started with foreign currency deposits in 1972 and gradually expanded to domestic yen deposits such as

Table 3.16. *City Bank Domestic Stockholdings*

Year	At cost (billion yen)	As % of total assets	Annual increase (%) [a]
1955	35	1.1	n.a.
1960	151	1.9	34.0
1965	389	2.1	20.8
1970	899	2.4	18.2
1975	1,992	2.5	17.5
1980	3,676	3.0	13.0
1983	5,207	3.3	12.3
1986	7,228	3.8	11.6
1987	8,761	3.5	21.2
1988	11,412	4.0	30.3
1989	15,062	4.6	32.0
1990	18,596	5.3	23.5
1991	20,207	5.8	8.7

n.a. Not applicable.

a. Compound annual rate for multiyear periods.

Source: Computed by authors from data in Bank of Japan, *Economic Statistics Yearbook,* 1992, p. 50 (total assets) and p. 51 (stockholdings at cost).

CDs, MMCs, and large-scale deposits. There was, however, no major change in balance sheet composition during the 1970s and 1980s, because of MOF's slow implementation and careful coordination. The only change on the liability side was a shift from borrowings, more than half of which were owed to the Bank of Japan, to call money—especially by regional, trust, and long-term banks.

As liberalization progressed, in May 1986 MOF revised restrictions on the minimum equity ratio—including unrealized securities gains—from 10 percent to a more realistic 6 percent for banks with foreign branches and 4 percent for those without them. Banks were also allowed, in July 1987, to issue convertible bonds to meet this requirement. BIS regulations regarding risk assets of commercial banks were applied to Japanese banks in June 1988: 7.25 percent equity by the end of March 1991 and 8 percent by the end of March 1993. The risk–asset ratio is calculated by taking all risk-related items whether on or off the balance sheet on the asset side and 45 percent of unrealized capital gains in securities on the equity side.

To help meet this requirement, banks issued some 5.5 trillion yen of equity and convertible bonds during 1985–89, representing over half the new issues on the Tokyo Stock Exchange. All 13 city banks, 3 long-term banks, and 7 trust banks met the interim requirement, and 16 met the 8 percent ratio in March 1989. The collapse of stock prices since February 1990 makes meeting the requirement for March 31, 1993 more difficult: In 1991 it was estimated that each 1,000-point drop in the Nikkei stock index reduces the overall bank equity ratio by 0.2 percentage point. When the March 1989 ratios were calculated, the Nikkei was at 32,839; 3 years later it was at 19,346. This translates into a 2.7 percentage point drop in the combined equity ratio. (Table 3.1 includes the 1992 BIS ratios.)

Mergers

There have been two types of mergers. First is the big-big—one city bank combines with another in a quest for economies of scale, scope, or regional coverage. The second, and more common, is the combining of a weaker bank with a stronger one, which is usually larger and of the same type.

There have been two periods of big–big, the early 1970s and the early 1990s. The earlier period sought scale economies. In 1971 Dai–ichi and Nippon Kangyo combined to form what has since been the largest bank (based on assets) in Japan and tenth in the world the year it was formed. As the yen appreciated it subsequently became the world's largest. In 1973 the merger of Taiyo and Kobe produced the bank with the largest network of branches, but right in the middle in asset size.

The two big–bigs in the 1990s—Mitsui Taiyo–Kobe (now Sakura Bank) in 1990 and Kyowa Saitama (now Asahi) in 1991—seem motivated by scope as well as scale, particularly the latter. For scope, Mitsui had a strong international presence (first worldwide in amount of loans in 1989), and Taiyo-Kobe had many domestic branches. As for scale, Sakura has by far the largest branch network in Japan, but Asahi has the largest in metropoitan Tokyo. Relative to the six largest city banks, Asahi remains small.

Examples of weaker banks combining with stronger are Seiwa–Hirosaki (to form Michinoku in 1976), Heiwa Sogo's absorption by Sumitomo (1986), and Iyo–Toho Sogo (1992). Iyo, the largest regional bank based on the island of Shikoku and in the forefront of installing ATMs in the early 1980s, was an archetypal candidate for absorbing a smaller bank.

As deregulation continues, we expect mergers of weaker into stronger banks to increase. A number of the smaller institutions—particularly the shinkin and even former sogo—are unlikely to survive. Thus, in October 1991 Tokai absorbed a credit association (Sanwa Shinkin), giving it 13 more branches in Tokyo.

New patterns are also emerging, particularly regarding shinkin. In 1990 Yachiyo Shinkin applied to be the first shinkin to become a commercial bank. MOF permission came in early 1991 and the change took effect that April 1. Yachiyo says it intends to continue in its old niches. In April 1991 Dai–ichi Kangyo and Jonan, one of the larger shinkin, established the first "cooperative tie-up" between a city bank and a credit association. Jonan is said to be healthy. The exact nature of the tie-up remains to be seen; initially it involves introducing the two banks' customers to one another and developing new products together. In the Osaka area, Daiwa, the only city bank allowed in the trust business, will offer trust services through 14 shinkin.

Among regional banks, two healthy banks with adjoining territories announced their merger in November 1990 (San-in Godo and Fuso, which had been a sogo bank). More such combinations—which can be likened to the emergence of super-regional banks in the United States—are possible. MOF drafted legislation in 1992 that will facilitate mergers and conversions (upgrading to commercial bank status).

Other Effects

Because of the slow pace of freeing bank deposit interest rates, insurance companies have accumulated more of the increase in savings than private banks have. From 1983 to 1986 72 percent of the increase in household savings was deposited in insurance companies, including pension funds run by insurance companies. Banks absorbed only 28 percent of the increase. City banks depended more on call money during this period than on loans from BOJ.

Although city and regional banks had declining shares of total assets, the trust banks increased share by taking in pension funds. City banks relied heavily on funds from international markets through the 1980s. BIS coordination induced the monetary authorities to allow Japanese banks to issue convertible bonds in order to improve their risk–asset ratio. Deposits in overseas branches and foreign subsidiaries increased primarily because the banks obtained permission to grant loans to nonresidents, there was a strong demand for impact loans by Japanese corporations, and especially, foreign transactions were liberalized (in principle) under the revised Foreign Exchange and Foreign Trade Control Law of December 1980. Table 3.17 has data on overseas deposits.

Japan's long-term capital outflow exceeded its current account surplus beginning in the 1980s—particularly in the latter part of the decade—although this was reversed in 1991, at least temporarily. In other words, Japan's financial institutions served as international intermediaries, lending long term and borrowing short term. This means Japanese banks were net borrowers of short-term capital in foreign markets. Thus, for example, by the end of September 1987 they had borrowed $157.6 billion from foreign banks and sent $144.0 billion to headquarters in Japan (Bank of England 1987, p. 520). Part of this money was borrowed because Japanese companies were seeking dollar-denominated liabilities to hedge their foreign exchange risk.

PROBLEMS AND PROSPECTS

The combination of gradual financial liberalization, continued rapid growth, and diversification of the banking and financial systems, and particularly the aftermath of bank financing of the real estate and stock market booms means that Japan's banking system will continue to undergo considerable further transformation in the years ahead.

One aspect of financial liberalization has been the decline in segmented markets and bank specialization. The shift away from a segmentation policy has taken place primarily because of changes on the asset side of the balance sheet. That is, the fact a number of large companies have become less dependent on bank financing simply by getting bigger and more liquid has rendered the financial

Table 3.17. *Deposits at Overseas Branches of City Banks* (*trillion yen*)

Mar. 31	Total [a]	Overseas branches	Overseas as % of total
1978	75.7	5.5	7.3
1979	85.7	6.9	8.1
1980	100.7	17.1	17.0
1981	113.1	22.2	19.6
1982	141.0	39.9	28.3
1983	153.5	46.7	30.4
1984	169.7	53.1	31.3
1985	195.1	69.3	35.5
1986	199.0	60.7	30.5
1987	230.3	79.6	34.6
1988	262.2	90.1	34.4
1989	304.4	117.3	38.5
1990	364.4	161,4	44.2
1991	353.5	130.0	36.8

Note: Includes CDs, a separate entry in the sources. From 1989 the BOJ series on total domestic deposits has been subtracted from the FBAJ series on total deposits to obtain overseas deposits. Before 1989 FBAJ published both series.

a. Total deposits at domestic and overseas branches.

Source: FBAJ *Analysis of Financial Statements of All Banks,* various issues (1991 edition, p. 16, has 1987–91), and Bank of Japan, *Economic Statistics Annual.* It does not say so explicitly in the English notes, but the BOJ series (e.g., 1990 edition, p. 49, table 16 (1)) is domestic deposits only.

structure of the high-growth period almost unworkable. At the same time, interest rate deregulation has meant growing competition for deposits. It has also deprived banks of ensured spreads, so the desire of banks to expand their deposits is no longer an automatic reflex. These changes therefore have caused banks to seek an "optimal" size rather than simply a larger one. A shift of promising bank personnel to competitive overseas markets, and increasing off-balance sheet businesses seem to be the examples of this behavior. The emphasis on loans to consumers and small and medium businesses, which began in the mid-1980s, is another aspect of the banks' seeking to reposition themselves and adjust.

All of this would have been difficult enough in a macroeconomic environment of continued real growth and solid asset markets. But the speculative bubble of the late 1980s and its bursting complicated the situation—in part by masking trends related to deregulation. In contrast to the U.S. savings and loan debacle, deregulation as such cannot be used in Japan as a scapegoat for the bubble and its aftermath, and the process is unlikely to be derailed or even slowed.

The overhang of potential bad loans to the real estate industry and to other firms using overvalued real estate as collateral has created severe problems for the banks in the early 1990s. A major difficulty has been the lack of information and transparency regarding the extent of the problem that each bank faced. This situation resulted in sharp declines in the prices of bank shares, especially in the first half of 1992. The system based on public trust in the banks and faith in the regulatory competence of MOF and BOF, was undermined. The authorities in the summer of 1992 were taking action to obtain more information on the bank debt situation and, of equal importance, to reduce the bad debt overhang by creating a special institution to buy up, at market prices, the real estate collateral underlying part of the nonperforming loans. Over time the bad loans will be written off and losses taken.

The decline in stock prices and likelihood of bad-loan write offs has put pressure on balance sheets, and the banks have cut back on their assets now that they are required to meet BIS capital adequacy standards. Banks will be able to raise capital through subordinate debt and even equity issues but only at globally competitive prices, unlike the halcyon days of the late 1980s.

As this chapter is being written in the late summer of 1992, Japan's city, long-term credit and trust banks, the largest of which had for some years ranked among the world's 10 largest banks (by assets), are seeing their credit ratings downgraded, a surcharge placed on some of their Euromarket borrowings, and their "hidden assets"—which were not only to help them easily meet BIS capital requirements but also (in a pinch) act as bad-loan reserves—shrink precipitously. Beginning with fiscal 1990 (which ended 31 March 1991) the city banks began to shrink their asset base.

As part of their retrenchment, banks are closing or downgrading their overseas offices—and even domestic branches that do not meet profitability goals (although the general trend continues to be for city banks to expand their branch networks). City banks also, on average, reduced their hiring of 1992 new college graduates into career track jobs by about 20 percent compared to 1991.

The situtation is somewhat different for smaller financial institutions. Because of the deregulation of deposit rates and the loss of their market niches, many smaller regional banks and credit associations lack sufficient scale and portfolio diversity to prosper in a competitive environment. The excesses of the speculative bubble have, in some instances, been combined with years of poor management to exacerbate these institutions' problems. MOF is predisposed to support consolidation of the industry, and the press abounds with speculation, but just what form this will take is so far unclear. Historically these institutions have absorbed one another, but it may become more common for them to be folded into the larger banks.

Nonetheless, it is highly unlikely the regulatory authorities will allow any bank to go bankrupt formally or any depositors to take losses. MOF and BOJ will not allow a financial crisis to occur. Rather, as in the past, weak banks will be merged into strong ones. This will involve not only small, local financial institutions but probably some large banks as well. The economy's growth, once the 1992 recession is passed, will bail out the system in the longer run—but not without pain for financial institutions (and, at least indirectly, taxpayers). The 1985–90 period of very low interest rates, easy money, and sharply rising asset prices is unlikely to be replicated. At home and abroad, Japanese banks instead face a competitive and noncozy world.

REFERENCES

(The word "processed" describes informally reproduced works that may not be commonly available through libraries.)

Adams, TFM and Iwao Hoshii [Peter J. Herzog]. 1972. *A Financial History of the New Japan*. Tokyo: Kodansha.

Bank of England. 1987. *Quarterly Bulletin,* November.

Fama, Eugene F. 1980. "Agency Problem and the Theory of the Firm." *Journal of Political Economy* 88.

Fuji Bank. 1967. *Banking in Modern Japan*, 2d ed. Tokyo: Fuji Bank.

Furukawa, Akira. 1985. *Gendai Nihon no kinyu bunseki*. Toyo Keizai Shinposha.

———. 1990. "Retail Banking and Consumer Choice in Japan." Processed.

Gerlach, Michael L. 1992. *Alliance Capitalism: The Social Organization of Japanese Business*. Berkeley and Los Angeles: University of California Press.

Goto, Shinichi. 1966 Jun. "City Banks." *Gendai kinyu Zenshu* 11.

Hadley, Eleanor M. 1970. *Antitrust in Japan*. Princeton, NJ: Princeton University Press.

Hasui, Akihiro. 1986 Apr. "Ginko no kenzensei to koteki kisei kantoku" (Sound banking and supervision by monetary authorities). *Kinyu kenkyu* 5(2) (Bank of Japan Institute for Monetary and Economic Studies).

Horiuchi, Akiyoshi. 1977 and 1978. *Madoguchi shido no yokosei*.

———. 1984 Aug. "Economic Growth and Financial Allocation in Postwar Japan." Discussion Papers in International Economics. Washington, DC: Brookings Institution.

———. 1988. "An Overview of the Japanese Financial System: A Perspective of the Economic Analysis of Information." Processed.

——— and Masayuki Otaki. 1987. "Finance: Importance of Government Intervention and Bank Lending." In Koichi Hamada, Masahiro Kuroda, and Akiyoshi Horiuchi, eds., *Macro Analysis on Japanese Economy*. Tokyo: University of Tokyo Press.

———, Frank Packer and Shinichi Fukuda. 1988. "What Role Has the 'Main Bank' Played in Japan." *Journal of Japanese and International Economies* 2 (2) 159–80. (Jun.).

Hoshi, Takeo, Anil Kashyap, and David Scharfstein. 1990. "The Role of Banks in Reducing the Costs of Financial Distress in Japan." *Journal of Financial Economics* 27: 67–88.

Izawa, Yuji, and Yoshiro Tsutsui. 1989. "Wagakuni ginkogyo ni okeru keieisha no mokuteki." Processed.

Jensen, Michael C., and William H. Meckling. 1976. "Theory of the Firm: Managerial Behavior, Agency Costs and Ownership Structure." *Journal of Financial Economics*. 3 (4) 305–60 (Oct.).

Kasuya, Munehisa. 1986. "Economies of Scope: Theories and Application to Banking." *Kinyu kenkyu* 4(2): (Bank of Japan Institute for Monetary and Economic Studies.)

———. 1989. "Ginkogyo no cost kozo no jissho bunseki." *Kinyu kenkyu* 8.

KGCK (Kinyu gyosei chosa kenkyukai). 1972. *Finance and Inspection*. Tokyo: KGCK.

Kusano, Atsushi. 1986. *The Showa 40.5.28. Yamaichi Affair and BOJ Emergency Loans.*

Nakamura, Takafusa. 1980. *Nihon keizai: Sono seicho to kozo* 2d ed. Translated in 1981 by Jacqueline Kaminski as *The Postwar Japanese Economy: Its Development and Structure*. Tokyo: University of Tokyo Press.

Nakatani, Iwao. 1984. "The Economic Role of Financial Corporate Grouping." In Masahiko Aoki, ed., *The Economic Analysis of the Japanese Firm*. Amsterdam: North-Holland.

Noma, Toshikatsu. 1986. "Scale Maximizing Behavior of the Japanese Banks; An Empirical Analysis." *Economic Studies Quarterly* 37.

Odaka, Konsuke, Keinosuke Ono, and Fumihiko Adachi. 1988. *The Automobile Industry in Japan: A Study of Ancillary Firm Development*. Tokyo: Kinokuniya.

OECD (Organisation for Economic Co-operation and Development). 1992. *Bank Profitability, Statistical Supplement 1981–90*. Paris: OECD.

Pettway, Richard H., Neil W. Sicherman, and Takeshi Yamada. 1990. "The Market for Corporate Control, the Level of Agency Costs, Corporate Collectivism in Japanese Mergers." In Edwin J. Elton and Martin J. Gruber, eds., *Japanese Capital Markets*. New York: Harper & Row.

Saito, Fuminori. 1983. *Comperative Japanese Companies: Banks*. Jitsumu Kyoiku Press.
Sheard, Paul. 1989. "The Main Bank System and Corporate Monitoring and Control in Japan." *Journal of Economic Behavior and Organization* 3:399–422.
Smitka, Michael J. 1991. *Competitive Ties: Subcontracting in the Japanese Automotive Industry*. New York: Columbia University Press.
Suda, Miyako. 1985. "Economies of Scale and Scope in Banking Industry." *Finance Kenkyu*
Suzuki, Yoshio. 1966. *Kinyu seisaku no Koka*.
———, ed. 1987. *The Japanese Financial System* (English ed. of *Wagakuni no kinyu seido*, 1986). New York: Oxford University Press.
Tachibanaki, Toshiaki, Kiyoshi Mitsui and Hiroshi Kitagawa. 1990. "Economies of Scope and Intercorporate Ownership." Processed.
Tsutsui, Yoshiro. 1988. *Kinyu shijo to ginkogyo*. Toyokeizai Shinposha.
Tsutsui, Yoshiro, and Shyoichi Royama. 1987. "Kinyugyo no sangyo soshiki." In Ryuichiro Tachi and Shoichi Royama, eds., *Nihon no kinyu*. Tokyo: University of Tokyo Press.
Williamson, Oliver E. 1975. *Market and Hierarchies*. New York: Free Press.
Yamashita, Kunio. 1986. Kinyu zaisei jijo, March 3, p. 16.
Yutaka, Inoue. 1990. Reporting in *Kinyu Journal*, July, p. 29, Table 3.18.

APPENDIX

Table 3.1A. *Financial Deregulation Measures in Japan, 1976–91*

Date	Instruments (minimum size in million yen)	Markets	Other
1976		Mar.: Official recognition of gensaki transactions.	
1977		Apr.: Government bonds allowed to be sold in secondary market.	
1978	Jun.: Medium-term (3-year) government bonds first sold (by bid).	Jun.: BOJ starts bid-based market operations in 20-year government bonds.	
	Oct.–Nov.: 7-day call loans allowed at free rate; 1-month bills with free rate created; rates liberalized on over-3-month-ends bills.	Jun.: Resale of bills allowed at free rate 1 month after purchase.	
1979	Apr.: Call rate liberalization; creation of 2- to 6-day call loans. May: CDs introduced (¥500, 3–6 mos) Oct.: rates liberalized on over-2-month-ends bills.	May: Liberalization of nonresident participation in gensaki.	Feb.: Lifting of all restrictions on nonresident acquisition of domestic securities.

Table 3.1A. (Cont'd.)

Date	Instruments (minimum size in million yen)	Markets	Other
1980	Jan.: *chukoku* (midterm government-bond funds) introduced. Jul.: First resident Euro-yen issue.	Apr.: Ceiling on gensaki sales (borrowing) by city banks abolished.	Nov.: Large security companies allowed to borrow in call market. Dec.: Amended Foreign Exchange Law goes into effect.
1981	Jun.: BIG and maturity-designated time deposits. Oct.: WIDE. Dec.: Corporate bonds with warrants.	Apr.: City banks permitted to be gensaki buyers (i.e., lenders). May: Start of BOJ sale of government bills in the market.	Dec.: Medium security companies allowed to borrow in call market, borrowing limits for large companies expanded.
1982			Apr.: New Banking Law and Securities and Exchange Law implemented.
1983	May: Floating rate housing loans.	Apr: OTC sales of longterm government bonds (by banks). Oct.: OTC sales of medium-term government bonds.	Jun.: Prohibition of short-term yen loans to nonresidents abolished.
1984	Jan.: CD minimum to ¥300. Dec.: Euroyen CDs allowed.	Jun.: Dealing in public bonds by 34 banks. Apr.: "Sweep" accounts combining *chukoku* and ordinary deposits. Jun.: Regulations on conversion of foreign funds into yen abolished (*enten*).	Apr.: Foreign institutions allowed to participate in government bond syndicates. Apr.: Transactions in foreign CDs and commercial paper allowed. Jun.: Liberalized short-term Euroyen lending to residents. Dec.: Euroyen bonds allowed nongovernment nonresidents.

Date	Instruments (minimum size in million yen)	Markets	Other
1985	Mar.: MMCs introduced (¥50, 1–6 mos). Apr.: CDs to ¥100 and 1 month minimum. Jun.: 5- to 6-month bill transactions introduced. Aug.: Sales of large-scale public bond investment trusts begin. Aug.: 2- to 3-wk call transactions introduced. Oct.: Large-scale deposits introduced (¥1000, 3–24 mos). Dec.: Ordinary money trust (a deposit instrument) introduced.	Jun.: Market established for yen-denominated bankers' acceptance. Jun.: Securities companies allowed to trade CDs. Jun.: Bond dealing by 44 local and 1 sōgō bank. Jul.: uncollateralized call money transactions allowed. Oct.: Government bond futures market started.	Apr.: First 3 bond rating agencies established. Apr.: Euroyen bonds allowed for residents and medium- and long-term lending to nonresidents liberalized. Jun.: MOF decided to allow 9 foreign banks in trust business (from 1986 May). Dec.: European banks licensed to deal in securities.
1986	Apr.: CD maximum term to 1 year. Apr.: Large-scale to ¥500. Sep.: Large-scale to ¥300. Sep.: MMC minimum to ¥30, maximum term to 1 year. Oct.: Variable insurance (hengaku hoken; payment based on market conditions).	Jan.: BOJ starts treasury bond (TB) gensaki. Feb.: Short-term government bonds (TB) issued by bid. Jun.: Government bond dealing by another 10 local and 29 sōgō banks, as well as 6 shinkin.	Feb.: Foreign brokers become Tokyo Stock Exchange members. Dec.: Establishment of offshore market in Tokyo.
1987	Apr.: MMC to ¥20, maximum term to 2 yrs. Apr.: Large-scale to ¥100. Oct.: MMC to ¥10. Oct.: Large-scale to 1 month.	Jun.: Osaka trading of stock options. Jun.: Government bond dealing by another 38 sōgō banks and 24 shinkin. Nov.: Commercial paper market established.	May: Rules for private placement of corporate bonds liberalized. Aug.: U.S. banks allowed into securities business. Nov.: Ban lifted on Euroyen commercial paper.
1988	Apr.: CDs to ¥50, minimum term 2 wks, maximum 2 yrs. Apr.: Large-scale to ¥50. Nov.: 1-wk and 1-month bills. Nov.: Large-scale to ¥30.	Government bond dealing by more shinkin (6 in Jun., 5 in Dec.). Sep.: Stock index futures begin trading.	Feb.: More foreign brokers join Tokyo Stock Exchange. Oct.: Shelf registration system for corporate bonds.

Table 3.1A. (Cont'd.)

Date	Instruments (minimum size in million yen)	Markets	Other
1989	Apr.: Uncollateralized call loans and bills term extended to 1 year. Apr.: Large-scale to ¥20. Jun.: Small-scale MMC introduced (¥3, 6 and 12 mos). Oct.: Small-scale MMC 3-month, 2- and 3-year terms introduced. Oct.: Large-scale to ¥10.	Apr.: Long-term government bonds issued by bids. May: 82 banks begin trading bond futures. Jun.: Tokyo financial futures exchange opens *and* Stock index options trading begins in Osaka. Oct.: TOPIX option trading begins in Tokyo. Jul.: Government bond dealing by another 4 shinkin.	Feb.: Beginning of conversion of sōgō to ordinary banks. May: Mid- and long-term Euroyen loans to residents liberalized. Jun.: Trading securities futures overseas allowed for 81 banks. Dec.: Trading foreign government bond futures allowed for 133 banks.
1990	MOF agrees to look into consumer complaints about the level of bank fees (very high by world standards) and the fact they are fairly uniform among banks. Nov.: Super MMCs with rates set as a percentage of unregulated large time deposit rates. Various maturities, ¥1–3.	Apr.: MOF speeds process for approving new branches. May: Government bond futures options trading begins on TSE, thus matching variety of instruments available in United States. Nov.: BOJ allows continuous bidding for interbank loans above ¥500 million, replacing system of 6 specialized firms setting a rate once daily.	Apr.: Domestic firms allowed to join Chicago MERC's GLOBEX 24-hour electronic financial futures trading network. Oct.: Two foreign firms licensed to enter investment trust management. Domestic and foreign investment advisory firms can accept corporate clients. Very strict requirements.
1991	MOF continues delay in deregulatory demand deposit rates.	Apr.: All government 10-year bonds to be auctioned.	Jul.: The last sogo bank to merge out of existence in Apr. 1992.

4

Korea: Development and Structural Change of the Financial System

YUNG CHUL PARK

After almost 15 years of uninterrupted rapid growth fueled by export expansion, Korea was running into an economic crisis of major proportions late in the 1970s. The crisis was precipitated by unfavorable external developments, but was certainly exacerbated by domestic economic mismanagement by an interventionist government that exercised tight control over the financial regime. The sheer size and growing complexity of the economy unquestionably reduced the government's ability to administer a system of rigid controls. Skepticism toward interventionist government grew deeper because of the massive investment in the heavy and chemical industries between 1975 and 1979 (which resulted in huge idle capacity in some of the targeted industries), accelerating inflation, and a growing current account deficit. In retrospect, it appears these macroeconomic developments, more than anything else, gave impetus to a surge of economic liberalism that culminated in a major stabilization program and in 1980–81 set in motion an attempt at economic liberalization.

Since the early 1980s, Korea has implemented a series of policy reforms to liberalize its trade and financial regime. It has also succeeded in lowering its rate of inflation below 5 percent per year while maintaining rapid growth. More significantly, Korea began accumulating a sizable surplus on its current account in 1986. These favorable developments and strong foreign pressures for economic liberalization should have made it much easier to implement financial reform measures. However, after some 10 years of attempts at liberalization, Korea's financial sector is still under rigid and pervasive government control and remains largely closed to foreign competition. Moreover, in the 1990s inflation has moved up and the current account is again in deficit, making the environment for continued reforms more difficult.

This chapter analyzes Korea's experience with financial development and liberalization since the 1970s with the purpose of identifying the sources of financial growth. It also looks at some of the factors that may have interfered with the financial liberalization process. (For a study of financial development in Korea during the postwar period until 1978 see Cole and Park 1983.)

The analysis, it is hoped, adds to our understanding of the causal relationship between financial growth and liberalization on the one hand and economic growth on the other. The first section summarizes the Korean macroeconomic context, and the second section provides an overview of the financial sector's evolution during the 1970s and 1980s.

The core of the chapter is the third and fourth sections, which examine—on both a theoretical level and for the Korean case—the relationship between financial deepening and domestic savings, and the effects of financial development on allocative efficiency.

After outlining the stabilization–liberalization program as set forth in the Fifth Five-Year Plan (1982–86), I examine the various reform measures taken for financial liberalization. Then I look at some of the economic forces and structural characteristics that have constrained liberalization efforts. Finally, drawing on the Korean experience, I analyze the role of finance in a rapidly growing economy.

MACROECONOMIC DEVELOPMENTS, 1973–81

Following a decade of rapid growth and industrialization through the promotion of exports during the first two Five-Year Development Plan periods (1962–71), Korea began in the early 1970s to experience a sharp increase in real wages and capital intensity in the manufacturing sectors that accounted for practically all exports. This increase undermined Korea's international competitiveness at a time when it faced growing competition from other developing countries emulating this export-led industrial growth, and it was viewed as a sign of change in Korea's comparative advantage to producing skill- and technology-intensive products such as machinery, ships, and sophisticated electronics. (For more on this period see Dornbusch and Park 1987.)

The Heavy and Chemical Industry Drive

To sustain rapid growth, therefore, it was believed major shifts in production and exports toward expansion of heavy and chemical (HC) industries were called for. A massive investment program for these industries, financed largely by foreign loans and central bank credit, was put into effect in 1973 and pursued vigorously until 1979. To the dismay of policymakers, this industrial restructuring through promotion of investment in HC industries ran into a host of financing, engineering, quality, and marketing difficulties. (HC includes six 3-digit industries, according to the Bank of Korea's classification: industrial chemicals; other chemicals; products of petroleum and coal; iron and steel; nonferrous metals; and machinery.)

The large investment in HC industries brought a sharp increase in the share of these industries in manufacturing output, employment, and exports. But it did not contribute to total export and output growth as much as was planned, and it complicated short-run management of domestic demand and the current account. Price increases, brought under control following two years of rampant inflation (1973–74) triggered by the first oil shock, began accelerating again due to the investment expansion in the HC industries—much of which took place during 1977–79. In 1980 the WPI (wholesale price index) jumped 40 percent.

The large increase in domestic demand generated by investment in HC industries and the associated expansion of liquidity, combined with a decline in export demand, resulted in a large deterioration in Korea's current account (which had shown a small surplus in 1977). The current account registered a deficit amounting to 2.1 percent of GNP in 1978, and two years later the deficit soared to 8.7 percent of GNP.

The Shocks of 1979–81

Strong inflationary pressures, coupled with a slowdown in growth, were exacerbated by a series of external and internal shocks that precipitated a recession and a huge accumulation of foreign debt. As a consequence of the second oil crisis in 1979—which doubled the price of oil within a year—the terms of trade deteriorated by 17 percent between 1978 and 1981. The cost of servicing the foreign debt, approximated by the 90-day Eurodollar rate, rose to more than 18 percent in 1980 from less than 8 percent three years earlier.

Grain imports rose by an annual average of 60 percent during 1979–81 because of poor harvests in 1978 and 1979 and the failure of the rice crop in 1980. Export earnings suffered from the deepening world recession and an erosion in Korea's export competitiveness caused by the sharp increase in unit labor costs. While Korea was beset by these problems it had to confront the social and political problems unleashed by the death of President Park Chung Hee in October 1979. The ensuring political turmoil and uncertainties clouded the business climate and further complicated management of the economy.

The hostile external environment and domestic political problems were much more dramatic than during the first oil crisis period. A rise in unemployment would pose a serious threat to an already shaky social stability. Nevertheless, it was evident to policymakers that the growth-first policy supported by foreign financing was simply not a viable alternative as it had been in 1974. The foremost reason was that availability of the external finance needed to lengthen the adjustment period was questionable. Indeed, it was obvious that any further deterioration in the current account would seriously undermine Korea's credit standing in international financial markets and would cripple its ability to borrow.

Most of all, it was inconceivable that exports would grow as fast as they had during 1976–77. This pessimism reflected the rise in trade protectionism and expectations of a deepening world recession. Persistently high interest rates and the diminished availability of external finance also raised the cost of borrowing abroad. Given the requirement for continuous external borrowing, the best policy alternative was to pursue stabilization policies in the hope of reducing the size of the current account deficit.

Confronting the Problems

Against this background of a deterioration in economic performance and a pessimistic future outlook, the Fifth Five-Year Economic and Social Development Plan was formulated in 1981. In describing the difficulties the economy was facing, the plan document states: "The causes of the current difficulties do not lie only in external economic factors such as the second oil shock, social unrest and a bad harvest. A more fundamental root can be traced to the fact that the government failed to properly reorient its economic management strategy to the changing economic and social environment" (Korea 1982, p. 10).

The document goes on to point out that the foremost cause of the problems was a chronic inflationary spiral and that the second was the inefficiencies embedded in the Korean economy. According to the document, government-initiated investment activities, protective measures such as import restrictions, and support for certain strategic industries all were necessary to sustain rapid growth during the earlier stages of development. As the economy grew in size, however, such active government intervention undermined the efficiency of resource allocation and impeded private initiatives, thereby impairing economic flexibility. These observations were made in reference to social and economic development that had been characterized by the strengthening—rather than relaxing—of government control over all facets of economic life during the latter part of the 1970s.

Poor economic performance and the inefficiency of government control convinced the Korean public—as well as planners—that a major shift in industrial policy was due. Reflecting this need for change, the Fifth Plan emphasized stability, efficiency, and balance among different geographical regions and income classes as the basic objectives of economic policy. The first priority was given to price stability, as it was then imperative to arrest the deterioration in Korea's export competitiveness. This objective was followed by economic liberalization intended to encourage greater openness, autonomy, and decentralization of authority in all sectors of the economy. Economic stabilization was also thought to be essential to fostering an environment conducive to economic liberalization.

Assessing the 1970s and 1980s

One presumed advantage of export promotion development over import substitution is that it allows the economy to operate closer to a free trade regime, because it provides uniform incentives to all export lines, relies less on controls, and encourages competition. With the promotion of heavy and chemical industries in the 1970s, this advantage to the Korean economy of an export-led development strategy either disappeared or became less visible than it had been earlier. Instead, economic policy became increasingly rigid and displayed many of the features usually associated with import substitution regimes.

Some control measures that should have been phased out were retained, and additional restrictions replaced incentives. In particular, Korean policymakers had to tighten their control over finance in order to allocate resources to the fledgling HC industries that private firms were reluctant to invest in because of their long gestation period and uncertain rates of return. To induce private investment in these industries, the government had to provide ever-more distorted incentives in the form of preferential loans. To facilitate such an allocation, government authorities had to keep nominal bank lending rates below market levels and to intensify credit rationing, resulting in negative real interest rates and rapid expansion of the curb market.

In retrospect, the economic liberalism that swept the nation in the early 1980s was a reaction to an interventionist regime that was becoming increasingly rigid and debilitating to the economy. Toward the end of the 1970s, setbacks in the HC industries and the associated drain on domestic resources prompted a debate on whether overall economic liberalization was needed. It was argued that such a massive misallocation of resources as had taken place in the HC industries could have been avoided had management of the financial system been left in the hands of the private sector.

The argument then went a step further by implying—and subsequently generating expectations that—economic liberalization could resolve many of the macroeconomic problems attributed to government intervention in the allocation of resources (Park 1985). In fact, an effective adjustment of investments in the HC industries would have required more aggressive intervention by the government, but this was not the course chosen until the mid-1980s. The delay of an industrial restructuring that was badly needed made it difficult to continue with economic liberalization.

AN OVERVIEW OF THE FINANCIAL SECTOR

During the 1970s and 1980s there was a rapid growth and modernization of Korea's financial sector (see Tables 4.1 and 4.A2). Measured by the ratio of M3 to GNP, Korea's financial system more than doubled in size between 1980 and 1989 (see the note to Table 4.1 defining what M3 is in Korea). The financial interrelation ratio (FIR—the ratio of total financial assets to nominal GNP) rose to over 4 in 1989 from less than 2½ before 1981. Although this ratio is much lower than Japan's, Korea's financial deepening has been comparable to that of Taiwan and the United States since the late 1980s.

What factors explain the rapid growth of Korea's financial sector in the 1980s? Simple inspection of the raw data and a more detailed study by Nam (1988) show the rise in the FIR has been closely related to the increase in real interest rates and economic growth. The causal nexus between financial and economic growth is discussed in some detail later.

Flow of Funds

Since the early 1970s a variety of nonbank financial intermediaries (NBFIs) have come into existence to complement and compete with the deposit money banks (DMBs). (DMBs include commercial banks, government-owned special banks, and the banking activities of three groups of primary sector cooperatives.) Cre-

Table 4.1. *Ratio of M2 and M3 to GNP*

Year	M2/GNP	M3/GNP	Year	M2/GNP	M3/GNP
1971	0.32	0.37	1982	0.38	0.59
1972	0.35	0.40	1983	0.37	0.61
1973	0.37	0.44	1984	0.35	0.64
1974	0.32	0.40	1985	0.37	0.70
1975	0.31	0.39	1986	0.37	0.78
1976	0.30	0.38	1987	0.38	0.87
1977	0.33	0.42	1988	0.39	0.94
1978	0.33	0.43	1989	0.42	1.07
1979	0.32	0.43	1990	0.40	1.15
1980	0.34	0.48	1991	0.41	1.18
1981	0.34	0.51			

Note: M1 is currency (including commemorative coins before Mar. 1986) plus demand deposits.

M2 is M1 plus savings and time deposits (but only if reserves must be held against them). A requirement to hold reserves is partly a function of the institution—rather than of the instrument—so some depositlike instruments do not require holding reserves. For example, money in trust is in practice a deposit equivalent but has no reserve requirement and is not counted in M2.

M3 is the sum of M2 and depositlike liabilities of nonbank financial intermediaries.

Source: Bank of Korea, *Monthly Bulletin.* In the Apr. 1992 issue, M2 and M3 for 1975–91 are on p. 7 and GNP for 1986–91 is on pp. 134–35.

ation of NBFIs and other efforts to develop money and capital markets have transformed a financial system that was dominated in the 1960s by commercial banking into one that is highly diversified and modern in terms of financial instruments, services, and institutions. This is reflected in Tables 4.A5 and 4.A6, which show the sources of external funds raised by nonfinancial sectors and how the funds were invested.

Financial services range from fixed rate deposits at local credit cooperatives to cash and asset management accounts for individual savers, as well as a range of services for institutional investors and investment banking. The financial sector now includes well-organized and fast growing money and capital markets through which corporations obtained more than half their financing needs in the 1980s. Some institutions and markets have been established in response to demand for new financial services, whereas others were created ahead of demand in order to develop a balanced and diversified financial system.

Deregulation in the 1980s

The monetary authorities embarked on a course of financial deregulation in 1981 as part of an overall liberalization of the economy. This deregulation has led to privatization of the then-existing four nationwide commercial banks (NCBs), as well as the creation of five new NCBs (three in 1989) and a host of nonbank financial intermediaries (NBFIs). To a considerable degree deregulation has also broken down the artificial segmentation of financial institutions by product and service, allowing even commercial banks (CBs) to underwrite securities and hold them for their own account.

Although it has been partial and marked by relapses, deregulation of interest rates has altered the behavior of CBs and NBFIs, as well as the modus operandi of monetary policy.

Encouraged by strong current account developments in the mid 1980s, the monetary authorities outlined a gradual decontrol of foreign exchange transactions and opening of capital markets to foreign competition. Commercial banking was further opened to foreign competition, followed by insurance. Barriers in these and other areas have been lowered, and will continue to be, although at a slower pace than originally envisioned. From 1992 foreigners have been able to buy and sell Korean securities, albeit within limits and under strict controls that, combined with lackluster expectations for Korean stocks, made the much-anticipated and delayed market opening something of a bust. Korean savers have been allowed to invest in foreign securities.

The World Bank highlighted Korea's experience as exemplifying a successful case of financial reforms for liberalization leading to rapid growth in the financial sector in the 1980s (1989, p. 126). The analysis in this chapter takes issue with this conclusion.

Structural Changes

Financial deepening and modernization have brought a number of changes in the structure of finance, the asset preferences of savers, and the financing behavior of business firms. Perhaps the most significant developments have been the rapid growth of credit extended by nonbank financial intermediaries (NBFIs) and direct financing through money and capital markets. NBFI 's' share in the financing of the nonfinancial sector almost tripled from 1970 –74 to 1989, when it stood at 33 percent. At the same time, the share of funds raised from securities issued in the money and capital markets also nearly tripled, to over 43 percent. Deposit money banks (DMBs) have lost share, but the largest decline has been in foreign financing. (See Table 4.A5; note the data do not include unregulated sources of funds.)

Tables 4.2 and 4.A12 show the structure and evolution of the Korean financial system, and Tables 4.A13 through A15 provide an overview of the size of the various components.

Nonbank Financial Intermediaries

NBFIs have grown at the expense of DMBs and informal borrowing from unregulated credit markets. The rapid growth of NBFIs can in large measure be attributed to the relatively free regulatory environment in which they have been allowed to operate. Unlike the DMBs, most of these institutions—such as investment and finance companies and merchant banking firms—have enjoyed con-

Table 4.2. *Government Financial Institutions* (as of July 1992)

Deposit Money Banks (DMB)

    Specialized Banks[a]

1961   Industrial Bank of Korea (small and medium enterprise financing)

1963   Citizens National Bank (small loans to households and small firms)

1967   Korea Housing Bank (housing loans)

1961   Credit and Banking Sector of the National Agricultural Cooperative Federation (NACF)

1962   Credit and Banking Sector of the National Federation of Fisheries Cooperatives (NFFC)

1981   Credit and Banking Sector of the National Livestock Cooperatives Federation (NLCF)

Non-Bank Financial Institutions (NBFI)

    Development Institutions[a]

1954   Korea Development Bank[b]

1967   Korea Long-Term Credit Bank[c]

1969   Export–Import Bank of Korea[d]

    Savings

1983   Postal Savings[e]

    Insurance

1983   Postal Life Insurance[e]

Funds[f]

1974   National Investment (to support heavy and chemical industries)

1981   National Housing[g]

1976   Credit Guarantee (to aid firms with inadequate collateral)

1987   Technology Credit Guarantee (to aid spread of new technology)

1988   Housing Finance Credit Guarantee[h]

Other

1983   Korea Nonbank Deposit Insurance Corporation

Note: Dates are year established.

a. Each established by specific legislation.

b. Role has evolved with the economy. From involvement in the heavy-industry push of the 1970s, in the 1980s the bank moved to fostering energy conservation industries and supporting cyclically depressed industries (e.g., shipping). Since 1986 the priority has been hi tech.

c. Name changed from Korea Development Finance Corp (KDFC) in 1980.

d. Operations handled by Korea Exchange Bank until Jul. 1976.

e. Resumed operations in Jul. 1983, after being abolished in 1977.

f. Korea is the first word of each name, Fund is the last.

g. Under Ministry of Construction, managed by Korea Housing Bank.

h. Function spun off from Housing Bank.

siderable discretion in managing their asset portfolios and setting their lending and borrowing rates at competitive market levels. This is because most NBFIs were created to compete with informal lenders in the unregulated money markets. This autonomy allowed them to grow rapidly by cutting into the market share of DMBs. Since the mid 1980s, however, the interest rate advantage has declined. This, together with financial reform toward multifaceted banking, has enabled DMBs to regain competitiveness and market share.

Expanding Capital Markets

To reduce the high degree of leverage and diversify sources of financing for corporations, Korean policymakers have since the late 1960s directed their efforts at developing capital markets. These efforts have been reinforced since the early 1980s in order to achieve a broader diffusion of corporate ownership through increased participation by the general public as a means of promoting distributive equity, as well as to prepare for opening of capital markets in the early 1990s. Tables 4.3 and 4.4 provide data on listed stocks and bonds, including funds raised during the 1980s.

Table 4.3. Capital Market Indicators
(billion won, except as indicated)

	1980	1985	1987	1989	1990	1991	1992
Stocks							
Companies listed on KSE	352	342	389	626	669	686	688
Capital stock	2,421.4	4,665.3	7,591	21,212	23,982	25,510	27,065
Market value	2,526.6	6,570.4	26,172	95,477	79,020	73,118	84,712
Market value as % of GNP	6.9	8.4	24.7	67.7	46.1	30.4	—
Value of stock traded	1,134.0	3,620.6	20,494	81,200	53,455	62,565	90,624
Stock price index[a]	106.9	163.4	525.1	909.7	696.1	610.9	678.4
Corporate bonds							
Issuers	434	1213	1,457	1,504	1,603	1,862	2,070
Face value	1,649.3	7,623.2	9,973	15,396	22,068	29,241	32,696
Value of bonds traded[b]	643.9	29,18.0	1,912	771	795	704	152
Public bonds							
Issuers	7	12	21	25	24	24	46
Face value	895.4	4,737.8	15,094	28,095	29,049	32,250	32,447
Value of bonds traded[b]	246.0	660.1	5,327	4,378	2,455	1,394	453

— Not available.

a. Korea Composite Stock Price Index (KCSPI) at year-end. Jan. 4, 1980 = 100. Measures the aggregate market value of all common stocks listed on the Korea Stock Exchange.

b. At market, which in most years has been less than the par (face) value of the bonds traded.

Source: Korea Securities Dealers Association, *Securities Market in Korea* 1988 (pp. 41 and 43 for stocks; p. 46 for bond issuers and face value; these tables have annual data for 1975–87 in million won and also include the number of issues). Korea Stock Exchange Fact Book 1990 (p. 24 for bond trading 1979–89 at both market and par values). Later data are from Korea Stock Exchange, *Stock* Jan., 1993, pp. 12–13 for stocks and pp. 71–71 for bonds.

Table 4.4. *Funds Raised by Listed Companies*
(billion won, except as indicated)

	1980	1985	1989	1990	1991	1992
Bonds	963.7	3176.7	6,959	11,084	12,741	13,726
Stock	171.1	294.6	14,669	2,917	2,687	1,798
Total	134.8	3471.3	21,628	14,001	15,428	15,524
Total as % of investment[a]	13.3	22.6	51.5	25.0	21.9	—
Disaggregaton of stock offerings						
Rights	170.8	259.5	11,124	2,582	2,460	1,716
General[b]	0.3	35.1	3,545	336	227	82

— Not available.

a. Private investment by corporate and noncorporate businesses.

b. Initial public and secondary offerings (called "new" and "outstanding" shares, respectively, in the source).

Source: Korea Securities Dealers Association *Securities Market in Korea 1988*, has annual data for 1975–87 in million won and also includes the number of issues (p. 38, Table 7). Later data are from Korea Stock Exchange, *Stock*, Jan., 1993, p. 65, and Bank of Korea, *Economic Statistics Yearbook*, 1992, p. 323.

During the first half of the 1980s capital markets remained depressed, largely because of the downturn of the economy. In the latter half of the 1980s the booming economy and large trade surplus generated optimistic prospects for the Korean economy in general. This optimistic economic outlook, coupled with tax and other incentives for holding equities, made the secondary and issue markets for equities hyperactive. Stock prices skyrocketed. The total market value of listed stocks almost doubled each year from 1986 through 1988 - and rose from less than 10 percent of GNP in 1985 to 68 percent in 1989. However, a slump set in toward the end of 1989 that continued into 1992.

Government policies for broadening and deepening the equity market have focused on encouraging and at times forcing large business groups (the *chaebol*) to go public. To this end, the major chaebol have been denied additional bank credits above a certain level and have been required to repay bank loans with the funds raised by issuing stocks and bonds, as is discussed in Chapter 5.

From 1984 the government encouraged corporations to go public, but there was only limited activity until 1987, when the regulations on public offering prices were changed to lower the cost of equity financing. From December 1983 companies had nominal legal authority to issue stock at other than par, but as a practical matter this was difficult to do. With the new rules, 44 companies made initial public offerings in 1987, the largest number in one year since 1978.

Rights issues are used in virtually all cases in which a listed company wishes to increase its capital. Nominally, from 1987 these can be at market price rather than at par. In practice, however, the exercise price is at a discount to market. The discounts, controlled by the Securities and Exchange Commission (SEC), have varied between 10 and 50 percent, "depending on market conditions," and were around 30 percent in mid-1992. The rights cannot be traded, and so failing to exercise them means a loss to the shareholder.

Growth of Financial Institution Assets

Since 1970 the growth of assets held by financial institutions has been phenomenal—and much faster than that of other sectors. Between 1970 and 1980, their assets as a percentage of GNP nearly doubled to 103 percent. During the 1980s, the ratio again nearly doubled. The faster growth of the assets of the financial sector as compared to other sectors means one thing: The expansion of financial layering is due to an increase in interfinancial transactions. As a result of this rapid growth, the financial sector has absorbed a growing share of the nation's resources. Its share of nominal GDP in 1985 was less than 4 percent; four years later it was 5½ percent. This is comparable to the level in many OECD countries (OECD 1989, p. 98). The relatively high share also raises an important question as to whether the amount of resources allocated to the financial sector has been excessive. This question is taken up later.

Financial Assets Held by the Nonfinancial Sector

The Government Sector

Financial assets held by the government fell sharply as a proportion of GNP between 1970 and 1980. The ratio in 1980 was less than one-third of what it had been a decade earlier. Since then the ratio has climbed slowly to about 0.25 in 1989. Much of the decline in government financial asset holdings was due to a cutback in lending and equity participation for development assistance. Since 1976 the government has consistently been generating a financial surplus. This surplus, which has grown in size since the late 1980s, has reduced the government's requirements for borrowing from the financial sector and has facilitated the implementation of financial reforms.

The Corporate Sector

Internal funds as a percentage of the corptorate sector's total financing rose steadily in the 1980s, exceeding the 40 percent level in 1988 from about 18 percent in 1980 (see Table 4.A10). Since the mid-1980s the proportion of direct financing also has risen markedly, to about 58 percent of total financing, whereas foreign borrowings have become a minor source of corporate funds. In the early 1990s, as in the 1970s, the corporate sector was obtaining more than 40 percent of its external credit from DMBs and NBFIs. All of these developments have been closely related to the substantial improvements in business profits and in the current account of the balance of payments.

Despite the increased availability of domestic finance and internal funds during the 1980s, there was a drop in the share of total financial assets held by corporations, although this simply returned the sector's share to the 20 percent it had been in 1970. This suggests that, unlike in other advanced countries, Korean firms have not been actively engaged in financial intermediation for their clients, subsidiaries, and subcontractors. Nonetheless, corporate holdings of securities, particularly stock and commercial paper, have increased as proportions of their total investment in financial assets, reflecting the relatively rapid growth of money and capital markets (see Table 4.A11).

The Individual Household Sector

As a result of a rapid accumulation of wealth, the individual sector (which excludes unincorporated businesses but includes noncorporate farms) accounted for more than 45 percent of total national savings in the late 1980s, up from less than 38 percent in the earlier part of the decade. Along with the rapid growth of savings, the individual sector's surplus of savings over investment climbed from around 6 percent of GNP during most of the early 1980s to 9 percent or more in the late 1980s (see Table 4.A3). This sector has recorded the highest rate of financial asset accumulation, reflected in the fact its FIR almost doubled—between 1980 and 1989 (see Table 4.A2).

Table 4.5 shows the division of the sector's savings between real and financial assets. There has been no clear trend, as the share held as financial assets varied over a wide range since 1975—from a high of 90 percent in 1982 to a low of 60 percent in 1979. Much of this volatility was caused by large fluctuations in agricultural inventories.

Perhaps the most significant financial development in the individual sector has been the marked increase in its borrowing from both the direct and the indirect securities markets—the result of the greater availability of housing finance and consumer credit. During the 1970s the share of the individual sector of funds raised by the nonfinancial sector was in the low teens. The percentage more than

Table 4.5. *Accumulation of Assets in the Individual Sector* (billion won)

Year	Total	Real assets	Financial assets Absolute	% of total
1975	1,483	312	1,171	79.0
1976	2,275	638	1,637	72.0
1977	3,428	668	2,760	80.5
1978	5,029	1,587	3,442	68.5
1979	5,608	2,234	3,374	60.2
1980	5,535	1,515	4,020	72.6
1981	8,262	1,217	7,045	85.3
1982	9,598	1,038	8,561	89.2
1983	9,624	2,700	6,924	71.9
1984	12,479	3,714	8,764	70.2
1985	14,436	4,129	10,306	71.4
1986	19,146	4,849	14,297	74.5
1987	25,996	5,891	20,097	77.3
1988	32,972	9,192	23,376	71.2
1989	41,488	10,040	31,448	75.8
1990	48,903	10,269	38,634	79.0

Source: Bank of Korea, *Flow of Funds* 1992, pp. 192–279 (financial assets) and pp. 59 and 62 (ratio of real to total assets) for 1970–91.

doubled between 1980 and 1985—to 28 percent—and it remained at or above that level throughout the rest of the 1980s. (See Table 4.A5.)

As in many advanced economies, increases in household income and wealth have altered savings and financial needs, and this is reflected in the sector's portfolio preferences, which are presented in Table 4.A9. Moving out of portfolios dominated by deposits at DMBs and equities in the 1970s, households have diversified their wealth holdings by adding a variety of new assets such as deposits at NBFIs, beneficiary certificates issued by investment trust companies, life insurance, and pension fund contracts.

In contrast to the rapid growth of money and capital markets, flow of funds data show that securities directly held by the household sector fell appreciably as a percentage of its total assets. Between 1980 and 1984 the average share was over 37 percent, while between 1985 and 1989 it dropped to below 30 percent. Much of the decline was caused by the fall in holdings of stocks. But this decline is a statistical artifice and its economic significance thus should be discounted: In valuing equities held by the household sector, the Bank of Korea uses issue price, which has been much lower than market price, particularly during the stock market boom of 1987–89.

Securities Holdings and Flow

Data are in Tables 4.A7 and 4.A8. Until the mid 1980s, the individual sector absorbed more than half the value of stocks issued by financial institutions and corporations. Absorption fell below 30 percent during the 1986–89 period. In what amounts to a complete turnaround in their portfolio behavior, financial institutions made a substantial investment in equities in 1986–89, purchasing 56 percent of the value of stocks issued during the period. These changes should be viewed with caution because of the use of issue rather than market price in valuing individual sector security holdings and the use of purchase price in valuing holdings by the other sectors.

In 1988–89 household savers bought more than half of total long-term securities issued. However, it should be noted that these were mostly public bonds and corporate bonds with bank payment guarantees. Household holdings of beneficiary certificates issued by investment trust companies (ITCs) in 1989 were three times as large as in 1980. It appears the household sector holds a larger share of its securities through ITCs than in the 1970s. There are indications this is being done to avoid some of the information problems encountered when purchasing directly from the markets—that is, households feel the ITCs have better information than they do.

Because the ITCs offer fixed yields on bond investment trust certificates with a high degree of liquidity, the risks of holding bonds are not shifted to the ultimate lenders (the household savers) but instead are assumed by the intermediating financial institution. This means that despite the rapid growth of money and capital markets, the importance of indirect finance has not decreased as much as the flow-of-funds data indicate. Banks and NBFIs use capital market instruments in their intermediation between saver-surplus and spending-deficit sectors more than before.

FINANCIAL DEEPENING AND DOMESTIC SAVINGS: THEORIES AND EVIDENCE

The 1980s witnessed a dramatic increase in domestic savings, a performance rivaling the doubling of the average propensity to save between 1965 and 1969. The decade began with a saving rate of 23 percent, 6 percentage points below the rate in 1978. Beginning in 1983, the savings to GNP ratio climbed rapidly, reaching an all time high of 38 percent in 1988 (see Table 4.A4).

During the same period, the ratio of M3 to GNP more than doubled, to 1.26, and the FIR moved up to 3.66 in 1989 from less than 3 in 1983. Is there any causal nexus between the increase in domestic savings and financial deepening? To what extent can the increase in both the savings ratio and FIR be attributed to liberalization of financial markets?

Theories

To answer these questions, we must first establish whether financial liberalization can, other things being equal, lead to financial growth and, if it does, the mechanism through which it does so. Starting from a repressive financial regime in a developing economy, deregulation of financial markets would raise the real rates of return on financial assets as the nominal rates of return on these assets are freed to be determined by market forces. Deregulation also generally increases the diversity of financial assets, which means there are more convenient vehicles for accumulating wealth. These developments then generate incentives for holding financial assets in preference to real ones, and hence result in financial deepening.

As for the positive effects of financial growth on savings, there are basically two arguments predicting a causality running from financial deepening to savings increases. The first stresses the saving incentives created by proliferation of financial assets—with high yields and low risks—that are convenient instruments for saving and which can satisfy diverse portfolio preferences of different savers. In other words, a large menu of financial assets and a large network of financial institutions can induce households to save more out of their incomes because it is now more convenient and profitable to save than when financial instruments were limited. Although this view is intuitively appealing, it essentially argues that financial deepening raises, other things being equal, interest rates on financial instruments adjusted for risk and liquidity, and that the higher rates stimulate saving. However, it is well known that the substitution effect and the income effect of an increased interest rate can cancel each other out, so the net effect is ambiguous in theory.

The second argument, advanced by McKinnon (1973), focuses on the complementarity between capital and money that is broadly defined to include time and savings deposits in developing economies. These two assets are claimed to be complementary because savers, who are often investors themselves, must accumulate savings in the form of deposits (the only readily available asset) until the amount required for a lumpy investment project is reached. Therefore, the higher the rate of return on deposits, the more willing savers are to engage in the accumulation process. As Dornbusch and Reynoso (1989) point out, it is difficult to differentiate this view from one that posits the positive effect of a higher interest rate on saving.

As opposed to these two arguments, one can contend that financial liberalization produces negative effects on household savings as it facilitates the financing of consumption through the use of credit. That is, as money and capital markets can be used more flexibly, current income becomes a less binding constraint on current consumption. Instead, permanent income becomes a more important determinant of consumption expenditure. In some cases liberalized financial markets may be associated with declines in household saving rates. An OECD study (1990) shows that the significance of transitory income declined slightly for the United States, Canada, and Japan in the 1980s.

The Korean Evidence

A number of empirical studies using Korean data provide conflicting results regarding the effect of real interest rates on savings. Depending on the choice of sample period and independent variables, the effect can be either positive or negative. Nam (1988) provides evidence showing savings responds to higher real interest rates. According to his estimation, the ratio of household savings to disposable income is explained mostly by the level and growth rate of per capita income during the 1964 – 84 sample period. The savings rate is also positively related to the curb market interest rate and negatively related to the ratio of financial assets to income. Others have estimated similar equations with different real interest rates but have not been able to duplicate Nam's results. On reason for this may be related to the observation that since 1981 the individual sector savings rate and the real interest rate have moved in opposite directions.

In contrast, the correlation between financial deepening (measured as M3/GNP) and the real interest rate appears to be greater than the correlation between savings and the real interest rate when a nominal deposit interest rate is used as the rate-of-return variable (see Nam 1988). However, it is easy to see that an increase in the ratio of M3 to GNP does not imply a corresponding increase in the savings rate because the increase could be brought about by a portfolio shift out of real assets without any change in the savings rate. Other financial asset to GNP ratios can be regarded as proxies for the wealth to GNP ratio. As Nam's finding shows, therefore, the savings rate may fall as the financial asset ratio increases.

Conclusion

In its *World Development Report 1989*, the World Bank highlights Korea's experience as one of the successful cases of financial reform—that is, liberalization—leading to rapid growth of the financial sector in the 1980s (p. 126). But the liberalization has in fact been relatively limited in important respects: Most interest rates continued to be controlled and, in particular, so was the asset management of financial institutions. In addition, the domestic money and capital markets were protected from foreign competition.

How then can we explain the marked simultaneous increase in the FIR, M3 to GNP ratio, and the savings rate in the 1980s? It is clear that the positive real interest rate throughout the period has been conducive to the accumulation of both savings and financial assets. But, I feel that the most powerful economic forces driving up the financial asset to GNP ratio and the savings rate have been the high rate of economic growth—over 10 percent a year on average—and price stability.

The high growth rate—which was not expected and was certainly higher than the target rate—is likely to have increased the transitory component of real income, while stable prices lowered the expected rate of inflation and hence increased real interest rates. Under these circumstances, households may have saved most of their transitory income increases or may simply have not been able to adjust their consumption to their rapidly rising income. In either case, it is likely they also found it attractive to keep their additional wealth in the form of financial assets. This argument is more realistic in view of later macroeconomic developments. The aggregate savings rate fell by 1.8 percentage points in 1989 and is expected to decline further with the deceleration of economic growth.

FINANCIAL DEVELOPMENT AND ALLOCATIVE EFFICIENCY

Financial deepening through financial liberalization may not necessarily contribute to a higher savings rate, but it can raise the proportion of savings channeled to investors through financial intermediaries and money and capital markets. Provided financial intermediaries and markets are more efficient in selecting viable investment projects, greater intermediation and more developed money and capital markets will ensure investment projects with high rates of return are financed and thereby increase the average productivity of investment and the rate of growth of output. By bringing together savers and efficient investors, financial markets in a competitive setting can improve the allocative efficiency of the economy because they allow deficit units to use borrowed funds to invest more than what they save. With scale economies in collecting and processing information and the ability to process risks, financial intermediaries can also alleviate financial market inefficiencies stemming from informational asymmetry between lenders and borrowers.

Compared to an individual saver, financial intermediaries can acquire more and better information about borrowers, and by pooling small savings, they can finance lumpy investment projects. Given these advantages, it is usual to expect financial intermediaries to be better at identifying viable projects than most individual savers are. However, this can be true only if financial intermediaries are operating in a competitive market environment. Thus, causality runs from financial development to economic growth if financial development is accompanied by financial market liberalization.

If instead the government controls the asset management and the lending and borrowing rates of banks and NBFIs, and it intervenes in financial markets, as is the case in most developing economies, financial deepening may not necessarily improve resource allocation. For example, an increase in controlled deposit rates will most likely increase demand for deposits and thereby expand the amount of savings allocated through financial intermediaries. If the allocation of that bank credit is determined not by the market mechanism but by the government to achieve its allocative objectives, there is no assurance that more intermediation will raise the average rate of return to investment.

One can argue that a higher deposit rate requires a higher lending rate in order for banks not to incur losses, and this means that, within the constraints of government priorities and excess demand for credit, on average relatively more efficient investment projects would be selected. To be tenable, this argument may require the assumption there is some interplay between the market and the government's allocation process. The Korean experience does not seem to support this argument, as evidenced by the excessive investment in heavy and chemical industries during the 1970s.

The Productivity Improvement Hypothesis

Since the mid-1960s, and in particular since the early 1980s, one can observe a close correlation of economic growth and financial deepening in the Korean economy. Korea has also followed a path of financial liberalization, although the path has been marked by interruptions and backsliding. Have liberal financial policies in the 1980s—interest rate deregulation and demolition of the walls separating NBFIs from DMBs—strengthened the linkage between economic growth and financial deepening through the improvement of productivity? If they have, can these effects be measured empirically?

I have tried. The results are not worth reporting here, other than to note the proxy for financial deepening (the ratio of corporate bonds and long-term borrowings from financial institutions to total assets) either has a wrong sign or is statistically insignificant.[1]

Allocative Efficiency

What would be the short-run and long-run effects of financial liberalization on the economy? In the short run, financial liberalization reduces the number of concessional interest rates and other subsidies (in the form of availability, collateral requirements, and terms of loans) and as a consequence could reduce dif-

---

1. Specifically, what I did to test the productivity improvement hypothesis is to assume, as Horiuchi andOtaki (1987) do, a Cobb–Douglas production function for the manufacturing sector expressed as

$$\log (y/l) - b \log (K/L) = \log A + (a+b-1) \log L$$

where Y is value added; L, labor; b, the income share of capital; K, capital stock; and A, total factor productivity. It is assumed A is positively related to financial deepening as measured by the ratio F of corporate bonds and long-term borrowings from financial institutions to total assets. Then the following equation is estimated:

$$\log (Y/L) - b \log (K/L) = a_0 + a_1 \log F + a_2 \log L$$

In this estimation I used cross-section–time series data for manufacturing subsectors for 1980 – 88 from BOK's *Financial Statement Analysis*. I also tried this and similar equations for different periods and different data on manufacturing subsectors.

ferences in lending rates of financial intermediaries to different sectors and industries.

Cho (1988) argues financial liberalization leads to similar costs of borrowing for different borrowers except for a risk premium and variable transaction costs. Using data from BOK's *Financial Statement Analysis,* he shows the variance of borrowing costs for the 68 4-digit manufacturing industries declined significantly—from over 43 in 1972 to fewer than 6 in 1984. I have run a similar test for a longer period—1971–88—for the 4-digit and 3-digit (28 industries) classifications using data from the same source and approximating the cost of borrowing as total financial expenses divided by total borrowings. In general the results confirm Cho's findings, but I am not certain this implies an improvement in the allocative efficiency of the economy.

Credit Availability

Even in a liberal financial regime, financial intermediaries differentiate among borrowers in terms of creditworthiness, ration credit among them, and charge different interest rates to different borrowers. If financial intermediaries indeed ration credit according to nonprice factors, the reduction in the differences in borrowing costs is not an adequate measure of the improvement in allocative efficiency associated with financial liberalization. This measure should be complemented by an estimation of the rates of return on investment in different sectors and industries, particularly over the long run. Reliable data for such estimation are not readily available.

As a proxy variable, I used the sectoral ratios of gross value added to capital from BOK's *Financial Statement Analysis* to examine changes in sectoral rates of return to capital in manufacturing industries classified at 2-, 3-, and 4-digit levels. Variances in the rates of return on capital for 3- and 4-digit industries declined in the 1980s. However, one should be cautious about accepting these results at face value because it is not clear how closely the rate of return data approximate the actual marginal rates of return to capital.

Market Integration

Another way of measuring the allocative efficiency of credit is to estimate the degree of integration of segmented financial markets along the path of financial liberalization. As a first approximation, deregulation of interest rates at financial institutions and market segmentation by product and service will, through financial market integration, tend to lower the differences between the interest rates prevailing in unregulated money markets and those in regulated markets. That is, through interest rate decontrol, some of the financial transactions in the unregulated markets will be absorbed by or integrated into the organized financial system. An expansion of the intermediation capacity of the organized financial sector following financial deregulation will be associated with smaller interest rate differentials between the regulated (organized) and the unregulated financial sectors. This financial integration will also stabilize the rate differentials between the two sectors.

I examined these hypotheses using 1971–88 data. The differences between the interest rate in the unregulated money market (i_U) and the bank lending rates

(i_B) and yields on corporate debentures narrowed sharply and are highly correlated with changes in the M3 to GNP ratio and FIR during the sample period
except for 1983. I also used estimates of the return to capital in manufacturing
instead of the bank lending rates. The result is the same: The rate differentials
moved closely with changes in the M3 to GNP ratio and FIR.

To show the stability of the rate differentials between the regulated and unregulated financial sectors, I calculated the standard deviation of the ratio of i_U to
i_B for 1971 to 1989. The differences between the two rates were large and moved
around a great deal between 1973 and 1984. Since then the differences have
become smaller and stable. The result is the same when the ratio of the unregulated market rate to yields on corporate debentures is used instead. Once again
this result does not necessarily support the efficiency improvement hypothesis
of financial liberalization, because the substantial fall in the expected rate of
inflation during the 1980s lowered the level of both rates, and the differentials
between them.

Conclusion

What can be said about the effects of financial liberalization on the allocative
efficiency of the economy from the evidence assembled? Largely because of data
problems and lack of confidence in the estimation results, I am not prepared to
reach any definite conclusions. One can always argue that the financial system
could have been more efficient but, in view of the super performance of the Korean economy, it is difficult to argue financial intermediaries and markets have
been inefficient in resource allocation, irrespective of the progress of financial
liberalization.

LIBERALIZATION AND INTERNATIONALIZATION, 1981–90

Efforts to improve overall economic efficiency through competition and private
initiatives have led to a series of liberalization measures in trade and finance
since the early 1980s. Economic liberalism was also instrumental in implementing the Anti-Monopoly and Fair Trade Act in 1981, and has contributed to
reducing tariffs and eliminating nontariff trade barriers. But despite numerous
and often confusing reform measures, deregulation of the financial sector has
been slow, uneven, and, most of all, limited in scope and degree.

The economic liberalization as set forth in the Fifth Plan (1982–86) did not
include any significant measures for removing exchange and capital controls.
Most of the measures for financial internationalization were initially aimed at
inducing foreign direct and portfolio investment. The Latin American fiasco and
Korea's experience with destabilizing capital inflows during the 1965–70 period
taught Korean policymakers to be extremely cautious about opening domestic
financial industries to foreign competition. However, with the emergence of a
current account surplus in 1986 and its subsequent growth, Korea came under
pressure to open its money and capital markets to foreign investors. This pres-

sure, together with the need for improving the efficiency of the financial sector, made policymakers much more receptive to financial internationalization. But the renewed inflationary pressure and a return to current account deficits in the 1990s have given policymakers an excuse to slow liberalization.

This section discusses some of the structural and macroeconomic changes that have been conducive for financial deregulation. I then survey some of the important reform measures that have been taken in pursuit of financial liberalization and internationalization.

Economic Forces behind Liberalization

Liberal ideology alone would not have been enough to push through deregulation. But Korean monetary authorities have been fortunate in that macroeconomic developments and changes in sectoral financial balances since the early 1980s have created a macroeconomic environment favorable to financial deregulation. Perhaps the most important developments have been the sharp drop in the rate of inflation and the related massive increase in domestic savings, which in turn led to a large accumulation of current account surpluses during 1986 –90. The excess of savings over domestic investment created strong downward pressures on market interest rates, including the curb market. Between 1980 and 1983 yields on government and public bonds fell 15 percentage points, to 13.8 percent, and the curb market rate fell 13 points, as shown in Table 4.6.

Inflation measured by the GNP deflator decelerated to about 5 percent in 1983 from a high of 24 percent in the aftermath of the second oil crisis. Throughout the rest of the 1980s policymakers were working in an environment of price stability and sustained rapid growth. This price stability no doubt contributed to bringing down interest rates and providing incentives for saving, in the form of financial assets. A major constraint blocking interest rate deregulation from the point of view of the monetary authorities had been the concern that deregulation would most likely jack up borrowing costs for business firms. The deceleration of inflation weakened this constraint considerably.

There was also marked improvement in the finances of the central and local governments. Budgetary squeezes and increases in tax revenues cut the size of government deficits and brought about a fiscal surplus from 1986 to 1988. At the same time, the government reduced the size of its lending to and equity participation in strategic industries. As a result, the need for the government sector to borrow from the BOK, DMBs, and capital markets declined substantially. Unlike in the 1960s and 1970s, monetization of public sector deficits shrank in size and did not pose an obstacle to the effective use of indirect instruments of monetary policy for demand management. The government has become a surplus sector in terms of flow of funds, and its surplus as a percentage of GNP has been growing.

An immediate impetus for financial deregulation came from a series of financial crises between 1982 and 1984, precipitated by financial fraud and distress borrowing by Kukje, at the time among the 10 largest *chaebol*, which met the fate of being broken up in 1985. (For further discussion of these crises, see Kim 1990, p. 32.)

These crises were blamed on the rigidity of the financial system, which had

Table 4.6. *Principal Interest Rates*
(percent per annum)

Year	Depositsª	Loansᵇ	Government bondsᶜ	Corporate bonds	Curb market	Increase in GNP deflator
1970	22.8	24.0	n.a.	n.a.	46.7	15.6
1971	20.4	22.0	n.a.	n.a.	46.1	12.5
1971	12.0	15.5	18.9	22.9	34.0	16.7
1973	12.0	15.5	16.7	21.8	39.4	13.6
1974	15.0	15.5	21.0	21.0	40.8	30.5
1975	15.0	15.5	21.1	20.1	40.4	25.2
1976	16.2	18.0	19.8	20.4	41.4	21.3
1977	14.4	16.0	20.8	20.1	34.1	16.6
1978	18.6	19.0	21.6	21.1	43.1	22.8
1979	18.6	19.0	25.2	26.7	42.7	19.6
1980	19.5	20.0	28.8	30.1	37.7	24.0
1981	16.2	17.0	23.6	24.4	35.4	16.9
1982	8.0	10.0	17.3	17.3	29.0	7.1
1983	10.0	10.0	13.8	14.2	24.7	5.0
1984	10.0	10.0–11.5	14.3	14.1	25.4	3.9
1985	10.0	10.0–11.5	13.9	14.2	23.4	4.2
1986	10.0	10.0–11.5	11.6	12.8	23.3	2.8
1987	10.0	10.0–11.5	12.4	12.8	22.2	3.5
1988	10.0	10.0–11.5	13.0	14.5	21.2	5.9
1989	10.0	10.0–12.5	14.4	15.2	18.9	5.2
1990	10.0	10.0–12.5	15.3	16.4	20.4	10.6
1991	10.0	10.0–12.5	16.7	18.8	21.2	10.9
1992	10.0	10.0–12.5	16.6	17.1	—	—

n.a. Not applicable.

— Not available.

Note: These are representative rates. The source provides greater detail, in regard to loans and deposits, see the 1990 edition on pp. 68–74.

a. Time deposits of 1 year or more.

b. General purpose loans up to 1 year with bank funds.

c. Government and public entities; average yield for the year.

Source: Bank of Korea, *Monthly Bulletin;* Ministry of Finance, *Public Finance and Financial Statistics;* and Korea Stock Exchange, *Stock.* The Jan. 1993 *Bulletin* has interest rates on deposits, loans, and commercial paper for 1975–92 on p. 9. GNP deflator is on pp. 107–8 of *Financial Statistics,* Aug. 1992, Government bond yields for 1987–92 are in *Stock,* Jan. 1993, p. 72.

become a hotbed of corruption and had spawned a large informal money market. The scandals generated a public outcry for reform in the direction of creating a liberal financial system. The monetary authorities responded to this by, among other things, lowering barriers of entry to the NBFI sector, introducing legislation that would end assumed-name accounts at financial institutions and anonymous transactions in money and capital market instruments. The authorities, however, also reduced the lending and deposit rates at DMBs, thereby sending out confusing signals as to their true intention for financial deregulation.

The Reforms

During the 1980 – 89 period, financial liberalization was directed at

1. Relaxing interest rate control gradually over time, including deposit and lending rates at DMBs.
2. Removing some barriers to entry into financial industries.
3. Giving financial institutions—both banks and nonbanks—more autonomy in their day-to-day operations and asset management—including reducing government control over management.
4. Moving toward universal banking and reduced specialization by institution in the nonbanking financial sector.
5. Relaxing restrictions on exchange rates and foreign exchange transactions.
6. Freeing capital movements.

Interest Rate Decontrol

In June 1981 a commercial paper market not subject to government control was created where investment, finance and merchant banking corporations were to serve as brokers and dealers. It was also expected that the CD market would function as a bridge between the curb market and the organized financial system and thus provide a reference point for setting official rates. The move was widely heralded as a first step toward a complete floating of interest rates.

In line with this direction of deregulation, yields on new corporate debentures were allowed to fluctuate 100 basis points above and below the banks' reference rates and differentials between interest rates on general loans and policy and directed loans were eliminated in June 1982. The importance of this measure should be discounted because in the same year the whole spectrum of bank interest rates was adjusted downward.

Early in 1984 DMBs established a band of lending rates within which they could charge different lending rates to different borrowers on the basis of creditworthiness. This has been followed by a series of measures decontrolling interest rates in the organized financial sector. The measures include lifting the upper limit on call rates in 1984, decontrolling yields on convertible bonds and debentures with bank payment guarantees in 1985, plus in 1986 freeing interest rates on CDs, on newly issued debentures with bank payment guarantees, and on financial debentures issued by deposit money banks. This series of liberalizations culminated in decontrol of bank lending rates in 1988. Unfortunately, however, the decontrol did not last very long and did not strengthen the price mechanism in financial markets as much as expected, as discussed later.

New Entrants and Privatization

In line with these reform objectives, the government divested its equity in one of the five nationwide commercial banks in June 1981. In the following two years three more banks were privatized. In addition, the government chartered two

joint-venture commercial banks with Korean and foreign partners in order to promote competition in the banking industry and to establish linkages with international financial markets. In 1986, the opening of branch offices of DMBs and
NBFIs was deregulated in order to give individual institutions more discretion in
setting up branch networks.

However, between early 1983 and 1987 no more new commercial bank charters were issued. Following the political reforms of 1987, the pace of this aspect
of liberalization has gathered momentum, and 3 new commercial banks were
established in 1989. In addition, 2 short-term finance companies and Korea
Exchange Bank (formerly a special bank) became commercial banks in 1989–91.

In July 1982 the government considerably relaxed requirements for establishing nonbank financial intermediaries—in particular, investment and finance
companies and mutual savings and finance companies. Within a year 12 new
short-term credit companies and 57 mutual savings and finance companies were
chartered. The period 1987–89 also saw a spate of new NBFIs as 5 new investment and finance companies were chartered and 12 new life insurance companies opened their doors.

MOF had announced plans to remove entry restrictions entirely for the leasing
business. During 1989–90 licenses were issued to many firms to operate outside
of Seoul, as part of developing regional finance. However, since then no new
licenses have been issued, and MOF does not appear likely to do so again soon.

Increased Management Autonomy

Denationalization of the nationwide commercial banks in 1982 was proceeded and
followed by abolishment and simplification of various government directives and
instructions regulating personnel management, budgetary, and other operational
matters of commercial banks. The General Banking Act also was amended to limit
ownership by any single shareholder of a commercial bank to 8 percent of total
shares, and guarantees and acceptances for an individual borrower to a maximum
of 50 percent of a bank's net worth. These limitations were intended to prevent
managerial control by a few individuals and large business groups.

At the end of November 1979, average required reserves stood at 23 percent
of deposits at DMBs. The ratio was gradually reduced to 3.5 percent a year later
before being raised to 5.5 percent. The substantial reduction was aimed at giving more freedom to the banks in their management of lendable resources and
easing the strain on bank profits. In January 1982 the monetary authorities
announced their plan for abolishing direct control (through credit ceilings and
quotas) over bank lending. Instead, there would be indirect control through
reserve requirements. This plan signaled the government's intention to refrain
from interfering with bank credit allocation, but as discussed later, this has never
been carried out to any meaningful degree.

Universal Banking

The authorities continued to move toward universal banking by broadening and
diversifying the financial services supplied by different financial institutions.
DMBs are now allowed to issue CDs as well as sell public debentures under repurchase agreements and commercial bills they discount. They offer trust services,
issue credit cards, and own NBFIs. They underwrite and own for their own

accounts government and corporate bonds, and many of them even have securities companies as subsidiaries. According to the Banking Law, DMBs can underwrite equity issues as well, but so far MOF has not allowed them to do so.

Reducing the segmentation of financial markets by activity took place mostly during the 1981–84 period. In 1980, one of the specialized banks offered credit card services to the general public for the first time; other banks followed in 1982. Also in 1982 DMBs were authorized to introduce money market instruments such as repurchase agreements (RPs) and marketable commercial bills, and local banks began trust businesses.

In 1984 cash management accounts (CMAs) were introduced to expand the scope of activities of investment and finance companies and, for a similar purpose, CDs were reactivated for DMBs. In the same year, securities firms began brokering and dealing in commercial paper and issuing payment guarantees for corporate debentures. These measures have been followed by the creation of a number of new deposit types at DMBs, broadening the kinds of institutions handling CMAs, and adding money trusts to the services offered by DMBs.

Foreign Exchange Control

The emergence of a surplus on the current account in 1986 and its increase until 1990 gave the monetary authorities confidence in deregulating a large array of foreign exchange transactions. So far, foreign exchange deregulation has been directed at abolishing, simplifying, and relaxing regulations on invisible trade transactions involving payments for travel and moving expenses, consulting services, and fees related to export and import brokerage. Businesses are also allowed to take out an unlimited amount in foreign currencies for the operational expenses of their foreign branches.

The Korean government acceded to the obligations of an IMF Article 8 country in November 1988, and plans to remove the other regulations on invisible transactions—aiming at the level of liberalization accepted among OECD member countries by 1992. Contracts for exports and imports can be denominated in won, although the actual receipts and payments must use a convertible foreign currency approved by MOF.

A forward exchange market was created in 1980. Since then, interest and currency swaps and financial futures have been introduced. In view of the deterioration of the current account in 1990, however, it is not clear whether the deregulation of foreign exchange will be carried out as planned, because the government plan is premised on the current account remaining strong.

Capital Account Liberalization

In promoting liberalization of capital account transactions, the monetary authorities sought first to deregulate foreign direct investment (FDI) into Korea and Korean direct investment into foreign countries. In 1984, the introduction of a negative system for FDI greatly increased opportunities for direct investment by foreigners. The list of nonpermissible businesses has been considerably shortened. At the end of 1989 all but 10 of 522 categories of manufacturing activity were open to foreign direct investment.

The plan for capital market liberalization announced by the government in 1981 envisaged four phases of gradual deregulation. During the first stage, from

1981 to 1984, the authorities promoted indirect investment in Korean securities by foreigners. For this purpose, two open-end international trusts were established in 1981 to serve European customers. Encouraged by the their popularity, each was increased in size about two years later, and three more trusts were sold to foreigners in 1985.

A more significant development from the point of view of capital market liberalization was the launching of the closed-end Korea Fund in New York in March 1984. Three years later as part of the second phase of liberalization (1985–87) Korea Fund raised additional money and a similar fund—the Korea Euro Fund—was created to serve the European market. After KEF's second tranche in July 1988, a total of $300 million of foreign funds was allowed into the Korean stock market, although all of it is managed at least in part by Koreans.

Since 1985 Korean firms have been allowed to issue convertible bonds (CBs) and bonds with warrants (BWs) in international financial markets. By September 1988 5 firms had issued CBs totaling $140 million, and 13 firms had issued $5.7 billion through the end of 1990.

During the third phase of deregulation, from 1987 to 1990, Korea's large securities companies were allowed to participate in syndicates underwriting foreign securities. Brokerage firms, investment trust companies, and insurance companies can invest up to $30 million in foreign securities.

The most significant measures for opening capital markets were implemented during 1991–92. In 1991 foreigners were allowed to purchase listed stocks, but only to the extent that shares had been converted from overseas CBs. Proceeds from selling shares converted from CBs also could be used to buy listed stocks. Since 1992 foreigners have been allowed to purchase Korean securities—but their holdings are subject to a predetermined ceiling of 10 percent and some issues remain off limits. The procedures are also quite cumbersome, to the point of having evoked complaints from foreign investors, which elicited a limited simplification.

Foreign securities companies can open representative offices and own up to 10 percent of the paid-in capital of Korean securities companies. In 1991 they were able to open branches. Since 1988 the markets for insurance and investment trusts also have been liberalized and opened to foreign firms.

Opening branches and representative offices of foreign commercial banks has been made easier. These branch offices have been allowed to offer a broader range of general banking services and were given national treatment in 1986. In June 1992 there were 51 foreign bank branch offices and representative offices, all in Seoul and Pusan. This was down from 75 at the end of 1989, reflecting the mergers and the worldwide retreat of marginal players.

Conclusion

These reform measures were significant and refreshing developments in a country long suffering from financial repression. Most of all, they reflected the government's determination to develop a freer financial system—one where the price mechanism reigns—and to open the financial industry to foreign competition.

Nevertheless, it should be pointed out that the various reform measures did not significantly alter the modus operandi of financial control. For example, although DMBs in theory can charge whatever interest rates they consider appropriate, in reality they have been colluding among themselves and are amenable to the wishes of the monetary authorities. As long as the monetary authorities feel that the rates are reasonable, they will maintain an attitude of benign neglect. If they feel otherwise, they certainly have the leverage to change the rates. For these reasons and domestic demand management, lending rates at DMBs remained virtually unchanged throughout 1989 and 1990, making one wonder about the seriousness of the government's intentions regarding interest rate deregulation. The monetary authorities presumably have less influence on the lending of NBFIs, but they have also directly or indirectly intervened to keep NBFI lending and borrowing rates in line with the rates at the DMBs.

Korean planners have taken a conservative step by step approach to liberalizing of the capital account of the balance of payments, with deregulation initially planned to be implemented over 15 years. Relatively free capital movements and complete removal of exchange rate controls will not be realized until after 1992.

CONSTRAINTS ON LIBERALIZATION

In the 1980s perhaps few other developing countries managed more durable and far reaching policy changes to promote economic liberalization than Korea. However, a number of studies have shown the role of the government in Korea has been and still is much more active than just correcting market failures and imperfections (for example, Kuznets 1988). In particular, the discussion in preceding sections indicates financial liberalization has been much more difficult than opening up the trade regime. This section and the next identify some of the structural and institutional characteristics that may have interfered with and constrained financial deregulation.

Conflicts with Monetary Policy

It was widely expected, and the monetary authorities made it clear, that quantitative restrictions on DMB lending would be eased out in favor of indirect credit control, with the overall deregulation of interest rates late in 1988. But, writing in mid-1992, one finds little change in the modus operandi of monetary policy at the MOF and BOK.

If there is any change, it is at most the degree of direct control. As before, DMBs are subject to direct quantitative ceilings on lending levels, and their lending rates have been kept artificially low and stable. Monetary authorities have attempted to lower market yields on short-term money market instruments through "moral suasion" and administrative guidance, thereby giving the impression of retreating from the policy of financial liberalization. A senior policymaker went so far as to say in late 1990 that financial deregulation could be put on hold if it interferes with the short-run management of the economy, and many in government feel the same way.

The supply of M2, which has been the intermediate target of monetary policy, is no more than an artificial grouping of some of the deposit liabilities of the DMBs. The rationale for sticking to this M2 as the quantitative target has been questioned, and debates for identifying a more appropriate target have been lively. Definitional problems aside, it has become much more difficult to control the growth of M2 because of the desegmentation of the financial market, which has led to a proliferation of new financial products—issued by both the DMBs and NBFIs—that are almost perfect substitutes for bank deposit liabilities.

As in other advanced economies, financial deregulation in Korea has considerably weakened the effectiveness of some indirect monetary policy instruments, because it has increased the credit creating capacity of NBFIs, the volatility of fund shifts, and created new markets that the monetary authorities cannot reach easily. In view of the uncertain effects of indirect control measures on the growth of M2, imposition of quantitative credit ceilings on DMBs was therefore claimed to be necessary.

Early in 1989 the Korean economy showed several symptoms of a classical stagflation—slow growth and a build up of inflationary pressures. To manage a reasonable rate of growth and price stability, the monetary authorities assigned to themselves the impossible task of controlling both M2 and market interest rates. M2 grew over the target level and was excessive, threatening price stability. Any further credit squeeze through, for instance, sale of monetary stabilization bonds would drive up the interest rates. Such an increase could discourage further business investment and foil the growth target. To achieve both targets, the monetary authorities had to force NBFIs to buy monetary stabilization bonds at a predetermined interest rate and to lower credit ceilings at DMBs.

Policy-Directed Loans

Although the monetary authorities have repeatedly expressed their intention of phasing out extension of subsidized policy-directed loans, they have not actually gotten very far in doing so. This has been another constraint compelling use of quantitative credit rationing. (Many of these loans were part of the heavy and chemical industries' drive and are nonperforming.) Policy-directed loans as a percentage of total DMB loans had fallen to less than 34 percent in 1983 from more than 42 percent throughout the 1970s. But since then the share, whether measured in terms of DMB total loans or assets, has not changed very much (see Tables 4.7 and 4.8).

The amount and terms of these loans are often determined independently of short-run monetary policy. They are always long-term and renewable, making DMB loan portfolios much more rigid than otherwise. Commercial banks have always placed expanding or at least maintaining their credit market share ahead of profits as their management goal. Thus, they resist cutting off or scaling down the supply of credit to their clients. Nothing short of direct control, many argue, can make DMBs respond to changes in monetary policy—all the more so since the late 1980s because of intensified competition as a result of increased interpenetration of markets by different types of financial institutions.

Table 4.7. *Loans and Discounts of DMBs by Fund Source*
(percent)

Source	1965–69	1970–74	1975–79	1980–84	1985–89	1990–91
Banking funds	85.5	92.1	92.1	92.3	92.7	93.7
Government	14.5	7.8	4.4	4.4	4.9	5.1
National investment fund	n.a.	n.a.	3.5	3.2	2.4	1.2
Directed loans (as % of total)[a]	35.2	38.6	40.6	39.8	34.6	30.6
Banking funds (as % of total)						
Loans[b]	56.3	49.2	49.6	47.4	53.2	47.4
Bills discounted	1.7	5.5	4.4	8.1	8.4	11.4
Overdrafts	6.7	6.7	5.4	4.6	3.8	4.7
Foreign trade	6.8	10.8	12.6	12.0	5.7	2.6
Housing	3.1	3.4	5.1	6.8	7.9	10.7
Other[c]	12.0	16.5	15.2	13.5	13.8	11.0

n.a. Not applicable.

a. Directed loans are the government and national investment fund categories plus foreign trade, housing, and other from banking funds.

b. Includes loans with installment savings and with workman's property formation savings; loans to small and medium industries made by the Small and Medium Industry Bank and the Citizens National Bank; and loans for low-income households made by the Citizens National Bank (from 1985).

c. Includes loans for equipment used by export industries and for energy conservation, agriculture, fishery, and livestock; loans with the Small and Medium Industry Promotion Fund, loans to the Korea Federation of Small Businesses; advances to factoring clients; and others.

Source: Bank of Korea, *Economic Statistics Yearbook.* The 1992 edition covers 1984–91 on pp. 60–61, Table 32.

Excessive Volatility

It should also be pointed out that the increasing volatility of financial markets has raised questions about the wisdom of leaving determination of financial market prices entirely to supply and demand. As several studies have shown (for example, Shiller 1981, 1990, Shleifer and Summers 1990, Stiglitz 1990), the variability of interest rates and stock prices can be excessive, given the flow of underlying information that markets are deemed to consider relevant. If asset prices do not reflect fundamentals, then one could make a persuasive case that market determination of financial asset prices does not necessarily increase the allocative efficiency of the economy. Although this does not mean bureaucrats can replace the price mechanism, nevertheless asset price volatility that has little to do with changes in the real sector of the economy has made monetary authorities less receptive to the idea of completely deregulating interest rates.

Since the mid-1980s, stock prices in Korea and elsewhere have bounced around in a wide range, responding to all sorts of political and economic developments at home and abroad. It is difficult to establish whether the deregulation of financial markets has contributed to the volatility of stock prices. However, to the extent it has become easier to purchase stocks and other financial assets with credit from commercial banks and other financial institutions, it would be fair to assume that stock market volatility has spilled over into other markets much more than was the case in the absence of asset price controls.

Table 4.8. Directed Loans by DMBs
(billion won and percent)

Source	1965–69	1970–74	1975–79	1980–84	1985–89	1990–91
Banking funds	51.0	449	1,756	6,356	11,310	19,829
Government	29.0	96	233	905	2,245	4,183
National investment fund	n.a.	n.a.	204	652	1,043	1,003
Foreign currency	30.5	136	804	2,961	4,942	9,317
Total directed	110.5	681	2,998	10,874	19,540	34,332
as % total assets	15.0	17.5	17.6	17.7	17.2	17.0
Acceptances[a]	223.7	1,215	5,767	19,254	20,615	29,650
Acceptances as % total assets	30.3	31.1	33.8	31.3	18.2	14.6
All directed as % total assets[b]	45.3	48.6	51.4	48.9	35.4	31.6
Total assets	737.7	3,905	17,081	61,563	113,472	202,470

n.a. Not applicable.

a. Acceptances and guarantees.

b. Loans, acceptances, and guarantees.

Source: Bank of Korea, *Economic Statistics Yearbook.* The 1992 edition covers 1984–91 on p. 31, Table 14, and pp. 60–61, Table 32.

Depositor Protection

Korea does not have an institutionalized system to protect depositors at DMBs. NBFI also have not developed any safeguards for their depositors even though they rely heavily on depository liabilities. Nonetheless, few depositors are worried about the possibility of failure and consequent loss because they have great faith in the notion that the monetary authorities are responsible for rescuing any bank that gets into trouble. And the record buttresses this belief.

To develop a safe and sound banking system, the authors of Korea's banking and other laws governing activities of DMBs and NBFIs instituted minimum capital requirements, chartering restrictions, and other regulations covering asset management. However, creation of a deposit insurance system has never been seriously debated in Korea, even when the nationwide commercial banks were privatized out in 1982–83. During the 1960s and 1970s, the idea of deposit insurance was moot—after all, the monetary authorities controlled every aspect of bank management.

Although the need for a deposit insurance system in a liberal financial environment was recognized, no one—depositors, banks, or government—was prepared to assume any part of the costs of creating and supporting such a system. Cynics would argue there was no need for an insurance system because the monetary authorities could not let any bank go under. According to this reasoning, it is cheaper to deal with a troubled bank individually before it becomes insolvent than to create an expensive insurance system.

The moral hazard problems of the U.S. FDIC and FSLIC in the United States are well known among the Korean public and obviously discouraged further debate on a governmental deposit insurance system. (Reading Adams' *The Big Fix* certainly affected my thinking on the matter.)

In refusing to pay the costs of institutionalizing a depositor protection system, the public has implicitly shifted responsibility for the safety of the financial system entirely to the monetary authorities and, in so doing, has given them much more regulatory power than otherwise would probably be the case. Moral hazard problems can be as serious in a government-controlled financial system as in a less regulated system with deposit insurance. Indeed, it appears that the possibility of moral hazard has been used to justify tighter control of financial institutions and markets in Korea.

Where does the prudential regulation needed for bank safety end and excessive regulation begin? This question has been raised in many countries, but drawing a line has been difficult. This ambiguity has given Korea's monetary authorities yet another excuse for vacillating between financial deregulation and reregulation.

Transactions under Assumed Names

In Korea until August 1993 it was legal to own deposit accounts and securities under assumed names. Before then owners of accounts under false names had taxes withheld at the source at higher rates than did real-name accounts, but the wealthy still paid less income tax than if the income was included in their overall taxable income. (To avoid the higher taxes, one could "borrow" a real name.) Furthermore, it is well known that lenders and dealers in the unregulated money market, speculators in real estate, and those engaged in dubious activities were the majority of anonymous holders of financial assets. From the point of view of the monetary authorities, there was no way of stopping money laundering or financial transactions related to underground and often criminal activities.

Because of anonymous transactions the monetary authorities felt they were deprived of essential information needed for safeguarding financial institutions and conducting monetary policy. Specifically, they claimed it was difficult to monitor the flow of funds between markets, institutions, and businesses. This lack of information, according to some, had forced the authorities to rely on other, often direct, means of regulation.

In 1972 in the aftermath of a financial scandal, the government introduced legislation making it compulsory to use real names for every financial transaction. These efforts ran into formidable opposition and the idea was scuttled. The government tried again in 1989, and once again the attempt was defeated by vested interests that included many politicians. Finally in a move that caught almost everyone by surprise, and that has disrupted financial markets, in August 1993 newly elected President Kim Young Sam decreed the use of real names.

STRUCTURAL CONSTRAINTS

There is an interlocking of financial liberalization on the one hand and a liberalization of trade and other factor markets on the other such that one regime cannot easily be liberalized independently of other, repressed sectors. For example, a restrictive trade regime is likely to justify and act to perpetuate a repressive financial system. The pace of financial liberalization is therefore contingent on liberalization in other sectors.

Financial deregulation, other things equal, leads to relatively prompt adjustments in financial markets. With trade restrictions, however, commodity markets send out wrong relative price signals and this induces investment in the wrong industries as long as the current account remains regulated. In fact, a liberalized domestic financial market can lead to the wrong investment decisions in such cases, because firms with good prospects artificially brought about by trade restrictions can borrow more easily than they could in an unrestricted environment (Park 1987).

Korea's trade sector became much more open during the 1980s with reductions of tariffs and removal of nontariff barriers, but it is far from an open regime. The protection of import-competing industries and export subsidies reflects an allocation of resources that government planners regard desirable on efficiency, equity, and other grounds. Unless the planners are assured a financial liberalization program will not interfere with achieving their allocative objectives, they will resist liberalization because they recognize if they do not, they will be following conflicting policies.

Agriculture is the most heavily protected industry in Korea—for instance, the price of rice in Korea is substantially more expensive than on international markets. At some price the authorities may find it more expedient and effective to support growers by intervening in financial and capital markets rather than raising the price further. Farmers are already favored borrowers, something they are hardly likely to be in a financially liberalized regime. But if farmers do not receive "adequate" credit (by political criteria), one can argue that the rate of protection can be raised to the point where financial resources will be channeled to them. In theory such a scheme is possible, but in practice it is unrealistic. The tradeoffs are obviously quite messy when the criteria include issues other than pure economic rationality.

The government controls finance in order to push the allocation of resources in a desired direction. Insofar as the government is prepared to intervene in the allocation of resources, the financial system is likely to be repressed—with government controls over interest rates and asset management of financial intermediaries to supplement or substitute in part for its intervention in commodity market. (Restrictions on commodity markets may not be efficient and productive methods of intervention. Depending on the sources of distortions, it might be more effective to intervene directly in the financial and capital markets to bring about a desired allocation of resources.)

Capital Movements

Restrictions on capital movements also constrain domestic financial deregulation. For a long time before the current account began to register a surplus in 1986, the Korean government played the role of a monopolistic intermediary for international financing. Nearly all foreign loans were guaranteed by the government directly or by financial institutions owned or controlled by the government. The guarantees meant the government borrowed foreign resources wholesale from international financial markets and then retailed them domestically. This intermediation role was necessitated by the private sector's inability to obtain a sufficiently high international credit rating and was in part chosen to reduce the cost of foreign borrowing.

The Chilean experience in the 1970s demonstrates that in regard to foreign borrowings, it is immaterial whether or not they are guaranteed by the state (see Diaz-Alejandro 1985, Edwards 1984). If a private borrower defaults, the state is in most cases liable for paying of the private foreign debt. The role of the government as the guarantor of foreign loans can then provide a practical rationale for its intervention in the domestic financial market.

In theory, there is no reason why the government cannot auction off proceeds of its foreign borrowings to the highest bidders or allow domestic financial institutions to allocate them at their own discretion. However, even when the loan market operates in a financing regime without any market impediments, financial institutions with incomplete information ration credit among their customers in order to minimize the riskiness of their loan portfolios (Stiglitz and Weiss 1981). So, the government will easily succumb to the temptation of having its hand in and will justify intervening in the allocation. After all, it is liable for the repaying of the loans.

Once the government starts intervening in the allocation of foreign loans, it will more or less automatically be drawn into the allocation of domestic currency loans as well, for two reasons. The first is that the government may find it necessary to help recipients of foreign loans secure domestic credit for the operation of the foreign-financed projects. Foreign loans have been used mostly to finance importation of foreign capital and intermediate goods. Foreign loan recipients therefore need domestic currency loans to finance, for example, working capital.

The second reason is that from the viewpoint of domestic borrowers, foreign loans can be and in fact are substitutes for domestic bank credit. Denied allocation of foreign loans by the government, a domestic borrower can attempt to obtain a domestic currency loan from a domestic bank and then convert it into foreign exchange to import equipment or intermediate inputs. If importation of particular equipment is an automatically approved item, the domestic borrower has no reason to prefer foreign loans over domestic loans insofar as there is no cost differential between them. This means the government may have to intervene in the allocation of domestic credit if it chooses to ration foreign credit. Otherwise, rationing foreign loans may not be effective.

If the real cost of borrowing abroad (adjusted for exchange rate depreciation) is lower than the cost from domestic sources, this rate differential provides the government with opportunities to subsidize industries regarded as strategic to economic development. In this regard, direct subsidization of strategic industries using the revenues the government could obtain from charging a domestic market rate of interest on its foreign currency lending may be more efficient than direct credit allocation. This point is generally recognized by the authorities. Nevertheless, when the state assumes the role of a financial intermediary in international financing, it often justifies its intervention on the grounds it must be current on its foreign debt servicing.

Industrial Restructuring and Nonperforming Loans

Perhaps the most important constraint on financial liberalization in the 1980s was the industrial restructuring necessitated by the unsuccessful program in the 1970s to develop heavy and chemical (HC) industries, which led to an accumulation of nonperforming loans at DMBs. Rationalization of these industries, first undertaken toward the end of the 1970s, has required continued government intervention in finance and no doubt interfered with financial liberalization.

Initially the government sought a market solution to restructuring the HC industries, with the expectation that the market would weed out inefficient firms and reallocate resources to sectors with higher rates of return to capital. As it turned out, however, the market mechanism was hardly adequate or capable of determining who was going to bear the adjustment costs, investment losses, and unemployment burden that restructuring was bound to create.

Much of the investment in HC industries was undertaken by chaebol, which dominate the manufacturing sector. Thus, a market solution as conceived by policymakers could not work because the chaebol, if left unchecked, could easily control financial as well as product markets. A substantial part of the investment in the 1970s that turned into idle capacity was carried out under the auspices of the government, and as such the government could not disavow at least some responsibility. The government has therefore had to play an important role and predictably has used finance as a means of facilitating industrial restructuring. There has been scrapping of unprofitable plants, mergers of duplicated investment projects, and postponements of other planned investments. (Studies of Korean industrial policy include Kim 1991 and Leipziger 1987.)

Restructuring HC industries was complicated by several other developments in the 1980s. The shipping industry, which invested heavily toward the latter part of the 1970s in purchasing old vessels at the height of the market as part of a national fleet-building program, suffered from the slow growth of the world trade volume. The decline in construction activities in the Middle East caused by softening oil prices hit the Korean construction firms that had moved aggressively into that market. To make matters worse, some light manufacturing industries, such as textiles and footwear, which traditionally have accounted for the bulk of Korea's exports increasingly priced themselves out of foreign markets and so had to be restructured.

Although there was a clear need for an overall industrial restructuring, the government was indecisive and slow in taking necessary measures until the mid-1980s, out of fear of the social and political problems—in particular unemployment—that restructuring might cause. Instead of undertaking a course of adjustment that might have been effective but was definitely bound to be painful, the government instead bailed out an increasing number of troubled firms by forcing the banks to assume their debts. The result was a marked increase in nonperforming loans held by the banks.

Once it became evident the government was likely to provide relief financing to bail out firms that would otherwise meet a sure bankruptcy, firms began to borrow heavily from many sources at any interest rate simply to remain in business. This increase in distress financing was partly responsible for high real interest rates in the secondary markets, which had been the major supply source of distress financing. The higher real interest rates in turn swelled the borrowing requirements of the troubled firms and subsequently increased nonperforming loans at the banks as some of these firms went bankrupt.

In pursuing a gradual financial liberalization, the authorities have taken a periphery-first approach in which interest rates in the secondary markets and rates at NBFIs, together with the asset management of these institutions, were deregulated first. As a result, NBFIs have enjoyed a competitive edge over DMBs and therefore have been able to increase their market share. Deregulation also allowed many inefficient high-cost firms to borrow heavily from NBFIs.

Because of these developments, commercial banks, which traditionally have catered to the credit needs of large industrial borrowers, saw a decline in their market shares at the same time they were experiencing an increase in their nonperforming assets and otherwise facing pressure on profits. To many observers the banks had become unable to compete without government support. Under these circumstances, it was believed a financial liberalization program could aggravate the distress-financing problem, as it was likely to increase interest rates. A marked increase in real interest rates associated with stable prices, it was feared, could result in a snowballing of the troubled firms' debt.

A disturbing question is why NBFIs, and investment and finance firms in particular, were willing to accommodate the needs of distressed borrowers. One answer is that they may have been convinced the government would continue to support troubled firms or, in any event, could not allow the bankruptcy of any financial institution, be it a bank or a small short-term credit company. It appears the moral hazard problem has posed a serious obstacle to domestic financial deregulation.

Industrial Organization

In the early 1960s when an export-led development strategy was formulated and promoted, Korea had to cope with a formidable array of structural and institutional problems. A low savings rate with a chronic current account deficit required a continuous inflow of foreign loans, which were not available without government guarantees. No matter what incentive system was instituted, it was believed the repressed financial system could not direct resources to export-oriented industries. There was no pool of entrepreneurs, managers, and traders who could initiate and lead development of export-oriented industries. An industrialist class that had been nurtured during the earlier import substitution period had little knowledge of foreign markets and experience in international marketing and hence was unprepared to undertake the higher risks of selling abroad.

In many cases, efficiency of export industries required adoption of increasing-returns technologies. This constraint conflicted with Korea's limited availability of domestic and foreign resources and forced policymakers to support a small number of large producers—in some cases one or two—in each of the industries promoted for exports. There is no market mechanism for concentrating resources in this way, so perhaps it was natural for the government to assume the task. The banking system was used to channel domestic and foreign savings to these large firms and, as a de facto partner, the government was drawn to participate in their business decisions. During the 1960s these firms become successful exporters and, with the growth of the economy, also developed into industrial groups—the chaebol that dominate the manufacturing sector.

The expansion and increase in the number of chaebol created a monopolistic or oligopolistic market structure in many industries. By 1977, for instance, the 30 largest groups accounted for 25 percent of employment and 34 percent of shipments in manufacturing. In 1982 the level was 41 percent of shipments; in 1987, 37 percent (Lee and Lee 1990). Moreover, despite continuing efforts to bring about a more balanced distribution of economic power, these large groups have been able to maintain their relative share of value added. *Dong-A Ilbo*, a daily newspaper, estimated these groups accounted for nearly half of manufacturing value added and a sixth of GNP in 1983 (August 22, 1984). Subsequent years have been about these levels. By international standards, these groups are small, but they are big fish in the Korean pond.

Concentration of economic power in the hands of a few conglomerates was deemed necessary for efficiency, but was recognized as highly undesirable for distributive equity. This dilemma created pressure for—and justified—government control of the industrial groups (Park 1990). With a protected trade regime and a closed financial system, the pricing and supply behavior of these groups simply had to be regulated. Moreover, the concentration of economic power by the chaebol has been a major constraint on financial liberalization.

Given this high degree of concentration, it is not at all surprising that these groups are also the major beneficiaries of domestic credit supplied by both banks and NBFIs, as discussed in Chapter 5. In the absence of any legal restrictions, the chaebol will not hesitate to acquire any financial institution they can to strengthen their fund-mobilizing capability.

When the denationalization of four nationwide commercial banks was first proposed, one of the most serious concerns was instituting safeguards to prevent chaebol from dominating the commercial banks and using them as private means of mobilizing funds. Ownership by any single shareholder was limited to 8 percent of total outstanding shares. However, it was not clear how effective this limitation would be in promoting diverse stock ownership. Through cross ownership and taking advantage of loopholes, industrial groups could control the management of these banks and also other financial intermediaries. Many people argue that short of direct government intervention, there are no adequate measures to prevent the chaebol from dominating the banking industry.

Local banks and NBFIs are not subject to the ownership limitation. As a result, most insurance companies, large investment and finance companies, and securities firms are owned or controlled by chaebol.

Insofar as the possibility of complete dominance of finance by the chaebol remains, bank denationalization and financial liberalization will not necessarily improve resource allocation because it will create an oligopolistic market structure. This widespread concern has not stopped, but certainly has not helped, the government's liberalization efforts.

The general public and political leadership are determined to prevent the concentration of resources in private hands, because such a concentration, it is believed, would worsen distributive equity and, in the end, destabilize the society. The general public also demands the government make sure the giants behave so that a balance between small and medium firms and industrial groups is maintained. Credit allocation has been the most effective means of keeping these conglomerates in line.

Broadly based ownership of DMBs may be desirable from the point of view of social equity, but it creates the problem of ensuring efficient and stable management. Chaebol-owned insurance companies are the largest equity holders in most denationalized DMBs, and the public would not allow the chaebol to choose the managers. Although reluctant, the general public seems prepared to give the government the power to make high level appointments at DMBs, even if that means compromising economic efficiency.

THE ROLE OF FINANCE: THE KOREAN EXPERIENCE

This chapter has analyzed the growth and structural change of Korea's financial industries during the 1970s and 1980s with a focus on identifying a causal nexus between finance and economic growth and development. Several salient features of financial development in Korea have been identified.

One feature is the predominance of indirect finance or intermediated credit markets. Although the business sector has come to rely more on direct finance and capital markets have grown in size and importance, direct holdings of stocks and bonds by household savers as a proportion of their total financial assets have not increased very much. Instead, investment trust companies and other NBFIs serve as intermediaries between issuers and holders of stocks and bonds, and in so doing, the risk of holding these assets is only partially shifted to the ultimate lenders. More than anything else, the problems of price volatility and informational asymmetry between lenders and borrowers in capital markets appear to be the main reason for savers' preference for indirect securities.

The repressive nature of the financial system is a second characteristic. Even after a decade-long promotion of liberalization, to die-hard liberalization advocates little has changed in the government's dominant role in managing the nation's finances. The government has not given up the idea of controlling interest rates and can and does interfere in the allocation of banks' loanable funds. The monetary authorities not only regulate entry but also determine the types of services and products banks, NBFIs, and securities firms can offer.

Financial industries are different from other industries. The payment system and the public confidence on which the financial system is built bear the qualities of a public good. Laissez-faire finance may not achieve or protect the positive externalities of a financial system. But one must wonder whether the degree of financial control exercised by Korean monetary authorities has been necessary or justifiable on efficiency grounds.

What is more puzzling is that financial repression, despite its severity and protraction, does not appear to have interfered with Korea's economic growth and industrialization. Or has it? I will return to this question later.

The closedness of Korea's financial sector has been a third feature. Korea has pursued an export-led development strategy ever since its first five-year development plan was launched in 1962. During almost three decades of successful promotion, Korea has developed a large and open trade sector. Export earnings accounted for almost 45 percent of Korea's GNP in the late 1980s. Yet the monetary authorities and the public are still debating whether Korea should open its money and capital markets to foreign investors. How should one explain this dichotomy between the real and the financial sector?

Dominance of the financial sector by a relatively small number of large financial institutions in both the banking and NBFI sectors has been a fourth feature. Despite the doubling of the number of nationwide commercial banks (NBCs) in the 1980s and new banks in 1989–90, the original five still control an oligopolistic market structure. Among NBFIs, ten large investment and finance companies, three large investment trust companies, and six large insurance companies dominate nonbanking financial intermediation.

The structure of banking and nonbanking financial intermediation and the pattern of ownership of financial institutions correspond closely to the pattern of distribution of economic power in other sectors. In other words, not surprisingly, the major chaebol are the largest borrowers at most DMBs and NBFIs; they have controlling interests in most NBFIs and securities firms; and they could easily control the management of the NCBs if the equity ownership restriction was removed.

Although the documentary evidence is limited, a large number of Korea's small and medium-size firms belong to subcontracting networks developed by or affiliated with chaebol, and they are known to obtain finance from or through these groups. Does financial concentration have anything to do with the growth of industrial groups in Korea? Or is industrial concentration responsible for financial concentration?

One can also observe in Korea a large increase in financial layering and financial interpenetration, as evidenced by the rapid growth of transactions among financial institutions including the central bank. The financial sector as a whole contributed almost 5½ percent of Korea's GDP in 1989, up from less than 4 percent four years earlier. This level of GDP contribution is close to that of many OECD countries.

Most financial institutions have been engaged in indirect finance through the issuance of deposits or depositlike liabilities. Is this allocation of resources to the financial sector "excessive"? Insofar as Korea's financial system consists of highly regulated and partially regulated sectors, there are arbitrage profits to be made by setting up institutions in the partially regulated sector, in order to exploit loopholes in the regulatory framework. This is likely to result in an excessive amount of real resources devoted to the supply of financial services, because there are fixed costs in establishing financial institutions.

Issues in the Role of Finance

The process of financial growth and liberalization in Korea during the 1970s and 1980s raises two important issues in regard to the role of finance in economic development. One issue is the extent to which liberal financial reform has contributed to growth in the financial sector and allocative efficiency in the economy. Korea's financial system was highly repressive until the early 1980s. Since then deregulation has been the manifest goal of financial policy, but it has been limited in both scope and degree. Is it possible to ascertain both quantitatively and qualitatively the effects of a repressive financial policy on economic growth and development in terms of Korea's experience? This is the second issue that requires careful analysis.

Financial liberalization since the start of the 1980s has been uneven and intermittent, and often relapsing into reregulation. Nevertheless, there is no denying that during the 1980s the financial environment became relatively free, with less government control over financial markets and institutions than in the past. Have financial reforms indeed led to rapid financial growth in Korea, as asserted by the World Bank in its *World Development Report 1989*?

Although limited in scope, interest rate deregulation and removal of restrictions on the types of services different financial institutions can offer appear to have induced household savers to move out of real assets (both stock and flow) and into financial assets. Although these portfolio shift effects are likely to be spread over a number of years, alone they cannot sustain rapid financial growth for any length of time. To sustain the rapid financial growth Korea has experienced, financial reforms must be able to promote real domestic savings and also improve the allocative efficiency of the economy. The empirical work, which suffers from a lack of reliable data, shows no evidence that the rise in the propensity to save is associated with the removal of financial restrictions.

The expansion of the financial sector has increased the proportion of investment resources allocated through financial markets and institutions. Once again, there is no convincing evidence this increased allocation capacity has led to any increase in the average productivity of investment. The conclusion is that the rapid financial growth in Korea should be explained by the high rates of growth of the economy, a rising propensity to save, and stable prices. The causality has run from changes in the real sector to the financial sector, not the other way around.

Does this evidence point to the conclusion that finance does not matter? In my view, finance may have been overwhelmed and dominated by powerful developments in the real sector in Korea—but it still mattered very much.

Neutrality of a Repressive Regime?

Economic orthodoxy tells us a liberal financial regime is likely to be more efficient in resource allocation because it stimulates competition. Judging from this norm, one must wonder how Korea could have maintained rapid growth and industrialization over the three decades after 1960 while overcoming all those inefficiencies the repressive and closed financial system produced. What have been, both quantitatively and qualitatively, the costs of financial repression? One hypothesis, which argues that Korea could have done even better in a more liberal financial environment, can be easily dismissed. Another hypothesis, which I elaborate on here, argues that Korea has been able to avoid much of the inefficiency cost by effectively supporting an export-led development strategy. I also argue that Korea might been able to avoid some of the undesirable macro-economic outcomes of market-oriented finance by maintaining a restrictive financial regime.

There is little doubt that the financial system in Korea has been geared to support the government's export promotion policy and has allocated the bulk of resources to export-oriented industries. Thus, exporters have always been most favored borrowers at both DMBs and NBFIs. Until the mid 1980s they were accorded an automatic short-term credit facility at a subsidized interest rate. The amount of short-term credit extended was directly tied to export earnings and did not require any collateral or domestic value–added content. Successful exporters have had easier access to other types of bank credit as well. For many small and medium firms, engaging in export and export-related activities has been the easiest way of gaining access to bank credit.

An important characteristic of the system was that export credit incentives did not discriminate between activities and exporters. Credits were contingent on export performance, which resulted in a uniformity of incentives across a wide range of industries producing potentially tradable goods. Foreign markets provided a test of suitability for other subsidized credit. The market test feature also made the cost of credit allocation to different industries and activities more apparent to policymakers and allowed them to reallocate resources whenever the costs became excessive. (See Hong and Park 1986, and Hong 1988.)

Exporting firms must compete with foreign producers in the international marketplace, which makes such firms more efficient than they otherwise might be. In an economy where bank credits are rationed and capital markets are small and underdeveloped, success and survival critically depend on a firm's access to bank loans. Exporters were no exception to this reality. They had to generate export earnings and hence had to be cost-efficient.

Under Korea's export promotion strategy, foreign competition has constrained the economic behavior of both firms and policymakers and provided feedback regarding policies' success or failure in reaching their objectives. Therefore, largely because of the relative efficiency of the export-led development strategy in resource allocation, the repressive financial system, which was passive and directed toward to the support of export-oriented industries, has been able to avoid large deadweight losses stemming from resource misallocation. (See Krueger 1980, 1981, 1985 on the efficiency of an export-promoting regime relative to that of an import substitution regime.)

Financial repression may have imposed substantial costs on the Korean economy—it certainly has been associated with government failures. At the same time, however, the restrictive financial regime may have offset some of these costs by minimizing the effects of financial market failures that could have been, among other things, serious obstacles to the promotion of export-led development.

Citing the development experiences of Hong Kong and Singapore, one might argue that a free market system can promote exports as efficiently as the interventionist regimes of Korea and Taiwan. I do not address this issue. Instead, I am examining whether a particular type of industrial policy—export promotion—can be consistent with market-oriented finance.

To appreciate this point, consider whether a market-oriented financial system could have supported Korea's export promotion policy as well as a repressive system. For a number of reasons, it may not have. Among the features of finance that may be responsible for financial market failures are externalities and coordination problems, financial price volatility, and short time horizons.

To remain competitive and cultivate new foreign markets, exporters often bear large costs gathering and processing information, advertising products, and other marketing activities. Learning and acquiring foreign technology and developing indigenous technology are vital to the very survival of many exporters. Investment in these activities generates significant externalities and is subject to economies of scale and scope in that such investment can reduce costs for new entrants in export-oriented industries. Because the returns to these types of investment are largely inappropriable, free market–financing arrangements may not result in an optimal level of investment in these activities. In this regard, Westphal (1990) argues that state intervention through credit rationing and import quotas may not be the appropriate means to ensure realization of the latent externalities unless it is combined with state actions to compel the warranted level of investment in these activities.

A coordinated investment program across sectors can lead to the expansion of markets in all sectors and hence be self-sustaining when no firm can make profits investing alone because of the presence of profit spillovers across sectors (Murphy, Shleifer and Vishny 1989). This big-push argument then suggests that developing economies could industrialize of each sector at a lower cost in tariffs and subsidies by implementing a coordinated investment program rather than undertaking piecemeal industrialization. The authors point to the Korean experience as a successful case of simultaneous industrialization.

Since 1962, the consecutive Five-Year Development Plans have provided a framework and detailed guidelines for Korea's industrial policy. Export promotion during the 1960s and 1970s was so intense that economic planners set the goal of making all industries export-oriented, as manifested by the slogan "export-orientation of all industries." To be successful, such a policy requires close coordination of investment in different industries.

I am not arguing that the big-push is a better strategy than others. Instead, I am making the point that a coordinated investment program is essential to a successful big push and that it is highly unlikely a deregulated financial system can support such a program without government intervention, because the short-run rates of return on investment differ considerably from sector to sector, particularly at an early stage of industrialization.

There are two characteristics of financial markets that are important to this discussion. One is that the speed of adjustment in financial markets is much faster than in product or labor markets. Another is that financial asset prices fluctuate much more than is warranted by changes in fundamentals, because they also respond to changes in investor sentiment and rumors. The combination of these two characteristics makes returns on assets more risky and hence raises the cost of financing. It also makes it more difficult to predict the cost and availability of financing in the future.

This volatility problem can be more serious to those producers specializing in export production. In addition to domestic news and events, exporters are exposed to developments in foreign markets, and these are harder for domestic financial markets to assess accurately. The high speed of adjustment and price volatility can then discourage physical investment, shorten the horizons of firms, and bias the choice of investment projects against long-term ones, particularly those for developing new products and technology.

This time horizon issue can be exacerbated by money managers who put more emphasis on the short-term prospects of their investments because they are themselves rewarded for short-term performance. Thus, an OECD study (1989) suggests that stock market volatility had a significant effect on investment and industrial production activities in the 1970s for Japan, the United States, and the United Kingdom. However, the significance of the effect disappeared in the 1980s, indicating that the real variables became more independent of price volatility.

In moving from a repressive to a liberal financial regime, one often encounters the virtual disappearance of long-term finance, as shown by the Southern Cone experience (see Diaz-Alejandro 1985). This problem appears to be more acute in an unstable environment with a high rate of inflation.

When market-determined interest rates are high and volatile, commercial banks—the traditional asset transformers—tend to match the maturities of their assets and liabilities and become more like information brokers. Householder savers become more sensitive to changes in interest rates and more receptive to new investments that are liquid and yield higher rates of return than existing ones. Commercial banks lend at the short end of the market as long as they borrow at the short end, and they often securitize their credit obligations to minimize the interest rate risk. One advantage of Korea's repressive financial system may have been its ability to supply long-term finance through a financial system dominated by commercial banks. This advantage was more critical during the 1960s and 1970s than it has been since then.

Commercial banks can and do transform assets and maintain mismatched balance sheets. But, the information asymmetries, political and social unrest, as well as the extra risks Korean firms were exposed to as exporters during the two decades of export promotion would have made the risks of extending long-term loans unbearably high to unregulated banks and NBFIs. In the absence of government intervention, the profit-oriented behavior of the commercial banks and NBFIs would have resulted in a dearth of long-term finance.

At an early stage of export promotion, exporters may find it difficult to establish themselves in new foreign markets and to learn to produce and market new products. Adjusted for these risk elements, the rate of return on investment in export-oriented industries, other things being equal, could be lower than on a similar investment aimed at the domestic market. To what extent would financial institutions in a laissez-faire financial environment assess the risks of operating in foreign markets and shift them efficiently to ultimate lenders? Would they not favor producers aiming at the domestic market and pay more attention to short-term profits? In Korea the heavily regulated financial system has been used to absorb these risks by providing subsidized credits and foreign loan guarantees and then to disperse them as widely as possible throughout the economy.

This risk absorption, mostly by the DMBs, raised the effective rate of return on investment in export-oriented industries. Together with the availability of long-term finance, this feature of the financial system has provided strong incentives to exporters. The costs of absorbing the risks were extremely high in some cases, as demonstrated by the costs of industrial restructuring in the 1980s. In other cases the costs have been manageable and been paid for by seigniorage, inflation, taxes, and forgone dividend payments to bank stockholders. The Korean government could have chosen a different system for absorbing and distributing the risk, but the use of the banking system has been least objectionable to the public and hence politically expedient.

CONCLUDING REMARKS

Although limited in scope, financial deregulation in the 1980s has helped strengthening competitive forces in Korea's financial markets. New financial and communications technologies have greatly reduced the costs of collecting and processing information. Despite these developments, I have not been able to identify any significant changes in the behavior of financial institutions or markets that indicate attempts to adjust to a changing financial environment. Nor do I see indications of changing relationships between the government and the financial institutions.

There is no evidence financial growth measured by the ratio of total financial assets to GNP has had any positive effects on savings behavior or has been associated with a higher average productivity of investment. It is more likely that the rapid growth of the financial sector has been the result of the high rate of growth of the economy, the rising propensity to save, and stable prices.

One could argue it is perhaps too early to detect any positive effect on the economy from financial liberalization. Others may claim financial reforms have been so uneven and protracted that this chapter's conclusions are hardly surprising. Although I do not dispute these views, the discussion here also casts some doubt on whether further deregulation could make any significant contribution to sustaining rapid financial growth.

Kim Dong Won of Suwon University and Kim Dong Wuk and others at the Korea Institute of Finance assisted in preparing the tables for the text and appendix.

REFERENCES

(The word "processed" describes informally reproduced works that may not be commonly available through libraries.)

Adams, James Ring. 1989. *The Big Fix: Inside the S&L Scandal.* New York: Wiley.

BOK (Bank of Korea). *Financial Statement Analysis.* Annual. An English summary appears in the September issue of the Bank's *Quarterly Economic Review.*

Cho, Yoon Je. 1988. "The Effect of Financial Liberalization on the Efficiency of Credit Allocation: Some Evidence from Korea." *Journal of Development Economics*, July.

Cole, David C., and Yung Chul Park. 1983. *Financial Development in the Republic of Korea 1945–1978*. Cambridge, MA: Harvard University, Council on East Asian Studies.

Diaz-Alejandro, Carlos F. 1985. "Good-bye Financial Repression, Hello Financial Crash." *Journal of Development Economics* 19(1/2):1–24 (Sept.–Oct.).

Dornbusch, Rudiger and Yung Chul Park. 1987. "Korean Growth Policy." *Brookings Papers on Economic Activity II.*

———, and Alejandro Reynoso. 1989. "Financial Factors in Economic Development." *American Economic Review* 79(2): 204 –9 (May).

Edwards, Sebastian. 1984 Dec. "The Order of Liberalization of the External Sector in Developing Countries." *Essays in International Finance* 156. Princeton, NJ: Princeton University.

Hong, Won Tack. 1988. "Market Distortions and Trade Patterns of Korea: 1960 – 85." Korea Development Institute Working Paper 8807 (Sep.).

———, and Yung Chul Park. 1986. "The Financing of Export-Oriented Growth in Korea." In A. H. H. Tan and B. Kapur, eds., *Pacific Growth and Financial Interdependence*. London: Allen & Unwin.

Horiuchi, Akiyoshi and Masayuki Otaki. 1987. "Kinyu: Seifu kinyu to ginko kashidashi no juyosei" (Finance: Government lending and the importance of bank loans). In Koichi Hamada, Masahiro Kuroda, and Akiyoshi Horiuchi, eds., *Nihon keizai no macro bunseki*. Tokyo: University of Tokyo Press.

Kim, Ji-hong. 1991. "Korea: Market Adjustment in Declining Industries, Government Assistance in Troubled Industries." In Hugh Patrick with Larry Meissner, eds., *Pacific Basin Industries in Distress: Structural Adjustment and Trade Policy in the Nine Industrialized Economies*. New York: Columbia University Press.

Kim, Pyung Joo. 1990. "Financial Institutions: Past, Present, and Future." Processed. Honolulu: East–West Population Institute.

Korea, Government of the Republic of. 1982. *The Fifth Five-Year Economic and Social Development Plan 1982–86*. Seoul.

Krueger, Anne O. 1980. "Trade as an Input to Development." *American Economic Review*, May.

———. 1981. "Export-led Industrial Growth Reconsidered." In Lawrence Krause and Won-tack Hong, eds., *Trade and Growth of the Advanced Developing Countries in the Pacific Basin*. Seoul: Korea Development Institute.

———. 1985. "The Experience and Lessons of Asia's Super Exporters." In Vittorio Corbo, Anne O. Krueger and Fernando Ossa, eds., *Export-oriented Development Strategies*. Boulder, CO: Westview Press.

Kuznets, Paul. 1988. "An East Asian Model of Economic Development: Japan, Taiwan, and South Korea." Economic Development and Cultural Change 36 (3): S11-43 (April supl.).

Lee, Kyu Urk and Je Hyug Lee. 1990. *"Industrial Groups and Economic Power Concentration."* Seoul: Korea Development Institute. In Korean.

Leipziger, Danny M. 1987. *Korea: Managing the Industrial Transition*. A World Bank country study. 2 vols. Covers through 1984.

McKinnon, Ronald. 1973. *Money and Capital in Economic Development*. Washington DC: Brookings Institution.

Murphy, K. M., Andrei Shleifer, and Robert W. Vishny. 1989. "Industrialization and the Big-Push." *Journal of Political Economy,* October.

Nam, Sang Woo. 1988 Dec. "The Determinants of National Saving in Korea—A Sectoral Accounting Approach." Korea Development Institute Working Paper 8821.

OECD (Organisation for Economic Co-operation and Development). 1989. *Economies in Transition: Structural Adjustment in OECD Countries*. Chap. 3: "Financial Markets: The Challenges of Modernisation." Paris: OECD.

———. 1990. *Macroeconomic Consequences of Financial Liberalization*. Paris: OECD.

Park, Yung Chul. 1985. "Economic Stabilization and Liberalization in Korea, 1980 –1984." In Bank of Korea, *Monetary Policy in a Changing Financial Environment*. Seoul.

Park, Yung Chul. 1987. "Financial Repression, Liberation, and Development in Developing Countries." In Lawrence B. Krause and Kihwan Kim, editors, *The Liberalization Process in Economic Development*. University of California Press.

————. 1990. "Development Lessons from Asia: The Role of Government in South Korea and Taiwan." *American Economic Review* 80(2): 118–21 (May).

Shiller, Robert J. 1981. "Do Stock Price Move Too Much to Be Justified by Subsequent Changes in Dividends." *American Economic Review* 71(3) (Jun.).

————. 1990. "Speculative Prices and Popular Models." *Journal of Economic Perspectives* 4(2): 55–66. (Spring).

Shleifer, Andrei, and Lawrence H. Summers. 1990. "The Noise Trade Approach to Finance." *Journal of Economic Perspectives* 4(3): 19–34 (Spring).

Stiglitz, Joseph E. 1990. "Symposium on Bubbles." *Journal of Economic Perspectives* 4(2): 13–18. (Spring).

————, and Andrew Weiss. 1981. "Credit Rationing in Markets with Imperfect Information." *American Economic Review* 71(3) (Jun.).

Westphal, L. 1990. "Industrial Policy in an Export-propelled Economy: Lessons from South Korea's Experience." *Journal of Economic Perspectives* 4(3) (Summer).

World Bank. 1989. *World Development Report 1989*. New York: Oxford University Press.

Table 4.A1. Korea: Macroeconomic Indicators (percent)

Year	Growth rate of real GNP	Gross investment (as % of real GNP)	Export of goods and services (as % of real GNP)	Current account as % of GNP Real	Current account as % of GNP Nominal	Household savings rate[a]	Rate of change in GNP deflator	Real interest rate[b] A	Real interest rate[b] B
1961	5.6	11.2	3.6	1.4	1.4	1.1	14.0	1.0	—
1962	2.2	8.3	3.9	−1.3	−2.0	−3.5	18.4	−3.4	—
1963	9.1	14.3	3.9	−3.4	−3.7	0.7	29.3	−14.3	—
1964	9.6	11.7	4.4	−0.7	−0.7	2.3	30.0	−15.0	—
1965	5.8	12.1	5.7	−0.1	0.3	0.3	6.2	20.2	—
1966	12.7	16.0	7.2	−2.8	−2.7	5.0	14.5	11.9	—
1967	6.6	15.9	9.0	−4.3	−4.0	2.5	15.6	10.8	—
1968	11.3	16.3	11.2	−8.3	−7.4	1.9	16.1	9.1	—
1969	13.8	21.5	13.4	−9.3	−7.3	7.7	14.8	8.0	—
1970	7.6	13.1	10.6	−7.6	−7.2	4.5	15.6	7.2	31.1
1971	8.6	12.1	11.9	−9.1	−8.9	4.8	12.5	7.9	33.6
1972	5.1	13.6	15.4	−5.1	−3.4	8.1	16.7	−4.7	17.3
1973	13.2	16.9	20.9	−4.4	−2.2	11.8	13.6	−1.6	25.8
1974	8.1	17.2	19.3	−8.7	−10.7	9.3	30.5	−15.5	10.3
1975	6.4	17.5	21.8	−6.0	−9.0	8.5	25.2	−10.2	15.2
1976	13.1	21.7	26.7	−2.6	−1.1	11.8	21.2	−5.0	20.1
1977	9.8	25.6	29.7	−2.4	0.1	16.5	16.6	−2.2	17.5
1978	9.8	27.7	30.7	−6.0	−2.2	17.8	22.8	−4.2	20.3
1979	7.2	26.4	29.2	−10.3	−6.5	16.5	19.6	−1.0	23.1
1980	−3.7	22.9	33.1	−7.5	−8.7	9.0	24.0	−4.5	13.6
1981	5.9	24.1	35.9	−5.2	−6.8	9.4	16.9	−0.7	18.5
1982	7.2	25.5	35.0	−4.0	−3.8	10.5	7.1	0.9	21.9
1983	12.6	27.5	37.1	−2.2	−2.0	10.9	5.0	3.0	19.7
1984	9.3	29.2	36.6	−2.1	−1.6	13.1	3.9	6.1	21.5
1985	7.0	29.3	35.8	−1.0	−1.0	13.6	4.2	5.8	19.2
1986	12.9	32.1	40.0	2.4	4.4	16.2	2.8	7.2	20.5
1987	13.0	35.6	43.0	4.6	7.6	18.0	3.5	6.5	18.7
1988	12.4	36.7	43.1	4.9	2.4	19.4	5.9	4.1	15.3
1989	6.8	33.1	38.8	−2.9	2.4	18.5	5.2	4.8	13.7
1990	9.3	32.4	37.0	−6.5	−0.9	19.1	10.6	−0.6	9.8
1991	8.4	31.8	37.5	−9.9	−3.1	—	10.9	−0.9	10.3

— Not available.

Note: Real GNP is at 1975 prices for 1961–69, then at 1985 prices.

a. The household savings rate equals individual savings divided by national disposable income, as reported in the national income accounts.

b. Real interest rates are the difference between the rate of change in the GNP deflator and, A, the time deposit interest, and B, the curb market interest rate.

Source: Various issues of Bank of Korea, *National Accounts,* and Ministry of Finance, *Financial Statistics,* as well as MOF, *National Income in Korea,* 1982.

Table 4.A2. Korea: GNP Per Capita, GNP, and Financial Assets Outstanding

Year	GNP per capita US$	GNP	Assets outstanding			Assets to GNP ratio		
			Total	Personal	Corporate	Total	Personal	Corporate
Billion won								
1965	105	806	630	162	56	0.78	0.20	0.07
1966	125	1,037	677	238	71	0.65	0.23	0.07
1967	142	1,281	1,374	353	127	1.07	0.28	0.10
1968	169	1,653	2,195	541	243	1.33	0.33	0.15
1969	210	2,155	3,469	858	417	1.61	0.40	0.19
1970	252	2,785	7,162	1,337	1,224	2.57	0.48	0.44
1971	289	3,417	9,075	1,782	1,622	2.66	0.52	0.47
Trillion won								
1972	319	4.2	11.7	2.3	2.1	2.78	0.55	0.49
1973	396	5.4	15.1	3.4	2.8	2.81	0.63	0.52
1974	542	7.6	20.7	4.4	3.6	2.73	0.57	0.47
1975	594	10.1	27.5	5.6	5.0	2.71	0.55	0.49
1976	803	13.9	35.9	7.3	6.8	2.58	0.52	0.49
1977	1,012	17.8	47.3	10.1	8.9	2.66	0.57	0.50
1978	1,396	24.0	62.7	13.6	12.5	2.61	0.57	0.52
1979	1,644	30.8	81.2	17.1	16.5	2.64	0.56	0.54
1980	1,592	36.7	114	21.2	22.8	3.09	0.58	0.62
1981	1,734	45.5	148	28.3	29.6	3.25	0.62	0.65
1982	1,824	52.2	189	36.7	37.4	3.63	0.70	0.72
1983	2,002	61.7	225	43.6	44.4	3.65	0.71	0.72
1984	2,158	70.0	265	52.5	50.7	3.78	0.75	0.72
1985	2,194	78.1	312	62.9	57.7	4.00	0.81	0.74
1986	2,505	90.6	355	77.3	66.9	3.92	0.85	0.74
1987	3,110	106	416	99	77	3.92	0.93	0.73
1988	4,127	126	498	112	89	3.94	0.95	0.71
1989	4,994	142	629	157	112	4.44	1.11	0.79
1990	5,659	171	772	196	134	4.50	1.14	0.78
1991	6,498	206	937	239	158	4.55	1.16	0.77

Note: Unincorporated businesses are included in coporate assets.

Source: Ministry of Finance, *Public Finance and Financial Statistics,* Aug. 1992; Bank of Korea, *Economic Statistics Yearbook* 1971; and *Flow of Funds in Korea,* 1992. Annual data for GNP and per capita GNP are summarized in *Financial Statistics* (pp. 107–8, Table 7–1, panel 1). Annual data for financial assets are in the *Yearbook* (for 1965–69, pp. 54–55) and Flow of Funds (for 1970–91, pp. 192–279).

Table 4.A3. *Korea: Financial Surplus or Deficit by Sector as Percentage of GNP*

Year	Government[a]	Corporate[b]	Individual[c]	Overseas
1970	0.52	−15.95	8.75	7.26
1971	−0.75	−15.82	9.96	8.49
1972	−0.41	−12.97	8.36	3.20
1973	0.21	−20.43	17.00	2.15
1974	0.56	−18.74	6.78	10.62
1975	−0.57	−18.45	8.93	9.59
1976	0.43	−12.31	8.70	1.93
1977	0.04	−14.51	13.35	0.05
1978	0.74	−13.98	10.04	2.82
1979	0.05	−15.76	6.88	7.04
1980	1.29	−17.04	5.69	9.38
1981	0.35	−15.65	6.91	7.54
1982	0.35	−13.43	9.03	5.53
1983	1.40	−9.98	5.62	3.20
1984	1.64	−10.75	6.12	2.61
1985	1.16	−10.05	6.71	1.94
1986	1.26	−6.82	8.79	−3.96
1987	3.09	−6.79	11.51	−8.52
1988	4.58	−7.04	9.37	−7.83
1989	3.18	−12.49	10.97	−2.62
1990	3.77	−17.11	11.48	1.71
1991	1.30	−15.40	10.90	2.99

Note: Before 1970, relevant data are not available. The sum of the columns is not zero because of statistical discrepancies in the underlying data.

a. The government sector includes the central and local governments, social security institutions, and public nonprofit corporations.

b. Includes "quasi corporations."

c. The individual sector includes households and private nonprofit institutions serving households. It also includes unincorporated businesses.

Source: Bank of Korea, *Flow of Funds* 1992, pp. 190–91.

Table 4.A4. Korea: Savings by Sector and Investment as Percentage of GNP

	Gross domestic savings					Gross domestic investment	Net foreign flow [b]
	Private[a]						
Year	Individuals	Corporations	Total	Government	Total		
1970	..	..	12.0	5.9	18.0	24.3	6.9
1971	..	..	11.0	5.0	16.0	24.8	8.5
1972	..	..	15.0	2.3	17.2	21.0	3.3
1973	..	..	19.6	3.0	22.6	25.2	2.2
1974	..	..	18.2	2.1	20.3	31.8	10.6
1975	7.6	8.0	15.6	2.5	18.2	28.8	8.9
1976	11.4	8.4	19.8	4.5	24.3	26.6	1.1
1977	13.3	9.9	23.1	4.4	27.6	28.3	−0.1
1978	15.2	9.4	24.6	5.2	29.7	32.6	2.1
1979	13.2	8.8	22.0	6.4	28.4	35.9	6.4
1980	8.9	9.0	17.9	5.2	23.1	32.0	8.5
1981	9.2	8.2	17.4	5.3	22.7	29.9	6.6
1982	9.7	8.8	18.5	5.7	24.2	28.9	3.7
1983	10.6	10.1	20.7	6.9	27.6	29.2	1.9
1984	12.1	10.8	22.8	6.5	29.4	30.3	1.5
1985	11.5	11.3	22.8	6.3	29.1	29.9	1.0
1986	14.6	11.9	26.6	6.2	32.8	28.9	−4.4
1987	16.1	13.3	29.4	6.8	36.2	29.6	−7.4
1988	17.2	12.8	30.0	8.2	38.1	30.7	−8.0
1989	16.7	10.4	27.1	8.3	35.4	33.6	−2.4
1990	17.2	10.1	27.3	8.8	36.1	37.2	0.9
1991	..	..	28.6	7.5	36.1	39.4	3.1

·· Not available.

Note: Gross domestic savings plus net foreign flow does not equal gross domestic investment because of statistical discrepancies in the various underlying data series. See Table 4.A3 for definition of sectors.

a. Disaggregation of private savings is unavailable for 1970–75, and for 1991 is not yet available.

b. Long-term capital account (direct investment plus loan disbursements minus loan repayments plus/minus minor items). Negative numbers represent capital outflows.

Source: Bank of Korea, *Economic Statistics Yearbook.* Using the 1992 edition as an example, data for 1986–91 are in Table 145 (pp. 322–23). Data for 1953–88 are in the 1990 *National Accounts,* pp. 14–35, except for the disaggregation of private savings.

Table 4.A5. *Korea: Source of External Funds Raised by Nonfinancial Sectors*
(percent)

	1970–74	1975–79	1980–84	1985–89	1985	1989
Distribution of funds by sector raising funds						
Corporate	73.9	79.9	72.9	67.6	69.7	70.3
Individual	13.5	11.9	21.2	30.5	27.9	28.6
Government	12.6	8.3	5.9	1.9	2.5	1.1
Distribution of funds by source						
Borrowing from financial institutions	53.1	48.0	50.0	55.5	61.4	50.2
Securities issued	16.2	20.1	25.1	31.1	19.8	43.4
Foreign borrowing	18.9	15.7	6.9	0.4	1.1	–1.3
Government loans	2.8	1.7	1.9	0.6	1.2	0.7
Trade credits	9.1	14.7	16.2	12.4	16.6	7.0
Borrowings from financial institutions (as % of total sources)						
Monetary institutions	40.8	30.9	25.5	25.2	32.6	16.9
Bank of Korea	5.8	2.4	1.9	–0.1	0.0	–1.7
Deposit money banks	35.0	28.5	23.6	25.3	32.6	18.5
Nonbanks	12.3	17.1	24.5	30.3	28.8	33.4
Insurance	0.5	1.8	4.3	6.7	4.0	7.7
Investment and finance companies	2.2	2.7	4.0	2.2	–1.5	4.2
Other[a]	9.6	12.6	16.2	21.4	26.3	21.5
Securities issued (as % of total sources)						
Government and public bonds	0.8	1.5	1.2	3.3	–0.8	5.1
Industrial paper	0.7	1.6	3.6	3.9	0.3	10.0
Debentures	1.0	3.8	7.5	7.6	11.2	10.1
Stock and equities	13.6	13.1	12.8	16.3	9.0	18.3

Note: Excludes miscellaneous sources and the informal sector.

a. Credits from development, savings, investment, securities, and public financial institutions.

Source: Bank of Korea, *Flow of Funds,* various issues.

Table 4.A6. *Korea: Uses of Funds by Nonfinancial Sectors*

	1970–74	1975–79	1980–84	1985–89	1985	1989
Distribution of funds by sector investing funds						
Corporate	30.8	40.6	39.8	33.0	39.1	35.2
Individual	50.5	47.5	49.6	57.2	53.4	56.2
Government	18.7	11.9	10.6	9.8	7.5	8.6
Distribution of funds by uses						
Currency	6.6	5.1	1.8	1.5	0.8	1.1
Deposits at financial institutions	48.8	43.9	42.9	56.6	52.5	54.0
Securities purchased	24.7	24.8	29.4	23.6	14.0	34.3
Foreign lending	−1.6	3.9	1.3	3.7	8.9	1.8
Government loans	9.0	3.8	4.8	2.6	4.7	2.1
Trade credits	12.5	18.6	19.9	12.0	19.2	6.7
Deposits at financial institutions (as % of total uses)						
Monetary institutions	35.9	29.4	20.1	21.6	22.3	16.1
Bank of Korea[a]	3.0	3.4	0.3	3.1	−0.1	2.5
Deposit money banks	32.9	26.0	19.8	18.5	22.4	13.6
Demand deposits	8.9	4.7	2.5	2.0	1.9	1.4
Time and savings	24.0	21.2	17.3	16.5	20.5	12.2
Nonbanks	12.9	14.5	22.8	35.0	30.2	37.9
Life insurance and pension funds	3.5	4.5	8.6	12.3	14.5	10.6
Trust	2.8	1.8	2.5	9.4	9.8	13.1
Investment and finance companies	2.7	3.2	3.5	1.1	−3.2	2.3
Other[b]	3.9	5.0	8.2	12.2	9.1	12.0
Securities purchased (as % of total uses)						
Government and public bonds	0.6	1.0	2.0	0.0	−1.4	2.5
Financial debentures	1.3	1.0	1.2	1.9	−0.8	1.9
Industrial paper	1.0	2.1	3.7	2.1	−2.5	7.0
Corporate debentures	0.3	1.4	1.0	0.2	1.1	1.3
Beneficiary certificates	0.1	1.5	4.9	8.3	8.2	8.9
Stock and equities	21.4	17.8	16.6	11.2	9.3	13.0

Note: Excludes miscellaneous uses and the informal sector.

a. All deposits at the Bank of Korea are government deposits.

b. Deposits at development, savings, investment, securities, and public financial institutions.

Source: Bank of Korea, *Flow of Funds,* various issues.

Table 4.A7. *Korea: Distribution of Purchases and Issuance of Debt Instruments and Equity by Sector*
(percent)

	1970–74	1975–79	1980–84	1985–89	1985	1989
Short-term securities						
Issuance by						
Financial sector	91.3	18.2	−22.7	59.8	100.9	15.2
Government	0	16.3	−6.7	8.9	0	11.8
Businesses	8.6	65.4	129.4	31.3	−0.9	73.0
Purchases by						
Financial sector	90.7	41.3	13.5	73.5	77.5	42.4
Government	0	0	1.1	0	−1.1	0.1
Businesses	2.1	22.8	56.5	17.4	10.3	48.0
Individuals	7.0	35.9	28.9	9.2	13.3	9.5
Long-term securities						
Issuance by						
Financial sector	63.0	59.0	48.4	65.9	42.2	51.3
Government	8.3	0.9	−0.7	2.8	−7.8	4.3
Businesses	28.8	40.1	52.4	31.3	65.3	44.4
Purchases by						
Financial sector	67.3	61.9	60.6	51.1	60.8	43.9
Businesses	7.9	8.2	7.7	4.7	5.1	8.1
Government	0.4	1.2	2.9	−0.6	4.2	−1.5
Individuals	24.6	28.6	28.8	44.2	30.0	49.5
Equity (stock)						
Issuance by						
Financial sector	14.2	13.1	19.9	32.5	13.8	53.0
Businesses	85.8	87.0	80.1	67.5	86.2	47.0
Purchases by						
Financial sector	15.9	20.4	18.4	56.1	40.1	69.8
Government	11.7	14.6	3.0	1.3	1.9	−7.0
Businesses	16.4	10.8	28.2	15.4	35.2	8.9
Individuals	56.0	54.2	50.4	27.2	22.9	28.3

Source: Bank of Korea, *Flow of Funds*, various issues.

Table 4.A8. *Korea: Distribution of Holdings of Outstanding Debt Instruments and Equity by Sector*
(percent)

	1970–74	1975–79	1980–84	1985–89	1985	1989
Short-term securities						
As an asset						
Financial sector	59.4	50.1	48.0	69.4	49.4	68.8
Government	0	0	0.2	0.2	0.7	0.1
Businesses	9.3	16.4	25.2	16.0	25.7	20.4
Individuals	31.4	33.5	26.6	14.3	24.2	10.7
As a liability						
Financial sector	59.2	29.6	38.0	55.1	31.0	52.5
Government	0	8.9	0.4	5.4	0	7.4
Business	40.8	61.6	61.6	39.5	69.0	40.1
Long-term securities						
As an asset						
Financial sector	62.9	65.8	61.2	59.8	60.8	55.8
Government	0.2	0.8	2.1	1.7	2.6	1.0
Businesses	10.4	7.0	7.0	4.8	7.3	4.8
Individuals	26.6	26.4	29.7	33.6	29.3	38.4
As a liability						
Financial sector	45.3	61.4	52.0	56.7	49.9	57.7
Government	33.5	5.0	2.6	1.1	0.4	2.0
Businesses	21.3	33.6	45.4	42.1	49.8	40.3
Equity (stock)						
As an asset						
Financial sector	13.2	16.0	16.6	37.6	17.9	58.5
Government	15.7	14.5	5.2	4.4	2.7	8.1
Businesses	14.8	13.6	19.5	18.5	23.9	10.4
Individuals	56.3	55.9	58.7	39.5	55.5	23.1
As a liability						
Financial sector	9.7	11.7	16.6	19.8	16.3	24.4
Businesses	90.3	88.3	83.4	80.2	83.7	75.6

Note: Financial sector holdings at purchase price.

Source: Bank of Korea, *Flow of Funds,* various issues.

Table 4.A9. *Korea: Composition of Financial Asset Holdings of the Personal Sector*
(percent)

	1970–74	1975–79	1980–84	1985–89	1985	1989
Currency	7.9	7.8	4.7	2.8	6.5	2.6
Deposits	51.7	47.9	46.7	49.8	45.9	50.5
Life insurance and pension funds	5.5	6.8	11.6	18.1	8.9	19.1
Securities	34.9	37.5	37.1	29.3	38.7	27.8
Deposits (as % of total holdings)						
Monetary institutions	43.1	34.4	30.4	27.4	30.6	25.0
Demand deposits	9.8	7.5	3.4	2.4	4.1	1.8
Time and savings deposits	33.3	26.9	27.1	25.0	26.5	23.2
Nonbanks	8.4	13.4	16.3	22.5	15.4	25.5
Trust	5.5	2.8	3.6	5.2	4.0	5.1
Investment and finance	0.6	3.3	2.0	1.8	2.5	6.7
Other[a]	2.3	7.3	10.7	15.4	8.9	13.7
Securities (as % of total holdings)						
Government and public bonds	1.4	0.9	1.6	0.5	1.1	0.7
Financial debentures	1.1	1.5	1.7	1.7	2.8	2.4
Industrial paper	0.3	2.2	3.6	1.7	3.5	1.2
Corporate debentures	0.3	0.5	0.7	0.3	1.0	0.2
Beneficiary certificates	0.0	1.1	5.9	9.8	2.9	12.1
Stocks and equities[b]	31.9	31.1	23.4	15.2	27.3	11.2

Note: Excludes miscellaneous holdings.

a. Deposits at development, savings, investment, securities, and public financial institutions not included elsewhere.

b. At issue price.

Source: Bank of Korea, *Flow of Funds,* various issues.

181

Table 4.A10. *Korea: Distribution of Source of Funds Raised by the Corporate Sector*
(percent)

	1970–74[a]	1975–79	1980–84	1985–89	1980	1985	1989
Internal[b]	—	26.6	28.2	39.7	18.3	39.8	27.1
Equity	18.6	13.4	12.5	15.5	8.9	7.8	19.2
Debt securities[c]	2.4	5.4	12.1	11.8	9.8	10.5	22.3
Borrowings from banks[d]	30.8	18.4	14.2	14.7	17.0	21.3	11.4
Borrowings from NBFI[e]	12.4	10.5	15.3	10.1	12.4	12.5	16.0
Government loans	4.1	1.3	1.7	0.2	2.2	0.1	−0.1
Foreign borrowings	20.0	11.8	4.1	1.3	13.6	0.4	−0.4
Trade credits	11.7	12.6	11.9	6.6	17.8	7.5	4.4
Amount raised (billion won) (annual average of multiyear periods)	1,519.5	6,133	16,873	31,640	14,238	21,043	31,640

— Not available.

Note: Covers the nonfinancial corporate sector, which includes both private and public enterprises. Disaggregate data are available in the sources for external financing, but not for internal funds. Excludes "other."

a. Internal funds data for 1970 –74 are not available. Data in this column show the total and distribution of *external* funds raised and thus are *not* comparable to the other columns.

b. Internal funds are savings, gross fixed capital depreciation, and capital transfer (net).

c. Includes bonds, industrial paper, and debentures.

d. Includes Bank of Korea loans, which are less than 0.4% in all periods.

e. Nonbank financial institutions includes investment and finance companies, as well as institutions for development, savings, securities, and investment.

Source: Bank of Korea, *National Accounts* 1990, pp. 62–75, for internal funds 1976 – 88. Bank of Korea, *Flow of Funds* 1992; Table IV– 6, p. 53, and Table IV–7, p. 57 (internal funds); liability side of the corporate sector in the annual transaction tables, pp. 104 –91, panel 16 (all else).

Table 4.A11. *Korea: Distribution of Uses of Funds Invested by the Corporate Sector*
(percent)

	1970–74 [a]	1975–79	1980–84	1985–89	1980	1985	1989
Real assets	—	70.8	67.5	69.1	65.4	71.4	62.0
Financial assets *(as % of total uses)*							
Currency [b]	20.8	3.3	1.8	1.7	1.6	2.4	1.2
Deposits at banks	25.5	6.4	2.5	3.3	4.4	3.7	4.6
Deposits at NBFI [c]	5.3	1.6	3.6	7.0	2.3	0.5	10.2
Equities	7.5	1.2	4.1	2.5	0.9	2.0	3.0
Debt securities [d]	3.4	1.1	3.4	3.0	3.7	–0.4	10.0
Foreign claims	–2.6	2.7	1.1	3.1	1.7	6.5	1.8
Trade credits	40.0	12.9	16.2	10.4	20.0	14.0	7.2
Amount invested (billion won) (annual average of multiyear periods)	262	6,129	16,792	32,038	13,042	21,544	50,066

— Not available.

Note: Covers the nonfinancial corporate sector, which includes both private and public enterprises. Disaggregate data are available in the sources for financial uses but not for real ones. Excludes "other," which is primarily statistical discrepancies. It is often a large category—e.g., 10% of the total including it in 1980.

a. Real-asset data for 1970–74 are not available. Data in this column show the total and distribution of financial assets used and thus are *not* comparable to the other columns.

b. Includes "transferable deposits," which are demand deposits and government enterprise deposits at the Bank of Korea.

c. Includes negotiable CDs and repurchase agreements (RPs) issued by investment and finance companies.

d. Includes bonds, industrial paper, debentures, and beneficiary certificates.

Source: Real-asset data are from Bank of Korea, *National Accounts* 1990, pp. 962–75. All other items are from the asset side of the nonfinancial corporate sector in the annual transaction tables of Bank of Korea, *Flow of Funds,* 1992. For example, 1989 data are on pp. 180–83.

Table 4.A12. *Korea: Number of Financial Institutions*

	First[a]	1960	1970	1980	1990
Commercial banks					
Nationwide	1945	5	9	10	10
Local	1967	n.a.	7	10	10
Foreign (branches)	1967	n.a.	6	28	66
Nonbank financial institutions					
Savings institutions[b]					
Trust accounts at a bank	1910	1	6	1	50
Credit unions	1960	1	1	1089	4606
Mutual credit facilities	1969	n.a.	1	1598	1696
Mutual savings and finance companies	1972	n.a.	n.a.	191	334
Investment institutions					
Investment trust companies	1970	n.a.	1	2	8
Investment and finance companies	1972	n.a.	n.a.	18	32
Merchant banking companies[c]	1976	n.a.	n.a.	6	6
Insurance institutions					
Life insurance	1946	n.a.	5	6	23
Non–life insurance[d]	1922	10	15	16	16
Quasi-financial institutions					
Securities companies	1949	13	21	25	25
Foreign securities companies[e]	1980	n.a.	n.a.	n.a.	22
Leasing companies	1972	n.a.	n.a.	3	20
Venture capital companies[f]	1974	n.a.	n.a.	1	51
Credit card companies[g]	1983	n.a.	n.a.	n.a.	6

n.a. Not applicable.

Note: See Table 4.2 for a list of specialized banks and development institutions.

a. Date the first institution of this type was formed.

b. 1980 data for savings institutions are as of Sep. 30.

c. All established in the period 1976 –79.

d. Includes foreign companies and joint ventures with foreign companies.

e. Representative offices.

f. Of these, 50 were formed in 1986 – 89. Because they were allowed to invest in listed securities while seeking actual venture capital investments, many of these became little more than fronts for foreign money to speculate in the Korean Stock Market.

g. Of these, 5 were formed in 1987– 88. Excludes international cards (such as American Express) that are accepted in Korea but do not have a Korean operation; includes local licensee of Visa and MasterCard.

Source: Bank of Korea, *Economic Statistics Yearbook,* various issues.

Table 4.A13. *Korea: Assets at Financial Institutions*

	Trillion won			Percentage distribution		
	1970	1980	1990	1970	1980	1990
Deposit money banks	1.989	38.27	173.1	72.10	67.21	42.68
Commercial banks	0.985	24.41	125.4	35.71	43.86	30.93
Specialized banks	1.004	13.87	47.6	36.39	24.35	11.74
Development institutions	0.630	9.43	32.3	22.85	16.55	7.97
Korea Development Bank	0.630	8.84	23.2	22.85	15.52	5.73
Export–Import Bank of Korea	0	0.59	2.7	0	1.04	0.67
Korea Long-Term Credit Bank	0	0	6.4	0	0	1.58
Investment institutions	0	2.43	54.1	0	4.27	13.34
Investment and finance companies	0	1.18	18.2	0	2.07	4.49
Merchant banking companies	0	0.55	5.2	0	0.96	1.28
Investment trust companies	0	0.71	30.6	0	1.24	7.56
Savings institutions	0.103	4.34	96.9	3.73	7.63	23.93
Mutual credits	0.004	0.89	13.8	0.14	1.56	3.41
Mutual savings and finance companies	0	0.53	10.9	0	0.94	2.69
Credits unions	0	0.21	3.6	0	0.36	0.89
Community credit co-ops	0	0.53	7.2	0	0.93	1.77
Trust accounts of banks	0.084	2.08	57.9	3.05	3.66	14.28
Postal savings	0.015	0.10	3.4	0.54	0.18	0.89
Insurance institutions	0.034	1.43	30.5	1.22	2.51	7.51
Life insurance companies	0.014	0.88	26.3	0.50	1.55	6.47
Non–life insurance companies	0.020	0.55	4.2	0.72	0.96	1.04
Securities institutions	0.003	1.04	18.7	0.11	1.82	4.62
Securities companies	0	0.91	15.6	0	1.59	3.85
Korea securities finance companies	0.003	0.13	3.1	0.11	0.23	0.77
Total	2.759	56.943	405.5			

Source: Bank of Korea, *Economic Statistics Yearbook;* Ministry of Finance, *Public Finance and Financial Statistics;* Securities of Supervisory Board, *Monthly Review;* National Credit Union; Federation of Korea, *The Statistics of Credit Unions.* All data for 1985–91 are in Tables 14 to 26 (pp. 30 –56) of the 1992 edition of the *Yearbook* except for securities companies which are in the *Review,* Dec. 1991 (pp. 44 – 45) for all years. For years before 1985, savings institutions data are in *Credit Unions,* 'Mar. 1986 (pp. 13 and 30 – 40), and other data are in various issues of the *Yearbook.*

Table 4.A14. *Korea: Loans and Investments of Financial Institutions*

	Trillion won			Percentage of total		
	1970	*1980*	*1990*	*1970*	*1980*	*1990*
Deposit money banks	0.842	16.86	97.50	75.37	60.98	30.88
Commercial banks	0.478	10.44	64.88	42.80	37.75	20.55
Specialized banks	0.364	6.42	32.62	32.57	23.23	10.33
Development institutions	0.186	4.24	22.52	16.70	15.34	7.13
Korea Development Bank	0.186	3.70	15.36	16.70	13.37	4.87
Export–Import Bank of Korea	0	0.54	2.61	0	1.97	0.83
Korea Long-Term Credit Bank	0	0	4.54	0	0	1.43
Investment institutions	0	2.05	41.58	0	7.42	13.17
Investment and finance companies	0	0.96	12.97	0	3.49	4.11
Merchant banking companies	0	0.48	2.47	0	1.73	0.78
Investment trust companies	0	0.61	26.14	0	2.20	8.28
Savings institutions	0.073	2.49	83.65	6.54	9.00	26.49
Mutual credits	0	0	12.73	0	0	4.03
Mutual savings and finance companies	0	0.48	9.86	0	1.75	3.13
Credit unions	0	0	2.78	0	0	0.88
Community credit cooperatives	0	0	4.88	0	0	1.55
Trust accounts of banks	0.073	2.00	51.80	6.54	7.25	16.40
Postal savings	0	0	1.59	0	0	0.50
Insurance institutions	0.015	1.06	25.19	1.39	3.85	7.98
Life insurance companies	0.009	0.80	22.62	0.79	2.89	7.16
Non–life insurance companies	0.006	0.26	2.58	0.60	0.96	0.82
Securities institutions	0	0.94	45.33	0	3.41	14.35
Securities companies	0	0.82	43.73	0	2.96	13.85
Korea securities finance companies	0	0.12	1.60	0	0.45	0.50
Total	1.117	27.648	315.773			

Note: Loans and investments = Loans and discounts + Due from banks in foreign currency + Securities + Investments.

Source: Bank of Korea, *Economic Statistics Yearbook;* Ministry of Finance, *Public Finance and Financial Statistics;* Securities of Supervisory Board, *Monthly Review;* National Credit Union Federation of Korea, *The Statistics of Credit Unions.* All data for 1985–91 are in Tables 14 to 26 (pp. 30 –56) of the 1992 edition of the *Yearbook* except for securities companies which are in the *Review* 1991 Dec. (pp. 44 – 45) for all years. For years before 1985, savings institutions data are in *Credit Unions,* Mar. 1986 (pp. 13 and 30 – 40), and other data are in various issues of the *Yearbook.*

Table 4.A15. *Korea: Indirect Instruments Issued by Financial Institutions*

	Trillion won				Percentage of total			
	1960	1970	1980	1989	1960	1970	1980	1989
Deposit money banks	0.025	0.79	12.42	84.05	88.6	83.1	70.5	39.5
Commercial	0.019	0.51	7.75	51.17	69.0	53.2	44.0	24.1
Specialized	0.006	0.28	4.67	32.88	19.6	29.9	26.5	14.5
Nonbank financial institutions	0.003	0.16	5.21	128.59	11.4	16.9	29.5	60.5
Development	0.002	0.04	0.17	8.43	6.8	3.8	0.9	4.0
Investment	n.a.	n.a.	1.80	36.26	n.a.	n.a.	10.2	17.1
Savings	0.001	0.09	2.32	55.52	1.8	9.8	13.2	26.1
Insurance[e]	0	0.03	0.92	28.38	2.9	3.2	5.2	13.3
Total	0.028	0.95	17.63	212.6				
Development institutions								
Korea Development Bank	0.002	0.04	0.17	6.03	6.8	3.8	0.9	2.8
Long-Term Credit Bank[a]	n.a.	n.a.	n.a.	2.40	n.a.	n.a.	n.a.	1.1
Investment institutions								
Investment and finance companies[b]	n.a.	n.a.	0.90	8.58	n.a.	n.a.	5.1	4.0
Merchant banking companies[a]	n.a.	n.a.	0.25	1.90	n.a.	n.a.	1.4	0.9
Investment trust companies[c]	n.a.	n.a.	0.63	24.18	n.a.	n.a.	3.6	11.4
Securities finance corporation	n.a.	n.a.	0.02	1.61	n.a.	n.a.	0.1	0.8
Savings institutions								
Trust accounts of banks[d]	0	0.08	1.04	29.17	0.4	8.4	5.9	13.7
Mutual savings and finance	n.a.	n.a.	0.28	8.50	n.a.	n.a.	..ɔ	4.0
Mutual credits	n.a.	n.a.	0.86	13.82	n.a.	n.a.	4.9	6.5
Credit unions	n.a.	n.a.	0.12	2.66	n.a.	n.a.	0.7	1.2
Postal savings	0	0.01	0.01	1.37	1.4	1.5	0.1	0.6
Insurance institutions								
Life insurance companies[e]	0	0.02	0.90	27.17	2.5	2.2	5.1	12.8
Postal life insurance[e]	0	0.01	0.02	1.21	0.4	1.0	0.1	0.5

n.a. Not applicable.

a. Deposits and debentures.

b. Bills issued and cash management accounts (CMAs).

c. Beneficial certificates and security investment savings.

d. Money in trust and security investment in trust.

e. Total assets.

Source: Bank of Korea, *Economic Statistics Yearbook,* various years. For example, the 1990 issue has annual data for these and other financial institutions for 1982–89 on pp. 30–56.

5

Korea: Development and Structural Change of the Banking System

YUNG CHUL PARK AND DONG WON KIM

Commercial banks are business firms engaged in the production and supply of intermediation services between savings-surplus units and spending-deficit units by combining labor, capital, and intermediate inputs. As financial intermediaries, they transform assets and serve as brokers of information. Like their counterparts in advanced economies, Korean commercial banks have undergone financial innovation and structural change in the process of deregulation. They have been transformed into multifaceted institutions supplementing their traditional role with securities business and a variety of fee-based activities considered outside the purview of commercial banking only a few years earlier.

Although there is a large and active curb (unregulated) money market in Korea, deposit money banks (DMBs) account for almost half of the supply of intermediated credit and constitute the core of the nation's payments system. For much of the postwar period until the end of the 1970s, nationwide commercial banks (NCBs) were under the tight control of the monetary authorities, namely, the Ministry of Finance (MOF) and the Bank of Korea (BOK, the central bank). During this period, the banks had only limited autonomy in managing their assets and liabilities and had to follow MOF guidelines and directives even for such internal operational matters as budgeting and staffing. Top managers were always appointed by the government.

Liberalization since the early 1980s has included privatizing of the nationwide commercial banks, lowering barriers to entry into the financial services industry, reducing segmentation of institutions by product and service, and partially deregulating interest rates—starting with rates at nonbank financial intermediaries (NBFIs) and on assets traded in money and capital markets. De facto control of many interest rates still exists, so yields on money market instruments and corporate bonds can respond to changes in market conditions only by moving within a limited range.

Korea has only gradually opened its financial markets to competition, particularly foreign competition. Still, whatever one may say about the macroeconomic effects, financial liberalization will continue in Korea. The internal and

188

external economic environment will not allow the monetary authorities to turn back to the repressive regime of the 1970s.

This chapter analyzes the behavior of commercial banks—particularly the five original nationwide ones— as banking firms, focusing on their pattern of adjustment to the changing financial environment in Korea. In a financially repressive regime such as Korea's until the end of 1970s, the management goal at financial institutions has been to maximize scale or market share, not profits. Have these banks adjusted their growth objective to any degree? Can one observe any improvement in cost-efficiency? These are some of the questions addressed.

The first section discusses the evolution of the regulatory system, while the second examines bank ownership and control. The third section provides an overview of risk taking by the commercial banks, which is then extended in sections analyzing bank asset and liability management. The sixth section looks at the ability of the monetary authorities to handle financial crises, by focusing on the problem of nonperforming loans at nationwide commercial banks. Bank operations, including sources of income, profitability, soundness, and cost-efficiency, are taken up in the seventh section. Table 5.1 provides data on the five NCBs established before 1983, which are the chapter's principal focus of attention.

REGULATION OF THE FINANCIAL SECTOR

Banking regulations may be classified into four types. The first category is entry—forming new banks, opening branches and representative offices, and the like. Regulation of asset and liability management is the second category. The third type is control of interest rates. The fourth relates to control over day-to-day management, including budgetary and personnel matters.

Among the four types of regulation, the objective of the entry and balance sheet types is to preserve the safety and soundness of the banking system, whereas the objective of interest rate and management control is to facilitate government intervention in the allocation of resources through the financial system. In line with the policy change to financial deregulation, formal control of the latter two has been gradually phased out, giving way to prudential supervision of banking institutions with emphasis on monitoring and examining banking activities.

The financial regulatory system in Korea is characterized by multiple regulatory agencies and overlapping jurisdictions. Authority is, in theory, divided between MOF and BOK, but in practice MOF has always assumed the highest regulatory authority.

Structural Regulations

Korea's commercial banks include 13 nationwide commercial banks (NCBs) with large networks of branches, 10 local banks, and 51 foreign bank branches (as of June 1992). Together with 3 specialized banks and the banking activities of 3 cooperative federations, they are classified as deposit money banks (DMBs). Of the 13 NCBs, 5 were founded in the 1980s (including 3 in 1989); Korea Exchange

Table 5.1. Major Nationwide Commerical Banks, 1989

	Commercial	Hanil	Korea First	Chohung	Bank of Seoul
Billion won					
Assets	14,402	12,957	13,270	13,161	12,887
Deposits[a]	6,585	6,775	6,320	6,269	5,464
Shareholder's equity	1,060	1,181	1,120	1,074	1,059
Net income	43.5	77.7	71.3	70.3	60.2
Percent					
Return on assets	0.30	0.60	0.54	0.53	0.47
Return on equity	4.1	6.6	6.4	6.5	5.7
Branches	239	235	232	246	260
Employees	8,550	8,820	8,964	9,146	9,593

Note: Data are as of year-end.

a. Includes deposits in foreign currency and CDs.

Source: Office of Bank Supervision 2nd Examination, *Bank Management Statistics* Oct 1990.

Bank coverted from a specialized bank in 1989; and 2 investment finance companies converted in 1991.

The Monetary Board (MB)—part of BOK—and the Office of Bank Supervision and Examination (OBSE) are responsible for overseeing and examining commercial banks. The MB approves their charters and the opening of their branches and representative offices, the latter on the recommendation of the superintendent of the OBSE. Table 5.2 outlines the domains of the regulatory authorities.

Specialized banks and the NBFIs fall directly in MOF's regulatory domain. Thus, branches of specialized banks are approved by the Minister of Finance. However, limits on staff size and expertise mean MOF's regulatory power and supervisory functions are in part delegated to OBSE and shared with the relevant industry associations. For example, regulation of specialized banks has been delegated to the OBSE. OBSE also examines the investment finance companies (IFCs), merchant banking corporations (MBCs), and mutual savings and finance companies (MSFCs).

Functional Regulations

Trust business at DMBs and investment trust companies (ITCs) has been under the direct supervision and control of MOF. In cooperation with the Securities Supervisory Board, MOF oversees the activities of securities firms and the Korea Stock Exchange. Insurance companies are subject to supervision and examination by the Insurance Supervisory Board and, of course, MOF.

As the BOK's governing body, the MB has the authority to set maximum rates of interest on bank deposits and loans. During the period of financial repression,

Table 5.2. *Supervision and Examination of Financial Institutions, 1990*

Ministry of Finance (MOF)

Office of Bank Supervision and Examination (OBSE)
Commercial banks
Specialized banks (see list in Table 4.2)[a]
Investment and finance companies (IFC)[a]
Merchant banking corporations[a]

Association of Mutual Savings and Finance Companies
Mutual savings and finance companies[a, b]

National Credit Union Federation
Credit unions[b]

Insurance Supervisory Board
Insurance companies (life and nonlife)

MOF directly
Trust business of banks

Securities and Exchange Commission (SEC)[c]

Securities Supervisory Board (SSB)
Securities companies
Korea Securities Dealers Association
Korea Securities Finance Corporation
Transfer agents (3 in Sep. 1992)
Korea Stock Exchange (KSE)[d]

SEC directly
Investment trust companies (ITC)[e]

---

a. Examination delegated by MOF to OBSE.
b. Also directly overseen by MOF.
c. MOF may repeal or suspend SEC resolutions.
d. Self-regulating within context of SEC and SSB regulation of security markets. Structured (from May 1988) as a nonprofit membership organization comprising all securities companies (31 as of Sep. 1992).
e. Examination delegated by MOF to SEC.
Source: More information can be found in BOK, *Financial System in Korea* 1990.

it was customary for MOF to determine deposit and lending rates at practically all financial institutions and to control yields on government and corporate bonds, debentures, and other money market instruments, and these would be duly set by the MB.

The monetary authorities began relaxing control over interest rates in 1981 by deregulating yields on money market instruments, deposit, and lending rates at NBFIs, as well as rates on long-term bonds. This decontrol was extended to the banking sector toward the latter part of 1988 when bank loan rates were decontrolled. Only a few months later, however, the authorities returned to the old regime of directly controlling bank lending rates for reasons of short-run macroeconomic management of the economy.

As for control over asset management, banks are allowed to issue no more than 20 times their net worth in the form of bankers' acceptances and guarantees. Commercial banks are qualified to underwrite stock issues, but so far they have not been allowed to do so. Among measures for bank safety, banks are prohibited from investing in corporate and other bonds with maturities longer than three years or to hold or purchase more than 10 percent of the shares in a single corporation or financial institution. A commercial bank's maximum lending to a single borrower cannot exceed 25 percent of the bank's net worth. The maximum a commercial bank can guarantee or underwrite in the way of securities issued by a single firm is 50 percent of the bank's net worth.

In 1981 MOF abolished the system of directives designed to control the internal management of commercial banks—including such matters as personnel assignment, salary levels, budgeting, and changes in the operational structure. But the monetary authorities still exercise considerable influence over appointment of top managers and even the day-to-day management of banks, through administrative guidance and moral suasion. Moreover, in February 1991 they stepped in to name the presidents of the five major banks.

Evolution of the Regulatory System

The regulatory system went full circle during the four decades after the Republic of Korea was formed in 1948. It began with a system structured primarily to develop market-oriented and sound banking; then it went through a period of repression; and then it reverted to an emphasis on competition and prudential regulation. This section briefly sketches the evolution of the regulatory system.

In 1950 a competitive, independent banking system was artificially grafted onto a war-torn economy dominated by agriculture. The economy had inherited a modern financial system from its colonial ruler, but it did not have the people who could run it. The system was restructured using reforms recommended by Bloomfield and Jensen of the Federal Reserve Bank of New York (1951), who envisioned an autonomous central bank and a privately owned commercial banking system. Consistent with this philosophy, a regulatory system was created basically to protect depositors by safeguarding banks against failure and runs. All one can say is that for the next 10 years the formal financial system functioned, but barely. The outbreak of the Korean War and the rampant inflation and social and political instability that followed constrained the system so much its role was supplanted to a considerable extent by informal money markets.

The military government that came to power in 1961 was determined to overcome the country's underdevelopment by implementing massive government-led programs. Thus, it was hardly prepared to entertain the idea of independent, market-oriented banking. To launch its development programs the new leaders lost no time bringing the banking system under tight government control through a series of measures, thereby opening the era of financial repression.

During the 1950s BOK had not really functioned as an autonomous central bank. In 1962 it was deprived of what formal authority it had as an independent institution, including managing foreign exchange, and it was further subjugated to MOF. The new government also suspended the voting rights of major stockholders in NCBs and repossessed the shares of commercial banks held by large stockholders on the ground they were illegally hoarded properties. At the same time, the superintendent of the OBSE was empowered to approve and dismiss the top managers of the banks. These measures were powerful enough to transform the commercial banks into de facto government agencies engaged in mobilizing financial savings and allocating them to support and carry out government development programs.

The government's domination of the banking system did not stop at controlling the existing commercial banks. During the 1960s, it expanded commercial banking by creating six specialized banks and seven local banks. The specialized banks were under the government's direct control and supervision. They were established to implement sector-specific allocation of resources and to develop specialized financial services such as foreign exchange and housing finance. The local banks were chartered for the purpose of promoting regional development. The government did not own a single share of any of the local banks, but it was able to control them much as it did the NCBs. (Subsequently, a seventh specialized bank and three more local banks were established.)

Repression continued throughout the 1970s. However, during this period, the government undertook a series of reforms aimed at developing NBFIs, fostering money and capital markets, and improving the allocative efficiency of DMBs. These reforms somewhat changed the structure of the regulatory system, but not its nature or purposes.

After a decade of directly managing financial institutions, in the early 1970s the monetary authorities began to realize that a financial system dominated by commercial banking had become too rigid to meet the growing and varied financial needs of an economy whose structure had become much more complex. Many parts of the economy, particularly small and medium firms, had little or no access to formal bank credit.

Much of the bank credit had been allocated to large industrial groups, the *chaebol*. Excessive reliance on intermediated credit, obtained largely from DMBs, made the chaebol highly leveraged and hence extremely vulnerable to cyclical fluctuations. Because each chaebol dealt with several different banks and NBFIs, there was a need to track their borrowing. To monitor their borrowing behavior and restrain their indebtedness to a manageable level, the government introduced a main bank system in 1976.

Chaebol, which we translate as (large) industrial or business groups, come in a wide range of sizes and diversity. The four largest are known worldwide (Samsung, Hyundai, Lucky-Goldstar and Daewoo) and have group sales of more than US $15 billion, making them large even by international standards. But after that, things taper off quickly. Lists in the press and elsewhere generally include 20 or 30 groups; the smallest group on the longer list had 1989 sales of around US $400 million.

In 1972, the monetary authorities made a bold attempt to decrease informal finance and integrate the huge unregulated money markets (UMMs) into the formal financial sector. They did this by decreeing a freeze on the UMMs and then creating a large number of NBFIs. Some of these NBFIs—such as investment finance companies and merchant banking corporations—were designed to take over curb market activities and, in so doing, to supply large firms with short-term working capital beyond what the commercial banking sector was able to provide. Since these new institutions had to compete with curb lenders and credit brokers and to serve as dealers of money market instruments, their success dictated that they be left alone in a competitive market environment. However, the government reneged on its promise of not controlling their lending and borrowing rates. But it did refrain from interfering with the management of their internal affairs.

Mutual savings and finance companies (MSFCs) were created in 1972 by consolidating some of the gray financial institutions operating in the curb market. They were intended to cater to the credit needs of small and medium firms and households. Numbering more than 300 in 1973, they were mostly owned and managed by those engaged in unregulated money market activities as lenders or brokers. This feature, coupled with the difficulty of regulating a large number of small MSFCs, made them prone to bankruptcy and financial fraud, and in general they were quite unstable. Still, the MSFCs enjoyed relative freedom of operation.

In contrast, the primary cooperatives of the national agricultural, fisheries, and livestock cooperative federations have been highly regulated by both MOF and the Ministry of Agriculture and Fisheries. Although organized as credit unions, they have developed into banking units, providing most banking services not only to their members but also to the general public. They are the principal financial institution in most rural areas, although in a country as compact as Korea, one is rarely very far from a DMB branch.

During the 1970s government policies for financial development were directed at improving the efficiency of the banking sector, complementing it with a variety of NBFIs, and fostering money and capital markets. The effects of these policies are difficult to evaluate, but from the point of view of regulation they complicated the task of supervising and examining financial institutions. Responding to this complication, the government created regulatory and semi-regulatory agencies for stock trading and issuing and for insurance. MOF assumed regulatory responsibilities for the NBFIs, but authority was delegated to the OBSE.

The financial liberalization set in motion in the early 1980s has changed the nature and (at least on a micromanagement level) the modus operandi of financial regulation. Requirements for entry have been eased, and OBSE regulations and directives for banks operations have been eliminated or relaxed to give the banks more day-to-day management autonomy. To encourage competition, the walls limiting each type of institution to specific financial markets have to a considerable extent been brought down. As a result, different institutions have been able to offer an increasingly similar array of products and services. Interest rate deregulation, after many years of procrastination, was speeded up in 1988. All in all, liberalization of financial services appears to be on course and moving along, although concerns have been raised about the speed of this process.

To what extent has this process promoted allocative efficiency in the economy and managerial efficiency of financial institutions? How has it changed the role of government in managing the financial system? These questions are discussed in the following sections.

OWNERSHIP AND CONTROL

As part of its liberalization, in 1982 the government began to divest its holdings in the NCBs. Almost three decades earlier the government had made a similar attempt to develop a commercial banking industry run by private shareholders. At that time, however, the shares were acquired by a small number of wealthy businessmen, giving them control of the banks. There was considerable concern that privately owned banks would contribute to the concentration of economic power, so in 1962 the military government took over the shares that the previous government had disposed of.

Under the 1982 rules, there is an 8 percent ceiling on ownership of an NCB by any single individual. This is defined in such a way that a single family or business group is barred from collectively owning more than the prescribed ceiling. The limit reflects ongoing concern over concentration of economic power, as manifested in strong public anathema to control of the banks by the chaebol. However, the holdings of life insurance companies are not included in the 8 percent group-ownership ceiling and the insurance companies own a lot of bank stock (as they do in most countries); the chaebol control the larger insurance companies, and thus it is very common in Korea to assert that the chaebol have significant ownership of the banks. Table 5.3 shows the ownership of the major NCBs.

Boram, one of the two investment finance companies that converted to commercial banks, has chaebol as its three largest stockholders, and their business has helped the bank establish itself quickly. The two converts were not made subject to the 8 percent ownership limit rule.

Not surprisingly, the groups are also large borrowers at banks where they are major stockholders. Under these circumstances, it has seemed obvious to the government that a statutory limitation alone is hardly adequate to keep the chaebol at arm's length from these banks. Perhaps this has given the monetary authorities an excuse for exercising influence beyond what may be considered prudential, in areas such as the appointment of top managers and the lending and borrowing activities of the privatized banks.

Despite the visible progress toward deregulation, there is a widespread perception that the banks remain subservient to MOF and BOK. Traditionally NCBs have relied heavily on central bank rediscounts for loanable funds. BOK is the cheapest source, and for liquidity management it can and does impose quantitative restrictions on the volume of credit extended by NCBs. Given this rationing power, it is hard to imagine the banks' ignoring BOK guidance or wishes. Another reason for the subservient relationship is that all five of the original NCBs are heavily burdened with nonperforming loans. Without BOK and other subsidies, the NCBs might not be able to post reasonable earnings, let alone expand lending and other operations.

Despite visible efforts to minimize the use of finance as a means of industrial policy, NCBs continue to serve as the major channel through which the bulk of policy-directed loans are distributed. Between 30 and 35 percent of the NCBs' loan portfolios in the late 1980s and so far in the 1990s can be classified as policy-directed lending. Because of this large scale of government intervention in

Table 5.3. *Ownership of Nationwide Commercial Banks by Chaebol, 1989* (percent)

Nationwide commercial bank[a]	Samsung	Hyundai	Lucky-Goldstar	Daewoo	Daelim	Shin Dong-ah[b]
Commercial Bank	10.66[c]*	n.r.	n.r.*	n.r.	n.r.	1.27
Hanil	4.69	1.37	2.23	n.r.	3.72*	n.r.
Korea First	5.52	1.29	3.08	n.r.*	5.60	n.r.
Cho Hung	7.64	n.r.	n.r.	n.r.	n.r.	5.97*
Bank of Seoul	3.20	2.17	n.r.	n.r.	n.r.	5.63
Shinhan[d]	n.r.	3.88	4.51	4.56	n.r.	n.r.
KorAm[e]	4.79	n.r.	n.r.	5.63	n.r.	n.r.

n.r. No reported holdings.

* An asterisk indicates the chaebol's "main bank" (as discussed in text). Hyundai's main bank is Korea Exchange Bank.

Note: These are, from left to right, the 4 largest chaebol (by sales) plus Daelim (13th, which is centered on a construction company) and Shin Dong-ah, which owns a lot of bank stock but is not one of the 30 largest chaebol. Various companies within each group, generally insurance companies, actually hold the stock. Samsung Life is the largest shareholder of Commercial and Hanil. Numbers from other sources may vary because of differences in which companies are included as being part of a chaebol.

a. The banks are listed in order of size by total assets. The five largest are the previously government-controlled banks that have been privatized. All seven trade on the Korea Stock Exchange, although it is not possible to determine the size of the float.

b. Includes holdings of Daehan Life Insurance, which is 50% owned by Shin Dong-ah. Daehan is the largest single holder in Korea First, Cho Hung, and Bank of Seoul.

c. Including: Samsung Life 7.58%, An-Kuk Fire Marine 1.87%, Samsung Co Ltd (a trading company) 1.21%.

d. Formed by Korean-Japanese and Koreans in 1982 as the first NCB founded with purely private capital.

e. Opened in 1983 as a joint venture between Bank of America (which initially owned just under 50%) and 10 other Korean companies besides Samsung and Daewoo.

Source: Maeil kyungje (Economic Daily) *1990 Annual Corporation Report.*

bank lending, the commercial banks have found themselves severely constrained in managing their assets. It has been difficult to extricate commercial banks from their preliberalization relationship with the government.

Because of simple inertia and the dependence of the large stockholders of these banks on the government for subsidies and other favors, NCBs have been unable to function as truly independent, privately run institutions.

The local banks, all privately owned and established between 1967 and 1971, are exempt from the 8 percent rule. As a result, local business elites have large shares in most of them, as do, in two cases, major chaebol. However, these large holders are barred from voting more than 8 percent of their stock.

There is no ownership restriction for NBFIs, including securities companies, and many chaebol have a controlling (although not necessarily a majority) interest in one or more of these institutions. For example, in the early 1980s Daewoo took over the then-largest securities firm (Sambo), and in September 1992 Samsung announced it was buying a controlling interest in a midsize broker. Such domination may at least in part explain why the general public has been willing to put up with tight, pervasive control of these institutions by the government for so long.

RISK TAKING BY COMMERCIAL BANKS

Although limited in scope and protracted in implementation, liberalization has helped to change the behavior of commercial banks. The effects deregulation has had on asset and liability management, whether banks have become more conscious about profits, compared to growth of deposits and loans, than they were in the repressive financial environment, and whether they have become more aggressive or conservative regarding risk taking are taken up in this and subsequent sections.

The success of a bank depends on its ability to manage risk. Changes in financial and information technology and liberalization have made it more difficult to manage risk because they have increased competition and multiplied the number of variables.

Financial liberalization, other things being equal, presumably induces commercial banks to take more risk than they would under a repressed financial regime as they move into new areas in competition with already established and experienced firms. The additional risk taking shows up as an increase in the number of bank failures and reduced bank profits. In Korea, however, although it may be too early to tell, there is no hard evidence that liberalization has significantly altered bank risk-taking behavior. There have been no bank failures and no discernible change in profitability or cost efficiency.

Most interest rates, including yields on short- and long-term bonds and money market instruments, have been controlled to varying degrees and have remained relatively stable even after deregulation, so risk due to changes in interest rates has been minimal.

Speculative dealing in foreign exchange and equities has posed a serious problem for bank safety, especially for smaller local banks. In 1989 a local bank almost went bankrupt as a result of large losses from speculative dealing in the forward exchange market.

Many local banks were lured into equity investment by the 1986 – 89 bull market as well as by a paucity of creditworthy borrowers in their localities. In absolute terms, stock holdings of local banks at the end of 1989 were more than 7½ times the level at year-end 1985. The proportion of equity holdings (valued at cost) in their securities portfolios shot from less than 2 percent before 1985 to over 10 percent in 1988 and 1989. Although the extent has not yet been reported, it is obvious that they sustained large losses on their holdings in 1990 and early 1991 when stock prices fell sharply. (When the market value of a specific stock held by a bank falls more than 30 percent from its book value—which is its purchase price—the bank must report the capital loss as an operating expense, even if it makes an overall gain on its securities holdings. In 1992 the Korean market generally (through September) traded in a range of 35 to 50 percent below its peak of 1989, making it likely that there were reportable losses.

The NCBs appear to have been somewhat more restrained in their securities speculation and investment during the stock market boom. Although the absolute amount of their stockholdings increased somewhat during the first two years of the boom, the share of equities in total NCB securities holdings actually declined.

However in 1988–89 the NCB went in with both feet—increasing the absolute amount of their holdings 2½ times and the proportional share by half. They also must have suffered losses from the stock market slide, but their losses are believed to be manageable. This assessment is supported by the fact that during the boom their holdings of securities as a proportion of total assets increased only modestly, going from about 6 percent in 1985 to 7.5 percent four years later. Also, NCBs' stockholdings remain well below the prescribed maximum of 25 percent of their demand deposits. Commercial banks are not allowed to hold more than 10 percent of a firm's shares.

NCBs have always been fully loaned up with little excess reserves. Given the strong demand for loans, they are unlikely to move out of lending in favor of investing in securities, except for managing short-term funds. The NCBs feel the need to nurture long-term relationships with their borrowers and, more important, to maintain and expand their loan market shares.

Liquidity Risk

Liquidity risk as a cause of bank insolvency has never been a serious concern to depositors in Korea. This is true even though there is no deposit insurance system or other institutional arrangements designed to protect depositors. Before the commercial banks were privatized, there was no need for such a system. After all, they were owned and controlled by the government. Even now that the commercial banks all are privately owned, few people entertain the possibility of a bank run. The privatization debate in the early 1980s led to a proposal for creating an institutional arrangement to protect depositors, but the proposal attracted little public support.

The prevailing argument has been that under no circumstances should these banks be allowed to become insolvent because of the significant externalities associated with their functioning and the systemic risk that their insolvency could entail. Indeed, unless absolutely unavoidable, the monetary authorities have been reluctant to let even a small MSFC go bankrupt. Under these circumstances, it has been rather difficult to draw the line between prudential and excessive regulation.

There have been a number of bankruptcies of small MSFCs, but in every case known to the public, depositors were paid the full amount of their deposits by the government, even though it had no legal obligation to do so. This practice has led to the public's belief that the monetary authorities will bail out any bank in trouble.

Assessment

By all accounts, in the 1980s the commercial banks were conservative and cautious about taking risks. This prudence may have been imposed by the government, but it could also in part be attributed to the hangover effect of nonperforming policy loans made when the banks were openly conduits for government-led investment.

Despite the government's continuing interference, there has been a growing consensus that the top managers of commercial banks should be held responsible for performance, at least much more than they were during the repressive regime. As a result, the commercial banks cannot shift blame onto the government for poor performance as readily as before.

Since the late 1980s commercial banks have been encouraged to expand their equity capital in an effort to improve their soundness and competitive strength. The increase in equity capital—which was significant in 1989, aided by the stock market boom—has enhanced the safety of these banks and at the same time may also have decreased the incentives for risk taking.

In the end, however, the conservativeness of commercial banks may simply mean deregulation has not yet been carried out to the point where weeding out inefficient banks is possible. The monetary authorities have yet to face the fact financial efficiency can mean instability.

BANK MANAGEMENT OF LIABILITIES

Changes in the liability structure of NCBs are shown in Table 5.4. The data reveal a number of interesting developments. Deposits of all kinds have always been the main source of loanable funds. The banks were losing out to NBFIs in competing for deposits until the mid-1980s, when their share had fallen below half of the deposit market. Since then their competitive strength has increased, as they have been allowed to market more attractive deposit instruments, so their share has recovered to some extent.

Certificates of deposits (CDs) were initially a lackluster mobilizer of funds. Although created to strengthen the banks' ability to compete with NBFIs in the short-term credit market and to pave the way for interest deregulation, the rates paid on CDs were controlled. The banks also had ceilings on CD issuance determined by BOK on the basis of their net worth and deposit liabilities. Since deregulation of CD interest rates in 1984, they have been used as means of increasing effective lending rates. Commercial banks often issue CDs to their borrowers, who in turn discount them for cash in the open market.

Borrowings from BOK shot up to 21 percent of total liabilities at NCBs in 1985 from a stable level of about 13 percent before. This increase was caused by an infusion of BOK funds related to the rescheduling of debt of bankrupt firms under the government's industrial restructuring scheme. This dependence on BOK declined markedly in the last half of the 1980s as improvement in the current account pumped money into the economy.

The current account surpluses have also been responsible for the marked decline in foreign borrowings by the NCBs. The large increase in their net worth reflects both new stock issues and accumulation of retained earnings since 1986. The increase also reflects successful efforts by the banks to improve their position vis-à-vis foreign financial institutions—including banks, insurance companies, and securities firms. Since the mid-1980s foreign firms have been making up a growing share of Korea's financial markets, as they have been accorded progressively more national treatment in many of the financial services they supply. The prospect of further opening up the money and capital markets beginning in

Table 5.4. *Liabilities and Net Worth of Nationwide Commercial Banks as Percentage of Total Liabilities and Net Worth*

	1975	1980	1985	1989	1990
Domestic liabilities	84.3	86.5	83.0	84.6	85.9
Foreign liabilities	10.2	8.6	12.8	2.4	3.7
Net worth	5.5	4.8	4.2	13.0	10.4
Domestic liabilities					
Deposits	52.7	54.7	49.1	53.2	46.8
CDs	n.a.	n.a.	1.8	1.1	4.5
Borrowings from ROK	13.0	13.9	20.9	10.3	9.8
Foreign currency deposits	7.3	4.8	1.0	6.4	9.5
All else	11.3	13.1	10.2	13.6	15.3
Foreign liabilities					
Borrowings[a]	9.3	8.4	10.3	2.1	2.9
Foreign currency deposits	0.8	0.1	1.9	0.1	0.1
Interoffice and all else	0.1	0.1	0.6	0.2	0.7
Net worth					
Paid-in capital	2.7	2.7	2.6	7.2	6.1
Surpluses	2.8	2.1	1.6	5.8	4.3
Total (billion won)	2,890	11,938	29,772	54,792	83,837

n.a. Not applicable.

Excludes guarantees and acceptances.

a. In foreign currency.

Source: Bank of Korea *Economic Statistics Yearbook.* The 1992 edition (pp. 34–35, Table 15(1)) covers 1982–89.

1991 made bank stocks popular. This, together with the strong stock market in 1988–89, made equity financing available and less expensive than before. At the same time, banks increased retained earnings by restraining dividend payments.

Financial institutions, be they commercial banks or NBFIs, have the same management goal of maximizing the scale or volume of deposits. In a regime in which interest rates are set below a market-clearing level, competition for deposits creates incentives for these institutions to make under-the-table payments to their depositors in cash or in kind to raise effective deposit rates closer to a market-determined level. It is common knowledge that both commercial banks and NBFIs offer their large depositors rates that are higher than the fixed rates or supply services free to compensate for the difference between the market and the fixed deposit rates.

When banks are allowed to do so, nonprice competition often takes the form of creating a variety of financial products differentiated by attributes other than yield. As Table 5.5 shows, the 1980s saw a proliferation of new deposit products issued by commercial banks. They offer seven different kinds of demand deposits and nine types of time and savings deposits, with varying maturities, yields, maximum sizes, and other restrictions. In fact, these instruments have become so similar in their attributes that it is no longer meaningful to distinguish between demand and other deposits. In addition to issuing CDs, during the 1980s the banks were premitted to sell commercial bills that they discount, as well as government and public bonds on repurchase agreements, to market bankers' acceptances, to offer factoring services, and most important, to engage in the money trust business, which has grown into a major activity.

The introduction of new financial products has been one of the consequences of desegmenting the of financial markets—the phenomenon of financial interpenetration—when interest rates are partially deregulated. That is, it has been the result of providing a more level playing field to different institutions, including commercial banks and NBFIs, without freeing interest rates. The proliferation has not been in response to changes in market demand but, rather, has been a bureaucratic response to maintaining a competitive balance between the commercial banks and the NBFIs.

Indeed, the process of creating new products and services has been disturbing. It often begins with the commercial banks' complaining of erosion in their competitive position and pressuring the monetary authorities to allow them to market more attractive instruments that could help restore their position in relation to the NBFIs in mobilizing funds. After a while, MOF and BOK usually succumb by permitting a new product with an effective yield, adjusted for risk and convenience, higher than those on existing similar products. Then comes demand and pressure mounted by the NBFIs to offset the competitive advantage they believe the commercial banks obtained by providing a new service. This game between the commercial banks and NBFIs has continued into the 1990s.

One could argue this is the incremental way liberalization occurs when the approach is piecemeal. But, product proliferation has not built up pressure for the decontrol of interest rates, which is the critical requirement for successful financial liberalization.

The multiplication of new products without interest rate deregulation has been the major cause of the large and often volatile shifts of funds among a large number of differentiated products, and for this reason it is not clear whether the expansion of the financial product menu has helped encourage financial savings. For example, commercial banks are allowed to issue money market instruments in direct competition with NBFIs. However, rates on CDs, repurchase agreements, and commercial bills have been kept in line with bank deposit rates, and well below the market rates on similar instruments issued by the NBFIs. As a result, the amount of loanable funds commercial banks have mobilized through issuing money market instruments has been small and declining relative to their total deposits. Table 5.6 gives data on money market instruments issued by NCBs.

Perhaps the most disturbing development from the point of view of financial deregulation has been the massive growth of money trusts at commercial banks. Local banks were first authorized to offer trust accounts in 1983, followed by

Table 5.5. Financial Products and Services Introduced in the 1980s

1980	Jan.	Securities savings for employees (securities companies)
	Feb.	Repurchase agreements (securities companies)
	Sep.	Credit cards (Citizen National Bank)
		Factoring (merchant banks)
1981	May	Factoring (IFCs)
	Jun.	Household checking (banks)
		Commerical paper (Seoul-area IFCs)
	Nov.	Beneficiary certificates for foreigners (investment trusts)
1982	May	Credit cards (nationwide commercial banks)
	Sep.	Sales of commerical bills (banks)
	Nov.	Repurchase agreements (banks)
1983	Feb.	Factoring (banks)
	Mar.	Repurchase agreements (post office)
	Apr.	Mutual installment deposits and loans (local banks)
	May	Money in trust (local banks)
	Sep.	Loans with securities as collateral (securities companies)
1984	Feb.	Money in trust (nationwide commercial banks)
	Mar.	International factoring (IFCs)
		Commerical paper (IFCs outside Seoul and securities companies)
		Commerical paper of small and medium firms (IFCs and merchant banks)
		Cash management accounts (CMAs) (large IFCs)
	Jun.	Certificates of deposit (CDs) (banks)
		CD brokerage (IFCs, merchant banks, and securities companies)
		CMAs (all IFCs)
1985	Mar.	Money in trust for households (banks)
	Apr.	Preferential savings accounts (banks)
		Preferential installment savings deposits for households (banks)
	Sep.	Money in trust (foreign banks)
1986	Sep.	Certificates of deposit (foreign banks)
1987	Jan.	Pension in trust for retirement (banks)
	Sep.	Money in trust for corporations (banks)
		Bond management funds (securities companies)
	Dec.	Savings deposits for housing for employees (banks)
1988	Feb.	Savings deposits for the purchase of "people's stocks"[a]
	May	"People's stocks" in trust
		Large-denomination repurchase agreements
		Preferential savings accounts for firms

a. People's stocks are shares of public enterprises held by the government that were sold to the general public.

other commercial banks the next year. The business of money in trust is the most important nonbank financial activity commercial banks have been allowed to move into. It includes nonspecific, development, household, and corporate types of trust accounts.

Returns on these trusts should correspond to the returns from the assets in which trust funds are invested, adjusted for the management costs. That is, they should shift risk to the trust beneficiaries. However, the banks offer fixed rates on them. Furthermore, in the case of household and corporate money trusts, ben-

Table 5.6. *Money Market Instruments Issued by Nationwide Commercial Banks*
(billion won and percent)

	Certificates of deposit	Commercial bills	Repurchase agreements	Total	As % of deposits	As % of assets
1982	n.a.	76.4	n.a.	76.4	0.7	0.4
1983	n.a.	60.8	n.a.	60.8	0.5	0.3
1984	490.0	57.8	n.a.	547.8	4.0	2.1
1985	533.5	42.5	n.a.	576.0	3.9	1.9
1986	685.5	18.0	597.5	1301.0	8.1	4.0
1987	669.7	2.7	426.5	1098.9	5.4	2.8
1988	596.3	6.4	264.2	866.9	3.2	1.9
1989	609.0	0.4	72.5	681.9	2.3	1.2

n.a. Not applicable.

Note: None of these instruments is classed as a deposit, which means none are part of the denominator of their total as a percentage of deposits.

Source: Bank of Korea, *Economic Statistics Yearbook*, pp. 34–35, Table 15 (1), except for CBs and RP.

eficiaries are free to withdraw any amount they wish at any time. These accounts are in fact indistinguishable from other deposit liabilities, except that they pay higher interest rates, so it would not be surprising if much of the growth of the trust business has been at the expense of the growth of other deposits at commercial banks. Nevertheless, the trusts are not subject to reserve requirements and hence are excluded from M2. Tables 5.7 and 5.8 have data on the trusts.

In Japan, money trust is a mechanism designed to secure longer-term funds for banks by paying higher yields to individual savers. The trust business was introduced in part for the same purpose in Korea, but mostly for strengthening the competitive position of commercial banks in relation to other financial institutions.

Table 5.7. *Volume of Trust Accounts as a Percentage of Total Deposits at Commercial Banks*

	1983	1985	1988	1989	1990
All	10.1	16.8	26.3	30.7	29.8
Five Nationwide	12.2	17.7	26.3	31.5	31.8
Shinhan and Koram	n.a.	13.3	41.9	41.4	36.8
Local	5.7	14.2	18.9	20.5	18.6

n.a. Not applicable.

Note: Total deposits = Deposits in won + Deposits in foreign currency + Mutual installment deposits + CDs + Money in trust

Source: Bank of Korea, *Statistics of Bank Management* 1991 (pp. 132–35).

Table 5.8. *Trust Accounts of Nationwide Commercial Banks*

	1983	1985	1987	1988	1989
Money in trust (billion won)					
Total	1,574	3,065	7,645	11,562	16,002
Household	n.a.	623	1,088	1,464	2,871
Corporate	n.a.	n.a.	1,932	3,402	4,405
Household and corporate as % of total in trust	n.a.	20.3	39.5	42.1	45.5
Distribution of tust account assets as % of trust assets					
Loans	71.8	73.7	51.6	38.7	35.3
Loans to banking accounts	6.5	8.7	3.7	2.0	3.1
Stocks	0.9	1.9	2.6	5.1	8.7
Bonds	8.4	6.1	29.8	17.4	18.8
Other securities	5.8	7.7	10.4	34.0	27.2
All else	6.6	1.9	1.9	2.9	6.9
Trust assets in billion won	1,574	3,077	7,835	12,138	18,135

n.a. Not applicable.

Source: Bank of Korea, *Statistics of Bank Management*, Oct. 1990. The *Economic Statistics Yearbook* has data for all banks (e.g., 1990 edition p. 55, for 1982–89).

ASSET MANAGEMENT

Table 5.9 presents an asset profile of NCBs for selected years since 1975. Loans and discounts, including foreign currency loans, have accounted for the bulk of commercial bank assets—from 51 to 54 percent. Cash items (which include checks and bills) more than tripled between 1975 and 1985. This jump reflects the growing use of checks for transactions. Domestic "due from" items—deposits with BOK and other banks, plus National Investment Funds (NIF)— varied a great deal, largely reflecting changes in reserve requirements and monetary policy. The volume of foreign assets declined substantially, largely because of decreased relending of borrowings from foreign banks secured by the NCBs. The share of securities holdings (which include stocks, debentures, and government bonds) grew rapidly in part due to increased holdings of monetary stabilization bonds (MSBs) but also because of increases in equity investment induced by the late 1980s boom in the stock market.

Lending Behavior

Lending rates at DMBs were partially deregulated toward the end of 1988. Since then banks can in theory charge different interest rates on loans to different borrowers on the basis of their creditworthiness, and they can vary their lending rates with changes in the demand and supply of loanable funds. In practice, however, rates have been set by the major DMBs in consultation with the monetary author-

Table 5.9. *Assets of Nationwide Commerical Banks*

	1975	1980	1985	1989	1990
Total (billion won)	2,890	11,938	29,772	54,792	83,837
Distribution as % of total assets					
Domestic	86.0	87.9	89.5	94.3	93.5
Foreign	14.0	12.1	10.5	5.7	6.5
Domestic as % of total assets					
Cash (checks and bills)	5.1	13.0	15.5	18.4	20.4
Due from banks	19.5	7.0	6.5	7.3	4.2
Securities	3.3	5.6	5.8	7.5	9.8
Loans and discounts	48.3	49.5	50.0	47.8	39.8
Loans in foreign currency	3.7	4.9	1.6	3.6	7.1
Fixed assets	3.0	3.5	4.2	3.6	3.3
All else	3.1	4.4	5.9	6.1	8.9
Foreign as % of total assets					
Foreign currency[a]	4.2	8.7	5.8	3.9	4.6
Due from banks[b]	9.5	2.6	2.3	0.8	0.7
Inter-office	0.3	0.7	2.3	0.1	0.2
All else	0.0	0.1	0.1	0.9	1.0

Note: Excludes guarantees and acceptances.
a. And bills bought.
b. In foreign currency.
Source: Bank of Korea, *Economic Statistics Yearbook.* The 1992 edition (pp. 34–35, Table 15(1)) covers 1982–89.

ities. For this reason, rates have been stable, similar among banks, and lower than those prevailing in money and capital markets. These rate differentials have generated a chronic excess demand for bank loans, and banks in turn have had to ration credit.

Banks have raised effective lending rates by charging up-front fees or by requiring their borrowing customers to maintain compensating balances. These practices can add 2 or 3 percentage points to the cost of a loan and may be used to screen borrowers on an ability-to-pay basis—a very rough proxy for creditworthiness. The extra income is used to attract deposits by paying more than what is allowed.

Increased competition resulting from deregulation may have changed the collateral policy and also strengthened the commercial banks' ability to assess the credit of their borrowing customers. Because of the nonavailability of data, it has not been possible to determine whether banks actually have devoted more resources to improving credit analysis. However, they have considerably relaxed their policy of requiring real asset collateral. As shown in Table 5.10, the share of DMB loans and discounts extended without real-asset collateral rose to almost half of DMB total lending in 1987 from about 30 percent in 1980.

This increase may in part reflect the effects of intensified competition or a

Table 5.10. Loans and Discounts of Commercial Banks by Type of Collateral

	1970	1975	1980	1985	1987	1989
Total (billion won)	389	1,645	6,861	17,788	21,287	31,900
Cases (thousands)	132	216	411	959	1,026	1,536
Type of collateral						
Distribution of amount (%)						
Real estate	61.8	48.7	54.6	44.8	40.6	42.7
Deposits	5.6	8.6	7.0	5.6	5.6	5.4
Other[a]	5.2	7.9	7.5	5.7	4.5	5.2
None[b]	27.5	34.9	30.8	43.8	49.2	46.7
Distribution of cases (%)						
Real estate	47.0	55.2	55.0	42.9	40.7	38.3
Deposits	11.3	12.2	9.3	9.4	12.1	10.5
Other[a]	3.8	2.1	1.9	1.2	1.2	7.4
None[b]	38.0	30.5	33.8	46.5	15.9	43.8

Note: Excludes trust accounts and foreign banks, as well as Daedong, Dongnam, and Dongwha banks, which were established in 1989. For 1970 and 1975 data are for Sep. 30; subsequent data are for Dec. 31.

a. Includes government bonds, stocks, debentures, etc., and other personal property.

b. Includes loans guaranteed by the Korea Credit Guarantee Fund, etc.

Source: Bank of Korea, *Economic Statistics Yearbook*. Data for 1977–89 are in the 1990 edition, p. 64, Table 31 (3).

response to the government's long-standing policy of replacing collateral requirements with better credit analyses and loan portfolio diversification. In our view, however, the increase has been mostly the consequence of the relative growth of policy loans that are not backed by any real-asset collateral.

Estimated Loan Supply Equation

We have examined the lending behavior of DMBs and NBFIs by estimating a somewhat ad hoc loan supply equation for eight manufacturing industries (2-digit classification) for 1974–87 and 1980–87. The model and results are presented in Tables 5.11 and 5.12.

Export performance and leverage are important determinants in bank credit allocation. Contrary to expectation, profitability and our proxy for collateral (the ratio of the industry's fixed real assets to its total bank borrowings), both expected to be positively correlated with lending, have either wrong signs or are statistically insignificant for both the entire and the subperiods. These variables appear to be more significant in the case of the NBFIs, however.

For what it is worth, our results imply financial liberalization has not altered the lending behavior of financial intermediaries to any significant degree. In a competitive environment, it is likely that the viability of investment projects would be one of the most important considerations for making loan decisions, but

Table 5.11. *Deposit Money Bank Loans*

	Constant	FBL (T–1)	NP (T–1)	DEBT (T–1)	ER (T–1)	LOAN (T–1)	R^2	DW
1974–87	3.127	–0.330	0.013	–0.0002	0.291	n.a.	0.19	1.97
	(29.2)	(–3.52)	(0.61)	(–2.72)	(3.34)			
	1.504	0.229	–0.35	–0.00002	0.065	0.727	0.82	1.21
	(4.81)	(3.85)	(–2.67)	(–0.46)	(1.25)	(20.0)		
	7.607	–0.342	–0.033	–0.00017	n.a.	–0.001	0.06	1.31
	(0.23)	(–2.42)	(–1.12)	(–1.85)		(–0.29)		
1980–87	6.437	–0.302	0.071	–0.0001	0.468	n.a.	0.47	1.98
	(38.1)	(–3.14)	(2.82)	(–2.09)	(5.11)			
	4.493	–0.019	0.019	–0.00009	0.359	0.245	0.50	1.80
	(4.84)	(–0.11)	(0.56)	(–1.55)	(3.40)	(1.96)		
	7.112	–0.747	0.104	–0.140	n.a.	0.105	0.42	1.82
	(39.4)	(–5.56)	(3.59)	(–2.28)		(4.48)		

n.a. Not applicable.

Note: Figures in parenthesis are *t* values.

In our specification, the share of the *i*th industry in total bank lending to the manufacturing sector; *Li*, is assumed to depend on the rate of profit (*NP*) measured by current profits divided by total capital, the ratio of total debt to paid-in capital (*DEBT*), total exports as a percentage of output (*ER*), and the ratio of fixed real assets to total bank borrowings (*FLB*) in the *i*th manufacturing industry (*FBL*).

FLB is used as a proxy for the collateral requirement and *DEBT* measures the degree of leverage. The sign of the coefficient of *FLB* is expected to be positive whereas that of *DEBT* is negative.

The estimation includes 8 manufacturing industries (2-digit classification). We estimated this equation using pooled cross-section time series data for the 1974–87 and 1980–87. We ran a similar test for the behavior of NBFIs.

our results do not support this view. Does this mean the extent of financial liberalization has been much less than it is claimed to be? Or should we question the reliability of our results?

The Main Bank System

The repressive financial regime institutionalized in the early 1960s and maintained for the following 20 years may have contributed to launching and then sustaining the export-led development strategy by supporting the government's allocation policy. However, some of the problems of a rigid system began to surface by the end of the 1970s. One of the monetary authorities' major concerns was the heavy reliance of Korea's major industrial groups on indirect financing—in particular, bank lending—which raised the leverage of these groups to dangerous levels, making them highly susceptible to business downturns.

Another concern was that a large proportion of bank finance was absorbed by some 20 of the largest chaebol, leaving very little for small and medium firms and other borrowers. The concentration of bank lending to chaebol was regarded as a cause of the concentration of economic power in chaebol hands, which is a major political issue. A third concern relates to management of bank lending,

Table 5.12. Nonbank Financial Institution Loans, 1980–87

Constant	FBL (T–1)	NP (T–1)	DEBT (T–1)	ER (T–1)	LOAN (T–1)	R^2	DW
3.940	0.116	0.107	–0.0002	0.430	n.a.	0.51	1.73
(29.5)	(1.01)	(3.83)	(–2.47)	(4.22)			
2.828	0.376	0.026	–0.00012	0.314	0.268	0.61	1.84
(6.72)	(3.00)	(0.76)	(–2.10)	(3.24)	(3.62)		
6.103	–0.141	0.132	–0.00016	n.a.	–0.005	0.40	1.42
(26.9)	(–0.86)	(3.79)	(–2.13)		(1.71)		

n.a. Not applicable.

Note: Figures in parenthesis are *t* values.

In our specification, the share of the *i*th industry in total bank lending to the manufacturing sector; *Li*, is assumed to depend on the rate of profit (*NP*) measured by current profits divided by total capital, the ratio of total debt to paid-in capital (*DEBT*), total exports as a percentage of output (*ER*), and the ratio of fixed real assets to total bank borrowings (*FLB*) in the *i*th manufacturing industry (*FBL*).

FLB is used as a proxy for the collateral requirement, and *DEBT* measures the degree of leverage. The sign of the coefficient of *FLB* is expected to be positive whereas that of *DEBT* is negative.

The estimation includes 8 manufacturing industries (2-digit classification). We estimated this equation using pooled cross-section time series data for the 1974–87 and 1980–87. We ran a similar test for the behavior of NBFIs.

including improving the allocative efficiency of policy-directed loans. Each chaebol usually consists of a number of manufacturing firms and their subsidiaries and affiliates. These firms have had access not only to bank loans but also to NBFI lending. As the number of firms in an industrial group increased as each group was expanding rapidly in the early 1970s, there was a critical need for information about the groups' indirect financing behavior.

To rectify these maladies of financial repression, the monetary authorities began monitoring—and in 1974 taking measures to restrain—the flow of bank credit to the large industrial groups. These measures were followed by introducing guidelines for implementing a main bank system in 1976. According to the guidelines, all chaebol, including related enterprises, with a total credit volume of 100 billion won or more (including acceptances and guarantees) from all financial institutions were required to participate in a main bank system.

Initially, all banks with loans to the larger groups were asked to assign a main bank to each group after consulting among themselves and with the respective groups. The main bank was then given a broad range of authority. It monitors and offers advice on all business activities, including borrowing and liability management. The main bank is also authorized to approve new investments, equity participation, mergers, and real estate acquisition plans. The monitoring role could place the banks in a powerful position, as they can obtain access to significant confidential financial and business information. In reality, however, the monitoring has been superficial and passive. Indeed, it has involved little more than collecting data that are forwarded to the Office of Bank Supervision. With these data, OBS controls the credit allocated to chaebol.

The main bank system has been complemented by a series of more direct measures aimed at preventing any further concentration of bank credit to chaebol. If deemed necessary, the superintendent of the OBSE can put a ceiling on the amount of additional credit that can be extended to any group. Banks and NBFIs are required to form a loan syndicate to meet a large credit demand by an industrial group.

In 1988, 177 enterprises with outstanding bank credit of more than 20 billion won were required to repay 10 percent of their debts. In 1989, the major chaebol were forced to reduce their bank credit by 5 to 10 percent, depending on their leverage and subject to a credit ceiling equal to their 1988 level.

How effective have these measures been in bringing about broader credit allocation? We do not have precise official statistics for the amounts and sources of borrowings of the large business groups. According to newspaper reports, however, it appears these measures have succeeded in reducing concentration. (See Table 5.13 for some of the details).

NONPERFORMING LOANS AT NCBs

Although no one knew (or wanted to know) the precise magnitude of the problem, in the early 1980s it was an open secret that Korea's commercial banks were awash in a sea of nonperforming loans that was growing day by day and which they could not write off. Some estimates were made in 1984 when the banks did begin to write them off. It became clear that if the normal criteria for a sound bank were applied, most of the banks were insolvent. At the end of 1984, according to BOK estimates, nonperforming loans at the five NCBs were close to 11 percent of their total loans and 2.6 times their total net worth. Since then the ratio has come down substantially, perhaps to a manageable level. The causes of the nonperforming loan problem are so complex they require a case study of their own. Much of the information needed for a careful study, including reliable data, are not available; here we are piecing together what information and statistics have become available.

Between May 1986 and February 1988, the Korean government designated 57 individual distressed enterprises for restructuring as part of its industry rationalization scheme. The government also took measures to restructure and rationalize the two most troubled industries—shipping and overseas construction— involving another 21 firms. When the government began surgery on these troubled firms, all on the verge of bankruptcy, their borrowings from financial institutions—mostly from DMBs—stood at 9,782 billion won, or 25 percent of total DMB loans and discounts. About 74 percent of these loans had to be rescheduled or written off. Some of the loans were assumed by firms that took over operations of the restructured firms, and others were classified as "recoverable."

What firms were insolvent, and how did they get into trouble? What was the government's policy response in the face of the growing insolvency problems? Of the 78 firms, 16 belonged to the Kukje group, one of the 10 largest chaebol at the time of its dissolution in February 1985 following its default on loan payments. In terms of industrial classification, some firms belonged to declining industries such as textiles and plywood, others were engaged in heavy industrial

Table 5.13. *Credit Extended to Major Chaebol as a Share of Total Credit*
(percent)

	1987[a]	1988	1989
Bank credit[b]			
Loans to			
Five major chaebol[c]	12.37	9.46	7.20
Thirty major chaebol	20.82	18.30	14.67
Total credit[d] to			
Five major chaebol[e]	13.40	11.13	8.37
Thirty major chaebol	24.43	23.25	18.29
Nonbank credit[d]			
Loans to			
Five major chaebol[c]	18.42	18.85	—
Thirty major chaebol	39.70	38.84	—
Total credit[d] to			
Five major chaebol[c]	17.62	17.28	—
Thirty major chaebol	37.88	36.50	42.1

— Not available.

Note: For comparison, in 1988 sales of the top 5 equaled 68% of the sales of the top 30, according to an Office of Bank Supervision and Examination (OBSE) survey. Thus, among the top 30, the second 25 have proportionately more credit than the top 5.

a. 1987 data for banks are as of Oct. 31. All other data are year-end.

b. Deposit money banks (DMBs), the Industrial Bank of Korea, the Citizens National Banks, the National Aricultural Cooperative Federation, the National Federation of Fisheries Cooperatives, and the National Livestock Cooperatives Federation.

c. The five largest, by sales are Samsung, Hyundai, Lucky–Goldstar, Daewoo, and Sunkyong.

d. Total credit is loans plus acceptances and guarantees issued.

e. Nonbanks include investment and finance companies, merchant banking corporations, and life insurance companies.

Source: Bank of Korea. BOK has been submitting to the National Assembly reports on the amount of credit extended to the 30 largest chaebol, and these are reported in the English-language press in Korea.

and chemical manufacturing (the HC industries). The most seriously troubled ones were in shipping and overseas construction.

Declining industries are not unique to Korea and include, as elsewhere, those unable to adjust to changes in comparative advantage. The HC industry enterprises were in part victims of the government's ambitious and reckless promotion in the 1970s. It appears firms jumped into investment in these industries with little understanding of the nature of the markets for these products but with the belief they would be supported to the end by the government.

Overseas construction firms, with business concentrated in the Middle East, saw their foreign contracts begin to dwindle in 1981 and then their earnings plummet, largely because of the drop in oil prices. Shipping is another industry that suffered from an ambitious government development plan and a sudden shift in the market. Beginning in 1976 shipping firms were encouraged to expand tonnage. Within four years they almost doubled capacity, to 5.2 million gross tons, by purchasing old and inefficient vessels with funds borrowed abroad and guaranteed by various DMBs. Following the second oil crisis in 1979, the volume of world trade, and thus of shipping, fell sharply. Unprepared for the downturn, these firms sustained huge losses and were faced with enormous debt they could not service.

Who should be blamed for the accumulation of nonperforming loans? Much of the blame must fall on the government. With tax and bank loan subsidies, it initiated and encouraged investment in many industries where Korea did not have comparative advantage in. The banks extended loans, acceptances, and guarantees. Even though they did so involuntarily, they should be held partly responsible because they did not carefully analyze the industries or the credit risks of their borrowers and they did not monitor the activities of their clients. In short, they did not try to make a bad situation less bad. The borrowers also must bear a large part of the blame. They plunged into new industries and investment without any experience or adequate preparation—like crass opportunists, not entrepreneurs or even competent managers—their only excuse was that if not they, then someone equally unqualified.

Korea's industrial restructuring problem had many causes. Unexpected changes in world market conditions and the slow adjustment to changes in comparative advantage by Korean industries were important ones. At the same time, the difficulties of adjustment were exacerbated by the moral hazard associated with government-led industrial development—the expectation the government will pay for the mistakes.

In executing the industrial restructuring program, the troubled firms' financial difficulties were directly shifted to the banks that had extended loans and issued guarantees. This was done in order to minimize the adverse effects on the economy from the restructuring. These loans became nonperforming and threatened not only the soundness of the banks concerned but also the stability of the financial system as a whole.

In managing the problems of the troubled firms, the government had three options. One alternative, the most drastic, was simply to declare the firms bankrupt and to reschedule and write off their debts. Another option was to continue to support them by infusing new credit in the hope they would soon recover. A third alternative was to sell the firms to third parties.

The first option was never seriously considered because of its contagion effects. Bankruptcy of these badly run enterprises was seen as certain to cause the insolvency of affiliates and subcontractors in the chain of industrial linkages. And the economic effects and social unrest from a domino effect were more than the government felt it could bear—it was the ultimate domino. But even short of a complete collapse, as an export-oriented economy, the spread of insolvency throughout the economy could damage the credibility and viability of Korean industries to an irreparable degree.

A key domino early in the chain—and thus the most serious immediate problem—was that bankruptcy of badly managed firms would lead to bankruptcy of most of the major banks, which would in turn cause a financial panic, not to mention damage Korea's international creditworthiness at a time when the country was burdened with more than $45 billion of foreign debt.

The government instituted a policy combining the second and third options, but initially opting more toward the second. Until the mid 1980s, the government kept supporting troubled firms and had the banks carry the bad loans on their books, hoping that at least some of the enterprises would recover and eventually pay off their debts. However, as hope for such a recovery dwindled, the volume of nonperforming loans at the banks grew. The troubled firms needed so much additional credit to stay alive that the banks could not maintain their normal lending to healthy firms. To relieve banks of the burden of nonperforming loans, the government implemented an industrial restructuring plan. The government's intention was to spread the actual and potential losses as widely as possible throughout the economy and to absorb these losses gradually over time to minimize the adverse impact of the restructuring.

The government first identified the troubled firms to be restructured, and then chose the takeover firms or groups. After scrutinizing the value of an insolvent firm's assets and liabilities, the conditions for the takeover were agreed to by the takeover firm and the main bank of the troubled firm. Usually, these included a tax subsidy and a rescheduling of the debt, which involved reducing the principal, forgoing and deferring interest, and providing fresh credit.

The rescheduled debts were then taken out of the category of nonperforming loans at the banks. At the same time, the banks were subsidized by BOK to compensate for some of their losses. At the end of 1987 BOK–subsidized loans to these banks amounted to more than 3 trillion won at interest rates of 3 to 6 percent per annum.

The third parties were often healthy companies in the same chaebol as the troubled firm. In such cases, the chaebol as a group had to absorb a significant share of the losses from the restructuring. Daewoo and its shipbuilding affiliate are perhaps the best publicized of these.

Two tables have been prepared showing estimates of nonperforming loans at NCBs. Table 5.14 shows loans classed as substandard, doubtful, assumed total loss, and an "especially mentioned" category (loans requiring more surveillance than the customary monitoring, according to the OBSE definition). These four groups of loans, which includes those accorded reduction and deferral of interest payments under the industry-restructuring scheme, accounted for more than 20 percent of NCB total credit in 1987. Including only the substandard, doubtful, and total loss categories, nonperforming loans were over 12 percent of NCB total credit. These numbers had fallen somewhat by the end of June 1988, the most recent data available.

Table 5.15 shows that nonperforming loans emerged as a serious threat to the soundness of Korea's commercial banks in 1981 when the ratio shot up to 7.25 percent of their total credit. After restructuring began in 1986 the ratio started down, falling below 6 percent in 1989. The data show the government kept supporting

Table 5.14. *Loans at the Five Major Nationwide Commercial Banks*
(billion won)

	1984	1986	1988	1989	1990
Total	284.4	348.0	367.5	440.0	534.3
Sound	225.4	259.6	344.3	423.7	520.2
Mentioned[a]	27.1	49.3	n.a.	n.a.	n.a.
Nonperforming	31.9	39.2	23.2	16.4	14.1
Nonperforming by type					
Substandard	8.9	9.7	n.a.	n.a.	n.a.
Doubtful	20.2	25.1	14.3	8.2	7.3
Estimated loss	2.8	4.4	8.9	8.2	6.8
Net worth	11.4	13.4	27.9	54.9	57.3
Nonperforming loans as a % of total loans	11.2	11.3	6.3	3.7	2.6
Nonperforming loans as a % of net worth	279.1	292.3	83.3	29.8	24.5

n.a. Not applicable.
a. Especially mentioned (see text explanation) not separately listed after Jun. 1988.

troubled firms for more than five years after their problems became obvious, thereby postponing the unavoidable restructuring. The result was simply to worsen the problem.

It is difficult to estimate the direct and indirect costs to the economy of the industrial restructuring. In 1987 alone, NCBs sustained losses amounting to 451 billion won stemming from restructuring nonperforming loans, twice their total profits that year. They received a subsidy of 189 billion won from BOK and absorbed the reminder. The effects of the restructuring on the economy could have been more severe if the economy had not rebounded in the late 1980s.

In 1986 few believed the restructuring would rescue the troubled firms and banks. Many thought restructuring was no more than temporary debt relief for the parties concerned, that it would contaminate the takeover firms, and in the end, that the government would fall deeper into the debt quagmire. Korea was, however, saved from the misery many people feared. Beginning in 1987, the economy entered an upswing phase lasting three consecutive years. Average annual growth was more than 12 percent. Many of the restructured firms not only managed to cut their perennial losses, they began posting profits. The shipping industry, once written off as hopeless, rebounded and became healthy.

The commercial banks have also benefited from the economic boom. The nonperforming loans are no longer considered a serious problem, and the available data support this view. With hefty profits, the banks have accumulated enough reserves and retained earnings to write off a large fraction of the remaining bad loans.

Table 5.15. *Nonperforming Loans as a Percentage of Total Banks Loans*

Year	NCBs	Local Banks		Year	NCBs	Local Banks
1962	0.50	n.a.		1976	2.87	1.46
1963	0.40	n.a.		1977	1.67	1.35
1964	0.20	n.a.		1978	1.08	1.43
1965	0.10	n.a.		1979	3.43	4.63
1966	0.10	n.a.		1980	2.74	8.89
1967	0.00	0.00		1981	7.25	6.85
1968	0.00	0.00		1982	6.95	5.51
1969	9.60	0.00		1983	8.57	6.90
1970	1.51	0.37		1984	10.85	8.47
1971	2.46	0.14		1985	10.22	8.18
1972	2.24	0.47		1986	10.53	8.54
1973	0.92	0.02		1987	8.42	7.36
1974	0.63	0.03		1988	7.44	6.16
1975	0.40	0.04		1989	5.86	4.11

n.a. Not applicable.

Note: Figures prior to 1976 exclude substandard loans.

This table differs somewhat from Table 5.14 because of a few differences in coverage of total credit and the fact it does not count the especially mentioned category as nonperforming loans.

Source: BOK Research Department for Kim 1990.

Does Korea's experience provide a model for other developing countries? The answer is a definite no. As they did during the first oil crisis, Korean policymakers took a gambler's approach to restructuring. They attempted to grow out of the problem, as they had tried to grow out of the oil crisis. In both cases they succeeded. So how should one evaluate Korea's approach to restructuring? The policymakers were lucky. In each case, an upturn in the world economy rescued the Korean economy from potentially disastrous consequences.

OPERATIONAL EFFICIENCY OF COMMERCIAL BANKS

Measured by several standard indicators, it is clear commercial banking has not been as profitable in Korea as it is in some other countries. The ratio of net profits to total assets of Korea's five NCBs in 1988 was one-sixth that of foreign bank branches in Korea and one-third that of U.S. banks. The picture is the same when the ratio of net profits to net worth is used. Table 5.16 presents another interesting development in commercial banking: Its profitability decreased before turning up in 1987. Is this phenomenon related in any way to financial deregulation?

During the period of financial repression, it is not an exaggeration to say that the commercial banks were little more than government agencies delegated the tasks of mobilizing savings and allocating them according to directives and guidelines issued by the government. The government maintained a controlling interest in the NCBs and exercised this control by appointing the top managers and interfering with asset and liability management. Bank managers were rewarded and promoted on the basis of the growth of deposits, not on overall balance sheet and income statement performance.

Under these circumstances it is of little interest to discuss cost-efficiency and profitability of individual banks, simply because the government was not concerned about profitability, or even safety, as much as private owners would be. Occasionally, the government would voice concern about management efficiency—usually when the banks could not make adequate dividend payments or when their international creditworthiness was at stake. But the government predictably responded to the situation by subsidizing (and thus artificially inflating) earnings rather than seeking ways to improve their quality.

Since the early 1980s, the NCBs have been in theory allowed to operate as privately owned institutions and have been subject to less government control. However, deregulation has not changed managers' goals. They continue with the sole objective of expanding market share.

Table 5.16. *Bank Soundness and Profitability*
(percent)

Year	Net worth to total assets	Net profits to net worth	Net profits to total assets	Noninterest expenses to Deposits	Noninterest expenses to Earnings
1965	7.37	24.67	1.80	8.16	41.94
1971	5.52	5.07[a]	0.28	4.49	19.63
1974	2.68	28.89[b]	0.78	3.92	18.45
1977	5.10	13.49	0.69	3.40	15.07
1980	5.47	14.36	0.79	3.90	11.12
1983	4.63	2.74	0.12	4.29	19.51
1986	3.95	4.04	0.16	4.03	18.14
1988	5.72	6.56	0.36	3.30	18.52
1989	10.83[e]	6.06	0.66	3.67	17.85

Note: Includes 7 nationwide, 10 local commercial banks, and 7 specialized banks. Daedong, Dongnam, and Dongwha Banks, established in 1989, are excluded.

a. The sharp drop reflects the increase in net worth from 23.2 billion won at the end of 1970 to 39.4 billion won at the end of 1971.

b. The jump was caused by a quadrupling of profits to 16.1 billion won, the result of a large increase in bank lending using funds borrowed from the Bank of Korea and foreign sources.

c. The decrease relates to a sharp reduction in profits following the lowering of bank lending rates.

d. The increase was due to the cut in deposit rate.

e. Banks issued a substantial amount of equity in 1989.

Source: This table, with annual data for 1965–89, was prepared by the Bank of Korea's Research Department for Kim 1990, who has kindly made it available.

Chapter 3 advances four hypotheses why Japan's banks are also expansion-oriented. One hypothesis relates to scale economies in banking. Although there is no convincing evidence, the cost function for these banks may exhibit an increasing return to scale. With the presence of scale economies, banks, other things being equal, continue to expand output until they reach the limit imposed by the monetary authorities through, for example, regulating branch openings. As Kitagawa and Kurosawa argue, under certain conditions, maximization of the volume of deposits may be rational and consistent in the long run with maximization of profits. There is almost an axiomatic view in Korea that in order to be competetive, banks should be big and grow, a view that must assume the existence of substantial scale economies in banking.

Sources of Income

Financial deregulation has definitely helped alter the relative importance of various sources of bank earnings, as it allowed the banks to add a variety of other financial services to their traditional intermediation business. A similar development has been observed in other countries.

Interest income from lending has declined in importance, although it continues to be the single largest source of income (see Table 5.17). The decline in the share of interest income has been offset by the increases in income from various off-balance sheet activities. Thus, beginning in the mid-1970s, there was a substantial increase in fees from foreign exchange transactions. In the mid-1980s much of the gains came in the "other" category, reflecting interest on reserve deposits and monetary stabilization accounts with BOK as well as income from trust and credit card business. Foreign exchange has diminished largely because of competition that led to a cut in various service fees.

Income from securities holdings—which includes dividends and interest, capital gains from the sale of securities, and fees from securities transactions—has made a significant gain as a source of bank income as banks actively cultivated their securities business to take advantage of the growing capital market.

Although there is clear evidence of an upward trend in off balance sheet activity income, it should be noted that the interest margin at NCBs fell sharply during 1981–85, to an annual average of about 400 basis points, from more than 600 during the preceding five-year period. The margin declined further in the late 1980s. The drop in interest income has in part been related to a government interest rate policy that has disregarded bank profitability. To compensate for the decline in lending margin, the monetary authorities may have encouraged NCBs to engage in a variety of off–balance sheet activities more than they otherwise would. Table 5.18 shows interest margins.

Soundness

Does a lack of equity capital cause banks to fail? Experiences in other countries suggest massive real or expected losses of earning assets or the loss of liquidity, not the lack of equity, are the main causes of bank failures. While inadequate

Table 5.17. *Income of Nationwide Commerical Banks, Distribution by Source* (percent)

| Year | Balance sheet items | | Off balance sheet sources | | | | Nonoperating[e] |
	Interest	Securities[a]	Fees[b]	Forex[c]	Other[d]	Total	
1965	74.3	3.5	3.3	4.9	10.9	19.1	3.1
1970	82.7	4.2	1.2	4.6	6.4	12.2	1.0
1974	77.0	4.5	0.9	11.6	1.8	14.3	4.3
1977	51.3	9.6	1.0	12.4	10.4	23.8	15.3[f]
1980	64.3	6.8	0.5	17.1	6.1	23.7	5.3
1983	59.7	11.4	0.8	11.1	16.2	28.2	0.7
1986	57.8	14.2	1.1	8.2	18.0	27.4	0.7
1989	56.8	12.3	1.9	5.9	22.3	30.1	0.8

Note: Includes all 7 nationwide commercial banks.

a. Realized gains from security holdings. Does not include unrealized gains or losses.

b. Primarily for payment services, such as remittances. Fees for foreign exchange transactions on behalf of clients are included under Forex, while those for credit cards are under Other.

c. Includes fees as well as gains (losses) from foreign exchange trading for the banks' own accounts.

d. Includes earnings from trust business and credit card operations, as well as interest on reserve deposits and stabilization accounts with the Bank of Korea.

e. Includes income related to real estate dealings.

f. During 1976–79 nonoperating income surged from revenue from issuing performance bonds for Korean construction companies, primarily in the Middle East.

Source: Bank of Korea.

equity does not necessarily precipitate failure, it is also true that banks stand a better chance of staying afloat if their capital is adequate. From this perspective, and judging a bank's soundness in terms of its ratio of net worth to total assets, one might argue that the safety of Korea's NCBs reached a precipitously low level during the 1971–75 period, when the ratio averaged 3.9 percent compared to 5.5 percent in the preceding five years. However, throughout the 1970s, the safety of NCBs was never questioned, simply because their ownership was in the hands of the government.

Deregulation and privatization have not changed the public belief in bank safety. In the process of writing off and rescheduling nonperforming loans, the ratio of NCB net worth to total assets went below 4 percent in 1985 and 1986, but few depositors were alarmed. Largely due to increased capitalization—NCBs and local banks raised 3 trillion won from stock offerings in 1989—the ratio jumped to 10 percent in 1989 and has remained at that level. This is a higher than the level required under BIS guidelines.

Korea's commercial banking system has operated under a tacit agreement between depositors and monetary authorities that the authorities will step in to rescue any bank in distress, whether it is small or large. For this reason, the safety of individual banks has never been questioned, irrespective of capital adequacy.

Table 5.18. *Spread at Nationwide Commercial Banks*

Year	Loans[a]	Cost of Funds[b]	Spread
1962	15.34	3.51	11.83
1963	15.79	3.23	12.56
1964	16.23	2.85	13.38
1965	19.47	5.44	14.03
1966	25.07	11.60	13.47
1967	23.97	12.65	11.31
1968	24.09	13.70	10.39
1969	22.31	14.87	7.44
1970	21.01	14.69	6.32
1971	19.13	14.42	4.71
1972	14.73	12.57	2.16
1973	12.72	9.57	3.15
1974	13.44	8.66	4.78
1975	13.91	9.28	4.63
1976	15.50	9.49	6.01
1977	14.47	9.03	5.44
1978	15.60	9.27	6.33
1979	16.89	9.89	7.00
1980	18.83	12.04	6.79
1981	16.92	12.18	4.74
1982	11.83	9.78	2.05
1983	9.78	6.36	2.88
1984	9.98	5.11	4.87
1985	10.08	5.08	5.00
1986	9.27	5.94	3.33
1987	8.92	5.62	3.30
1988	9.41	5.43	3.98
1989	10.54	5.86	4.68

a. Interest received as a percentage of total loans.
b. Interest paid on deposits as a percentage of total deposits.
Source: BOK, Research Department, for Kim 1990.

Profitability

In this chapter, NCB profitability is measured by the ratios of net profits to net worth and of net profits to total assets. Whichever is used, it is clear profitability has fluctuated over a wide range since the early 1960s (see Table 5.16). One interesting observation is that NCBs enjoyed their highest profit rates from 1973 to 1981, a period encompassing the two oil crises and often characterized by a high degree of financial repression. This is not surprising. In a banking system where the management goal is growth, profitability can be a secondary consideration and in fact can be easily manipulated. For example, much of the increase in bank profits during the 1970s came from maintenance of relatively large interest margins—facilitated by heavy reliance on borrowings from BOK and foreign sources—and the increase in fee income from foreign exchange transactions.

In 1982 bank profits plummeted and remained depressed until 1988. The major culprit in the dismal performance was, of course, the hemorrhaging caused by carrying a large volume of nonperforming loans. This difficulty was further aggravated by narrowing interest margins beginning in 1982.

Have NCBs been as unprofitable as their income statements seem to indicate? What about the hidden subsidies they have been accorded? If one takes into account the subsidies (adjusted for implicit taxes) does the profit profile change very much? In fact, a study by Kim (1990) shows the two profitability measures adjusted for taxes and subsidies looked substantially better throughout the 1980s and the high profitability shown on NCB income statements during 1973–81 was overstated, as Table 5.19 shows.

Cost Structure

Financial deregulation strengthens competitive forces in financial markets. This, together with reductions in information-gathering and -processing costs due to advances in communication technology, should improve cost efficiency. The cost of attracting and handling a unit of deposits has declined some since 1981, but on average it was higher in the 1980s than in the 1970s. The ratio of total expenses to total earnings was also higher and changed very little throughout the 1980s as compared to the 1970s.

Gross earnings and operating costs as a proportion of intermediated assets show little change since 1984 (see Table 5.20). But, we should be cautious about interpreting these results. To evaluate cost efficiency we need to estimate a cost function and have a definition of output. However, there is no operational definition of bank output. This means little can be said about the effects of deregulation on cost-efficiency in terms of standard measures.

Largely due to the unavailability and unreliability of detailed banking data, it is difficult to estimate the cost functions for banking firms in Korea. According to estimations by Hwang (1988), the cost functions for both NCBs and local banks display significant economies of scale for two outputs— earnings from lending operations and other earnings—and also economies of scope. We have estimated similar equations for a longer period up to 1989, but we were not able to obtain results consistent with Hwang's. This does not mean his results should be questioned but, rather, that estimation of a reasonably realistic cost function requires more accurate data and better functional specification.[1]

1. Hwang (1988) assumes the following cost function of a multiproduct banking firm using a number of inputs:

$$C(y,p.) = \min p \cdot x = V(y)$$

where y, p., and x are vectors for outputs, input prices, and inputs. Taking a translog of this function

Table 5.19. *Commerical Bank Net Profits to Total Assets, Adjusted for Subsidies and Taxes*
(percent)

Year	Reported profitability			Adjusted by[a]		Difference from average using	
	NCB	Local banks	Average[b]	Call[c]	Bills[d]	Call	Bills
1965	1.80	n.a.	1.80	2.02	2.16	0.22	0.36
1966	0.88	n.a.	0.88	0.92	−1.75	0.04	−2.63
1970	0.39	1.80	0.48	0.58	1.34	0.10	0.86
1971	0.28	1.98	0.39	0.48	1.10	0.09	0.71
1972	0.21	1.10	0.29	0.10	4.24	0.11	3.95
1973	0.30	1.04	0.39	0.19	3.73	−0.20	3.34
1974	0.78	1.13	0.83	1.30	2.98	0.47	2.15
1975	0.62	1.06	0.68	1.06	2.10	0.38	1.42
1976	0.99	1.66	1.03	1.22	2.15	0.19	1.12
1977	0.69	0.60	0.77	0.78	1.41	0.01	0.64
1978	0.84	1.43	0.93	0.82	0.93	0.09	0.20
1979	0.70	1.29	0.79	1.29	3.50	0.50	2.71
1980	0.79	1.38	0.86	0.72	3.51	−0.14	2.65
1981	0.64	0.90	0.67	0.67	3.01	0.00	2.34
1982	0.23	0.35	0.24	0.63	4.58	0.39	4.34
1983	0.12	0.25	0.14	0.42	3.40	0.28	3.26
1984	0.30	0.68	0.35	0.86	3.27	0.51	2.92
1985	0.15	0.47	0.19	0.56	2.41	0.37	2.22
1986	0.16	0.39	0.19	0.43	1.62	0.24	1.43
1987	0.19	0.27	0.20	0.52	1.79	0.32	1.59
1988	0.36	0.50	0.39	0.69	2.66	0.30	2.27
1989	0.66	0.60	0.65	0.89	3.15	0.24	2.50

n.a. Not applicable.

a. Profitability adjusted for implicit taxes and subsidies. Subsidies are computed in two ways (see notes c and d). Implicit taxes has 2 parts. The first involves deposits in monetary stabilization accounts, and is computed by applying the difference between a market rate of interest and the rate actually paid by BOK. The second applies the difference between the yield on corporate debentures and the yield on monetary stabilization bonds to the amount of outstanding stabilization bonds.

b. Weighted average of nationwide commercial and local banks.

c. Subsidy computed using the difference between the call rate and the BOK lending rate, applied to the volume of BOK lending.

d. Subsidy computed using the difference between the discount rate for commmercial bills and the BOK lending rate, applied to the volume of BOK lending.

Source: BOK, Research Department, for Kim 1990.

and expanding it, he estimates the following equation for 1981–86 with pooled time series and cross-section data for both NCBs and local banks.

$$\ln C = A_0 + \Sigma A_i \ln y_i + \Sigma B_j \ln p + 0.5\,(C_{ij} \ln y_i \ln y_j)$$
$$+ 0.5\,(D_{ij} \ln p_i \ln p_j) + E_{ij} \ln y_i \ln p_j$$
$$C_{ij} = C_{ji} \text{ and } D_{ij} = D_{ji}$$

Table 5.20. *Commercial Bank Income and Costs as a Percentage of Intermediated Assets*

	1984	1985	1986	1987	1988	1989
Interest margin[a]	2.007	2.252	1.557	1.680	1.802	2.297
Gross earnings[b]	4.250	4.288	3.522	3.117	3.567	4.104
Operating costs	2.634	2.541	2.388	2.282	2.365	2.163
Net earnings[c]	1.616	1.747	1.113	0.835	1.205	1.940
Net worth	7.00	6.14	6.44	7.29	10.64	17.45

Note: Intermediated assets = Loans + Foreign currency loans + Local import usance + Advanced payment + Call loans + Local letter of credit bills bought + Factoring bills +Securities.

a. Interest received minus interest paid.
b. Interest margin plus fees and commisions.
c. Gross earnings minus operating costs.

Source: Bank of Korea, *Statistics of Bank Management,* Oct. 1990, pp. 215, 221.

CONCLUDING REMARKS

Financial liberalization has strengthened competitive forces in financial markets by lowering entry barriers, deregulating interest rates, and easing market segmentation. New financial and communications technologies have greatly reduced the costs of collecting and processing information. Despite these developments, we have not been able to identify any significant changes in the behavior of the commercial banks that may be related to increased competition. The relationship between the government and financial institutions remains essentially unchanged. In managing their assets and liabilities, commercial banks have not deviated very much from the pattern of the 1960s and 1970s. There is no evidence competition has helped improve the cost-efficiency of commercial banks.

One might argue that it is perhaps too early to detect any effects of financial liberalization on the behavior of commercial banks. Others may claim the scope of financial liberalization has been so limited that our conclusions are hardly surprising. The answer may lie somewhere between these two views.

REFERENCES

BOK (Bank of Korea), Research Department 1990. *Financial System in Korea.* Seoul: BOK.
———. Savings Planning and Payment Systems Department. 1991. *Financial Instruments in Korea.* Seoul: BOK.
Benston, George J., and others. 1986. *Perspectives on Safe and Sound Banking: Past, Present and Future.* American Bankers Association in cooperation with MIT Press.
Bloomfield, Arthur I., and John P. Jensen. 1951. "Banking Reform in South Korea." New York Federal Reserve Bank. (Reprinted in 1963 by BOK.)
Cole, David, and Yung Chul Park. 1983. *Financial Development in Korea 1945–78.* Cambridge, MA: Harvard University Press.
Hwang, Kyu Bong. 1988. "An Analysis of the Cost Structure of Nationwide Commercial Banks in Korea." *Bank Information.* July. In Korean.
Kim, Pyung Joo. 1990 Aug. "[Korean] Financial Institutions: Past, Present, and Future." Honolulu: East–West Population Institute.

6

Taiwan: Development and Structural Change of the Financial System

JIA-DONG SHEA

The development experience of Taiwan has generally been regarded as spectacular. The growth of the economy, price stability, and income distribution equality over the past four decades leave little doubt that the praise is deserved. Development of the financial system certainly contributed to making this possible, by stimulating and mobilizing savings and allocating investment funds because success was greatly dependent on a high domestic savings rate and the use of those savings for productive investments. Nonetheless, the financial system has often been criticized as being underdeveloped and inefficient and, in the 1980s, was even regarded as a major obstacle to further economic growth. Much of the financial inefficiency and underdevelopment were blamed on the high degree of government intervention in interest rate determination, as well as in financial intermediation, market structure, and banking operations.

This chapter reviews the structure, development, and performance of the financial system in Taiwan, and discusses its impact on economic growth. The focus is on the efficacy of the system in stimulating and mobilizing savings and its efficiency in allocating loanable funds. The first two sections provide a brief overview of the structure and evolution of the financial system in Taiwan, and the third looks at its performance in stimulating and mobilizing savings and in allocating funds. Models to test criticisms of the formal system's credit allocation and the contribution of the informal system to allocative efficiency also are included in the third section.

The government's financial policies are divided into interventionist, growth promotion, and stabilization, and their impact on the development and efficiency of the financial system is analyzed in the fourth through sixth sections. The seventh section discusses the causes of liberalization during the 1980s, and the eighth and ninth section look at two aspects of liberalization—deregulation and internationalization—including policies and their consequences. Taiwan's experience suggests several lessons regarding financial development and financial policies, which are presented in the final section.

Macro Overview

From 1951 to 1991, Taiwan's real GNP increased 28.5 times—an average annual growth rate of 8.9 percent—and per capita GNP grew 10.9 times in real terms, reaching US $8,815 in 1991. Prices remained relatively stable. From 1953 to 1991 the average annual growth rate of the GNP deflator was 6.4 percent; the wholesale price index grew 5.0 percent; and the consumer index, 6.6 percent. If we exclude 1973–74 and 1979–80, periods in which prices were highly affected by the energy crises, the average annual growth rates were only 5.0 percent for the GNP deflator, 2.7 percent for wholesale prices, and 5.0 percent for consumer prices.

Income distribution became steadily more equal throughout the 1950s, 1960s, and 1970s. Although the trend reversed in the 1980s, the level remains one of the most equal by world standards. (The Gini coefficient was 0.326 in 1968, 0.277 in 1980, and 0.308 in 1991. By comparison, the number for the United States was 0.412 in 1980, and for Japan was 0.338 in 1979.)

The financial system in Taiwan is summarized in Table 6.1. One of the most important features of the system is "financial dualism," which means that in addition to the formal (organized, regulated) financial system, there is an informal (unorganized, unregulated) system that also plays an important role. The formal system includes all institutions and markets established according to financial laws or rules and subject to regulation by the financial authorities. The informal system is composed of all the markets not set up according to financial laws or rules, and it engages in lending and borrowing activities without being under the direct regulation or supervision of financial authorities.

THE FORMAL SYSTEM

The formal system is supervised and regulated by the Ministry of Finance (MOF) and the Central Bank of China (CBC). The former is in charge of matters relating to administration, and the latter is responsible for the banking operations of financial institutions. The system consists of institutions and markets.

From 1961 to 1990 the number of financial institutions increased by about 28 percent—to over 480—while the number of locations (head and branch offices) almost tripled, to over 4,000 (see Table 6.2). (In the same period the population increased about 80 percent.) Although the number of persons served per location is still much larger than in developed countries, the network of financial institutions is nonetheless a dense one when the fact Taiwan has one of the highest population densities in the world is taken into account. Table 6.A12 gives the number of financial institutions in various years, and data on the number of banks and branches are in Table 7.6. The distribution of assets, loans and investments, and deposits among the different types of institutions is shown in Tables 6.A13–A15.

As for the geographical distribution of financial institutions, not surprisingly, bank branches are concentrated in the major cities, particularly Taipei. Nonethe-

Table 6.1. *The Financial System in Taiwan*

Formal-system organizations	Formal system	Informal system
Monetary institutions[a]	*Market-specific institutions*	*Market-specific organizations*
Central Bank of China (CBC)	Money market	Installment credit
	Bills finance companies	Leasing
Full-service domestic banks	Capital market	Investment
Commercial banks	Taiwan Stock Exchange Corporation	Rotating credit co-ops
Specialized banks		Credit unions
Foreign banks (local branches)	Fuh-Hwa Securities Finance	*Other types of transactions*
Medium and small business banks	Securities dealers	Unsecured credit
	Brokers	Secured credit
Cooperatives[b]	Traders	Loans on post-dated checks
Credit co-op associations		Deposits with firms
Credit departments of farmer associaions	*Offshore banking centers*	
	Units of domestic banks	*"Unorganized" participants*
Credit departments of fisher associations	Units of foreign banks	Moneylenders
		Pawnbrokers
Other financial institutions	*Others*	Others
Postal saving system	Foreign exchange market	
Investment and trust companies	Foreign currency call loan market	
Investment and trust companies		
Units of commercial banks		
The China Development Corporation		
Insurance companies		
Life		
Property and casualty		
Central Reinsurance Co[c]		

a. Audited by the Central Deposit Insurance Corporation, by the authority of MOF and CBC.
b. The Cooperative Bank of Taiwan acts as the central bank and auditing agency for co-ops.
c. Does not do business with the general public.

less, in part because the various cooperatives are primarily rural and the postal savings system is ubiquitous, banking services are fairly evenly distributed on the island, so all residents have adequate access to them. Interestingly, the data suggest the distribution of financial institutions became more geographically equal through the 1970s, but this trend reversed in the 1980s. The reason for this needs further study.

Table 6.2. Number of Units of Financial Institutions

End of year	Total units[a]	Full service banks[b]		Foreign bank branches		Medium and small business banks		Credit cooperative associations	
		Units	%	Units	%	Units	%	Units	%
1961	1,359	260	19.1	1	0.1	84	6.2	153	11.3
1970	1,821	393	21.6	7	0.4	118	6.5	222	12.2
1980	2,830	536	18.9	21	0.7	165	5.8	274	9.7
1989	3,834	708	18.5	38	1.0	269	7.0	432	11.3
1990	4,012	738	18.4	43	1.1	283	7.1	473	11.8

End of year	Credit departments of farmer and fisher associations		Investment and trust companies[c]		Postal savings system		Insurance companies	
	Units	%	Units	%	Units	%	Units	%
1961	385	28.3	1	0.1	451	33.2	24	1.8
1970	393	21.6	1	0.1	610	33.5	77	4.2
1980	724	25.6	26	0.9	952	33.6	132	4.7
1989	992	25.9	52	1.4	1,181	30.8	162	4.2
1990	1,053	26.2	54	1.3	1,202	30.0	166	4.1

Note: For the number of institutions of each type, see Table 6.A12.

a. Units are physical locations—head offices and branches. The percentages are of total units. The Central Bank of China, Central Reinsurance Corporation, and postal agencies—which do not do business with the general public—are excluded. The source provides data on these and on bills and securities finance companies.

b. Domestic commercial (10) and specialized (6) banks, government (12) and privately (4) owned. These are called "domestic banks" in the source. Table 7.6 has additonal data on branches.

c. Includes China Development Corporation, which in some places is classified as a full-service bank.

Source: Yearbook of Financial Statistics of the ROC 1990, pp. 467–69, which gives annual data.

Monetary Institutions

Monetary institutions accept demand deposits and checking deposits, and therefore have the power to create deposit money. In addition to the central bank, there are four types of monetary institutions: full-service domestic banks, local branches of foreign banks, medium- and small- business banks, and cooperatives. (CBC 1984 describes the various types of financial institutions.)

The Central Bank of China (CBC) did not resume operation in Taiwan until 1961. After the government retreated from mainland China in 1949, the Bank of Taiwan, a commercial bank controlled by the Taiwan provincial government, performed most of the functions of a central bank. The decision to reactivate the CBC was motivated by a desire to fine-tune monetary policy and to promote economic development.

From 1961 to 1979 the CBC was under the direct supervision of the president of the Republic of China. It enjoyed a high degree of independence and usually dominated the Ministry of Finance. Then in 1979 the CBC was put under the jurisdiction of the Executive Yuan (the cabinet) to better coordinate with the cabinet on economic policies, despite strong warnings from scholars such as SC Tsiang that this move would create the danger of monetary policies being determined largely by popular clamor rather than by more dispassionate opinion. The CBC's diminished status—exacerbated by the declining seniority and influence of the govenor of the central bank within the ruling party and the political liberalization movement—did indeed lead CBC policies to be more influenced by the cabinet and legislators in the late 1980s. As a result, promoting economic and export growth supplanted financial stability as the CBC's primary policy goal.

Full-Service Domestic Banks

There were 16 full-service domestic banks in Taiwan at the end of 1990, with 738 locations around the island. Aside from commercial banking operations, most of them operate savings and foreign exchange departments, and some have trust departments. Among them are 6 government-owned specialized banks—3 of which originated on the mainland. They were established mainly to facilitate the government's growth promotion polices. (Chinese-language sources on the activities and history of the specialized banks are their annual reports, Bank of Communications 1987, Central Trust 1985, Cooperative Bank 1976, Farmers Bank 1983, Land Bank of Taiwan 1981, Lin 1988.)

The Export–Import Bank of China was established in 1979 to provide export and import financing; it does not accept deposits from the public. The other specialized banks engage in a mixture of functions beyond their specialized purposes, including commercial and savings banking.

The Land Bank of Taiwan, reorganized in 1946 from the local office of a colonial-period Japanese bank, specializes in real estate and agricultural loans. It was intimately involved in the land reform that followed retrocession. The Farmers Bank of China, specializing in agricultural financing, was founded on the mainland in 1933 and resumed operations in 1967. Originally intended mainly to provide working capital, it also handles mortgages. The Bank of Communications, which originated on the mainland in 1907, began operations in Taiwan in 1960 with a changed purpose—specializing in venture capital investments and medium- and long-term loans to industries, mining, transportation, and other public enterprises. From 1992 it has been called Chiao Tung Bank in English as well as Chinese.

The Cooperative Bank of Taiwan, reorganized from a colonial-period bank, is designated by MOF to provide agricultural finance and is authorized to examine and supervise the operations of credit cooperatives. The Central Trust, founded on the mainland in 1935 and moved to Taiwan in 1949, is responsible for cooperating with the government in its purchasing, trade, banking, trust, insurance, storage, freight, and other related needs. It also operates as a commercial bank and as an investment and trust company.

Domestic banks represent only about 20 percent of the total number of locations of financial institutions, but they have always been the backbone of the financial system in Taiwan. The role of domestic banks has decreased steadily since the 1960s. Still, they accounted for the majority of assets, loans, and investments—as well as almost half of deposits—of all financial institutions in 1990. The main reason domestic banks have lost share is that they have long suffered from severe restrictions on their operations, including the opening of new branches and (until 1991) new banks, while other financial institutions and the informal market have been less, or at least differently, constrained.

Foreign Banks

Before 1965 the monetary authorities hesitated opening the domestic market to foreign banks. But when U.S. economic aid ended in 1965 and official diplomatic relations suffered contractions in the late 1970s, the authorities changed their attitude and allowed foreign banks to open branches in Taipei. This was intended to encourage foreign investment, strengthen ties with the outside world, and improve domestic banking operations through competition and the transfer of know-how. The number of local branches of foreign banks therefore rose dramatically from 1 (Japan's Dai–ichi Kangyo) in 1964 to 38 branches (33 banks) at the end of 1989. However retrenchment (including mergers of overseas parents) reduced the number to 35 in 1990.

Operational restrictions on foreign banks have been eased since the late 1980s. Initially foreign banks could locate only in Taipei, but they can now branch to Kaohsiung and Taichung. They are authorized to handle foreign exchange transactions, extend loans to firms as well as individuals, and engage in trust business. They can also accept local currency deposits—checking, demand, savings, and time—although the total is subject to a ceiling of 15 times paid-in capital. (Before April 1990 the ceiling was 12.5 times.) In general, foreign banks enjoy the same range of activities as domestic banks although, their role is still limited.

Medium- and Small- Business Banks

MSBBs were developed in 1978–79 from privately owned mutual savings and loan companies, which provided rotating credit. At the end of 1979 mutual savings accounted for almost one-fifth of the MSBBs' deposits, and mutual loans represented more than half of their loans. Since then, these two figures have declined rapidly, representing just 3.9 percent and 3.0 percent, respectively, of their total deposits and total loans at the end of 1990. (Data on mutual loans and savings is found in the *Taiwan Community Financial Journal*, published in Chinese by the Research and Training Center of Community Finance.)

Under the Banking Law of 1975, MSBBs are identified as specialized banks that extend medium- and long-term credit to small and medium businesses. With the exception of the government-owned Medium Business Bank of Taiwan, which operates with branches throughout the island, the other seven, still privately owned, are restricted to nonoverlapping regions, and thus do not compete with one another.

Since the early 1960s—even though the number of units has been stable at 6 to 7 percent of all financial institution units—the MSBBs' share of assets, and of loans and investments, more than doubled, while their share of total deposits increased by about half.

Cooperatives

There are three types of cooperatives in Taiwan: credit cooperative associations, credit departments of farmers' associations, and credit departments of fishermen's associations. They accept deposits from and grant loans to their members. They do not offer preferential terms, but it is easier for members to obtain loans from cooperatives than from other financial institutions because the people involved generally know one another. Credit availability is one of the main incentives for joining a co-op. Each co-op operates in a fairly small geographic area, but they compete by branching. As a result, although representing about one-third of locations, cooperatives are small scale. Although their market share has risen somewhat, they account for less than 16 percent of total assets and of total loans and investments, and less than 20 percent of total deposits.

The cooperatives' perations are examined and supervised by the Cooperative Bank of Taiwan, a government-owned commercial bank authorized by MOF and the CBC to act like the central bank for cooperatives. The Cooperative Bank must report any wrongdoing to the authorities, who then decide how to deal with the problem. It also is required to accept the co-ops' surplus funds as redeposits.

Other Financial Institutions

Other financial institutions include insurance, investment and trust companies, and the postal savings system. They cannot accept demand and checking deposits—in other words, they cannot create deposit money—but they can mobilize public funds to finance investments.

Investment and Trust Companies

Before 1971, there was only one investment and trust company (ITC), the government-owned China Development Corporation. In 1971–72 the market was opened in order to increase the sources of long-term loans, and seven private ITCs were allowed to set up. Since then, in order to prevent fierce competition, no new licenses have been granted. The operations of ITCs include trust deposit management, direct and syndicated medium- and long-term loans and investments, securities underwriting, and the like.

In the 1970s ITC market share increased very rapidly. However, in the first half of 1980s three of them got into trouble from over-investing in the real estate market (which was in a recession at the time) or from making loans to badly managed firms in their same conglomerate group. After this, the operations of ITCs became less expansionary, and therefore, their shares in total assets, total loans and investments, and total deposits were lower in 1990 than in 1980. In 1992 China Trust, the largest ITC, was allowed to convert to a commerical bank.

Postal Savings System

The postal savings system (PSS) is a legacy of the Japanese colonial period. Its functions are overseen by the Directorate General of Remittance and Savings Banks (DGRSB). In addition to remittance services conducted inside and outside the country, the PSS accepts savings deposits and conducts life insurance business through its extensive network of post offices, which have separate windows for financial operations. The term "postal savings system" is used to distinguish DGRSB's financial operations from its other business and services.

Operating units of the PSS have accounted for about a third of all financial institutions since 1961. The PSS accepts the same kinds of savings deposits and pays the same interest rates as other financial institutions. However, it enjoys the advantages of a longer business hours and income-tax free interest on passbook savings up to certain amount, so the system has been very effective in mobilizing savings through its widespread post offices.

Because the PSS is prohibited from lending, initially most deposits were redeposited with the CBC. The CBC paid PSS according to the one, two, or three-year deposit rate, plus a 0.18 percent premium. CBC used the money to extend medium- and long-term credit at a preferential interest rate to certain investment projects, using full-service domestic banks, especially the specialized banks, as an intermediaries.

In March 1982 this redeposit policy was modified. Incremental savings deposits accepted by the PSS were redeposited in four of the specialized banks, in order to supplement their loanable funds. These four were the Bank of Communications, Farmers Bank, Land Bank, and Medium Business Bank. Since October 1984 the ratio of redeposits with these banks has been adjusted downward or upward by the CBC on several occasions. The CBC retained what was not redeposited. Redeposit policy was a powerful tool for the CBC to control the money supply and ration credit selectively.

Insurance Companies

There were 8 (for a while, 9) life insurance companies and 14 property and casualty insurance companies in Taiwan before 1989 when 3 foreign life insurance companies and 5 foreign property and casualty insurers (all from the United States) were allowed to set up branches. This was a direct response to U.S. pressure. At the end of 1990 Taiwan had 15 life and 19 property and casualty insurers.

Insurance companies had a limited role in Taiwan before 1980. Strong family ties, which includes providing emergency help, was one of the limiting factors. The superstition that insurance brings bad luck was another. But, the breakdown of the traditional family structure and the increasing amount of education per capita are benefiting the insurance companies. Their reserve funds are used primarily for loans and real estate and securities investments.

Financial Markets

Financial markets channel funds from lenders to borrowers by expediting the creation and trading of financial instruments, and they include all the mechanisms for issuance, trading, and redeeming claims. They are classified as money or capital markets according to the maturity of the financial instruments they handle. The money market deals with instruments due in one year or less, while the capital market deals with longer maturities.

Money Market

Before the first bills finance company was established in 1976, the money market in Taiwan was not well developed. In 1977 and 1978 two more bills finance companies were set up. They advise firms on the use of money market instruments, and act as the dealers, underwriters, and brokers as well as guarantors or endorsers of many kinds of money market instruments. In addition to creating a primary market, the bills finance companies also participate in the secondary market to promote the negotiability of bills and notes.

The major market instruments and their shares of total outstanding volumes of money market bills in 1991 (1990) are treasury bills, 15 percent (3 percent);commercial paper, 38 percent (42 percent); bankers' acceptances, 7 percent (10 percent); and negotiable certificates of deposit, 40 percent (45 percent).

Although no new bills finance companies have been allowed since 1978, by the end of 1991 the number of branches had increased to 20, and the size of the market had grown rapidly—in 1991 outstanding money market instruments had reached 15.9 percent of GNP and over 12.5 percent of the total loans and discounts of financial institutions, as Table 6.3 shows.

Capital Market

The capital market is composed of the bond market and the stock market. Both are regulated by Securities and Exchange Commission (SEC), and neither is fully developed. At first, because bond issuing costs (including interest and administrative costs) were usually higher than bank financing costs, and the issuing procedure was complicated and time-consuming, firms preferred bank-financing. Most corporate bonds have been issued by public enterprises and bought by financial institutions. Deposit money banks started issuing debentures in 1980: By the end of 1988 the amount outstanding was NT$21 billion and reached NT$59 billion at year-end 1990. Table 6.4 has bond market data.

The lesson of hyperinflation on mainland China during 1945–49, caused by printing money to finance deficits, taught the government to maintain a balanced budget. This fiscal prudence has worked against development of a government bond market. However, to sterilize the impact of the huge balance of payments surplus on the domestic money supply in the late 1980s, the CBC issued tremendous

Table 6.3. *Money Market Instruments Outstanding*

End of year	Amount in million NT$	As a % of GNP	As a % of loans
1976	7,474	1.06	1.66
1980	86,613	5.82	8.47
1985	309,816	12.32	16.84
1989	580,347	14.63	13.27
1990	662,016	15.22	13.29
1991	766,576	15.87	12.52

Note: Loans means total loans and discounts of financial institutions.
Source: Central Bank of China, *Financial Statistics Monthly*, various issues.

Table 6.4. *Corporate and Government Bonds Outstanding*
(million NT$)

	1961	*1970*	*1980*	*1989*	*1990*	*1991*
Corporate[a]	107	480	25,008	45,429	51,600	64,118
Government[b]	776	9,030	18,432	208,695	188,774	347,647
Total	883	9,510	43,440	254,124	240,374	411,765
as % of GNP	1.3	4.2	2.9	6.4	5.5	8.5
as % of loans[c]	4.6	10.1	4.2	5.8	4.8	6.7

a. Public and private enterprises.

b. Excludes savings bonds and CDs issued by CBC for sterilization purposes, as discussed in the text.

c. Denominator is total loans and discounts of financial institutions.

Source: Central Bank of China, *Financial Statistics Monthly*, various issues.

amounts of CDs and savings bonds through the bond market, thereby greatly expanding the size of the bond market. By the end of 1987 the sum of CDs and savings bonds issued by the CBC reached a peak of NT$1.123 trillion, more than 6 times the level of outstanding corporate and government bonds. By the end of 1989 it still amounted to NT$382 billion, about 1.5 times outstanding corporate and government bonds. In 1989 the CBC shifted its sterilization policy from issuing CDs and savings bonds to raising the required reserve ratio. Thus, the CBC's outstanding CDs and savings bonds dropped sharply in that year and in 1990.

There was no formal stock market in Taiwan until the Taiwan Stock Exchange Corporation (TSEC) began operating in 1962. Although there had been over-the-counter (OTC) markets operated by securities brokers and traders before then, the number of traded companies and the level of transactions were rather small. When the TSEC began operations, OTC transactions were prohibited, although since the end of 1989 they have again been allowed.

In 1980 the Fuh-Hwa Security Finance Company was established to increase overall market liquidity and the marketability of individual securities by providing margin loans and stock loans for securities transactions and serving as a securities custodian. Before 1980 the Bank of Taiwan, Bank of Communications, and Land Bank had provided loans for security purchases. With Fuh-Hwa's establishment, they discontinued this activity.

To promote listing, the authorities provided incentives such as a 15 percent reduction on corporate income tax for three years and, for shareholders, up to NT$360,000 of dividends plus interest free from income tax. The listing criteria set by the authorities also are high, however, as an application for listing must pass examination by the Securities and Exchange Commission.

The traditions of a low proportion of equity funding, a reliance on bank borrowing, and the desire for close management control and little public disclosure have impeded the growth of the stock market. By the end of 1986, when the number of so-called big companies—assets over NT$100 million (about US $2.8 million at 1986 exchange rates)—reached 5,062, there were only 130 listed companies. At the end of 1991 dealers and brokers had 470 branches, compared to just 221 listed companies. Data are in Table 6.5.

Since the mid-1980s, Taiwan's economy has been troubled by excess liquidity due to the huge trade surplus and speculative capital inflow. This contributed to a virtually vertical ascent in the stock price index—from 945 in 1986 to 9624 at the end of 1989—when the price–earnings ratio reached over 55. The index peaked at 12,495 in February 1990 and then fell almost 80 percent to a low of 2560 in October, mainly due to the unsustainability of the market bubble and the contractionary monetary policy adopted by the CBC. By March 1991 it had recovered to 5000 and has traded in the 4500 to 5500 range from then until now (September 1992).

During the boom the number of brokerage accounts leaped from 634,000 in 1987 to 1.6 million in 1988 and by 1990 exceeded 5 million, or one account for every four people in Taiwan! Many clients have multiple accounts, however, so the actual percentage of the population directly involved in transactions is lower. At the end of 1989 the number of investors was 2.8 million, or 13.9 percent of the total population.

The stock market is full of small, uninformed investors who can be easily manipulated by a small group of large investors and insider traders. For many reasons the Securities and Exchange Commission does not have the capacity to prevent insider trading or market manipulation. First, regulations on such activities

Table 6.5. *Stock Market in Taiwan*
(billion NT$ except as noted)

Year	Broker locations[a]	Listings[b]	Total par value[c] NT$	%[d]	Total market value NT$	% of GNP	Stock price index[e]	Turnover[f]	Trading values[g]
1962	n.a.	18	5.9	23.1	6.8	8.9	n.a.	n.a.	0.6
1970	n.a.	42	8.4	9.0	20.0	8.8	134	160	4.8
1980	68	102	108.7	10.6	219.1	14.7	547	108	10.9
1986	67	130	240.9	21.0	548	19	945	162	23
1987	67	141	287.3	11.9	1386	42	2135	267	81
1988	149	163	343.6	10.2	3383	94	5202	295	219
1989	307	181	421.3	9.6	6174	156	8616	524	641
1990	452	199	506.4	10.2	2682	62	6775	459	438
1991	470	221	616.7	12.8	3184	66	4929	285	201

n.a. Not available.

a. Number of brokers, dealers, and broker branches.

b. Number of listed companies.

c. Number of shares times their par value, which is NT$10 in all cases.

d. As a percentage of total loans and discounts of financial institutions.

e. 1966 = 100.

f. Percentage of shares outstanding traded during the year.

g. As a percentage of GNP.

Source. *Securities and Exchange Commission Statistics*, various issues.

are not clear, particularly in regard to the definitions of such activities. The Judiciary Department often has different opinions and reaches different conclusions than does the SEC. And unless the Judiciary Department confirms an SEC verdict, a finding of manipulation or insider trading cannot be sustained. Second, the widespread use of borrowed-name accounts hinders effective implementation. (Such an account is opened in the names of a real person, but not that of the person who actually owns and controls the account.) The stock market in Taiwan is thus not so much a vehicle for investment as a paradise for gamblers.

THE INFORMAL FINANCIAL SYSTEM

The composition of business sector financing sources given in Table 6.6 shows the relative roles of the formal and informal financial systems. Clearly, the informal financial system has played an important role.

The system includes the markets and mechanisms where borrowing and lending activities by businesses and households occur without the direct supervision and regulation of the financial authorities. Most market players (such as moneylenders, pawnbrokers, and rotating credit cooperatives) have no formal organization and therefore are fragmented. The exceptions are credit unions and companies engaged in installment credit, leasing, or investments.

Financial installment credit companies, leasing companies, and investment companies are licensed by the Ministry of Economic Affairs, but they extend credit to or accept deposits from the general public without otherwise being regulat-

Table 6.6. *Composition of Business Sector Financing by the Financial System* (percent)

	1964–90	*1964–70*	*1971–75*	*1976–80*	*1981–85*	*1986–90*
Financial institutions	54.5	57.1	67.4	57.2	52.2	54.1
Money market[a]	7.3	—	0.0	4.5	10.6	6.9
Capital market[b]	14.4	15.7	9.8	13.9	13.9	15.1
Curb market[c]	23.8	27.2	22.8	24.4	23.3	23.9
Total in billion NT$[d]	968.9	52.4	205.5	650.8	1514.6	2787.6

— Not applicable.

Note: The business sector includes both private and public enterprises.

The percentages are computed from totals over the entire period. The NT$ amounts in the last line are averages of annual data.

a. The money market was established in 1975.

b. The amount of financing from the capital market is defined as the sum of the accumulated net amount of stock issued by listed companies and the outstanding volume of corporate bonds.

c. Data about the size of the curb market (informal system) are compiled by the Central Bank of China from sample surveys of the financial condition of enterprises.

d. Average of annual data.

Source: Computed by the author from data in CBC, *Flow of Funds in Taiwan District, ROC* 1991, and Ministry of Finance, *1990 Securities and Exchange Commission Statistics.*

ed. Credit unions were introduced into Taiwan by the Roman Catholic church in 1964. MOF has allowed them to operate under certain limits on an experimental basis since 1968, but so far they have not been legalized under the banking laws and therefore have not been formally regulated.

Types of Informal-Market Transactions

In addition to installment credit, leasing, and mutual savings and loans, the more commonly observed types of financial transactions in the informal market are rotating mutual credit, deposits with firms, loans against post-dated checks, and secured and unsecured borrowing and lending. The Central Bank collects data on interest rates for deposits with firms, on unsecured loans, and on loans against post-dated checks, and publishes them in its *Financial Statistics Monthly*.

Rotating mutual credit (commonly called *hui* or *biao-hui* in Taiwan) has been the most popular practice in the informal market. This involves a group of members, each of whom contributes a fixed amount. The size and practices of these groups vary widely. Typically, the groups meet at regular intervals (usually monthly) and lend out their collected pool by means of competitive bidding. Those who currently have outstanding loans generally cannot borrow more, and the expectation is that each member will be able to borrow at some point. Repayment is usually in installments over several years, depending on the group's size. Groups vary from a few friends to as many as several dozen people.

Many firms take deposits from their employees at favorable interest rates so as to give them an incentive to support the company and also to avoid having to seek outside financing. Some companies accept deposits from relatives and friends of employees, and even the general public. Until 1990 the income tax laws gave an incentive to employees to participate because interest earned up to a certain amount was excluded from taxable income. Although the 1989 Banking Law tightened the prohibition on deposit taking by nonbanks, in practice it is difficult to prevent firms from continuing to take deposits from the public. The practice remains legal in regard to employees and their families.

Loans against post-dated checks are common because they usually are eligible for discounting at banks. Thus, a check's payee (lender) can accept a check from the payer (borrower) and either hold it until the stated date or present it to a bank for immediate (albeit discounted) payment. Before 1986, loans against post-dated checks were protected by criminal law: A person who bounced more than three checks was subject to criminal penalities. The removal of criminal sanctions has increased the risks, but the loans remain common. The payee now depends on civil law, collateral, the credit record of the payer, or even professional money collectors (including gangsters) to protect the claim.

Pawnbrokers and moneylenders operate in a fairly competitive environment, often advertising their services in newspaper classified sections. One can discount post-dated personal checks and borrow against cars and even real estate.

There are no official published statistics regarding loans to the household sector. The general impression is that, except for loans collateralized by real estate, households usually find it very difficult to borrow from financial institutions. Based on a survey by the Chung-Hua Institution for Economic Research, my colleagues and I estimated that in 1982 the household sector obtained between 45 and 52 percent of its borrowing from the informal financial system in 1982 (Shea and others 1985). Other surveys made by academic institutions have had similar results.

During the period 1964 –90, financial institutions provided the business sector with 55 percent of its total domestic financing. The informal system (curb markets) accounted for 24 percent, capital markets 14 percent, and the money market 7 percent. Further decomposing the business sector into public enterprises and private enterprises (including incorporated and unincorporated businesses), public enterprises depended primarily on financial institutions as the source of their borrowing, while private enterprises borrowed only slightly more than half from financial institutions and over one-third from curb markets. (Public enterprises are those in which more than half of the shares are controlled by the government.) Tables 6.7 and 6.8 show annual data for sources of borrowing.

Table 6.8 shows the curb market share of private enterprise financing clearly declined in the periods 1964 –73, 1981– 84, and from 1987 and rose during 1975– 80 and 1985– 86. The 1964 –73 fall could have been a natural result of the development of the formal financial system. The comeback in 1975– 80 was partly the result of controls on bank interest rates. Also, 1973– 80 was a period with a higher inflation rate. A controlled bank interest rate could not be adjusted to depositors' expectations regarding inflation, thereby widening the gap between it and the curb market rates. As a consequence, funds shifted from financial institutions to the informal system, and the curb market became more important.

Following decontrol of bank interest rates, starting in 1980, the curb market's share dropped steadily until 1984. The reasons for the resurgence of curb market financing in 1985– 86 are closely related to the economic recession in 1985 and the remaining interventionist policies adopted by the financial authorities, which are explained later.

Some comments on the accuracy of data on the informal market are in order. Information is collected each year by the CBC using a questionnaire on enterprises' assets and liabilities. The sampling and estimation procedures can be found in CBC's "Report on the Survey of Financial Conditions of Public and Private Enterprises in the Taiwan Area." Some informal market activities, such as usury, are illegal. This, and the desire to evade taxes on income from legal curb market activities, means there is probably some bias toward understatement. On the other hand, borrowing from the owner of a firm is included as part of the firm's informal-market borrowing, a debatable procedure.

Sampling error may also be present. Table 6.8 shows the informal system's share of private-enterprise borrowing was much lower in 1987 and 1988 than in 1986. This flies in the face of the general perception that 1987– 88 were boom years for financial investment companies (FICs). If any of the big FICs had been included in the sample, the resulting informal-sector share might have been much larger.

Table 6.7. Composition of Sources of Domestic Borrowings by Public Enterprises (percent)

End of year	Formal system				Informal system		
	Financial institutions	Money market	Bond market	Subtotal	Households	Other	Subtotal
1964	97.7	n.a.	1.8	99.5	0	0.5	0.5
1965	97.5	n.a.	1.7	99.2	0	0.8	0.8
1966	97.7	n.a.	1.6	99.3	0	0.7	0.7
1967	98.7	n.a.	0	98.7	0	1.3	1.3
1968	94.8	n.a.	0	94.8	0	5.2	5.2
1969	96.1	n.a.	0	96.1	0	3.9	3.9
1970	98.2	n.a.	0	98.2	0	1.8	1.8
1971	98.5	n.a.	0	98.5	0	1.5	1.5
1972	98.3	n.a.	0.5	98.8	0	1.2	1.2
1973	98.6	n.a.	0.4	99.0	0	1.0	1.0
1974	97.2	n.a.	2.7	99.8	0	0.2	0.2
1975	95.8	n.a.	4.1	99.9	0	0.1	0.1
1976	94.0	1.0	4.8	99.8	0	0.2	0.2
1977	91.5	2.4	6.0	99.9	0	0.2	0.2
1978	86.3	3.3	10.3	99.9	0	0.1	0.1
1979	84.5	2.0	11.9	98.3	1.1	0.5	1.7
1980	86.3	1.3	10.6	98.2	1.2	0.6	1.8
1981	82.0	4.8	10.1	96.9	2.9	0.2	3.1
1982	82.1	3.7	10.1	96.0	3.7	0.3	4.0
1983	82.2	4.6	9.2	96.0	3.3	0.7	4.0
1984	79.0	7.6	10.2	96.9	1.9	1.2	3.1
1985	77.6	10.0	9.5	97.2	1.6	1.2	2.8
1986	76.4	9.1	12.1	97.6	1.3	1.1	2.4
1987	71.7	7.6	17.0	96.3	0.5	3.2	3.7
1988	73.2	5.5	16.7	95.4	4.0	0.6	4.6
1989	75.0	4.6	13.0	92.6	6.4	0.9	7.3
1990	64.2	17.8	11.1	93.1	5.9	1.0	6.9

n.a. Not applicable.

Note: Data on the size of the informal system are compiled by the central bank based on sampling results of surveys on financial conditions of enterprises. Sampling bias naturally distorts the results.

Source: CBC, *Flow of Funds in Taiwan District* 1991.

Although some of the informal system's activities are unlawful, the authorities usually have refrained from suppressing it. They recognize it has contributed to the stimulation and mobilization of savings as well as to the allocative efficiency of loanable funds. In addition, the informal system is the last resort of households and medium and small businesses when seeking funds. Watched but not much meddled with, the informal system has played an important role in Taiwan.

Table 6.8. *Composition of Sources of Domestic Borrowings by Private Enterprises*
(percent)

End of year	Formal system				Informal system		
	Financial institutions	Money market	Bond market	Subtotal	Households	Other	Subtotal
1964	51.5	n.a.	0.8	52.3	45.5	2.2	47.7
1965	55.5	n.a.	0.7	56.2	42.1	1.8	43.9
1966	53.8	n.a.	0.9	54.8	43.9	1.4	45.2
1967	60.0	n.a.	1.0	61.0	35.2	3.8	39.0
1968	64.3	n.a.	1.1	65.4	28.2	6.4	34.6
1969	64.0	n.a.	0.9	64.9	28.9	6.1	35.1
1970	61.9	n.a.	0.8	62.7	31.4	5.8	37.3
1971	63.7	n.a.	0.7	64.4	31.3	4.3	35.6
1972	67.9	n.a.	0.6	68.5	27.4	4.1	31.5
1973	72.5	n.a.	0.4	72.8	24.1	3.0	27.2
1974	69.5	n.a.	0.6	70.1	28.3	1.6	29.9
1975	69.6	0.1	0.5	70.2	27.7	2.1	29.8
1976	67.1	0.3	0.6	68.0	29.5	2.5	32.0
1977	62.9	2.9	0.6	66.4	31.1	2.5	33.6
1978	59.6	4.0	0.5	64.2	33.8	2.0	35.8
1979	56.9	8.1	0.5	65.4	32.3	2.3	34.6
1980	54.7	8.9	0.5	64.0	33.6	2.3	36.0
1981	52.5	11.6	0.5	64.7	33.3	2.0	35.3
1982	53.2	13.3	0.5	67.0	30.5	2.6	33.0
1983	54.5	14.2	0.7	69.4	28.1	2.5	30.6
1984	54.1	15.0	1.0	70.1	27.1	2.8	29.9
1985	51.2	13.1	1.0	65.3	31.1	3.6	34.7
1986	50.2	8.4	0.8	59.3	37.9	2.8	40.7
1987	55.9	6.6	0.6	63.1	34.0	2.8	36.9
1988	63.3	5.7	0.6	69.6	27.9	2.5	30.4
1989	64.7	7.3	0.4	72.4	24.0	3.6	27.6
1990	66.1	10.0	0.4	76.5	19.3	4.2	23.5

n.a. Not applicable.

Note: Data on the size of the informal system are compiled by the central bank based on sampling results of surveys on financial conditions of enterprises. Sampling bias naturally distorts the results.

Source: CBC, *Flow of Funds in Taiwan District* 1991.

Financial Investment Companies

Financial investment companies, which had been prospering during the mid- and late 1980s but finally ceased operation in 1990, collected funds from the general public by paying monthly returns of as much as 9 percent, although 4 percent was the usual level. They used the funds to speculate in the stock, foreign exchange, and real estate markets, or else were pure Ponzi schemes. By accepting funds from the public and investing them in real and financial assets, the companies played a role similar to mutual funds.

In 1989 the revised Banking Law prohibited these companies from collecting additional funds from the public. The ending of new cash infusions and the cooling of the stock and real estate markets in 1990 eventually brought about the collapse of the financial investment companies.

PERFORMANCE OF THE FINANCIAL SYSTEM

The role of the financial system in economic growth is well understood in the literature. According to the Harrod–Domar growth model, the growth rate of an economy equals the investment rate divided by the marginal capital-output ratio. Stimulating and mobilizing savings can provide more funds for investment purpose and therefore raise the investment rate, while more efficient allocation of loanable funds can lower the marginal capital-output ratio.

Stimulation of Savings

As Table 6.9 shows, the share of gross domestic savings in Taiwan's GNP has risen steadily from 15 percent in 1951–60 to 33 percent in 1981–90. In the late 1980s Taiwan had one of the highest savings ratios in the world. Because of this, Taiwan's rapid growth has been accompanied by much less foreign borrowing than other developing countries. Although the savings rate over the 1951–70 period was slightly less than the investment rate, investment since has effectively been financed entirely out of domestic savings. Taiwan is in fact a net creditor to the outside world.

There are many reasons for Taiwan's high savings rate. The most important are a high growth rate in real GNP, a stable price level, large government savings

Table 6.9. *National Savings, Investments, and Net Foreign Borrowings as Percentages of GNP*

Period	Gross domestic		Net foreign borrowing[a]
	Investment	Savings	
1951–60	16.08	14.91	1.17
1961–70	21.89	21.07	0.82
1971–80	30.48	31.85	–1.37
1981–90	22.26	33.28	–11.02
1991	22.23	29.45	–7.22

Note: Data in this table are simple averages of annual data.

a. Net foreign borrowing is gross domestic investment (column 1) minus gross domestic savings (column 2).

Source: Directorate-General of Budget, Accounting and Statistics (DGBAS), *National Income in Taiwan Area, ROC*, 1991.

(21 percent of national savings and 20 percent of government current revenue over the period 1951–90), an underdeveloped social security system, low accessibility to consumer financing, the tradition in Chinese culture of frugality, and a strong desire to establish an independent family business. In addition, the policy of high real rates of interest on deposits, tax exemption for interest income on most bank deposits, vigorous savings promotion campaigns by financial intermediaries in the early years, and easy access to financial institutions certainly also helped. A widespread and convenient informal financial system providing high returns was another factor. (For a discussion of these factors see Sun and Liang 1982 and Scitovsky 1985.)

Tables 6.9 and 6.A4 show the investment ratio fell sharply in the 1980s, although it was still above the levels of the 1950s and 1960s. The reasons include rising labor costs, environmental considerations, unavailability of land, and social and political unrest.

The bank deposit rate, curb market interest rate, and inflation rate are reported in Table 6.10. The real interest rate on one-year savings deposits has been positive since 1961 except for the first oil shock period, and the average was about 6 percent between 1961 and 1990. The real curb market interest rate has averaged as high as 21 percent in the same period. There was a persistent gap between the curb market and the savings deposit rate (between 11 and 18 percent), regardless of whether the supply of loans from the banking system was in shortage (before 1982) or in surplus (after 1983). A large part of this gap may represent the higher default risk and transaction costs in curb market lending.

Mobilization of Savings

The absolute amounts of savings, investment, and financial surplus or deficit of households, government, public enterprises, and private enterprises are given in Table 6.A3. Between 1951 and 1989, private and public enterprises generated internal savings equal to about 65 percent of their investment funds. The household sector put 26 percent of its savings into housing, vehicles, and other durables. However, it always has been the most important source of surplus. The government, has also provided a huge financial surplus, although it has invested a large proportion (some 60 percent) of its savings in infrastructure.

Based on flow-of-funds statistics, the sources and uses of funds of households, private enterprises, public enterprises, government, and financial institutions from 1970 to 1989 are reported in Tables 6.A5 and 6.A6.

A few comments on the data. The government made extensive direct investment in infrastructure and purchased significant amounts of corporate stocks (mostly shares of public enterprises). Accumulation of foreign assets, almost entirely held by the CBC, constituted a large proportion (almost 37 percent) of the total uses by financial institutions.

The major source of external funds for private enterprises was issuing stock, but most of the shares were not issued to the public. Private enterprises were more dependent on financial institutions and the curb market than were public enterprises, which depended on internal savings and stock issued to the government for most of their investment funds.

Table 6.10. *Interest Rates and Inflation*
(percent per annum)

| Year | Nominal Interest Rate | | | Real Interest Rate[b] | | |
	Curb[a]	1-year savings deposit	Change in WPI	Curb	1-year savings deposit	Difference
1961	33.51	15.60	3.22	30.29	12.38	17.91
1962	30.97	13.92	3.04	27.93	10.88	17.05
1963	23.87	12.72	6.48	21.89	6.24	15.65
1964	24.53	11.04	2.48	22.05	8.56	13.49
1965	23.76	10.80	−4.66	28.42	15.46	12.96
1966	23.82	10.20	1.49	22.33	8.71	13.62
1967	23.85	9.84	2.53	21.32	7.31	14.01
1968	23.89	9.72	2.97	20.92	6.75	14.17
1969	25.42	9.72	−0.27	25.69	9.99	15.70
1970	21.25	9.72	2.73	18.52	6.99	11.53
1971	21.49	9.48	0.03	21.46	9.45	12.01
1972	21.85	9.00	4.45	17.40	4.55	12.85
1973	22.45	9.36	22.86	−0.41	−13.50	13.09
1974	29.15	14.40	40.58	−11.43	−26.18	14.75
1975	27.26	12.33	−5.07	32.33	17.40	14.93
1976	27.53	11.83	2.76	24.77	9.07	15.70
1977	26.61	9.90	2.76	23.85	7.14	16.71
1978	25.99	9.50	3.54	22.45	5.96	16.49
1979	28.96	10.98	13.82	15.14	−2.84	17.98
1980	30.63	12.50	21.54	9.09	−9.04	18.13
1981	30.96	13.59	7.62	23.34	5.97	17.37
1982	28.28	11.18	−0.18	28.46	11.36	17.10
1983	26.69	8.80	−1.19	27.88	9.79	18.09
1984	25.97	8.31	0.48	25.49	7.83	17.66
1985	24.98	7.23	−2.60	27.56	9.83	17.73
1986	22.51	5.52	−3.34	25.85	8.86	16.99
1987	22.90	5.00	−3.25	24.15	8.25	15.90
1988	20.87	5.12	−1.56	22.43	8.68	15.75
1989	21.74	8.09	−0.38	22.12	8.47	13.65
1990	23.42	9.50	−0.61	24.03	10.11	13.92

a. Interest rates on unsecured loans and loans against post-dated checks in Taipei and Kaohsiung Municipalities and Taichung City, weighted by the amount of each.

b. Nominal rate minus the WPI (wholesale price index).

Source: CBC, *Financial Statistics Monthly*, various issues, except the WPI is from DGBAS, *Commodity Price Statistics*, Jul. 1992.

In sum, the main function of Taiwan's financial system has been to channel household savings to finance the investment by private enterprises, and this function was performed reasonably well until the mid-1980s. At that time a large share of domestic savings began to be used to finance the accumulation of foreign exchange reserves, which statistically are classified as foreign investment, with the result that a large proportion of deposits have turned into foreign assets.

The success of the financial system in mobilizing savings is also evidenced by the steady increase of the ratio of M2 to GNP, as shown in Table 6.11. This ratio was only 28 percent in 1961–65, almost doubled in 1971–75, and reached 130 percent in 1986–90. Another indicator can be found in Table 6.12, which shows the share of deposits with longer maturities has been rising.

Allocation of Loanable Funds

As far as economic growth is concerned, efficient allocation of loanable funds is as important as the availability of loanable funds per se. Although the financial system in Taiwan has a good record of stimulating and mobilizing domestic savings, the performance of financial institutions in allocating funds has often been criticized. The criticisms include that collateral was emphasized rather than the profitability or productivity of the borrowers; that medium- and long-term loans were in short supply; that public enterprises and large firms were favored over private enterprises and medium and small businesses; that export industries were privileged in obtaining bank loans and preferential loans, compared to import-competing industries and the nontradable sector; and that consumption finance was purposely neglected.

The emphasis on collateral in bank lending is illustrated in Table 6.13. Secured loans accounted for about three-fifths of the loans made by domestic banks at both the beginning and end of the 1961–90 period, although there was a dip in between.

Loans by domestic banks having a maturity of more than one year have steadily increased share. Note that the total loans of domestic banks includes lending to private enterprises, public enterprises, and households. Lending to the last two is more likely to be long-term. In the 1980s banks were troubled by excess liquidity, and so started to expand consumer loans. A major part of

Table 6.11. *M2 as Percentage of GNP*

Period	Percent	Period	Percent
1961–65	28.4	1976–80	65.3
1966–70	37.7	1981–85	83.5
1971–75	49.6	1986–90	132.6

Note: Data are averages of annual figures.

M2 includes currency, checking accounts, passbook deposits, time deposits, negotiable CDs, time savings deposits, foreign currency deposits, foreign exchange proceeds deposits, foreign exchange trust funds, and CDs in foreign currency held by enterprises and individuals.

Source: CBC, *Financial Statistics Monthly*, various issues.

Table 6.12. *Maturity Structure of Deposits with Domestic Banks* (percent)

	1961–70	1971–80	1981–90
Checking and passbook deposits	38.6	37.9	33.2
Time deposits of less than 1 year	16.5	13.6	15.3
Time deposits of 1 year or more	44.9	48.5	51.5

Note: Data are averages of annual shares within the period.

Source: Computed from table of deposits with domestic banks and appendix table of analysis of time deposits and time savings deposits with domestic banks by maturity, in CBC, *Financial Statistics Monthly*, various issues.

these loans, almost always secured by household real estate, was used to speculate in the real estate and stock market booms. Mostly long-term, these loans contributed to the sharp increase in the shares of secured and longer-term loans during the 1980s.

Public enterprises have an advantage in obtaining bank loans. Financial institutions funded about 88 percent of public enterprise domestic borrowing over the 1964–90 period, but provided only 60 percent of private enterprise domestic borrowing. Until the mid-1980s, public enterprises had always been granted more loans by financial institutions per unit of production value or GDP than had private enterprises. Over the 1965–88 period the ratio of loans from financial institutions relative to gross value added averaged 47 percent for public enterprises but only 29 percent for private enterprises.

Table 6.14 shows the distribution of net value added and loans from financial institutions between public and private manufacturing between 1980 and 1988. Public manufacturing enjoyed a share of loans from financial institutions much larger than its share of net value added (domestic factor income) except in 1987 and 1988. Because public enterprises engage in more capital-intensive production, one might expect them to have a higher proportion of borrowing. However, even after making this adjustment the system's bias toward financing public enterprises seems to remain strong.

Table 6.13. *Secured Loans and Medium- and Long-Term Loans as a Percentage of Total Loans of Domestic Banks*

Period	Secured	Medium- and long-term	Period	Secured	Medium- and long-term
1961–65	61.1	30.1	1976–80	54.0	35.2
1966–70	63.9	31.4	1981–85	55.8	50.1
1971–75	55.4	31.8	1986–90	61.1	63.0

Note: Discounts and advances on imports are not included in total loans.

Source: Computed from table of loans and discounts at domestic banks, in CBC, *Financial Statistics Monthly*, various issues.

Table 6.14. *Distribution between Public and Private Manufacturing of Net Value Added and of Loans from Financial Institutions*
(percent)

Year	Net value added		Loans[a]	
	Public	Private	Public	Private
1980	9.36	90.64	21.67	78.33
1981	9.49	90.51	23.85	76.15
1982	11.04	88.96	25.29	74.71
1983	11.77	88.23	25.16	74.84
1984	10.92	89.08	21.64	78.36
1985	9.12	90.88	18.31	81.69
1986	10.09	89.91	15.26	84.74
1987	10.54	89.46	10.45	89.55
1988	11.80	88.20	7.03	92.97
Averages				
1980 – 85	10.28	89.72	22.65	72.85
1980 – 88	10.46	89.54	18.74	81.26

a. By way of estimating average outstanding balances during the year, loans from financial institutions are the average of the year-end loans for the current year and the previous year.

Source: Unpublished DGBAS data on GDP and factor income by kind of economic activity; and CBC, *Report on the Survey of Financial Conditions of the Public and Private Enterprises in Taiwan Area, ROC*, various issues.

In Taiwan, only large private firms with good credit were qualified to borrow from the money market, where interest rates were generally lower than the bank loan rate. Bank loans were the first choice for other private enterprises and the rest of the large firms' financial needs. Borrowers went to the curb markets as a last resort. To compare the availability of loans from financial institutions by company size, Table 6.15 shows the composition of domestic borrowing of private enterprises classed by asset scale in 1983. Clearly, the larger the firm, the greater the ability to obtain financing from both financial institutions and the money and bond markets; and the fewer assets a firm had, the more it depended on high-cost curb market financing.

The impact of all this on the allocative efficiency of loanable funds was that loan applications for investments that were profitable but could not meet collateral requirements might have been rejected by financial institutions. The shortage of longer-term loans must have forced enterprises to curtail their long-term investments or, at best, to roll over short-term loans for such purposes, a common phenomenon in Taiwan that increases firms' liquidity risk. The preferences for exporting industries are generally regarded as successful policy measures to stimulate exports and economic growth. In the 1980s, however, they also distorted

Table 6.15. *Percentage Distribution of Sources of Domestic Borrowings by Private Enterprises in 1983, by Scale of Assets*

Assets (million NT$)	Source		
	Financial institutions	*Money and bond market*	*Curb market*
under 1	10.5	0	89.5
1–5	31.0	0	68.9
5–10	44.1	0	55.9
10–40	50.9	0.3	48.8
40–100	59.3	1.0	39.7
100–500	66.4	4.4	29.2
500–1000	65.8	15.9	18.3
over 1000	70.1	19.6	10.3

Source: Derived from Liu 1988, Table 4, which is compiled from data from a 1983 CBC survey of the financial conditions of private enterprises in Taiwan.

fund allocations among the exporting, import-competing, and nontradable sectors, and contributed, together with the policy of discriminating against consumption financing, to a huge trade surplus.

The preference of financial institutions to lend to public enterprises and large businesses also distorted the allocation of investment funds. Public enterprises in Taiwan have often been criticized for their low efficiencies in operations and investment. The prosperity and importance of medium and small businesses also indicate that large businesses are probably not superior to medium and small businesses in operational or investment efficiencies. For instance, in 1987 medium and small businesses, defined as those with a capital of less than NT$40 million, made up 98 percent of all firms and accounted for 67 percent of total exports. Taking just manufacturing in 1987, medium and small firms accounted for 99 percent of the number of firms, 71 percent of the value of manufacturing exports, and 47 percent of total manufacturing sales in Taiwan.

Easier access to bank loans by public enterprises and large firms inevitably induced them to adopt more capital-intensive technologies, the result of which is a higher productivity for labor and a lower productivity for capital in public and large enterprises relative to private and medium and small enterprises. If we could reallocate resources in such a way as to shift some capital from public and large enterprises to private and medium and small enterprises in exchange for some labor, the total productivity of the whole economy might increase.

In short, the allocation of investment funds has not been completely satisfactory from an efficiency point of view. The efficiency loss can be attributed to four main factors: government ownership of major banks, strict entry regulations, interest rate control, and selective credit-rationing policies. All these factors are related to the financial policies discussed later.

Testing Criticisms of Credit Allocation

To capture the behavior of financial institutions in rationing their loanable funds and thus test the criticism of that behavior, I have estimated two credit allocation equations, one for five sectors (for 1965–88) and the other for 11 manufacturing industries (private enterprises only, 1974–88). The results support the criticisms. Financial institutions emphasized collateral more than the productivity of borrowers when rationing loans, and exporting industries were favored. In a similar study, which did not include the general availability of bank loans and the export ratio as explanatory variables, Shea and Kuo (1984) also obtained the result that collateral rather than profitability was the key factor considered by financial institutions in granting loans, based on pooling the data on 19 industries over the period 1975–82.

In the model here, the bank-financing ratio—that is, the proportion of loan demand actually financed by financial institutions (BL/DL)—is used as the dependent variable. The explanatory variables are the general availability of bank loans relative to total market demand (TBL/TDL), collateral (FA/DL), capital productivity (KI/TA), and previous relationship with financial institutions (which is measured by the previous year's bank-financing ratio). In the manufacturing equation, the export ratio is included to capture the effect of export promotion policies. The regression equations and data sources are in Table 6.16; and the results are presented in Tables 6.17 and 6.18.

The results show the general availability of bank loans and the previous year's bank-financing ratio have significantly positive impact on the current year's bank-financing ratio, which is as expected. When testing the validity of each of the three criticisms, the regression should show significantly positive coefficients for collateral, and it does. Also as it should be if the criticism is correct, capital productivity has insignificantly positive or even negative coefficients. However, the export ratio, which also should have significantly positive coefficients, does so only at the 10 percent level.

A specific sector or industry has been disproportionately favored in the credit-rationing process if it has a larger sectoral or industrial dummy coefficient. The regression coefficients of sectoral dummy variables show the manufacturing sector was favored when applying for loans from financial institutions, while the mining sector and the communication, transportation, and storage sector were discriminated against. (The other two sectors—construction; and wholesale and retail trade, restaurants, and hotels—had neutral results.) Because manufacturing also has been the major exporting sector in Taiwan, this result supports the assertion that exporting industries were privileged in obtaining bank loans.

The favored private manufacturing industries are food and beverages, chemicals, basic metals, and transport equipment. Those not favored are lumber and furniture, nonmetallic mineral products, fabricated metal products, machinery, and electrical and electronic machinery and equipment. The other two industries—textiles and apparel, and paper and printing—were treated neutrally when applying for loans.

Table 6.16. *Credit Allocation Equations*

The equations showing credit allocation by financial institutions among 5 major private sectors and among 11 private manufacturing industries, respectively, are specified as

Sectoral credit allocation equation

$$\left(\frac{BL}{DL}\right)_{it} = a_1 = \sum_{i=2}^{5} a_i D_i + b_1\left(\frac{TBL}{TDL}\right)_t + b_2\left(\frac{FA}{DL}\right)_{it} + b_3\left(\frac{KI}{TA}\right)_{it} + b_4\left(\frac{BL}{DL}\right)_{i,\,t-1} \tag{1}$$

Manufacturing industrial credit allocation equation

$$\left(\frac{BL}{DL}\right)_{it} = c_1 + \sum_{i=2}^{11} c_i DM_i + d_1\left(\frac{TBLM}{TDLM}\right)_t + d_2\left(\frac{FA}{DL}\right)_{it} + d_3\left(\frac{KI}{TA}\right)_{it} + d_4 ER_{it} + d_5\left(\frac{BL}{DL}\right)_{i,\,t-1} \tag{2}$$

where subscript *i* denotes private sector (or industry) *i* and *t* is the year,

BL_i Loans by *i* from financial institutions

DL_i Domestic borrowings by *i* from financial institutions and curb market

TBL_t Total loans from financial institutions by all private enterprises in year *t*

TDL_t Total domestic borrowing of all private enterprises from both financial institutions and curb markets in year *t*

$TBLM_t$ Total loans from financial institutions by the entire private manufacturing sector in year *t*

$TDLM_t$ Total domestic borrowings of the entire private manufacturing sector from both financial institutions and curb markets in year *t*

FA Fixed assets

KI Before tax income of capital (the sum of rent, interest, and profit, net of depreciation)

TA Total assets

ER Export ratio

Di Dummy variable for sector *i* (no dummy variable is defined for the mining sector, which is the reference sector).

DM_i Dummy variable for industry *i* (no dummy variable is defined for food and beverages, which is the reference industry).

Note: For manufacturing, annual data over the period 1974 – 88 are pooled. The ordinary least squares method is applied to estimate the equations. The estimated values of b_1, b_4, d_1 and d_5 are expected to be positive. If the criticisms mentioned in the text are true, the regression result should also show significantly positive values for b_2, d_2, and d_4, and insignificantly positive or even negative values for b_3 and d_3.

Source: Loans from financial institutions and curb markets, fixed assets, and total assets of each sector and industry were obtained from the "Report on the Survey of Financial Conditions of the Public and Private Enterprises in Taiwan Area" published by the Central Bank of China. Data on capital income are from unpublished Directorate-General of Budget, Accounting and Statistics (DGBAS) material. The export ratio of each industry is roughly measured by the ratio of export value relative to production value of the whole industry (including both public and private firms). Export value is compiled from the "Monthly Statistics of Exports and Imports" published by the Ministry of Finance, and production value comes from national income statistics compiled by DGBAS.

Table 6.17. *Credit Allocation Equations, Five Major Private Sectors*

Explanatory variable	Coefficient	t value
Constant	0.08758	1.100
TBL/TDL	0.22918	1.768[a]
FA/DL	0.03744	1.953[a]
KI/TA	−0.54153	−4.137[b]
$(BL/DL)_{t-1}$	0.50974	6.069[b]
D2 (manufacturing)	0.12191	4.441[b]
D3 (construction)	0.03976	1.966[b]
D4 (trade, restaurants, hotels)	0.05550	2.659[b]
D5 (communications, transportation, storage)	−0.00895	−0.302

$R^2 = 0.8385$.

a. Significantly positive at 5% level.

b. Significant at 2.5% level.

Table 6.18. *Credit Allocation Equations, Eleven Private Manufacturing Industries*

Explanatory variable	With ER $R^2 = 0.8479$		Without ER $R^2 = 0.8462$	
	Coefficient	t- value	Coefficient	t- value
Constant	0.05387	0.858	0.10862	2.350[a]
TBLM/TDLM	0.29085	3.563[a]	0.25131	3.316[a]
FA/DL	0.05755	2.699[a]	0.05613	2.630[a]
KI/TA	0.07478	0.805	0.04693	0.519
ER	0.09075	1.285[c]	n.a.	n.a.
$(BL/DL)_{t-1}$	0.54153	9.577[a]	0.53169	9.470[a]
DM2 (textiles and apparel)	−0.05027	−1.875[b]	−0.02223	−1.425[c]
DM3 (lumber and furniture)	−0.07482	−2.175[b]	−0.03497	−2.343[a]
DM4 (paper and printing)	−0.03795	−2.070[b]	−0.04708	−2.871[a]
DM5 (chemicals)	−0.02358	−1.358[c]	−0.01462	−0.917
DM6 (nonmetalic mineral)	−0.07649	−2.850[a]	−0.07294	−2.726[a]
DM7 (basic metals)	0.00186	0.130	−0.00216	−0.154
DM8 (fabricated metal)	−0.13220	−5.521[a]	−0.11352	−5.955[a]
DM9 (machinery)	−0.08156	−3.153[a]	−0.05811	−3.162[a]
DM10 (electrical[d])	−0.07770	−2.568[a]	−0.04352	−3.016[a]
DM11 (transport equipment)	−0.01241	−0.817	−0.00695	−0.475

n.a Not applicable.

a. Signficant at 1% level.

b. Signficant at 5% level.

c. Signficant at 10% level.

d. Includes electronic machinery and equipment.

247

Although the factors affecting financial institution preferences among industries still needs further investigation, banks do not appear to have allocated loans according to growth potential. This conclusion is supported by a Spearman's Rank Correlation Coefficient test of the relationship between bank credit allocation preferences and the average production growth rates of private manufacturing industries. The result, although positive, was insignificantly small.

The Informal System's Contribution to Allocative Efficiency

The performance of financial institutions in allocating funds was far from satisfactory. Fortunately, however, the authorities did not intend to suppress the informal financial system by seriously implementing the usury law and related prohibitory rules. By offering higher interest rates, the informal system competed away loanable funds that would otherwise have been used by financial institutions, using them to fund investment projects that had been rejected for loans by financial institutions simply because the prospective borrower could not provide sufficient collateral or meet the government's credit rationing criteria. Thus the informal financial system improved the allocative efficiency of investment.

Both the extent to which productivity was a criterion for loans from financial institutions, and the efficiency contribution of the informal system from 1965 to 1982 were measured by a model developed by myself and Kuo. Our results support the criticism that the efficiency of financial institutions in allocating loanable funds has been far from satisfactory—productivity of borrowers had not been an important consideration in rationing credit. (The model is presented in the Appendix.)

We also estimated that the total productivity of total loans was increased about 6 percent and that the level of GDP rose by 1.23 percent on average during 1965–82 because of the existence of a curb market. (It is assumed the curb market rate purely measures only the marginal productivities of curb market borrowers. In reality, however, part of the rate reflects higher default risk and transaction costs. Therefore, our results overestimate the actual efficiency contribution of the informal system.)

GOVERNMENT INTERVENTION

Growth promotion and stabilization are two reasons governments intervene in financial markets. In Taiwan such good intentions have been at the forefront, but as means to the ends the authorities adopted several interventionist policies harmful to the development and allocative efficiency of financial institutions—and thereby indirectly promoted the growth of the informal system. The four interventionist policies were government ownership of major banks, strict entry regulations, interest rate control, and selective credit-rationing policies.

The financial system in Taiwan has been noted for its active curb markets, and financial institutions have not allocated loanable funds according to the productivity or growth potential of borrowers. In addition to the interventionist policies, there have been other factors responsible for these phenomena. On the borrower side, the traditions of high debt to equity ratios and the indifferent accounting at private enterprises, especially medium and small businesses, reduced the propensity of financial institutions to lend money to them. Table 6.19 shows the debt to equity ratios of private enterprises and private manufacturing.

Government Ownership of Banks

The government owns and manages most of the domestic banks. Of the 16 domestic full-service banks, only 4 are less than half owned by the government. At the end of 1990, these 4 private banks had only 10 percent of total assets, 9 percent of total deposits, and 8 percent of total loans of domestic banks.

Some of the government banks were transferred from the Japanese in 1945 and thus are government-owned for historical reasons. Besides specialized banks that are usually also government owned in other countries, the authorities kept ownership for reasons of equity and stability. That is, government-owned banks are more willing to cooperate in implementing monetary policies, and putting the major banks under its direct control meant the government could keep them from being part of any concentration of private economic power. The profits of a protected banking industry have been a source of revenue for the government.

However, government ownership caused great damage to the economic efficiency of the banking industry. In addition to financial regulations, government banks are subjected to the same administrative control as other government agencies. All their directors and senior management are appointed by the government. Numerous regulations and restrictions on personnel, accounting, budgeting, and auditing have turned government banks into bureaucracies which operate inefficiently and are sluggish in bringing in financial innovations.

Pressure or lobbying for loans from representatives or government officials has distorted credit policy. Loans are viewed as government assets by the auditing agency, and getting permission from auditors to write off bad loans therefore is difficult. Under such a system, loan officers are unwilling to take risks, and collateral is emphasized when granting loans.

Table 6.19. *Total Liabilities as a Percentage of Shareholder Equity of Private Enterprises (average for each period)*

Period	Overall	Manufacturing only	Period average	Overall	Manufacturing only
1964–70	114	135	1981–85	160	175
1971–75	135	148	1986–90	151	151
1976–80	150	164	1964–90	140	153

Note: In US accounting terminology, this is called the debt–equity ratio.

Source: CBC, *Report on the Survey of Financial Conditions of the Public and Private Enterprises in Taiwan Area, ROC*, various issues.

Regulation of Market Competition

To prevent instability caused by competition among financial institutions, the authorities have maintained strict regulations on setting up new institutions and branches. Bank deposit and lending rates were set or fully controlled by the CBC before 1980. To reduce the cost of funds and thus stimulate investment, the CBC often sets bank interest rates lower than a market equilibrium, although the real deposit rate has usually remained positive. These factors weakened market competition, which in turn reduced the role of the price mechanism in allocating investment funds.

Lin and Shea (1983) applied disequilibrium econometric techniques to show the supply of loanable funds of financial institutions often was less than demand during the period 1962–82. To resolve the problem of excess demand, criteria other than the productivity of borrowers were applied. Inefficient allocation of loanable funds, compensating balance requirements, commission requests, and a prosperous informal system were among the consequences. Although no direct data are available on compensating balance requirements, Shea (1984) estimated that on average 20 to 25 percent of private enterprise loans from banks were used as compensating balances over the period 1965–82. When this result was presented to a seminar of the Bankers Association of ROC, some participants suggested the ratio was at the lower end of the range.

Selective Credit-Rationing Policies

The need for nonprice credit rationing has invited further intervention and guidance from the government. MOF and CBC often have ordered financial institutions to expand or restrict loans to certain economic activities, industries, or borrower groups. The purpose was usually to promote economic growth or to stabilize the economy. To some extent, it was also to equalize the availability of bank loans among business groups. For example, financing real estate transactions was limited or even forbidden when property markets were considered speculative. Growth promotion policies, discussed in the next section, routinely use selective credit.

GROWTH PROMOTION POLICIES

To promote economic growth, the government adopted policies to accommodate the financing needs of specific industries and economic activities. These policies include export financing, industrial financing, machine-import financing, strategic-industry financing, emergency financing, and the establishment of specialized banks. Among these policies, export, strategic-industry, and emergency financing policies deserve more discussion; the others can be summarized as special loans.

Export Financing

Taiwan is a small open economy with a high degree of trade dependency. Because export promotion was proposed as the nation's economic development strategy in the 1960s, export financing has been important, in addition to other incentives such as rebates of custom duties and commodity taxes on imported raw materials, tax exemptions, and allowing retention of foreign exchange earnings to be used for importing raw materials and machinery.

Exporting firms could apply for short-term loans as preshipment working capital based on letters of credit. After the products were shipped, firms were eligible for loans based on letters of credit, documents against acceptance or payment, and shipping documents. Since 1978, local branches of foreign banks have been allowed to extend preshipment export loans in foreign exchange.

In addition, the CBC provided a special low rediscount rate to designated domestic banks for export loans. These banks were permitted to charge borrowers an annual rate that was usually just 1 percentage point higher than the rediscount rate. The difference between the export loan rate and the minimum interest rate for secured loans is illustrated in Table 6.20.

As the trade surplus started to pile up foreign exchange reserves in the late

Table 6.20. *Interest Rate Subsidy on Export Loans*
(percent)

Year	Export rate	Minimum[a]	Difference	Year	Export rate	Minimum[a]	Difference
1963	7.50	14.94	7.44	1978	6.50	10.50	4.00
1964	7.50	14.04	6.54	1979	8.75	11.98	3.23
1965	7.50	14.04	6.54	1980	10.53	13.50	2.97
1966	7.50	14.04	6.54	1981	11.55	14.19	2.64
1967	7.50	13.63	6.13	1982	9.79	11.18	1.39
1968	7.50	13.32	5.82	1983	8.05	8.60	0.55
1969	7.50	13.32	5.82	1984	7.86	8.31	0.45
1970	7.50	13.30	5.80	1985	7.41	8.08	0.67
1971	7.50	12.25	4.75	1986	5.79	7.20	1.41
1972	7.50	11.63	4.13	1987	5.50	6.75	1.25
1973	8.17	11.81	3.64	1988	5.50	6.87	1.37
1974	10.99	15.89	4.90	1989	7.54	9.22	1.68
1975	7.80	13.48	5.68	1990	8.75	10.23	1.48
1976	7.00	12.83	5.83	1991	8.31	9.56	1.25
1977	6.62	10.91	4.29				

a. Minimum rate for secured loans. The prime rate is used after the prime rate system was set up in March 1985. Monthly data are averaged to get annual data.

Source: CBC, *Financial Statistics Monthly*, various issues.

1970s, the CBC gradually reduced the rate differential. Moreover, because the margin between the rediscount rate and the export loan rate was only 1 point, the banks had no particular desire to apply for rediscounts. Most export loans by domestic banks were therefore financed by their own loanable funds rather than accommodated by the CBC. Thus, the actual benefit of export loans to exporting firms came mainly from the availability of funds rather than the interest subsidy, even in the 1960s and 1970s.

Special Loans

The CBC has often adopted a special loans policy to accommodate financing needs and to direct the allocation of funds, using both government commercial and specialized banks. After extending special loans, the banks could rediscount them at a preferential rate at the CBC.

Agriculture, various industries, exporting, and machinery imports are the major categories of recipients. In addition, there was the "medium- and long-term credit special fund" of the CBC set up in 1973 to finance basic construction and long-term investments. Funds came mostly from redeposits of postal savings and the Cooperative Bank of Taiwan, which was receiving redeposits from the extensive network of co-ops.

Finally, six government banks were set up or designated to specialize in industrial, agricultural, real estate, medium and small business, and export–import financing; and special loan programs for agriculture, medium and small business, venture capital, and the like, have been implemented. More extended discussions on the special loans policy can be found in Lee and Chen (1984).

Emergency Financing

In 1974 and 1979, when the energy crises caused GNP and export growth to slow, the CBC provided various special loans and rediscounts to relieve the financial difficulties of exporting firms and medium and small businesses. When the domestic economy again suffered from stagnation in 1982 and 1985, the CBC turned to special loan and expansionary monetary policies. MOF even allowed firms with financial problems to extend the due date of bank loans, and it granted some firms an extension of the redemption period for their dishonored checks.

Strategic Industry Financing

In the 1980s upgrading the industrial structure became an important policy goal. Therefore, measures to promote strategic industries were promulgated in 1982. The industries were selected based on six criteria: linkage effects, market potential, technology intensity, value added, energy intensity, and pollution—with high levels of the first four and low levels of the last two being considered desirable. Selected at that time were electrical and nonelectrical machinery, information, and electronics. Later, the list was extended to include the biotechnology and material industries.

The government provided strategic industry firms with special medium- and long-term, low-interest loans. These were extended by the Bank of Communications and the Medium and Small Business Bank of Taiwan, with 20 to 25 percent of the funds provided by the Development Fund of the Executive Yuan and the rest by the two banks. The rate difference between strategic loans and the prime rate was between 175 and 275 basis points. Preferential loans later were expanded to finance the purchase of automation equipment and domestically produced machines, as well as for investment projects for environmental protection.

From the beginning, the preferential loan policy has been severely criticized by scholars. It is regarded as a distortional policy, and some of the selection criteria are seen as improper or inconsistent with one another.

Conclusion

In sum, the government tried hard to influence the allocation of available investment funds and to create additional funds for specific industries and activities through selective credit control policies. In the 1950s and early 1960s, the Taiwan economy was short of investment funds; the private sector lacked experienced entrepreneurs; and industries with comparative advantage could be easily identified. Under such circumstances, a strategy to depend on selective credit control policies rather than the price (interest rate) mechanism to allocate investment funds to public enterprises, exporting activities, and industries supposed to have comparative advantages might not cause much harm.

By the 1970s and 1980s, however, when Taiwan's economy had more investment funds and entrepreneurs, and industries with comparative advantage were no longer easily identifiable, the government's dependency on such policies naturally invited distortions and criticisms. Thus, although some studies—such as Kuo (1983)—emphasize the success of industrial policy in the early period, others—such as Hsing (1988)—argue that the economy could have performed even better had more market-oriented policies been adopted as early as the 1960s.

STABILIZATION POLICIES

In the early years after World War II until around 1952, Taiwan suffered high inflation. Its ending is generally attributed to currency reform, the introduction of gold savings deposits and preferential rate deposits, and the arrival of aid from the United States. (For details on stabilization policies and their impact, see Tsiang 1982 and Lee and Chen 1984.)

During the decades of rapid economic growth since the mid-1950s, Taiwan has enjoyed relatively stable prices. The exceptions are 1973, 1974, and 1980, when the change in the GNP deflator was over 15 percent, and in 1955, 1960, 1979, and 1981, when the GNP deflator grew by more than 10 percent. All but the two earliest of these can be related to the oil shocks.

Because the 1945–49 hyperinflation in mainland China is viewed as one of the major factors causing the KMT government to lose the battle against the communists, stabilization of prices in Taiwan has been a national goal with very high priority since 1952. In addition to maintaining the government budget in balance or in surplus, several major policies have been adopted to stabilize domestic prices.

The Financial Development of Japan, Korea, and Taiwan

Money Supply Policy

During the period 1962–89, the money supply (M1B, defined as the sum of currency, checking account deposits, passbook deposits, and passbook savings deposits) increased at an average annual rate of 22 percent, much greater than the average growth rate of real GNP (9.4 percent). However, due to a high income elasticity of money demand, estimated to be 1.3 to 1.5, prices remained quite stable. Scholars have put forward different views to explain the high income elasticity of money demand. Tsiang (1977) argues that import and export transactions create extra demand for money that is not taken care of by the national income variable. Shea (1983b) shows the process of monetization, financial development, and specialization of the production process all have contributed to the high income elasticity.

The increase in money supply from 1962 to 1989 is decomposed into four sources in Table 6.21. The government budget has in fact been a contractionary factor over the period. Excess credit expansion to the general public was the most important source of increase in the 1960s and 1970s. Accumulation of net foreign assets by the banking system also contributed to money creation in the 1960s and 1970s, and was the primary cause of the rapid increase in the 1980s.

Before the money market became effective and of substantial scale, the CBC depended on a required reserve ratio, control of the rediscount rate, redeposits from the postal savings system and the Cooperation Bank, accommodations to domestic banks, and moral suasion to control the money supply. Since 1979 open

Table 6.21. *Growth Rate of the Money Supply (M1B) and Contributions of Different Sources to the Increase* (percent)

Period	Money supply growth rate[a]	Percentage of money supply growth caused by [b]			
		Government budget	Credit expansion[c]	Foreign assets[d]	Other
1962–65	19.8	–30.6	47.4	84.8	–1.7
1966–70	16.9	–25.6	85.8	57.8	–18.1
1971–75	28.5	–33.2	136.3	28.7	–31.8
1976–80	24.2	–19.4	101.8	51.7	–34.1
1981–85	13.8	–1.2	–121.5	269.0	–46.2
1986–90	22.6	–10.9	27.1	127.8	–44.0

a. Averages of the annual growth rates within each period.

b. Each row adds to 100%. The distribution is for the total money supply increase during the period.

c. Excess credit expansion to the general public (households and enterprises) is defined as monetary institutions' claims on households and enterprises minus quasi money (mainly composed of time deposits and time savings deposits) and pre-settlement requirements for imports.

d. After 1976 the valuation changes resulting from fluctuations in the exchange rate of the NT dollar against foreign currencies are excluded.

Source: CBC, *Financial Statistics Monthly*, various issues.

market operations through the money market have become an additional tool. For example, in 1986 and 1987, when Taiwan's huge trade surplus caused the supply of high-power money to expand very quickly, the CBC issued treasury bills, CDs, and savings bonds equal to well over half the money supply of the previous year in order to sterilize the impact of the trade surplus on the money supply.

Interest Rate Policy

Interest rate policy is an effective instrument for fighting inflation. Scholars such as McKinnon (1973) and Tsiang (1979) have advocated the policy of raising the deposit rate in order to end inflation. Taiwan is probably the first developing country to set an example by doing this successfully. In the early 1950s, preferential savings deposits offering a very high interest rate were introduced to stabilize domestic prices. The result was indeed very prompt and successful. (For details, see Irvine and Emery 1966, Chandavarkar 1971, and Tsiang 1979, 1982).

This early experience did not, however, lead the authorities to accept the principle of letting interest rates balance the demand and supply of loanable funds. Instead, before 1980 bank interest rates were kept strictly under the control of the CBC and were usually set at levels lower than market-clearing rates in order to stimulate investment. Still, most of the time the CBC did set the rates above inflation. The CBC also used raising bank interest rates as part of its stabilization package when the economy faced the threat of inflation.

Exchange Rate Policy

In its early years of development, Taiwan was seriously troubled by a shortage of foreign exchange. The authorities therefore imposed strict exchange controls and at various times adopted dual and multiple exchange rate systems. In September 1963, a dual rate system was replaced by a fixed uniform system. Subsequently, the New Taiwan dollar appreciated relative to the U.S. dollar only once—from 40 to 38 in February 1973. However in July 1978, the NT dollar moved to 36, and a floating exchange rate system was adopted.

The purpose of introducing a floating exchange rate was to make the economy less vulnerable to external disturbances. Huge trade surpluses in 1972 and 1973 resulted in 33 and 45 percent increases in the money supply, which contributed to a 32 percent jump in the GNP deflator in 1974. Trade surpluses in 1977 and 1978 helped increase the money supply by 34 and 35 percent, thereby intensifying the severe inflation of 1979 and 1980, when the GNP deflator rose 11 percent and 16 percent.

As Table 6.21 shows, after floating rates were introduced in 1978, the accumulation of net foreign assets by the banking system turned out to be the primary source of the rapid growth of money supply in the 1980s. The reason is that the authorities still regarded the exchange rate as an important policy instrument to promote exports.[1]

1. This is demonstrated in Shea (1988), where I applied quarterly data from 1979Q1 to 1987Q4 to study exchange rate determination under floating rates. The ordinary least squares method was used to obtain the regression:

In the mid 1980s, as the domestic investment ratio was dropping dramatically and the trade surplus was growing year after year, the CBC intervened in the foreign exchange market to slow appreciation of the NT and thus maintain the profitability of domestic products in the export market. As a result, the huge trade surplus and the speculative capital inflow caused the money supply to expand very quickly.

TRANSITION TO A LESS REGULATED REGIME

In the late 1970s the authorities embarked on a road toward financial liberalization—including both domestic deregulation and internationalization. The factors forcing and opposing this move are reviewed in this section. The actual policies are presented, and their consequences discussed, in Section 8 (deregulation) and Section 9 (internationalization).

Domestic Causes of Liberalization

Bad experience with past intervention and changes in the domestic economic and political environments were two major driving forces for liberalization—and there is a general consensus that intervention had resulted in a backward financial system and a misallocation of funds. Continuous complaints and criticism from the general public and scholars put pressure on the authorities to make changes.

President Chiang Ching-Kuo relaxed social and political control to a great extent in the mid-1980s, and this spilled over into economic and financial affairs. Thus there was a favorable overall environment for the voices asking for financial liberalization and internationalization.

Some specific events focused the issues. In the late 1970s and early 1980s, there were several major defaults and bankruptcies. Some of these were outright frauds, while the others were caused by bad management or economic recession. One common element of the bankruptcies was that the suppliers of curb market credit suffered great losses. For example, there were many cases of rotating credit cooperatives' losing money to the organizers' fraud. Although no specific instance was massive, their repetition over several years attracted the attention of the general public, as well as the executive and legislative branches of government, to problems with the financial system.

The private sector had accumulated great wealth through its high savings rate during the previous 40 years. The excess of domestic savings over domestic

---

$$R(NT/U.S.) = -0.0229 - 0.3264R(U.S./SDR)_{-1} + 0.0542(BOT/NGNP)_{-1} + 0.3376GRGNP_{-1}$$
$$(3.553) (2.212) (3.543)$$
$$R^2 = 0.625 \qquad DW = 1.785$$

where $R(NT/U.S.)$ is the appreciation rate of the NT relative to the U.S. dollar, $R(U.S./SDR)$ is the appreciation rate of the U.S. dollar relative to special drawing rights, $(BOT/NGNP)$ represents the ratio of the balance of trade to nominal GNP, GRGNP is the growth rate of real GNP, and subscript $_{-1}$ denotes the previous quarter.

investments in the 1980s, accompanied by a huge trade surplus and a rapid expansion of the money supply, created a serious excess liquidity problem. The limited variety of financial assets and investment channels could no longer satisfy the demands of asset holders.

The excess liquidity led to dramatic rises in the prices of stocks and real estate. Financial investment companies appeared that collected funds from the general public by paying monthly interest as high as 9 percent, and they expanded quickly. This not only threatened financial stability, it also endangered social justice, unbalanced income and wealth distribution, and facilitated speculation. To resolve these problems, providing additional legal instruments and investment channels became a necessary policy.

Foreign Contributing Factors

In the 1970s and early 1980s, deregulation had gradually become fashionable in the international community. This certainly strengthened the morale of reformers and put pressures on decisionmakers in Taiwan. More important, the huge trade surplus in the 1980s invited pressures from the outside world to open domestic financial markets, to intervene less in determining the exchange rate, and to relax exchange controls. Because a major part of the trade imbalance was with the United States, it was the predominant outside voice. Frankly speaking, without foreign pressure, deregulation would have proceeded at a much slower pace.

Opposition

The financial system in Taiwan was under strict control for almost 40 years. The controls can hardly be said to have been without any merit, and some vested interest groups had been created under the system, so decontrol naturally encountered resistance. The arguments included stability and equity, as well as direct attempts to protect vested interests.

Financial stability had long been an important concern to the authorities. It justified the controlled bank interest rate, strict barriers for new entry, and government ownership of most of domestic banks. Experience also showed that private institutions (particularly trust and investment companies) had bad records in complying with the prudential rules set by the authorities. The authorities therefore moved slowly and cautiously in privatizing government-owned commercial banks and allowing establishment of new private financial institutions.

Under the Three Principles of the People, the guideline and philosophy enunciated by Sun Yat-Sen in the 1920s, the government should develop public rather than private capital. The idea was to prevent the concentration of economic power and to equalize income distribution. This consideration was another justification for government ownership of the major banks and limited entry, and it is a principal argument of those who have continued to oppose privatization and setting up of new private banks even after the government's decision to do both.

Government ownership of the major banks created at least two vested interest groups. One was the officials and legislators who influenced or directly controlled the banks, and the other was the bank employees. Because of their power, the former had privileges in applying for loans, introducing relatives and friends to become bank employees, and possibly serving as top managers or on the boards of directors. The latter could enjoy an easier life and a more secure job as a government employee. This explains why the decision to privatize the three most influential commercial banks, which were mainly controlled by the Taiwan provincial government, faced strong opposition from assembly members and some of the employees in 1989.

LIBERALIZATION POLICIES

The authorities in Taiwan have realized the backwardness of the financial system and adopted several measures to improve it. Interest rate decontrol, market entry deregulation, and privatization of major banks have been the principal elements of liberalization—with the major effort focused on interest rate decontrol. The problem of government ownership remains essentially untouched due to opposition from vested interest groups. Concerns about financial stability and distributional equity, as well as the intention to protect government-owned banks, have also slowed the process of entry deregulation. In addition, the monetary authorities have not allowed creation of a wide range of financial instruments for depositors.

Some observers, such as Chang (1989) and Kuo (1989), consider converting to a floating exchange rate system in 1978 as a liberalization. However this policy change was intended to ease the pressure of the trade surplus on the money supply and to speed the balance of payment adjustment so it is better viewed as a stabilization policy.

Interest Rate Decontrol

By far the most significant progress has been in the area of interest rates, although decontrol has been gradual. There have been six major steps. In 1976 a formal money market was established. Its unregulated rates were used as an indicator for the adjustment of regulated bank rates. In November 1980 the CBC promulgated the Essentials of Interest Rate Adjustment, which allowed banks to set their own interest rates on negotiable CDs and debentures, as well as on bill discounts, and enlarged the spread between the maximum and the minimum regulated lending rates.

Banks were required to set a prime rate in March 1985. Under this system the range of lending rates was further expanded. Moreover, banks were allowed to set their own rates on foreign currency deposits in September 1985, and the range of interbank call rates was gradually allowed to widen. The regulations prohibiting the maximum deposit rate from exceeding the minimum loan rate also were abolished in September 1985. In January 1986 the CBC reduced the categories of deposit rate ceilings from 13 to 4. This forced banks to set their own rates for various kinds of deposits.

The Banking Law was revised, effective on July 20, 1989—deleting the remaining regulations controlling maximum deposit rates and maximum and minimum loan rates. This revision nominally closes the history of interest rate control in Taiwan. In principle, rates on loans, deposits, and other financial instruments can be determined by markets. However, since most of the major banks are government-owned and no new banks would be operating until late 1991, the banks were reluctant to compete with one another and have continued to be easily influenced by the CBC.

Still, what actual decontrol there has been has had some positive effects on the banking system. The most visible is the fact that the share of private enterprise borrowing from curb markets declined from 36 percent in 1980 to 30 percent in 1984.

According to Kuo (1989), the upper limit on the loan rate set by the CBC has not been a binding constraint since 1984, as the gap between realized loan rates and the maximum widened under the pressure of excess liquidity caused by the huge trade surplus, and the difference between average loan rates and average deposit rates narrowed from 356 basis points at the end of 1984 to 268 in December 1988.

Promotion and expansion of consumer loans in the mid- and late 1980s also benefited greatly from interest rate decontrol. Of course, the pressure of excess liquidity also was important. Without the widening of the gap between maximum and minimum loan rates, however, the banks might not have felt that the risk premium was high enough to justify such loans.

Market Entry Deregulation

Several measures have been adopted to lower entry barriers. In 1984 regulations governing branching by existing banks were relaxed, allowing each qualified bank to set up three full-service branches and three limited-service agencies per year, as compared with two of each previously. The 1989 revised Banking Law liberalized the establishment of new private banks and granted MOF the power to authorize new banking products.

MOF intends to open the market to new banks gradually by limiting the number of licenses in each round. After the Guidelines for the Establishment of Commercial Banks was approved by the Executive Yuan, the MOF started accepting applications in April 1990. Of the 19 applicants, 15 were granted charters in June 1991. One more was added to the list in 1992. In addition, the largest investment and trust company was allowed to convert to a commercial bank in July 1992.

The authorities adopted several measures to address the effects of entry deregulation on stability and equity. The Guidelines set the minimum amount of capital at NT$10 billion and require that at least 20 percent of the shares be issued to the general public. The revised Banking Law limits individual ownership stakes to 5 percent and group shareholdings to 15 percent of any newly established private bank. It also sets stringent limits on related-party lending to prevent financial scandal. The law requires a capital ratio of at least 8 percent, as recommended worldwide by the Bank for International Settlements, and provides for strict prudential supervision, with heavy penalties for offenders.

The Securities and Exchange Law was amended in January 1988 to lift restrictions on establishment of new securities companies. Since January 1988 licenses have been made available to any firm meeting a basic set of financial and operating requirements. The revised law also permits qualified integrated securities firms to provide margin financing directly to customers. After drafting detailed regulations governing margin financing, Fuh-Hwa's monopoly was broken in October 1990.

Stock market disclosure requirements have been strengthened and tighter insider trading regulations introduced, although these regulations are still far from satisfactory and have not been implemented very effectively.

Privatization of Major Banks

To improve the efficiency of government banks, so they can survive the fierce competition expected from the new private banks, the authorities decided to reduce the government's equity in the three most influential commercial banks (First, Hua-Nan, and Chung-Hwa) to below 50 percent, by offering part of the stock in the market. However, this idea was strongly opposed by the members of Taiwan Provincial Assembly (the provincial government controls more than half the stock of each of the three) and some bank employees. A sharp drop in the stock market after February 1990 delayed sale of the shares owned by the central government. So the three banks remain controlled by the government, although in 1991 some government-owned shares were sold. Knowing it had hardly any chance of achieving the goal of privatizing the three banks before the end of 1992, MOF began planning to privatize some of the central government–owned specialized banks.

Consequences

As many economists in Taiwan predicted, deregulating bank interest rates while keeping the other two key interventions of entry regulation and government ownership essentially untouched would not contribute much to the development and the efficiency of the financial system. One clear indicator of this lack of success was the prospering and rapid expansion of investment finance companies in the mid- and late 1980s. Also, the share of private enterprise borrowing from curb markets rose in 1985–87, even though the banks were swamped with excess reserves.

The recovery of curb market financing clearly indicates curb market borrowers simply had no way to obtain loans from financial institutions. In other words, there was a severe problem of market segmentation. The formal financial system in Taiwan mainly serves the financial needs of public enterprises and large private enterprises, while medium and small private enterprises depend heavily on the informal system. According to the second-best theory, deregulating interest rates under market segmentation may actually cause more harm than good to the economy.

I have investigated the impact of interest rate liberalization on output, using a model incorporating the market segmentation phenomenon. The results show that, whether loanable funds in the banking system are in shortage or in surplus, interest rate liberalization does not necessarily have a positive effect on the total output of the economy (Shea 1989).

Of course the authorities do have reasons to be cautious in privatizing banks and allowing the establishment of new private financial institutions. The unpleasant record of private financial institutions in complying with prudential rules certainly constitutes a severe threat to the system's stability. The majority of the 19 applicants to set up new banks are conglomerates. Their intentions are generally believed to be making speculative profits from issuing bank stock when prices are rising, and using the banks as cash cows for their other businesses. To prevent this, limits on individual and group ownership and related-party lending must be strictly observed, and the CBC's examination department as well as MOF's Department of Monetary Affairs ought to be expanded.

In 1991 in compliance with political pressure, MOF surprisingly granted new-bank charters to almost all the applicants. The intense competition for market share after the banks opened in early 1992 has meant reductions in lending rates, increases in deposit rates, improved customer service, and development of new financial services. The resultant rapid expansion of total bank credits has led the CBC to implement some curbs on credit expansion and to continue closely monitoring the situation.

INTERNATIONALIZATION

Internationalization was declared in 1984 to be one of the major guidelines for Taiwan's future economic development. In the first few years, however, progress was rather slow. After the exchange controls were relaxed in July 1987, internationalization has speeded up. The important measures adopted by the end of 1990 fall under five headings: capital flow deregulation, access to the domestic financial market, creating an offshore banking center, setting up financial institutions abroad, and establishment of the Taipei foreign currency call loan market.

Capital Flow Deregulation

Strict foreign exchange control characterized the early years of development. A fixed exchange rate system was adopted in 1963. Strict control created an active—and fairly open—black market, and invited under–invoicing of exports and over–invoicing of imports, reflected in huge discrepancies in Taiwan-United States trade statistics.

In July 1978, to make the economy less vulnerable to external disturbances, the authorities introduced a floating system. However, the CBC continuously intervened in the mid 1980s, thereby nullifying the purpose of a floating rate system. The trade surplus, short-term speculative capital inflows, and the balance of payments surplus were continuously expanding, so foreign exchange reserves and the money supply increased too rapidly.

To reduce the pressure on the domestic money supply and the value of the NT dollar, as well as eliminate the efficiency cost associated with foreign exchange control, the authorities phased out most of the controls on July 15, 1987. Under the new system, current account transactions have been completely liberalized.

As for capital account transactions, an adult or a company was allowed to remit outward up to US$50 million annually, and the ceiling on inward remittances was US$50,000 per person per year.

The purpose of the lower inward ceiling was to fend off hot money that had been entering Taiwan in 1986–87. The aim of the broad relaxation on outward remittances was to encourage investment abroad and capital outflow, so the balance of payments surplus and money supply growth could be reduced. But the strong appreciation expectations regarding Taiwan's currency—caused by the central bank's controlled crawling appreciation strategy in 1986–87—not only handicapped capital outflow but also attracted speculative capital, which came into Taiwan through both legal and illegal channels.

In 1987 the CBC decided to let the NT dollar appreciate more rapidly, which finally stopped the speculative inflow in 1988. (During 1987–90 the exchange rate remained within 5 percent of 27.5 to the US dollar.) In 1988–90, there was a substantial net capital outflow. In August 1989 the central bank raised the ceiling on foreign liabilities of both local and foreign banks by 30 percent of the original ceiling, which had been set in October 1987 as part of the attempt to keep out hot money. The ceiling on inward remittances was raised incrementally. Both inward and outward remittance limits were set at US$3 million in March 1991, and further raised—to US$5 million—in October 1992.

With the relaxation of exchange controls, individuals and firms are free to hold and use foreign exchange. In addition, the authorities have devised two channels for people to invest in foreign securities. One is the Designated-Purpose Trust Program, under which more than 10 local banks and trust companies have been authorized to acquire shares in mutual funds issued by well-known foreign securities firms. Private investors can either invest in the mutual funds through these institutions or entrust them to purchase other foreign securities on their behalf as a broker. Since January 1986 the other channel has been four securities investment trust companies that have been authorized to issue open-end beneficial certificates to the public. These funds are used to invest in foreign securities. The four companies also offer domestic open-end and closed-end funds.

Foreign investors have been allowed since late 1983 to make indirect security investments through the purchase of four funds issued abroad by the same four securities investment trust companies. At the end of 1990, the total amount issued was US$151 million. Two of these are closed end and are listed in New York.

McKinnon (1982) and others suggest it is better to liberalize the domestic financial market before liberalizing capital flows. In Taiwan the domestic financial system is not well developed and is still under strict control, so whether lifting foreign exchange controls has been a wise policy remains an open question.

Access to Domestic Financial Markets

In 1985 foreign banks with branches in Taipei were authorized to open branches in Kaohsiung, and in late 1990 in Taichung. In addition to banking, the insurance market and the securities market have been opened to foreigners. Since 1986, each year two life and two property insurance firms from the United States have been allowed into Taiwan.

Under the 1988 Securities and Exchange Law, foreign investors may participate in the securities business through investment in and management of local
securities firms. In addition, there is no restriction on foreign investment in securities–investment consulting companies. In June 1989 the SEC took a further step
by accepting the applications of foreign securities firms to set up branches in Taiwan to engage in local brokerage business and overseas securities transactions.
In 1991 foreign investment institutions were allowed, with SEC permission, to
invest in local securities.

To protect domestic banks and maintain financial stability, the authorities in
Taiwan have kept the operations of foreign banks under strict control. However,
following relaxation of entry barriers and because of pressure from the United
States, some of the restrictions were gradually lifted in the 1980s. According to
the revised Banking Law of July 1989, foreign banks are permitted, on approval
by MOF, to set up savings and trust departments, through which they can accept
passbook savings and time savings deposits, extend long-term loans, and apply for
licenses as securities underwriters, brokers, and dealers. At this stage, foreign
banks have been accorded "national treatment," in the sense that they are treated
in the same way as domestic banks in all of their operations. In February 1989
branches of foreign insurance companies were allowed to invest a maximum of 35
percent of their capital and reserves in the local securities market.

Although some of the deregulation policies were adopted under pressure from
foreign countries, they have nonetheless contributed to the development of Taiwan's financial system, by enhancing market competition and introducing financial know-how. More important, the opening of domestic financial markets has
also provided an equity argument for local scholars and the general public asking
the authorities to open markets for local participants as well.

Establishing an Offshore Banking Center

Establishing an offshore banking center was a major step toward financial internationalization. The idea was initiated to improve the managerial efficiency of
domestic banks by learning from international financial markets and to provide
training and education for the staffs of domestic banks to familiarize them with
the procedures of international finance. The final goal was to promote Taiwan as
a financial center for the western Pacific.

In June 1984 the International Commercial Bank of China established the
first offshore banking unit. By the end of 1991 (1989) there were 30 (23) offshore banking units, established by 15 (11) domestic banks and 15 (12) foreign
banks. Total assets of the units reached US$23.5 billion in 1991, still relative-
ly small.

The structure of assets and liabilities shows that the development of offshore
banking units has not been satisfactory. Interbank transactions have constituted
the major activity. About 95 percent of liabilities have been owed to financial institutions, and the share of claims on financial institutions on the assets side has
never been less than 75 percent. Deposits by and loans to nonfinancial institutions have been relatively limited.

By definition, an offshore banking center is an outside-to-outside market; that is, the participants are supposed to use foreign exchange collected from abroad to finance the needs of the outside world. However, before 1986 the major function of offshore units in Taiwan was simply to redeposit the foreign exchange of domestic banks into foreign financial institutions.

Since 1986 offshore banking units have borrowed heavily from foreign financial institutions to meet the demand of domestic banks. Notice that from 1984 to 1989, financial institutions in Taiwan were inundated with deposits because of the huge trade surplus. The offshore banking units set up by domestic banks therefore naturally became the channel to make use of this accumulated foreign exchange. But when the CBC's intention to maintain a slow and steady appreciation of the NT dollar against the US dollar became clear in 1986–87, domestic banks began borrowing from abroad through their offshore units. Thus the units became simply a tool for foreign exchange speculation.

Setting up Financial Institutions Abroad

Domestic financial institutions going abroad is normally the most effective means to internationalize the financial sector. Unfortunately, Taiwan's achievement in this respect has been unsatisfactory. At the end of 1989, there were only five banks—with 15 branches, 3 subsidiaries and 6 representative offices—operating abroad. However, in 1991 the numbers reached 10 banks with 27 branches, 5 subsidiaries, and 14 representative offices. Of these, 17 (up from 8 in 1989) are in the United States; 5 in the Netherlands (all opened in 1990–91); 4 in the United Kingdom; 3 each in Japan and Hong Kong (all opened in 1991); 2 each in Panama, Singapore and Germany; and 1 each in Australia, Benin, Canada, France, Indonesia, the Philippines, Saudi Arabia, and Thailand. Their major operations are providing trade-related financial services for domestic trading firms, and most of their customers are overseas Chinese. In addition, some banks are owned by overseas Chinese and Republic of China nationals as individuals in New York and California.

Several factors have contributed to the limited foreign presence of Taiwan's financial institutions abroad. Most of its major trading partners and the countries where major international financial centers are located have no formal diplomatic relationship with the Republic of China. Therefore, domestic banks lack official channels to negotiate with foreign authorities about opening branches.

Until the mid-1980s, direct investment abroad was not encouraged. Consequently, the demand for services from overseas financial institutions was limited. Even with the growing need, the authorities have remained very conservative in promoting the establishment of overseas financial institutions. No guidelines for screening and approving domestic bank applications to establish overseas financial institutions have ever been provided. Nor has the government vigorously applied the reciprocity principle to force countries allowed into Taiwan to accept financial institutions from Taiwan.

Most of the banks capable of setting up overseas branches are government owned. For political reasons, some countries do not welcome government-owned banks from Taiwan in their territory. But even where they are not unwelcome, the bureaucratic nature of the government banks handicaps their ability to compete effectively.

In November 1988 MOF lifted restrictions limiting where overseas branches can be located and the number of branches that can be established in a given foreign city. Since then several banks from Taiwan have been actively exploring the possibility of opening more branches or subsidiaries in major foreign financial centers. The intention is to meet the demand for financial services of domestic nationals in the wake of the relaxation of foreign exchange controls. In particular, some banks want to enter Hong Kong before 1997. However, if the system of government ownership has not been changed, the prospects for overseas financial institutions can hardly be optimistic.

Establishing the Taipei Foreign Currency Call Loan Market

The Taipei foreign currency call loan market was set up on August 7, 1989, to better use the foreign exchange reserves held by the CBC, to improve the efficiency of the management of foreign exchange funds held by authorized foreign exchange banks, and to promote Taipei as an international financial center. The CBC designated part of its foreign exchange reserves (US$3 billion and 500 million deutsche marks initially, plus a subsequent US$4 billion) to finance authorized foreign exchange banks through the call loan market. Many local branches of foreign banks participate, and nonresident banks have been allowed to take part since August 1990. The number of tradable currencies has expanded from just U.S. dollars to include the 13 others listed on the foreign exchange market. Maturities range from overnight to 12 months. Total transactions in December 1991 were equivalent to US$24.3 billion.

LESSONS AND CONCLUSION

The formal financial system in Taiwan is underdeveloped, but the participants—including the regulatory and policymaking authorities—recognize this and have endeavored to deal with it. The resulting experience offers several lessons about financial development and financial policies.

On the negative side, strict entry regulations and government ownership of financial institutions are adversely affecting Taiwan's financial development and the allocative efficiency of its investment funds. Interest rate control, which set bank rates lower than market clearing rates, reduced allocative efficiency. Selective credit control policies, although they may not have severely distorted resource allocation at the earlier stages of economic development, cannot be recommended at later stages. Finally, for a small open economy unable to control capital inflow and outflow effectively, intervening in foreign exchange markets may be disastrous for controlling the domestic money supply, so it, too, cannot be recommended as a policy.

On the positive side, the widespread systems of postal savings and credit departments of farmers' associations, associated with the policies of a balanced government budget, money supply control, and a positive real interest rate on deposits, have proved beneficial to the stimulation and mobilization of savings. When interest rate control, fund shortages, or an underdeveloped formal financial system exists, allowing an informal financial system to be active is helpful in mobilizing savings, financing the needs of those discriminated against by the formal system, and improving the allocative efficiency of loanable funds.

The search for a balance among prudence, stability, and efficiency is never-ending. Taiwan has traded a lot of efficiency for stability in the course of its economic growth. What remains unclear is how large these efficiency costs were, and thus whether this trade-off was worthwhile. Although it is clear that Taiwan must now address the rigidities and inefficiencies of its financial system, concerns for stability and opposition for vested interest groups will undoubtedly slow the process of financial deregulation.

The author would like to thank Hugh Patrick, Yung Chul Park, Aris Protopapadakis, and Ramon Moreno for valuable comments, and Larry Meissner for editorial assistance and comments. Financial support from the National Science Council of the Republic of China is greatly appreciated.

REFERENCES

(The word "processed" describes informally reproduced works that may not be commonly available through libraries.)

Asian Development Bank. 1985 Sep. *Improving Domestic Resource Mobilization through Financial Development*. Manila. Asian Development Bank.

Bank of Communications. 1987 Mar. *Eighty Years of the Bank of Communication of China*. Taipei: Bank of Communication of China. In Chinese.

CBC (Central Bank of China). 1984 Feb. *Financial Institutions in Taiwan*. Taipei: Central Bank of China. In Chinese.

Central Trust of China. 1985 Oct. *Fifty Years of the Central Trust of China*. Taipei: Central Trust of China. In Chinese.

Chandavarkar, Anand G. 1971 Mar. "Some Aspects of Interest Rate Policies in Less Developed Countries: The Experience of Selected Asian Countries." International Monetary Fund Staff Papers.

Chang, Chi-Cheng. 1989. "Financial Liberalization in the Republic of China." Keynote address at the First Annual Pacific Basin Finance Conference in Taipei, Mar. 13.

Cheng, Hang-Sheng. 1986. "Financial Policy and Reform in Taiwan, China." In Hang-sheng Cheng, ed., *Financial Policy and Reform in Pacific Basic Countries*. Lexington MA: Lexington Books.

Chiu, Paul CH. 1981. "Performance of Financial Institutions." In Kwoh-Ting Li and Tzong-shian Yu, eds., *Experiences and Lessons of Economic Development in Taiwan*. Taipei: Institute of Economics, Academia Sinica.

Cooperative Bank of Taiwan. 1976 Oct. *Thirty Years of the Cooperative Bank of Taiwan*. Taipei: Cooperative Bank of Taiwan. In Chinese.

Farmers Bank of China. 1983 Apr. *Fifty Years of the Farmers Bank of China*. Taipei: Farmers Bank of China. In Chinese.

First Commercial Bank of Taiwan. 1979 Nov. *Eighty Years of the First Commercial Bank of Taiwan*. Taipei: First Commerical Bank of Taiwan. In Chinese.

Galenson, Walter, ed. 1979. *Economic Growth and Structural Change in Taiwan*. Ithaca, NY: Cornell University Press.

Hsing, Mo-Huan. 1988. "Could the Taiwan Economy Have Performed Better?—An Appraisal of Economic Policies Adopted by the Government since the 1950s." Taipei: Institute of Economics, Academia Sinica. Processed.

Irvine, Reed J., and Robert F. Emery. 1966. "Interest Rates as an Anti-inflationary Instrument in Taiwan." *National Banking Review*, Sep.

Kuo, Shirley WY. 1983. *The Taiwan Economy in Transition*. Boulder, CO: Westview Press.

———. 1989. "Liberalization of the Financial Market in Taiwan in the 1980s." Keynote address at the First Annual Pacific Basin Finance Conference in Taipei, Mar. 14.

Land Bank of Taiwan. 1981 Sep. *Thirty-five Years of the Land Bank of China*. Taipei: Land of China. In Chinese.

Lee, Yung-San and Shang-Cheng Chen. 1984 Dec. "Financial Development in Taiwan: Review and Prospective." *Proceedings of the Conference on Financial Development in Taiwan*. Taipei: Institute of Economics, Academia Sinica. In Chinese.

———, and Tzong-Rong Tsai. 1988 Jun. "Development of Financial System and Monetry Policies in Taiwan." *Conference on Economic Development Experiences of Taiwan and Its New Role in an Emerging Asia-Pacific Area*. Vol. 1. Taipei: Institute of Economics, Academia Sinica.

Lin, Pei-Chow. 1988 Jun. "A Study on the Specialized Bank System in Taiwan." In *The Reform of [the] Financial System in Taiwan*, Chung-Hua Institution for Economic Research, *Research Project Report* (77): 92–194. In Chinese.

———, and Jia-Dong Shea. 1983 Nov. "A Disequilibrium Econometric Analysis of the Bank Loan Market in Taiwan." *The Chinese Economic Association Annual Conference Proceedings*. Tapei: Chinese Economic Association. In Chinese.

Liu, Shou-Hsiang. 1988. "The Development and Prospect of Financial Institutions in Taiwan." *Proceedings of the Conference on the Modernization of Service Industries in ROC*. Taipei: Chinese Economic Association. In Chinese.

Lungberg, Erik. 1979. "Fiscal and Monetary Policies." In Walter Galenson, ed., *Economic Growth and Structural Change in Taiwan*. Ithaca, NY: Cornell University Press.

McKinnon, Ronald I. 1973. *Money and Capital in Economic Development*. Washington DC: Brookings Institution.

———. 1982. "The Order of Economic Liberalization: Lessons from Chile and Argentina." In Karl Brunner and Alan H. Meltzer, eds., *Economic Policies in a World of Change*. Amsterdam: North-Holland.

Scitovsky, Tibor. 1985. "Economic Development in Taiwan and South Korea." *Food Research Institute Studies, 19(3): 214–64.*

Shea, Jia-Dong. 1983a Mar. "Financial Dualism and the Industrial Development in Taiwan." *Proceedings of the Conference on Industrial Development in Taiwan*. Taipei: Institute of Economics, Academia Sinica. In Chinese.

———. 1983b Sep. "The Income Elasticity of Money Demand in Taiwan." *Academia Economic Papers*. Taipei: Institute of Economics, Academia Sinica. In Chinese.

———. 1984 Sep. "Compensating Balance Requirements and the Money Demand of Private Enterprises in Taiwan." *Academia Economic Papers*. Taipei: Institute of Economics, Academia Sinica.

———. 1988 Jan. "The Factors Affecting the Exchange Rate of NT Dollars." *Money Market Briefing*. January, pp.1–5. In Chinese.

———. 1989 Jan. "The Output Effects of Interest Rate Liberalization with Market Segmentation." *Taiwan Economic Review*. Taipei: Department of Economics, National Taiwan University. In Chinese.

———, and Ping-Sing Kuo. 1984 Dec. "The Allocative Efficiency of Banks' Loanable Funds in Taiwan." *Proceedings of the Conference on Financial Development in Taiwan*. Taipei: Institute of Economics, Academia Sinica. In Chinese.

———, Ming-Yih Liang, Ya-Hwei Yang, Shou-Hsiang Liu, and Kun-Ming Chen. 1985 Jun. "A Study on the Financial System in Taiwan." *Economic Papers* 65. Taipei: Chung-Hua Institution for Economic Research. In Chinese.

———, and Ya-Hwei Yang. 1989 Dec. "Financial System and the Allocation of Investment Funds in Taiwan." Paper presented at the Conference on State Policy and Economic Development in Taiwan, held by Soochow University in Taipei.

Research and Training Center of Community Finance. *Taiwan Community Financial Journal*. (This provides data on mutual loans and savings.) In Chinese.

Sun, Chen, and Ming-Yih Liang. 1982. "Savings in Taiwan, 1953–1980." In Kwoh-Ting Li and Tzong Shian Yu, eds., *Experiences and Lessons of Economic Development in Taiwan*. Taipei: Institute of Economics, Academia Sinica.

Tsiang, Shoh-Chieh. 1977. "The Monetary Theoretic Foundation of the Modern Monetary Approach to the Balance of Payments." *Oxford Economic Papers*, November, pp. 319–38.

————. 1979. "Fashions and Misconceptions in Monetary Theory and Their Influences on Financial and Banking Policies." *Zeitschrift für die gesamte Staatswissenschaft*, December, pp. 584 – 604.

————. 1982. "Monetary Policy of Taiwan." In Kwoh-Ting Li and Tzong-Shian Yu, eds., *Experiences and Lessons of Economic Development In Taiwan*. Taipei: Institute of Economics, Academia Sinica.

Yang, Ya-Hwei. 1982. "An Economic Analysis of Exports Financing System in Taiwan." *Economic Papers* 13. Taipei: Chung-Hua Institution for Economic Research. In Chinese.

APPENDIX: CREDIT CRITERIA AND THE EFFICIENCY CONTRIBUTION OF THE INFORMAL SYSTEM

To measure demand for funds in the formal and informal markets, investigate the extent to which the formal sector used productivity as a criterion in extending credit, and to estimate the contribution of the informal system in improving allocative efficiency, Shea and Kuo (1984) set up a theoretical model and applied 1965-82 data.

THE BASIC MODEL

We specified the equation of the demand for bank loans by private enterprises as

$$L_b\,(r_b,\,V,\,D,\,\varepsilon) = \exp\,[\alpha_0 + \alpha_1 r_b + \alpha_2 \ln V + \alpha_3 D + \varepsilon\,] \qquad (1)$$

$$\ln L_b = \alpha_0 + \alpha_1 r_b + \alpha_2 \ln V + \alpha_3 D + \varepsilon \qquad (2)$$

where L_b denotes private enterprise demand for bank loans, r_b the interest rate charged by banks, V the nominal gross value added produced by private enterprises, D is a money-market dummy variable (0 for years before 1977 when the money market had not yet been set up, 1 for the years since), and ε is the disturbance term.

The setting up of the money market provided a new source of funds through issuing commercial paper and bankers' acceptances. Thus, the money market and the bank loan rate should have negative effects on the demand for bank loans. The more gross value added that private enterprises produce, the more financing they need. Therefore, we expect $\alpha_1 < 0$, $\alpha_2 > 0$, $\alpha_3 < 0$.

Let actual bank loans available to private enterprises be L_a. The bank loan rate (r_b) is purposely set below the market clearing rate by the authorities in order to stimulate investment. Therefore, $L_b > L_a$. The loan demand not met by financial institutions then shifts to the informal system in search of loans. However, only demand that has a productivity as high as the curb market rate can become an actual borrower in the curb markets. Thus, effective demand for curb market loans can be defined as bank loan demand that has a marginal productivity greater than or equal to the curb market interest rate, and has not been financed by a financial institution. Therefore, the allocative efficiency of financial institutions, or in other words, the proportion of high-productivity demand financed by financial institutions, is a key factor affecting private enterprise demand for curb market loans. Two extreme cases are illustrated below.

Most Efficient Credit Rationing

In this case, all the loanable funds of financial institutions are allocated to the most productive borrowers. Denote the curb market interest rate as r_c. Then, demand for curb market loans by private enterprises can be expressed as

$$L_c (r_c, V, D, \varepsilon; \; L_a) = L_b (r_c, V, D, \varepsilon) - L_a \qquad (3)$$

In Figure 6.1, line ABC denotes the demand curve for bank loans. The vertical line $L_b = L_a$ intercepts the bank loan demand curve and horizontal axis at points B and $0'$ respectively. If financial institutions have allocated loanable funds to the most efficient users, then loan demand located on AB, which has a productivity higher or equal to r_b, has been financed by the financial institutions.

Use $0'$ as the original point and vertical line $L_b = L_a$ as the vertical axis measuring r_c. Then line BC represents the demand curve for curb market loans. For example, if $r_b = \alpha$ and $r_c = \beta$, then among the total bank loan demand $0D$, $00'$ is financed by financial institutions and demand for curb market loans is $0'E$.

Efficiency-neutral Credit Rationing

In this case, loanable funds are rationed by financial institutions according to criteria unrelated to productivity. The possibility of getting credit from financial institutions can be measured by $L_a/L_b(r_b, V, D, \varepsilon)$. Therefore, curb-market loan demand, which is composed of bank loan demand that has a marginal productivity at least equal to the curb market interest rate and has not been financed by financial institutions, can be written as

$$L_c (r_c, V, D, \varepsilon; \; L_a) = L_b (r_c, V, D, \varepsilon) \; [1 - (L_a/L_b (r_b, V, D, \varepsilon)] \qquad (4)$$

In Figure 6.2, line $ABCD$ is the bank-loan demand curve. When $r_b = \alpha$, each point on line ABC has possibility $00'/0E$ of getting bank credit. Thus, the loan demand actually financed by banks is line AF. The horizontal difference between ABC and AF, which is line $A'C$ using $0'$ as the original point, represents the demand curve for curb market loans. For instance, if the curb market rate is B, loan demand with a marginal productivity at least equal to B is $0G$. Of this demand, $0H$ ($0H/0G = 00'/0E$) is financed by banks, the rest (HG or $0'I$) constitutes demand for curb market loans.

TESTING WHETHER PRODUCTIVITY MATTERED

In the case of most efficient credit rationing, financial institutions take productivity as the unique criterion in rationing credit; while in the efficiency-neutral case, productivity is an irrelevant factor. Actual allocative efficiency lies between the two extreme cases. Therefore, define a parameter θ, $0 \leq \theta \leq 1$, and take the

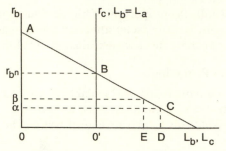

Fig. 6.1. The demand curve for curb-market loans: the most-efficient credit rationing case.

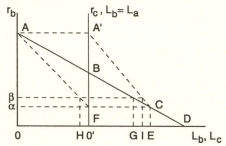

Fig. 6.2. The demand curve for curb-market loans: the efficiency-neutral credit rationing case.

weighted average of equations (3) and (4), using θ and $1-\theta$ as weights, to obtain the following general form for private enterprise curb-market loan demand:

$$L_c\,(r_c,\,V,\,D,\,\varepsilon;\,L_a)$$

$$= \theta\,[L_b\,(r_c,\,V,\,D,\,\varepsilon) - L_a] + (1-\theta)L_b(r_c,\,V,\,D,\,\varepsilon)\,[1 - (L_a/L_b\,(r_b,\,V,\,D,\,\varepsilon)]$$

$$= L_b(r_c,\,V,\,D,\,\varepsilon) - L_a[\theta + (1-\theta)L_b(r_c,\,V,\,D,\,\varepsilon)/L_b(r_b,\,V,\,D,\,\varepsilon)] \tag{5}$$

Note that if $\theta = 1$ or 0, equation (5) degenerates into equation (3) or (4). Thus, the value of θ can be used as a measure of the allocative efficiency of financial institutions. The higher θ, the more efficiently financial institutions allocate loanable funds.

Substituting equation (1) into equation (5) and simplifying yields

$$\ln(L_c + L_a\{\theta + (1-\theta)\,\exp[\alpha_1\,(r_c - r_b)]\})$$

$$= \alpha_0 + \alpha_1 r_c + \alpha_2\,\ln V + \alpha_3 D + \varepsilon \tag{6}$$

Empirical Results for Productivity

We applied annual data for 1965-82 to estimate equation (6). The search method was used to estimate θ, and the nonlinear ordinary least-squares method was employed to estimate other parameters. It turned out the best estimate for θ is zero, and the corresponding regression result when $\theta = 0$ is

$$\ln\{L_c + L_a \exp[-2.04859 (r_c - r_b)]\} \tag{7}$$

$$(-2.91)$$

$$= 5.24868 - 2.04859 r_c + 1.37112 \ln V - 0.16873 D$$

$$(-16.92) \quad (-2.91) \quad (45.11) \quad (-3.44)$$

$R^2 = 0.9981$; the figures in parentheses are t values.

The result that $\theta = 0$ indicates productivity of borrowers had not been an important consideration in rationing credit. This result supports the general criticism that the efficiency of financial institutions in allocating loanable funds has been far from satisfactory.

THE CONTRIBUTION OF THE INFORMAL SYSTEM

Given that financial institutions were not allocating loanable funds according to the productivity of borrowers, the existence of the informal system has contributed to allocative efficiency by attracting savings away from bank deposits and making those funds available to more productive users. The contribution of the informal system to the allocative efficiency of loanable funds is illustrated in Figure 6.3.

Because the estimated value of the bank allocative efficiency parameter θ is zero, we can follow Figure 6.2 to draw the demand curves for bank loans and curb market loans when the bank loan rate $r_b = \alpha$ as AC and $A'C$ respectively. Assume the loanable funds of the informal system are L_c. Then, the equilibrium curb market interest rate is r_c^*, and the total productivity of curb market loans is $\square 0'A'MN$.

Because AF is the loan demand actually financed by financial institutions in the efficiency neutral case, total productivity of bank loans L_a is $\square 0AF0'$. Therefore, total productivity created by loans from both financial institutions and the informal system is $\square 0AF0' + \square 0'A'MN$.

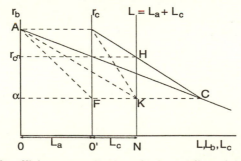

Fig. 6.3. The efficiency contribution of informal financial system.

If the informal financial system did not exist, all loanable funds $L_a + L_c$ are at financial institutions and are allocated by them. Based on the same reasoning as above, bank loan demand actually met by financial institutions is AK when the productivity of borrowers is not considered, and total productivity created by total loans $L_a + L_c$ is $\square 0AKN$.

Note the area $\triangle AFK$ equals area $\triangle A'FK$. Thus, comparing the total productivities of the same total loans $L_a + L_c$, total productivity is raised by the area $\triangle A'KM$ if the informal system is allowed to exist. That is, the area $\triangle A'KM$ represents the contribution of the informal system to the allocative efficiency of loanable funds.

Empirical Results for the Informal System

We applied the estimated loan demand equation (7) to measure the efficiency contribution of the informal system for the period 1965-82. Our results show the total productivity of total loans was increased 6.03% and the level of GDP increased by 1.23% on average during this period. (It is assumed the curb market rate purely measures the marginal productivities of curb market borrowers. However, in reality, part of the rate reflects higher default risk and transaction costs. Therefore, our results overestimate the actual efficiency contribution of the informal system.)

Table 6.A1. Taiwan: Macroeconomic Indicators
(percent)

Year	Growth rate of real GNP	Gross investment (as % of real GNP)	Export of goods and services (as % of real GNP)	Current account as % of GNP Real	Current account as % of GNP Nominal	Household savings rate[a]	Rate of change in GNP deflator	Real interest rate[b]
1955	8.1	9.2	6.9	−4.2	−4.3	9.1	10.1	5.1
1956	5.5	10.0	7.3	−5.0	−6.9	7.6	8.8	8.9
1957	7.3	9.5	7.8	−3.8	−5.1	7.6	8.7	13.6
1958	6.6	9.8	7.4	−4.8	−6.4	8.9	4.8	19.4
1959	7.8	11.5	8.4	−4.8	−8.3	8.9	7.1	6.8
1960	6.4	13.8	8.8	−4.8	−7.5	11.0	13.6	2.9
1961	6.8	13.9	10.5	−4.3	−7.1	11.8	4.8	12.4
1962	7.9	13.0	10.0	−4.0	−5.3	8.7	2.1	10.9
1963	9.4	14.1	11.8	−2.4	−1.2	13.0	3.4	6.2
1964	12.3	14.1	13.5	−1.8	−0.8	14.4	4.2	8.6
1965	11.0	16.5	15.0	−2.1	−3.0	14.8	−0.7	15.5
1966	9.0	16.0	16.3	0.1	0.3	16.5	2.8	8.7
1967	10.6	19.0	16.9	−2.0	−2.0	17.3	4.5	7.3
1968	9.1	20.3	19.6	−3.0	−2.9	16.6	6.7	6.8
1969	9.0	20.2	22.3	−2.4	−0.7	18.0	6.4	10.0
1970	11.3	22.0	25.7	−1.8	−0.0	19.7	3.4	7.0
1971	13.0	23.0	30.3	0.7	2.5	23.1	3.0	9.4
1972	13.4	22.7	35.7	3.7	6.2	26.4	5.8	4.6
1973	12.8	24.1	39.3	3.8	5.3	29.0	15.0	−13.5
1974	1.2	31.6	36.0	−3.8	−7.8	26.0	32.4	−26.2
1975	4.4	26.3	35.0	−0.7	−3.3	20.6	2.2	17.4
1976	13.7	26.3	41.7	2.4	2.2	26.4	5.4	9.1
1977	10.2	25.0	42.6	5.1	4.9	26.4	6.4	7.1
1978	14.0	24.9	45.5	8.0	6.5	28.3	5.3	6.0
1979	8.4	28.0	44.5	3.6	1.1	27.4	11.5	−2.8
1980	7.1	28.4	45.0	4.3	−1.2	26.4	16.2	−9.0
1981	5.8	27.0	46.4	7.2	2.0	25.0	12.0	6.0
1982	4.0	23.8	45.6	9.0	5.2	23.4	3.5	11.4
1983	8.6	22.4	48.9	11.6	8.6	25.6	1.9	9.8
1984	11.6	21.2	51.5	13.6	11.1	27.5	0.9	7.8
1985	5.6	18.3	50.0	15.6	13.6	26.9	0.6	9.8
1986	12.6	17.1	56.7	19.3	19.3	32.7	3.3	8.9
1987	11.9	20.0	60.3	17.5	17.1	33.0	0.5	8.2
1988	7.8	22.6	59.1	12.0	10.8	28.9	1.1	6.7
1989	7.3	22.2	58.1	9.6	7.6	24.9	3.1	8.5
1990	5.0	21.9	56.0	7.6	5.3	23.3	4.1	10.1

a. Net household savings as a percentage of household disposable income.

b. The real interest rate is calculated as the 1-year savings deposit rate (before 1955, the preferential interest rate on 1-year savings deposits) minus the rate of change in the wholesale price index.

Source: DGBAS, *Statistical Abstract of National Income, Taiwan Area, ROC, 1951–91*, Tables 1, 4, 5 and 8; *Financial Statistics Monthly*, various issues, for interest rates and wholesale price index.

Table 6.A2. Taiwan: *GNP Per Capita, GNP, and Financial Assets Outstanding, 1965–90*

Year	GNP per capita US$	Billion NT$				Assets to GNP ratio		
		GNP	Total	Personal	Corporate	Total	Personal	Corporate
				Assets outstanding				
1965	217	112	181	66	19	1.61	0.59	0.17
1966	237	126	226	82	24	1.80	0.65	0.19
1967	266	143	270	98	29	1.89	0.69	0.20
1968	303	168	356	127	59	2.12	0.76	0.35
1969	344	191	417	150	83	2.19	0.79	0.44
1970	388	218	484	181	86	2.22	0.83	0.39
1971	442	261	580	219	110	2.22	0.84	0.42
1972	745	307	750	280	154	2.44	0.91	0.50
1973	695	389	1,034	322	244	2.66	0.83	0.63
1974	920	525	1,467	493	232	2.80	0.94	0.44
1975	964	560	1,657	581	277	2.96	1.04	0.50
1976	1,132	656	2,028	698	321	3.09	1.07	0.49
1977	1,301	754	2,372	835	375	3.15	1.11	0.50
1978	1,573	968	3,242	1,147	463	3.35	1.19	0.48
1979	1,917	1,164	3,809	1,336	561	3.27	1.15	0.48
1980	2,343	1,441	4,821	1,651	691	3.35	1.15	0.48
1981	2,664	1,694	5,608	2,078	830	3.31	1.23	0.49
1982	2,635	1,828	6,473	2,374	874	3.54	1.30	0.48
1983	2,794	1,998	7,359	2,767	954	3.68	1.38	0.48
1984	3,093	2,368	8,472	3,225	1,111	3.58	1.36	0.47
1985	3,362	2,515	9,683	3,905	1,147	3.85	1.55	0.46
1986	4,566	2,926	11,251	4,978	868	3.85	1.70	0.30
1987	5,657	3,289	13,849	5,941	1,165	4.21	1.81	0.35
1988	6,376	3,585	16,510	7,086	1,354	4.60	1.98	0.38
1989	7,478	3,969	19,492	8,454	1,611	4.91	2.13	0.41
1990	7,887	4,327	21,548	9,313	1,786	4.97	2.15	0.41

Note: Unincorporated businesses included in Corporate assets.

Source: IMF, *International Financial Statistics*; CBC, *Financial Statistics*; Taiwan Statistical Data Bank.

Table 6.A3. *Taiwan: Financial Surplus or Deficit by Sector as a Percentage of GNP*

Year	Government General	Government Enterprises[a]	Private Enterprises[a]	Private Households[b]	Rest of the World
1951	1.99	−3.83	−0.32	3.40	−1.23
1960	1.69	−2.78	−3.89	2.55	2.43
1965	0.25	−1.28	−7.81	6.84	2.00
1970	0.53	−2.72	−6.94	9.14	−0.01
1971	1.28	−3.62	−5.49	10.41	−2.58
1972	3.76	−3.45	−4.92	11.10	−6.50
1973	3.74	−4.76	−6.66	12.96	−5.28
1974	4.95	−8.14	−15.20	10.70	7.70
1975	2.62	−9.21	−4.97	7.77	3.79
1976	3.52	−7.20	−3.14	8.39	−1.57
1977	2.34	−4.67	−3.06	9.70	−4.31
1978	4.38	−4.20	−3.32	9.27	−6.13
1979	5.33	−4.74	−8.58	8.49	−0.50
1980	3.35	−7.02	−4.88	6.99	1.56
1981	2.29	−5.27	−4.32	8.62	−1.31
1982	0.66	−4.99	−1.99	9.74	−4.84
1983	1.90	−2.41	−1.98	10.62	−8.70
1984	2.24	−0.45	−2.51	11.39	−11.87
1985	1.69	0.13	−0.91	13.13	−14.82
1986	0.40	0.98	0.97	18.24	−21.35
1987	2.51	−0.19	−3.86	19.24	−18.40
1988	2.22	0.10	−6.80	15.85	−11.69
1989	−4.94	−1.57	−6.20	20.47	−8.51
1990	−1.09	−2.99	−4.31	14.95	−7.29

Note: Rows do not sum to zero because of statistical discrepancies in the underlying data.

a. Includes corporate and noncorporate enterprises.

b. Households, farmers, professionals, other self-employed (vocational households), and nonprofit organizations.

Source: Computed by author from underlying data in *Flow of Funds in Taiwan District* 1991, accounts 4–7 (financial surplus by sector from 1965); *National Income in Taiwan Area, ROC* 1987, Tables 6 and 7 (financial surplus by sector 1951 and 1960); *National Income in Taiwan Area, ROC* 1991, ch 3 Table 16 (overseas sector) and ch 2 Table 1 (GNP).

Table 6.A4. *Taiwan: Saving by Sector and Investment as a Percentage of GNP*

	Gross domestic savings						
	Private		Government			Gross domestic	Net
Year	Households[a]	Enterprises[b]	General	Enterprises[b]	Total	investment[c]	foreign flow[d]
1955	2.7	4.5	5.1	2.3	14.6	13.3	−1.2
1960	4.8	4.9	4.0	4.1	17.8	20.2	2.4
1965	8.2	6.2	2.6	3.7	20.7	22.7	2.0
1970	11.0	6.4	3.6	4.6	25.6	25.6	− 0.0
1971	13.0	7.4	4.2	4.2	28.8	26.2	−2.6
1972	13.7	7.9	6.5	4.0	32.1	25.6	− 6.5
1973	16.0	9.2	6.2	3.0	34.4	29.1	−5.3
1974	13.6	6.1	8.3	3.5	31.5	39.2	7.7
1975	11.0	4.6	7.1	4.0	26.7	30.5	3.8
1976	11.7	7.8	8.3	4.5	32.3	30.8	−1.6
1977	13.3	7.2	7.7	4.3	32.5	28.3	−4.3
1978	13.4	8.0	8.6	4.4	34.4	28.3	− 6.1
1979	12.9	6.8	9.7	4.2	33.6	32.9	− 0.5
1980	11.5	8.0	7.9	4.9	32.3	33.8	1.6
1981	13.6	6.4	6.6	4.7	31.3	30.0	−1.3
1982	13.8	6.1	5.1	5.1	30.1	25.2	−4.8
1983	14.4	6.7	5.6	5.4	32.3	23.4	− 8.7
1984	15.4	6.6	5.7	6.0	33.7	21.9	−11.9
1985	16.3	6.5	5.2	5.5	33.5	18.7	−14.8
1986	19.4	9.8	4.3	4.9	38.4	17.1	−21.3
1987	19.4	8.4	6.3	4.3	38.4	20.1	−18.4
1988	16.3	6.6	7.2	4.3	34.3	22.8	−11.7
1989	13.6	5.7	7.8	3.7	30.8	22.3	− 8.5
1990	14.1	5.7	5.8	3.6	29.2	21.9	−7.3
1991	15.2	7.2	2.6	4.4	29.4	22.2	−7.2

a. Includes corporate and noncorporate enterprises.

b. Households, farmers, professionals, other self-employed (vocational households), and nonprofit organizations.

c. Gross domestic fixed capital investment plus increase in stocks (inventory).

d. Long-term capital account (direct investment plus loan disbursements minus loan repayments plus/minus minor items). Negative numbers represent capital outflows.

Source: Computed by author from underlying data in *National Income in Taiwan Area, ROC* 1991, ch. 3, Table 16. NT$ data are also available (for 1951–89) in an English-language source: DGBAS, *Statistical Abstract of National Income, Taiwan Area, ROC*, Feb. 1991, p. 51, Table 13, for savings and net foreign investment; p. 49, Table 12, for investment; p. 1, Table 1, for GNP.

Table 6.A5. *Taiwan: Sources of External Funds Raised by Nonfinancial Sectors*
(percent)

	1970–74	1975–79	1980–84	1985–89	1985	1989
Distribution of funds by sector raising funds[a]						
Government	3.2	2.3	4.8	8.9	5.7	19.0
Public enterprises	20.4	30.6	25.4	8.7	15.4	8.0
Private enterprises	53.5	43.2	44.2	51.6	45.0	45.4
Households[b]	22.9	24.0	25.6	30.8	33.9	27.5
Distribution of funds by source[c]						
Borrowing from financial institutions	42.1	40.8	40.9	50.3	28.8	60.4
Securities issued	22.6	33.7	35.0	32.4	46.7	28.7
Foreign capital[d]	2.1	1.2	1.3	2.3	4.1	2.5
Domestic trade credits[e]	24.1	22.2	21.3	11.8	11.6	7.8
Foreign trade credits	8.6	1.5	0.2	3.1	4.4	0.8
Government loans	0.4	0.6	1.3	0.2	4.4	−0.2
Borrowings from financial institutions (as % of total sources)[f]						
Nonbanks	3.3	2.4	1.9	2.8	2.0	3.2
Monetary institutions	38.9	38.4	39.0	47.5	26.8	57.2
Central bank	0.9	−0.2	−0.1	0.0	−0.3	0.0
Full-service domestic banks	30.0	26.8	26.2	32.6	22.0	38.6
Foreign banks	4.1	2.9	1.4	1.8	−2.4	2.7
Medium and small business banks	1.0	2.5	4.1	5.1	4.1	5.6
Credit co-op associations	2.1	3.9	3.6	5.4	−0.2	6.3
Credit departments[g]	0.7	2.5	3.8	2.6	3.7	4.0
Securities issued (as % of total sources)[c]						
Government	0.2	1.0	1.0	3.4	7.7	2.3
Corporate bonds	0.3	1.4	1.0	0.1	−1.0	−0.4
Commercial paper	n.a.	3.5	2.2	0.8	−1.9	2.9
Domestic bills accepted by banks	n.a.	0.3	4.4	−0.9	1.9	0.8
Stock and equities[h]	22.1	27.6	26.4	29.0	40.0	23.0

n.a. Not applicable.

Note: Multiyear figures are computed by averaging the annual distributions.

Excludes miscellaneous sources and the informal sector.

a. Calculated from *Flow of Funds*, pp. 28–59, accounts 4–7.

b. Includes nonprofit institutions.

c. Compiled from *Flow of Funds*, pp. 60–109, Financial Assets and Liabilities summary tables.

d. Excludes direct investment.

e. Notes and accounts receivable.

f. Compiled from *Flow of Funds*, pp. 112–63, Outstanding Amounts of Domestic Financial Assets and Liabilities summary tables, except that the data on the 5 types of deposit money banks are from *Financial Statistics Monthly* Appendix Tables of Assets and Liabilities of Various Financial Institutions. The *Flow of Funds* and *Monthly* have different numbers for total loans; it is assumed that the difference is proportional among the types of bank.

g. Credit departments of farmers' and fishermen's associations.

h. Corporate stocks and shares of noncorporate enterprises.

Source: CBC, *Flow of Funds in Taiwan District, ROC, 1965–90,* and *Financial Statistics Monthly,* Jan. 1982 and Jan. 1991.

Table 6.A6. *Taiwan: Uses of Funds by Nonfinancial Sectors*

	1970–74	1975–79	1980–84	1985–89	1985	1989
Distribution of funds by sector investing funds[a]						
Government	18.1	18.4	11.4	9.7	8.8	8.8
Public enterprises	3.5	5.1	8.0	6.2	10.4	6.4
Corporate	22.9	14.5	13.0	21.5	12.9	25.4
Households[b]	55.5	62.0	67.5	62.6	67.9	59.5
Distribution of funds by uses[c]						
Currency	3.9	4.2	2.8	2.6	1.9	1.7
Deposits and similar	39.4	45.7	55.3	58.7	74.0	60.3
Securities purchased	29.9	27.8	23.2	23.7	16.2	17.0
Government loans	0.4	0.5	1.0	0.1	1.9	−0.2
Foreign lending[d]	3.6	1.2	1.3	6.0	0.9	13.1
Trade credits	22.9	20.6	16.4	8.8	5.0	8.1
Deposits and similar claims on financial institutions (as a % of total uses)[e]						
Monetary institutions	32.2	35.8	40.1	46.9	57.2	51.2
Central bank	3.3	2.7	−1.0	3.5	0.4	3.8
Deposit money banks	28.8	33.1	41.1	43.4	56.8	47.3
Demand deposits	9.0	12.4	9.0	17.5	8.8	5.6
Time savings and foreign currency	15.5	16.4	29.7	22.6	46.4	36.2
Government deposits	2.4	3.6	2.0	3.0	1.4	5.2
Other	2.0	0.6	0.4	0.2	0.2	0.3
Nonbanks	7.2	10.0	15.2	11.8	16.9	9.1
Time and savings	3.5	5.7	9.8	6.7	15.3	1.2
Trust funds	2.8	2.8	2.8	1.4	−3.2	4.0
Life insurance reserves	0.9	1.5	2.5	3.8	4.7	3.9
Securities purchased (as % of total uses)[c]						
Government securities	−0.2	−0.0	0.1	1.0	0.9	1.9
Financial Debentures[f]	0.2	−0.1	0.1	0.2	0.4	−6.9
Other debt[g]	0	0.9	1.1	0.6	−2.1	0.1
Corporate stock	28.1	25.5	21.2	16.8	16.4	18.1
Shares of noncorporate enterprises	1.8	1.5	0.7	5.1	0.6	3.8

Note: Multiyear figures are computed by averaging the annual distributions.

Excludes miscellaneous uses and the informal sector.

  a. Calculated from *Flow of Funds*, pp. 28–59, accounts 4–7.

  b. Includes nonprofit institutions.

  c. Compiled from *Flow of Funds*, pp. 60–109, Financial Assets and Liabilities summary tables.

  d. Includes investment abroad and foreign trade credits.

  e. Compiled from *Flow of Funds*, pp. 112–63, Outstanding Amounts of Domestic Financial Assets and Liabilities summary tables.

  f. Includes Central Bank securities and bank debentures.

  g. Includes commercial paper, domestic bills accepted by banks, and corporate bonds.

Source: CBC, *Flow of Funds in Taiwan District, ROC, 1965–90.*

Table 6.A7. *Taiwan: Distribution of Purchases and Issuance of Debt Instruments and Equity by Sector*
(percent)

	1970–74	1975–79	1980–84	1985–89[a]	1985	1989[a]
Short-term securities						
Issuance by						
Financial sector[b]	92.2	0.3	35.6	−88.3	100.2	−165.6
Private enterprises[c]	7.8	95.6	51.4	23.8	−12.4	66.4
Public enterprises[c]	0.0	4.1	13.0	−35.4	12.2	−0.8
Purchases by						
Financial sector	..	63.9	98.6	−212.5	133.0	−99.7
Private enterprises	..	17.5	−0.6	63.0	1.7	−0.3
Public enterprises	..	2.1	−0.1	5.2	−4.1	−0.4
Households	..	16.6	2.0	44.2	−30.5	0.4
Long-term securities						
Issuance by						
Financial sector[d]	17.2	8.8	34.2	69.4	57.3	−124.8
Government	−0.2	28.0	51.3	29.3	49.2	29.9
Private enterprises	19.0	7.5	9.0	−0.5	0.5	−1.5
Public enterprises	64.0	55.7	5.4	1.7	−6.9	−3.6
Purchases by						
Financial sector	121.1	98.1	85.2	84.7	79.9	−10.4
Government	0	0	0.5	0.3	−0.4	−6.5
Private enterprises	−3.9	0.8	0.5	2.8	1.2	−25.3
Public enterprises	3.7	−0.2	4.3	0.3	6.5	−52.9
Households	−20.9	1.3	9.6	11.8	12.8	−5.0
Equity (stock)[e]						
Issuance by						
Private enterprises	71.4	75.5	68.2	83.7	69.6	90.8
Public enterprises	28.6	24.5	31.8	16.3	30.4	9.2
Purchases by						
Financial sector	2.2	2.2	4.7	4.6	1.4	10.0
Government	20.2	23.1	29.9	15.6	26.0	6.4
Private enterprises	5.5	4.6	4.3	19.1	2.0	32.1
Public enterprises	0.5	1.2	1.2	0.1	3.1	−0.3
Households	71.6	69.0	59.9	60.6	67.5	51.7

· · Not available.

Note: Multiyear figures are computed from the totals for the period. (This approach is used rather than averaging the annual distributions because of the frequency of negative values in many categories and years.)

a. Short-term securities for 1986 – 89, as well as both short-term and long-term securities for 1989, had net redemptions. As with other years, negative numbers represent redemptions (disinvestment), with the result that the sum of the distribution is –100%.

b. Treasury bills-B issued by CBC.

c. Commercial paper and domestic bills accepted by banks.

d. CDs and SBs (savings bonds) issued by CBC, plus bank debentures.

e. Excluding stock issued by financial institutions and shares of noncorporate enterprises.

Source: Computed from absolute data in CBC, *Flow of Funds in Taiwan District, ROC, 1965–90*, pp. 60 –109 ("Summarized Tables on Changes in Financial Assets and Liabilities"); and DGBAS, *Statistical Yearbook of ROC 1990*, p. 193, Table 99. In the *Flow of Funds* "CBC securities" is a single-line item, so the *Yearbook* was used to obtain disaggregate data on treasury bills, savings bonds, and CDs.

Table 6.A8. *Taiwan: Distribution of Holdings of Outstanding Debt Instruments and Equity by Sector (percent)*

	1970–74	1975–79	1980–84	1985–89	1985	1989
Short-term Securities						
As an asset						
Financial sector	94.4	73.8	81.6	70.3	90.1	64.8
Private enterprises	5.6	12.3	2.2	12.4	1.3	14.0
Public enterprises	0.0	2.2	4.6	2.8	1.6	3.0
Households	0.0	11.7	11.6	14.5	7.0	18.1
As a liability						
Financial sector[a]	..	11.1	30.9	42.3	27.3	24.4
Private enterprises[b]	..	81.8	45.5	42.8	62.4	47.1
Public enterprises[b]	..	7.1	23.6	15.0	10.4	28.5
Long-term securities						
As an asset						
Financial sector	63.1	93.4	87.9	82.8	87.0	85.2
Government	0	0	0.3	0.6	0.3	0.3
Private enterprises	8.1	1.7	1.9	3.8	1.5	2.5
Public enterprises	1.4	0.4	1.4	3.8	3.0	0.9
Households	27.5	4.5	8.5	8.9	8.1	11.0
As a liability						
Financial sector[c]	14.4	5.6	14.2	75.0	25.8	60.0
Government	72.7	50.4	49.8	18.4	47.3	33.2
Private enterprises	6.7	7.8	8.1	1.3	8.6	1.4
Public enterprises	6.1	36.3	28.0	5.2	18.4	5.3
Equity (stock)[d]						
As an asset						
Financial sector	2.8	2.4	2.8	3.0	3.1	3.6
Government	24.3	24.4	24.4	22.2	23.9	20.3
Private enterprises	4.4	3.7	3.6	6.6	3.6	9.9
Public enterprises	0.4	1.0	0.9	0.8	1.0	0.6
Households	68.1	68.5	68.3	67.4	68.4	65.6
As a liability						
Private enterprises	74.3	74.1	74.2	77.7	74.6	78.6
Public enterprises	25.7	25.9	25.8	22.3	25.4	21.4

.. Not available.

Note: Multi-year figures are computed from the totals for the period. (This approach is used rather than averaging the annual distributions because of the frequency of negative values in many categories and years.)

a. Treasury Bills-B issued by CBC.

b. Commercial paper and domestic bills accepted by banks.

c. CDs and SBs (savings bonds) issued by CBC plus bank debentures.

d. Excluding stock issued by financial institutions and shares of noncorporate enterprises.

Source: Computed from absolute data in CBC, *Flow of Funds in Taiwan District, ROC, 1965–90*, pp. 112–63 ("Summary Tables on Year-end Outstanding Amounts of Domestic Financial Assets and Liabilities"); and *Financial Statistics Monthly*, various issues. In the *Flow of Funds,* "CBC securities" is a single line item, so the *Monthly* was used to obtain disaggregate data on treasury bills, savings bonds, and CDs.

Table 6.A9. *Taiwan: Composition of Financial Asset Holdings of the Personal Sector*
(percent)

	1970–74	1975–79	1980–84	1985–89	1985	1989
Currency	5.8	5.7	4.6	3.6	3.6	3.3
Deposits	44.9	52.3	53.8	59.7	59.9	61.0
Life insurance reserves	1.7	2.1	2.9	4.7	4.0	5.1
Securities[a]	47.6	39.9	38.8	31.9	32.5	30.6
Deposits and similar claims on financial institutions (as % of total holdings)						
Demand	8.8	13.3	10.6	14.6	9.2	15.5
Time, savings and foreign currency	33.7	34.7	38.8	42.2	47.5	42.4
Trust funds	2.5	4.3	4.4	2.9	3.2	3.1
Securities (as % of total holdings)[a]						
Bonds of						
Government	1.3	0.2	0.2	0.4	0.2	0.8
Financial debentures[b]	0.2	0.0	0.1	0.7	0.1	0.1
Nonfinancial corps	0	0.0	0	0.1	0.0	0.1
Commercial paper	0	0.2	0.5	0.2	0.2	0.2
Domestic bills accepted by banks	0	0	0.4	0.4	0.4	0.4
Corporate stock	42.6	36.6	35.4	25.8	29.8	23.3
Shares of noncorporate enterprises	3.5	2.9	2.1	4.3	1.8	5.7

Note: Multiyear figures are computed by averaging the annual distributions.

Excludes miscellaneous holdings and informal sector credits.

The source contains 25 categories, 16 of which are relevant to this sector, and 13 of which are included in this table. Because households includes farmers, professionals and other self-employed (vocational households), the sector holds a significant amount of "notes and accounts receivable." "Loans to households" is also a large category. Neither is included here. In 1989 the excluded categories (these two plus "all else, net") were 12.1% of a total that included them in the denominator.

a. Bonds are included at face value. Stocks and equities are valued at cost.

b. Includes central bank securities and bank debentures.

Source: Computed from absolute data in CBC, *Flow of Funds in Taiwan District, ROC, 1965–90*, pp. 112–63 ("Summarized Tables on Year-end Outstanding Amounts of Domestic Financial Assets and Liabilities").

Table 6.A10. *Taiwan: Distribution of Sources of Funds Raised by the Private Corporate Sector*
(percent)

	1970–74	1975–79	1980–84	1985–89	1980	1985	1989
Internal[a]	25.2	29.4	29.6	29.8	24.4	37.1	17.3
Equity[b]	25.9	28.0	28.3	42.1	32.8	40.0	34.7
Debt securities[c]	0.1	4.4	7.4	0.1	4.2	–1.4	6.0
Borrowings from							
Financial institutions	19.3	16.6	17.0	29.1	16.7	7.2	30.8
Government	0.0	0.1	0.2	0.7	0.0	1.7	1.2
Foreign sources[d]	5.8	2.8	1.6	8.2	1.2	9.1	6.0
Trade credits (domestic)[e]	23.6	18.7	16.0	–10.0	20.7	6.3	3.9
Amount raised, in billion NT$ (annual average of multiyear periods)	104.6	208.4	382.7	661.6	491.2	370.5	1,023

Note: Includes both corporate and noncorporate private enterprises. Multiyear figures are computed by averaging the totals for the period. Excludes miscellaneous sources and the informal sector.

    a. Internal funds are savings and gross fixed capital depreciation.

    b. Corporate stock and shares of noncorporate enterprises.

    c. Bonds, commercial paper, and domestic bills accepted by banks.

    d. Includes foreign trade credits.

    e. Includes notes and accounts receivables.

    Source: Computed from absolute data in CBC, *Flow of Funds in Taiwan District, ROC, 1965–89*. Internal funds ("gross savings" in source): pp. 36 – 43 (account 5); foreign claims: pp. 60 –109 ("Summarized Tables on Changes in Financial Assets and Liabilities"); all else: pp. 112– 63 ("Summary Tables on Year-end Outstanding Amounts of Domestic Financial Assets and Liabilities").

Table 6.A11. *Taiwan: Distribution of Uses of Funds Invested by the Private Corporate Sector*
(percent)

	1970–74	1975–79	1980–84	1985–89	1980	1985	1989
Real assets	62.0	60.9	61.1	60.6	56.3	65.6	28.5
Financial assets (as % of total uses)							
Currency	1.4	2.3	1.6	2.6	2.8	3.6	3.0
Deposits[a]	8.1	8.9	11.2	24.2	9.3	16.6	15.5
Equities[b]	1.9	1.6	1.8	9.0	1.5	2.2	16.7
Debt securities[c]	−0.1	0.8	−0.1	1.9	0.8	−0.2	−3.6
Foreign claims[d]	4.8	1.8	2.6	18.3	1.9	2.1	35.5
Trade credits (domestic)[e]	21.8	23.8	21.7	−16.5	27.5	10.1	4.4
Amount invested, in billion NT$ (annual average of multiyear periods)	93,038	170,207	279,720	451,971	342,333	243,933	621,578

Note: Funds invested are taken as the differences between year-end figures of outstanding absolute amounts, except direct data are available for investment in real assets and foreign claims. Multiyear figures are computed by averaging the totals for the period. Excludes miscellaneous uses and the informal sector.

a. Demand, time, savings, and foreign currency deposits, plus trust funds and presettlement requirements for imports.

b. Corporate stock and shares of noncorporate enterprises.

c. Central bank securities, bank debentures, government securities, commercial paper, domestic bills accepted by banks, and corporate bonds.

d. Includes foreign trade credits.

e. Includes notes and accounts receivables.

Source: Computed from absolute data in CBC, *Flow of Funds in Taiwan District, ROC, 1965–89.* Investment in real assets; p. 36 (account 5); foreign claims; pp. 60 –109 ("Summarized Tables on Changes in Financial Assets and Liabilities"); all else; pp. 112– 63 ("Summary Tables on Year-end Outstanding Amounts of Domestic Financial Assets and Liabilities").

Table 6.A12. *Taiwan: Number of Financial Institutions*

	Goverment-owned				Privately owned			
	1960	*1970*	*1980*	*1990*	*1960*	*1970*	*1980*	*1990*
Domestic banks								
Commercial	4	5	5	6	0	2	4	4
Specialized[a]	6	6	7	7	7	7	7	7
Other institutions								
Foreign banks	0	0	0	0	1	6	22	35
Credit cooperatives	0	0	0	0	80	76	75	74
Farmer associations[b]	0	0	0	0	290	296	278	285
Fisher associations[b]	0	0	0	0	0	0	4	24
Investment and trust companies	1	1	1	1	0	0	7	7
Insurance companies								
Life	2	2	2	2	0	6	7	13
Property and casualty	2	2	2	2	0	11	12	17
Totals[c]	16	17	18	19	378	404	420	466

Note: Data are year-end.

For the number of branches of these institutions, see Table 6.2.

a. Includes 1 government and 7 private medium business banks in all years; before being reorganized in 1977–79 these were mutual savings and loans.

b. Credit departments of the associations.

c. Totals include the government-owned postal savings system, as well as (1980 and 1990) the privately owned Fuh-hwa Securities Finance Company and 3 bills finance companies.

Source: CBC, *Financial Statistics Monthly* and *Annual Report of the Operations of Financial Institutions, Taiwan District*, various issues.

MOF *Yearbook of Financial Statistics* 1990 (pp. 466–58, Table 129); DGBAS *Statistical Yearbook of the ROC* 1990 (p. 202, Table 102); and *Taiwan Statistical Data Book* 1990 (pp. 149–50, Table 8–2a) give number of financial institutions. Unfortunately they do not agree in all cases and do not separate private from government banks.

Table 6.A13. Taiwan: Assets of Financial Institutions

	Billion NT$				As % of total			
	1961	1970	1980	1990	1961	1970	1980	1990
Full-service banks	21.0	96.0	1,099.2	4,842.8	80.2	70.5	64.5	53.3
Foreign banks	1.2	4.0	93.4	265.5	0.9	2.9	5.5	2.9
Small business banks[a]	0.8	5.9	63.2	667.1	3.1	4.3	3.7	7.3
Credit co-ops	2.0	10.8	116.6	834.9	7.5	7.9	6.8	9.2
Credit departments[b]	1.4	6.9	85.5	622.2	5.2	5.1	5.0	6.8
Investment and trust companies	0.3	2.0	73.0	394.7	1.3	1.5	4.3	4.3
Postal savings	0.2	8.0	141.8	1,059.4	0.8	5.9	8.3	11.7
Insurance companies	0.2	2.6	30.6	400.7	0.9	1.9	1.8	4.4
Total	26.1	136.2	1,703.3	9,087.3				

Note: Excludes Central Bank of China.

a. Medium and small business banks.

b. Credit departments of farmers' and fishermen's associations.

Source: CBC, *Financial Statistics Monthly* Oct. 1982 and Jun. 1991 (Appendix Tables of Assets and Liabilities of Various Financial Institutions); MOF, *Yearbook of Financial Statistics of the ROC*, 1975 and 1990 (Assets and Liabilities of Property and Casualty Insurance Companies).

Table 6.A14. *Taiwan: Loans and Investments of Financial Institutions*

	Billion NT$				As % of total			
	1961	*1970*	*1980*	*1990*	*1961*	*1970*	*1980*	*1990*
Full-service banks	14.4	74.7	164.6	3,748.6	82.0	76.4	67.5	68.3
Foreign banks	0.1	3.0	85.8	202.5	0.4	3.1	7.6	3.7
Small business banks[a]	0.7	4.8	54.6	509.6	3.8	4.9	4.8	10.0
Credit co-ops	1.2	6.9	79.6	507.2	7.1	7.1	7.0	9.2
Credit departments[b]	0.8	4.3	53.4	347.1	4.7	4.4	4.7	6.3
Investment and trust companies	0.3	1.9	71.5	329.5	1.6	1.9	6.3	6.0
Postal savings	0.1	0.5	1.8	10.3	0.3	0.5	0.2	0.2
Insurance companies	0.1	1.7	20.9	303.3	0.3	0.7	1.8	5.5
Total	17.7	97.8	1,132.2	5,490.9				

Note: Excludes Central Bank of China. Includes loans, discounts, portfolio investments, and real estate.

a. Medium and small business banks.

b. Credit departments of farmers' and fishermen's associations.

Source: CBC, *Financial Statistics Monthly* Oct. 1982 and Jun. 1991 (Appendix Tables of Assets and Liabilities of Various Financial Institutions); MOF, *Yearbook of Financial Statistics of the ROC*, 1975 and 1990 (Assets and Liabilities of Property and Casualty Insurance Companies).

Table 6.A15. *Taiwan: Deposits at Financial Institutions*

	Billion NT$				As % of total			
	1961	*1970*	*1980*	*1990*	*1961*	*1970*	*1980*	*1990*
Full-service banks	14.1	62.4	560.2	3,241.5	75.6	66.5	55.3	46.2
Foreign banks	0.0	0.1	3.2	77.2	0.0	0.1	0.3	1.1
Small business banks[a]	0.9	5.0	45.8	519.7	4.9	5.3	4.5	7.4
Credit co-ops	1.8	10.0	107.4	806.0	10.1	10.6	10.6	11.5
Credit departments[b]	1.1	5.1	70.2	579.2	5.9	5.4	6.9	8.3
Investment and trust companies	n.a.	n.a.	62.5	363.4	n.a.	n.a.	6.2	5.2
Postal savings	0.6	9.2	137.5	1,044.4	3.4	9.8	13.6	14.9
Insurance companies	0.0	2.1	25.4	388.5	0.1	2.2	2.5	5.5
Total	18.5	93.9	1,012.2	7,019.9				

n.a. Not applicable.

Note: Excludes Central Bank of China. Includes deposits held by individuals and enterprises, government deposits, trust funds, and insurance reserves.

a. Medium and small business banks.

b. Credit departments of farmers' and fishermen's associations.

Source: CBC, *Financial Statistics Monthly* Oct. 1982 and Jun. 1991, (Appendix Tables of Assets and Liabilities of Various Financial Institutions); MOF, *Yearbook of Financial Statistics of the ROC*, 1975 and 1990 (Assets and Liabilities of Property and Casualty Insurance Companies).

7

Taiwan: Development and Structural Change of the Banking System

YA-HWEI YANG

The financial system in Taiwan has not been a perfect bridge for transferring funds between savers and investors, but it is improving gradually. The system's role in Taiwan's economic development has been studied fairly extensively in such works as Shea and Yang (1989) and Lee and Tsai (1988), but these are primarily on a macro level. There is little analysis at the micro level—even in Chinese. This chapter seeks to fill that void.

To analyze the financial system on a micro level, two viewpoints must be considered: that of the banking firms and that of the banking industry. Individual banking institutions, when put together, make up the banking industry. Safety, liquidity, and profitability are the fundamental principles in operating a banking firm and these are matters of concern to the managers of any firm. Cost-efficiency is the most important criterion for evaluating the soundness of an industry, and banking is no exception.

The performance of specific banking firms and the banking industry as a whole can be distorted by regulations and other intervention by the government. One of the arguments for regulation is that it increases stability. On the other hand, it leads to a loss of efficiency. Achieving both stability and efficiency during financial liberalization is a social objective that should be pursued. This chapter analyzes the levels of both in Taiwan's regulated and liberalizing system. In addition, I look at the behavior of different banks and compare them using both theoretical and empirical approaches.

First I present a general model for explaining the behavior of different types of banks and then derive and test several themes from the model. The general regulatory environment and deregulatory steps that have been taken also are discussed in the first section, with particular attention paid to interest rate controls. Ownership and specific aspects of regulation are taken up in the second section.

The operations of banks are then analyzed in sections on liabilities and assets. I then assess nonperforming loans, and Taiwan's experiences with financial crises. Next, the operational efficiency of financial institutions is evaluated, including off balance sheet activities and cost structure. I then analyze how the banking industry was fundamentally changed in 1992 by the entry of 16 new commercial banks.

Creating financial stability, accommodating industrial policy, and avoiding an overly unequal income distribution have been economic (and socio-political) factors in Taiwan's control of its financial system. Satisfying interest groups in particular and (more recently) voters in general have been political factors affecting policy. These factors have been manifested most explicitly in controls of interest rates and bank ownership.

Political and Economic Factors in Financial Regulation

Baltensperger and Dermine (1987) mention three motives for banking regulation: bank safety and overall financial stability, monetary control, and prevention of monopoly activity and concentration (promotion of competition). Stigler (1971) was the first to state that regulation does not maximize industry revenue because the political process automatically admits powerful outsiders (government officials) to the industry's councils. Peltzman (1976) extended this argument with the empirical proposition that "regulation will tend to be more heavily weighted toward 'producer protection' in depressions and toward 'consumer protection' in expansions. Neither group achieves all that it wants from regulation in the sense that the price consistent with political equilibrium is neither the monopoly-profit-maximizing price nor the competitive price."

Baldwin (1984) summarizes seven models to explain industry protection, three of which can be applied to banking: the interest-group, equity-concern, and status-quo (historical) models. The interest-group model is probably the best known: Those industries (owners, workers, suppliers and the like) benefiting from protection organize politically to pressure for protection. The objective of ensuring that low-income groups are not hurt by economic change is the basis for the equity-concern model (which is often used as a disguise for nonpoor interest groups). The status-quo model sees government officials as exercising general caution in the face of the uncertain consequences of change, including a desire to avoid large adjustment costs and maintain existing property rights (even in the form of rents generated by protection). Later, Baldwin (1989) suggests two approaches to analyzing the political economics of protectionism: the economic self-interest of participants in the political process and the broad social concerns of voters and public officials.

Theoretical Framework for Bank Behavior

This study establishes a theoretical framework for analyzing bank behavior. Banks in Taiwan can be characterized as government-owned commercial banks, government-owned specialized banks, domestic privately owned commercial banks, and local branches of foreign banks. Each group has a slightly different behavior pattern depending on how it weights the pursuit of each of the following five objectives:

1. Profit maximization. This is a common objective of all banks, but government banks do not care much about the final profit figure.
2. Bad-debt minimization. Keeping the bad-debt ratio low is important at government banks.
3. Policy loans. Government-owned specialized banks have a responsibility to provide low-interest preferential loans to specific types of businesses.
4. Related-business loans. Private banks may have a preference for related companies when extending loans.
5. Enlarging staff. For a manager, utility comes not only from maximizing profit but also from increasing staff. A larger staff is generally seen as meaning that the manager has more power.

These goals can be used to specify a complete model of general bank behavior, which is presented mathematically in Table 7.1. The utility of the owner or manager of a bank is a function of the five goals. Profits are a function of the size of the loan portfolio, the interest earned on it—in this model we are considering three loan types: general, related-party, and policy-directed—offset by the bad debts that each type generates, the total deposits and their cost, the capital employed and its cost, and labor and the wage rate.

Managers at each of the four types of bank have subsets of the overall utility function—that is, they are concerned with only some of the variables. Thus, for a government-owned commercial bank, the utility function reflects concern with profit maximization, bad-debt minimization, and staff enlargement; the other two factors are not important. But for a government-owned specialized bank—which has the additional responsibility of providing special loans to specific businesses—the utility function adds that variable. The utility function for a domestic private bank includes increases in loans to related businesses and profitability, while a local branch of a foreign bank simply wants to maximize profit and thus has a one-variable utility function.

The model generates several themes—predictions about bank behavior—that are analyzed in this chapter:

1. The bad debt ratio for domestic banks, especially government banks, is lower than for local branches of foreign banks.
2. Asset management at foreign banks is more intense than at government banks. Given a certain amount of loanable funds, foreign banks extend more loans and make more investments than do domestic banks.
3. The major characteristics of customers differ among types of banks. For example, borrowers at specialized banks are mostly from specific kinds of businesses designated by the government as favored recipients of credit. The borrowings of businesses related to a domestic private bank tend to be with the related bank, and conversely, there is some concentration of loans by the private banks to their related businesses.
4. The productivity of foreign banks, given the same factors of production, is higher than that of domestic banks. In other words, foreign banks are more cost-efficient than government banks.

Table 7.1. *Bank Behavior Model*

The utility function of the owner or manager of a bank can be expressed as:

$$U = U(\pi, N, Q_1, Q_2, L) \tag{1}$$

where (as discussed in the text) π is profit; N, bad debt; Q_1 are loans to related business firms; Q_2, low interest policy loans; and L, labor; and

$$\delta U / \delta\pi > 0, \quad \delta U / \delta N < 0, \quad \delta U / \delta Q_1 > 0, \quad \delta U / \delta Q_2 > 0$$

The profits function is

$$\pi = i_1(Q_1) + i_2(Q_2) + i_3(Q - Q_1 - Q_2) - N_1(Q_1) - N_2(Q_2) - N_3(Q - Q_1 - Q_2) - i_0D - rK - wL$$

where i_0 is the interest rate for deposits; i_1 for related-business loans; i_2 for policy loans; and i_3 for general loans; Q is total loans; Q_1 are loans to related business firms; and N_1 is the related bad-debt ratio; Q_2 and N_2 relate to policy-directed loans; N_3 is the bad-debt ratio on loans other than related-firm and policy-directed loans; D is total deposits; r is the cost of capital; K is the amount of capital; L is the amount of labor; and w is the wage rate.

$$N = N_1 + N_2 + N_3 \tag{3}$$

Bank output (total loans) can be expressed as a function of capital and labor:

$$Q = Q(K, L) \tag{4}$$

The amount of total loans is limited by the total amount of total deposits:

$$Q \leq D \tag{5}$$

Combining Equations 1 to 5 gives us a complete model. However, for different kinds of banks, variations of the model are needed. The major difference is in the utility functions.

$$U\text{gc} = U\text{gc}(\pi, N, L) \quad \text{government-owned commercial bank} \tag{6}$$

$$U\text{gs} = U\text{gs}(\pi, N, L, Q_3) \quad \text{government-owned specialized bank} \tag{7}$$

$$U\text{p} = U\text{p}(\pi, Q_2) \quad \text{domestic private bank} \tag{8}$$

$$U\text{f} = U\text{f}(\pi) \quad \text{local branch of foreign bank} \tag{9}$$

The model and themes it represents can be related to the work of several scholars. Williamson (1963) analyzes the behavior of managers whose utility function considers profits plus scale of staff and the manager's own rewards. Migue and Belanger (1974) analyze the behavior of government officials whose utility function considers product level plus budget surplus. Combining related viewpoints, Orzechowski (1977) leads to the intuitively obvious point that once government officials (or other decisionmakers) pursue objectives other than profit, production deviates from profit maximization and cost minimization. The themes (utility functions 6 – 8) can be seen as pursuits of multiple objectives.

5. Foreign banks have higher profit ratios than domestic banks, because profit maximization is their most important—the only—goal.
6. Government banks tend to hire more workers than private banks.

REGULATION

The full scope of previous and continuing regulation is too broad and too comprehensive to describe completely in the space available, but a general grasp is possible. Major regulations can be grouped into three categories. Factors affecting the industry's operating environment—primarily interest rate controls—are the first group. The second group is regulations applying to industry practices, such as covering loan standards. The third group pertains to industry structure, including ownership and branching. Following an overview of the regulatory environment, this section looks at loan standards and interest rate regulation, including the liberalization of rates. Policy loans (government-directed loan allocations) are discussed with other bank assets in the fourth section.

Evolution and General Environment

The financial system in Taiwan has been under central and provincial government control since the end of World War II. For 40 years, change was cautious, and steps toward liberalization were usually slow. But since the mid-1980s the pace has picked up. The New Banking Law of 1989 is an important step toward financial liberalization.

Under the tightly regulated system that previously existed, formal institutions could not meet the needs of the economy so an informal network of financial activities and institutions came into being. This included a curb market for borrowing and lending funds. Even the government recognized the value of this gray market in promoting economic development and (most of the time) financial stability and so largely left it alone.

The Ministry of Finance (MOF) holds administrative power over all financial institutions, including chartering, branching, top manager assignment, and punishment. The Central Bank of China (CBC) checks bank operations to ascertain whether the bank is complying with central bank policy, such as interest rate management, and helps MOF examine bank records. Punishment power rests with MOF. The only penalty the central bank can impose for violating regulations is raising a bank's cost of capital.

Government-owned financial institutions constitute the bulk of Taiwan's financial system: They hold some two-thirds of the formal system's deposits and have made some two-thirds of the loans. Government banks, including commercial and specialized banks, are the core of the system. Specialized banks were established to assist specific categories of users, usually through preferential interest rate loans. Businessmen cannot dominate the behavior of government-owned banks, but the business sector may influence banks through representatives or other indirect channels. Some of the privately owned financial institutions have close relationships with business groups. If a private financial institution concentrates its loans on a particular group and the group defaults, the institution can run into trouble. Usually, financial crises are calmed by direct or indirect government intervention. In the future the Central Deposit Insurance Corporation will take the place of the government in handling such situations.

Overall, MOF and the CBC supervise, regulate, and examine the behavior of financial institutions; businesses influence the operation of financial institutions through direct and indirect channels; and all units in the regulatory environment are closely related.

Financial examination originally was to have been done by the MOF. However, due to limited staff, the ministry has not been able to do this by itself. Therefore, in 1962 it entrusted examination activities to the CBC. In turn, in the 1970s the CBC delegated to the Cooperative Bank of Taiwan the task of examining the books of the over 300 credit cooperatives and credit departments of farmer and fishery associations. Since the Central Deposit Insurance Corporation (CDIC) began operating in 1985, I also have examined some insured institutions. Thus, although MOF is responsible for financial examinations, they are actually carried out by other units, which then report the results to MOF.

To improve monitoring, econometric models that were developed as part of the world wide application of such methods, locally modified for Taiwan's conditions, are being adopted as a "financial early warning system." These models analyze the financial status of institutions and presumably can spot problems at an early stage. The system has been adopted by the CDIC, and MOF plans to use it for all types of financial institutions. MOF will closely watch any institutions that might have trouble, in order to resolve any problems before they become serious.

Since the Mid-1980s

Since 1986 there has been excess supply in the funds market, and the excess money has flooded into all kinds of speculative activities. Many of the activities were illegal under the laws existing at the time. So-called underground investment companies popped up to provide services to those wishing to speculate in the stock market and real estate booms spawned, at least in part, by the excess liquidity. These phenomena greatly disturbed MOF, and the 1989 reforms were partially the result of this concern.

The New Banking Law has three main purposes: privatization of banks, liberalization of interest rates, and punishment of illegal financial activities. In a sense, the third purpose is a nonliberalizing one, as it is intended to bring into the regulatory system some previously illegal and gray areas providing desirable financial services and then stamping out those still outside the system. But if the authorities restrict themselves to keeping the system honest and audited, the third purpose can be viewed as a part of liberalization, because liberalization needs the company of a good regulatory system.

There have been no major financial crises since 1986, so the protective function of deposit insurance has not been tested. As new private banks open, MOF definitely faces difficulties in controlling and advising them. Maintaining a stable and safe financial environment in a freely competitive financial sector has become an important but difficult goal. In order to achieve it, the deposit insurance system is expected to play a much more important role than it has. In addition, a sound examination system is also urgently needed.

Loan Standards

To ensure the soundness of the financial system, the monetary authorities have imposed some restrictions on bank portfolios. For example, to ensure liquidity, the ratio of liquid assets to deposits must be 7 percent or more. The ratio of "risky" assets to owner equity must be less than 8 percent, although as of the end of 1990 just what constitutes a risky asset had still not been announced.

To diversify risk, the government limits the total of all loans to a specific customer to 25 percent of a bank's net worth. Sometimes, however, customers borrow through subsidiaries controlled by affiliates (including relatives or friends). Thus, the actual loans to specific customers may be over the 25 percent limit. There are no relevant data, but it is believed there are instances of the limit being exceeded.

The Ministry of Audit, part of the Control Yuan, examines the process of extending loans to see whether there have been violations of the rules. This applies to both private and government banks. The penalties are more serious for employees at government banks because they are subject to other regulations that add punishment for rule violations. The process is quite strict and complicated when a bad loan is found on the books of a government-owned bank. All Taiwanese bankers, but particularly government ones, are therefore rather conservative in extending loans and do not actively seek customers. At the same time, financial institutions with higher profit ratios usually receive higher evaluations from administrative authorities.

Interest Rates

The government controlled bank interest rates rather tightly from the 1940s until 1986 and then somewhat more loosely until 1989. Before 1975 the government prescribed rates for loans and deposits that all banks had to follow. Then the CBC was given the authority to prescribe uniform interest rates for deposits, while a newly created Interest Rate Recommendation Committee (IRRC) of the Banks Association, composed of representatives from the banks, set floor and ceiling rates on loans, subject to the approval of the CBC. The permitted range for loan rates was allowed to widen progressively during the 1970s.

In 1980 the rates paid by banks for debentures, negotiable CDs, foreign currency deposits, and interbank call loans all were allowed to fluctuate freely. In 1985 banks were allowed to fix their own rates on loans within the prescribed range, and in 1986 the ceiling was removed. Also in 1986, deposit rates were decontrolled except for a ceiling.

Ceilings and floors on both deposits and loans were abolished by the New Banking Law that took effect in July 1989, and the IRRC was disbanded. Before interest rate liberalization, banks pursued a variety of approaches to avoid rate-limiting regulations. For example, banks requested compensating balances and tied loans to agreements to use fee-based bank services. In tight-money periods, instead of lending money directly, banks would guarantee bankers' acceptances and then buy them back from the borrower in the money market at a discount, in effect giving the bank a higher interest rate. With this and other strategies, Taiwanese banks were routinely able to circumvent the ceiling on bank loan rates , so the actual cost of a loan usually has been different—higher—than the posted cost.

After interest rate liberalization there have not been any significant differences among the banks in interest rates, particularly for deposits, because the bank fund market has had an excess supply. The three government commercial banks still act as market leaders, and because they have similar cost structures, significant variations should not in fact be expected, at least in the beginning stage of interest rate liberalization. But this situation is changing somewhat as the new banks seek to gain market share, as is discussed later.

Interest Rate Liberalization

Two indexes can be used to measure the degree of interest rate liberalization. One is the difference between the interest rate on loans and that on deposits. The second is the difference between the bank interest rate and the market rate.

As a rule of thumb, the smaller the spread between the rates charged for loans and paid on deposits, the more competitive the financial market is. During the period of controlled rates, the government never announced the spread, just the floor and ceiling for interest rates. Thus it is necessary to estimate the actual spread. This has been done by inferring effective interest rates on deposits and on loans from reported interest income and expense and reported levels of deposits and loans. The method is not precise, but the result is consistent with a declining spread, and there is other evidence to support such a conclusion. Table 7.2 provides my estimates of the spread.

The second index is used to measure deviation from the equilibrium rate and to identify the adjustment speed and flexibility of bank interest rates. The closer the bank rate is to the market rate, the greater the degree of financial liberalization.

A money market, that is, a short-term bills exchange market, was established in Taiwan in 1976. Its interest rates have been flexible—not under the control of the government—so changes in the bill rate can quickly reflect the demand and supply of loanable funds. Therefore, this money market interest rate is usually taken as a proxy for an equilibrium market rate. The curb rate is another representative proxy for the market interest rate. These two rate series plus a representative bank interest rate are plotted in Figure 7.1.

Between 1978 and 1989 all three series moved in the same direction, but bank rates had the smallest range, and the changes lagged behind the money market rate. The 1978–89 period was a tight one, and 1981–89 was a loose period.

The difference between the bank interest rate and the curb market interest rate has not changed very much. There is a straight-forward reason for this. Usual-

Table 7.2. Bank Interest Revenue, Cost, Rates, and Spread

Year ending Jun. 30	Interest revenue	Interest cost	Interest rate on		Spread[c]
	Million NT$		Loans[a]	Deposits[b]	
1968	5,972	3,886	15.31	8.38	6.93
1969	7,296	4,510	14.90	8.20	6.70
1970	9,022	5,623	14.81	8.67	6.14
1971	10,813	7,033	14.48	8.99	5.49
1972	12,799	8,575	13.96	8.62	5.34
1973	17,247	11,089	14.38	8.42	5.96
1974	33,174	23,087	19.59	13.45	6.14
1975	40,118	25,928	16.64	10.56	6.08
1976	41,311	27,554	12.98	7.50	5.48
1977	42,141	28,992	10.97	5.77	5.20
1978	54,757	35,819	11.55	5.39	6.16
1979	76,214	44,008	12.82	5.70	7.12
1980	102,329	61,915	14.28	8.10	6.18
1981	138,419	83,253	16.34	10.13	6.21
1982	146,568	103,784	14.93	10.38	4.55
1983	136,301	104,873	12.03	8.43	3.60
1984	142,635	126,221	10.92	8.16	2.76
1985	158,100	145,363	10.83	7.64	3.19
1986	144,374	140,472	9.01	6.00	3.01
1987	152,105	139,259	8.45	4.84	3.61
1988	178,016	146,221	8.17	4.17	4.00
1989	305,337	261,106	10.89	6.15	4.74
1990	416,097	374,657	12.04	7.50	4.54
1991	450,770	435,891	11.09	7.55	3.54
1992	508,430	480,524	10.30	7.09	3.21

Note: Includes the local branches of foreign banks.

a. Interest revenue as a percentage of total loans; see note d.

b. Interest cost as a percentage of total deposits; see note d.

c. Difference between rate on loans and rate on deposits.

d. Data on total loans and total deposits are available only for the calendar year-ends, while interest revenue and cost are fiscal years. To adjust for this, the denominators used for computing the interest rates are the result of averaging the total deposits (loans) of two consecutive years, then averaging two consecutive results of the first averaging. Mathematically, this is $(A_{t-2} + 2A_{t-1} + A_t)/4$ where the subscript t is the year of the entry and A is total deposits (loans) at the end of that calendar year.

Source: Central Bank of China, *Annual Report of Financial Activities.*

ly those firms capable of obtaining funds from banks can also get funds from the money market—but they will go to the banks first because the money is less expensive. On the other hand, even when the banking system has excess loanable funds, some firms do not have access to banks—they simply do not qualify. Therefore, the demands for funds in the banking sector and in the curb market do

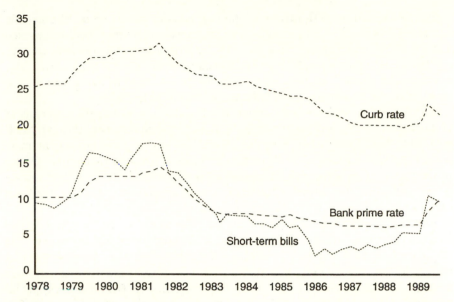

Fig. 7.1. Interest rates 1978–89, quarterly.

not shift very much and the risk premium and transaction cost premium stay pretty much the same.

To test causality in the interest rate structure, I used the Vector ARIMA model. The results show that until 1980 the bank rate adjusted about 3 months later than the money market rate did, and after 1981, about 1 month later. In other words, the speed of adjustment for bank rates quickened. (See Yang 1990a for a fuller discussion.)

OWNERSHIP AND CONTROL

MOF controls the creation and ownership of banks. There are several reasons for this, including ensuring financial stability, keeping track of the sources and uses of funds, avoiding a concentration of wealth, being pressured by vested interest groups, and the like. In 1989 restrictions on creating new banks were abolished. The chartering process was complex, and applications were still being processed two years later. Many observers were surprised when the results were announced in late 1991—few expected so many newcomers to be allowed, as is discussed later.

Ownership of the equity of any one bank by any one person is limited to 5 percent by the 1989 law. The percentage of any one bank owned by related persons may not exceed 15 percent. The rules are somewhat complex, as they seek to prohibit indirect holdings, and the term "persons" thus is used in its legal sense of including corporations and other such legal entities as well as actual people. No accurate data have been disclosed, however.

Before the end of 1991 Taiwan's banking industry consisted of 10 domestic commercial banks, 33 foreign banks, and an assortment of other institutions (see Table 6.A12). As discussed later, in 1991–92 16 new privately owned commercial banks were created and China Trust became a commercial bank. Generally references to "banks" in this chapter refer to the 24 listed in Table 7.3 plus the new banks (which are discussed later and listed in Table 7.22).

Most of the stock in six of the commercial banks is owned by the government of Taiwan Province, and some is held by the central government through MOF (see Table 7.4). Chang-Hwa, First, and Hua-Nan—as the three largest commercial banks—have played the role of market leaders since World War II. Of the others, two initially were regional (based in the two largest cities, but now island-wide), and one is the successor to the Japanese colonial period central bank for the island.

Of the four older privately owned commercial banks, three were founded by overseas Chinese during the 1970s. As part of maintaining ties to the overseas Chinese community, the government provided preferential measures to attract their investment in Taiwan. This applied not just to banks but to other activities as well. The International Commercial Bank of China (ICBC), deserves special mention. Created in 1912 as the government-owned Bank of China, its opera-

Table 7.3. *Principal Banks in Taiwan, 1991*

Government-owned	Privately owned
Commercial banks	*Commercial banks*
First Commercial Bank	International Commercial Bank of China
Hua-nan Commercial Bank	United World Chinese Commercial Bank
Chang Hwa Commercial Bank	Overseas Chinese Commercial Banking Corp
Bank of Taiwan	
City Bank of Taipei	Shanghi Commercial and Savings Bank
City Bank of Kaohsiung	
	Medium business banks
Specialized	Taipei Business Bank
Export–Import Bank of China	Medium Business Bank of
Chiao Tung Bank[a]	Hsinchu
Farmers Bank of China	Hualien
Central Trust of China	Kaohsiung
Cooperative Bank of Taiwan	Taichung
Land Bank of Taiwan	Tainan
Medium Business Bank of Taiwan	Taitung

Note: The 10 (6 government and 4 private) commercial banks plus 6 of the specialized banks (all but the Medium Business Bank) are considered full-service banks.

There were 35 foreign banks from 13 countries at the end of 1990: the United States (12), France (5), Singapore (3), the United Kingdom (4), the Netherlands and Canada (2 each), and 1 each from Australia, Germany, Hong Kong, Japan, the Philippines, South Africa, and Thailand.

a. Called Bank of Communications until 1992.

Table 7.4. Ownership of the Three Major Commercial Banks (August 1991)

Bank	Total capital[1]	Percentage of shares held		
		Private	National treasury	Provincial treasury
First	7.344	30.21	1.56	68.23
Hua Nan	7.257	42.34	1.78	55.88
Chang Hwa	6.525	48.44	1.45	50.05

1. Par value of stock in billion NT$.

tions on the mainland had been necessarily abandoned when the Kuomintang (KMT = Nationalist) government moved to Taiwan. When the Republic of China (based in Taiwan) was displaced at the United Nations by the People's Republic of China (based on the mainland), the latter began taking possession of Chinese government properties around the world. To avoid seizure of the Taiwan-based Bank of China's overseas assets, it was privatized as the ICBC in December 1971. It remains closely associated with the government, however, through the KMT's direct and indirect holdings.

The KMT, which has been in power on Taiwan since the end of World War II, owns stock in Central Investment Holding (CIH) and seven financial institutions, as shown in Table 7.5. CIH owns 25 percent of the International Commercial Bank. Fuh-Hua Securities Finance is a monopoly, and the bills companies are two of just three such firms. The KMT also has a high degree of control in the insurance industry and the investment and trust business. The KMT firms generally cooperate with government financial institutions and government enterprises, and receive support from the government. Other political parties do not own any financial institutions.

Although many private financial institutions exist besides the major banks, their scale is quite small. Private insurance, investment, and trust companies

Table 7.5. Kuomintang Ownership of Financial Businesses, 1988

Company	After-tax profit (million NT$)	Par value of stock (billion NT$)	Shares KMT owns as % of total
China Investment and Trust	1,796	3.00	3.26
China Development Corp	244	1.05	17.08
China United Trust and Investment	621	1.00	52.21
Fuh-Hua Securities Finance	339	1.25	47.20
China Bills Finance	183	0.90	36.70
Chung-Hsing Bills Finance	316	1.50	58.20
Central Property and Casualty Insurance	73	0.36	100.00

Source: Finance Information. Nov. 1989

outnumber the government institutions in these fields. In other words, until 1991 the government has kept tighter control on the number of privately owned banks than on the number of any other type of financial institution.

In May 1990 the central government sold part of its equity in each of the three major banks, but the provincial councillors have not yet agreed to sell their part. The offering was by lottery in an attempt to ensure broad distribution. However the sale was not well received in the stock market because the price had been set on April 1, and market conditions had deteriorated substantially by May. Continued weakness in the Taiwanese stock market has led to postponement of other offerings.

Branches

The number and specific location of branches have also been subject to government approval, for the expressed purpose of protecting existing branches from competition. Foreign banks have been the most restricted, being allowed just one office (which had to be in Taipei) until 1985, at which point a branch could be opened in Kaohsiung (a major port and industrial center, and Taiwan's second-largest city). It was 2 years before Hollandsche Bank received permission to open the first foreign branch in Kaohsiung, followed by Citibank. In 1990 Taichung, Taiwan's third largest city, was opened to foreign branches, and Citibank opened there the following year. Government banks generally have more branches than private banks.

Control of branching has been used to maintain market shares and promote "orderly" growth. Thus, banks have been limited to no more than three new branches a year. Banks that violated regulations in the previous year have not been allowed to establish branches in the current year, a regulation set in 1984. The approval rate for branch applications has been 70 to 80 percent. Table 7.6 provides data on branches.

The dominant role of government financial institutions and the three big commercial banks is apparent in their share of deposits and loans. There has been an increase each year since 1963 in the absolute amount of total loans and loans by each institution type shown. Government institutions had a generally declining share of loans in the 1970s, but since recovering from a low in 1981 they have had a fairly stable two-thirds share. Data are in Table 7.7.

On the deposit side, banks experienced disintermediation in 1980—although it was equal to only some 1.6 percent of their 1979 deposits. For government financial institutions (including nonbanks), deposits fell for two years, standing in 1980 at just 72 percent of their 1978 level. For the three major government commercial banks, however, the decline was less than 10 percent. In 1981 deposits for both categories recovered to record high levels. The timing was different for private institutions, as their deposits dropped only in 1978—a year deposits were swelling at government institutions—but recovered in 1979, reaching new highs in 1980 even as government institutions continued to lose deposits. Market shares have been quite volatile, but over the entire period the general trend seems to have been a rising share for private institutions, from less than one-fourth before the late 1970s to one-third or more during the 1980s.

Table 7.6. *Number of Banks and Branches*

	Government owned				Privately owned				
	Specialized		Commercial		Specialized		Commercial		Foreign
Year	Banks	Branches[a]	Banks	Branches[a]	Banks	Branches[a]	Banks	Branches[a]	banks[b]
1978	6	198	5	340	5	88	4	23	13
1979	7	207	5	346	7	89	4	23	13
1980	7	216	5	347	7	91	4	24	21
1981	7	230	5	363	7	92	4	29	24
1982	7	242	6	366	7	97	4	31	25
1983	7	243	6	370	7	102	4	31	28
1984	7	243	6	371	7	110	4	35	31
1985	7	248	6	386	7	117	4	37	32
1986	7	257	6	389	7	124	4	43	32
1987	7	282	6	391	7	139	4	47	32
1988	7	293	6	406	7	152	4	52	32
1989	7	301	6	424	7	170	4	58	33
1990	7	311	6	433	7	164	4	68	35

a. Number of branches includes home office. For additional data on the number and branches of financial institutions, see Tables 6.2 and 6.A12.

b. The number of branches is the same as the number of banks until 1987. In 1989, 5 of the 33 banks had a second branch. See discussion in text.

Source: Central Bank of China, *Financial Statistics Monthly,* various issues.

Employees

Employees of government-owned banks are government employees, just as if they worked at a government ministry. To qualify for employment, they must pass a test held by the Examination Yuan. Many kinds of tests are held. Some are annual general civil service exams taken by prospective government employees regardless of what part of the government they are going to work for. Occasionally, tests are arranged for a specific bank.

The chairman of the board and the general manager of government banks are appointed by MOF for 3-year terms that can be renewed once. The advantage of the limit on tenure is that it prevents top managers from becoming entrenched at a specific bank. (This is analogous to the Chinese imperial practice of rotating magistrates from place to place every 3 years.) The disadvantage is that few of the managers are willing to be forceful leaders, instead they just sit there, hoping that nothing bad occurs during their term.

Staff at MOF, CBC, and government-owned financial institutions move around among the various entities. In other words, positions at any given bank are filled from both internal promotion and recruitment from other government agencies. The staffs are in effect permanent employees of the government until they retire. Moreover, bank board members may be retired bureaucrats from any government institution—not just a financial one. As the number of private banks and other financial institutions increases, the government employee pool has been tapped to staff the new banks. During the late 1980s' stock market boom, several senior managers left government service to take positions with security companies.

Table 7.7. *Percentage of Total Loans Made by Different Types of Banks*

Year	Government institutions 3 major CBs[a]	Total	Private banks	Foreign banks	Total loans (billion NT$)
1962	23.7	97.0	3.0	0	16.2
1963	26.8	96.4	3.6	0	17.3
1964	25.8	95.6	4.4	0	21.0
1965	24.6	94.0	5.3	0.7	26.1
1966	26.0	92.8	6.0	1.2	30.2
1967	30.1	93.0	5.5	1.5	37.3
1968	32.9	93.7	4.1	2.1	47.0
1969	34.7	92.3	4.7	3.1	59.5
1970	33.8	92.0	4.8	3.1	71.8
1971	34.6	90.8	5.5	3.7	88.7
1972	35.6	89.9	6.0	4.2	109.2
1973	29.9	88.2	6.4	5.4	163.2
1974	26.6	87.2	6.1	6.7	230.9
1975	26.8	88.3	6.3	5.4	305.5
1976	29.4	87.2	6.6	6.2	382.7
1977	30.4	87.1	6.5	6.4	473.9
1978	34.8	86.7	6.9	6.4	586.8
1979	29.7	82.3	11.4	6.3	742.3
1980	26.1	73.4	17.3	9.3	918.8
1981	25.4	76.9	11.7	11.4	990.2
1982	23.6	79.7	11.2	9.1	1,151
1983	24.0	82.2	10.3	7.5	1,341
1984	23.8	83.0	10.1	7.0	1,501
1985	23.4	84.1	09.8	6.2	1,613
1986	25.6	83.0	10.5	6.5	1,810
1987	26.5	82.6	11.0	6.4	2,112
1988	28.9	83.2	11.5	5.3	2,853
1989	29.9	82.7	11.9	5.4	3,611
1990	29.4	82.3	12.5	5.1	3,976

Note: Postal savings system data are excluded.
a. The 3 major commercial banks are First, Hua Nan, and Chang Hwa.
Source: Central Bank of China, *Annual Report of Financial Activities*, various issues.

The three major banks had over 5,500 employees each at the end of 1991, while employment at medium business banks ranged between 266 (Taitung) and 1,770 (Taipei). With 15 percent of the staff, Taitung had only some 5 percent of the assets of Taipei. Similarly, Taipei had 30 percent of the staff but just 15 percent of the assets of First (one of the three major commercial banks). During the 1980s domestic bank employment increased about 3.5 percent a year, with the pace in the last part of the decade running at close to 4 percent. The average foreign bank had just 93 employees (but then it also had only one office) in 1990, compared to 70 in 1977.

LIABILITIES

Domestic banks obtain most of their funds from deposits, but foreign banks have had to rely more on funds provided by their parents and borrowing from domestic financial institutions, because of restrictions on their deposits. Government deposits are made only in domestic banks and typically receive low interest rates. A time series on bank deposits is in Table 7.8, and liabilities and owner equity by category of bank in 1980 and 1990 are given in Table 7.9.

Table 7.8. *Percentage of Total Deposits Held by Different Types of Banks*

| | Government institutions | | | | Total |
Year	3 major CBs[a]	Total	Private banks	Foreign banks	loans (billion NT$)
1962	32.5	99.5	0.5	0	16.8
1963	32.5	99.2	0.8	0	20.6
1964	33.1	99.2	0.8	0	24.6
1965	35.0	97.3	1.2	1.4	28.0
1966	37.4	97.8	1.4	0.9	35.0
1967	39.9	98.4	1.3	0.3	42.1
1968	40.2	97.7	1.3	1.0	49.8
1969	42.6	98.0	1.4	0.7	58.1
1970	42.1	98.5	1.3	0.2	67.7
1971	43.0	98.1	1.5	0.4	84.2
1972	41.9	97.9	1.8	0.3	115.1
1973	38.9	97.2	2.2	0.6	153.5
1974	42.2	97.2	2.1	0.7	164.0
1975	34.8	97.2	2.3	0.5	240.9
1976	33.5	95.9	3.3	0.8	321.2
1977	34.3	95.4	3.8	0.7	401.1
1978	36.4	94.4	4.7	0.8	518.7
1979	32.4	90.0	9.1	0.9	601.1
1980	31.7	90.0	9.5	0.5	689.1
1981	31.0	89.4	10.0	0.6	813.0
1982	30.2	89.3	9.9	0.8	984.9
1983	30.4	89.2	9.8	1.0	1,229
1984	30.1	88.9	9.9	1.2	1,477
1985	30.2	88.3	10.0	1.6	1,813
1986	31.3	89.2	9.6	1.2	2,185
1987	31.2	88.1	10.3	1.6	2,698
1988	33.4	86.7	11.7	1.6	3,355
1989	31.1	85.7	12.8	1.6	4,237
1990	29.7	84.0	14.2	1.8	4,601

Note: Postal savings system, Central Bank of China, and interbank deposits data are excluded.

a. The 3 major commercial banks are First, Hua Nan, and Chang Hwa.

Source: Central Bank of China, *Annual Report of Financial Activities*, various issues.

Table 7.9. *Balance Sheet Structure by Type of Bank: Equity and Major Liability Items as a Percentage of Total*

	Government			Medium	
Year and item	Specialized	Commercial	Private[a]	business	Foreign
1980					
Deposits[b]	62.1	50.4	45.8	81.1	2.8
Government deposits	0.9	10.8	0.2	0.0	—
Foreign currency deposits	0.1	0.6	0.8	0.0	1.0
Other financial instutions[c]	6.1	16.3	7.6	2.0	5.0
Borrowings	14.1	10.1	22.2	1.8	75.9
Bankers' acceptances	0.3	0.8	1.5	0.0	6.1
All else	10.1	5.7	14.7	5.8	5.8
Equity	6.3	5.2	7.3	9.4	3.4
Balance sheet total in billion NT$	373.5	622.2	139.8	37.2	96.4
1990					
Deposits[b]	68.7	72.1	76.8	89.7	19.6
Government deposits	1.7	7.9	0.2	0.0	0.0
Foreign currency deposits	0.5	1.0	2.1	0.0	6.8
Other financial institutions[c]	12.2	5.2	2.0	0.2	3.0
Borrowings	6.4	3.1	1.6	0.0	46.3
Bankers' acceptances	0.2	0.6	0.4	0.0	15.1
All else	6.8	5.8	8.8	3.6	4.4
Equity	3.5	4.3	8.0	6.4	4.8
Balance sheet total in billion NT$	2,391	2,681	822	339	314

Note: Distributions may not add to 100% due to rounding.

a. Excludes medium business banks.

b. Except deposits by the Central Bank of China, other financial institutions, the government, and in foreign currency.

c. Deposits by the Central Bank of China and other financial institutions

Source: Central Bank of China, *Statistics of Important Activities for Financial Institututions,* various issues.

Because most deposit interest rates were set by the government until 1986 and then were subject to a ceiling until July 1989, banks could not use rates to manage the level and structure of their deposits. When loan opportunities are limited, as they were during part of the 1980s, deposits can be larger than loans. This imposes a heavy interest expense burden on the banks. Thus, although banks were supposed to absorb deposits without resistance at the regulated rates, in the early 1980s a few banks rejected some large-denominated deposits. This led to negotiations between depositors and banks that resulted in effective rates lower than the regulated deposit interest rates.

The volume of negotiated CDs increased sharply after 1988 because banks raised interest rates on them to attract funds and to comply with CBC requests to contract the money supply.

Deposits in foreign banks are explicitly restricted by the government to lessen their ability to compete with domestic banks. Foreign banks can accept demand deposits but not time savings deposits. Until 1990 their demand deposits could not be over 12.5 times the amount of paid-in capital, with a ceiling of NT$1 billion. In 1990 the absolute ceiling was removed, and the relative ceiling was raised to 15 times paid-in capital.

The postal savings system (PSS) collects less than 3 percent of total deposits, and they all are redeposited in four specialized banks (the Medium Business Bank of Taiwan, the Bank of Communications, the Land Bank of Taiwan, and the Farmers Bank of Taiwan). Originally, the specialized banks were not supposed to absorb deposits, but they were allowed to accept them beginning in the late 1980s. The PSS is an important source for them—some two-thirds in the case of the Bank of Communications at the end of 1988.

There are few bank debentures, as the bond market is still in an early stage of development and its scale is too small to attract many buyers. Foreign banks that issue debentures in their home country or the Euromarket have not issued any in Taiwan. Between 1980 and 1990, owner equity increased substantially in absolute terms for all four types of banks but declined as a percentage of the balance sheet.

To summarize the differences between domestic and foreign bank liabilities in mid 1991, the latter do not have government or PSS deposits, NT dollar time deposits, debentures, foreign exchange trust funds, or CDs denominated in foreign currencies. Foreign banks obtain their local currency primarily through the interbank call market.

BANK ASSETS

Loans are the banks' most important bank asset. Table 7.10 show data on assets by type of bank for 1980 and 1990 and reveals that the ratios of investment and loans to assets decreased while medium- and long-term loans increased for all banks.

In the decisionmaking process used by bankers in extending loans, the so-called five Ps—person, purpose, payment, protection, and perspective—are, on the surface, the principal criteria. In practice it is somewhat different. For a survey conducted by myself and others, questionnaires were distributed to Taiwanese firms asking them to rank what they considered important to a bank's decision to make a loan (Yang and others 1987). The responses were used to create two indexes: importance (weighted) and universalism (the number of respondents listing a factor). The results are in Table 7.11.

Collateral heads both lists, suggesting that safety is the main factor considered by bankers, because collateral can enable them to avoid the risk of no return on a loan. (Foreign banks are not allowed to make equity investments in real estate, but they can lend against real estate as collateral.)

Table 7.10. *Balance Sheet Structure by Type of Bank: Asset Items as a Percentage of Total*

Year and item	Government		Private[a]	Medium business	Foreign
	Specialized	Commercial			
1980					
Cash and interbank deposits	16.2	21.7	11.4	11.3	2.7
Government securities	1.0	1.5	0.6	0.7	0.0
Other investments	6.0	4.8	7.2	9.1	0.6
Loans and discounts	73.6	68.3	70.9	73.1	88.7
All else	5.1	5.2	11.8	6.8	9.8
Reserves for losses	−1.9	−1.6	−1.8	−1.0	−1.8
1990					
Cash and interbank deposits	22.0	19.3	20.4	17.8	17.0
Government securities	1.0	1.5	0.9	0.4	0.2
Other investments	11.9	8.8	12.6	8.6	2.0
Loans and discounts	62.3	66.6	60.5	69.6	65.1
All else	3.7	4.6	6.7	4.3	17.5[b]
Reserves for losses	−0.8	−0.8	−1.0	−0.8	−1.8

Note: Distributions may not add to 100% due to rounding.
a. Excludes medium business banks.
b. Bills receivable were 15.1% of 1990 total assets.
Source: Central Bank of China, *Statistics of Important Activities for Financial Institutations,* various issues.

The banks' loan-extending attitude may be measured approximately by the ratio of actual loans and investments to the available amount of loanable funds. The volume of loanable funds can be measured as net worth plus liabilities minus required reserves. The ratios for domestic banks and foreign banks are shown in Table 7.12.

Foreign banks have a higher percentage of their available funds out in loans and investments. In other words, foreign banks are more active in loan extension and portfolio investment than domestic banks, which is what is expected from theme 2 of my model.

Special Loans

Preferential financing helps decrease the costs facing firms. Common instruments of such a policy are special loans, investment, and insurance provided by specialized financial institutions. Loans are the most frequently adopted of the three instruments. Beneficiaries of the policy include strategic industries, small and medium businesses, and exporters.

The government's export-financing policy has been important since the 1960s when export orientation was proposed as the economic development strategy.

Table 7.11. *Ranking of Determinative Factors in Lending*

Importance	Universalism
Collateral	Collateral
Relationship[a]	Relationship[a]
Scale of firm	Guarantor
Guarantor	Scale of firm
Debt ratio	Debt ratio
Interest rate	Interest rate
Length of loan	Length of loan
Transaction costs	Transaction costs

a. Between the borrowing firm and the bank.
Source: Yang and others, 1987.

After the 1970s, as the ever-increasing trade surplus resulted in tremendous foreign exchange reserves, export subsidies were reduced. After the 1980s, in order to upgrade production technology, the government selected specific strategic industries and gave them preferential loans.

Table 7.12. *Indexes of Bank Liability Utilization*

Year	Index 1		Index 2	
	Domestic banks	Foreign banks	Domestic banks	Foreign banks
1978	67.4	94.0	96.4	103.8
1979	70.5	94.6	99.1	104.2
1980	78.5	96.7	100.2	103.6
1981	89.7	94.7	100.7	104.6
1982	86.9	90.6	99.2	105.6
1983	86.6	94.0	100.0	105.2
1984	85.7	87.1	99.4	101.5
1985	77.2	79.6	97.6	102.2
1986	65.0	83.1	89.4	103.9
1987	59.7	66.5	89.8	104.4
1988	74.7	83.2	92.7	106.0
1989	83.9	93.9	94.6	112.2

Note: Index 1 = (Loans and discounts + Portfolio investment) as a percentage of (Deposits + Bank debentures issued + Foreign liabilties + Due to financial institutions + Others − Required reserves).

Index 2 = (Loans and discounts + Portfolio investment + Foreign assets + Real estate + Claims on financial institutions except central banks) as a percentage of liabilities.

Portfolio investment = Government securities + Stocks and bonds.

Source: CBC, *Financial Statistics Monthly,* various issues.

Strategic Industry Loans

In the 1980s improving the industrial structure became an important policy issue. Therefore, several measures intended to promote the growth of so-called strategic industries were taken in 1982. These industries include machinery, and the information and electronic industries.

The government provided firms in these designated industries with special low-interest medium- and long-term loans. Collateral requirements are also somewhat more lenient for these industries, in that firms often can use the machinery being purchased as security, rather than providing a mortgage, as is the case with most commercial loans.

The loans are extended by Chiao Tung Bank (formerly the Bank of Communications) and the Medium Business Bank of Taiwan, with 20 to 25 percent of the funds coming from the Executive Yuan Development Fund and the rest provided by the two banks. The difference between the strategic loan rate and the prime rate has been 175 to 275 basis points. Loans have also been made to nonstrategic industries to finance automation equipment, domestically produced machinery, and environmental protection projects. Indeed, the targets of and budgets for subsidized credit have been continually modified, as has the terminology. "Rising star industry" and "important industry" were phrases being used in the early 1990s as alternatives to "strategic industries." Table 7.13 has data on the various kinds of preferential loans in 1988.

In a questionnaire-based study of the effects of preferential loans on strategic industries, I found that they had had little impact (Yang 1990b). Most subsidized firms would have made investments even without the preferential loans; the loans did not significantly reduce the cost of capital; and they were not important to firms' operational efficiency.

Table 7.13. *Distribution of Preferential Medium- and Long-Term Loans Outstanding, 1988*
(percent)

Category	Medium Business Bank	Bank of Communications[a]	Total
Strategic industries	20.3	35.6	32.1
Automated equipment	29.4	32.4	31.7
Domestically produced machines	36.3	26.3	28.5
Protect environment, prevent pollution	—	5.0	3.9
"Good manufacturing product" projects	—	0.1	0.0
Co-operational export and new product development	14.1	0	3.2
Projects supported by the Council for Economic Planning and Development	—	0.6	0.5
Total amount in million NT$	23,997	82,110	106,107

a. The Bank of Communications became Chiao Tung Bank in 1992.
Source: The two banks.

The Bank of Communication has extended its financing activities beyond the communication industry since its founding in 1907. It was reorganized in 1979 to play the role of a development bank. This involves medium- and long-term credits and venture capital (including equity positions). Strategic industries have received most of the development credits. Tables 7.13 and 7.14 show the bank's investments by category.

Aid to Small and Medium Businesses

Medium business banks are required to extend at least 70 percent of their total loans to small and medium businesses, and they have in fact generally exceeded this minimum. Although both these specialized banks and general banks (the 16 full-service banks listed in Table 7.3) lent declining shares to small and medium businesses in the late 1980s, the absolute amount of loans increased, as shown in Table 7.15. This is evidence for theme 3 of the model, that the borrowers from specialized banks are mostly some specific kinds of businesses. (As of 1991 small and medium businesses are officially defined as, for manufacturing: owner's capital less than NT$ 40 million, assets under NT$ 120 million; for general business: latest year sales of NT$3.5 million to NT40 million; and, for small-scale commercial: latest year sales less than NT$2.5 million.)

There are eight medium business banks, one of which is government-owned—the Medium Business Bank of Taiwan (MBBT). Each of the seven private ones is based in a specific region of the island, a fact reflected in their names (see Table 7.3), and are much smaller than the island-wide government bank. The MBBT offers strategic industry loans as well as many special loans to small and medium businesses (SMBs), such as the SMB Development Loans program and three Sino-American Fund loan programs. These are listed in Table 7.16.

A variety of other aid is offered to SMBs as part of an integrated system dating from 1967 when the Executive Yuan promulgated Regulations Governing Assistance to SMBs as a policy guidance tool. Although they have been revised several times, the regulations are still in effect. A number of organizations have been created, with the MBBT, the SMB Credit Guarantee Fund, and the Small Business Integrated Assistance Center as the core of the system, which operates under the regulation of MOF.

Table 7.14. *Loans and Investments of the Bank of Communications at June 30 Fiscal Year-end*
(Billion NT$)

Type of credit	1985	1986	1987	1988	1989
Development	76.28	80.95	81.53	87.19	110.05
Nondevelopment	22.23	24.84	29.86	31.57	32.81
Equity[a]	1.76	1.89	2.52	3.15	3.87

The Bank of Communications became Chiao Tung Bank in 1992.

a. Includes venture capital.

Source: BOC, *Annual Report.*

Table 7.15. *Loans to Small and Medium Businesses
and Their Percentage of Total Loans*

	1987		1988		1989	
Type of Bank	NT$[1]	%	NT$[1]	%	NT$[1]	%
Medium business	150.7	78.1	207.9	75.7	267.8	72.6
Other general[2]	496.6	33.1	683.2	34.8	952.9	31.4
Total	644.3	38.2	891.1	39.9	1220.7	35.9

Note: Data are for June 30 of year shown (fiscal year-end).

1. In billions.

2. Domestic commercial and specialized banks (see Table 7.3) and local branches of foreign banks.

Source: Small Business Integrated Assistance Center.

The Credit Guarantee Fund was founded in July 1974 with grants from government agencies and related financial institutions. The fund is basically intended to offer its guarantee on behalf of firms considered to perform well but lacking the collateral needed to obtain loans under the usual lending rules. In other words, those firms whose credit evaluation by banks is on the margin can seek the help of the Credit Guarantee Fund.

The Integrated Assistance Center started to serve SMBs in July 1982. It provides financial diagnostic services and helps firms secure financing when they encounter difficulties doing so on their own. The Center also helps firms implement sound accounting systems. Cases accepted by the Center come from banks, government agencies, or firms themselves. Its annual report (in Chinese) is a useful reference on small business in Taiwan.

Table 7.16. *Distribution of Preferential Loans
of the Medium Business Bank of Taiwan by Loan Program*
(percent)

Loan program	1986	1987	1988	1989
Small and medium business development loans	93.68	93.67	92.51	93.62
Sino-American Fund loans				
Promotion of S&M business	4.09	4.27	2.85	2.61
Pollution-prevention equipment	0.49	0.50	0.65	0.46
Automation	n.a.	n.a.	0.21	0.37
GMP loans	0	0.90	0.85	n.a.
Business credits	1.74	0.66	0	n.a.
Youth business adventure	n.a.	n.a.	2.94	2.94
Total loans in NT$ billion	6.356	8.727	11.828	14.150

n.a. Not applicable.

Note: Data are for fiscal years ending Jun. 30 of year shown.

Source: Medium Business Bank of Taiwan, *Annual Report*, various years.

The SBA (Small Business Administration, part of the Ministry of Economic Affairs) was established in January 1981. In coordination with several other government and private organizations, the SBA has set up programs to provide advice on finance, management, production technology, and marketing. In addition, the MBBT has a SMB Service Center for assisting such businesses in solving their financial problems.

Specialized Banks

In executing financial policy, specialized banks always face a dilemma. They must satisfy two objectives: profit and policy. To achieve profits, banks prefer loans collateralized by mortgages; to satisfy policy, banks must make loans for risky projects. Bankers are subject to scrutiny from the auditing authority if a loan goes bad, even if the loan was made because of policy considerations. So there is a conflict between the profit objective and the policy objective.

The Medium Business Bank of Taiwan (MBBT) and the SMB Credit Guarantee Fund usually argue about which is responsible for bad debts. The Fund allows the MBBT to decide whether to lend money up to a (fairly low) limit per firm. If the loan is defaulted, the MBBT asks the Fund for compensation, at which point the Fund might charge the MBBT with not having been careful enough in following the rules regarding selection of firms. Such disputes, if not settled by the two principals, are arbitrated by a committee consisting of five members, each from a different financial institution.

NONPERFORMING LOANS

Bad loans, called accounts, and overdue loans, are collectively called nonperforming loans. Data by type of bank are in Tables 7.17 to 7.18.

The government prescribes procedures for all domestic banks for handling such loans under the Act on Handling of Overdue Loans, Called Accounts, and Bad Loans, which was promulgated in 1960 and modified in 1972, 1978, 1981, and 1985. Several important parts of the act follow.

1. "Overdue loans" are those late in being paid.
2. "Called accounts" are overdue loans meeting one or more of the following criteria:
   a. 6 months overdue.
   b. Less than 6 months overdue but the loan's collateral is claimed by creditors. (The rights of creditors follow the priority of their credits. Those with first priority can claim all assets until their claims are satisfied. Only then can the next tier of creditors recover, and so on down to unsecured creditors, who have the lowest claim.)
3. Overdue loans and called accounts are handled as follows:
   a. The finances and performance of the firm are evaluated. If the firm is considered worthy of continuing operations, repayment terms are renegotiated.

Table 7.17. *Nonperforming Loans at Government Banks,
by Type as a Percentage of Total Loans*

Year	Specialized banks					Commercial banks				
	Total loans[1]	Nonperforming loans				Total loans[1]	Nonperforming loans			
		Overdue	Called	Bad	Total		Overdue	Called	Bad	Total
1977	146.2	3.41	0.83	2.31	6.55	237.2	2.76	1.08	2.04	5.38
1978	180.8	2.19	0.72	2.56	5.47	301.0	1.54	0.95	2.03	4.52
1979	189.3	1.12	2.44	2.86	6.42	346.0	0.50	1.89	2.43	4.81
1980	230.0	0.67	2.41	2.87	5.96	416.0	0.32	1.74	2.33	4.39
1981	259.4	0.49	2.00	2.62	5.12	441.0	0.34	1.53	2.05	3.91
1982	413.0	0.35	1.59	2.09	4.03	487.3	0.39	1.93	2.09	4.42
1983	516.0	0.41	1.67	1.77	3.86	563.9	0.50	2.05	2.06	4.60
1984	604.8	0.51	1.53	1.49	3.53	616.4	0.39	2.14	1.89	4.42
1985	736.1	0.62	1.75	1.48	3.85	631.6	0.61	2.63	1.77	5.02
1986	759.8	0.34	2.34	1.64	4.32	784.1	0.27	2.39	1.79	4.45
1987	895.0	0.17	1.73	1.77	3.67	894.3	0.13	1.96	1.90	3.99
1988	1,167	0.11	1.04	1.71	2.86	1,272	0.08	1.12	1.75	2.95
1989	1,547	0.02	0.72	1.39	2.13	1,665	0.07	0.68	1.58	2.33
1990	1,710	0.12	0.88	1.16	2.16	1,806	0.11	0.94	1.12	2.18

1. In billion NT$

Source: MOF, *Summary of Financial Statistics*, various issues.

    b. If the debtor is considered incapable of repaying the loan in full, it should at least try to make partial repayment. The bank should seek to recover at least the principal.

4. Overdue loans and called accounts are deemed "bad loans" (to the extent they are not expected to be repaid) in the following situations:

    a. The loan cannot be paid back.

    b. The loan is two years overdue, having been called but not paid.

    c. The value of the collateral is not enough to cover the balance remaining on the loan.

5. Once regulations have been violated, the responsibility is to be assumed by the person who made the loan and by the managers of the bank. The matter is to be investigated by the administrative authority.

    Both government and private banks are allowed a 1 percent bad-loan ratio on secured loans and a 3 percent ratio on unsecured loans. Ratios in excess of this invite careful scrutiny by the banking authorities, at least at government-owned banks, and the bankers involved can face serious penalties. These include requiring the individuals who made a bad loan to repay it; some bankers who could not make restitution have been jailed. Not surprisingly, it is quite common for a loan

Table 7.18. *Nonperforming Loans at Private and Foreign Banks, by Type as a Percentage of Total Loans*

Year	Total loans[1]	Domestic private banks				Total loans[1]	Foreign banks			
		Nonperforming loans					Nonperforming loans			
		Overdue	Called	Bad	Total		Overdue	Called	Bad	Total
1977	18.89	1.32	0.97	4.55	6.85	31.01	1.60	3.20	2.51	7.31
1978	58.40	0.60	0.36	2.14	3.10	38.99	0.98	1.89	2.30	5.17
1979	76.97	0.88	0.37	2.56	3.80	47.19	0.66	1.51	2.29	4.47
1980	100.6	0.39	0.43	2.65	3.47	66.01	0.62	0.91	2.32	3.85
1981	116.4	0.52	0.59	2.71	3.83	101.87	0.24	0.41	1.90	2.54
1982	129.0	0.55	0.67	2.84	4.07	97.82	0.96	0.77	2.97	4.70
1983	136.4	1.19	1.12	2.70	5.00	96.73	1.97	1.90	3.42	7.29
1984	148.1	1.52	2.01	2.98	6.50	96.31	3.75	7.67	3.15	14.57
1985	144.0	1.55	2.72	2.66	6.93	85.88	8.11	9.34	5.87	23.33
1986	117.2	1.32	3.28	0.99	5.59	107.4	4.63	3.64	5.81	14.08
1987	221.5	0.82	2.33	2.16	5.31	128.4	3.18	3.15	4.92	11.25
1988	318.2	0.46	1.14	1.60	3.20	146.0	0.47	2.66	4.00	7.13
1989	425.8	0.32	0.91	1.34	2.57	190.4	1.82	2.02	3.40	7.24
1990	491.8	0.39	0.80	1.33	2.52	201.3	0.56	0.79	1.99	3.34

1. In billion NT$

Source: MOF, *Summary of Financial Statistics,* various issues.

to be renegotiated and extended rather than being listed as a bad loan, and the published bad loan ratio of government banks is always low and stable.

If the employees of government banks make more profit for their bank, they do not get any monetary reward for themselves. But if they make mistakes in extending loans, serious penalties are almost certain. The asymmetry between rewards and penalties distorts the system by creating tremendous incentive for loan officers in particular and banks in general, to be quite conservative in their loan decisions.

Foreign banks tend to take write-offs on nonperforming loans more quickly, usually in less than two years. They otherwise use a similar accounting process. Since the mid-1980s foreign banks have had higher bad loan ratios than domestic banks. This is because they had confidence in local firms. However, because small and medium firms tend not to keep good accounts, it is hard to tell how well they are actually doing. When the economy prospers, they appear to flourish. But once the economy slows, especially as it did in the early 1980s, their situation can turn to one of financial distress. As the foreign banks took their write-offs in 1985–88, they turned more conservative in their lending attitude.

The data in Tables 7.17 and 7.18 show that the bad-loan ratios and nonperforming loan ratios of foreign banks are higher than those of domestic banks. This demonstrates theme 1 of the model.

HANDLING FINANCIAL CRISES

Government financial institutions are particularly averse to default risk; their operational risk is covered by government protection. Private financial institutions are not explicitly supported by the government. However experience shows that any possible financial crises are usually solved by the government, at least implicitly. Thus, the government will negotiate with the relevant institutions to help stabilize their financial status. There are a number of examples of this, particularly in the early 1980s when the system was severely strained. These include the Asia Trust case of 1982 and three 1985 cases: Tenth Credit Co-op, Cathay Investment, and Overseas Investment. Each was handled differently.

In 1982, the Asia Trust and Investment Corporation invested heavily in real estate and stocks, thereby violating the regulations. Slumps in both the construction and stock markets led to the company's funds being frozen. Asia Trust's loans were illegally concentrated in related businesses, a fact the CBC uncovered and which was reported in the press. Consequently, thousands of depositors rushed to Asia Trust, and bankruptcy seemed imminent. But the authorities decided to provide NT$4.3 billion through the CBC and the Taiwan Bank to stem the run. They also asked the International Commercial Bank of China (ICBC) to invest NT$200 million in Asia Trust and take over its operations for two years. This stabilized the situation, stemmed the run, and thus eliminated the crisis. With an ICBC man as general manager, Asia Trust's operations recovered, and at the end of the two years, ICBC withdrew and the original owner regained control of Asia Trust.

The Tenth Credit Cooperative Association case exploded in 1985. The Association extended a lot of credit indirectly to related businesses in the Cathay group. Cathay did not do well, however, leading depositors to lose faith in both the group and the Association. Anxious depositors crowded at the gate of the Association's compound. The government immediately asked the Cooperative Bank of Taiwan (CBT) to provide help. The CBT totally took over the Tenth Co-op, operating it, handling its clearing activities, and paying its debts. (The CBT simply absorbed the resulting losses.) All Tenth Co-op managers were replaced by CBT staff. No new loans were issued, but deposits operated as before. The Tenth Co-op in effect swallowed up by the CBT. The quick decision by the government averted financial panic.

In the wake of the Tenth Credit case, the situation of Cathay Investment and Trust Company (CITC), another affiliate of the Cathay group, became very dangerous. CITC had guaranteed large amounts of commercial paper and bankers' acceptances for other Cathay companies, and it looked as though CITC would have to make good on much of this paper. The government immediately organized a group of three other banks to manage CITC, which defused the situation. In 1989 CITC was taken over by another business group.

Overseas Investment and Trust Company officials used trust funds to speculate illegally in foreign exchange trading, accruing substantial losses. MOF asked the United World Chinese Commercial Bank to take over the management of Overseas Investment, and it is now part of United World.

These four examples follow the same model. Illegally operated financial institutions precipitated a financial crisis. The government gave support and had the institutions taken over by others. In all cases, however, the illegal activities had been going on for some time before panic occurred. Officials delayed penalizing the wrongdoers because they felt doing so would itself incite a panic. Thus the problem became more and more serious, until it was impossible to hide it any longer, and a serious financial crisis was the result. The government officials who had decided to delay action until there was a crisis were criticized, and were also penalized to some degree. Two ministers of finance were forced to resign because they allowed these situations to get out of hand.

Deposit Insurance

After the financial crises of the early and mid-1980s, there was discussion of establishing a deposit insurance system, and enabling acts were promulgated in 1985. The Central Deposit Insurance Corporation (CDIC) was organized by MOF and CBC with NT$2 billion in capital. The maximum protection afforded each depositor at an insured institution is NT$1 million. (A depositor can have accounts at several banks and thereby have more than NT$1 million insured.)

The banks pay premiums of 0.15 percent annually. Participation is voluntary, but as of March 1990, among private institutions all 4 commercial banks, all 7 medium business banks, and all 6 trust and investment companies were members, as were 27 of the 33 foreign banks. (Some of the foreign banks have comparable coverage from other sources.) Among the smaller institutions, participation is less common: 37 of 94 credit co-ops, 51 of 285 farmer association credit departments, and 14 of 23 fishery association credit departments are part of the CDIC. Some of the co-ops have alternative insurance through other channels, such as the Farming Insurance Program, but most have simply been waiting to see what happens. Only 3 of the 11 major government banks joined—they are already backed by the government, and the Taiwan provincial councillors who exercise voting control at many of these banks do not feel the cost is justified.

Curbing the Informal Sector

Underground investment companies became pervasive in the early 1980s, having found a loophole in the old banking law. They asserted they were obtaining funds by issuing certificates and were not taking deposits as financial institutions did. This obviously troubled the authorities, because MOF could not regulate or close them down. Therefore, in the 1989 Banking Law a broadly worded clause (Article 29–1) was included declaring that states collecting funds from the public at large are considered to be absorbing deposits. After announcement of the new law, many underground investment companies went bankrupt because of the rush to withdraw cash from them. Hung Yuan was one of the biggest such companies. Three of its organizers were prosecuted and in May 1992 received jail sentences of 1 to 7 years; two were fined NT$300 million each (the amount set by statute).

OVERALL PERFORMANCE

A commercial bank in Taiwan usually has the following departments and activities:

1. Operations, handling short-term loans and deposits. All commercial banks have this department.
2. Savings, including issuing financial debentures and extending medium- and long-term credits. All commercial banks have this department.
3. Trust department, investing in securities, issuing guarantees, and the like, as listed in Article 101 of the Banking Law. Most older banks have this department. A new bank must be more than a year old before it can apply.
4. Foreign department, dealing with foreign exchange activities and export and import advances. Requirements are set by the CBC. In general, it will be around 2 years before new banks are allowed in this area.
5. Bill activities. MOF approved secondary market transactions by banks in July 1992, with six private banks receiving permission. Primary market transactions are not allowed yet.

Table 7.19 presents key ratios for the four major categories of banks between 1977 and 1988. Several observations can be made about bank financial ratios. First, foreign banks have tended to be more liquid than domestic ones. Because of their limited access to local currency, foreign banks generally hold higher levels of vault cash than do domestic banks. In 1979 and 1982 foreign banks were particularly liquid, which reflects their willingness to have liquid assets on hand to speculate on future interest revenues when they expect interest rates to rise sharply in the short run. This demonstrates that foreign banks have been much quicker to react to changes in actual and perceived opportunities than have domestic banks.

Second, specialized banks have the highest liquidity among domestic banks. They obtain funds from the government and from deposits by the postal savings system, plus a small amount from the public, and thus do not need to worry about sudden withdrawals. At the same time, they make longer-term loans. Portfolio management does not seem to be an important consideration for the specialized banks. Specialized banks are the least profitable of the domestic banks, but this is a direct consequence of their policy of making low-interest loans in relatively risky situations even while facing a cost of funds that is not very different from other banks.

Because of the restrictions on NT dollars in foreign banks, these banks have tended to make their loans in US dollars. Foreign banks had higher profits in the 1970s, although, their profitability dropped to a low level after 1981, especially in 1985 and 1986. In the 1970s their attitude toward extending loans was more aggressive than domestic banks. Any firm with the potential for success had access to foreign banks. Foreign banks profited from their liberal lending policy during the growth period of the 1970s, but they suffered for it in the 1980s when the pace of economic growth slackened and many firms faced financial difficulty. Because many of the loans had little or no collateral, the resulting write offs caused the profitability of foreign banks to fall sharply.

Table 7.19. *Financial Ratios by Type of Bank*

	Owner equity as percent of loans and investments				Net pretax profits as percent of operating revenues			
	Government-owned				Government-owned			
Year	Specialized	Commercial	Private	Foreign	Specialized	Commercial	Private	Foreign
1977	5.8	5.2	11.7	3.7	6.8	14.0	17.7	20.3
1978	5.3	4.5	10.7	4.0	8.0	13.2	16.6	14.6
1979	7.7	4.8	9.8	3.0	12.6	14.1	17.9	11.9
1980	7.8	7.0	9.2	3.8	11.2	20.7	17.1	13.5
1981	7.9	7.6	9.7	3.9	8.4	17.4	14.6	9.1
1982	6.4	8.8	10.0	4.9	5.7	14.3	13.6	7.6
1983	5.0	7.0	9.7	6.0	2.9	8.8	15.9	8.6
1984	4.6	6.7	9.6	6.5	5.4	12.5	14.0	11.3
1985	4.5	7.2	10.3	7.2	5.3	12.8	12.8	−13.1
1986	4.1	4.0	8.5	5.7	5.4	9.4	10.6	−12.0
1987	4.0	2.8	7.2	4.7	8.5	7.4	16.1	12.7
1988	4.1	4.4	7.9	7.0	11.5	15.4	24.5	11.9
1989	4.2	4.5	11.4	7.0	8.2	9.4	34.2	8.4
1990	4.7	6.0	10.8	7.2	10.0	14.9	22.5	8.5

Source: CBC, *Statistics of Important Activities for Financial Institutions,* various issues.

It seems theme 5 of the model is not supported. According to the model, foreign banks are supposed to be more profitable than domestic banks, but this is not consistently the case. Although the risks the foreign banks took paid off when times were good, they did not when times were not. In part this reflected the foreign bankers' failure to understand the actual local situation, in particular the inadequacy of the acounting systems of most firms. Bankers—U.S. bankers in particular—have frequently been rewarded for simply shoveling money out the door without too much regard for whether it comes back. When this was going on in the 1970s (worldwide, not just in Taiwan), it was observed that many of the individual senior and loan officers did not care much whether the loans could be repaid—they would have their bonuses, and possibly even different jobs, before any problems had to be addressed. This was quite a contrast to the Taiwanese banker who can go to jail for lending that was far more responsible but nonetheless never repaid! Our model assumed compctent loan officers who are compensated to consider more than their own near-term bonuses.

Off Balance Sheet Activity

Trading financial instruments and generating fee income affect bank profits but are not visible on balance sheets. Except for bankers' acceptances and backup credit lines, none of these have been major items in Taiwan. Backup credit lines—including guarantees of commercial paper—have contributed to financial crises in Taiwan, as discussed earlier.

Interest rate swaps for US dollar–denominated debt are executed, but not for NT dollars because there is no financial instrument for hedging the transaction. Futures markets are not legal, and the cash market for financial instruments is not efficient, being limited primarily to the banks for their own speculative purposes. Currency options are sometimes undertaken by banks, but in general they are seldom used.

Banks actively extend loans against exporters' letters of credit (see Table 7.20), and they also issue bankers' acceptances (BAs, which are a bank's promise to pay the interest and principal if the issuing party cannot). BAs are off the balance sheet. The extensive use of these two operations has made BAs an important part of the money market, at times exceeding commercial paper in volume (see Table 7.21).

BAs first became important in Taiwan not so much for the fee income they generated as for the opportunity they offered foreign banks to get around their lack of domestic currency. A foreign bank can issue a BA, which can be discounted in the money market, thereby giving the borrower local currency.

Domestic banks also have used BAs to increase revenue. During the tight period around 1980, bank interest rates moved more slowly than money market rates. As a result, banks would not lend to firms; instead, they issued BAs. When the

Table 7.20. *Letters of Credit and Percentage Issued by Domestic Banks*
(billions)

	Imports				Exports			
	Issuing		Advising		Loans		Advances	
Year	US$	%	US$	%	US$	%	US$	%
1975	3.9	84	5.2	69	1.1	63	4.7	78
1976	4.5	84	7.0	71	1.6	60	6.7	83
1977	5.2	82	7.9	70	1.7	71	7.9	85
1978	7.8	82	10.5	71	2.5	74	10.9	88
1979	10.5	81	13.0	71	2.2	66	14.3	88
1980	12.3	80	14.8	70	3.2	68	17.2	88
1981	12.3	81	15.7	67	3.4	65	19.3	87
1982	11.5	81	15.1	68	3.3	79	18.1	88
1983	13.5	81	18.2	71	4.7	87	20.9	90
1984	14.4	81	20.5	70	5.4	96	24.7	90
1985	13.6	84	21.4	68	4.8	97	24.7	90
1986	18.2	86	27.5	70	5.0	75	31.5	86
1987	25.3	85	34.4	68	6.8	63	40.3	85
1988	32.2	85	40.9	65	8.4	71	43.0	88
1989	35.1	84	42.4	66	7.7	66	43.4	87
1990	32.8	83	42.8	65	6.3	78	41.7	88

Source: Yearbook of Financial Statistics of the ROC.

Table 7.21. Money Market Bills Outstanding (billion NT$)

Year	Treasury bills	Commercial paper	Bankers' acceptances	Negotiable CDs	Total
1978	7.40	14.91	2.46	22.42	47.195
1979	2.00	42.72	3.69	20.86	69.277
1980	1.60	59.30	6.62	19.10	86.613
1981	1.40	84.66	25.11	56.04	167.206
1982	2.00	72.94	60.35	42.73	178.015
1983	14.60	73.72	85.71	48.54	222.570
1984	24.00	92.08	103.83	44.20	264.106
1985	78.28	85.32	110.10	36.12	309.816
1986	79.80	82.91	71.60	18.74	253.046
1987	65.63	78.82	59.24	25.81	229.510
1988	197.00	85.82	43.48	153.61	479.915
1989	34.00	134.75	57.02	354.58	580.347
1990	18.00	282.05	65.06	296.90	662.016

Source: CBC, *Financial Statistics Monthly,* Aug. 1991.

would-be borrowers sold their BAs in the money market, the banks bought them back at discounts reflecting the market rate of interest (in other words, at a higher cost of funds to the borrower than the fixed controlled rate).

Cost Function

Through the estimation of a cost function one can analyze the relative efficiency of different banks and observe their economies of scale. Liu (1988) and Juang and Gueih (1989) made empirical studies of Taiwan's banking industry. They adopted a dual-theory developed-cost function (see Benston, Hanweck, and Humphrey 1982, and Kolari and Zardkoohi 1987 for an explanation of this approach).

Liu collected annual data for 1981–85 from 47 banks (including government and private commercial, specialized, and foreign banks). The cost for each branch is the explained variable and the four kinds of banks are the dummy variables. He drew three conclusions.

1. Foreign banks have lower operating costs than domestic private banks. Government specialized banks and government commercial banks have similar operating cost levels. As predicted by theme 4, private banks and foreign banks are more productive—more cost efficient—than government banks.
2. Almost all banks are in a stage of scale economies. Government banks are very close to having constant returns to scale.
3. Multiple products are complementary and reduce operating costs. Therefore, economies of scope exist.

Juang and Gueih (1989) used a translog cost function to evaluate the performance of 47 banks during 1982–86. Instead of using dummy variables, they estimated three sets of simultaneous equations for total banks, government (commercial and specialized) banks, and private (domestic and foreign) banks. Their conclusions are similar to Liu's.

THE NEW BANKS

In response to the New Banking Law of 1989, by July 1992 16 new private banks had been established. In 1990, of 19 groups that applied to MOF, 15 were authorized. Each is initially allowed to open 5 branches (as well as operating and savings departments, for a total of 7 units). The first new bank opened in December 1991, while the other 14 started operations in the first half of 1992. In addition, privately owned China Trust Company applied for and received permission to convert to a commercial bank, which it did in July 1992. In the second run of applications, just one bank applied, and it was authorized in June 1992.

The major characteristics of the newly formed banks are summarized in Table 7.22. Most have their headquarters in Taipei. The owners and managers include business group owners, former politicians, and managers of financial institutions.

The new private banks have affected several areas: interest rates, services, deposits, loans, and profits. Each of these, and public confidence in the new banks, is discussed next.

After the new banks were authorized, but before they started operating, interest rate competition started. Some banks lowered their rates for loans, and others raised their rates for deposits. Dah An, one of the new banks, set a prime rate lower than had ever appeared before. Most banks have followed the trend of lowering loan rates. On the other hand, Union Commercial Bank set the highest interest rate for passbook savings deposits. Many banks followed. As a result, overall loan rates are lower and deposit rates are higher, which means the spread—the difference between loan and deposit rates—has become smaller.

Domestic banks started to set their own prime lending rates in April 1991. Immediately after deregulation there was not a lot of difference among the banks in the interest rates they paid and charged, and movements in rates tended to be similar. This is consistent with collusion. However, after the new banks were authorized in mid-1991, interest rate competition started and there were more differences in the banks' primes. Although financial liberalization has enlarged the variance of interest rates among banks, there is some degree of co-movement in adjusting interest rates. In a competitive market, similar prices and a tendency for prices to move together follow by definition. The key question is whether we are seeing the effects of competition or whether there is price leadership.

There has certainly been nonprice competition, as the new banks maneuver for market share and the critical mass of customers necessary to become viable long-run players. The new banks have sought to emphasize various services. For example, Eastern Sun developed a computer system providing financial information about personal accounts and the economic environment. Grand's strategy is to provide high-quality counter service. Baodao provides an account manager sys-

Table 7.22. *Banks Formed During 1991–92*

Name and opening date	Capital (billion NT$)	Chair	General manager
Asia Pacific 1992 Feb. 12	10.0	Former manager of Bank of Taiwan	Former manager and director of Bank of Taiwan
Baodao 1992 Apr. 09	10.0	Business group owner	Former manager of the Cooperative Bank of Taiwan
The Chinese Bank 1992 Jan. 25	10.0	Business group owner	Former vice manager of Overseas Chinese Commercial Bank
Chung Shing 1992 Mar. 12	13.5	Mayor of Kaohsiung City	Vice manager of City Bank of Taipei
Cosmos 1992 Feb. 12	12.0	Business group owner	Former director of the Bureau of Wine and Tobacco Monopoly; former vice manager of the Land Bank of Taiwan
Da An Commercial 1992 Jan. 4	10.0	Former minister of finance	Former vice manager of Chiao Tung Bank
Eastern Sun 1992 Jan. 21	10.0	Professor at Taiwan University	Vice manager of Hua-Nan Commercial Bank
Far East International 1992 Apr. 11	10.0	Business group owner	Former vice manager of International Commercial Bank
Fubon Commercial 1992 Apr. 21	10.0	Business group owner	Former manager of Hua-Nan Commercial Bank
Grand Commercial 1991 Dec. 30	12.6	Business group owner	Manager of First Commercial Bank
Our Commercial 1992 Apr. 4	10.5	Councilman in Kaohsiung	Former vice manager of Medium Business Bank
Sino Pac 1992 Jan. 28	10.0	General manager of Overseas Chinese Commercial Banking Corporation	Vice general manager of the Bank of Taiwan
Taishin Intl 1992 Mar. 23	10.0	Business group owner	General manager of the Central Deposit Insurance Corp; former vice manager of City Bank of Taipei
Tan Asia 1992 Mar. 4	10.0	Former general manager of the Bank of Taiwan	Former vice manager of the Medium Business Bank of Taiwan; business group owner
Union Commercial 1992 Jan. 24	12.0	Controller of another bank	Former vice manager of the First Bank

Note: All of these had 5 branches (the maximum allowed) as of July 1992, except Far East Intl had just 1 and Our Commercial had 4. All were based in Taipei except Kaohsiung is home to Chung Shing and Our Commercial, while Asia Pacific and Tan Asia are headquartered in Taichung.

322   *The Financial Development of Japan, Korea, and Taiwan*

tem to help customers in their financing arrangements, and it was the first to adopt on-line counters. Our Commercial Banking Corporation stresses regional service, especially in Tainan. Many banks plan to issue negotiable CDs, so the outstanding amount of such instruments is expected to increase significantly. In addition, credit cards for consumers and car loans are becoming more common.

On the asset side, potential loan customers who were not welcomed by government banks in the past are being pursued by the new banks. The managers of the new banks may even visit potential customers instead of waiting for borrowers to come to them. Banks are also providing financial consulting services to businesses.

The deposits taken in by the new banks during their first months of operation did not match their loan volume. This shortfall is one reason they are offering high deposit rates and negotiable CDs. Deposits had reached almost 90 percent of loans by the end of July 1992.

At the time applications were being made, many people believed operating a bank was very lucrative. When 15 new banks opened at the about same time, it was quickly realized that their profits would not be as high as expected. There are two reasons for this. First is the narrowing of interest rate spreads. Second, some banks are reported to have purposely overestimated their potential profits during the beginning stage in order to attract stockholders.

To the public, the new banks are generally felt to be not as reliable as the established government banks. Some people are standing aside, waiting to see how the private banks perform—including whether they are run honestly and effectively—which is one reason they have not obtained as much in deposits as they have lent out. No one seriously expected them to become big quickly, and their combined initial market share has indeed been small, but growing. Thus, at the end of December 1992, the new banks had 2.76 percent of deposits and 3.90 percent of loans of full-service banks, compared to 1.52 percent and 2.51 percent six months earlier. (China Trust's data are not included.)

Because it was already a member when it was China Trust, China Trust Commercial Bank, has become a member of the CDIC. None of the other new banks had joined CDIC, as of July 1992, although two, Grand Commercial and Sino Pac, had applied. Membership requirements include being in business over 6 months; activities fulfilling the operation program at the time of establishment; no operating loss without compensation in the month immediately before application; no violations of relevant laws; and no excessively large loans to related companies.

The sort of expansion taking place in banking in Taiwan is unprecedented. As the process unfolds, analyzing and assessing it will attract the attention of policymakers, regulators, and academics (not to mention shareholders and bankers).

Privatization of Government Banks

Privatization of government banks has been discussed and suggested by many people in Taiwan. However, the process in regard to the three major commercial banks (First Commercial, Hua-Nan, and Chang-Hwa) has been delayed. Their shares are held primarily by the Taiwan provincial government, and the Provincial Council must approve any sale. This is something council members are reluctant to do because their authority over the banks gives them the ability to meddle, in particular in the loan-extending process. This is understandably something they are reluctant to give up, which means privatization of the three banks is improbable any time soon.

Shares in the Chiao Tung Bank (formerly the Bank of Communications), the Farmers Bank of China, and the Chung Kuo Insurance Company, which are mostly held by the Ministry of Finance, will be sold to the public, although no timetable has been set.

CONCLUSION

Four general themes proposed for explaining bank behavior are supported by the evidence available. Restated for Taiwan specifically, these are

1. The bad-debt ratio for domestic banks, especially government banks, is lower than that for local branches of foreign banks.
2. Asset management at foreign banks is more intense than at government banks. That is, given a certain amount of loanable funds, foreign banks extend more loans and make more investments than domestic banks do.
3. The major characteristics of customers of different banks are not the same. For example, the borrowers of specialized banks are mostly from specific kinds of businesses designated by the government as favored recipients of credit. For a domestic private bank, loans to related businesses are usually greater than loans to nonrelated businesses.
4. The productivity of foreign banks, given the same factors of production, is higher than that of domestic banks. In other words, foreign banks are more cost-efficient than domestic banks. Generally speaking, government banks usually maintain operational stability and keep away from the threat of financial crisis. However, government banks are less efficient than private banks.

The privatization of banks began in 1990. Achieving both stability and efficiency through an insurance and examination system is an important problem still to be solved. Regulations governing some bank activities still need to be eliminated, in order to create a more market oriented financial services industry. Financial liberalization and financial internationalization are part of the financial revolution. The speed of financial revolution, although faster than before, needs to be mastered in order to match the needs of economic development.

Because financial liberalization was slow until the late 1980s and the new private banks began operation only in 1992, it is too early to evaluate the full impact of financial liberalization. The extensive regulations governing various institutions and activities are still in force, and some international financial instruments, such as futures and options, do not yet exist in Taiwan. In the 1990s, making Taiwan an international or even an Asian financial center is a long-term target, and this country's financial liberalization still has a long way to go.

I have benefited greatly from the comments of the other authors and discussants at the conferences held as part of this project, especially Hugh Patrick, Yung Chul Park, and Jia-Dong Shea. Research and financial support were provided by the Chung-Hua Institution for Economic Research and the National Science Council of the Executive Yuan, for which I am grateful.

REFERENCES

Amacher, Ryan C., Richard S. Higgins, William F. Shughart II, and Robert D. Tollison. 1987. "The Behavior of Regulatory Activity over the Business Cycle: An Empirical Test." In Robert J. Mackay and others, eds., *Public Choice and Regulations*. Stanford, CA: Hoover Institution.

Baldwin, Robert E. 1984. "Trade Policies in Developed Countries." In Ronald W. Jones and Peter B Kenen, eds., *Handbook of International Economies* vol. 1. Elsevier Scientific Publishers.

———. 1989. "The Political Economy of Trade Policy." *Journal of Economic Perspectives* 3(4): 119–35.

Baltensperger, Ernst, and Jean Dermine. 1987. "The Role of Public Policy in Ensuring Financial Stability: A Cross-Country, Comparative Perspective." In Richard Portes and Alexander K. Swoboda, eds., *Threats to International Financial Stability*.

Benston, G. J., G. A. Hanweck, and D. B. Humphrey. 1982. "Scale Economies in Banking: A Restructuring and Reassessment." *Journal of Money, Credit, and Banking* 14: 435–56 (Nov.).

Chou, Tein-chen. 1991. "Measurement of Market Share in the Banking Industries." *Bank of Taiwan Quarterly* 42 (2): 40–56. In Chinese.

Juang, C. R., and S. C. Gueih. 1989. "A Study on the Scale Economies of Taiwan's Financial System." *Fundamental Finance* 18: 61–78 (Mar.). In Chinese.

Kolari, James, and Asghar Zardkoohi. 1987. *Bank Costs, Structure and Performance*. Lexington, MA: Lexington Books.

Lee, Yung-San, and S. C. Chen. 1983. "The Influence of Financial Policy on Industrialization in Taiwan." Conference on Taiwan's Industrial Development, Academia Sinica, Taipei. In Chinese.

———, and Tzong-Rong Tsai. 1988 Jun. "Development of Financial System and Monetary Policies in Taiwan." Conference on Economic Development Experiences of Taiwan.

Liu, J. L. 1988. "The Cost Function of Financial System in Taiwan." In *The Revolution of Taiwan's Financial System: A First-Stage Study*. Taipei: Chung-Hua Institution for Economic Research. In Chinese.

Migué, Jean-Luc and Gérard Bélanger. 1974. "Toward a General Theory of Managerial Discretion." *Public Choice* 17: 147–62 (Spring).

Orzechowski, William. 1977. "Economic Models of Bureaucracy: Survey, Extension, and Evidence. In Thomas E. Borcherding, editor, *Budgets and Bureaucrats: The Sources of Government Growth*. North Carolina University Press.

Peltzman, Sam. 1976. "Toward a More General Theory of Regulation." *Journal of Law and Economics* 19: 211–40 (Aug.).

Shea, Jia-Dong, and Ya-Hwei Yang. 1989 Dec. "Financial System and the Allocation of Investment Funds." Conference on State Policy and Economic Development in Taiwan; ROC. UCLA and Soochow University. Published as Chung-Hua Institution for Economic Research Occasional Paper 9001.

Stigler, George J. 1971. "The Theory of Economic Regulation." *Bell Journal of Economics and Management Science* 2 (Spring).

Williamson, Oliver E. 1963. "Managerial Discretion and Business Behavior." *American Economic Review* 53: 1032–57.

Yang, Ya-Hwei. 1982. *An Economic Analysis of Exports and Financial System in Taiwan*. Chung-Hua Institution for Economic Research, Economic Papers 13. In Chinese.

———. 1990a Jun. "An Analysis on Structure of Interest Rates of Banks, Money Market and Curb Market: A Vector ARIMA Approach." Conference on Financial Situation and Price Problems in Taiwan, Academia Sinica, Department of Economics, Taipei.

———. 1990b. "The Influence of Preferential Policies on Strategic Industries: An Empirical Study of Taiwan." Chung-Hua Institution for Economic Research Discussion Paper 9003.

——— and others. 1987 Apr. "The Influence of Financial Liberalization on Domestic Industries' Financial Structure." Chung-Hua Institution for Economic Research. In Chinese.

8

Comparisons, Contrasts, and Implications

HUGH T. PATRICK

The financial systems of Japan, Korea, and Taiwan have not just grown; they have been profoundly transformed over time. The process has been evolutionary and incremental, driven by real economic growth and the attendant growth and change in demand for various types of financial services. The most momentous change was triggered by a conscious government decision in each country—in Japan in the 1970s and in Taiwan and Korea in the 1980s—to liberalize and make more market-competitive what had been heavily regulated, domestically closed, and somewhat repressed financial systems.

To draw out some significant comparisons and contrasts and to reflect on their implications, this chapter first considers four aspects of the countries' systems. These are structure, the stress on the safety of the system, financial repression (the definitional result of below-market interest rate policies), and the ownership and control of commercial banks. This provides a context for analyzing the liberalization process, bank behavior, and the efficiency and effectiveness of finance, including the relationship of financial policies to the more comprehensive industrial policies of each country. The chapter concludes with an overall evaluation.

Financial Deepening

Financial development has been driven, or pulled, by increasing demands by savers and borrowers for more services—both more scale and more types. Although some of the measured increases in financial assets have been due to financial layering—transactions among financial institutions—most reflect provision of funds to business. An indicator of financial development is the level of financial deepening—the ratio of total financial assets to GNP, termed the "financial intermediation ratio" (FIR).

Two points about financial deepening as a measure of, or proxy for, successful financial development. First, as Cole and Slade (1991) stress, a financial system has multiple functions and so has to be evaluated by a number of criteria. This is done in the country chapters and elsewhere in this chapter.

Second, as considered in Chapter 1, is the direction of causality. Did finan-

The Financial Development of Japan, Korea, and Taiwan

cial deepening cause more rapid real economic growth, or did rapid growth bring about financial deepening? The issue is complex, and there are no definitive models or tests. In Shea's judgment, deepening in Taiwan did lead to a more efficient use of investment funds and, accordingly, accelerated growth. Teranishi leans toward a similar view for Japan. For Korea, Park sees the causal flow running from real to financial. At the very least, finance accommodated real growth in all three countries. Without financial deepening (and the underlying behavior it proxies), real economic growth would not have been as rapid. In other words, even if simply accommodating rather than causal, financial development is essential to achieving rapid real development and growth.

Figure 8.1 shows that very substantial deepening took place between 1965 and 1990. For Japan the ratio rose from 3.66 to 6.62; for Taiwan the increase was from 1.61 to 4.95, and for Korea from 0.89 to 4.55. The comparisons are somewhat misleading because time is only a rough proxy for economic growth, and more important, Japan's GNP per capita was always substantially higher at any given point in time.

A more interesting comparison is the level of financial development for any given level of economic development. Figure 8.2 provides this. GNP per capita is converted to U.S. dollars on the reasonable assumption that the exchange rate's degree of deviation from purchasing power (and hence level of development) is comparable across these countries for any given level of development. A general financial deepening over the course of economic growth is apparent, but the gaps and divergent patterns of change indicate clearly that forces in addition to the level of economic development were important.

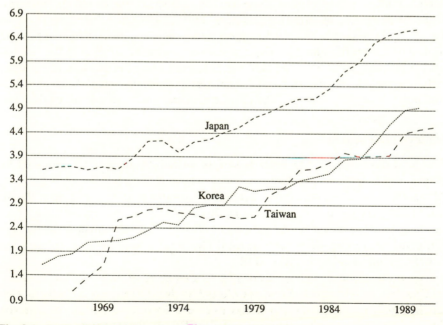

Fig. 8.1. Ratio of financial assets to GNP (FIR), 1965–90

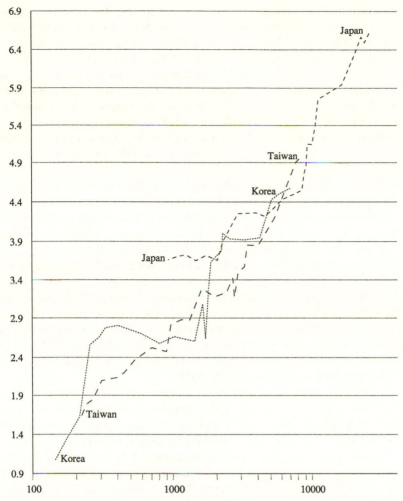

Fig. 8.2. Financial intermedition ratios to US$ GNP per capita, 1965–90.
Note: Underlying data are found in Tables 2.A2, 4.A2, and 6.A2.

The Korean ratio was flat for a long period (1972–78) during which GNP per capita in U.S. dollars quadrupled (and in won rose almost six-fold). This was when inflation was rapid and real interest rates were negative. Once financial policy changed so as to bring inflation under control and to initiate the process of financial liberalization, financial deepening jumped sharply and then continued an upward course.

Japan in the 1960s is a seemingly surprising case. The level of financial deepening was high relative to that later exhibited by Taiwan and especially Korea at the same income level. But it did not increase at all, despite a doubling of GNP per capita during 1965–70. Then from the late 1970s, it began to rise sharply relative to per capita GNP. Two main forces were at work: financial deregulation, which made financial assets more attractive, and the speculative bubble in stocks and real estate during the easy money period to 1989. The bursting of the bubble ended the rise in the FIR, and it will probably decline into the early 1990s.

In contrast, Taiwan's deepening is manifested as a generally smooth curve over time and relative to the level of development. Taiwan did not allow inflation to occur, as Korea did. Moreover, it had substantially higher real interest rates on deposits than either Japan or Korea. Although initially lower than Japan's at the same income levels, Taiwan's FIR rose steadily, and from the late 1980s the ratio was similar to what it had been for Japan at comparable income levels (from the mid-1970s). Rapid increase in the FIR is unlikely to persist in the 1990s.

The differences in patterns are due mainly to differences in the respective financial behavior of the personal and business sectors in the three countries. Japanese corporate holdings of financial assets relative to GNP have been remarkably high, at least twice the ratio in Taiwan or Korea at the same income levels. There were three principal reasons for this. Japan has had a high degree of interbusiness trade credit, reflecting subcontracting and wholesaler–retailer relationships. Firms held substantial compensating deposit balances (a financial asset) against borrowings. Finally, firms tended to hoard financial assets for precautionary purposes or to seize new investment opportunities as they arose. In addition, in the 1980s Japanese firms engaged in financial arbitrage and speculation. As a result, after being roughly constant until the mid-1980s, the ratio of corporate sector financial assets to GNP increased from 1.16 in 1985 to a peak of 1.71 in 1989, then dropped to 1.50 in 1990.

Throughout the 1965–90 period Taiwan's personal sector holdings of financial assets were higher than Japan's at the same levels of GNP per capita; indeed, the gap widened as growth proceeded. Put another way, Japan from the late 1970s has had the same personal sector ratio of financial assets as Taiwan had had but, at per capita income levels, some three times higher. Why Taiwan's personal sector has had consistently higher rates of financial assets accumulation at much lower levels of income than Japan is a puzzle, probably explained only in part by the relative importance of unincorporated business. Korea initially had a very low ratio of personal assets to GNP, which persisted, not surprisingly, until inflation was brought to a halt in the early 1980s, whereupon it increased rapidly to reach, by the late 1980s, Japanese ratios at comparable income levels. (Because Korea includes unincorporated businesses in the corporate sector—while they are included in the personal sector for Taiwan and Japan—the disaggregated flow of funds data are not directly comparable.)

STRUCTURE

Commercial banks have been and continue to be the core of the financial system in these three countries. This is typical of most financial systems, although in contrast to the British and American cases of an early and important role for capital markets. The financial systems of Japan, Korea, and Taiwan have been characterized by separation between commercial and investment banking, and within banking by segmentation by borrower and function.

These financial systems were dramatically transformed over the four decades under consideration here. In addition, the patterns of financial development were, in a broad sense, remarkably similar. Each moved from a highly regulated and moderately repressed to a considerably less regulated and much more competitive, market-based system. At the same time, by virtue of history, the Japanese financial system has always been more developed than those of Taiwan or Korea.

The discussion in this section compares the following basic structures as they existed before the process of liberalization: formal and informal markets, insulation of the system from direct foreign influence, and segmentation of the domestic market.

Formal and Informal Sectors

As the systems evolved from the initial establishment of banks and other modern financial institutions in the nineteenth and early twentieth centuries, the traditional financial system of moneylenders and the like became integrated into the modern system. Gradually, modern financial institutions penetrated traditional markets and supplanted them and their institutions. Many traditional players became modern. Thus, moneylenders established banks, money market companies and investment and trust companies, and rotating credit cooperatives became credit associations or mutual savings banks.

This interplay took place in all three countries, but in two important distinguishable patterns. First, in Japan the process of displacing the traditional sector for virtually all business loans by a panoply of modern financial institutions permeating every part of the economy was completed by the early 1950s (Teranishi 1990), although moneylenders and pawnshops for consumer credit have persisted in a minor way. Second, in Taiwan and Korea part of the traditional financial sector evolved into an unregulated, informal (curb) market. This was a direct consequence of financial repression and credit rationing in organized finance. The curb market comprises a considerable range of more or less segmented activities and participants but is essentially short-term. It is a gray area: Technically illegal, most of the time it has been tolerated by the monetary authorities.

The interplay between organized and informal financial sectors has been important to the financial system's operation and credit allocation in both Taiwan and Korea. Shea stresses the importance of the informal market in Taiwan in providing funds to small firms lacking access to loans from the commercial banks. This improved the allocative efficiency of the overall financial system. Cole and Park (1983) describe a similar role and process in Korea, although the government was more ambivalent about the benefits of the curb market. Korean authorities attempted in the 1980s to absorb its activities into the organized financial sector by means of higher real rates on deposits and, probably more important, the transformation of curb market dealers into investment and finance companies and other nonbank financial intermediaries. A similar policy—to pull to the surface so-called underground financial institutions—was initiated in Taiwan in the late 1980s.

Insulated Systems

The governments created essentially closed financial systems, insulated from foreign financial markets and players. Controls were imposed on both outflows and inflows of capital, as well as on foreign exchange. Foreign exchange controls initially were used to control both imports and capital flows. A few foreign banks were allowed to establish branches or representative offices, primarily to finance foreign trade, because U.S. and later Eurocurrency interest rates were lower than domestic rates until the 1970s in Japan and considerably later in Taiwan and Korea. However, foreign financial institutions were, and are, essentially niche players with small market shares. Japan was the earliest in allowing its banks to operate abroad, but initially mainly as listening posts and to serve the overseas operations of their Japanese business clients.

Japan was, by the late 1950s, the second-largest borrower from the World Bank—the only long-term foreign capital source to which it had access—but overall the amounts were modest. It did rely on foreign financing for foreign trade and on modest amounts of domestic corporate loans made by foreign banks in yen (impact loans). Taiwan, for political reasons, was never a real participant in international financial markets until it accumulated huge foreign exchange reserves in the 1980s, and then its participation was predominantly by the central bank until the early 1990s.

Korea differs dramatically from Taiwan and Japan in its reliance on foreign borrowings; they averaged close to 5 percent of GNP from the late 1960s to the early 1980s. But this did not occur in a way that undermined the closed nature of the system, because the government kept tight control over the process. All loans had to be made directly to the government or guaranteed by the government and were channeled through the financial system. Interest rates on foreign borrowings were substantially below domestic market rates, which made them a particularly attractive source of funds.

Segmented Markets

As a result of historical development and government policy, the financial systems of Japan, Korea, and Taiwan not only were specialized by type and size of borrower and type and size of depositor, but the loan and deposit markets were segmented as well. Government regulation shaped the financial framework and determined the conditions for its operation—and in the perceptions of policymakers, banks, especially big banks, were the foundation of the system, although the relative share of smaller financial institutions increased steadily over time.

One important distinction is between wholesale and retail financial markets. In wholesale markets, transaction units are large, and the players (governments, big business, big financial institutions) are relatively knowledgeable and sophisticated about costs, risks, and alternatives. Retail transactions are in small units and typically involve households and small businesses. Wholesale banking generally is more competitive than retail banking. There are substantial economies of scale in making transactions and in amassing information to assess creditworthiness. Typically, large banks dealt with large customers, other institutions with smaller customers.

Thus in each country, commercial banks are divided into two groups. The first is the powerful, large, and (in principle) nationwide ones, making loans to (typically large) corporations. The second group is smaller banks serving local and regional markets. Specialized financial institutions grew up or were created to provide services to (usually unincorporated) small family businesses and agriculture. The governments established specialized institutions to provide funding for exports and long-term finance for domestic investment in priority industries, plus (to a limited extent) private housing.

In all three countries, nationwide commercial banks were severely limited in the number of branches they could open. Financial markets were thus segmented geographically, so that in each local market for small borrowers there are only a few banks and other competing financial institutions. This localism, combined with the policy-regulated gap between deposit and loan interest rates and the limitations of competition among different types of lending institutions, meant that in each country even the most marginal institution was profitable enough to survive. It has also meant that effective interest rates to small borrowers have been relatively high, presumably reflecting some oligopoly rent over and above risk premiums.

An important additional form of institutional specialization and prescriptive market segmentation lay in the provision of longer-term credit to finance business plant and equipment. The governments recognized the importance of high fixed investment and high capital formation rates to achieve rapid growth. Yet as Teranishi (1990) has stressed, there was a mismatch between the desire of entrepreneurs to borrow long-term funds and that of savers to hold their (at earlier stages of development, relatively limited amounts of) financial assets in short-term maturities. This preference for short-term assets no doubt reflected not only the small amounts of family wealth in financial form but also the history of inflation and domestic economic and political uncertainties. The preference was reinforced by the lack of secondary bond markets and other financial alternatives to savings deposits and by the characteristics of financial repression. The governments addressed this mismatch by creating and financially supporting special long-term lending institutions. Their loans went primarily to large industrial enterprises, especially in the early years.

SAFETY OF THE SYSTEM

The abiding, indeed overwhelming, concern of the financial authorities in all three countries has been the safety of the financial system. All their regulations and controls may be seen in that light. Thus safety and the related topics of prudential supervision, moral hazard, and incentives are issues that appear throughout this chapter.

The concern with safety can be posed as a question: Who and what is to be protected? First, the system itself. Second and related, the depositors: Their reactions are the stuff of financial panics, so their protection is in itself an important social objective. In principle it is system stability, not the guarantee of individual institutions against failure, that is the object. In practice, the stability of the system has implicitly meant that individual banks were guaranteed against bankruptcy. The occasional insolvent small bank in Japan has been merged into a stronger bank. In Korea, where the government forced the main banks to make policy loans that subsequently went bad, the monetary authorities have stepped in to refinance the loans and protect the banks. The authorities in Taiwan have allowed a few major marginal nonbank financial intermediaries to fail, with losses to the depositors, and from time to time there have been crackdowns on the curb market in Korea.

Stability has been achieved in two ways: limitations on competition among financial institutions and prudential supervision of the banks. Competition was restricted through interest rate ceilings, segmented markets, and restrictions on entry. Banks nonetheless competed to collect deposits, since deposit maximization led directly to profit maximization. Once the system was established, it was very difficult to obtain permission to enter any given category of institution. No new banks have been chartered in Japan since the mid-1950s, and only a limited number have been permitted in Korea. Taiwan allowed few entrants until the early 1990s. The authorities did not permit new financial instruments that would undermine the rather simple menu of deposits of various maturities.

Information

Uncertainties and thus the costs of financial intermediation are reduced by "good" information. However, it is difficult to obtain sufficient, accurate credit information about virtually any but the largest borrowers in any of these countries. Public disclosure is required only of the small number of companies—substantially greater in Japan than in Korea or Taiwan—listed on stock exchanges, and that disclosure is much less than required in the United States. Only in the 1980s have listed corporations in Japan been required to present consolidated balance sheets. (At the same time, Japan virtually mandates management forecasts of earnings, something severely restricted in the United States.)

Accounting and auditing are fundamental tools not only for lender evaluation of credit risk but also for management decisions. Yet the reliability of the financial data available even to insiders of private unlisted companies is open to question in all three countries, especially given the widespread propensity to evade taxes, particularly by the myriad of small businesses. Even for large companies it is unclear to what degree the accounting and auditing systems in Korea and Taiwan are reliable providers of information; Japan is somewhat better. Credit rating agencies have only recently begun to operate in Japan, and they have barely begun to play a role in Korea or Taiwan.

In the absence of publicly available information on company performance, prospects, and hence creditworthiness, it is not surprising that banks have been the primary collectors of information and the monitors of borrower performance and behavior. Nor is it surprising that in all three countries banks typically require loans be heavily collateralized, usually by specific real assets.

Banks and the regulatory authorities in the three countries have responded somewhat differently to the problems of assessing creditworthiness. Relationship banking—getting to know and trust each other through repeated transactions over time—is highly developed in Japan, epitomized by the main banking system. In Taiwan, banks have been highly risk-averse, so relationship banking has been constrained to a relatively small number of large private and state enterprises, with much less involvement in information gathering and monitoring. In Korea the financial authorities in 1976 initiated a lead bank arrangement more or less modeled on the Japanese main bank system, to control the allocation of credit to the 30 major business groups (*chaebol*). Autonomous monitoring and loan syndication have not yet developed because of continuing strong government control over the banks.

Inevitably, knowledge is asymmetric: Borrowers know more about their own conditions and prospects than do their creditors. Moreover, the regulatory, information, and financial systems persist in being opaque—they are far from being transparent. Insiders (by definition) know what is going on; outsiders know much less. As in many countries, insider use of information for corporate or personal benefit is tolerated much more than in the United States and the United Kingdom.

FINANCIAL REPRESSION

The most important domestic regulations were government-established or sanctioned ceilings (and in Taiwan, floors) for interest rates on deposits, loans, and new bond issues—indeed on every financial instrument. These ceilings were below market-clearing rates: "Financial repression," so defined, has thus been a feature of all three economies. Nonetheless, compared to many developing countries, especially those experiencing high inflation, the interest rate gap (degree of financial repression) was modest. It was lowest in Japan, somewhat higher in Taiwan, and especially wide in inflation-prone Korea before the 1980s. In addition, real interest rates on loans were positive in Japan and quite high in Taiwan. In all three countries the profitability (marginal productivity) of investment was high. The of ceiling interest rates in the organized financial sectors of these countries may have been imposed in part to ensure safety of the system, but the reasons and rationale went far beyond prudential concerns.

More broadly defined, financial repression encompasses a range of policies designed to limit competition in financial markets. These include entry restrictions, market segmentation, limitations on creation of financial instruments, and constraints on development of securities issues and secondary markets. The monetary authorities in all of these countries pursued such policies, both formally and through administrative guidance. Moveover, they did not discourage cartel-like behavior among the major banks.

Financial repression is certainly not an optimal policy instrument for resource allocation; the standard case against it is well known and easily summarized. As Shaw (1973) and McKinnon (1973) stressed in the early finance development literature, repression adversely affects the quantity and especially the quality of real capital accumulation through distorted incentives for investment allocation.

Investment projects are undertaken to fulfill a concept of what ought to be done, whether or not it makes real economic sense. The choices made by planners in allocating capital have meant that excessively high capital–labor ratios are chosen because low interest rates make capital appear abundant and cheap rather than scarce and valuable. Whenever possible, savers seek real alternatives to financial instruments—inventories, precious metals, foreign assets. Because the demand for loans exceeds the supply of loanable funds at ceiling interest rates, credit must be rationed by managerial or bureaucratic fiat. (For further discussion, see McKinnon 1991, Gelb 1989, World Bank 1989, Fry 1988.)

Nonetheless, all three countries made finance the handmaiden of development policy—albeit in rather different ways and to substantially different degrees—to achieve similar objectives: to promote exports; to make long-term funds available at a relatively low cost to finance business fixed investment (primarily in heavy industry); to build infrastructure (power, water, transport, communications); and to implement other sector-specific industrial policies. All three countries grew rapidly while repressing their financial systems, so it was easy to believe that these policies were having the intended positive, causal effect. (A more detailed discussion and my own evaluation appear in the concluding section.)

If certain categories of activities merit preferential treatment to achieve development or social welfare objectives, they are more efficiently supported by direct subsidy payments. However, low interest rates are politically attractive. They are a less obvious subsidy instrument because their costs do not appear explicitly in the government budget. And Ministries of Finance like low interest rate policies in order to reduce the cost of funding the government debt, although government debt was not large in Taiwan or Korea and became so in Japan only from the mid 1970s. In bureaucratic politics, policymakers appreciate the power embodied in regulatory systems, and especially in situations of financial repression where they influence—if not determine—credit allocation decisions.

Government policies to provide preferential credit for selected activities do not necessarily require ceiling interest rates, financial repression, and direct allocation programs. Virtually all advanced industrial countries, even those with market-based competitive financial systems, have preferential funding programs for certain activities that are deemed socially important—housing, rural electrification, student education, local governments, and so on. Japan, Korea, and Taiwan used such mechanisms in addition to their overall systems of low interest rates to channel funds to priority uses, and undoubtedly they will continue to do so when even their systems are more fully liberalized and based on competitive financial markets.

Level of Repression

Compared to most developing countries—many of which have high inflation rates and negative real (ceiling-constrained) interest rates—Japan, Korea, and Taiwan have been only moderately repressed. Both Taiwan and Korea have significant informal financial markets in which rates are determined through demand and supply. Curb rates incorporate somewhat higher risk premiums and perhaps some element of market power than would probably prevail in an unrepressed freely competitive formal system, but they nonetheless are a useful measure of the degree of financial repression.

Korea has been the most repressed of the three. The interest rate gap between bank and curb market loans was 15 to 25 percentage points, and bank real interest rates tended to be slightly negative until the 1980s, when the halting of inflation resulted in positive and fairly high real rates and a narrowing of the bank–curb differential to about 10 percentage points.

Taiwan was somewhat less repressed. The gap between bank and curb loan rates has regularly been 10 to 15 percentage points, while real interest rates on bank deposits and loans have been positive and high. Formal ceilings were terminated in 1989 but financial dualism has persisted: The bank loan market has been limited primarily to large corporate borrowers while, with the important exception of export credits, small enterprises have had to borrow in the curb market at much higher interest rates.

The degree of repression was substantially less in Japan. The gap between official ceiling loan rates and estimates of market-clearing rates until the mid-1970s was 5 to 10 percentage points (depending on the firm's size and creditworthiness), and real interest rates were positive, although low. The use of compensating deposit balances raised effective loan rates, thereby narrowing the repression gap. From the mid-1970s, with the emerging surplus of domestic savings over the demand for private investment as well as the gradual removal of ceiling rates as the system embarked on its liberalization process, repression on the loan side virtually came to an end.

In all three countries, ceiling deposit rates were substantially below loan rates, providing a spread sufficient to make banks profitable even at ceiling lending rates. Deposits have been the last category to be deregulated. As of 1992 ceiling rates continue on all deposits in Korea and on demand and smaller savings deposits in Japan. Since 1989 there have been no formal controls in Taiwan, but initially the rates did not move very much, suggesting some ongoing combination of government informal administrative guidance and oligopolistic or cartel-type bank behavior.

In all three countries the low interest rate policy emerged out of the early postwar period of confusion and disruption. Direct controls were at first extensive, and their removal and a return to market prices and mechanisms have been less rapid in finance than in the real sectors of the economy. Bureaucrats quickly found market imperfections and failures to justify intervention, even as they came to accept the efficiency and effectiveness of market forces in principle.

Consequences of Low Deposit Interest Rates

Low interest rates and rationed credit benefit those who can borrow on these terms, and they impose an implicit cost on those who provide the funds. Returns on assets in the organized financial sector—such as deposits, government and corporate bonds, insurance, and pension funds—were lower than they would

have been in a competitive general equilibrium. In addition, borrowers excluded from the organized market have had to borrow in the curb market or not borrow at all, thereby bearing the burden of substantially higher interest costs or
exclusion from access to credit.

It is difficult to estimate what market deposit rates would have been in each
country in a fully competitive financial system in general equilibrium. The partial evidence—curb market rates in Taiwan and Korea, the compensating-bal-
ance deposit requirements and the secondary market in NTT bonds in Japan in
the 1960s—are almost surely overestimates.

The low interest rates on financial assets imposed a loss of income on savers.
In the heyday of repression—until the early 1970s in Japan and a decade or so
later in Korea and Taiwan—my rough calculations suggest such lost income was
on the order of 1 to 3 percent of GNP annually in Japan, somewhat more in Taiwan, and even higher in Korea, where the inflation tax was the most severe. These
were mainly distributional, not deadweight, losses. How the benefits of repression were distributed is discussed later. These losses decreased over time in each
country, as a consequence of both liberalization and the pragmatic development
of loopholes and offsetting adjustment mechanisms, especially in wholesale
deposit markets.

Deadweight losses from low interest rates are reflected in lower savings rates.
The theoretical presumption is that low interest rates constitute a disincentive to
personal and household savings; that is, the price effect outweighs the income
effect. On the other hand, to the extent low interest rate policies actually increase
real growth, households are indirectly compensated. So long as real rates are
not negative, the economic growth compensation may be sufficient to generate a
high savings rate. In any case, the empirical evidence on the elasticity of saving
to real interest rates is mixed and unclear. In none of the three countries is there
strong evidence of any significant effect of interest rates on savings behavior.

Despite deposit interest rates below a market equilibrium, savings rates and
the holding of household savings in financial assets increased as a percentage of
household income and GNP during the high-growth periods in Taiwan and Japan.
Other forces clearly were at work: the rapid growth in real incomes, relative price
stability, lack of alternative financial or other instruments in which to hold savings, and indivisibilities (as in housing markets). Apparently policymakers in
Japan believed, with some correctness, that savings rates would be high and savings would be channeled through the banking system without substantial interest rate incentives as long as real rates were not negative. In Taiwan real deposit
rates were considerably higher and nominal rates remained quite constant; policymakers evidently surmised that interest rate elasticity was low.

The personal savings rate rose substantially in Korea in the 1980s during a
period when real interest rates increased. However, this does not provide definitive evidence either way as regards the elasticity of personal saving to changes
in real interest rates, because so many other factors were involved. In particular, there was the virtual ending of inflation in the mid-1980s, for the first time
since the Korean War, and the financial reform policies themselves must have
had a profound impact on Korean thinking and behavior. Moreover, the observed

increase is to some degree probably an artifact of the national accounts data, because previously unrecorded savings, hidden in informal market assets and in unrecorded small business and housing investment, were surfacing and entering the estimations.

Low Loan Interest Rates and the Distribution of Rents

Low loan interest rates relative to market-clearing rates have two effects: Credit has to be rationed to handle the excess demand of borrowers, and rents are created (the difference between ceiling loan rates and market rates). The rents can be huge. They result not only from the implicit transfer from depositors but also from central bank credit (additions to base money made on preferential terms) and, important in the case of Korea, foreign funds borrowed and relent at interest rates substantially below market rates. To illustrate, if rationed credit amounts to 50 percent of GNP and the interest gap is 10 percentage points, credit rents are 5 percent of GNP each year. This is in effect a redistribution from savers and taxpayers to those who obtain rents. And the static costs are surely smaller than the dynamic consequences of inefficient investment allocation.

The power to allocate credit on preferential terms and to determine who receives the rents creates a potential for abuse, one type of moral hazard. It can be significant at both individual and systemic levels, although individual instances of such misuse of power, while important, are not the main issue. Rather, it is the corrosive effects on the political economy. It is not coincidental that in all financially repressed economies, recipients of rationed credit are major financial supporters of the political apparatus in power.

Theoretically and conceptually such rent seeking (termed corruption by some) is well understood. In the case of loan markets and credit rationing, the rent must be divided among the borrower, its customers (if its prices are thereby lower than they otherwise would be), the lending institution, the loan officer, and those determining basic policies (bureaucrats, politicians, the political party in power). This is the central political economy issue of finance, but it has not been subject to much empirical research, for obvious reasons. Relationships and arrangements are densely opaque; information is particularly difficult to obtain; and research is not encouraged.

Several general observations about these political economy issues are in order. First, to the extent lending institutions evade interest rate ceilings by requiring compensating balances or loan-related fee income, effective interest rates for the borrower are raised closer to a market level, and the possibilities of inefficient credit allocation and rent-seeking activities are reduced accordingly. The prevailing interpretation for Japan is that such requirements by commercial banks were high enough to create competitive markets, especially for large, creditworthy borrowers. Thus the rents accrued to the banks in the form of higher profits, higher wages, less efficient management, and perhaps less risk taking in loan portfolios than would otherwise have been the case.

Analysis of the distribution of rents from financial repression in Korea and Taiwan is difficult because hard information is sparse. Occasional scandals and anecdotal evidence (a useful source is the *Far Eastern Economic Review*) suggest only some of the rents went to lending institutions and their borrowing clients. That is, a considerable portion appears to have gone to support the state apparatus—the political parties and leadership in what were, after all, rather authoritarian regimes. The massive building of family business groups in Korea (chaebol) and their increasing importance in Taiwan can be attributed in substantial part to favorable government policies, of which access to cheap credit was one important instrument.

Second, low interest rates were only one among several sources of regulatory rents to be allocated. As elsewhere, foreign exchange controls and import licensing provided opportunities. Government construction projects and procurement have also constituted significant channels for the flow of rents. The existence and utilization of insider information have been taken for granted and perhaps are the quintessential manifestation of these as insider societies.

Third, politics is expensive, both in democratic countries facing recurring elections and in authoritarian countries—especially as they make the transition to more democratic regimes. It appears that through various murky channels the financial systems in these three countries have been significant conduits for the funding of politics. How politics will be paid for in the more liberalized financial regimes of the 1990s remains to be seen.

OWNERSHIP AND CONTROL OF BANKS

Much of the discussion and analysis in this book focuses on the nature, characteristics, and role of the large, nationwide commercial banks. Their number is small: depending on definition and time periods, there were from 6 to 10 in Taiwan (before 1991), 5 to 7 in Korea, and 11 to 15 in Japan. Market size in Korea and Taiwan, and economies of scale and scope in all three countries, suggest continuation of this oligopolistic market structure over the longer run.

The key issues for any country are the structure of ownership and, even more important, the control of its banks, indeed of all financial institutions. These have been fundamental concerns in the liberalization process in Korea and Taiwan, although not in Japan. Japan, Korea, and Taiwan exemplify quite different cases of ownership and control.

Entry and participation of foreign-owned commercial banks are irritants in the relations of each country with the United States and Western Europe. The governments in Taiwan, Korea, and Japan appear committed to overwhelming domestic ownership of their banking systems, although this is certainly not stated explicitly. U.S.-based Citibank's strategy of developing retail banking globally will be an interesting test, as it has announced plans to open additional branches in Japan and Korea and presumably in Taiwan once that is allowed.

None of the major banks in these three countries is controlled by private shareholders, although some smaller and local banks are. Rather, control largely rests with management in Japan and with government in Korea (through intrusion, although this is less true of the two newer, smaller, nationwide banks). Until 1991 government entities majority-owned and controlled the major banks in Taiwan, while ownership of the four smaller commercial banks was concentrated in a few individuals who appointed management and otherwise exercised control. In 1991–92 16 new private commercial banks were licensed, presaging a major transformation of the banking system.

Ownership of commercial banks in Japan and Korea is widely dispersed among industrial enterprises, other domestic institutions, and individuals. Government divestiture is supposed to take place in Taiwan, but the provincial government, which actually owns most of the shares, has been reluctant to cooperate in this with the central government. The intention is that while owners will control the private banks chartered to open from 1992, they will be constrained by regulation and supervision from lending disproportionately in support of their own business ventures. Ownership patterns in Korea and Japan appear stable, despite reports that in 1992 holdings in Japanese banks by clients, including group-related firms, were being reduced.

In Korea, stock ownership is dispersed, and no one conglomerate (or anyone else) can officially own more than 8 percent of a bank. At the same time, following a 1976 government policy decision, all chaebol and their main firms were assigned a lead bank. The balance of power appears to lie with the companies rather than the banks. But real control over the banks emanates from the Ministry of Finance and, to a lesser extent, the Bank of Korea. The Bank Supervisory Board uses the banks for information-gathering purposes.

Authorities in both Korea and Taiwan want to create more efficient management and a more competitive banking environment, but are proceeding gingerly in light of ownership issues. Wealthy entrepreneurs and their family-based conglomerates are the likely entrants as new banks are allowed and government-owned banks are privatized. The concern is that they will use their financial institutions to finance excessively their own or related business activities, as happened under "organ banking" in prewar Japan. There are three sorts of problems: credit risk from loans being concentrated to a few borrowers; opportunities for fraud, corruption, and internalization of rents; and pricing of loans and services in a way that shifts profits away from the banks. There have been enough such cases throughout the world that regulatory authorities are appropriately concerned.

There is also a broader set of social concerns, related to the concentration of power in the hands of a few families who own financial–industrial conglomerates. Their economic power is seen as being used not only to gain excess profits directly but also for activist rent-seeking—influencing the government to distort markets—as well as acquiring political power for its own sake.

How big is too big? The structure and market power of (family-owned) conglomerates is an important issue that has yet to be well researched. The Korean government focuses its policies on the top 30 chaebol, but only the top 5 or so appear disproportionately large for the size of the economy. In early postwar Japan, Occupation authorities identified 83 "holding companies" and 10 family conglomerates (*zaibatsu*, including Mitsui, Mitsubishi, Sumitomo, and Yasuda) as representing potentially excessive power. Share ownership was taken away from the major zaibatsu families, and holding companies were made illegal and dissolved. However the final action taken on most large Japanese industrial companies was less drastic than originally envisioned, as it was decided that sheer size was less undesirable than some of the probable consequences for economic recovery of plans to break up operating companies.

Two things are particularly interesting about the Japanese case. One is that the banks have neither captured corporate businesses (in the manner alleged for German universal banking) nor been captured by them—the existence of *keiretsu* notwithstanding. Another is that peer pressure—bank reputation and credibility with the financial and business communities—seems to be a major external force operating on management. The government role is modest compared to Korea and Taiwan. Regulatory authorities have intervened in bank management only in instances of serious difficulty, which generally has involved smaller institutions.

Japan is an unusual case as regards ownership. Bank shares are widely dispersed among a large number and wide variety of industrial corporations and other financial institutions, and all but one city bank has less than 9 percent of its shares directly in the hands of individual stockholders. Moreover, cross-holdings between banks and their corporate borrowers and allied financial institutions (such as trust banks and insurance companies) have been the norm. These long-term relationships appear in their most archetypal form as horizontal keiretsu, in which a city bank plays a major role. Nonetheless, members collectively own less than a third, often much less, of the group bank's equity.

Horizontal keiretsu are cited in some of the recent literature on industrial organization as an efficient and effective form of business organization, intermediate between the corporate conglomerate and the marketplace; others view them as a structural impediment restricting access to the Japanese market. (See Sheard 1991.) There is little apparent concern among Japanese over keiretsu economic and political power, in great part because ownership and control are separated. That is, there is not the concentration of both in the hands of a few families that there was in the prewar period.

It appears keiretsu are generally accepted in Japan because they are adequately constrained. The groups compete with one another, and moreover, within each group power is diffused among the presidents of the member companies. A group does not pursue a well-articulated, well-defined, common business strategy. Rather, their political activities, including contributions, are subject to considerable scrutiny—probably more so than most other players in Japan's quite democratic and competitive political system.

Bank Employees

For somewhat different reasons, the effects of the labor market and employment system are to bind most lower and middle management to their employing bank through late middle age, if not for their entire career. In Japan it is the so-called permanent employment system. In Taiwan it is the government civil service system, of which bank employees are members. In Korea it is apparently an incipient permanent employment system, somewhat less formalized than in Japan. As a general rule it is difficult for bank managers in any of the three countries to quit and find comparable or better jobs elsewhere. As a consequence, bank employees have good reasons to fit in, perform well (however defined by senior management), and follow orders. Specific financial rewards for individual performance—selective wage increases or bonuses—have not been used as significant incentive mechanisms. Instead, the main reward is promotion to higher positions, which of course means higher salaries as well as greater status and power. Promotion is based on merit (performance) as well as seniority, especially for higher positions, not unlike other very structured bureaucracies everywhere.

The realities of the ownership and control systems are, of course, very important, especially to top management. In Korea and for the government-owned banks in Taiwan, senior bank managers have to be responsive to the government (the financial authorities), since that is who appoints and removes them. Some rise through the ranks in banking careers, but others are placed there from the outside, including from the government bureaucracy. In Japan, bank presidents and chairmen are almost always promoted from within, although in a few cases they served previously as senior officials in the Ministry of Finance. Typically the president (the CEO) selects his successor and then becomes chairman.

LIBERALIZATION

The process of financial deepening—the increasing demand for and supply of funds, and additional types of financial services—tended to undermine the regulatory framework. This was particularly true in wholesale markets, where financial institutions and their large clients developed strategies to get around interest rate ceilings. Smaller financial institutions, less closely watched by the authorities, also developed new ways of doing business.

This nibbling away at the regulated and market-constrained set of arrangements was an important component of what became a more comprehensive set of domestic and to varying degrees, foreign pressures to end financial repression and to engage in market-oriented financial reform. The self-interest of some major private participants in the financial system changed: In the evolving environment they came to perceive benefits from a liberalized market.

Policymakers in each country have had to adjust to this dramatically altered environment. At some point the monetary authorities decided to liberalize. In Japan the process began seriously in the mid-1970s, and in Taiwan and Korea, in the early 1980s.

Liberalization is both a goal and a process. The objective is to achieve a market-based financial system in which institutions compete and prices (interest rates) are determined in competitive markets. Deregulation—the removal of government-imposed restrictions on competitive practices—is more than simply eliminating rules. Rather, it is redefining the rules so that prudential objectives continue to be met and cartel-like private market power is prevented, even as regulatory control over interest rates is ended.

In all three countries the initial steps toward liberalization were small and halting, and the entire process has been gradualist and piecemeal. This reflected a combination of bureaucratic reluctance to proceed other than incrementally, the power of (and need to buy off) interest groups benefiting from their special market niches and rents under the old system, some lack of consensus on ultimate objectives, and considerable policy inertia. Nonetheless, over time the degree of liberalization has been substantial, at least in Japan and Taiwan, as shown in Table 8.1.

A slow, incremental approach had both benefits and costs. The benefits were that everyone had time to adjust; the general contours of the process were more or less transparent and predictable; and there were no major mistakes or calamities. There were two major costs: The inequities and inefficiencies of repression persisted that much longer. In addition, the opportunities for financial arbitrage created by the coexistence of regulated and deregulated financial instruments, although profitable for the sophisticated, had little social benefit and were a distraction.

Financial liberalization does have costs. Market interest rates are more volatile than controlled ones, and this generates swings in asset prices. Hedging is feasible for individual players, but not for the system as a whole. The possibility of individual financial institution failure increases. And macroeconomic stability becomes even more important for the stability of the financial system.

Common Causes

There are a number of common elements in explaining why policymakers in Japan, Korea, and Taiwan decided to end interest rate ceilings, deregulate domestically, and open the economy to international financial flows. First and foremost, the shift was a pragmatic response to changing circumstances—primarily domestic, but to some extent external. Quite simply, repression was less effec-

Table 8.1. *Indicators of Relative Financial Liberalization*

	Japan		Korea		Taiwan	
Indicator	*1965*	*1990*	*1965*	*1990*	*1965*	*1990*
FIR[a]	3.62	6.62	0.89	4.55	1.61	4.95
Overall level						
Domestic	low	high	low	medium	low	high
International	low	high	low	low	low	medium
Government involvement in						
Ownership of banks	low	low	high	low	high	medium
Credit allocation	medium	low	high	high	high	medium
Interest rate controls	high	low	high	high	high	low
Possibility of new bank entry	none	none	none	low	none	high

Note: These judgments are relative to one another. Compared to all developing countries in 1965, these three were only mildly repressed.

a. Financial intermediation ratio (ratio of financial assets to GNP).

tive. The economies had grown dramatically and become more complex, and private businesses were larger and more self-confident. The Korean curb and Taiwanese informal markets had increased in significance, and in Japan the *gensaki* market essentially undermined the regulated short-term loan market, while the explosive expansion of government debt and trading in government bonds undermined the regulated long-term market. New and rising current account surpluses created domestic liquidity, reduced market interest rates, and generated pressures from the domestic financial system to relax interest rate controls, ease restrictions on financial services development, and similar steps.

Common Aspects

Deregulation and liberalization had three related but distinct components, all aimed at creating a more competitive, market-based financial system. The first, and most important, was ending of controls over *interest rates*. Market-determined rates are essential for competition. The second element was ending, or at least easing, the restrictions on creation of *financial instruments*.

Third, the authorities permitted *market entry* into previously segmented markets, mainly by allowing existing institutions to expand their scope of activities beyond their traditional markets. The authorities have been largely unwilling to allow newcomers, although Taiwan licensed 16 new banks in 1991–92. Also, as a consequence of intense foreign pressure, all three countries have allowed the limited entry of foreign financial institutions.

Country-specific Aspects

The specific causes, timing, form, and pace of financial liberalization have differed in each country. Each macro chapter contains a fuller discussion, so only a few points are made here to summarize how far each country had come by mid-1992.

In Japan liberalization was a direct consequence of changed domestic economic conditions: the slowing of growth from the mid-1970s, with the attendant Keynesian surplus of private savings and massive government deficit spending financed by bonds sold to the public. Repression through interest rate controls has ended for all financial instruments except, significantly, small savings and demand deposits—and those restrictions are scheduled to be lifted by 1993. Financial markets are essentially highly competitive, and international transactions have been liberalized. Entry and increases in branch offices remain restricted, however, and the domestic corporate bond market has yet to develop fully due to policy and institutional constraints.

Liberalization began in Taiwan in the 1970s with small, halting steps. From the mid 1980s the pace and intensity of reform built up because of both domestic and foreign pressures, reaching a crescendo of changes in 1989–90. Decontrol of interest rates proceeded rapidly, and by 1989 deposit and loan rates were, in principle, free. In this formal sense, Taiwan's financial liberalization has progressed further than Japan's—and both are far ahead of Korea, which retains controls over most rates. The stickiness of deposit rates, however, suggests that highly competitive markets have yet to emerge. It appears bank collusion in setting rates, probably with the tacit support of the monetary authorities, has replaced formal government controls. In 1990 Taiwan initiated a major reform of its commercial banking system, including the licensing of 16 new private banks with large capital requirements and the privatization of some government-owned banks.

In Korea financial liberalization was an important component of the 1980–81 shift in government economic policy toward price stability, mobilization of domestic saving, trade liberalization, and a winding down of the heavy and chemical industry policy. The most important step was reducing inflation, with an attendant rise in real interest rates. But beyond that and privatizing the major banks, steps to eliminate financial repression by ending interest rate controls faltered, and little progress has been made since the mid-1980s. Most change has come through market-induced loopholes as participants have played arbitrage games, much as Japan did in the early 1980s. The overhang of nonperforming loans in bank portfolios, financed with cheap Bank of Korea credit, constitutes a continuing, albeit diminishing, problem for Korea's Big Five commercial banks, inhibiting the liberalization and competitiveness of commercial banking. Rather than focusing directly on the banking sector, the monetary authorities' approach to institutional reform was to encourage development of nonbank financial intermediaries in order to attract funds from the curb market.

Sequence

Financial liberalization is appropriately carried out in steps, and the sequencing is important. Conventional wisdom says it should take place in the context of a liberalized, or liberalizing, real economy: real reform before financial, domestic reform before international opening. Where domestic prices are distorted by price controls or protection, a liberalized financial system will more effectively allocate resources—but to the wrong uses.

Japan, Korea, and Taiwan have more or less followed the conventional sequence. Fortunately, there are few serious price distortions. A few prices are regulated, mostly in basic grains and nontradables such as utilities and transport, but on the whole the domestic price system is market-determined. Agriculture, in which Japan and Korea are extreme cases of (high) price distortion, is the major exception, followed by the remaining protection from manufactured imports in Korea and Taiwan.

By definition of financial liberalization, the first priority is to let interest rates be determined in markets. Next comes encouraging competition among existing financial institutions. This means preventing cartels from mimicking government-controlled interest rates, allowing institutions to do business across a wider range of financial activities (which is particularly important in specialized systems where segmented markets and niches are significant), and making bureaucratic, risk-averse management systems and cultures flexible, profit-oriented and competitive. The independence of the management from specific, intrusive government policy guidance is essential.

In concentrated financial systems, new entry should be allowed, indeed encouraged, subject to normal prudential and social equity requirements. New entrants can provide the competitive drive to force change in existing institutions. Similarly, everything we know about state-owned banks indicates they are much less efficient than privately owned banks, and much more the prisoners of the allocational priorities of government bureaucrats and leaders. Although commercial banks were privatized in Korea in the early 1980s and are being privatized in Taiwan in the early 1990s, banking behavior has continued to be bureaucratic and oligopolistic. Although competition is increasing, financial markets are not yet highly competitive.

Internationalization

The pace and process of domestic liberalization in each country have been intertwined with the liberalization of international transactions. Internationalization has three areas in which controls must be removed and competitive opportunities and forces made possible: inflows and outflows of capital, the activities of institutions handling these flows, and the opportunities for foreign financial institutions to operate in the domestic markets (as well as for domestic institutions to operate in the home markets of foreign countries).

Domestic opening to foreign institutions has lagged far behind liberalization of financial flows. Whether by policy design or structural conditions and costs of entry, foreign firms have small shares of the domestic loan, deposit, and other financial markets in all three countries.

During the 1980s most Japanese financial markets became highly integrated with global financial markets, as foreign transactions and foreign asset holdings were freed. The sheer size of Japan's economy, financial system, and cumulated current account surpluses made Japanese institutions major players in international finance. By the late 1980s Japan had replaced the United States as the world's largest net creditor nation, and Japanese banks, which dominated listings of the world's largest, had a larger share of the international loan market than did U.S. banks. Its banks engaged in classic intermediation, lending long-term and borrowing short-term. Thus, Japan's international financial role is and will be quantitatively and qualitatively different from that of Taiwan and Korea.

The monetary authorities kept Taiwan insulated from international finance until the late 1980s, despite its huge cumulated current account surplus, which was held predominantly as foreign exchange reserves by the central bank. Capital inflows were restricted. So too were outflows, until liberalization started in the early 1990s. It has been politically difficult for Taiwan's government-owned banks to establish overseas branches.

Liberalization has proceeded even more slowly in Korea, despite the earlier reliance on foreign loans, a pattern reappearing in the early 1990s at least temporarily. Given ongoing high interest rates and a continued net international debtor position, domestic pressure to free up international transactions has been less strong. The government has continued to control and constrain capital inflows and the activities of foreign financial institutions. Korean banks have few offices abroad.

Securities Markets

With economic growth, the emergence of large companies, and financial liberalization, it is natural that securities markets—for equities and equivalents (convertible and warrant bonds), corporate bonds, and corporate paper—have come to play an increasing role. This natural evolution is essentially market-driven (demand-following), although the regulatory authorities can and did, particularly in Korea and Taiwan, provide tax and other incentives for companies to list their shares on the stock exchange. They also encouraged the supervisory and information-gathering infrastructures essential to the effective operation of securities markets.

A well functioning securities market makes several important contributions to the financial system: It is potentially a less expensive alternative source of funds for larger firms; by generating market values of financial assets and their yield, it provides objective information on market-clearing interest rates that served as a basis for evaluating loan and deposit rates; and it enhances the competitiveness of the financial system by providing an alternative source of funding. It is not evident that the markets in Japan, Korea, and Taiwan have provided good information and pricing signals. While the experiences of Japan, Korea, and Taiwan are different, all share the occurrence of speculative bubbles in their stock markets during 1986–90, which is taken up in the next section.

The corporate bond market remains underdeveloped in all three counties. Bond issuance has long been restricted to government enterprises, public utilities, and a few other selected corporations. Bonds have been placed through negotiation rather than competitive bidding, with financial institutions and others pressured to purchase them. Despite liberalization, bonds continue to be only a negligible source of funding in Taiwan. In Japan the need to raise external funds to refinance maturing convertible bonds and to ease domestic regulatory barriers suggests a continued growth of the straight domestic bond market in the 1990s. In Korea, short-term corporate bonds did become a significant source of external funds in the late 1980s. However, they were guaranteed by banks and involved special placement rather than open market sale—in effect a mechanism for evading interest rate ceilings on bank loans.

As a general rule, statistics on stock, bond, and corporate paper issuance in all three countries combine data on negotiated private placement with financial institutions (relationship transactions) and arms-length, competitive, market transactions. The data do not readily lend themselves to a simple measure of the relative proportions of negotiated finance and open market finance; the Gurley–Shaw distinction between direct and indirect finance is blurred in practice.

Implications of the 1986–90 Stock Market Booms and Subsequent Crashes

The three countries shared certain major common elements in their boom and bust experience. From the mid-1980s each was running a large current account surplus, not fully sterilized by their central banks; monetary policy was expansive, and inflation rates were low; currencies appreciated relative to the dollar; and nominal interest rates decreased, dramatically so in Japan as a deliberate policy to encourage direct real investment and capital outflow. Each economy was awash with ample domestic liquidity, and the process of financial and trade liberalization was under way. Money flowed into major asset markets: stocks and real estate. Speculators used gains in each market as collateral both to pyramid and to invest in the other market. Prices, as measured by price–earnings ratios and rental yields on real estate, came to be excessively high. Each market found itself in a speculative bubble.

The Tokyo, Seoul, and Taipei stock market booms were dramatic. Between the beginning of 1986 and the all-time peak in 1989 or 1990, the stock price index tripled in Tokyo, went up six times in Seoul, and an amazing fifteen times in Taipei. And the subsequent crashes were equally dramatic. The 1990 trough was 48 percent below the peak in Tokyo, 44 percent in Seoul, and an astounding 80 percent in Taipei. The markets all rebounded fairly quickly and with some vigor, but then Tokyo and Seoul resumed declines that have taken their markets below the 1990 lows. As of August 1992 Seoul languished around half its high, Tokyo around two-fifths. The Taipei index was just one-third of its peak (but 60 percent above its trough).

Inevitably, the wake of such sharp declines has exposed the debris of failed deals, collateral no longer of sufficient value to cover loans, insider behavior, outright fraud, and inadequate regulation and supervision of stock markets, securities companies, banks, and other financial institutions.

It is too early to fully evaluate the effects and implications of these stock market bubbles and their bursting; they are different for each country. For Japan unrealized capital gains on stock portfolios of banks count in part toward meeting BIS capital adequacy requirements, which made it easier for the banks to expand loans rapidly. As these so-called hidden gains have sharply decreased, the banks are shrinking their asset base and scrambling to raise capital.

During the boom, the major commercial banks in Japan and Korea raised substantial additional equity capital. Japanese companies seized the chance to obtain extraordinarily cheap loans and equity capital, issuing securities both domestically and abroad. Korean firms similarly took advantage of their stock market's surge, and a few companies issued convertible bonds overseas. Few companies or banks in Taiwan raised capital through the stock market during the speculative boom, although it had the greatest rise of the three. The crashes ended opportunities for raising capital inexpensively.

The effects of the stock market booms and subsequent crashes on real economic performance in each country so far do not appear to have been great. Economic growth was not only stronger than expected, it accelerated in 1990 in both Korea and Japan. Only in Taiwan was it slower, absolutely and relative to expectations. The 1991–92 passing of Japan's longest postwar expansion was due primarily to an ending of the huge business fixed investment boom that had fueled domestic growth, combined with inventory adjustment. Korea's growth problems were associated primarily with a government-sponsored housing construction boom and renewed inflationary pressures in the complex political environment leading up to the year-end 1992 presidential elections. However, both real economic performance and asset market prices are affected by the same macroeconomic policy variables, particularly changes in interest rates and credit availability, as well as confidence factors, so it is difficult to disentangle the autonomous effects of asset market changes.

BANK BEHAVIOR

Bank behavior and performance have been substantially conditioned by rapid economic growth, which reduced the chances of a loan going bad, and the authorities' stress on safety, which has had several effects.

Through the 1980s only a few banks in each country got into serious trouble. They were bailed out by the authorities; managers were sacked; and in a few instances in Japan troubled banks were merged into (absorbed by) other banks. A few smaller nonbank financial intermediaries went under, seemingly as object lessons to others on the costs of mismanagement or fraud. This implicit guarantee against bank failure has not only reassured depositors, it has also provided a very comfortable safety net for bank managers and owners.

At the same time, as U.S. experience demonstrates, de facto guarantees provide an incentive for banks to take excessive risks. Yet apparently in general they did not behave that way in any of the these countries, at least in the era of financial repression. In part, given the excess demand for loans under a policy of financial repression, the available credit was fully absorbed by the demands of creditworthy borrowers. In general, there were few opportunities, and little if any reward, for a loan officer taking extra risk—and definite disincentives. In Taiwan bank officials are subject to severe penalties if loans are defaulted. In all three countries a mistake can lead to a loss of reputation, and this matters.

Rankings of banks by size scarcely changed except by merger (which has occurred only in Japan)—demonstrating the general presumption that market shares would be relatively stable. This is consistent with the implicit rule that before liberalization banks were supposed to refrain from price competition and to limit nonprice competition.

A stated major objective of financial liberalization has been to promote greater competition among banks. However, even under full liberalization, the small number of banks may result in oligopolistic competition. It is the degree of market power that is important. In my judgment, collusive behavior is more likely to inhibit competition than are market imperfections deriving from imperfect information. There is also the danger of exploitative behavior of those (notably business group owners) who control banks. Clearly the need for prudential regulation and supervision is crucial under a financially liberalized regime.

As the country chapters show, banks have a more complex set of goals than short-run profit maximization. Profits certainly are important—to maintain the bank's viability, reputation, and ability to reward its stakeholders, both shareholders and employees. Maximization of the long-run growth of bank size (usually measured by assets) has been a major objective in all three countries. As Kitagawa and Kurosawa point out, in a system of interest rate ceilings this is equivalent to both long-run profit maximization and deposit growth maximization. Private stockholders of bank shares in all three countries are, of course, interested in dividends and stock price appreciation, but they are not able to influence bank management substantially. The main exception is stockholder-owners that control management, namely, some small banks in Japan, the private commercial banks in Taiwan, and the two newer nationwide commercial banks in Korea.

Japan provides the clearest example, since financial liberalization has proceeded fairly far, of how banks and bankers respond as risks and rewards are altered through the competitive market process. Banks have come to give considerably higher priority to profit maximization. Ranking banks by profits, rather than simply asset size, is becoming an important new measure of bank performance, reputation, and status. Japanese banks have taken on more risk in order to increase profits. Indeed, some traders and middle managers from time to time have taken on excessive risk in order to demonstrate superior performance; their occasional huge losses indicate Japanese banks have yet to install satisfactory systems of internal controls.

With financial liberalization, the banking metaphor in Japan has shifted from cruising in government-protected convoys to racing in more individually designed yachts of different capabilities. In the progressively more competitive, liberalized markets since the late 1970s, each Japanese bank has developed its own, more distinctive, strategy. This has meant variations in bank profitability and performance not seen earlier. Japanese banks took much higher degrees of risk in the mid- to late 1980s than they realized. This includes helping finance the domestic real estate boom, directly and indirectly (by loans to affiliated nonbank financial intermediaries). In addition, a number of major banks internationalized by making foreign real estate and merger and acquisition bridge loans in the United States and Europe. Still, it is unlikely any major bank will collapse and very unlikely overwhelming systemic problems will emerge. Nonetheless, bank growth and profitability will be low, and banks are likely to behave considerably more cautiously.

In Korea the metaphor for commercial banks has been that of handmaiden serving the government and its industrial policies, and the chaebol that carried those policies out. The heyday was the mid- to late 1970s when the government's development strategy to create heavy and chemical industries was at its peak. Policy loans were made to designated industries and even specific firms. Bankers had every incentive to follow government lending directives—and little incentive to develop bank internal information-gathering, credit evaluation, and lending appraisal capabilities. From the mid-1980s the banks have begun to build up these skills. Yet they remain handicapped both by the overhang of policy loans gone sour—such loans continue to comprise about one-third of their loan portfolios—and by the continuing government intrusion into their lending policies and management. In February 1991 the government appointed new presidents for five of the commercial banks, a reminder that top bank management serves at government sufferance, even a decade after the banks were privatized.

The most appropriate metaphor for the major commercial banks in Taiwan has been that of bureaucratic steward for the state. Their stock is owned by governmental authorities, so senior managers are appointed by the government and the staff is civil service. The first claimants on their loans are state enterprises. Only in the early 1990s is this changing.

Risk

The standard approach to protecting against borrower default is credit appraisal. This requires adequate information about a (potential) borrower's business situation and intentions, as well as the bank's capability of assessing that information. The essence of banking is to get to know the borrower well and to engage in repeated loan transactions; the costs of obtaining information and monitoring performance are at least fully covered in the terms of the loans and related fee business. Most banking in every market economy is of this relationship type. This is most true of Japan, with its main bank system. Government–chaebol arrangements in Korea and the role of state-owned enterprises and state-owned banks in Taiwan fundamentally affect not only the intensity but also the very nature of bank relationships with corporate clients.

In the absence of good information about the borrower, banks in Japan, Korea, and Taiwan have found it cheaper and safer to require specific collateral against loans. Thus, it has been the availability of good collateral, rather than the business performance of borrowers, that has determined much bank lending. To term this "pawnshop" banking, as has been done from time to time in these countries, is to denigrate the significance of the very real problems of lack of information about borrowers. Nonetheless, using collateral as the basis for loan decisions does not generate allocational efficiency: Those who have assets are not necessarily those with the most productive and profitable projects or business activities.

To be acceptable, collateral must be difficult to destroy or dispose of surreptitiously and must have alternative uses so as to be salable. Not surprising, real estate is commonly employed. One of the problems banks created for themselves in the speculative stock and real estate booms of the late 1980s was to make loans close to inflated values placed on the collateral.

Legal recourse on a defaulted loan is possible, but time-consuming and expensive. Discussion of the legal systems of Japan, Korea, and Taiwan and their mechanisms for enforcing financial contracts is well beyond the scope of this book. In general these societies do not rely much on litigation to resolve conflicts. As elsewhere, such problems are typically settled by negotiations. Nonetheless, legal sanctions can be important, as they provide a basis for negotiated settlements. The Korean authorities have used them in the occasional crackdowns on the curb market. And the possibility in Taiwan, until 1987, of criminal prosecution and imprisonment of debtors defaulting on post-dated checks must have been an effective deterrent. Business reputation, and its loss when checks are not honored, continues to be a factor. In Japan, two defaults on short-term promissory notes (trade bills) within six months brings an automatic cessation of clearing privileges, loss of liquidity, and quick bankruptcy or reorganization.

From the viewpoint of banks, ironclad government guarantees of their loans to specific companies are even better than collateral. However, the governments in Japan, Korea, and Taiwan have formally guaranteed commercial bank loans only to state-owned enterprises, not those to private companies. Some observers argue that the government's de facto guarantee that large banks will not be allowed to go bankrupt implies banks can make excessively risky loans to large borrowers (a moral hazard problem). The experience in each of the three countries has been different, as the country studies treat in some detail.

Taiwan's banking has been so conservative that no commercial bank has ever been faced with major potential losses from its private sector loans. In Japan the monetary authorities have long made it clear that banks will have to absorb loan losses without government subsidies, although they stand ready to assist in the merger of a troubled bank. At the same time, government policies allowing industries in cyclical trouble to establish antirecession cartels, primarily in the 1960s, substantially reduced potential loan losses by their banks; and government policies smoothing out and slowing down the decline of structurally depressed industries have mainly benefited their banks and other creditors.

The most problematic case has been Korea. The government forced the banks to make huge numbers of policy loans to selected firms in designated industries, as Park discusses in the country chapters. Some borrowers subsequently could not repay the principal; others, in slightly less serious straits, could not service their loans. The amounts involved were far greater than the net worth of the five commercial banks caught up in these policy loans. The banks quite naturally argued that since the government had made the loan decisions, it should be responsible for the losses. And that is more or less what happened, in a complex, case-by-case bargaining of the sharing of losses among the governmental authorities, the lending banks, and the (typically chaebol) borrowing companies and their owners.

Accurate assessment of the quality of an individual bank's loan portfolio is one of the most difficult tasks facing bank management itself, the supervisory agency, and the financial markets at large. Data are available on the actual losses banks have written off, net of collateral sale. Loss rates thus far have been very low in Japan and Taiwan; they have been considerably higher for Korean banks, in large part because partial write-offs have been one component of the rescue package for policy loans that went bad. However, bankers routinely renegotiate the terms and conditions of problem loans, frequently reducing interest rates and extending terms of repayment so the loans will not be defined as nonperforming. The hope is that conditions will improve eventually and the loans can be repaid; and in many instances this hope has been fulfilled by the country's rapid GNP growth in a nondeflationary environment.

Renegotiations between banks and their problem borrowers are not transparent, at least to the general public. Presumably the supervisory authorities are able to monitor such arrangements and know each bank's actual condition well, but the supervisory process in each country itself is not very transparent. Apparently the rationale has been not to disturb financial stability by making bad news public until absolutely necessary while quietly requiring banks facing such difficulties to improve their performance in fairly standard ways.

Banks, of course, face other risks in addition to that of borrower default. As already stressed, bankers in Japan, Korea, and Taiwan have been well protected by the monetary authorities from systemic risk—financial panics and the spread of runs on banks. Another major risk for banks lies in the volatility of the prices of their assets, relative to deposits and other liabilities, as interest and foreign exchange rates change. Asset price swings provide opportunities for gain as well as prospects of loss. Bankers in all three countries have had to learn how to manage interest rate and exchange rate risk as financial liberalization has proceeded. Their learning process has not always been smooth. Many banks have been slow to develop adequate internal procedures for risk management, and market instruments for hedging have not been allowed to develop fully or rapidly by the still quite cautious and control-oriented regulatory authorities in each of the three countries.

The internal operations of individual commercial banks remain very much a black box in all three countries. One reason is that little research has been done on bank managements and especially on the details of internal decisionmaking processes, systems of internal control to ensure staff behavior falls within bank guidelines and norms, and the like. The occasional banking scandal does provide flickers of illumination in a generally opaque set of banking arrangements. Such events suggest the banks in all three countries need to improve both their risk management procedures and their ability to monitor and control their own behavior in order to prevent excessive risk taking (as reflected, for example, in the occasional huge losses some banks have had in government bond or foreign exchange trading) and to prevent fraudulent activities of bank staff members. In general banks are responding to their respective new financial environments, most rapidly in Japan, by enhancing credit evaluation and risk management capabilities. But many of the banks apparently still have a considerable way to go.

Prudential Supervision

To be effective, supervision has to be regular, to anticipate potential problems, and to be armed with mechanisms to prevent bank capital depletion. At the same time, a system that results in no defaults or losses at all is excessively risk averse.

It is difficult to evaluate the quality and effectiveness of the monetary authorities in Japan, Taiwan and Korea. On the one hand, there have been no bankruptcies of banks, no depositor losses, not even significant government bailout costs except in Korea. The few crises have been dealt with swiftly and without spilling over into more general financial panics. Troubled financial institutions have been warned, loans restructured, dividend payments restricted, management changed. Where necessary, banks have been merged into other institutions, appropriately lubricated with central bank credit and other subsidies.

However, supervisory capabilities have not yet been severely tested in Taiwan or in Japan, although the rash of scandals surfacing in the aftermath of the bursting of the speculative stock market and real estate bubbles may change that in Japan. Deregulation, liberalization, and heightened competition mean problems—including management inefficiency, excessive risk taking, and even ex post "mistakes"—will take place in entirely different environments, although Korea must be considered separately because of the particular difficulties of the huge policy loans made by commercial banks that have become nonperforming or outright bad debts.

While the protection of depositors has been paramount, in none of these countries have the authorities provided significant government-sponsored deposit insurance. The major reason is that it was popularly (and correctly) perceived that the authorities would not allow any bank to fail. Moreover, the lessons of the U.S. savings and loan experience have made deposit insurance a much less attractive instrument of protection. Rather, monetary authorities in all three countries are increasing capital-asset requirements and strengthening supervision.

Moral hazard is a potentially serious problem in any financial system. Aside from issues regarding safety (notably excessive risk taking and fraudulent behavior), there is information asymmetry. One aspect of this is the ability of insiders to take advantage of their favorable access to information about the prospects for their business enterprise, exemplified by investing in the stock market for personal gain. Japan, Korea, and Taiwan are insider societies, and there are few efforts to prevent taking advantage of special knowledge and few penalties for misuse. In this they are like most societies—the United States and United Kingdom are exceptional in their degree of concern (a concern I share).

The package of ceiling interest rates, market and institution segmentation, restrictions on entry, and close supervision of the limited number of banks made for a very safe but not very competitive system in all three countries. Moreover, the incentive structures typically encouraged ongoing risk aversion and rewarded asset growth rather than profit maximization. It was almost always beneficial to follow, and dangerous to challenge, the rules and administrative guidance of the monetary authorities. Smaller financial institutions took advantage of loopholes or new, gray-area opportunities as they arose, but the main financial institutions cooperated rather closely with the regulatory authorities. This made sense; they were players in a cozy game.

The degree of emphasis on safety by policymakers in all three countries has, however, led to societal costs in the form of inefficiencies in financial intermediation and credit allocation. This is not to say governments should be limited to prudential regulation. They should take an active part in the design and maintenance of the financial system and are especially well placed to help the financial sector overcome ignorance and lack of information, as indeed they did in all three countries. Japan's prewar experience is an example of such government involvement without resorting to financial repression.

THE EFFICIENCY AND EFFECTIVENESS OF FINANCE

Evaluation not only of the economic efficiency but also of the overall effectiveness of the performance over time of the financial systems of Japan, Korea, and Taiwan and their financial institutions does not readily lend itself to modeling or quantitative testing. The causal patterns are too complex and intertwined, the dynamics too difficult to specify, and the available data too weak. Nonetheless, we have accumulated a great deal of knowledge and analytical insight, and evaluative judgments are possible, indeed necessary.

The criteria for economic efficiency are, in principle, direct and obvious. In terms of Pareto optimality and market-efficient results, there are two major questions. How successfully has the financial system enhanced and mobilized domestic (and foreign) savings, especially from households and individuals? To what degree has it allocated those savings to the most efficient uses? Conceptually, of course, externalities—both benefits and costs—should be included in the calculus, but in practice that is difficult to determine. At a more micro level, how efficiently have financial institutions provided their intermediation services?

Evaluation of economic efficiency is the domain of the economist, whereas effectiveness is the domain of the economic historian. Effectiveness is a more comprehensive (and vaguer) concept than allocative efficiency. Basically, it asks such questions as, Did the economy grow rapidly? Did it create a system of self-sustained growth? Was overall resource allocation reasonably good? Was the resultant industrial structure reasonably efficient? Did standards of living improve significantly? Were social welfare objectives met? Were the imperfections and failures both of markets and of bureaucratic and policy decisionmaking mechanisms overcome?

Analysis and appraisal start with financial markets and financial institutions but must delve beyond these. The role of the state is a key ingredient. At a minimum, its monetary authorities set the rules and engage in prudential oversight. In Japan, Korea, and Taiwan, the government has played a direct role in credit allocation, albeit to varying degrees over time and by country. After a general overview, the following discussion focuses on government influence on the allocation of credit, with particular attention to the goal of achieving rapid economic growth.

Careful econometric tests of the financial system's contribution to the development of high savings rates in all three countries produce results that are mixed and unclear. We do not know for sure to what extent the increases in savings rates and their mobilization through the financial system were due to real per capita income growth, reductions in the rates of inflation, positive (and, in Taiwan, high) real interest rates, the spread of financial institution offices, or other variables. Perversely, a moderately repressed financial system may have induced a higher savings rate by small businesses and households that wanted to invest but had to rely primarily on their own savings because of credit rationing or very high borrowing costs.

These financial systems were relatively successful in mobilizing domestic savings, although there are significant differences. In both Korea and Taiwan the large share and active role of curb markets indicate their modern financial sectors were substantially considerably less involved than Japan's in mobilizing private savings and allocating them to productive investment. In broad sectoral terms, all three systems channeled credit to infrastructure and productive business uses, and away from provision of credit to consumers and housing. This certainly resulted in more rapid growth, given the high investment demand, but at some welfare cost.

The preference in lending and the wide differential in effective interest rates charged implies that in a static sense capital was misallocated, going excessively to large firms and insufficiently to small ones. In a dynamic context the conclusions are less clear-cut, at least in the cases of Japan and Korea where large firms were the technology importers and innovators, engines of the economic growth process.

Government Involvement in Credit Allocation

In each country, policymakers have presumed they (the government) should take an active role in promoting economic development. The key issues have been the type and degree of intervention. Policymakers were quick to realize that control of access to preferential (low-cost) credit is a powerful form of control. They also understood that markets replace decisionmaking bureaucrats. So, in each country the government intervened in the allocation of credit and otherwise strictly controlled most financial markets. The objectives were to promote exports, finance productive fixed investment, build infrastructure, and implement sector-specific industrial policies. However, the degree of government intervention and support differed substantially: It was by far the greatest in Korea, less so in Taiwan, least in Japan.

Despite rhetoric about helping small business, the central focus of government credit programs in all three countries was big enterprises and big projects. But government involvement went beyond purely developmental objectives to income distribution and other implicitly political rationales. Thus, all three countries created government financial institutions providing house ownership mortgages, even though housing as such was not a favored activity. The government encouraged development of specialized, small-scale financial institutions (credit associations and cooperatives) for agriculture, forestry, fisheries, and small businesses. In the early phases of economic growth, when credit was tight and larger business investment demand was high, not much credit was channeled to these sectors, especially relative to their contributions to GNP. Rather, these institutions were relatively self-contained; the deposits of farmers or businesses were lent to their counterparts. Later, as credit demands eased and political pressures by these interest groups became more pronounced, government credit was made more available.

Small businesses have been important contributors to GNP growth—probably most in Taiwan, next in Japan, and least so in Korea—but we know relatively little about their operations and especially their financing. In Taiwan and Korea small enterprises have had limited access to bank loans and have relied heavily on informal markets. In Japan small businesses had greater access to credit but at high effective interest rates in oligopolistic markets. Given the information costs of determining the creditworthiness of small business borrowers, it is not surprising that in a system with regulated interest rates, banks and other lenders preferred to lend to presumably less risky large firms and to require specific collateral.

A government has two ways to alter credit allocation: It can lend its own funds, and it can influence how financial institutions lend theirs. The government plays a direct financial role by generating funds in three ways: running a financial surplus in the public sector, serving as a domestic financial intermediary (borrowing from the private sector and relending), and borrowing from abroad. In each country the authorities created a panoply of specialized government financial institutions to lend to business, especially development banks and export–import credit banks.

Government Financial Institutions

Although the nature and extent of the government as a financial intermediary have not been a central focus of these country studies, they do provide interesting and useful evidence. The government financial institution share of corporate finance as a whole was modest and declining in Japan, although significant in the high-growth era for certain industries. The shares have been much higher in both Korea and Taiwan.

In all three countries government financial institutions naturally were important to the implementation of government policies to fund long-term investment in infrastructure and those industries targeted for development priority. In addition to their own loans, they had signaling and syndication leadership roles for commercial banks. This was of some importance in the 1950s and 1960s in Japan, but in Korea and Taiwan, direct government intervention in commercial bank lending made it less significant.

The sources of funds for government financial institutions have differed somewhat among the three countries. In all three the public sector as a whole—central government, local government, and state enterprise—was a modest net borrower until the mid-1970s. When government enterprises are excluded, it appears the public sectors ran budgetary balances or, in the case of Taiwan, even surpluses. After 1975 the patterns diverged. In Japan, pursuant to its Keynesian and structural deficit financing, the public sector deficit rose sharply before subsiding in the 1980s and turning to surplus in 1988. Korea's public sector had a small surplus from the mid-1970s until the late 1980s, when it increased significantly. In Taiwan, the public sector has generated a relatively small surplus from the late 1970s.

Postal savings have been particularly important in Japan and to a lesser extent in Taiwan. In both countries they comprised a significant share of total private deposits and were the major source of funds for government development finance institutions. In Korea they have not played a major role in government financial intermediation.

In Korea, foreign loans, typically with government guarantees and in many instances channeled through government financial institutions, were an important (and relatively very cheap) source of investment funds in the 1970s and early 1980s. The borrowing of the Japanese government and its financial institutions was much more limited. Most were World Bank loans in the late 1950s and early 1960s, for which the Japan Development Bank on occasion served as the conduit. In the 1960s Japanese government financial institution loans from foreign borrowing were limited, especially after the U.S. Treasury in 1963 applied an interest equalization tax and administrative guidance to halt such plans. Taiwan, like Korea, a major recipient of U.S. foreign aid in the 1950s, was not able to borrow in international capital markets for political reasons.

The State Enterprise Sector

An important function of government financial institutions, as well as the government budget, has been to finance the state enterprise sector. There are considerable differences in the size and scope of this sector among these three countries, and differences in their financing. In Taiwan, reflecting the ideological heritage of Sun Yat-sen's thinking, defense needs, and the colonial heritage, the government owns a fairly wide range of enterprises in key basic industries, as well as public utilities, communications, and transportation. The sector is relatively considerably smaller in Korea and Japan, limited mainly to infrastructure. Analysis of the financial impact of state enterprises—as investors, savers, and borrowers—is complicated by the fact their financial condition is largely determined by government policy rather than business performance: They receive subsidized credit, and output pricing can be high (taking advantage of monopoly power) or low (reflecting social policy).

The evidence suggests state enterprises in all three countries have been relatively bureaucratic and inefficient, and would benefit from reform. In Taiwan the sector remains large, although it is decreasing in relative importance. Firms have generated large internal reserves but their investments were even larger, and they were heavy borrowers from the government's specialized financial institutions as well as the government-owned commercial banks.

Influence on Other Financial Institutions

The major difference among the countries in their government's involvement in credit allocation has been the nature, extent, and form of government influence over lending by commercial banks. The Korean government was the most intrusive and relied the most on direct controls for subsidized credit allocation. The banks were mere conduits, and the amounts were huge, especially during the 1970s. In Taiwan the government pursued similar policies but somewhat less obviously; after all, the relevant commercial banks were government-owned, and state enterprises constituted a large share of targeted firms. But it was more a matter of availability of credit than of particularly low interest rates relative to those paid by private business borrowers from banks.

By the mid-1950s in Japan the monetary authorities had stopped targeting priority sectors for loans by private commercial banks or other private financial institutions. Subsequently, through monetary policy they determined the supply of credit and relied on the banks and market signals to determine which industries and firms borrowed. The central bank's attempts to channel bank lending were infrequent and in the form of negative injunctions: restrictions on lending to trading companies engaged in speculative activities in the 1973 oil crisis and to real estate companies in 1989–92.

In addition to direct controls—regulation, directive, and administrative guidance—central bank lending, rediscounting, and reserve requirement policies affect the flow of funds. In all three countries, increases in base money commensurate with real economic growth were made available to the financial system on more or less preferential terms. In Japan, only the city banks were able to borrow from the central bank, and at low rates that in turn benefited their large corporate clients. In Korea the central bank imposed relatively high reserve requirements, which channeled private funds to the central bank to relend under preferential programs; the Bank of Korea paid interest on those reserves when it was deemed necessary to bolster the profits of banks.

Low Interest Rate Policies

The most important domestic regulations of the financial systems in all three countries were the ceilings set on interest rates—deposits and loans, as well as other financial instruments such as bond issues. When the low interest rate policy is evaluated in conjunction with government preferential allocations in imperfect markets of limited information and some private risk aversion, the authors of the country studies reach somewhat different conclusions about the consequences.

Shea argues that the combined system of low interest rates in the modern sector and government preferential allocations resulted in a suboptimal pattern of credit allocation in Taiwan; the informal market was an important mechanism for funding small business, which has been the engine of Taiwan's rapid economic growth. Park contends that in Korea on net balance credit directed and subsidized by government policy was effective if not optimally efficient. There is evidence that in Japan low nominal interest rates on loans were offset in large part by compensating deposit balances, which leads Teranishi to argue that funds were allocated relatively efficiently across sectors and large firms.

Export Credits

Probably the most successful program of subsidized credit by developmental criteria in all three countries was for exports and export production, mainly through central bank rediscount of export trade bills at low interest rates. Korea and Taiwan are outstanding examples of an export-led development strategy, and cheap and available credit was a major policy instrument. (Hong Kong and Singapore achieved very successful export-oriented economic growth without financial repression or subsidized export credits.) Japan's development strategy in the high-growth era also gave priority to exports, albeit primarily to reduce the balance of payments (import) constraint on what was primarily domestic demand–based growth. These programs were especially effective because they clearly signaled that stable supplies of credit were available for this purpose. In Taiwan especially, but Japan as well, this was an important incentive for small firms, otherwise denied ready access to bank credit, to become competitive in export markets.

Channeling substantial resources into export production was an efficient allocation both by static criteria (overcoming other distortions in resource allocation) and in a dynamic growth context. Importantly, the export credit system left it to the competitive marketplace to determine which industries and firms would receive credit, based on performance. It was the antithesis of sector-specific industrial policies. However, the subsidy programs may have persisted too long, resulting in some overallocation of resources to export production. Taiwan's huge current account surpluses since the mid-1980s can be interpreted in this way. It is most unusual for a country at Taiwan's GNP per capita level, with a high return on domestic investment and burgeoning unmet infrastructure investment needs, to be such a large capital exporter.

The export surpluses eventually resulted in a substantial appreciation of Japan's and Taiwan's exchange rates since 1985 and in resultant huge losses in the domestic currency values of their accumulated foreign assets. Still, as a development strategy it is better to overshoot than undershoot on export growth. And one of the more important consequences of export success is that it enables, and indeed generates pressure for, reduction of high import barriers and the international liberalization of the financial system.

The degree of credit subsidy differed greatly among the countries in the 1960s and 1970s. In Japan the gap between regular and export interest rates was not large (although it was at times as much as 7 percentage points below the effective rate at which small firms could borrow for domestic purposes). In Korea the export credit rate was very low relative to official rates, and much more so compared to curb market rates (some 20 to 30 percentage points); and the amounts were so generous that export-based firms engaged in arbitrage by relending some of their export-related borrowings in the curb market (Cole and Park 1983). In Taiwan, too, the gap between the bank-subsidized export credit rate and the informal market rate was high (10 to 15 percentage points).

Long-term Finance

A general theoretical case has been made that developing countries have inadequate supplies of long-term finance relative to their need to finance business fixed investment and capital-intensive infrastructure. On the one hand the uncertainty of success of investment projects and the inadequate information to evaluate project feasibility and firm creditworthiness make long-term commitment of funds appear even more risky than they are. On the other hand, most savers— it is asserted—prefer relatively short-term financial assets, especially when secondary markets are poor and inflationary fears persist (as they did, based on the historical experience in each of these countries). As a consequence, there is a term mismatch.

Dealing with this mismatch has been a central concern in all three countries. The most direct response was to establish specialized government financial institutions whose main purpose was to make long-term loans for fixed investment. But that was by no means sufficient. Two other approaches were also followed: the creation or encouragement of (private) financial institutions to provide long-term funds and the encouragement or at least toleration of commercial banks' rolling over short-term loans (de facto term lending). The three countries differ somewhat in how these approaches have been applied.

Postwar Japan inherited government-controlled long-term credit banks. They were privatized but continued in the business of term lending. They raised funds by issuing debentures that were purchased by commercial banks, other financial intermediaries and their borrowers, and, for the one-year maturity, wealthy individuals. The Bank of Japan also, in effect, provided funds by accepting the debentures as collateral for central bank loans to the city banks. There were no comparable private long-term credit banks in Korea or Taiwan.

In the normal process of financial development and deepening, a range of thrift and other specialized institutions offering some long-term loans have emerged and grown: trust accounts of banks, insurance companies, and specialized institutions for agriculture and small business. In none of the countries did the government encourage the development of a corporate bond market; on the contrary, they introduced all sorts of regulatory barriers to the issuance of bonds. A secondary bond market, by generating market-determined interest rate yields, would have fundamentally undermined the low interest rate policy.

The commercial banks have also been a major source of long-term finance in all three countries. They made term loans, particularly in Taiwan, and they virtually automatically rolled over short-term loans to their best clients. In Japan, however, term lending by private financial institutions was based on profitability and creditworthiness criteria, even with the main bank system and relationship banking, implying those funds were efficiently allocated. In contrast, in Korea and Taiwan the commercial banks were subject to strong guidance, even regulation, so most of their term lending went to priority sectors and even designated large firms.

In general, the credit subsidy element was greater for long-term than short-term loans in all three countries. The main beneficiaries of this were infrastructure enterprises and large manufacturing firms, particularly in priority industries.

Subsidized credit for infrastructure is much less controversial than that for implementation of manufacturing industrial policy, since the positive externalities are more direct and obvious. Infrastructure includes utilities, communications, and transport. In all three countries the government has engaged directly in many of these activities. Because the main thrust of economic growth lay in manufacturing, there probably was not serious overinvestment in infrastructure; indeed, from time to time the supply of infrastructure services lagged behind the demand for them.

Industrial Policy

All three countries have pursued, although with substantially differing intensities and degrees of specificity, policies to promote certain manufacturing industries regarded as crucial to rapid growth. Preferential credit allocation at subsidized interest rates was part of a package of policy instruments to promote these industries. Thus, to evaluate credit policies, what is required is a comprehensive evaluation of the efficiency and effectiveness of the industrial policy programs themselves. That goes beyond the purpose of this book—indeed, definitive comparisons of the nature and effectiveness of industrial policy in Japan, Korea, and

Taiwan are not yet possible, and there is not even a consensus evaluation of each country's experience. But some general observations can be made.[1]

Industrial policy is essentially sectoral policy—choosing certain industries for support using sector-specific measures. It is the differential nature and degree of support that are the essence. When certain industries receive preferential treatment, then inevitably other industries are relatively disadvantaged in the resource allocation process. The basic issue is how the process of industrial development took place in each country. Was it state-led, with business following the leadership and the initiative of government bureaucrats? Or was it a process shaped essentially by decentralized private business decision making, with government measures helpfully supporting implementation? The answers vary—country by country, industry by industry, and even by types of scholars. (Economists tend to emphasize the role of business while political scientists emphasize the leadership of the government bureaucracy.)

A central issue is the nature of the government–big business relationship. In all three countries that relationship has been positive and cooperative. At the very least it can be said that the government provided a supportive environment for the development and growth of business, through general policies that benefited all manufacturing sectors. Probably the most important policy instrument until development was well under way (and foreign pressures mounted) was the protection of nearly all manufacturing from import competition while trying, more or less, to encourage domestic competition.

The industries selected for government support, and the reasons for choosing them, were similar among the three countries. Initially selected were basic industries that symbolized a "developed" status and had important linkages to other sectors: steel, coal mining, petroleum refining, petrochemicals, and fertilizer. From that emerged a more general emphasis on heavy and chemical industries, first in Japan and then in Korea, though much less so in smaller Taiwan. In other words, this was not picking "winners" in terms of globally new industries—it was catching up with the existing industrial structure of more economically advanced countries.

The degree and nature of industrial policy, and concomitantly the role of preferential finance, differed significantly, but in all three countries, elements of the financial system were mobilized. Policy was applied most extensively, intensively, and directly in Korea. The government took a strong leadership role from the president on down through an interventionist bureaucracy. Korean industrial policy reached its peak in the 1970s when the economic development strategy shifted from market-based light industries to the creation of new heavy and chemical industries. This strategy was also critically shaped by defense priorities in

---

1. The following are useful studies of industrial policy. For Japan, Komiya, Okuno and Sazumura (1988) is a comprehensive overview; see Patrick (1986) on high technology; Johnson (1982) and Okimoto (1989) on MITI; Anchordoguy (1989), Friedman (1988), Genther (1990), Okimoto Suzano, and Weinstein (1984), and Samuels (1987) for industry case studies. For Korea see Song (1990), Stern (1990), Amsden (1989), and Leipziger (1987). For Taiwan see Wade (1990) and Li (1988). Patrick (1991) covers declining industries in all three.

light of the threatened withdrawal of U.S. troops. The selected industries were capital-intensive and had significant economies of scale.

The government in effect sought to create private firms of sufficient scale and intensity. It was decided that certain family-owned conglomerates (chaebol) were the most efficient instruments. The argument was that the chaebol had already assembled the best available management; had greater capabilities of obtaining access to and effectively utilizing foreign technologies; could more readily transfer capital within the conglomerate, and offered economies of scope. In other words, they were better able than others to overcome market imperfections in technology and information—and the government would provide them access to cheap capital. The financial system was duly mobilized, as already discussed.

In Japan the range of industries supported was equally wide, but the degree of credit subsidy was far less than in Korea. Moreover, the policies were aimed at the industry level; they were not targeted specifically to individual groups or firms as such. In fact, the share of the Big Six keiretsu in total manufacturing declined modestly over time. New entrants were encouraged both by government technology importation licensing policy and by the growing domestic market. In general, government direction of business was less important than voluntary, mutually agreed programs from which both benefited. The interplay between Ministry of International Trade and Industry (MITI) officials and large business was complex and nuanced and evolved over time as business became more powerful, independent, and autonomous. As MITI lost its controls over foreign exchange, import licenses, and tariffs and as cheap credit became much more available in the surplus-savings era from the mid-1970s, it became mainly a coordinator and distributor of information among major firms.

Japan's financial system supported the government's industrial policy, but the extent of private financial institution involvement was relatively small and indirect. They usually gave priority to targeted industries, but the extent of subsidy was small since effective interest rate differentials were modest, particularly for bank loans. The government did not intervene directly in the loan policies of commercial banks and other private institutions. The Japan Development Bank (JDB) and other government financial institutions played a leading role in industrial policy financing, and their signaling effects were important. Nonetheless, banks did not follow the signals blindly; their support was conditional on their own credit evaluations. For example, even in the 1950s and 1960s banks refused to lend much to the targeted shipping industry, which they viewed with some skepticism; as a result, as much as half of JDB loans went to shipping firms. Moreover, the banks sought clients in industries not targeted by MITI, such as household durables, automobile assembly, and consumer electronics, and financed their rapid growth. In this the banks bypassed MITI, backing on their own the industries that had already begun to reshape the Western economies MITI was trying to catch up with.

The Taiwan case is quite different. The focus was on a narrower range of industries, not surprising given the smaller population and the smaller potential domestic market. The development of defense industries was a high priority, increasingly so as Taiwan's international political position became more difficult. Industrial policy was implemented mainly through state enterprises, as well as a few large private firms controlled by or close to the governing political party and its leaders. State enterprises, producing only one-tenth of GNP, engaged in one-quarter to one-third of fixed investment. In general the relationship between the government and the private business sector, especially small business, was not positive and close; there were two distinct sectors—state and private—somewhat mistrustful of each other.

State enterprises received first priority in funding from both government specialized development banks (such as the Bank of Communications) and government-owned commercial banks. Large private enterprises came next. Smaller firms have had to rely mainly on the informal market, except for export credits. Because credit demand exceeded supply from the formal sector, even big businesses had to go to the informal market for some of their needs.

Evaluation

A comprehensive, definitive evaluation of the industrial policies of Japan, Korea, and Taiwan, and the subsidized credit programs to support them, will come only after many more empirical industry studies and further historical perspective. Much depends on the criteria for evaluation. Analysis of efficiency is made difficult by externalities, price distortions in goods markets, imperfect factor markets, insulation from world markets, the hiding of true economic costs by debt rescheduling at low interest rates, inadequate evidence as to what would have been a market equilibrium interest rate for evaluating the profitability of investment projects, and other forms of imperfect information.

In each of these countries, there are cases of successful industrial policy and cases of failure. Traditionally, the literature has paid more attention to the successes. However, investments in certain industries were outright mistakes; examples include aircraft and aluminum in Japan, shipping and power-generating equipment in Korea, and automobile assembly and certain state enterprises in Taiwan. The timing was wrong in other industries—too early relative to capital shortages, technological capabilities, and the general level of development.

My assessment is that the record of industrial policy is spotty and mixed in these countries. In Japan there was less industrial policy than meets the eye, or than MITI claims for itself. In all three countries the most important policy instrument was protection from imports. Whatever one's assessment of their past industrial policy successes, extensive protection is not politically feasible for these countries and has been reduced steadily and substantially in most areas (agriculture and, to a lesser extent, finance being major exceptions).

Each author has evaluated, implicitly or explicitly, the country's program of government-directed credit. As noted earlier, our evaluative criteria include effectiveness as well as economic efficiency. Simply put, did the economic system work, despite whatever inefficiencies there were? By these criteria, the economic development and growth of Japan, Korea, and Taiwan have been remarkably successful. Mistakes in credit allocation and in other policies have been swept away (often under the rug) by this overall, long-run economic success.

From the perspective of policymakers, such a historical judgment is not very satisfactory. After all, if one is to learn from these experiences, the myriad forces at work bringing about successful economic development need to be disentangled and understood. Successful policies have to be identified, and so too do policy mistakes and failures. Finance is important, but it is by no means the determining factor in economic success or failure. Efficient and effective finance ensures that the best investments are made, but what makes investments successful depends on a host of real factors: technology, management, labor skills, factor proportions, and output demand.

CONCLUDING REFLECTIONS

The financial development of Japan, Korea, and Taiwan since the 1950s has been very successful from a 40-year perspective: Whatever the problems, difficulties, deficiencies and costs, it worked. Much of the success can be attributed to factors external to finance: unprecedentedly rapid rates of real economic growth and structural transformation, largely successful macroeconomic policies and performance, and personal savings rates that, beginning low, rose to very high shares of income. The experience of these three countries demonstrates the centrality of price stability—control over inflationary pressures—to successful financial and real development. The financial system was rather more the accommodator of this real economic performance than its instigator. It participated centrally in this dynamic real economic growth through its own growth, structural change, and institutional development.

The financial systems of the three countries continue to be quintessentially banking-based systems. That should not be surprising. The development of capital markets to the point that issuing stocks or bonds become a significant source of external funds even for large corporate borrowers typically occurs only when reliable information becomes available, capital market institutions are created, and a certain level of economic development and size is attained. Only Japan has reached the point where finance through autonomous domestic capital markets is a real option for its large firms.

The three financial systems are similar in their general lack of transparency. In this respect they are more akin to continental Europe and most developing market economies than to the Anglo-American market-oriented models of relatively high degrees of disclosure and transparency. Part of this has to do with the inadequacies of reporting requirements and accounting and auditing institutions, practices, and performance. The implicit or informal rules of the game apparently are as important as the explicit, formal rules—and are not well defined, described, or understood by those not directly involved.

The path of evolution of financial institutions, markets, and government policies in each country probably will end up in the same place in its general contours, although not in its specifics. The trend in each country is from a segmented, regulated, and protected credit-rationing system of financial markets and institutions to a deregulated, market-oriented, competitive financial system linked to global financial markets. This process has already taken considerable time and promises to take even more time. Relaxation of the regulatory authorities' hold has been slow, gradual (if abrupt on occasion), and piecemeal. Japan started earliest and has achieved the most; then Taiwan; Korea still has a considerable way to go. There has not been a "grand design" to be implemented quickly through sudden, comprehensive deregulation—although the United States and United Kingdom provide, as they did in industrialization, a model of what a liberalized system entails, and what prudential problems the monetary authorities should seek to avoid. Nonetheless, the pressures of market forces, changing domestic political constituencies and concerns, and foreign governments keep moving the liberalization process forward in all three countries.

Two Conundrums

Two themes have guided the thinking of the authors of this book.

1. How could these economies grow rapidly while their financial systems were repressed?
2. With the economies growing so successfully, why move to a more liberalized, deregulated, market-oriented financial system?

There are no simple answers, although the second question is less difficult to answer than the first. Each author has made judgments, and we agree generally, although we are not in complete agreement on all our conclusions.

Given that there are going to be government policies to direct credit to preferred activities, the issue is the means by which objectives are implemented. Basically the choice is between the government using market-conforming incentives and mechanisms or some form of direct credit allocation. Subsidization of selected activities is involved in both. It is possible to combine elements of financial repression with generic market-conforming interest subsidies, as exemplified by the successful export credit programs in all three countries. In general, credit directed toward broadly defined goals—exports, fixed investment, pollution controls—appears to have been more market-conforming and effective than that directed toward specific industries or firms.

The results of credit programs to support sector-specific industrial policies are mixed: There have been cases of success, of long and expensive gestation periods before industries succeeded, and of outright failure. It is difficult to imagine that an unrepressed, market-based, competitive, allocatively more efficient financial system would have generated growth rates even more rapid than actually occurred. Indeed, all three economies were operating flat-out in their high-growth eras (which continue in Korea and Taiwan). The key lies in the basic strategies of development and the overall effectiveness of resource allocation in these economies, less in microefficiency at the margin.

These systems on the whole were effective in transferring resources to productive uses—to business investment and to exports. The efficiency costs of financial repression probably have been more in the form of less rapid improvements in welfare—less housing and consumption—than in measured GNP performance. Surely owners of small businesses would have had to save less, and been able to live better, if they had had better access to credit at more reasonable interest rates. This raises a second criterion for evaluating the effectiveness of policies of financial repression: the effects on the distribution of income and wealth.

Financial repression probably widened income and wealth distribution in all three countries; that is, companies benefited at the expense of savers. The direct effects may have been relatively modest, although this is not a well-researched topic. Wealth distribution has widened dramatically with the huge increases in real estate prices in all three countries, and those rises have been abetted by/from banks and other financial institutions credit to real estate purchasers. This is true for the entire period (for stock prices as well) despite the sharp declines in the early 1990s. Only relatively recent entrants have actual losses; the great majority have simply seen staggering paper gains reduced to merely outstanding gains. A plausible case can be made that low yields on deposit and bonds made real assets more attractive, but the empirical evidence is unclear. The asset market bubbles of the late 1980s occurred in a quite liberalized Japan, a liberalizing Taiwan, and a still financially repressed Korea.

A third criterion in evaluating financial repression is its effects on the sociopolitical system. Finance is a very powerful instrument. How is that power utilized, and how is it constrained? There are two major points about financial repression. First, the power to allocate credit lies in the hands of the political and government bureaucratic authorities. Do they use that power for the sake of national welfare or for their own purposes? Do they recognize a difference between these? Second, interest rate ceilings create rents. Who obtains these rents, and for what purposes? Political scientists and others critical of the governments in each of these three countries have pointed to the use of finance to support the political apparatus in power, to finance elections, and to reward supporters. Evaluation of these questions is largely outside the boundaries of this book.

The second question—why liberalize the financial system when the economy is growing so rapidly—can be answered in either of two ways. For those who conclude that the earlier policies of financial repression were, on balance, not efficacious in Japan, Korea, and Taiwan—using some combination of criteria of allocational inefficiencies, worsening of income and wealth distribution, and political economy costs—then a policy shift toward a liberalized, market-oriented, competitive financial system was desirable all along.

Even those who promoted policies of low interest rates and credit directed to priority purposes came to realize that at some point the costs of financial repression outweigh the allocational benefits, at least as they perceived them. As these economies grew and developed, they became more complex and sophisticated and more difficult to micromanage. Information was better, and markets worked better. Government officials came to realize they could not readily pick winner industries, much less firms, better than the market could. Earlier mistakes in credit allocations became evident with the passage of time; and periodic financial scandals exposed credit misallocations as well as instances of fraud and corruption, thereby generating pressures for reform. Thus financial liberalization, in this way of thinking, is associated with ongoing economic development—both part of an evolutionary process, with each reinforcing the other, at least after some level of real development.

New Challenges

Although we did not anticipate it when planning this analytical history of the financial development of Japan, Korea, and Taiwan, it ends at a time when each country's financial system appears to be entering a major new phase, each for quite different reasons. There are real problems that will have to be confronted in the 1990s if truly market-oriented and effectively competitive financial systems are to prevail.

In Taiwan the banking system will be fundamentally transformed by the entry of 16 newly licensed, large, well-capitalized banks, almost all owned and controlled by identifiable private business groups. Moreover, in principle the hitherto dominant, government-owned, commercial banks are to be privatized. Will this create a more dynamic and competitive, less risk averse banking system? Will it enable the integration of the informal market into the formal financial sector? To what degree will the government's pervasive control of the management and operations of the formerly government-owned banks, and indeed all financial institutions, be attenuated? Will prudential regulation and supervision prevent the banks' misuse by their owners? What can be said is that the comprehensive liberalizing policies set in place in 1989 hold out prospects for a major improvement in the competitiveness, efficiency and effectiveness of Taiwan's financial system.

For Korea, the central problem is implementing the financial liberalization policies initiated in the early 1980s but subsequently stalled. The government in 1991 and 1992 announced comprehensive schedules for deregulating domestic finance and increasing international openness during the 1990s. Will they be carried out? There are other major questions. How will the potential for cartel behavior among the small number of banks be constrained? Will the commercial banks succeed in developing an independent relationship, based on their own monitoring capabilities, in relation to both the chaebol and the government? Will the government really retreat from its hitherto heavily interventionist role in credit allocation? The government will have to undertake two major policies if its professed goal of financial liberalization is to be achieved. Inflation must be kept under control in a political environment that generates demands for expansionary macroeconomic policies and cheap credit. And use of government-directed credit programs—policy loans and the like—through the commercial banks will have to be greatly reduced. Ultimately this requires altering the arrangements among the chaebol, the government, and the financial system.

Japan's financial system faces a completely new and unexpected challenge: a large overhang of bad loans, especially for real estate development. This has put the banks on the defensive, domestically and internationally. There are two sources of these sour loans: the bursting of the asset bubble in the early 1990s and poor bank management. A number of smaller local banks and credit associations have been poorly managed for years and suffer from a lack of scale and portfolio diversity. Deregulation of deposit rates and other losses of market niches in a competitive environment have exposed their fundamentally unsound positions.

Real estate and stock speculation in the late 1980s generated huge volumes of loans that cannot be serviced by the cash flow of their borrowers, and because real estate and stock prices have dropped precipitously, the collateral cannot be sold to cover the loan. All financial institutions suffer from these problems, but they are most severe for those located in urban areas (notably Tokyo and Osaka) and those specializing in real estate development finance (trust banks and long-term credit banks). The lack of transparency of these bank bad debt problems—how severe they really are—makes objective evaluation difficult.

There is an irony here. In the past the monetary authorities and banks disclosed little about nonperforming loans and other difficulties because there was no need. Rapid economic growth limited the consequences of problem loans, and all financial institutions were profitable. Lack of transparency was accepted because the public fundamentally trusted the regulatory authorities and the banking system; apparently everyone agreed disclosure would have caused only needless concern. The persistence of this opaque system in the early 1990s has meant balance sheet quality has been generally assumed by outside specialists and even the general public to be far worse than it may in fact be. This distrust has hampered the task of dealing with what have been very real problems. It has increased the cost of raising capital for the banks, and has even led to the frightening thought that some banks might actually fail.

These problems, together with highly publicized bank and securities company scandals, have created an unprecedented decline in public confidence in stock brokers, bankers, and even the regulatory authorities. A systemic crisis is highly unlikely, and hardly anyone seriously expects the authorities to allow any banks to go formally bankrupt or any depositors to take losses. Nonetheless, attitudes have become more cautious and concerned.

De facto failures will occur, but they will be handled. A raft of forced mergers, of large financial institutions as well as small ones, is likely. Failing banks will be merged into more successful ones, with subsidized credits (low interest rate central bank and deposit-insurance fund loans, government deposits, tax concessions) that may be less than fully transparent lubricating the process.

The bad debt overhang will plague the Japanese financial system for much of the 1990s. Although many loans are nonperforming and the collateral impaired, renewed growth of the economy, with concomitant recoveries in asset markets, will make them less of a burden. Actual ultimate total losses (at least to the banks) may not be large. Rather, the problem for the banks is reduced profits during the process.

In all three countries the financial trends set in motion in the 1980s will continue in the 1990s, albeit at different rates and from different levels. Domestic financial deregulation will persist; it is difficult to conceive of realistic scenarios in which this process is reversed. Similarly, the trend toward liberalizing international finance transactions and increasing financial integration with global markets will continue. Domestic capital markets will become stronger—broader and deeper—and hence a more attractive source of finance for large corporations.

Deregulation of interest rates is a necessary but far from sufficient condition for financial liberalization. The dangers of oligopolistic, even cartel-like, behavior persist. Thus, an ongoing challenge in each country is how to create truly competitive financial institutions and markets. The financial authorities will have to tread the fine line between effective prudential regulation and financial market freedom and competition.

What Do These Development Experiences Tell Us?

There are lessons from the financial development experiences of Japan, Korea, and Taiwan that are relevant to other economies, but they have to be teased out. And policymakers in other countries will have to apply those lessons in light of their own country's institutional structure, policy objectives, and means of implementation. I see five broad generic truths emerging from these three country studies.

First, successful economic performance over the long run depends on a host of real factors: labor skills, human capital formation, and entrepreneurial drive; productive investment and the savings to finance it; innovation and improvement in products and processes; active interaction in the world economy; organizational, decisionmaking, and policymaking capacities; appropriate price signals and other incentives; and control over inflation.

Second, finance and the financial system have an important role to play in economic development and growth. They are not necessarily an engine of growth, and they do not have to be. Rather, they have to be the fuel-injection system—mobilizing savings and pumping them into the investment engine, the more efficiently the better.

Third, the financial system works best in a stable macroeconomic environment; price stability is especially important. In all three of these countries, fiscal policy was conservative, and budget deficits were not a source of inflationary pressure. Their financial systems were effective mobilizers of savings and allocators of funds only after inflation was brought under control. Rapid, steady economic growth, combined with mild and brief slowdowns in economic activity, makes financial and real activity easier and more effective; that is, success begets success.

Fourth, the difficulties financial institutions and others in these countries have in terms of inadequate information, and their mechanisms for coping, highlight the importance of developing adequate accounting, auditing, legal, and prudential supervision capabilities. Yet the reality is that the provision of these services is likely to lag well behind the need. Banks in each country have responded to information deficiencies and asymmetries in different ways along a similar spectrum, depending on the particular time: Lend on the basis of safe collateral; lend to larger, well-established enterprises while ignoring smaller borrowers; develop sustained relationships with clients and invest in gathering information about them and monitoring them.

Fifth, policymakers do have alternative ways to channel credit to priority uses. But if a country does decide to adopt financial repression, those policies should be mild, modest, and generic rather than narrowly focused. A key variable is having positive real interest rates: Even under financially repressive policy regimes, they are associated with higher rates of mobilization of savings and effective if not optimally efficient financial intermediation.

There are significant topics we have not been able to deal with fully here. These are of two types: those needing further research and those beyond the boundaries of this book. The micro chapters on commercial banking substantially extend the frontiers of the knowledge available in English, yet the authors make clear how much more empirical research needs to be done in any language. Of particular importance is the internal management of banks and other financial institutions, including their actual decisionmaking processes and abilities to gather and use information about clients, monitor them, and exercise control when there are problems. Similarly, while such topics as the information infrastructure or the political economy of allocating and utilizing rents generated by either financial repression or limited information in these insider systems are important, they require skills and knowledge beyond those in the usual tool kits of economists.

We thus end this book with a call for further research, empirical and theoretical, on the far-ranging topics and issues of the financial development of Japan, Korea, and Taiwan and, by extension, other countries as well. Throughout this book we have identified—frequently explicitly but sometimes implicitly—an agenda of research topics. No doubt the reader will think of others. Many require the skills of specialists in disciplines other than economics, including business management, accounting, law, political science, and indeed all the social sciences. We have much to learn, together.

This chapter benefits greatly from the research of my colleagues in this project and their constructive criticisms and thoughtful insights. Inevitably we have some differences in interpretation, mainly of nuance and emphasis. I am solely responsible for the views and judgments presented in this chapter. I am particularly thankful to Larry Meissner for his skill in the excising, reorganizing, and editing of an all-too-long earlier draft, and to Nicole Domencic for her research assistance.

REFERENCES

Amsden, Alice. 1989. *Asia's Next Giant: South Korea and Late Industrialization*. Cambridge: Cambridge University Press.

Anchordoguy, Marie. 1989. *Computer, Inc: Japan's Challenge to IBM*. Cambridge, MA: Harvard University Press.

Cho, Lee-jayu, and Yoon-hyung Kim, eds. 1991. *Economic Development in the Republic of Korea: A Policy Perspective*. Honolulu: University of Hawaii, East–West Center.

Cole, David C. and Yung Chul Park. 1983. *Financial Development in the Republic of Korea 1945–1978*. Cambridge, MA: Harvard University, Council on East Asian Studies.

———, and Betty F. Slade. 1991. "Reform of Financial Systems." In Dwight Perkins and Michael Roemer, eds., *Reforming Financial Systems in Developing Countries*. Cambridge, MA: Harvard Institute of International Development.

Friedman, David. 1988. *The Misunderstood Miracle: Industrial and Political Change in Japan.* Ithaca, NY: Cornell University Press.

Fry, Maxwell J. 1988. *Money, Interest and Banking in Economic Development.* Baltimore: Johns Hopkins University Press.

Gelb, Alan. 1989. "Financial Policies, Efficiency and Growth: An Analysis of Broad Cross-Section Relationships." World Bank.

Genther, Phyllis. 1990. *A History of Japan's Government–Business Relationship: The Passenger Car Industry.* Ann Arbor: University of Michigan, Center for Japanese Studies.

Johnson, Chalmers. 1982. *MITI and the Japanese Miracle.* Stanford, CA: Stanford University Press.

Komiya, Ryutaro, Masahiro Okuno, and Kotaro Suzumura, eds. 1988. *Industrial Poicy of Japan.* Academic Press.

Kuo, Shirley, Gustav Ranis, and John Fei. 1981. *The Taiwan Success Story: Rapid Growth with Improved Income Distribution in the Republic of China 1952–1979.* Boulder, CO: Westview Press.

Leipziger, Danny M. 1987. *Korea: Managing the Industrial Transition.* A World Bank country study. 2 vols.

Li, Kuo-ting. 1988. *The Evolution of Policy behind Taiwan's Development Success.* New Haven, CT: Yale University Press.

McKinnon, Ronald I. 1973. *Money and Capital in Economic Development.* Washington, DC: Brookings Institution.

———. 1991. *The Order of Economic Liberalization: Financial Control in the Transition to a Market Economy.* Baltimore: Johns Hopkins University Press.

Okimoto, Daniel I. 1989. *Between MITI and the Market.* Stanford, CA: Stanford University Press.

———, Takuo Sugano and Franklin B. Weinstein, eds. 1984. *Competitive Edge: The Semiconductor Industry in the U.S. and Japan.* Stanford, CA: Stanford University Press.

Patrick, Hugh, with Larry Meissner, eds. 1986. *Japan's High Technology Industries: Lessons and Limitations of Industrial Policy.* University of Washington Press.

———, with Larry Meissner, eds. 1991. *Pacific Basin Industries in Distress: Structural Adjustment and Trade Policy in the Nine Industrialized Economies.* New York: Columbia University Press.

———, and Henry Rosovsky, eds. 1976. *Asia's New Giant: How the Japanese Economy Works.* Washington, DC: Brookings Institution.

Samuels, Richard J. 1987. *The Business of the Japanese State: Energy Markets in Comparative and Historical Perspective.* Ithaca, NY: Cornell University Press.

Shaw, Edward S. 1973. *Financial Deepening in Economic Development.* New York: Oxford University Press.

Sheard, Paul. 1991. "The Economies of Japanese Corporate Organization and the 'Structural Impediments' Debate: A Critical Review." *Japanese Economic Studies* 19 (4), (Summer).

Song, Byung-Nak. 1990. *The Rise of the Korean Economy.* New York: Oxford University Press.

Stern, Joseph J. 1990. "Industrial Targeting in Japan." Harvard Institute of International Development (HIID) Discussion Paper 343.

Teranishi, Juro. 1990. "Financial System and Industrialization of Japan: 1900–1970." Banca Nazionale del Lavoro *Quarterly Review*, September.

Wade, Robert. 1990. *Governing the Market: Economic Theory and the Role of the Government in East Asia Industrialization.* Princeton, NJ: Princeton University Press.

Woo, Jung-en. 1991. *Race to the Swift: State and Finance in Korean Industrialization.* New York: Columbia University Press.

World Bank. 1989. *World Development Report 1989.* New York: Oxford University Press.

Yamamura, Kozo and Yasukichi Yasuba, eds. 1987. *The Political Economy of Japan.* Vol.1: *The Domestic Transformation.* Stanford, CA: Stanford University Press.

Index

Credit associations and unions (continued)
Taiwan, 228, 234
Credit cooperatives
mergers in Japan, 113
Taiwan, 228
Credit information-gathering, country
comparisons, 332–33
Credit rationing, Taiwanese government, 250
Cross-shareholding, Japanese *keiretsu*, 94, 95
Curb market
country comparisons, 329, 343
Taiwan, 235, 260, 292, 295–97

Daewoo, 193, 196, 212
Dah An Commercial Bank, 320
Dai-ichi Kangyo Bank, 94, 120
cooperative tie-up with Japan, 120
foreign branches, 227
Daini chigin, 31
Daiwa, 120
Defense expenditures, 7
"Delegated monitors," 12–13
Japanese banks, 98, 99
Demand deposits
Korean banks, 201
Taiwan banks, 305
Demand-following finance, 10
Deposit Insurance Corporation (Japan), 88–89
Deposit insurance programs, 15
financial crises in Taiwan and, 315
Japan, 88–89
Korea, 157–58
Taiwan, 293, 294
Deposit money banks (DMBs)
Korea, 133, 135, 137, 153–54, 188
collateral requirements, 205–6
deregulation, 154–55
interest rate decontrol and, 150
lending behavior, 202–6, 207, 208
loans and discounts, 156
policy-directed loans and, 155, 157
regulation, 189–90
Taiwan, 230
Deposits and deposit rates
Japanese banks
deregulation, 91–93
long-term, 30
as source of funds, 102
Taiwan banks, 303, 305
Deregulation
country comparisons, 341–47
efficient resource allocation and, 58
Japan, 47–62, 51–58
banks (1976–91), 125–28
characteristics, 58–59

consequences, 59–62
interest rates, 122
international financial markets, 55–56
Korea, 134–35, 147–54, 188
bank lending rates, 204–6
Taiwan financial system, 256–61
United States, 58
Designated-Purpose Trust Program, 262
Developing countries
financial liberalization in, 11
monetary reform and, 16–18
role of banks in, 13–14
Development plans and strategies
export-oriented, 6, 7
Korea, 132
Direct financing
Korea, 139
in postwar Japan, 37
Directorate General of Remittance and Savings
Banks (DGRSB) (Taiwan), 228
Domestic banks (Taiwan), 290, 299–300, 320.
See also other types of banks e.g., City
banks, Commercial banks, etc.
bankers' acceptances and, 318–19
cost function, 319–20
employment in, 302
full-service, 226–27
nonperforming loans, 313
performance, 316, 317
regulation, 294
Domestic savings
financial reform and, 166
Korea, 142–44, 176
Taiwan, 238–41, 275, 276, 277, 278

Eastern Sun Bank, 320
Economic development
country comparisons, 4–8
financial deepening and, 325–26
financial factors in, 8–11
Japan's financial system and, 41–47
Korea, role of finance in, 165–66
Economic liberalization, in Southern Cone, 11
Economies of scale
Japanese banks, 114–15
Taiwan banks, 319
Economies of scope, Japanese banks, 116
Education, 6
Embezzlement, Japanese banks, 111, 112
Emergency financing, Taiwan Central Bank of
China, 252
Employees, banking system
country comparisons, 340–41
Japan, 45
Taiwan, 301–2

"Window guidance," 40, 41, 42
  effectiveness of, 87
  Japanese banks, 86 – 87
World Bank, 38
  Japanese economic development and, 38
  loans from, 356

Yachiyo Shinkin, 120
Yamaichi Securities, 113

Yang, Ya-Hwei, "Taiwan: Development and
  Structural Change of the Banking
  System," 288–324
Yen-Dollar Committee, 59

Zaibatsu, 7, 94
  bank ownership and control, 339– 40
Zaitech, 116
Zenkoku banks, 30